ONE KIND OF FREEDOM

The economic consequences of emancipation

ONE KIND OF FREEDOM

The economic consequences of emancipation

ROGER L. RANSOM
PROFESSOR OF ECONOMICS
UNIVERSITY OF CALIFORNIA, RIVERSIDE

RICHARD SUTCH
PROFESSOR OF ECONOMICS
UNIVERSITY OF CALIFORNIA, BERKELEY

CAMBRIDGE UNIVERSITY PRESS
CAMBRIDGE
LONDON NEW YORK MELBOURNE

Published by the Syndics of the Cambridge University Press
The Pitt Building, Trumpington Street, Cambridge CB2 1 RP
Bentley House, 200 Euston Road, London NW1 2DB
32 East 57th Street, New York, NY 10022, USA
296 Beaconsfield Parade, Middle Park, Melbourne 3206, Australia

First published 1977

Printed in the United States of America

*Typeset by the Fuller Organization, Inc.,
Philadelphia, Pennsylvania*

*Printed and bound by Vail-Ballou Press, Inc.,
Binghamton, New York*

Library of Congress Cataloging in Publication Data
Ransom, Roger L 1938-
One kind of freedom.

Bibliography: p.
Includes index.
1. Southern States — Economic conditions.
2. Southern States—History—1865–1914
3. Afro-Americans — Southern States — Economic conditions.
I. Sutch, Richard, joint author.   II. Title.
HC107.A13R28   330.9′76′04   76-27909
ISBN 0 521 21450 5 hard covers
ISBN 0 521 29203 4 paperback

This book is dedicated to our families,
who shared our year in Berkeley
when work on this volume was begun.

CONTENTS

Contents

STATISTICAL APPENDIXES

DATA APPENDIX

PREFACE

The SOUTHERN ECONOMIC HISTORY PROJECT was established in 1968 when the authors of this volume were both in Berkeley, California. Supported that year by funds from the Institute of Business and Economic Research at the University of California, Berkeley, we began an investigation into the post-Civil War economic history of the American South. We were intrigued, first, by the fact that while economists had given considerable attention to the institution of slavery and the economic exploitation of blacks before the Civil War, they had virtually ignored black history in the post-Civil War period. It seemed obvious to us that the economic institutions that replaced slavery and the conditions under which ex-slaves were allowed to enter the economic life of the United States for the first time as free agents were of crucial importance to an understanding of the Afro-American experience.

We were intrigued, also, by an as yet unresolved paradox in American economic history. The period between the Civil War and World War I was one of unparalleled economic growth and development for the United States as a whole. Yet the South did not share equally in this expansion. Southern agriculture stagnated while an agricultural revolution transformed the rest of rural America. The South's industrial sector remained small and backward during the age of American industrial growth. And southern people – white as well as black – were among the poorest, least educated, and most deprived of all Americans at a time when America was becoming the richest, best educated, most advantaged nation in the world.

Our joint investigation into these two issues has continued from 1969 to the present with the financial support of the National Science Foundation. The Southern Economic History Project has made the findings of this research available through a series of working papers, by presentation at scientific meetings, and in professional journals. It seemed to us that the best format for reaching a wider audience would be a book addressed to historians, economists, and others interested in this critical period of American history. Hence, the present volume.

Our intent is to provide a historical narrative describing and interpreting the economic changes that swept the South following emancipation. Simultaneously we wish to acquaint the reader with the variety of information and statistical data upon which we have drawn to support our interpretation. We felt it was essential to do the latter, since the strengths and weaknesses of our methodological approach could be judged only by a reader acquainted with the details of our research. We have tried throughout the book to strike a balance between the narrative and these details. Whenever our statistical procedures required such lengthy description that our narrative would be seriously interrupted, we relegated them to statistical appendixes at the end of the volume. At the same time, we have made a conscious effort to keep the reader of the main text fully aware of the logic of our research methodology and the statistical evidence upon which we draw. Thus, a reader less interested in the methodological or statistical details may skip the appendixes without forgoing the information necessary to form his own judgments. Nevertheless, we hope we have succeeded in making these appendixes accessible to the general reader, and in particular those who are reluctant to work through pages of mathematical formulations. Our appendixes may be dull, but we trust they are comprehensible.

In a longer data appendix (Appendix G) we have different objectives in mind. That appendix describes the statistical data we have collected from a variety of archival sources. It includes a discussion of the manner in which we narrowed the scope of our study to focus on the cotton-producing regions of the South. After examining data from each county of all eleven former Confederate States, we were able to establish the boundaries of a large geographic region within which economic and social conditions were sufficiently homogeneous to enable us to make broad generalizations concerning the economic life of the people living there. We call this region the Cotton South; its boundaries are shown on the map opposite the opening page of Chapter 1. The map also locates twenty-seven counties within the Cotton South that we have selected to represent the larger region. A number of systematic statistical samples have been drawn from the historical records of these counties. These samples, when appropriately aggregated, form the basis for many of the quantitative generalizations we present. The procedures used to select the representative counties, collect the samples of data, and aggregate the statistics are described in the data appendix.

The Cotton South covers an area of more than 200,000 square miles, ranging from the Carolinas through Georgia, Alabama, Mississippi, and westward into the prairies of Texas. More than half of the black population of the United States lived in the Cotton South in 1880, and nearly three-fourths of the country's cotton was grown there. Whenever possible, the results of our study have been based on data from this region. Where it was impossible to obtain data for the individual counties in the Cotton South, we have based the arguments of the text on data for five cotton-producing states: South Carolina, Georgia, Alabama, Mississippi, and Louisiana.

Because we are economists by training, not historians, a characteristic of our work perhaps requires a few words of explanation. As economists, we have tried to understand the complex workings of the southern economic system by reducing it to a few bare essentials. We have studied the history of this period and believe we have identified the major forces at work. We then developed what might be termed an abstract model of the postemancipation economy. This model brings into sharp focus the interrelationships of those factors which we believe are central to the two issues under study. In the process, we have eliminated what we believe are minor or irrelevant details. We devote considerable attention to justification of the plausibility of our analyses – the inclusion of some factors as critical, the exclusion of others as of less importance – and to demonstrations that both our assumptions and the implications of our models are consistent with the historical evidence.

A serious danger which accompanies any attempt to theorize about human behavior and social institutions is that the theories and the models are likely to depict experience *too* starkly. They may stereotype individuals and situations, while paying insufficient attention to the variety of experiences and the deviations from the norm. Though we have been critical of this tendency in the work of others, we have not completely avoided the same distortion in our own work. Ultimately, it is impossible to obtain the insight which comes with abstraction and simultaneously retain the full richness of detail and variety that is the reality of human experience.

As economists our interest and our analysis naturally focus upon the economy of the postemancipation South. At the same time, whenever we thought it relevant and important to do so, we have attempted to show how noneconomic forces impinged upon the economy, how they helped to direct the evolution of economic institutions, and how they constrained the alternatives available to the South. On the other hand, we have not tried to reverse this procedure. We do not examine the impact of economic events upon the other dimensions of southern life. The demographic, political, social, and cultural histories of the South are beyond the scope of this study. For this reason we make no pretense to have written a general history of the South. We offer our analysis of the southern economy instead as a contribution to the study of that history.

While we hope we have contributed to the understanding of postemancipation history, we know that we have drawn heavily from that history. Indeed, our reliance upon works of the numerous historians who have addressed their attention to the same problems we are examining here is greater than our citations and footnotes might suggest. Whenever possible, we have returned to original sources and the accounts of contemporaries rather than relying upon the work that first called a document to our attention. We are also indebted to the work of several of our colleagues in economics who, in the last several years, have written on the postemancipation economy. Where their research parallels our own work, we have taken notice in the text of our book. We have eschewed, however, debates that would substantially digress from our own analysis.

The organization of this book reflects our analytical, rather than a chronological, approach to the material. Much of our story focuses on the momentous changes that occurred immediately after the end of the Civil War. The emancipation of the slaves in 1865 shattered the economic system of the Old South. Southerners, both black and white, had to build a new society with new institutions. The economic institutions established at that time shaped in large measure the course of subsequent economic development in the South. We begin by examining the legacy which slavery left southerners and the impact of the Civil War. We then turn to an examination of those changes that proved most influential: the demise of the plantation system, the rise of tenancy, the rearrangement of the financial and marketing structures that supplied southern agriculture. This task accomplished, we are able to explain both the mechanisms through which southern farmers were exploited and the dynamic forces that retarded southern development.

Roger L. Ransom
Richard Sutch

Gloucester, Massachusetts
June 1977

ACKNOWLEDGMENTS

This book is more than the product of its two authors. It is the joint product of its authors and the many people who aided our efforts. We cannot hope to express our full sense of gratitude here, but we can acknowledge our debt and offer our thanks to all the people who have aided our efforts, provided encouragement, and offered advice.

We share a common mentor in economic history: Douglass C. North was Roger Ransom's thesis adviser at the University of Washington in Seattle, and it was in North's seminars on American economic history that Richard Sutch first became interested in the subject. Later as a Ph.D. student in economics at the Massachusetts Institute of Technology, Sutch was able to pursue this interest in Alexander Gerschenkron's economic history seminar across Cambridge at Harvard University. Between them, these two scholars have trained more economic historians of recent generations than (we would venture to guess) the rest of the profession combined. Our debt to them is nonquantifiable – but extremely large.

When we first considered a joint research project on southern economic history, we received early encouragement from Joseph Garbarino, Director of the Institute of Business and Economic Research at Berkeley, who provided not only kind words and advice, but a grant of money to get us started. Jim Blackman, John Meyer, and Paul Taylor, all three of whom are themselves interested in southern economic history, also offered encouragement and help at the outset of our venture.

The Southern Economic History Project could not have pursued its research without generous financial assistance. Our greatest debt in this regard is to the National Science Foundation, which has, at various times, provided three major grants.[1] We have also received assistance from the Institute of Business and Economic Research at Berkeley, which housed the project for five years, and the Center for Social and Behavioral Science Reseach at Riverside, where the project is currently operating. Without the

[1] The following projects were funded by the National Science Foundation: GS 2668: Agriculture, Credit, and the Position of the Negro Farmer: 1865–1900; GS 3263: Agriculture and Economic Growth in the American South: 1865–1940; and SOC74–09457: Merchant Monopoly in the Rural South: 1865–1900.

aid of a computer, our task would have been greatly lengthened, and we appreciate the access to their facilities which the Berkeley Computer Center granted us. The distance between Riverside and Berkeley was made less of an obstacle by travel funds made available by the Riverside Academic Senate. Professor Sutch was granted a Ford Faculty Fellowship for the academic year 1970 – 1971 which allowed him more time than he would otherwise have had to devote to this project. We appreciate the investments made by each of these groups.

Assembling the vast array of data that provided the foundation for this book was a task that rested largely on the shoulders of our research staff. It has been our great fortune to have the assistance of extraordinarily capable and meticulous people working with us.

Sheila Moffett Rubey joined the project at its outset and supervised the collection of data from the manuscript census schedules, a task that took three years to complete. She was quite literally indispensable to the project. At various times she was assisted by Lynnae Wolin, Wendy Barnes Schonfield, Deborah Doyle, Barbara Robbins, and Sue Boutin.

The checking of our data was largely the responsibility of Wendy Barnes Schonfield, and our failure to uncover errors in the course of our subsequent use is eloquent testimony to the care with which she carried out that task.

Lynnae Wolin deserves a very special mention. She spent many hours collecting and collating the sample from the Dun and Bradstreet Archives, an assignment she carried out with incredible meticulousness and with a devotion that can only be appreciated by those who have worked with microfilms of handwritten documents.

Lynnae Wolin and Deborah Doyle collected several of the supplemental samples, helped us to compile tables, and assisted various phases of the library research. DiAnne Dwyer and Edgar Breffitt compiled the extensive data we drew from the Mortality Census.

We are extremely grateful for the care and devotion our data collection staff has shown. We hope this book is a worthy testimonial to *their* accomplishment.

Our research assistants, Arden Hall and Charles Wolin, were both graduate students in economics at the University of California, Berkeley, when our project began. While Arden Hall spent many late-night hours nursing our programs through the computer, Charles Wolin spent equally many hours searching in the library for obscure books and documents for which our appetite must have seemed insatiable. We are deeply indebted to each of them. At various times the Southern Economic History Project has also called upon John Lyons, Bruce Vermuellen, Michael Boskin, Pauline Andrews, Michael Hurd, William Compton, Arif Waquif, Sandor Fuchs, Michael Herschberg, George Boutin, Martha Chase, and Barbara Dewald for research assistance.

Several people went to considerable effort to assist us in our search for materials. Lucia Dunn went out of her way during a trip to Georgia to collect documents and locate records we required. Robert Rubey assisted in the microfilming of documents in New York. Professor Joseph Reid generously allowed us to examine his extensive collection of labor and tenancy contracts gathered from archives in the South. We have reproduced several of these contracts in our text. Mrs. Crerar Bennett of Milford, Delaware, allowed us to read her private collection of letters. Mathea Falco helped us locate a particularly rare document in Washington. Without the aid of these friends, our work would have been less complete.

We were fortunate to have had available some of the best libraries in the world. We are particularly grateful to Berkeley's library system, which is so comprehensive that very little traveling to other libraries seemed necessary. Particularly helpful were the excellent collections and staffs of the university's Agricultural and Government Documents Libraries. The Interlibrary Loan Service at both Berkeley and Riverside proved most helpful in our search for written knowledge.

When we did have to travel to other libraries, we benefited from generous assistance in each case. The material from the Dun and Bradstreet collection was obtained from the companies' library in New York and from the Baker Library at Harvard University. We are grateful to Charles F. G. Raikes, Frederick Staats, and John J. Pemrick of Dun and Bradstreet Companies, Inc. for permission to examine and quote from these records and for extending to us the courtesy of the corporation to aid our research. Roberta J. Gardiner of the Dun and Bradstreet Library was most helpful in facilitating our examination of those archives. Robert W. Lovett and Lawrence Kipp of the Baker Library helped us enormously in our examination of the Mercantile Agency collection at Harvard. Ann Campbell of the National Archives assisted us in locating materials at the Archives' San Francisco branch. Ruth Cory and her staff at the Georgia State Archives in Atlanta were both helpful and hospitable when we visited there.

At other times we have used collections at the New York City Public Library, Widner Library at Harvard, the University of North Carolina Library, the National Archives in Washington, the Library of Congress, and the National Agricultural Library.

Any university research project requires bookkeeping and administrative assistance. In our case these tasks may have been more than doubled since the project had two investigators on two campuses. We were fortunate to have the bureaucratic know-how and skills of Virginia Brainard and Virginia Douglas at the Institute for Business and Economic Research at Berkeley, Sharon Vander Veen of the Center for Social and Behavioral Science Research at Riverside, and Eva Ewen and Lee Smith of the departments of economics at Berkeley and Riverside.

Typing, proofreading, and correcting the mountains of working papers, monographs, and drafts that preceded this book were ably performed by Connie Harrison, Jan Sibert, Sharon Vander Veen, Kathleen Cinelli, Pat Chatham, Helen Way, and Lee Smith, with occasional assistance from the staffs of the departments of economics at both Riverside and Berkeley.

Once typed, we imposed our working papers, monographs, memos, and drafts upon our colleagues. They responded most generously with advice, suggestions, and criticisms. Our list of debts in this regard is so extensive that we can only spotlight the tip of an iceberg. Paul David, Stanley Engerman, Robert Fogel, Robert Gallman, William Parker, Joseph Reid, Peter Temin, Harold Woodman, and Gavin Wright have from the beginning been our best and most constant critics. Each has caused us to rework our arguments, rethink our positions, rewrite our prose. We believe the final product was much improved in this process. If so, each deserves a share of the credit.

All our colleagues in economics at the University of California have been free with their advice and encouragement. Carlo Cipolla, Albert Fishlow, Richard Roehl, and Thomas Rothenberg at Berkeley; and William Brown, Kay Hunt, and Morgan Reynolds at Riverside each merits special attention. Colleagues elsewhere who have been of particular assistance include Stephen DeCanio, James Foust, Claudia Goldin, Stewart Greene, Herbert Gutman, Mark Hopkins, Kenneth Stampp, Richard Sylla, and Gary Walton.

The penultimate draft of this book was read by Elizabeth Block, Stanley Engerman, Carl Degler, William Parker, Joseph Reid, Peter Temin, Jonathan Wiener, Harold Woodman, and Gavin Wright, each of whom provided detailed comments that helped us to perfect the ultimate draft.

The antepenultimate, penultimate, and ultimate drafts were typed and assembled by Sharon Vander Veen with an assist from Poinka Patuscha and Lee Smith. Sharon Vander Veen kept her wit and humor throughout this process of perfection despite the fact that she was content with the first draft. The index was prepared with the assistance of DiAnne Dwyer. The maps and figures were drafted by Sheila Moffett Rubey, Edgar Breffitt, and DiAnne Dwyer.

We also wish to thank the Economic History Association, Academic Press, and the Agricultural History Society for permission to draw from our previously published work.[2]

[2] Roger L. Ransom and Richard Sutch, "Debt Peonage in the Cotton South After the Civil War," *Journal of Economic History* 32 (September 1972); idem, "The Ex-Slave in the Post-Bellum South: A Study of the Economic Impact of Racism in a Market Environment," *Journal of Economic History* 33 (March 1973); idem, "The Impact of the Civil War and of Emancipation on Southern Agriculture," *Explorations in Economic History* 12 (January 1975); and idem, "The 'Lock-in' Mechanism and Overproduction of Cotton in the Postbellum South," *Agricultural History* 49 (April 1975).

A NOTE TO THE READER

One minor problem created by our frequent use of contemporary citations deserves a brief comment. Some of the quotations we have reproduced use expressions that reflect the racism of the times. They refer to individuals as "niggers" or "sambos." Contemporary whites frequently ridiculed and exaggerated the black dialect or made light of the freedman's inexperience with (and presumed ignorance of) free society and the free economy. Moreover, the conclusion these contemporaries reached regarding black behavior were often based upon a blatantly racist outlook. In repeating these contemporary statements, we do not support either the style of presentation or the conclusions reached. However, we feel it is essential to quote these passages rather than to paraphrase them. Indeed, by presenting the quotations in their original form we hope to convey one of the ways in which racism permeated the outlook and thinking of nearly everyone at the time. We trust that modern readers will understand the importance of our point and not be offended by the passages in question.

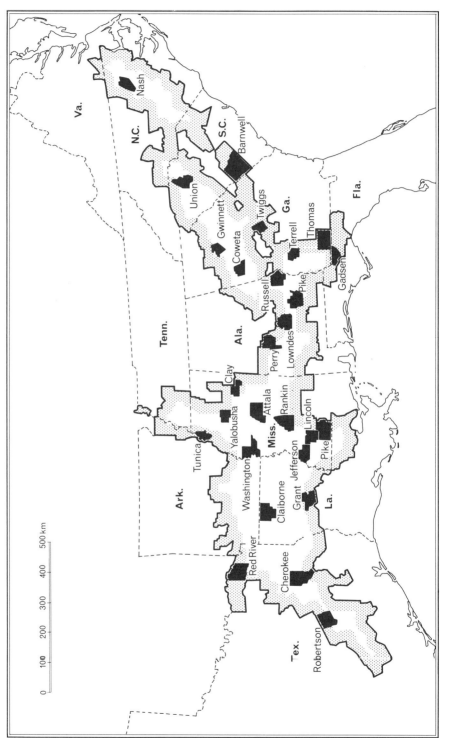

The Cotton South and twenty-seven counties chosen to represent the region.

CHAPTER 1

WHAT DID FREEDOM MEAN?

1. Neither slavery nor involuntary servitude, except as a punishment for crime whereof the party shall have been duly convicted, shall exist within the United States, or any place subject to their jurisdiction.

2. Congress shall have power to enforce this article by appropriate legislation.

Constitution of the United States, Amendment XIII,
ratified December 6, 1865.

At the conclusion of a long and bloody civil war, with their emancipation from slavery and involuntary servitude, over 4 million Americans were permitted a kind of political and economic freedom for the first time in their lives. Beyond doubt, this change in the status of black Americans was accompanied by an unambiguous and substantial improvement in their economic well-being. It is also probable that most blacks were emboldened and enheartened by emancipation. But whatever the ex-slave's initial reactions to freedom – with its opportunities, its responsibilities, and its uncertainties – the material gains were real and stimulated an optimistic view of the potential for further economic advancement. This optimism was further reinforced when black workers found that they possessed the power, not only to shape their own destinies within the society in which they found themselves, but also to change that society, at least in a limited way.

For nearly two and one-half centuries, black slave labor had been an integral part of southern life. Emancipation had destroyed the foundations of the southern economy and southern society. Freedom meant that the immediate postwar years had to be literally years of reconstruction, and freedom meant that the new economy and the new society that were to be constructed on the site of the old could not be patterned on the old design. Although new institutions emerged, they were fashioned in haste and in a climate of racial animosity, and as a result they emerged deeply flawed. The black had gained his political freedom, but he was soon effectively disenfranchised. He had gained his social freedom, yet he remained an outcast in white society, discriminated against because of the color of his skin. He had

Notes to Chapter 1 appear on pages 317–319.

gained his economic freedom, but the southern economy emerged poor and stagnant, and the black man was the poorest of southerners. Blacks gained much with emancipation, but that gain represented a single step from slavery to freedom. Further advancement was effectively curtailed. The optimism with which the ex-slave confronted freedom was soon extinguished. Black Americans would have to wait many decades before the next step toward economic equality could be taken.

This tragedy need not have occurred. It is our thesis that the lack of progress in the postemancipation era was the consequence of flawed economic institutions erected in the wake of the Confederate defeat. This book is our attempt to identify these flaws and to assess the price southerners paid as a consequence. Our focus throughout is on the economic aspects of the transformation brought on by emancipation. If we seem preoccupied with the material side of life, with agricultural productivity, with the distribution of income, and with economic growth, it is not only because our own training as economists naturally drew us to those topics, but also because we believe that an untangling of the economic history of this period is a necessary prerequisite for a reexamination of the political, social, and psychological histories of the postemancipation South. Since we believe the southern economy can be fully understood only in the context of southern society, we have tried to supply that context. We believe economic history should not be divorced from political, social, demographic, psychological, or intellectual history. Accordingly, we have attempted to avoid distorting our analysis by undue neglect of these dimensions of the story. Nevertheless, our lack of expertise in these disciplines has kept us from venturing very far into areas separate from the object of our economic research. An analysis of the influences the economic realities of the period had on these aspects of society is a task for other social science historians.

The welfare gains associated with emancipation

American slavery had been a viable economic institution because the value of the slaves' labor exceeded the value of the provisions they consumed. The southern slaveowner had been expropriating the entire product of the slaves' labor and in return provided only the food, shelter, and clothing necessary to keep the slaves healthy and hardworking. The freedmen, on the other hand, possessed the legal right to the entire product of their own labor and could consume or dispose of it as they wished. Provided productivity did not fall substantially, their potential income as free workers would exceed the value of their consumption as slaves.

This potential gain in material income was not insignificant, as can be seen in the high prices slaves brought in the slave market. The market price of a slave had represented the value to the owner of the legal right to exploit the slave's labor. A prime field hand sold for $1,650 to $1,800 at the end of the 1850s, a time when the annual output achieved on slave farms was less than $260 per working hand.[1] The fact that someone would pay over six times an individual's annual gross output for the legal right to expropriate all but the income necessary for subsistence testifies both to the productivity of slave labor and to the potential gain to the slave from his own emancipation.

We can make a first approximation of the economic value of freedom by calculating the rate of exploitation of slave labor. *Economic exploitation* is the expropriation of the product of labor without compensation.[2] The *rate of exploitation* is the fraction of that total product of labor which is exploited. By the term *the product of labor* we do not mean the average total annual output per slave (as might a Marxist), but rather that amount *less* the share of output paid to capital, land, and management personnel, where these other shares are figured at the market rate of return earned by capital, the market value of land rent, and the competitively determined salary earned by managers.

We have utilized the manuscript records of the Census of Agriculture for 1859 to estimate the average total output per slave in the cotton regions of the United States; the value of the output attributable to capital, land, and management; and the value of output attributable to labor. We have also utilized the extensive literature on the treatment received by American slaves to estimate the value of the food, clothing, shelter, and medical care with which they were provided. These estimates are presented in Table 1.1. The methods used (and the assumptions we made) to calculate these estimates are discussed at length in Appendix A. Our calculations suggest that slaves received only 21.7 percent of the output produced on large planta-

Table 1.1. *Estimates of total output, labor's product, slaves' consumption, and total exploitation per slave: 1859*

	Average per slave, all farms	Average per slave, plantations with 51 or more slaves
Total output ($)	127.55	147.93
Less		
Interest and depreciation		
due to capital	13.99	11.32
Rent due to land	46.10	52.83
Salary due to management	5.00	5.00
Product of labor ($)	62.46	78.78
Less slaves' consumption	28.95	32.12
Total exploitation ($)	33.51	46.66
Rate of exploitation (%)	53.7	59.2

Source: Tables A.1, A.4, A.6. See Appendix A for details of these estimates.

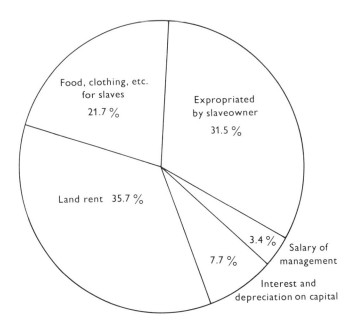

Figure 1.1 Distribution of output on large slave plantations: 1859. (*Source:* Table 1.1.)

tions, and well over one-half of their potential income was expropriated from them without compensation (see Figure 1.1). Provided productivity was unaffected and no new forms of exploitation arose, freedom would allow blacks to claim this previously exploited income.

There can be no doubt that the blacks actually did receive a larger fraction of the income generated in agriculture following the Civil War. Their share of output rose from the 22 percent provided slaves on large plantations for their subsistence to the approximately 56 percent of output we calculate was received by black sharecroppers and tenant farmers in 1879. This estimate, reported in Table 1.2, is based on the manuscript records of the 1880 Census of Agriculture, and its derivation is explained in detail in Appendix A. Had there been no decline in output per capita, this dramatic shift in the distribution of output would have more than doubled the potential consumption of black Americans. As it was, material income increased by nearly 29 percent.

Of even more significance, perhaps, than the increase in material income received by black labor is the fact that, when free, the ex-slaves were able to make their own consumption decisions. Before the war, nearly everything consumed was selected and provided by the master. The foods eaten, the clothes worn, the size, style, and furnishing of the slaves' cabins, were all determined by the owner according to his own, rather than the slaves', best interests. Not surprisingly, the slaves' diet was crude and monotonous, and their shelter and clothing were no more than barely adequate. Only rarely did luxuries enter slave life; almost never were slaves allowed to refine their

Table 1.2. *Comparison of per capita output and material income measures, slaves on large plantations in 1859 with black sharecroppers in 1879*

	Plantations with 51 or more slaves, 1859	Black-operated sharecropped family farms, 1879	Percent change, 1859–1879
Expressed in 1859–1860 dollars per capita[a]			
Total output	147.93	74.03	−50.0
Product of labor	78.78	41.39	−47.5
Material income	32.12	41.39	28.9
Expressed as percent of total output			
Product of labor	53.3	55.9	4.9
Material income	21.7	55.9	157.6

[a] The value of output in 1879 is calculated by deflating the current dollar figures using a cash price index devised for this purpose in Appendix A.
Source: 1859: Table 1.1; *1879:* Tables A.8, A.9, A.10. See Appendix A for details.

tastes.[3] Free to spend their incomes where and when they wished, the freedmen could, even if constrained to the same level of expenditures, markedly increase their economic well-being by purchasing what they liked rather than what their former master had provided.

The freedmen quickly took advantage of this opportunity. The slave cabins were abandoned and new dwellings were constructed more to the liking of black families than the old slave quarters. A contemporary observer, David Barrow, recalled that the Negroes on his family's Georgia plantation moved, rebuilt, and expanded the old slave cabins in order to gain "more elbow-room."[4] "Luxuries" such as hams, tinned fish, cheese, and candy entered their diets – in some cases, for the first time in their lives. New clothes, particularly brightly colored articles of apparel, were immediately in great demand by the newly freed blacks. Whitelaw Reid observed that "calicoes, cottonades, denims, shoes, hats, brass jewelry, head handkerchiefs, candy, tobacco, sardines, cheese, and whisky were the great staples" traded to freedmen along the Mississippi River in 1865.[5] Whites did not always view such expenditures with approval. "Look how Ben. has wasted his money," said one plantation operator to Reid. He proceeded to list Ben's purchases: boots, mackerel, sardines, rings, shirting, candy, cheese, breastpins, earrings, whiskey, tobacco, candles, a hat, and a skillet.[6] Indeed, there were many reports, immediately after the war, of the "extravagance" of freed blacks who added luxuries to their consumption. Regardless of what white observers thought of these expenditures, it cannot be denied that black people found great enjoyment in the purchase of such items. It was an important way they exercised their new freedom.

Not the least of the changes blacks made in their consumption patterns was sharply to increase their consumption of "leisure." As slaves, blacks were compelled to work long hours with few days off. Women, adolescents, and the aged were all expected – and forced – to work as long and as often as the men. When free to set their own hours of work, the ex-slaves, quite predictably, chose to exchange a fraction of their potential income for "free" time: time for leisure, housekeeping, child care – in short, time for all the activities of men and women other than those designed to earn a material income. They duplicated (perhaps emulated) the work-leisure patterns of other free Americans. Adolescents in their early teens, women with children, and elderly men and women all worked significantly fewer hours per day and fewer days per year than had been the standard under the oppression of slavery. Even the adult men chose to work less. The cumulative effect was quite spectacular; the decline in the hours worked by the black population ranged between 28 and 37 percent per capita.[7]

The withdrawal of such a significant fraction of the potential labor supply was a voluntary response to the new patterns of incentives in the postemancipation economy. Had they chosen to do so, blacks could have worked more hours on their tenant farms than they did. Presumably such extra efforts would have produced additional output and income. Since they chose not to work longer hours, they must have valued the free time more than the income forgone. The ex-slaves' preference for leisure was an obvious manifestation of their improved condition. Too often this perfectly normal response to emancipation has been taken as "evidence" to support racist characterizations of blacks as lazy, incompetent, and unwilling to work without compulsion.

It is possible to be more precise about the value of this released labor time. If we evaluate the released time by the magnitude of the income forgone (it must have been worth more than this in the view of the blacks) and estimate the output forgone at the average productivity per hour, our measure of material income would have to be increased by 40 to 60 percent to yield an appropriate measure of potential "welfare" for sharecroppers comparable to the material income received by slaves. This calculation and comparison are carried out in Table 1.3. Relative welfare, according to these measures, increased by nearly 80 percent and perhaps by as much as 105 percent between 1859 and 1879.

The reduction in the black labor supply has another important implication: the figures on per capita output and the per capita product of labor in Table 1.2 cannot be taken as measures of labor productivity. Less output per capita was produced in 1879 than in 1859 partly because less labor per capita was devoted to production. When the per-capita-product-of-labor figures are converted to a per-effective-worker basis, a decline in labor productivity of between 16.3 and 26.7 percent is implied by our calculations. However, these productivity estimates undoubtedly exaggerate the actual decline that accompanied emancipation; the 1859 output figures reflect the spectacularly high productivity of the most prosperous agricultural

Table 1.3. *Comparison of per capita material income and relative welfare measures, slaves on large plantations in 1859 with black sharecroppers in 1879, expressed in 1859–1860 dollars per capita*

	Plantations with 51 or more slaves, 1859	Black-operated sharecropped family farms, 1879	Percent change, 1859–1879
Material income	32.12	41.39	28.9
Value of released labor time			
Low estimate[a]	—	16.34	—
High estimate[b]	—	24.52	—
Value of welfare relative to slavery			
Low estimate	32.12	57.73	79.7
High estimate	32.12	65.91	105.2

[a] Calculated assuming a 28.3 percent reduction in labor time per capita between 1859 and 1879; see Table 3.3. [b] Calculated assuming a 37.2 percent reduction in labor time per capita; see Table 3.3.
Source: Table 1.2.

year the South had experienced before that date. Cotton output in 1859 was 25 percent higher than in the previous year, which in turn was 17 percent above the previously recorded high in 1855. The cotton crop in 1859 was 31.3 percent above a simple trend line extrapolating the annual crop production recorded between 1849 and 1858.[8] One could argue from this that our 1859 estimate of output per effective worker exaggerates labor productivity in a typical antebellum year by as much as 25 to 30 percent.[9] If so, the decline in the product of labor per capita should be revised downward even further. If our minimum estimate of the decline in labor supply is accepted, the fall in productivity after this adjustment is reduced to only 4.7 to 8.4 percent. If the labor decline was as much as 37.2 percent (our high estimate), it seems quite possible that there was no decline at all in the productivity per man-hour of black agricultural labor following the Civil War. Our calculations suggest an increase of between 4.6 and 8.8 percent.[10]

The potential for economic development

More central to our concern than the improvements in economic welfare and productivity that accompanied emancipation, and also more relevant to the concerns of the freedmen themselves, was the potential provided by emancipation for continued economic development. An appraisal of the South in 1865 from the perspective of modern-day economic theory seems to justify optimism on the part of the ex-slaves as well as their former masters. The region possessed all the requisite conditions for rapid economic growth over the subsequent decades. There was an abundance of both improved and virgin land, and a rural population of 4 million whites and free blacks provided an agricultural labor force.[11] Despite the loss of life and the physical damage of the war, the South retained both its supply of labor and its heritage of market institutions that had allowed the plantation economy to prosper before the Civil War. These positive conditions for growth were reinforced by the rapid expansion of the rest of the American economy in the postwar era.

Before the war, white southerners advanced themselves economically through the acquisition of farmland; by obtaining management positions in farming, business, and commerce; by organizing their own businesses; or by obtaining the education necessary to practice professions. Once free, blacks hoped for the same. For a very few, emancipation did bring considerable gains in a reasonably short time. A few black spokesmen gained political office, and a select few achieved prominence as lawyers, educators, and businessmen. Less spectacular examples of early success were those ex-slaves who, through a combination of good fortune, hard work, and frequently an assist from the Union military government, acquired title to farmland and became successful farmers. Larger numbers secured at least some degree of independence and managerial responsibility in the early postwar years by agreeing to become tenant farm operators for white landlords. While these families had not realized their hope of landownership, the freedom associated with the operation of a family farm seemed enormous compared with the regimentation under slavery. Additionally, some of the blacks who had been fortunate enough to acquire artisan skills as slaves managed, once free, to pursue their trades as independent craftsmen.

The success some blacks had in securing the fruits of their freedom provides a measure of the potential that was the basis for hope on the part of all blacks. Unfortunately, for the vast majority of freed slaves, those who had toiled most of their lives as field hands on a plantation, such opportunities never materialized. Emancipation offered the slaves the right to buy land for the first time, but it provided no money with which to purchase it. Apart from the handful who were given farms in the early years of Reconstruction, the promise of land for freedmen proved illusory. Unable to acquire land, blacks still hoped for an opportunity to acquire education. Yet the rewards for those who did overcome the opposition of whites and attend public school proved small. As the balance of the nineteenth century unfolded, the actual progress of American blacks was agonizingly slow, particularly in the eyes of those who had hoped for so much.

The failure of American blacks to make more rapid progress was part of a larger failure – that of the southern economy to grow and develop during the forty-year period following the Civil War. For the balance of the century the ex-slaves and their descendants remained in the South and they remained in agriculture. Yet southern agriculture stagnated. There was little advance in productivity; there were no improvements in technology. Southern industry fared somewhat better, but it remained a small sector on the periphery of the agrarian economy. As a result, per capita incomes in the Cotton South barely changed between 1880 and 1900. According to the estimates of Richard Easterlin (the only regional income estimates we have), they grew at less than 1 percent per year.[12]

Without economic growth no group can advance its position except at the expense of other groups. In the late nineteenth century ex-slaves were in no position to demand a larger share of the South's economic output, and southern whites were certainly unwilling to see their own positions deteriorate further to benefit the blacks. Per capita output had already fallen sharply with the Civil War, and, as we have seen, the material incomes of blacks had actually increased. Whites had therefore borne the full brunt of that loss.

The record of economic growth

There is no doubt that agricultural production per capita immediately following the war was significantly below the standards achieved during the prosperous years of the 1850s. We have constructed an index of crop output deflated by the rural population for each year from 1866 to 1900, which we present in Figure 1.2. These annual estimates include the production of all major crops in the Five Cotton States of South Carolina, Georgia, Alabama, Mississippi, and Louisiana. Table 1.4 presents three-year averages of per capita crop output centered on the census years of 1869 through 1899, together with a single-year estimate for 1859. In both the figure and the table, the estimates are evaluated at constant (1899–1908) prices to remove the effects of price changes over the period.

The initial fall in production relative to the pre-Civil War standard of 1859 is apparent from the per capita measures. In 1866, the first postwar year for which we have estimates, the value of per capita crop output was only 29.8 percent of the 1859 level. Per capita output rebounded sharply from this prewar low and expanded steadily until it reached approximately 57 percent of the 1859 level in the early 1870s. It is likely that this resurgence represented a full recovery to parity with prewar levels of labor productivity. It will be recalled that two factors would have precluded a return to the level of per capita output of 1859. First, the 1859 standard reflected a physical productivity that was as much as 25 to 30 percent above yields that might be considered typical of the late antebellum era. Second, the decline in the supply of black labor would by itself reduce per capita output by as much as 26 percent.[13] The combined impact of these two effects suggests that an output level of 57 to 59 percent of the prewar level could be considered as the postwar equivalent of antebellum productivity.

After the initial recovery, only slow progress was recorded. As late as 1878–1880, per capita crop output was only 63.5 percent of the 1859 level. By the turn of the century, per capita production had reached three-fourths of the level achieved in 1859; but, as the data in Table 1.4 reveal, the annual

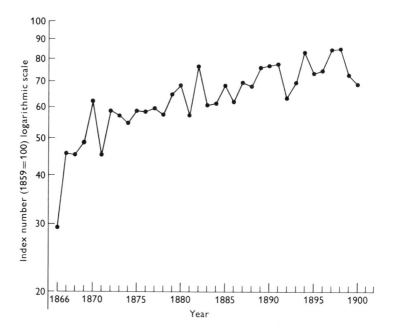

Figure 1.2 Index of physical crop output per capita, Five Cotton States: 1866–1900 (1859= 100). (*Source:* Appendix F, Table F.3.)

Table 1.4. *Estimates of per capita crop output and its rate of growth, by decades, Five Cotton States: 1859–1900.*

| Year(s) | Physical crop output per capita[a] | | Annual growth rate (%) |
	1899–1908 Prices ($)	Index (1859=100)	
1859	71.39	100.0	
			−6.3
1868–1870	37.14	52.0	
			2.0
1878–1880	45.33	63.5	
			1.4
1888–1890	52.33	73.3	
			0.3
1898–1900	53.73	75.3	

[a] Population used to deflate crop output includes only rural population; see Appendix F, Table F.2.

Source: Appendix F, Table F.3.

rate of growth in per capita crop output fell in each of the last three decades of the nineteenth century. During the 1870s, growth of output averaged 2.0 percent per year; in the 1880s it was 1.4 percent; and in the 1890s it was virtually at a standstill, 0.3 percent per year.[14]

Black southerners were less fortunate than even the unimpressive record of southern agricultural progress during this period might first suggest. Based on our sample of 4,695 farms from the Cotton South drawn from the manuscript records of the 1880 Census of Agriculture, we estimate that in 1879 black-operated farms produced only 62 percent as much output as white-operated farms. Yet the black farmer had to support an average family of 5.6 individuals, while white farm families had an average of 5.1 members. The published returns of the 1900 Census of Agriculture indicate that black-operated farms in the Five Cotton States were still in 1899 producing only 62 percent as much output as white-operated farms.[15] The progress made by black farmers had been no greater over those twenty years than that made by whites; their relative position was unchanged. Since agricultural output per capita for the Five Cotton States grew at only 0.56 percent per year between 1879 and 1899, the income of black farmers could hardly have grown much faster.[16]

Apparently the cotton economy failed to provide blacks with an opportunity to make additional headway after the first gains from freedom. In 1900 the black people of the Cotton South still depended upon farming for their livelihood.[17] Evidence on housing conditions for black farmers in the cotton belt at the turn of the century suggests that although the ex-slaves and their decendants had more space than their parents had been given on the antebellum plantation, the quality of housing was not much better. A study for the U.S. Department of Agriculture by W. O. Atwater and Charles D. Woods reported that in 1895–1896 around the Tuskegee region of Alabama

practically all the negroes live in cabins, generally built of logs, with only one, or at most two rooms. The spaces between the logs were either left open, admitting free passage of the wind in winter as well as in summer, or were chinked with earth or occasionally with pieces of board. The roofs were covered with coarse shingles or boards and were apt to be far from tight. The windows had no sash or glass, but instead, wooden blinds, which were kept open in all weather to admit the light.[18]

Though the diet was probably a bit more varied than the rations of slaves forty years earlier, it still consisted primarily of corn and pork. Summarizing the findings of their detailed dietary studies, Atwater and Woods concluded that "the field laborer was both underfed and overfed, since the food contained too little protein and too much fuel value."[19] The dietary studies indicated that working members of tenant farm families fared even less well than did hired field laborers. Their diets were more imbalanced, and they included fewer calories.[20] Cooking habits of black families did little to improve the nutritional value of their food. The Department of Agriculture study reported:

The daily fare is prepared in very simple ways. Corn meal is mixed with water and baked on the flat surface of a hoe or griddle. The salt pork is sliced thin and fried until very brown and much of the grease tried out. Molasses from cane or sorghum is added to the fat, making what is known as "sap," which is eaten with the corn bread. Hot water sweetened with molasses is used as a beverage. This is the bill of fare of most of the cabins on the plantations of the "black belt," three times a day during the year.[21]

These descriptions of conditions at the end of the nineteenth century suggest the lack of any substantial progress for blacks beyond the initial gains of emancipation. Of course, the black farmer of 1900 was better off than an antebellum slave. He achieved a higher material standard of living with less work effort than was required of a slave, and he enjoyed the privilege of spending his income as he pleased. Yet that privilege was obviously constrained by the poverty of southern agriculture. Carl Kelsey presents several lists of the incidental purchases made by typical black families in the central cotton belt that show an average expenditure of less than $5 per family member on clothing, tobacco (considered, according to Kelsey, a "necessity"), and other "cash items." Excluding clothing, the annual amount spent ranged from $1.09 to $4.48 per family member.[22]

The institutional constraints to progress

It might be argued that the hopes for a rapid rise from slavery were extravagant and unrealistic from the beginning. Before the Civil War the rate of economic growth in southern agriculture lagged behind the pace established by the rapidly industrializing northeastern economy. Perhaps the postwar stagnation was merely a continuation of the prewar trends. Although the data are rather crude, income estimates for 1840 and 1860, based upon the work of Richard Easterlin, suggest that agricultural output per worker only grew at between 0.40 and 0.48 percent per year in the South. At the same time, the average per capita income in the Northeast grew at 1.7 percent, and in the West, at 1.6 percent.[23] On the other hand, historians have generally suggested that the lagging economic progress of the antebellum South is attributable to the retarding influence of slavery.[24] Once unfettered, the South might presumably have fashioned superior and more modern institutions. Certainly that was the basis for many of the hopes expressed after emancipation.

In fact, as we shall show, institutional change and reorganization did come to the South, and they came with remarkable swiftness. The new institutions did not require generations to develop; the structure of the postemancipation economy was established well within the decade following the Civil War. The root of the problem was not, therefore, that the transition from slavery to freedom necessarily took time, but that the institutions established after the war effectively prevented the blacks from progressing beyond the first step taken with emancipation.

The financial and marketing intermediaries so crucial to staple agriculture were destroyed by war and the collapse of the Confederate government. As they struggled to regain their footing in the years following, these intermediaries were confronted with the problem of dealing with hundreds of thousands of small farms. The old system proved unable to cope with this situation, and a new system evolved. Small rural merchants scattered throughout the South advanced supplies to the cotton farmers on loans secured by the forthcoming crop. But the new arrangement had a serious drawback. Merchants quickly gained a position of considerable monopoly power within a small radius of their stores. This power allowed them to extract a monopoly return on the credit they advanced their customers, as well as to force the small farmer to concentrate on the production of cotton at the expense of food production.

The fact that emancipation was unaccompanied by a redistribution of land meant that a large landless class of free laborers came into being. When it became apparent that the plantation gang-labor system could no longer work using free labor, cultivation was continued by tenant farmers working small-sized one-family farms they did not own. By itself, this development might not have proved a serious obstacle to recovery and subsequent growth. However, in the context of reorganized credit institutions and widespread illiteracy among southern farm operators, the prevalence of tenancy did impede southern agricultural progress.

The difficulties posed by adjustment to a monopoly over credit and a detrimental system of land tenure faced all farmers in the Cotton South. For blacks, the impact of these factors was magnified by their inauspicious legacy from slavery, their position in postbellum society, and the racial barriers erected against them by white southerners. The ex-slaves were thrown into a market environment with which, for the most part, they had had no contact as slaves. Without an endowment of land, capital, or specialized skills, blacks sought to establish their credit in a market controlled by monopolists who refused to accept the possibility that black farmers could be as successful as whites. Seeking to gain title to the land and access to the education they needed for economic advancement, blacks encountered the unyielding and frequently violent hostility of whites who tried to deny them both.

The success blacks were able to achieve in the face of such odds is testimony to the effort they made to become free and equal Americans. That the gains were so small and the successes so few can be attributed to the failure of the southern economy to develop a set of institutional arrangements that might have allowed the freed slaves to participate fully in American society.

CHAPTER 2

THE LEGACY OF SLAVERY

> We have turned or are about to turn loose four million slaves without a hut to shelter them or a cent in their pockets. The diabolical laws of slavery have prevented them from acquiring an education, understanding the commonest laws of contract, or of managing the ordinary business of life.
>
> > Thaddeus Stevens, Congressman from Pennsylvania, speech to the House of Representatives, December 18, 1865. Quoted in James G. Blaine, *Twenty Years of Congress* (Norwich: Henry Bill, 1886), 2, p. 129.

Defenders of black slavery in the United States claimed that Afro-Americans gained much from being enslaved under the "civilizing" influence of the "advanced" society of whites. "No fact is plainer," claimed Albert Taylor Bledsoe in 1856, "than that the blacks have been elevated and improved by their servitude in this country. We can not possibly conceive, indeed, how Divine Providence could have placed them in a better school of correction."[1] In the eyes of these apologists, slavery in the southern states was an "apprenticeship" that could prepare the blacks for freedom. "The truth is," asserted Chancellor Harper in the 1840s,

that supposing that they are shortly to be emancipated, and that they have the capacities of any other race, they are undergoing the very best education which it is possible to give. They are in the course of being taught habits of regular and patient industry, and this is the first lesson which is required.[2]

It is easy to dismiss these arguments as the blatantly racist rhetoric of southern slaveholders or to ridicule their logic by pointing out that American slavery was an "apprenticeship" for life, not a "preparation" for freedom. Nonetheless, freedom did come to all black Americans in 1865, and well prepared or not, the ex-slaves entered the economic life of the South. There remains, then, a point in this defense of slavery that is crucial to an understanding of the impact of emancipation. Did American slavery provide the slave with, or did it deprive him of, skills and knowledge that might be usefully applied in the free economy that was to come?

Notes to Chapter 2 appear on pages 319–323.

We shall argue that slavery proved a poor preparation for freedom. The slave had never negotiated a contract, borrowed on credit, determined the crop mix, marketed a cotton crop, or read an agricultural journal. Slaves were universally illiterate and without the benefit of formal education. They typically possessed no skills beyond those of a field hand. They entered life as free workers without possession of land or assets of any kind. Indeed, it is difficult to imagine an apprenticeship less valuable or a legacy less auspicious than that of American slavery.

Slave literacy

Formal education for slaves was almost nonexistent. In most slave states it was actually illegal to educate a slave. Apparently such laws were passed in the 1820s and 1830s in the belief that an illiterate slave population would be more docile and less subject to revolt. The fear of black education had been intensified by the fact that the leaders of several famous insurrections and conspiracies were, in fact, literate. Denmark Vesey was a free Negro whose role in the 1822 plot in Charleston was apparently inspired by his reading of abolitionist literature. Nat Turner was also literate, and it was claimed, though never proved, that he was inspired by the writings of David Walker, another educated slave. Historian Richard Wade reports that the Charleston City Council, four years after the Vesey episode, wrote that the ability to read and write would enable slaves "to carry on illicit traffic, to communicate privately among themselves, and to evade those regulations that are intended to prevent confederation among them."[3]

There are no tabulations of slave literacy from the antebellum period. Contemporaries suggest that in the countryside illiteracy was universal among the slaves. Only in the cities were educated slaves observed, and it is doubtful that even there the proportion was very high.[4] Probably no more than 2 to 5 percent of adolescent and adult slaves could read and write on the eve of the Civil War, and those were largely self-educated.[5] In 1870, after emancipation, less than 10 percent of blacks over the age of twenty could read and write in the Five Cotton States. By contrast, over 80 percent of adult whites in those states were literate.[6] Slaves were typically unable to read or write; it goes almost without saying that they were also without formal education in arithmetic, science, and the classical humanities.

Slave occupations

It is clear that occupational training was also systematically denied rural slaves. There is enough evidence to conclude that only about 6 percent of adult male slaves held occupations above those of agricultural worker, unskilled laborer, or house servant. By contrast, 24.5 percent of free white males were employed as skilled artisans or professionals or were engaged in commercial or managerial activities. Based on a sample of 1,422 gainfully occupied slaves from predominately rural counties in South Carolina, Geor-

Table 2.1. *Estimated occupational distribution of males, slave and white, rural districts, Five Cotton States: 1860*

| | Percent in each occupation class | |
| | Rural slave population | Rural white population |
Occupation[a]		
Agriculture	88.7	70.8
Field hand	88.5	11.6
Driver, overseer	0.2	4.3
Farm operator	0.0	54.9
Service	2.9	0.0
Unskilled labor	2.8	4.8
Artisan	5.6	7.5
Blacksmith	2.0	0.4
Carpenter	1.9	3.3
Other	1.7	3.7
Managerial, commercial	0.0	9.8
Professional	0.0	7.2
Total gainfully occupied	100.0	100.0

[a] See Appendix B for a precise definition of occupations and a description of the estimation procedure.

gia, and Louisiana, we have estimated the occupational distribution of slaves for the Five Cotton States presented in Table 2.1.[7] When these figures are contrasted to those for white males in the same counties of the South, the differences are striking. No slaves held professional occupations. None were doctors, lawyers, or manufacturers. No slaves were engaged in commercial occupations. There were no slave peddlers, merchants, bookkeepers, or clerks. The absence of slaves in these occupations is clearly related to the high levels of formal education required. But absence of formal education does not preclude the possibility that the slave might be taught some specific skill. Even in the industrial North illiterate workers could function at many jobs as effectively as literate workers.[8] Despite this possibility, only 5.6 percent of the male slaves represented in Table 2.1 possessed artisan skills, and these were primarily plantation crafts such as carpentry and blacksmithing. More than two-thirds of the black artisans fell into these two categories. The situation among slave males was dismal enough; the occupational distribution of slave women was even less open. Virtually no slave women held jobs beyond those of field hand or servant.

Education and training of slaves

The facts of the case are clear enough. What is difficult to understand is why slavery should have produced a laboring class so bereft of formal education and advanced skills. Slavery was a system that vested the ownership of one person's labor in another. Yet it is not immediately obvious why this arrangement should have inhibited formal education or training for the slaves. Why did not slavery lead to the exploitation of the blacks' talents as well as their brawn?

It was not the laws against teaching slaves to read and write that made literacy among slaves so rare. It is difficult to believe that laws prohibiting education of slaves would have been enacted and enforced had the slaveowners perceived substantial gains from such activity. There is no evidence that slaveholders vigorously protested these laws or that the laws were enforced against masters who deliberately chose to educate their slaves.[9] We feel these laws ought to be viewed as evidence of the owners' economic disinterest in education, rather than as an explanation of slave illiteracy.

Nor was it the blacks' disinterest in education that explains the low level of slave literacy. To the extent that slaves had a desire to see themselves or their children acquire education or special skills, they needed the assistance, or at least the acquiescence, of their master. On a typical plantation only a rudimentary education could have been obtained clandestinely. Apparently a good deal of such secret activity took place, but the low incidence of literacy among slaves indicates that very little progress in black education was achieved in this way.[10] It was essentially the master's unwillingness to allow education to interfere with the daily work routine that was the true explanation for this failure.

The master was unwilling to invest the time of his slaves in their education because of the small size of the productivity gain to be expected from the education of field hands. A productive field hand was one who worked diligently, hard, and long at hoeing or picking cotton, not one who could read or make management decisions. While an educated, literate field hand might be more productive than an illiterate one, the difference was likely to be small and far outweighed by the costs of providing the requisite education.[11] In fact, the costs of educating slaves were high. Slave children were put to work at a very young age, usually between six and twelve.[12] Education would detract from this work effort and lower the immediate return to the child's owner. The loss of earnings to the slaveowner would have to be justified by the prospect of increased productivity during the working years.

Two objections might be raised to this line of argument. First, it should apply with the same force to free unskilled workers as to slave unskilled workers. If there were low returns to literacy, why did the free workers of the nineteenth century attain such high levels of education? The second objection questions why the slaveowner viewed all his slaves as field hands. Why could he not envision greater potential for at least some of his slaves? Both these questions have essentially the same answer: there was an important distinction between the perspective on education held by free workers on the one hand and by slaveowners on the other. We see three separate elements to account for this distinction.

The free person who was a field laborer could aspire to a better occupation (no matter that his chance of actually obtaining one might have been slim), or he could hope that his children might achieve a higher status for themselves. Because the surest way of rising above the level of the common laborer in the free enterprise economy of nineteenth-century America seemed to be through education, the benefits of literacy to a free worker went well beyond the productivity gains obtainable in agricultural field work. Upward mobility in the labor force – the basis of the American Dream – provided a constant impetus for education of free children. Not so for the American slave. He and his family could not afford such aspirations or such dreams; his master made all such decisions for him.

To the extent that the slaveowner did invest in slave education, he was apt to be selective in his choice of candidates and specific trades to be taught. To the best of his ability, he would attempt to distinguish those who had aptitude from those who did not. As a profit maximizer, he would seek to be as objective as possible. Individuals find such objectivity more difficult when evaluating their own talents. They would also view the risk of failure differently. Individuals value the *opportunity* to succeed in and of itself; slaveowners would calculate only the expected outcome. A slave's death, for example, might deny a slaveowner the return to his investment, and therefore the master should weigh the risk of such an occurrence before educating his slave. The free person, too, might die before reaping the full benefits of his education, but from his own perspective, the threat of death, while ever present, would be no reason to stint his own future.

Finally, the returns to education are also said to include nonpecuniary benefits. The ability to read and write has benefits unrelated to economic productivity. The educated man is more cultivated, less afraid of the world, and more confident in his ability to adjust to changes within it. The educated man is said to be happier. While such gains might have great appeal to an individual, even a slave, a slaveowner would have little interest in such nonpecuniary gains and would seldom be willing to finance their acquisition. In fact, these benefits of education were a liability in the eyes of white slaveholders, who felt that educated slaves would prove more difficult to control.

The free worker, in short, saw returns to education that did not interest the owner of slaves. The slaveholder saw no reason for providing the potential to take up opportunities he did not intend to give his slaves; he was inclined to take an objective, actuarial view of the probability of failure and death; and he had little reason to value (and some reason to fear) the psychological benefits of education. By contrast, free workers had a greater demand for education than would be warranted by a simple dollars-and-cents calculation. They accordingly invested – some might say overinvested – in education for themselves and their children beyond what could be justified by the expected rate of return.

This tendency of the free worker to invest in education beyond the point that would be considered optimal by a businessman is the real explanation for the failure of slaveowners to educate their slaves. Because free individuals perceived benefits to education that went beyond those seen by slaveowners, educated free workers were in abundant supply. They could, as a result, be hired for wages that were not sufficiently greater than the pay of an unskilled worker to justify the time and expense they had invested in their own education. On the plantation, only a small number of literate managers and artisans was needed, and they could be hired from the free population more cheaply than a slave could be educated to provide such services.[13]

These arguments apply, we feel, with great force to the issue of formal education of slaves. But literacy was not the only skill that could be obtained less expensively from the free labor market. A slaveowner would find little incentive to train slaves in specialized artisan skills that would compete with those of free labor, since the costs of training would usually not be repaid by the expected increase in the income generated by the slave's labor. As we have noted, the only apparent exception to the denial of education and training for slaves was in the case of plantation crafts such as blacksmithing and carpentry. In the plantation environment, the cost of training such craftsmen was reduced by the fact that such training could be accomplished on the job. Moreover, a field hand who had attained the skills of a carpenter or a blacksmith would have an advantage over his free competitor whenever his owner found it unnecessary to have a full-time skilled artisan on his plantation. It is unlikely that white artisans would be willing to do field work when there was no need for their special skills. Yet the status of slave field hands who had learned a craft was not so high that they could object to working in the fields.[14]

The slave work ethic

If the legacy of "human capital" (that is, education, literacy, and skills) left by slavery was marginal, the legacy of physical capital left to blacks was nonexistent.

At the time of his emancipation, the freedman had none of the capital requisites for agriculture. He did not own land, work stock, or farming implements. Set free without human or physical capital, the black nevertheless had one possession he could rely upon to provide income for himself and his family and over which he had a virtual monopoly in the agricultural South. This was his labor.

This asset was not, to be sure, a legacy of slavery; black labor had been forcibly imported from Africa generations before. However, southerners, in retrospect at least, held that those generations of slavery had taught the slave how to work and how to live. Seventeenth- and eighteenth-century Africans were viewed by nineteenth-century southerners as primitive savages, uncivilized, and undisciplined.[15] Two hundred and fifty years of slavery, it was argued, at least prepared the freedman for hard work and

predisposed him to social tranquillity. Hollis Burke Frissell, a prominent
southern educator, apparently thought this was the case. In Montgomery,
Alabama, in 1900 he said during a speech:

It is only fair to call attention to the part which the South performed in the education
of the barbarous people forced upon her. The Southern plantation was really a great
trade school where thousands received instruction in mechanic arts, in agriculture,
in cooking, sewing, and other domestic occupations. . . . The training which the
black had under slavery was far more valuable as a preparation for civilized life,
than the freedom from training and service enjoyed by the Indian on the Western
reservations. For while slavery taught the colored man to work, the reservation
pauperized the Indian with free rations; while slavery brought the black into the
closest relations with the white race and its way of life, the reservation shut the
Indian away from his white brothers and gave him little knowledge of their civilization, language or religion. As a consequence the Indian gains the habits of civilized
life much more slowly than the Negro.[16]

Frissell's suggestion that slavery imbued the slave with a work ethic
indispensable to success as a free laborer has recently reappeared in the
work of Robert Fogel and Stanley Engerman. These authors insist that the
American slave internalized the "Protestant work ethic." Slaves were
"diligent," "responsible," and "hardworking," "virtues" they presumably
carried with them into freedom.[17] Upon closer examination, however, Fogel
and Engerman's argument has been shown to amount to nothing more than
a curious interpretation of the well-known fact that slaves were worked
hard.[18]

There is no question that slaves worked hard; they were forced to. The
high level of slave productivity, the long hours of work demanded, the
amount of caloric energy supplied by their diet, descriptions of the work
gang, and the ever-present threat of physical punishment all testify to
that.[19] Contemporary descriptions of slave workers as "shirkers" and their
manner as "slow," "plodding," and "lazy" were obviously colored by racist prejudice. Nevertheless, they are not inconsistent with the fact that
slaves worked hard. As historians of slavery have emphasized, shirking
was one of the few expressions of "day-to-day resistance" and independence available to slaves who chose to strike out against their bondage.[20]
The reports that slaves were slow in movement, unenergetic, and prone to
fatigue, even if exaggerated, need not be incorrect. Such behavior would be
the natural outcome of long hours, backbreaking work, and a diet short of
the calories necessary to fuel both labor and leisure activities.

By modern standards the slave diet was enormous, providing over 4,000
calories per day to the adult field hand, but this was merely a reflection of
the amount of work extracted from him. The diet provided actually had
little food energy to spare after deducting reasonable allowances for the
calories required for work, sleep, and light personal activities.[21] If this is
so, then slaves, during the hours they were not forced to work hard, would
naturally appear to be "slow" and "plodding" in their movements. Paul

David and Peter Temin have suggested that the stinting of the diet may have proved economical from the master's point of view, who not only economized on food, but also "could have effected a saving of supervisory and police costs – without entailing much loss in routine work performance."[22]

There is, to repeat ourselves, no question that slaves worked hard. They worked hard, however, not because they internalized the Protestant work ethic, as maintained by Fogel and Engerman, but rather because they lived with the constant threat of physical punishment. This is not to deny the existence of a positive incentive system for slaves. Rewards of extra food, assignment to choice tasks, and even in some instances small amounts of cash were offered by planters to promote diligent labor.[23] However, the more powerful incentives that generally operate with free labor – the hope of economic advancement, the desire to excel in the eyes of fellow workers, the goal of providing a headstart for one's children or a retirement for one's self – were not generally characteristics of the slave economy.

This interpretation leaves open the possibility that slaves, who viewed shirking as a positive act and who were provided only a minimal standard of living irrespective of the amount or quality of the work performed, began their careers as freedmen without a positive work ethic. In other words, slaves might have internalized poor work habits that would seriously affect their productivity once free. This was apparently the belief of many plantation owners in 1865. "Labor can be extracted from the Negro only by compulsion" asserted the *Southern Cultivator* in that year.[24] Carl Schurz made a more systematic canvass of white opinion for his report to President Andrew Johnson:

In at least nineteen cases of twenty the reply I received to my inquiry about their views on the new system was uniformly this: "You cannot make the negro work without physical compulsion." I heard this hundreds of times, heard it wherever I went, heard it in nearly the same words from so many different persons, that at last I came to the conclusion that this is the prevailing sentiment among the southern people.[25]

Planters apparently were convinced that force would be required to make the freedmen work because its use was "required" when they were slaves. To them it appeared as a characteristic of the race, not of the economic system. Accordingly, they predicted a gloomy future for the blacks. "No longer protected by his subordinate position," said the *Southern Cultivator* of 1865, "his future course is downward."[26] The freedmen would "do precisely as all the race have done who have gone before them. They [will] sink down into idleness, filth, disease and death."[27]

Such fears were, fortunately, unwarranted. The ex-slaves did work hard and well. Peter Kolchin, in his careful study of the response of Alabama's blacks to emancipation, found that "to the astonishment and relief of whites, freedmen rushed to contract during the first few days of 1866 and then settled down to work."[28] Kolchin went on to quote a planter: "One thing is obvious, the negroes, who are hired are farming and working much better than anyone predicted they would work." A Freedmen's Bureau agent wrote his superior: "Planters say to me [']my negroes have never done so well as they are doing now[']." In 1867, the report was that "the freedmen, according to universal testimony, are working better than they did last year."[29] Joel Williamson's study of South Carolina produced similar conclusions.[30]

Of course, the first few years of experience with free labor were not without their disruptions, disputes, and disappointments (subjects we shall take up in later chapters), but these problems were not generally caused either by poor work habits on the part of the freedmen or by their belief that they would be provided for by others. On the other hand, freedmen worked hard, not because they had actually been imbued with the Protestant work ethic as slaves, but because of the powerful influence of self-interest. As General Wager Swayne, head of the Freedmen's Bureau in Alabama, remarked: "The true incentives to labor in the free States are hunger and cold."[31] In the first years of freedom it was enough for the ex-slaves to know that the product of their labor would be proportional to the effort they exerted for them to shed the work ethic of slavery and adopt the positive habits of free laborers. The freedmen were the beneficiaries of emancipation, not of slavery.

The legacy of slavery: racism

While the freed people were willing to work hard, their lack of capital, education, and experience was a severe obstacle to success. In the postbellum period, this obstacle was magnified by a legacy slavery had left, not to the ex-slave, but to the white southerner. This was a firmly entrenched, universally held, and passionately defended belief in the inherent inferiority of the black race. The doctrine of Negro inferiority had been one of the cornerstones for the "moral" justification of the enslavement of blacks propounded by the apologists for slavery, and once established, this racist belief had an insidious way of reinforcing itself. A slaveholder who was convinced that the black race did not have and could not develop the capacity to advance beyond that level already achieved with slavery would see no point in investigating the potential gains from allowing his slaves to educate themselves, acquire advanced skills, or work independently. He then viewed the absence of educated, skilled, and independent Negroes as *proof* that his belief in Negro inferiority was well founded. This circular reasoning was astutely noted by Benjamin Truman during his visit to the South in 1865: "Inheriting his slaves, and finding them always brutish, stupid, and slow of understanding, [the planter] committed the logical inaccuracy of preventing them from ever becoming anything else, and proceeded to argue that they never could become so."[32]

While the Thirteenth Amendment legally ended the South's "peculiar institution," and the southerners' acquiescence closed further debate on the question of slavery, a new and equally sensitive issue arose to take its place. The position of the ex-slave in the economic, social, political, and legal systems of the country had yet to be defined. While the southern white was willing to concede the black's freedom, he was – with rare exceptions – unwilling to concede his equality in any of these realms.[33] The freeing of the slaves did nothing to change the whites' opinion of the Negro. The doctrine of Negro inferiority infected every aspect of southern life in the postwar period. Arguing that blacks were incapable of benefiting from education, occupational skills, or managerial independence, whites resisted the freedmen's attempts to acquire them.

The tenacity with which the whites defended this illogical doctrine suggests a deeper motivation for placing barriers in the way of Negro economic advancement. If the blacks had been truly incapable of becoming educated or acquiring skills, white supremacists would have had little reason to oppose Negro schools. If the Negro had been truly incapable of independent farming, white supremacists would have had little reason to oppose landownership by blacks. But such was not the case. White opposition to both education and landownership reflected a strong undercurrent of fear. They feared economic competition from the blacks; they feared that their social position in southern society would be eroded by the existence of educated, independent, landowning blacks. They feared, in short, that the Negro might not prove to be inferior. These fears, above all else, created the racial animosity that became so important in the reshaping of the social and economic institutions of the South. The white southerner was dedicated to putting the black "in his place" and keeping him there. In 1865 the ex-slave's place was, unquestionably, to be in the cotton fields. Not in the schools. Not in the cities and towns.

Black education in the postwar period

The individual who must operate in a society where other citizens are literate is burdened with a crippling disadvantage when he is unable to read or write. This was exactly the position of the Negro in 1865. Slaves had been denied education as a matter of both principle and law. The importance of education to the future of the black race in America was apparent to all: the northerners interested in the Negro's progress, whites in the South, and most of all, the Afro-American himself. The blacks' enthusiastic desire for education was commented upon by observers throughout the South. The blacks, remarked one letter writer in 1865, "generally desire instruction, and many seize every opportunity in intervals of labor to obtain it. . . . Only an enthusiastic desire for improvement could lead any people to put forth the efforts which the freed people are making to procure instruction."[34] Whitelaw Reid declared:

Of the great masses of negroes whom we did see in May and June [1865], two general statements may be safely made:

They were as orderly, quiet, and industrious as any other class of the population; and,

They were far more eager than any others to secure the advantages of education for themselves, and especially for their children.[35]

Northerners were encouraged by this enthusiasm. "The most hopeful sign in the Negro was his anxiety to have his children educated," was the way one officer in the Freedmen's Bureau expressed an almost unanimous view of northern observers.[36]

Despite the eagerness of the ex-slaves to learn, the problems confronting Negro education were formidable. Nowhere in the South did a statewide system of public education exist before the Civil War. Except in a few of the large cities, public schools were unknown. The establishment of an extensive rural system of primary education necessary for any real and rapid improvement in black literacy would have been expensive and, in any case, was not of high priority to white legislators who sought to rebuild the South.

A few southern landowners did set up their own schools for the freedmen employed on their plantations. But from the outset, these efforts ran into strong opposition from the white community. An illustrative incident was related by James Atkins, of Henry County, Georgia, who described his father's attempt to establish such a school: "As soon as the war closed, or in 1865 or 1866, he built a school-house, and employed a colored man to teach. His neighbors, as respectable men as I know, burned the school-house, so that he had to abandon the project of having colored schools."[37] Such violence was seldom necessary, of course, to dissuade most southern planters from efforts like that of Atkins's father. The incident demonstrates, however, the extremes to which whites were willing to carry their opposition to black education.

This did not mean that freedmen were left without assistance in obtaining education. They were supported by a unique alliance between the Freedmen's Bureau and enthusiastic northerners, who organized themselves into societies dedicated to the "elevation of the Negro."[38] Such groups enlisted northern schoolteachers and provided funds for their salaries, while the Freedmen's Bureau undertook the construction of school facilities. As early as 1866 the Freedmen's Bureau reported 975 schools "regularly organized" under its supervision, with enrollments totaling about 90,000 black students. This figure ignores "many schools not regularly reported;" overall, the bureau estimated that "there are now 150,000 freedmen and their children who are earnestly occupied in the study of books."[39] By 1869 (the peak of the bureau's operation of schools in the South), 3,000 schools were run directly under the auspices of the bureau, with 150,000 students – adults as well as children – in the former slave states. In all, over 4,000 schools enrolling over 250,000 students were reporting to the bureau in 1869.[40]

This intense effort by the Freedmen's Bureau provoked a violent response from the southern whites. They viewed the schools as a double threat: not only were they educating the blacks, but the suspicion was widespread that the teachers were espousing the doctrine of racial equality. General Oliver O. Howard, director of the Freedmen's Bureau, characterized the way bureau teachers were received in the South:

It is difficult to describe the odium with which the excellent self-denying school teachers are met. Doubtless the treatment to which they are subjected arises in part from the feelings engendered by the war, but it is mostly due to prejudice against educating the blacks, and the belief that the teachers are fostering social equality.[41]

Moreover, unlike the southerners' experience with the privately established school, informal social pressure had no effect on the Freedmen's Bureau agent or the Yankee schoolteacher. Accordingly, schools operating under the auspices of the bureau were targets of numerous acts of violence.[42] Although the army stood ready to protect the schools, it frequently proved incapable in rural areas of providing sufficient security to the schoolteacher, who was both ostracized and threatened by a hostile white community. John A. Minnis, U.S. district attorney for northern Alabama, testified that "when reconstruction first took place, in most portions of the State where I was, it was dangerous to talk about even attempting to educate the negro at all. . . . They would hardly allow such a man as a teacher to go there. If he did he could not get board in a white man's house."[43]

Thus, while the number of schools established by the Freedmen's Bureau was impressive, the majority were located in towns, rather than in rural districts, where the bulk of the black population resided. Any attempt to expand the network of schools was effectively ruled out by the limited resources of the bureau, which were continually strained by the more urgent need to provide rations and protection to the destitute. The bureau did well with the resources at hand, but the task was enormous. The bureau superintendent for Alabama reported: "But little has been accomplished compared with the magnitude of the undertaking. It is safe to say that there are 100,000 children in the State who have never learned the alphabet nor been inside of a school house."[44] The most liberal estimates of enrollments suggest that only a small portion of the black population attended bureau schools. The enrollments reported for 1869 represented only about 7 percent of the school-age black population in the Five Cotton States.[45]

Most of the responsibilities of the Freedmen's Bureau were allowed by Congress to expire at the end of 1869. A limited effort was maintained in education, but by the end of the following year even this was abandoned. General Howard noted in his 1871 report: "The school funds having all been expended or promised previous to July, 1870, no new appropriations have been made. . . . To the numerous applications for help, I have been obliged to return only words of advice and encouragement."[46]

While direct federal support for education was limited and short-lived, it left a very important legacy in the South. The idea of free public schools had been planted in the minds of blacks and poor whites alike. Although both groups favored publicly supported schools in principle, the whites saw no benefits to themselves in education for the blacks. In many cases, they viewed black education as a distinct threat to their economic and social position. There were, of course, white southerners – primarily the educated and wealthy – who were willing to support the principle of universal education, including schools for blacks. But even they were opposed to an integrated system. Invariably the hostility and antagonism of the whites led to a de facto segregation of public schools.[47]

Segregating the public school system was not sufficient to quiet the objections of whites to general education for the Negro; there remained the problem of financing. By 1872 every southern state had established a state-financed and state-organized school system. Under these new state systems, the cost of providing education was met through property taxation. Since public education involved substantial expenditures, property taxes in the Reconstruction Period were substantially higher than those levied before the war. Predictably, the education tax became the target of bitter opposition.[48] Yet the taxes were apparently not the only issue. Witnesses familiar with the situation insisted that racist views formed the real objections to education for Negroes – not the level of taxes. The following exchange occurred between the Select Congressional Committee and a public school teacher from Chickasaw County, Mississippi.

Question. The great bulk of the property there [Chickasaw County] is held by the white people?

Answer. Yes, sir.

Question. Does not this school tax bear very heavily upon the people, this keeping up of two hundred schools, the machinery of school boards, and all that?

Answer. I never heard any one object to it because it was a burden to them, but because it was introduced there against their wishes. Every man I have talked to, who is opposed to the present system, says that it is cheaper for them than the private school system. . . .

Question. What ground of objection had they against it? You say they objected to it because it was put there against their will; was it not put there by the legislature of the State?

Answer. The ground of objection is this: Under this free-school system the colored people would be taught. If it was a private-school system, the whites would not teach colored schools, . . . They object to paying for the education of colored people, inasmuch as they do not believe in educating them; that is the majority do not.[49]

The landed classes were joined in their opposition to colored schools by the poor whites, who saw the Negro as a direct economic threat. The county superintendent of education for Perry County, Alabama, observed: "The uneducated white man, and the man who in his sphere of life is brought nearer to competition with the negro – that class of men are, in my opinion, opposed to the education of the negro."[50] The strength of these objections to black education was so great that whites did not hesitate to employ violence in an attempt to prevent the Negro from having schools. In counties throughout the South schools were burned and teachers threatened, whipped, beaten, and in some cases murdered. Sometimes these assaults were carried out by members of the Ku Klux Klan, which singled out black education as a particular target for their violence.[51] When a probate judge from Greensboro, Alabama, was asked what the sentiments of the people in his county were toward the establishment of Negro schools, he replied: "Well, sir, it meets with the bitterest opposition on the part of the people; as an evidence of it, a large number of the school-houses in Hale County have been burned down."[52]

There is no question that this violence succeeded in reducing the opportunity for blacks to attend school and substantially increased the risks for those who did. It is testimony to the importance the blacks placed upon education that Negro education was not completely extinguished. Scattered statistics, collected from state documents on enrollment in schools, are presented in Table 2.2 for four southern states between 1871 and 1880. The data indicate that a sizable proportion of the black school-age population was enrolled at that time and that the absolute level of enrollments increased substantially over the entire decade. Nevertheless, black enrollment would probably have been substantially higher had the freedmen been provided with more schools. Statistics in Table 2.3 reveal a great disparity in the number of schools provided for whites and blacks in the three states for which such data are available. In these states, the school-age black population was approximately equal to the school-age white population; yet in the data presented, white schools outnumbered those for blacks by more than two to one. The much higher ratio of children per school for blacks than for whites reflects this unequal provision of school facilities for black students.

There are few reliable data on expenditures for education disaggregated separately for white and black schools. Knight, in a study of education during Reconstruction, reported figures implying that the annual expenditures per student for teachers' salaries in black schools in North Carolina between 1871 and 1875 averaged about three-fourths of that spent per student for white teachers.[53] It is probably true that the black schools were distinctly inferior to those provided for whites. A public school teacher in Mississippi testified that colored schools were routinely assigned "third-class teachers," who were paid substantially less than the "first-class teachers" assigned to most white schools.[54] A black woman recalled her experience in a black school as follows: "When nigger chillun did get to go to school dey wasn't 'lowed to use de old blueback spellin' book 'cause white folks said it larn't them too much."[55]

Probably the best measure we have of the effectiveness of the educational effort of the southern schools is the statistics on literacy obtained from the census reports and presented in Table 2.4. It is apparent that only minimal progress had been made by the end of the Reconstruction period. In 1870,

Table 2.2. *Public school enrollment of blacks in four Cotton States: 1871–1880*

	Number of students	Enrollment as percent of school-age population[a]	Enrollment as percent of colored population 5–17[b]
South Carolina			
1871	33,834	27.0	23.2
1875	63,415	41.6	36.9
1880	72,853	43.4	34.5
Georgia			
1873	19,755	13.2	9.5
1874	42,374	24.2	19.8
1880	86,399	37.4	33.7
Alabama			
1871	54,336	33.7	32.8
1875	54,595	31.6	29.6
1880	72,007	42.3	34.1
Mississippi			
1871	45,429	n.a.	29.0
1875	89,813	50.8	48.2
1880	123,710	49.2	53.3

[a] The school-age population was estimated by the state reporting to the U.S. Commissioner of Education. The definition of school ages was given as: South Carolina, 6–16 years; Georgia, 6–18 years; Alabama, 5–21 years (7–21) for 1880); Mississippi; 5–21 years.

[b] The "colored" population includes Chinese and Indians as well as Negroes. The colored population 5–17 years old for each year was interpolated between census figures assuming a constant growth rate.

Source: U.S. Department of the Interior, "Report of U.S. Commissioner of Education," *Report of the Secretary of the Interior, 1880,* House of Representatives, Executive Document Number 1, 46th Congress, 3rd Session (Washington: GPO, 1882), 3, Part 5, pp. 4, 5, 58, 59, 178, 179, 290, 291. Georgia, Department of Education, *Report of the State School Commissioner of Georgia to the General Assembly [1877–1878]* (Atlanta: James P. Harrison & Co., 1881), p. 5. U.S. Census Office, Ninth Census [1870], *The Statistics of the Population of the United States* (Washington: GPO, 1872), p. 618. U.S. Census Office, Tenth Census [1880], *Statistics of the Population of the United States* (Washington: GPO, 1883), p. 646.

nearly 80 percent of black children aged ten to fourteen could neither read nor write, and the percentage was higher still among the fifteen- to twenty-year-old group. Ten years later the illiteracy rate in these age groups was still nearly 75 percent. Literacy among blacks was undoubtedly higher in the towns than in the rural districts, so we may safely conclude that in 1880 over three-quarters of the black children in rural districts were not learning to write. Because of the failure to educate the black children, illiteracy remained over 80 percent in the adult population in 1880, and over 75 percent as late as 1890. Such a failure is not surprising; all the actions by whites to resist black education tended to increase the implicit costs of

Table 2.3. *Public schools by race of students and number of children five to seventeen years old in Alabama, Georgia, and Mississippi: 1871, 1873*

State, year	Whites			Blacks		
	Number of public schools	Number of children aged 5–17	Number of children per school	Number of public schools	Number of children aged 5–17	Number of children per school
Alabama, 1871	2,399	184,441	76.9	922	165,601	179.6
Mississippi, 1871	1,742	131,570	75.5	860	156,424	181.9
Georgia, 1873	1,392	228,866	164.4	360	207,167	575.5

Source: Number of public schools for Alabama and Georgia is from U.S. Department of the Interior, "Report of the U.S. Commissioner of Education," *Report of the Secretary of the Interior, 1880*, House of Representatives, Executive Document Number 1, 46th Congress, 3rd Session (Washington: GPO, 1882), 3, Part 5, pp. 4, 5, 58, 59; the Mississippi figure is from Vernon Lane Wharton, *The Negro in Mississippi, 1865–1890* (New York: Harper & Row, 1965), p. 246, originally published in 1947. The number of children aged 5 to 17 was interpolated from census figures (see Table 2.2).

Table 2.4. *Percent of persons unable to write, by race and age group, Five Cotton States: 1870, 1880, 1890*

Age and race[a]	1870	1880	1890
10–14 years			
Colored	78.9	74.1	49.2
White	33.2	34.5	18.7
15–20 years[b]			
Colored	85.3	73.0	54.1
White	24.2	21.0	14.3
Over 20 years			
Colored	90.4	82.3	75.5
White	19.8	17.9	17.1

[a] "Colored" includes Chinese and Indians as well as Negroes; "white" includes both native and foreign-born whites.   [b] Illiteracy in 1890 is given for ages 15–19 and over 19, rather than 15–20 and over 20.
Source: U.S. Census Office, Ninth Census [1870], *The Statistics of the Population of the United States* (Washington: GPO, 1872), pp. 396–397, 560–567. Idem, The Vital Statistics of the United States (Washington: GPO, 1872), pp. 608–612. U.S. Census Office, Tenth Census [1880], *Statistics of the Population of the United States* (Washington: GPO, 1883), pp. 919–925. U.S. Census Office, Eleventh Census [1890], *Report on the Population of the United States* (Washington: GPO, 1895), Part 1, pp. 104–113, 204–219.

schooling. Coercion and outright terror meant danger to students and teachers alike. The smaller number of schools and their absence in some rural districts meant that many students had to travel long distances to attend school. Finally, the inferior quality of the black schools must have discouraged many a potential young scholar. The inevitable outcome was the gradual extinction of the blacks' once fervent desire for schooling. As early as 1871 an observer remarked on this effect: "I cannot say that the negroes are quite so keen for education as they were. The discouragements they have met with have caused them, to some extent, to abandon the idea of getting an education."[56] The effect of racism, then, had caused the costs of schooling for blacks to increase – both directly and indirectly. As a result, only one-quarter of black children in 1880 had received enough education to be able to write. While racial prejudice is by no means the sole explanation for this failure, it must certainly have been a dominating force in the extinction of black enthusiasm for education.

The precise impact an inadequate investment in education would have on agricultural productivity – and hence on the economic welfare of the black – is difficult to assess. However, even if literacy were irrelevant to the level of agricultural output, it cannot be denied that the inability to read and write would severely limit an individual's opportunities outside the agricultural sector. Quite apart from the fact that many nonagricultural jobs presupposed an ability to read and write, the illiterate farmer would be less likely to learn of job opportunities for which he did qualify. Illiteracy, if it did nothing else, helped to trap the black farmer in southern agriculture.

The black artisan and professional in the postwar period

One potential escape from an agrarian future existed for those few ex-slaves fortunate enough to have been trained in slavery as skilled artisans. Throughout the South there were black carpenters, blacksmiths, masons, and painters who established themselves following emancipation. But, as indicated in Tables 2.5 and 2.6, their numbers were small. In the rural dis-

Table 2.5. *Occupations reported by black males, selected rural areas, Five Cotton States: 1870*

Occupation	Number	Percent
Farmer[a]	151	5.7
Farm laborer[a]	1,997	75.6
Laborer[b]	392	14.8
Servant	29	1.1
Other unskilled	31	1.2
Lumberman	10[c]	
Railroad hand	7	
Teamster/drayman	4	
Worker in grist mill	3	
Boatman	2	
Other[d]	5	
Artisan[e]	39	1.5
Carpenter	18	
Blacksmith	6	
Shoemaker	4	
Miller	2	
Tanner	2	
Basket maker	2	
Other	5	
Other skilled[g]	3	0.1
Total	2,642	100.0

[a] The census enumerators did not make a careful distinction between farmers and farm workers. They recorded the occupational description given them by the respondents. See Chapters 4 and 5 for a discussion of black farm tenure and farm labor. [b] It is likely that some farm laborers were recorded as simply "laborers" or "day laborers." [c] Includes "getting timber for railroad" (7) in Taylor, Ga. [d] Includes ditcher (1), "works in blacksmith shop" (1), "works in tannery" (2), and "works in shoeshop" (1). [e] Includes apprentice artisans. [f] Includes 1 each: cooper, wheelwright, sawyer, steam engineer, and butcher. [g] Includes 1 each: minister, clerk in store, and gardener.
Source: Manuscript Census of Population, 1870. See Appendix B.

Table 2.6. *Occupations reported by black males, six selected towns: 1870*

Occupation	Selma, Dallas County, Alabama	Thomasville, Thomas County, Georgia	Newnan, Coweta County, Georgia	Cahawba, Dallas County, Alabama	Kosciusko, Attala County, Mississippi	Bastrop, Morehouse Parish, Louisiana
Farmer[a]	7	—	—	—	13	—
Farm laborer[a]	59	50	102	45	8	—
Laborer[b]	314	43	17	13	4	8
Servant	120	10	35	9	—	11
Other unskilled	172	73	31	2	5	1
Drayman, teamster	71	12	4	—	4	1
Porter	40	3	1	—	—	—
Waiter	29	4	5	—	—	—
Railroad hand	—	27	6	—	—	—
Worker in						
Blacksmith shop	5	5	5	—	1	—
Boot and shoe shop	2	5	2	—	—	—
Iron foundry	6	—	—	—	—	—
Other mills and shops[c]	13	7	5	—	—	—
Digger, ditcher[d]	3	7	—	—	—	—
Miscellaneous[e]	3	3	3	2	—	—
Artisan[f]	240	58	28	2	6	1
Carpenter	96	32	10	—	4	1
Blacksmith	24	8	7	—	2	—
Mason	19	2	—	—	—	—
Painter	17	4	3	—	—	—
Boot and shoemaker	11	4	4	—	—	—
Barber	14	—	2	1	—	—
Plasterer	8	—	—	—	—	—
Baker	4	—	—	—	—	—
Butcher	3	1	—	—	—	—

Railroad worker						
Fireman	17	—	—	—	—	—
Brakeman	7	—	—	—	—	—
Engineer	5	—	—	—	—	—
Other[g]	15	7	2	1	—	—
Commercial	45	17	7	1	—	—
Hotel, saloon, restaurant						
Keeper	12	—	—	—	—	—
Cook	11	1	4	—	—	—
Grocer[h]	10	—	—	—	—	—
Clerk	2	9	1	—	—	—
Huckster	4	—	1	—	—	—
Hostler[i]	1	2	1	1	—	—
Watchman	2	1	—	—	—	—
Cotton sampler	3	—	—	—	—	—
Public gardener	—	4	—	—	—	—
Professional	13	5	2	4	1	—
Minister	5	3	—	1	—	—
Policeman	5	—	—	—	—	—
Schoolteacher	1	1	2	1	1	—
Nurse[j]	1·	1·	—	1	—	—
Bookkeeper	1	—	—	—	—	—
Clerk of courts	1	—	—	—	—	—
Postmaster	—	—	—	1	—	—
Total gainfully occupied	970	256	222	76	37	21
Total population	6,484	1,651	1,917	431	577	521
Total black population	3,660	985	847	302	183	139

Notes to Table 2.6 appear on page 34.

tricts only 1.5 percent of gainfully occupied black males were professional artisans in 1870. A sample of 2,642 employed black men, drawn from the manuscript 1870 Census returns from the rural districts of thirteen counties, is reported in Table 2.5. Over 81 percent were farmers or farm laborers, and another 17.1 percent were day laborers, servants, or unskilled workers.[57]

On the other hand, these rural districts were not the place to find black artisans in 1870, as our tabulation of the occupations of the employed black male population of six Cotton South towns (Table 2.6) makes clear. Selma, Alabama, the eighth largest town in the Cotton South, had 24.7 percent of her 970 black male workers recorded as artisans in 1870. (The average for all six cities taken together is 21.2 percent. If other skilled workers, including professionals, are added, the percentage rises to 27.2.) However, only 9.9 percent of the black population of the Five Cotton States resided in cities and towns in 1870.[58] It would seem, therefore, that no more than 3.5 percent of black males managed to pursue the occupation of a skilled artisan.[59] This is only two-thirds of the proportion we estimated for male slaves in rural districts in 1860 (see Table 2.1).

The explanation of this apparent disappearance of black skills is not clear. Joel Williamson has suggested that whites would not deal with black artisans and quotes a flour mill owner as rejecting a black miller on this account: "I have an idea of puting Paschal to the mill. But some say a negro will drive all the customers away."[60] While such discrimination was undoubtedly present and would serve to restrict employment opportunities for blacks, there is also the likelihood that many of the slaves whose occupations were recorded as carpenters, blacksmiths, and the like, in 1860 did not actually possess sufficiently developed skills to earn their living as artisans once they were free. As W. E. B. Du Bois said:

Notes to Table 2.6.

[a] The census enumerators did not make a careful distinction between farmers and farm laborers. They recorded the occupational description given them by respondents. See Chapters 4 and 5 for a discussion of farm tenure and farm labor.
[b] It is likely that some farm laborers were recorded as simply "laborers" or "day laborers."
[c] Includes cotton-seed-oil mill (3), gas works (3), car shop (2), tin shop (2), stable (2), grist mill, planing mill, saw mill, tailor's shop, wheelwright's shop, butcher shop, barber shop, wagon shop, harness shop, brickyard, cotton yard, foundry, turpentine still, and "store."
[d] Includes well diggers and grave diggers.
[e] Includes woodcutter (3), lamplighter (2), mail rider (2), messenger in depot, cabin boy on steamboat, bootblack, and pinsetter in tenpin alley.
[f] Includes apprentice artisans.
[g] Includes car builder (3), coopersmith (3), wheelwright (3), harness maker (2), wagon maker (2), confectioner, railroad route agent, steamboat engineer, pressman, chair maker, boiler maker, tailor, wagon painter, dyer, brick maker, coach maker, and fireman.
[h] Includes "fruitner."
[i] Includes livery stable keeper.
[j] Probably "nurses" should be more properly referred to as servants than medical nurses.
Source: Manuscript Census of Population, 1870. See Appendix B.

The slave artisan . . . was rather a jack-of-all-trades than a mechanic in the modern [1902] sense of the term – he could build a barn, make a barrel, mend an umbrella or shoe a horse. Exceptional slaves did the work exceptionally well, but the average workman was poor, careless and ill-trained, and could not have earned living wages under modern competitive conditions.[61]

The slaveowner would have had an obvious incentive in characterizing such handymen as artisans. Not only might such exaggeration add to their market price should they be sold, but it would also tend to inflate the (self-perceived) economic importance of the planter as well. We conjecture that, once free, these semiskilled artisans turned their energies to farming and thus were recorded in the 1870 Census as "farmers."

It is also likely, as we have pointed out, that many slave "artisans" were illiterate. While not a serious disadvantage to the slaveowner, the skilled freedmen probably found illiteracy a major obstacle to pursuing artisan trades independently. The need in these occupations to communicate with distant suppliers and customers, to keep books, and to make financial arrangements meant that those who could not read and write would, in most cases, have to work for others. Even then, illiteracy would hinder artisans from attaining great proficiency.[62] That such was the case is suggested by the postwar literacy rates reported in Table 2.7 for black workers in various occupations. The literacy rate among artisans was four times higher than that among farm laborers.

Table 2.7. *Literacy rates of gainfully occupied black males: 1870*

Occupation[a]	Sample[b]	Sample size	Percent literate
Farmer	Rural	151	8.2
Farm laborer	Rural	1,997	5.0
Laborer	Rural	392	7.1
Laborer	Urban	399	12.0
Servant	Urban	185	7.0
Other unskilled	Urban	284	16.2
Artisan	Urban	335	21.8
Carpenter	Urban	143	18.9
Blacksmith	Urban	41	19.5
Commercial	Urban	70	30.0
Professional	Urban	25	80.0
All occupations	Rural	2,642	5.7
All occupations	Urban	1,582	14.9

[a] The definition of each occupation class is given in Table 2.5 for the rural sample and Table 2.6 for the urban sample.   [b] These are the same samples used to prepare data for Tables 2.5 and 2.6.
Source: Manuscript Census of Population, 1870. See Appendix B.

A related factor helping to explain the nominal decline in black skills was also suggested by Du Bois. Slavery had not given black artisans experience in business – only in craftsmanship. Slave carpenters and blacksmiths, save in very rare instances, never had to solicit customers, make bids, set prices, hire help, or order supplies. "His business," noted Du Bois, "had been to *do* work but not to *get* work."[63] For many ex-slaves, such competitive skills were doubtless easy to acquire, but for others the lack was sufficiently detrimental to cause them to abandon their trades, except perhaps as sidelines.[64]

A final point that must be made is that aspiring black artisans met with both competition and hostility from established white tradesmen. As slaves, skilled blacks worked under the protection and patronage of their white owners, who were typically important and powerful men in their communities. Had they remained in the rural areas, skilled blacks might have retained the patronage of their former masters. But the demand for skilled work was greatest in the towns and cities. Blacks who migrated in search of urban employment not only encountered the direct hostility and competition of whites, they also severed their ties to their former masters.

A few attempts were made to prohibit or establish restrictions on blacks seeking employment in towns. Thus, for example, South Carolina passed a law in December 1865 which provided that "no person of color shall pursue or practice the art, trade, or business of an artisan, mechanic, or shopkeeper, or any other trade, employment, or business . . . on his own account and for his own benefit . . . until he shall have obtained a license . . . which license shall be good for one year only."[65] Shopkeepers and peddlers were required to pay $100 a year for a license; artisans, $10. White men paid no such fee, nor had free blacks before the war.[66] The infamous Black Codes, passed in virtually every southern state immediately after the war, sought to limit the mobility of the blacks. Artisans seeking skilled employment were particularly victimized by the "vagrancy" regulations, which treated any "person of color" without an employer as a vagrant, subject to fine and imprisonment. These codes were soon overturned, but the sentiment behind them was not forgotten.

Such coercive measures must have had a depressing effect on the number of practicing artisans. They also discouraged development of skills and may explain why blacks worked for lower wages than whites. Ironically, the blacks' willingness to work for less only increased the white workers' opposition to black competition and ultimately led to organized attempts to exclude blacks from labor unions and from certain occupations altogether.[67]

By 1890, the year in which the first published census data on occupation by race are available, these forces had been powerful enough to have an observable effect on the occupational status of blacks in the Five Cotton States. In Table 2.8 the occupations reported in the census are listed in descending order of their racial composition. Our index of racial balance is a standardized measure that indicates the extent to which a given racial composition within an occupation deviates from what would be expected if there

were no racial bias to occupational choice. (This index is derived and defined in Appendix B.) It can range from a value of +1 (complete exclusion of
whites) through zero (exact integration of the employment category) to −1

Table 2.8. *Racial balance index for various occupations, Five Cotton States:
1890*

Occupation[a]	Sex	Percent of blacks in occupation class	Racial balance index
Whites excluded			
Laundress	F	.968	.813
Black occupations			
Servant	M	.906	.796
Laborer, not specified	F	.934	.629
Laborer, not specified	M	.779	.526
Porter	M	.776	.499
Barber	M	.718	.398
Agricultural laborer	F	.886	.393
Agricultural laborer	M	.694	.349
Teamster	M	.641	.239
Servant	F	.837	.180
Open occupations			
Lumberer	M	.610	.176
Railroad employee	M	.569	.093
Other factory operative	M	.545	.044
Mason	M	.522	−.002
Gardener	M	.516	−.014
Clergyman	M	.512	−.022
Saw-mill operator	M	.487	−.072
Iron- and steel-mill operator	M	.457	−.132
Not specified	M	.444	−.157
Farm operator	M	.441	−.163
Other laborer	M	.439	−.167
White occupations			
Blacksmith	M	.410	−.224
Shoemaker	M	.409	−.226
Hotel, etc., keeper	M	.372	−.299
Carpenter	M	.355	−.332
Other skilled occupation	M	.349	−.344
Painter	M	.341	−.359
Teacher	M	.325	−.390
Nurse, midwife	F	.660	−.395
Engineer, fireman	M	.299	−.440
Butcher	M	.285	−.467
Farm operator	F	.545	−.639
Other service occupation	F	.540	−.647
Miller	M	.150	−.723
Cotton-mill operator	M	.143	−.736
Foreman	M	.130	−.760
Other laborer	F	.446	−.787

Table 2.8. *(cont.)*

Occupation[a]	Sex	Percent of blacks in occupation class	Racial balance index
Blacks excluded			
Government official	M	.073	−.866
Printer	M	.066	−.879
Other skilled occupation	F	.346	−.881
Surveyor	M	.065	−.881
Manufacturer	M	.063	−.885
Merchandiser	M	.054	−.901
Machinist	M	.047	−.914
Seamstress	F	.304	−.921
Bookkeeper	M	.036	−.934
Hotel, etc. keeper	F	.276	−.938
Not specified	F	.269	−.942
Banker	M	.032	−.942
Physician	M	.021	−.962
Lawyer	M	.019	−.965
Teacher	F	.209	−.970
Merchandiser	F	.173	−.982
Other factory operator	F	.172	−.983
Clerk	F	.048	−.999
Government official	F	.033	−.999
Cotton-mill operator	F	.019	−.999

[a] See Appendix B for definitions of occupations.
Source: Appendix B.

(complete exclusion of blacks). Rather arbitrarily, we have characterized occupations according to the grading system indicated in the table. Under these definitions only one occupation, that of laundress, effectively excluded whites. "Black occupations" included servant, agricultural laborer, common laborer, porter, barber, and teamster. Only male occupations were in the "open" category. Among others, they included lumberman, railroad employee, mason, gardener, clergyman, saw-, iron-, and steel-mill operative, and farm operator. All the skilled occupations other than masonry were predominately white. (Printer, machinist, and seamstress were almost exclusively white.) All, or nearly all, of the professional, mercantile, and commercial occupations effectively excluded blacks.[68] Nevertheless, even this situation represented an improvement over slavery, when such occupations were *never* held by bondsmen. Despite their small numbers, the black occupational elite was very significant. To a large extent the leaders of the black community were to come from this tiny minority.

Emancipation, it would seem, freed the slave, but offered only restricted employment opportunities outside agriculture. Slavery left the blacks uneducated, illiterate, and untrained. Racism in the post-Civil War period then curtailed both the education of blacks and the free exercise of skills they possessed. The black man began his career as a free man heavily handicapped. Nevertheless, he still held high hopes for the future. After all, agriculture and black labor had been the source of the South's wealth before the Civil War. All that seemed necessary for black prosperity was to reorganize agricultural production to accommodate the new system of labor. But no one foresaw how difficult that would be.

The problems encountered were not those most southerners had anticipated in the wake of the South's defeat. The blacks, who had been expected to prove unable to cope with freedom and to emerge as a liability to the southern economy, quickly responded to the incentive freedom made available. They went to work, and they worked hard. The destruction and disruption of the Civil War, which were expected seriously to hinder economic recovery, were, as we shall argue in the next chapter, quickly repaired. The difficulties engendered by the war and emancipation were of an entirely different nature than expected. The physical damage of the Civil War proved to be of far less consequence than the less visible but irreparable damage to the financial and merchandising system wrought by the cessation of commerce. Emancipation proved to be a cause of friction, not because blacks were incapable of establishing their independence, but because they asserted their independence and insisted upon institutional arrangements more to their liking than those envisioned for them by whites.

CHAPTER 3

THE MYTH OF
THE PROSTRATE SOUTH

Even the most sanguine are astonished at the zeal and energy displayed by our people in reconstructing their private fortunes. Our railroads have been repaired, commercial intercourse with the world reopened, cities and villages which were but a few months since masses of charred ruins rebuilt as if by magic, and our planting interest, though less prosperous than heretofore, owing to the change of labor and unpropitious seasons, has not been less active. We have every reason to hope that this is but the beginning, the ground swell of a great and glorious future, if fortune will continue to favor us.

> John T. Burns, Comptroller General, State of Georgia, *Annual Report of the Comptroller General of the State of Georgia . . . October 16, 1866* (Macon: J. W. Burke & Co., 1866), p. 28.

The American Civil War devastated the South; the loss of human life, work animals, and other livestock was enormous; the destruction of houses, barns, fences, bridges, railroads, and levees paralyzed agriculture; the burning of cities, factories, warehouses, and wharves crippled the southern economy. The well-known stories of Sherman's march to the sea; the burning of Richmond, Atlanta, Columbia, and Charleston; the raids into northern Alabama; and other, less dramatic, incidents add to the popular image of widespread destruction. Every account of the Reconstruction Period comments on this devastation, and a number of historians and economists have asserted that the loss of southern capital from the war severely affected the economic recovery of the South.[1]

If the destruction of the Civil War was responsible for both the initial fall in output and the subsequent inability of the South to rebuild quickly, then the relative economic backwardness of the South during the half-century following the war could be attributed, at least in part, to the wartime devastation. James Sellers made this thesis quite explicit:

Chronologically, the economic incidence of the war did not fall upon one generation. . . . The evidences of the devastation produced by the Civil War still remain [in 1927] in the economic life of the South. The Census of 1900 showed that after the lapse of a full generation the South had hardly recovered the economic development of 1860.[2]

Notes to Chapter 3 appear on pages 324–329.

This picture of southern postwar developments, on the other hand, stands in sharp contrast with the typical experience of other war-devastated economies. Even before the Civil War, John Stuart Mill had noted "the great rapidity with which countries recover from a state of devastation."

An enemy lays waste a country by fire and sword, and destroys or carries away nearly all the moveable wealth existing in it; all the inhabitants are ruined, and yet in a few years after, everything is much as it was before. . . . The possibility of a rapid repair of their disasters, mainly depends on whether the country has been depopulated. If its effective population have not been extirpated at the time, and are not starved afterwards; then, with the same skill and knowledge which they had before, with their land and its permanent improvements undestroyed, and the more durable buildings probably unimpaired, or only partially injured, they have nearly all the requisites for their former amount of production.[3]

This comment, written in 1848, suggests that the economic resurgence of West Germany, Italy, and Japan following World War II was not a phenomenon peculiar to modern times.[4] If rapid economic recovery was the rule, even with pre-Civil War economies, a closer examination of the asserted connection between the physical destruction and the subsequent economic performance of the South seems in order. Notwithstanding the extensiveness of the war, the South was not "depopulated" or "laid waste"; nor had all the "moveable wealth," as legend would have it, "gone with the wind." The South retained the skills and knowledge embodied in its population and its land remained relatively unharmed.

The recovery of the southern economy

A closer look at the southern economy reveals that the transportation and manufacturing sectors, at least, did experience a rapid regeneration. Despite the fact that the rolling stock of southern railroad companies was decimated during the fighting, and that much of the existing track was in disrepair, the railroads of the South, aided by northern capitalists and the Union Army, were quickly restored to operating order. Northern journalists traveling in the South during late 1865 and early 1866 complained about the frequent delays in service and the dilapidated equipment. Nevertheless, they were often surprised by the success of efforts to repair facilities so soon after the end of hostilities. "I found the railroad in better condition than I supposed that I should," reported Sidney Andrews in 1865. "The rails are very much worn, but the roadbed is in fair order for nearly the entire distance."[5] Whitelaw Reid felt that railroads were "rapidly getting into running order, and old lines of travel were reopening," an opinion that seems to reflect the view of most travelers in 1866.[6] By the following year James De Bow could claim that "the railroads between Washington and Charleston, S.C. are all in good operating condition and make as good time as they did before the war."[7] "By 1870," concludes historian John Stover, "the physical restoration and rehabilitation of southern railroads was practically complete."[8]

The manufacturing sector of the South, like the railroads, was crippled by the destruction consequent upon the war. Yet, after only a few years of peace, much of the damage seems to have been repaired. Table 3.1 presents several measures of manufacturing activity in the Five Cotton States for 1859 and 1869. Expressed in currency prices, all the measures – total output, value added, and capital investment – greatly exceeded their prewar level by 1869. Even in terms of gold prices, which experienced almost no inflation between 1859 and 1869, the value of the capital stock and the value of output had returned to and exceeded their 1859 levels only four years after the end of the war. Since the 1869 figures may well be understated relative to the prewar numbers by the Ninth Census tabulations,[9] we can safely conclude that the manufacturing sector of the Five Cotton States had regained its prewar level of activity by 1870.[10]

Once the damage from the war was repaired, manufacturing in the Five Cotton States continued to expand rapidly. Table 3.2 presents data on manufacturing activity from 1869 to 1899 in these states.[11] The total gold value of output and the total value added in manufacturing rose more than sixfold over this thirty-year period. Capital investment expanded even more, increasing by a factor of 10. Perhaps the best measure of labor productivity we have – the value added per worker – increased by more than 50 percent. Between 1869 and 1889 value added per worker grew at the average rate of 2.5 percent per year.[12] Manufacturing clearly prospered in the South after the war. Yet, the effect of this recovery and subsequent growth in manufacturing on the economic expansion of the southern economy as a whole should not be exaggerated. Manufacturing employment in 1870 was only 3.8 percent of the total labor force in the Five Cotton States that year. Even by the end of the century, manufacturing employed only 6.5 percent of the labor force.[13] It was agriculture that dominated the economic life of the South throughout the nineteenth century and that provided a means of livelihood for virtually every family of ex-slaves. Unlike southern manufacturing, however, the agricultural sector did not completely recover in the years following the war and, as we have seen in Chapter 1, exhibited virtually no growth during the remainder of the century. It is therefore clear that an explanation for the poor performance of the southern economy in the postemancipation era, and for the slow pace of black economic advancement over the same years, will have to be sought in a study of the economic institutions of southern agriculture.

The rapid resurgence of the manufacturing sector, on the other hand, does not rule out the possibility that the destruction produced by the conflict of the Civil War was a major influence on the course of agricultural development. Economists and historians who accept the damage produced by war as an explanation for southern backwardness have emphasized that the Cotton South lost a significant fraction of its agricultural factors of production. The loss of life among the black population was said to be high as a

Table 3.1. *Indexes of manufacturing activity, Five Cotton States: 1859, 1869*

	Value in currency millions of dollars		1869 as percent of 1859	Value in gold prices[a] millions of dollars		1869 as percent of 1859
	1859	1869		1859	1869	
Value of output	58.3	86.4	148	58.3	68.5	117
Value added	25.4	33.6	132	25.4	26.5	105
Capital investment	34.8	46.1	132	34.8	36.5	105

[a] In 1859, gold and currency values were at par. The currency figures for 1869 were deflated using the November 1869 price of gold in terms of currency (1.262) as reported in Ainsworth R. Spofford, ed., *American Almanac and Treasury of Facts . . . 1889* (New York: American News Co., 1889), p. 341, to obtain the 1869 gold values. We have not used price deflators, such as Robert Gallman's ("Commodity Output, 1839–1899," in National Bureau of Economic Research, *Trends in the American Economy in the Nineteenth Century* [Princeton: Princeton University Press, 1960], p. 28), since they are based upon national data and are weighted by the components of manufacturing production in national output. These national component weights were quite different from those for southern output.

Source: U.S. Census Office, Eighth Census [1860], *Manufactures of the United States in 1860* (Washington: GPO, 1865), pp. 14, 32, 203–204, 294, 559. U.S. Census Office, Ninth Census [1870], *Statistics of the Wealth and Industry of the United States* (June 1, 1870), (Washington: GPO, 1872), Table IX(B), pp. 493–494, 507–508, 522–523, 537–538, 568–569.

Table 3.2. *Indexes of manufacturing activity, Five Cotton States: 1869, 1879, 1889, 1899*

	1869 currency prices	1869 gold prices[a]	1879	1889	1899
Value of output (millions of dollars)	78.3	62.0	91.6	195.7	364.8
Value added (millions of dollars)	32.5	25.8	32.5	83.0	142.1
Capital invested (millions of dollars)	42.9	34.0	53.5	158.0	340.8
Value added per worker[b] (dollars)	514	407	523	663	648

[a] See footnote *a*, Table 3.1.　[b] The series developed by Easterlin on average number of wage earners in manufacturing was used to compute the value added per worker.

Source: Richard A. Easterlin, "Estimates of Manufacturing Activity," in Simon Kuznets and Dorothy Swaine Thomas, eds., *Population Redistribution and Economic Growth, United States, 1870–1950,* 3 vols. (Philadelphia: American Philosophical Society, 1957), 1, pp. 684, 692–697.

consequence of war, disease, and starvation. Also, according to some accounts, the southern supply of agricultural capital, particularly working stock, was substantially reduced. This decline in the supply of labor and these capital losses would explain the decline in agricultural output, and the South's slow recovery could be understood as a consequence of the difficulties in restoring the depleted stock of inputs.

This interpretation seems to us unfounded. It can be established fairly conclusively that the destructive impact of the Civil War on southern agriculture has been greatly distorted and exaggerated. The failure of the southern economy to return rapidly to its prewar potential cannot be adequately explained by the loss of capital, work stock, or transportation facilities. As we shall show, the failure of per capita output to recover its prewar level by the end of the century is explained by the withdrawal of black labor and not by the physical damage wrought by the war.

The withdrawal of black labor

Emancipation gave the ex-slave the freedom to lighten his burden and, for the first time, reserve a portion of his time for himself. The slave was literally worked to the limit of his economic capacity. Once free, he quite naturally chose to work less, so that he might reserve a portion of each day within which to enjoy the fruits of his labor, fruits that had previously been taken from him by his master. The result was that the amount of labor offered by each freedman and his family was substantially less than when slavery forced every man, woman, and child to work long hours throughout the year. Rather than work like slaves, the freedmen chose to offer an amount of labor comparable to the standard for free laborers of the time.[14]

To indicate how substantial this decline in the labor supply was, we have constructed a conjectural estimate of the decline in the man-hours per capita supplied by the black population to agriculture. We have tried to make a conservative estimate, one that can be considered a lower limit to the actual decline. Our estimate takes account of the reduction in labor force participation (particularly noticeable among women and children) and the general declines in both the number of days of work and the number of hours worked each day. We made no attempt to estimate the reduction in the intensity of work performed each hour. While the estimate is conjectural, it is nevertheless solidly based on an extensive review of contemporary commentary as well as census samples and contemporary agricultural surveys. A more complete discussion of our estimating procedure is offered in Appendix C. Our estimates are summarized in Figure 3.1, which contrasts the number of hours worked per year before and after emancipation separately for men, women, and children. In each case both a high and a low estimate is offered. In Table 3.3, we partition the total percentage decline into the three components we were able to estimate: decline in labor force participation, decline in number of days worked, and decline in length of work day.

Table 3.3. *Percent decline in man-hours per capita offered by the rural black population as a consequence of emancipation*

	Percent decline	
	Low estimate	High estimate
1. Fraction of rural population employed in agricultural occupations	17	24
2. Average number of days worked per year	8	11
3. Average number of hours worked per day	9	10
Cumulative effect of 1 through 3	28.3	37.2

Source: Appendix C.

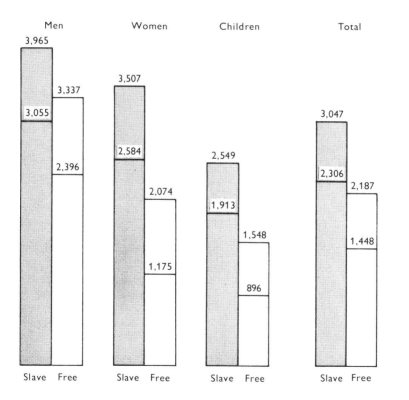

Figure 3.1 Maximum and minimum estimates of the number of hours worked per year by the black population over ten; as slaves in 1850s and freedmen in 1870s. Total presented is the male-equivalent hours supplied per person ten years old or older. (*Source:* Appendix C, Table C.1.)

The effect of freedom was dramatic. The number of man-hours per capita supplied by the rural black population fell by an amount between 28 and 37 percent of the quantity of labor that had been extracted through the coercion of slavery. This decline in the labor provided by blacks after emancipation must have created a bottleneck that was particularly constraining to the plantation economy. Plantations had relied exclusively on black slave labor before the war, and with emancipation the supply of this labor fell to two-thirds its previous level. Moreover, there is no evidence that white workers who had been engaged in nonplantation agriculture before the war joined the plantation work force to help alleviate this bottleneck created by the withdrawal of black labor.[15] Perhaps one reason why white labor could not be easily substituted for black labor on the plantation was the attitude whites had developed during slavery against working in a subordinate position for another man. Before the war, Frederick Law Olmsted observed that "to work industriously and steadily, especially under directions from another man, is, in the Southern tongue, to 'work like a nigger.'"[16] Moreover, according to Olmsted, "the employment of whites in duties upon which slaves are ordinarily employed is felt to be not only humiliating to the whites employed, but also to the employer."[17]

The reduction in the black labor supply did not go unnoticed. Throughout the South there were frequent complaints from planters of a "labor short-age." Most contemporaries estimated that the decline was even greater than our own conjecture presented in Table 3.3. A Georgian thought that "fifty per cent, more than fifty per cent, of black labor has disappeared from the fields. The negroes are not dead, nor gone . . .; but they have very much quit the fields."[18] An agent of the U.S. Department of Agriculture, report-ing on the conditions in the South during the first half of 1867, estimated the "effective labor" supply at less than one-third the prewar level and quoted the opinion of "careful and experienced men" that it had fallen to one-quarter the previous level.[19] A survey of planters taken early in 1869 by the Boston cotton firm of Loring and Atkinson produced numerous comments on the labor scarcity. The editors summarized the results of their canvassing:

Our correspondents are unanimous in showing that there was a decided difficulty in obtaining hands in 1868, and that although not universal, yet it was felt more or less all over the South. . . . As additional evidence of the dearth of labor, the burden of the answers to the question, "What are the chief needs of your neighborhood?" is, Laborers, laborers, reliable laborers. . . . It can be safely stated that the labor power at present is not more than one-half what it was in 1860.[20]

The newspapers and magazines of the times were full of complaints about the difficulty of hiring black workers. Typical is the comment of a corre spondent of the *Rural Carolinian*, from Anderson County, South Carolina, in 1870:

Labor is very scarce in this section, and, I think, over the county there is not more than one farmer in ten with hands enough. I know several plantations on which there is not a hand. I do not know of one but would employ one or more additional hands if they could get them.[21]

Impact of the supply of black labor on agricultural production

This shrinkage of the effective labor supply had a profound impact on the ability of the South to produce cotton. With the technology of the time, there were only limited possibilities in the short run for substituting other factors of production, such as work stock, land, or capital, for labor. In the nineteenth century, cotton production was a labor-intensive process, and in the land-abundant American South, the available labor supply had always been the constraining factor limiting cotton production.[22]

If we make the extreme assumption that the ratios with which black labor was combined with other factors were fixed by technological and sociological considerations, then the fall of 28 to 37 percent in the per capita supply of black labor could explain, by itself, almost all the 36.5 percent decline in per capita crop production discussed in Chapter 1.[23] This being the case, the impact of the Civil War on the southern capital stock can be ruled out as a significant contributor to the reduction in per capita output. The argument is based on the fact, which we shall establish below, that the percentage decline in labor supply *exceeded* the percentage reduction in the supply of the other factors of production. Therefore, it was impossible for the land-labor ratio, the work-stock-labor ratio, or the capital-labor ratio to have fallen. If anything, these ratios rose. After emancipation each man-hour of labor had more (not less) land, working stock, and capital with which to work. This should have made labor after the war more productive rather than less productive. This being the case, the fall in per capita output can be explained only by a reduction of the labor supply offered by blacks, or indirectly, through a reduced efficiency of production.[24] We shall discuss the latter possibility in succeeding chapters; our concern here will be with the effects of a reduced supply of labor.

The situation in the South after the Civil War was exactly the reverse of that confronting most war-ravaged economies. In the typical situation, the destruction of capital outweighs the loss of life, causing a *fall* in the ratio of capital to labor. The mechanism of regenerative growth in such economies is the extremely high rate of investment stimulated by the abnormally high rates of return to new capital formation, which are in turn a reflection of the relative scarcity of capital.[25] In the South, the decline in labor relative to other factors of production presumably increased the relative return to labor,[26] but this shift could not stimulate a sufficient increase in the quantity of labor supplied to offset the withdrawal of labor that accompanied the removal of coercion. Therefore, if it can be shown that the physical destruction from the war did not result in lower factor-labor ratios, we can be confident that further expansion of agricultural output would depend upon population growth or technological change. It is to this task that we now turn.

Impact of the war on the factor-labor ratios

The war did not, of course, literally destroy the land.[27] Therefore, with the decline in the labor supply it is obvious that the land-labor ratio must have risen.

Despite the fact that the South's endowment of land was not substantially affected by the war, the reduction in the labor supply apparently significantly reduced its utilization. Contemporary reports mention acreage left uncultivated "for the want of labor."[28] These reports are not contradicted by the 1870 Census. Compared with 1860, the Five Cotton States reported a decline exceeding 20 percent in "improved acres," which include, in addition to tilled land, land left fallow or devoted to meadows or pastures.[29] The extremely high agricultural prices in the first years after the war should have encouraged farmers to plant as much acreage as possible.[30] The decline in land cultivation suggests that only limited scope existed for increasing the land-labor ratio.[31]

According to the popular account, the conflict between the two armies decimated the South's livestock population. Working animals were withdrawn from the farms by the Confederate Army for use as draft animals and mounts. Not only was mortality among these animals quite high, but breeding would have been curtailed, affecting the usual rate of increase. Also, according to popular accounts, the Union Army confiscated or destroyed those animals it found in its path. The most infamous example, and probably the most extreme, was Sherman's general order before his troops entered Georgia that "the army will forage liberally on the country during the march." Regarding work stock, Sherman's orders read: "As for horses, mules, wagons, &c., belonging to the inhabitants, the cavalry and artillery may appropriate freely and without limit."[32]

It is probably true that the loss of livestock was substantial throughout the Cotton South. The 1870 enumeration indicates a fall of nearly one-third in the number of horses, asses, and mules between 1860 and 1870 in the Five Cotton States.[33] Surprisingly, while they are quite vocal regarding the scarcity of labor, contemporary observers are silent regarding any shortage of working stock. It seems that the shortage of labor, and the relatively fixed work-stock-labor ratio, meant that the disappearance of animal power went largely unnoticed.

That there was no relative shortage of work animals in the years following the Civil War is made evident by the fact that the market price of mules was actually *less* at that time than before the war. Throughout the mid-1850s, the price of a mature working mule seems to have been approximately $100. By the end of the 1850s the price had risen to around $150.[34] By contrast with these prewar prices, in 1868 the average value of mules in the Five Cotton States ranged between $52 in Mississippi and $61 in South Carolina. Postwar gold prices for mules in these states reached a peak in 1870, when they averaged $115 per head, a level not surpassed during the balance of the nineteenth century.[35]

Most of the mules used in the Cotton South were bred in Kentucky, Missouri, and Tennessee. A comparison of selling prices in these states before and after the war is provided in Table 3.4. So as not to exaggerate the decline in prices, we report the postwar prices for 1870, the peak year for mule prices in the Cotton South. Had a mule shortage existed, a substantial increase in price, not the observed decrease, should have been exhibited by the statistics. This decline in the prices of work stock is even more noteworthy in view of the high prices paid for cotton in the period 1867–1870 relative to its prewar price level. When the price of mule colts is expressed in terms of the amount of cotton they were worth, the decline in relative mule prices is dramatic. In 1859 a mule colt was worth 1.03 bales of cotton, while in 1870 a colt was equivalent to only 0.54 bale.[36] Standard economic reasoning would suggest that this relative price should have risen, not declined, had a shortage of mules constrained production.

The substantial fall in the relative price of mules reflects a relative abundance of working animals and a limited ability to substitute draft animals for human labor. As one observer explained in 1869: "Some planters are also increasing their teams to substitute for manual labor, but this will be only a partial good, for the crops cannot be gathered by mule power, and the gathering is always the great difficulty."[37]

Table 3.4. *Comparison of mule prices in mule-raising states: 1859, 1870*

	Gold price ($)	
Animal	1859	1870
Colt	50	40
Two-year-old	66–130	58–82
Three-year-old	120	82–104

Source: 1859: The American Farmer, Fourth Series, 14 (1859), p. 251. The source reported averages at a sale of 800 mules of "inferior quality." *1870:* U.S. Department of Agriculture, *Monthly Report,* February 1870, p. 68. The prices reported for Kentucky, Missouri, and Tennessee were weighted by the number of mules estimated for those states on January 1, 1870, given in U.S. Department of Agriculture, Bureau of Agriculture Economics, *Livestock on Farms, January 1, 1867–1919* (Washington: U.S. Department of Agriculture, January 1937), pp. 74, 100, 102. The currency prices were deflated to a gold basis using the average value of the dollar for the month of January 1870 as reported in Ainsworth R. Spofford, ed., *The American Almanac and Treasury of Facts . . . 1889* (New York: American News Co., 1889), p. 341. This is the same deflation index used by the U.S. Department of Agriculture, *Livestock on Farms.*

While working stock was clearly the most important form of agricultural capital, farm implements, plows, wagons, harrows, hoes, and the like were also necessary factors of production. While direct destruction of agricultural implements in the course of the warfare must have been quite small,[38] the neglect of four years probably took a substantial toll. Nevertheless, the capital outlay required for these implements was a relatively small amount. By a liberal estimate, a large prewar plantation required $25 worth of implements per working hand.[39] Nor should all the cost of re-equipping a farm be attributed to the direct effects of the war. Depreciation of farm implements used or neglected during the war would have required some replacement of capital in any event. Contemporary estimates of the rate of depreciation seem to range from 10 to 25 percent per year.[40] At that rate of depreciation, four years of normal use would have reduced the value of farm implements by one-third to two-thirds even in the absence of destruction from military action.

Depreciation may have required replacement or repair of buildings, wagons, and fences on the farm. But the same regenerative mechanism that prompted the rapid rebuilding of the South's manufacturing sector would have accelerated the replacement of agricultural capital worn out of lost during the war. Even in those regions where the loss of this form of capital was extensive, much of the damage could have been repaired during the first year of operation. D. Wyatt Aiken, a prominent farmer, wrote that on his own farm he spent three months in the summer of 1866 to put his plantation in shape: "land was cleared, rails were mauled, fences renewed, old houses torn down and rebuilt; the dilapidation consequent upon the war was wiped out, and by 1st January, 1867, the marketable value of my plantation had increased to an amount equal to the value of a good crop."[41]

It seems quite plausible to assume that the loss of farm capital due to the war could have been replaced within the course of a single season. Of course, with the substantial decline in labor, it would not have been necessary, or even economically wise, to replace all that was lost. As in the case of the work animals, failure to restore completely the capital stock to a prewar level would not imply that a capital shortage existed.

The destructive effects of the war were, in an economic sense, largely irrelevant because of the impact emancipation had on the supply of labor. Within a few years the damage had been repaired, the capital replaced, and the livestock restored at least to the extent that labor productivity equaled, and perhaps exceeded, its prewar standard. Historians and economists alike have paid too little attention to this decline in labor brought about by emancipation. This phenomenon not only goes a long way in explaining the aggregate economic performance of the post-Civil War South and the frequent complaints of a labor shortage, but it also helps to explain the otherwise puzzling postwar decline in land values.

The decline in land values

The fall in tilled acreage accompanying the reduction in the labor supply created a supply of "redundant" land that acted to depress land prices. According to a survey made by the United States Department of Agriculture in 1867, the value of farmland had declined from the 1860 level in every one of the former Confederate States. The depreciation in land values was greatest in the Five Cotton States, ranging from a 55 percent decline in Georgia to a 70 percent fall in Louisiana.[42] The reasons for the sharp reductions in land value were, according to the department's correspondents: "general indebtedness, scarcity of money, want of reliable laborers, great loss of capital in slaves, want of [financial] capital, unsettled condition of the country, general poverty of the people, fear of confiscation, and negro dominion."[43] Apparently, the much lower values of land were not the result of wartime destruction. Neither were they the result of temporary disorganization and disruption following the end of the war, since the survey just cited was taken in 1867, two and one-half years after the close of hostilities. Two years later, another survey quoted farmland prices ranging from $2 to $8 per acre. In the years before the war average cotton land had been valued at between $15 and $25 per acre.[44] If Georgia is taken as typical, the value of improved farmland had not recovered even by the mid-1880s.[45]

Some historians have claimed that crop yields per acre fell following emancipation. Paul Gates attributed the "low-yield basis" of postwar crop production to "row cropping, failure to rotate, and soil depletion."[46] It is more likely that any decline in crop yields per acre was the logical consequence of the decline in land values and the scarcity of labor. With cheap land, agriculturalists would attempt to cultivate as extensively as possible, sacrificing yield per acre to increase yield per man-hour. This effect would explain the scattered references to the effect that the yield of a given field was less than before the war. However, in the aggregate, this depressing effect on yields would have been at least partially offset by the fact that the land that remained in production should have been the most productive. The least fertile land would have been left uncultivated.

The myth of the prostrate South

The hypothesis we have advanced accounts for a complex sequence of events following the Civil War entirely by the decline in the labor supply that accompanied emancipation. The decline in per capita output, the decline in land values and mule prices, the reduction of acreage planted in crops, and the decline in work stock employed in agriculture are all seen as a consequence of the change in labor supply. But perhaps some will feel that the story all fits together rather too well. If we are correct, then why did previous investigators neglect this explanation? And what led them to exaggerate the destructive impact of the Civil War on postbellum agriculture?

The answer, we think, has three parts. First, historians and economists were too quick to generalize from the numerous individual reports of family destitution and personal bankruptcy to a sweeping conclusion that the South was a devastated and bankrupt economy. Second, because these generalizations seemed confirmed by comparisons of the 1870 Census of Agriculture with agricultural statistics from the 1860 Census, they were often accepted uncritically. Finally, because contemporary comments and complaints of a labor shortage were frequently couched as assertions that blacks would not, or could not, work without compulsion, they were either dismissed as racist slander or offered merely as evidence of the discontent consequent upon the South's defeat, overlooking the possibility that an actual permanent decline in the South's supply of labor had occurred.

The use of individual reports of financial ruin to support claims of a general disaster, we are sure, embodies a common fallacy. For the most part, white plantation owners did not experience the destruction of their capital assets so much as they experienced the confiscation of them. It was the loss of their slaves that they lamented, not the loss of their lands, buildings, and farm implements. Of course, from the point of view of a slaveowner, there can be no question that the abolition of slavery was a severe financial blow. Slaveholders had a considerable fraction of their wealth invested in slave "capital." According to Lewis Gray, the investment in slaves for a typical cotton plantation of sixty hands would amount to at least 50 percent of the total investment required.[47] Our own estimate places the proportion at an even higher fraction of the required investment: 58.6 percent.[48] We estimate the market value in 1860 of the 2 million blacks in the Five Cotton States conservatively at $1.6 billion.[49] Accepting the census enumeration of total real and personal property in 1860, reproduced in Table 3.5, the holdings of slaves by our estimate would have represented 45.8 percent of the *total* wealth held by all residents of the Five Cotton States. The value of slaves was nearly 60 percent of the total capital invested in agriculture and completely overshadowed the minuscule $38 million invested in the manufacturing establishments of the five states.

No wonder the abolition of slavery was viewed by the slaveholders as a disaster of the first order of magnitude. Nevertheless, the outlawing of slavery did not destroy the "capital" embodied in the black population. The apparent disappearance of nearly one-half of the southern capital stock represented, not a loss to the South, but a transfer of the ownership of "capitalized labor" from the slaveholders to the ex-slaves themselves. As free agents, the former slaves "owned" themselves and the right to profit from their own labor as they saw fit. Apparently, it is because so much of southern history has been written from the perspective of the slaveowner that this transfer of ownership has been incorrectly viewed as a loss to the southern economy. Former slaveowners' laments about their financial losses cannot be generalized and used as evidence of the destructive impact of the Civil War.

Table 3.5. *Composition of wealth, Five Cotton States: 1860*

Asset	Value (millions of dollars)	Percent of total wealth	Census source (volume, page)[a]
Slaves	1,589	45.8	*Population*, pp. 592–597[b]
Farmlands and buildings	868	25.0	*Agriculture*, p. vii
Farm animals	172	5.0	*Agriculture*, p. cxxvi
Farm implements	48	1.4	*Agriculture*, p. x
Manufacturing capital	38	1.1	*Manufacturing*, p. 729
Other real estate	364	10.5	*Statistics*, p. 319[c]
Other assets	393	11.3	Residual statistic
Total	3,472	100.0	*Statistics*, p. 319

[a] Source references are from U.S. Census Office, Tenth Census [1860].   [b] See note 49, for details.   [c] Estimated by subtracting the value of farmland and buildings from the total value of real estate given in the source cited.

Historians and economists have also been misled by the 1870 Census. Because of serious deficiencies in that enumeration of the South, comparison of aggregates for 1870 with corresponding figures from prewar censuses greatly exaggerates the postwar economic decline.[50] In particular, census figures on the population and the level of agricultural output of the South in 1870 are substantially below their true values. The deficiencies of the Ninth Census first became apparent when it was established that the population was substantially undercounted in the former Confederate States in 1870. These deficiencies were not fully apparent at the time of the census. At first, the slow rate of population increase measured between 1860 and 1870 was attributed to higher mortality during the war decade. In the introduction to the population volume of the 1870 Census, the low rate of increase in the South's black population was explained in a single cumbersome sentence:

Drawn largely from the plantations, where their increase was natural, rapid, and sure, to cities and camps, where want, vice and pestilence made short work of the multitudes hastily gathered, inadequately provided for, and left for the first time to their own control, while so much of the impulse to procreation depended on the profits of slave-breeding was withdrawn by the abolition of chattelism, it is only to be wondered at that the colored people of the South have held their own in the ten years since 1860.[51]

There was also authoritative contemporary support for such an interpretation. General O. O. Howard, the superintendent of the Freedmen's Bureau, estimated "the loss of African life by the war" at 25 percent.[52] Others placed the death rate even higher. A Mississippi planter estimated that along the Mississippi River, 50 percent of the Negroes had died in epidemics during 1863–1864.[53] While there is no question that mortality, among whites as well as blacks, was considerable during the war, these contemporaries were undoubtedly misled by the complaints of labor shortages to exaggerate the true losses.

After the results of subsequent censuses were published, it became clear that the 1870 population counts for the former Confederate States were much too low. And in 1890 the Census Office officially acknowledged that a serious undercount had occurred.[54] Elsewhere we have estimated the extent to which the 1870 Census undercounted the population of the southern states. Based on our estimate of the true black population in 1870, we concluded that the census enumeration was 6.6 percent below the mark.[55]

Our estimate of the Negro population in 1870 also allowed us to infer the war-related mortality among blacks. The original enumeration, if accepted, would imply that approximately 10 percent of the black population died as a direct result of the war and its immediate aftermath. Our adjusted population estimate suggests a more reasonable, though still enormous, death rate of 1.6 percent.[56] We can confidently reject the contemporary notion that 25 to 50 percent of the blacks were killed or died in epidemics during the Civil War decade.

The fact that there was a substantial undercount of population in the Ninth Census casts considerable doubt on the accuracy of the Census of Agriculture taken at the same time. The superintendent of the Ninth Census cautioned readers of the problems of collecting agricultural data in the South, specifically referring to the "great number of farms in each of the former slave states, of undetermined acreage."[57] It is apparent from his discussion that the statistics on total acreage were not adjusted to account for those farms that did not report their size. Our examination of the original manuscripts of the census forms returned by the assistant marshals confirms the superintendent's suspicions about the completeness of the returns. We have also noticed that there is a substantial nonreporting problem in addition to the one alluded to by the Census Office. The value of the farm, the value of farm implements, the number and value of livestock, and other information seem frequently to have gone unrecorded.[58]

The only piece of concrete evidence we have found on the magnitude of the underreporting and underenumeration problem of agricultural statistics suggests that the extent of omissions in the 1870 Census may have been substantial. The cotton firm of Latham, Alexander and Company estimated the production of cotton each year based on shipments of the crop to major ports. Their figures imply that the cotton crop of 1869 was understated in the 1870 agricultural returns by approximately 12 percent.[59] The skepticism of the superintendent and the implications of the cotton production figures lead us to conclude that any evidence based on the 1870 Census of Agriculture must be handled with great care. The huge fall in the aggregate magnitude of such variables as tilled acreage, value of farms, number and value of livestock, and the number and value of work stock that is frequently cited from that census surely exaggerates the true change over the decade between 1860 and 1870.

The decline in the labor supply brought about by emancipation was viewed by most white southerners, not as a natural expression of freedom, but as confirmation of their racist contention that free blacks would be lazy, carefree, and incapable of working diligently without physical compulsion. This prejudice, built up during years spent in the self-serving defense of slavery, was retained intact through the war. Whitelaw Reid reported the words of a "young Alabamian" in 1865:

I tell you, the nigger *never* works except when he is compelled to. It is n't in his nature, and you can't put it in. He'll work a day for you for good wages, and then will go off and spend it; and you'll not get another lick out of him till he's hungry, and has got nothing to eat.[60]

When black men sought to free their wives from dawn to dusk labor in the fields so that they might better care for their children and the household, *De Bow's Review* reported the change in words that did not imply the editor's admiration. "Most of the field labor is now performed by men, the women regarding it as the duty of their husbands to support them in idleness."[61] Whites typically resented the blacks' new freedom, which allowed them to set their own hours of work. "Emancipation does confer real, actual liberty on negroes," conceded *De Bow's Review,* "liberty which they know how to enjoy, in which they luxuriate, and which they mean to retain. The negro slave worked eight or nine hours a day; the negro freedmen will not average three hours a day."[62] Resentment was so strong that it is difficult to find a southern white's comment on the labor shortage that is free of racist overtones.

The racial slurs apparent in contemporary comments on the labor situation should not blind the modern reader to the fact that the removal of compulsion produced a permanent, substantial, and economically far-reaching decline in the supply of labor. On the other hand, our own preoccupation with the economic impact of this change in the labor supply is not intended to minimize the importance of racist misconceptions in determining the outcome of the dispute between white landowners and black laborers over the form of agricultural organization that would be adopted.

It is obvious that some agreement between the races had to be reached. Freedmen were without land or other assets, and the plantation was without labor. It is our contention, which we shall develop in Chapter 4, that the blacks were able to prevent the creation of a labor system that would have replaced the exploitation of slavery with some other form of labor exploitation. At the same time, landowners successfully retained their ownership and control of the soil, and thereby prevented a collapse of the social and political hegemony that was their own legacy from the world of slavery.

CHAPTER 4

THE DEMISE OF THE PLANTATION

A share in the crop is the universal plan; negroes prefer it and I am forced to adopt it. Can't choose your system. Have to do what negroes want. They control this matter entirely.

> Response of a farmer to the survey conducted by F. W. Loring and C. F. Atkinson, *Cotton Culture and the South Considered with Reference to Emigration* (Boston: A. Williams & Co., 1869), p. 32.

One of the most dramatic and far-reaching developments of the postemancipation era was the decline of the plantation system of agriculture and its replacement by tenant farming. The reorganization of the antebellum plantation into smaller tenancies, each operated by a single family, was both swift and thorough. We know that by 1880 the plantation system had ceased to exist. In fact, as early as November 1869 the editor of the *Rural Carolinian* felt that this transformation was well under way. "That the old plantation system of farming must now be generally abandoned throughout the South is too obvious to require argument. In fact it has, in the main, and as a matter of necessity, been already laid aside."[1] As sudden and complete as it was, the abandonment of the old system and the fragmentation of farm operation in the Cotton South came about only after an attempt had been made to restore the prewar organization.

The revival of the plantation system

The antebellum plantation system depended upon the use of forced labor, so that the granting of freedom to the slaves undermined the primary economic advantage of this form of agricultural organization. Nevertheless, since few large landholders in the South had experience with any other system, it was only natural that they attempt to recreate the plantation regime as nearly as possible. While the planter had little experience dealing with free labor, he could at least draw upon an established technology familiar to himself, his overseer, and the laborers.

Notes to Chapter 4 appear on pages 329–335.

So it was that in 1865 and 1866 most of the prewar plantations were reestablished. The freedmen were hired for fixed wage payments, and the work-gang system was reintroduced with only minor modifications from the slave regime. The following description of the Barrow plantation in central Georgia during this period illustrates the similarity between the old and the new forms of organization:

For several years after the war, the force on the plantation was divided into two squads, the arrangement and method of working of each being about the same as they had always been used to. Each of these squads was under the control of a foreman, who was in the nature of a general of volunteers. The plantation was divided into two equal parts, and by offering a reward for the most successful planting, and thus exciting a spirit of emulation, good work was done, and the yield was about as great as it had ever been.[2]

Though this account does not specify the value of the "reward" to the superior work gang, we can speculate that it was probably similar to the Christmas feast or suit of clothes offered to the slaves who exceeded their picking quotas.[3]

Of course, the postwar version of the plantation system had its points of difference from that of the slave era. The use of whips and other forms of corporal punishment was deemphasized – but by no means eliminated. The overseer was frequently renamed "manager" or "agent" or, in the case of the Barrow plantation, "supertender." Yet, while the overseer's name had been changed to indicate the new order, his duties remained virtually the same.[4]

The laborers were provided housing and rations in addition to their fixed monthly wages. The housing provided was typically the old slave quarters – small cabins or barrackslike buildings with little privacy and no amenities.[5] The weekly ration differed little, if at all, from that offered slaves. Gray stated that during slavery "there was considerable uniformity in the rations allowed, especially in the cotton producing regions. The standard ration was 1 or $1^{1}/_{2}$ pecks of [corn] meal and $3^{1}/_{2}$ pounds of bacon per week for each adult. About half a ration was allowed for a child."[6] Loring and Atkinson put the postbellum standard at 4 pounds of mess pork or bacon, 1.5 pecks of cornmeal, and 1 pint of molasses, based on their extensive survey in 1868. Nonworking family members had to be supported from the rations or earnings of the workers.[7] In January 1866, A. H. Arminton of Nash County, North Carolina, drew up "articles of agreement" between himself and Calvin, "formerly the property of said Arminton but now a freedman." Calvin and his wife, Penny, were to receive for themselves and their children "eight pounds of meat and two pecks of meal pr. week."[8] Alonzo T. Mial's contract with twenty-one workers, reproduced as Figure 4.1, provided each male worker with 15 pounds of bacon and 1 bushel of meal each month; about 3.75 pounds of meat and 1 peck of corn per week. The women generally received only 12 pounds of bacon each month (ap-

We Alonzo T. Mial of the County of Wake State of North Carolina of the one part, and the undersigned freed laborers of the other part have entered into the following Contract here in and after mentioned.

Witnesseth. That the Said laborers have agreed to work on the plantation of the Said Mial in the County of Wake and State aforesaid, from the date which Stands opposite their respective names to the 31st day of December 1865. That we will rise at day brake and attend to all duties preparatory to getting to work by Sun rise, and work till Sun Set, and when ever necessary even after Sun Set to Secure the Crop from frost, or taking up fodder or housing Cotton in picking Season after the days work is over, or any other Small jobs liable to loss by not being attended to the night before. Stoping in the Spring and Summer months for dinner one hour and a half, at 12 O'C. and in the Fall and Winter [and] Spring months one hour.

That we will do our work faithfully and in good order, and will be respectful in our deportment to the Said Mial and family or Superintendent. That we will work under the directions and management of the Said Mial or any Superintendent whose Services he may employ. That we will attend to all duties necessary to the plantation on Sundays, and will be responsible for the loss or damage from neglect or carelessness of all tools placed in our possession. The ordinary ware and tare of the Same excepted. And we further agree that time lost by idleness or absence without leave shall not be paid for, but for all time So lost we agree to pay double the amount of our wages and that all loss of time from Sickness or absence with leave will not be paid for. Also That we will pay for our rations advanced during all lost time. And we further agree That one half of our monthly wages Shall be retained by The Said Mial till the end of the year, and the amount So retained Shall be forfeited by a violation of this Contract on our part.

The Said Mial has agreed on his part in Consideration of the faithful performance of the above obligations of the undersigned freed laborers to pay the Said laborers the amount of money pr. month which stands opposite their respective names, or in no event payment to be delayed longer than three months, reserving one half however of the above amount till the end of the year which amount shall then be paid if not forfeited by a violation of this Contract by the Said freed laborers. I also agree to furnish the first day of every month free of charge to every full hand fifteen lbs of Bacon and one Bushel of meal pr. month or as pr.

No.	Name	Age	Wages	Ration	Date
7	Scott X Miles (his mark)	37	$10.00	15lbs Bacon 1 Bush Meal	1st Jan. 1866
8	Short X Alston (his mark)	63	$10.00	15lbs Bacon 1 Bush Meal	1 Jan. 1866
9	Frances X Alston (her mark)	20	$6.00	12lbs Bacon 1 Bush Meal	1 Jan. 1866
10	Elizabeth X Alston (her mark)	18	$5.00	12lbs Bacon 1 Bush Meal	1 Jan. 1866
11	Stetler X Alston (his mark)	15	$4.00	12lbs Bacon 1 Bush Meal	1 Jan. 1866
12	Wiston X Miles (his mark)	47	$10.00	15lbs Bacon 1 Bush Meal	10th Jan. 1866
13	George X Miles (his mark)	16	$6.	12lbs Bacon 1 Bush Meal	10th Jan. 1866
14	Chapman X Miles (his mark)	14	$6.	12lbs Bacon 1 Bush Meal	10th Jan. 1866
15	Joseph X Miles (his mark)	51	$10.00	15lbs Bacon 1 Bush Meal	1 Jan. 1866
16	Robert X Miles (his mark)	20	$10.00	15lbs Bacon 1 Bush Meal	8th Jan. 1866
17	Barnet X Miles (his mark)	17	$6.00	12lbs Bacon 1 Bush Meal	8th Jan. 1866

amount which Stands opposite their respective names. I also agree to Sell to them for their family Support not in my employ provisions Such as I may have to Spare at the retail Shop price in the City of Raleigh. I also agree to give them half of every other Saturday between the 1st day of March and the 1st day of August, and will furnish them land for a Small Crop. Also will furnish the teams and tools for the cultivation of the Same provided the teams and tools are not abused by Them. To all of which we do this day mutually agree. This the 29th day of January A. D. 1866.

Witness

Malcolm Hinton [signed]

A. T. Mial [signed]

No.	Names of Freed Laborers	Age	Pay pr. Mo.	Amount of Rations pr. Mo.	Date of Commencement
1	John X Miles *his mark*	29	$10.00	15lbs Bacon 1 Bush Meal	8th Jan. 1866
2	Lewis X Miles *his mark*	63	$10.00	15lbs Bacon 1 Bush Meal	22nd Jan. 1866
3	Dick X Miles *his mark*	68	$10.00	15lbs Bacon 1 Bush Meal	1st Jan. 1866
4	Allen X Miles *his mark*	39	$10.00	15lbs Bacon 1 Bush Meal	1 Jan. 1866
5	Joseph X Rhodes *his mark*	21	$10.00	15lbs Bacon 1 Bush Meal	1 Jan. 1866
6	Seaton X Hinton *his mark*	18	$10.00	15lbs Bacon 1 Bush Meal	30th Jan. 1866
18	Rheubin X Miles *his mark*	15	$6.00	12lbs Bacon 1 Bush Meal	8th Jan. 1866
19	Rebecca X Miles *her mark*	11	$3.	10lbs Bacon 1 Bush Meal	8th Jan. 1866
20	John X Miles *his mark*	9	$2.	10lbs Bacon 1 Bush Meal	8th Jan. 1866
21	Calvin X Miles *his mark*	48	$10.00	15lbs Bacon 1 Bush Meal	1 Jan. 1866
22	Alex Miles	12	$2.00	10lbs Bacon 1 Bush Meal	1 Jan. 1866
23	Isaac High	21	$10.00	15lbs Bacon 1 Bush Meal	5th Feb. 1866
24	Haywood Whitley	25	$10.00	15lbs Bacon 1 Bush Meal	27th Feb/66
25	Amanda Whitley	22	$5.00	12lbs Bacon 1 Bush Meal	19th Mar/66
26	Mary Whitley	38	$5.00	furnished from table	5th Mar/66
27	Henry Whitley	21	$	12lbs Bacon 1 Bush Meal	2nd Ap/66

Figure 4.1 Contract between Alonzo T. Mial and twenty-one freed laborers; January 1866. (*Source:* Alonzo T. Mial and Millard Mial Papers, North Carolina Department of Archives and History.)

proximately 3 pounds per week) to supplement their bushel of meal. No
allowance was made for the workers' children, although Mial agreed to
"Sell to them for their family Support not in my employ provisions Such as
I may have to Spare at the retail Shop price in the City of Raleigh" (see
Figure 4.1).

The wages offered freedmen varied considerably. Whitelaw Reid reported hearsay evidence of blacks working for food and rations alone, and
the Freedmen's Bureau noted wage offers as low as $2 per month in Georgia
during 1865.[9] By contrast, in the delta areas along the Mississippi River,
Reid observed that, "twenty dollars per month, with rations, lodging, etc.,
was a common offer; and some went as high as twenty-five."[10] Loring and
Atkinson's survey of planters in 1869 reported that most workers probably
were offered between $5 and $15 a month.[11] The Freedmen's Bureau sought
to ensure a wage contract of between $8 and $10 per month in 1865 and
1866.[12] A survey taken by the Department of Agriculture reported an average annual wage for "full hands" in 1867 varying from $100 in South
Carolina to $150 in Louisiana. Women received between one-half and two-
thirds the pay offered "full hands"; a youth received one-third of a man's
wages.[13] Arminton agreed to pay Calvin $120 and his wife $80 for the year
1866, and in January of that year, Alonzo T. Mial offered the workers who
signed with him wages varying from $10 a month for full hands down to $2
for nine-year-old John Miles. Very frequently, only a portion of the wages
was paid monthly, the balance being reserved to guarantee the laborer
would stay with the plantation through the season.[14]

A serious problem that plagued planters attempting to reestablish the
plantation system was the almost total lack of circulating currency in 1865–
1866. The Confederate issue was worthless, and the Federal issue had not
yet reappeared in sufficient quantities.[15] As a result, some planters who had
contracted to pay money wages found it impossible to obtain the necessary
cash. Payments had to be deferred, made in kind, or paid in private scrip.[16]
One response to the lack of currency was to offer a share of the year's crop
as wages rather than a fixed sum of money. References can be found in the
assistant commissioner's reports to General Howard for 1866 to the practice
of paying shares, rather than wages, to plantation labor.[17]

Initially, the fraction of the crop offered to the laborer in lieu of cash
wages was quite small. A. R. Lightfoot reported that in 1865 the hands
"were contented with a share in the cotton and corn crops, ranging from an
eighth to a twelfth."[18] As with cash wages, housing and rations were also
provided, in addition to the interest in the crop. However, as soon as the
freedmen began to exercise their bargaining power, the share they received
was increased. Lightfoot continued: "In 1867, they again demanded a share
in the crops. But their estimate of the value of their labor had risen, instead
of an eighth of the cotton and corn, they demanded a *fourth* of everything
raised on the plantation."[19]

It should be emphasized that this system was not a tenancy arrangement.
Rather, it was the plantation system employing the work-gang system of

organization in which the worker received his wages at the end of the season as portion of the crop. Although share wages were not uncommon for several years, they became less frequent as the improving credit system and expanding currency supply began to make payment in kind unnecessary.[20]

The planters' efforts to reestablish a facsimile of the prewar plantation were encouraged by the Freedmen's Bureau. The bureau's strong advocacy of wage contracts was undoubtedly an important factor in establishing an organized market for free labor in a situation where neither employer nor employees were accustomed to dealing with contracts and wages. Having encouraged the Negro to sign, the bureau stood ready to assist both in drawing up the contract and in enforcing the agreement when necessary.[21]

In the first few years of freedom, the wage payment system was, from all indications, universally adopted both by the plantations and by those smaller farms that required a hired hand or two. The reports of the Freedmen's Bureau and the testimony of planters and travelers all agree that any other system of compensating labor was so rare as to constitute an isolated experiment. The Freedmen's Bureau makes only infrequent reference to tenant farming in its extensive reports of 1866 on the reorganization of agriculture and labor, and in one such reference the Mississippi assistant commissioner described a proposed sharecropping agreement as an "undeveloped idea."[22] Travelers in the South during the period also reported the wage system as the universal choice of the landlords. Whitelaw Reid visited the South from May 1865 through May 1866. He discussed the reorganization of the plantation system extensively in his account of the journey, but he made only one reference to sharecropping and that in a chapter on "labor experiments."[23] John Trowbridge, another traveler, recorded hearing of two similar experiments with sharecropping during his visit from August 1865 to February 1866.[24]

Black labor in the new system

In 1865, white southerners worried aloud that their former slaves might not work effectively or might quit the plantation for some other life. These pessimistic views were reinforced by the actions of many blacks in the months immediately following the news of their new status. The first response of many slaves upon learning of their emancipation was to test the extent of their liberty. When it became known "that their liberation was no longer a mere contingency, but a fixed fact," Carl Schurz observed:

Large numbers of colored people left the plantations; many flocked to our military posts and camps to obtain the certainty of their freedom, and others walked away merely for the purpose of leaving the places on which they had been held in slavery, and because they could now go with impunity.[25]

More than idle curiosity prompted this migration. A powerful force motivating those blacks whose families had been broken by slavery was the desire to reunite their families. "In Louisiana," wrote John Dennett, "I met men and women who since the war had made long journeys in order to see their parents or children. I dare say there must have been thousands of such cases."[26]

The aspect of blacks' migration most troubling to white contemporaries was an exodus from agricultural areas to the urban regions. "The cities and towns are full of labor, but it is next to impossible to get them to leave these places," complained one planter in his response to the Loring and Atkinson survey.[27] The reports of other contemporaries agree that immediately after the war southern towns, particularly the larger ones, experienced substantial influxes of newly freed slaves; often the towns became overcrowded with blacks. Shantytowns and tent cities were constructed on the outskirts of virtually every major southern city to accommodate the influx.

The freedmen's motives for taking up such residences seem again to be a combination of the natural desire to demonstrate their freedom and an attempt to seek employment in a life away from the old plantation. Towns appeared to offer the greatest hope for a new life. When Whitelaw Reid queried a resident of a Negro settlement outside Selma, he was told: " 'I's want to be free man, cum when I please, and nobody say nuffin to me, nor order me roun'.' "[28]

At least two points should be considered before concluding from this evidence that a substantial number of blacks left agricultural occupations for the city. In the first place, much of this migration was unquestionably temporary. There were insufficient job opportunities in the urban areas to accommodate all who moved into the towns in the wake of freedom. Necessity ultimately sent many back to the rural areas where employment could be procured. This return to the land was encouraged by both the Freedmen's Bureau and the hostile white population of the towns. The bureau reports suggest that by the end of 1866 the situation had stabilized. The report of a bureau officer in Vicksburg, Mississippi, observed that the freedmen had "gone to the Plantations," and "the number still remaining around towns is not excessive."[29] Nevertheless, towns in the Cotton South *did* experience a marked increase in colored population between 1860 and 1870. Table 4.1 presents data for the forty-five towns in the Five Cotton States with 1,000 or more people in 1870 for which 1860 population returns are available. Negro population in these towns grew by 72 percent, while the white population remained relatively unchanged. The figures suggest that blacks were attracted to large towns; the twenty-one small towns reporting data experienced a 15 percent fall in Negro population.[30]

A second point should be noted when assessing the impact of black movement to the cities and towns. Since the South was a predominantly rural region, even an influx of blacks that was very large relative to the white urban population would have represented a tiny fraction of the rural population. The growth in urban black population implied by Table 4.1 was less than 4 percent of the rural Negro population in 1870. It amounted to no more than 75,000 people in the Five Cotton States.[31]

Table 4.1. *Urban population, Five Cotton States: 1860, 1870*

Population of town, 1870	Number of towns, 1870	Urban population, 1870 (thousands)		Number of 1870 towns reporting data for 1860	Percent change in population for reporting towns, 1860–1870[a]		
		Black	White		All	Black	White
1,000–2,500	56	40.5	47.2	21	− 0.5	− 14.6	+16.5
2,500–10,000	19	45.0	43.4	15	+23.9	+ 62.3	− 0.8
10,000–50,000	8	87.0	93.2	8	+32.8	+ 78.5	+ 7.2
50,000 and over	1[b]	50.4	141.0	1	+13.5	+109.6	− 2.5
All cities	84	222.9	324.8	45	+20.5	+ 72.0	+ 0.5
Total rural population	—	2,022.0	1,870.2	—	—	—	—
Precent urban in 1870	—	9.9	14.8	—	—	—	—

[a] Includes only those towns that reported population in both 1860 and 1870. [b] New Orleans was the only city with over 50,000 people in 1870.
Source: U.S. Census Office, Ninth Census [1870]. *Statistics of the Population of the United States* (Washington: GPO, 1872), Table 3.

Occasional complaints by southerners that their former slaves had "emigrated North and West" also seem to have been overstated.[32] The first postwar census contains no evidence that an exodus of blacks had substantially affected the population of the southern states. There was apparently some migration to the frontier regions of the South – particularly to Texas and Florida – between 1860 and 1870. Nonetheless, only 9 percent of all blacks born in the Five Cotton States lived outside those states in 1870, and many of these had been taken out of the region as slaves before the Civil War.[33]

The motives of the freedmen for relocating themselves and their families were widely misinterpreted by their former masters. Their movement was not an attempt to avoid work or to enter a life of idleness. "At no time," concluded John Dennett, after an extended tour of the South, "has anything like a majority of the Negroes thought that freedom meant exemption from labor."[34] In our research into the contemporary documents, we have uncovered no reliable testimony to suggest that blacks as a group refused to work, worked grudgingly, or worked unsatisfactorily when fairly treated by white employers. As we noted in Chapter 2, as early as 1866 the freedmen signed labor contracts and went to work.

Economic setbacks in 1866 and 1867

Although the landowners contracted for wage labor in 1866 and 1867 and the blacks agreed to work for the wages offered, many planters apparently lost money in those years. Much of the blame for this situation was laid elsewhere than on the plantation system. The enormously high price of cotton in 1864–1865, induced by wartime shortages, encouraged extravagant plans.[35] The high demand for labor and the labor shortage produced by emancipation, coupled with the pressure from the Freedmen's Bureau, resulted in a high level of wages in 1866–1867. When the cotton stocks hoarded during the war reached the market, and cotton production resumed, prices collapsed and many planters found themselves unable to meet their commitments at the end of the season. The price fall was dramatic: in 1864 the New York price was $1.02 per pound; it fell to 83 cents in 1865, to 43 cents in 1866, and to 32 cents in 1867.[36] Throughout much of the South the loss caused by the unexpectedly rapid decline in cotton prices was aggravated by a protracted drought in 1866 and again in 1867. The United States Department of Agriculture reported that "the results of planting in 1866 and 1867 were, in most cases, disastrous to planters. . . . In some sections, the entire crop, as is asserted of the majority of plantations, did not suffice to pay laborers and their food and clothing."[37]

These losses were in turn compounded by the inexperience of most planters with free labor and its proper management. "A lack of the ability or skill to judiciously manage *free* negro labor," wrote the editor of the *Rural Carolinian,* was one of the "true causes why the large plantation system . . .

[was] generally impracticable, rather than the inherent unreliability of [black] labor."[38] Many planters, however, were reluctant to accept any blame for themselves or to find fault with the system. Rather they attributed their problems to ill luck and the supposed inferiority of the Negro.

The widespread crop failures in 1866 and 1867 turned the climate of optimism into one of pessimism. In the words of the official report to Congress, "loss and bankruptcy were rife, and gloom overspread the planting community."[39] One reflection of this change in outlook was a sharp fall in the wages offered for the 1868 season. According to the information provided to the Department of Agriculture by its county correspondents, wages in the Five Cotton States fell by as much as 25 to 40 percent between 1867 and 1868. The annual wages earned by ablebodied men are presented in Table 4.2. The incomes of women and children, also reported by the USDA, show similar changes.[40]

Nevertheless, it is unlikely that a technique of production that had evolved and developed over sixty years of experience would have been abandoned simply because of one or two years of losses. Planters of the South had seen hard times before without abandoning the plantation system. But they began to do so in 1867–1868. The difficulties we have been discussing here were significant, not because they soured the planter on the practicality of using wage labor, but because they placed him in a weak position to resist another powerful force: dissatisfaction of blacks with the old system.

Black dissatisfaction with the plantation system

From the outset, the workers had expressed their displeasure with the wage plantation. The wage system as practiced by the large landowners bore an uneasy resemblance to slavery. The work gangs, the slave quarters, the overseers, the use of corporal punishment, all led to the suspicion that little

Table 4.2. *Annual wages earned by black males,*
Five Cotton States: 1867, 1868

State	Annual wage ($)		Percent decline
	1867	1868	
South Carolina	100	93	7.0
Georgia	125	83	33.6
Alabama	117	87	25.6
Mississippi	149	90	39.6
Louisiana	150	104	30.7

Source: U.S. Department of Agriculture, *Report of the Commissioner of Agriculture for the Year 1867* (Washington: GPO, 1867), p. 416.

had been gained with freedom beyond wages. Workers, according to a contributor to the *Southern Cultivator* in 1869, were "anxious to rid themselves of all supervision on the part of the white race, and to look upon it as a sort of continued badge, or remembrancer, of their former condition of servitude."[41] From the beginning, the blacks resisted and complained about attempts to revive the prewar arrangements. Despite the reservations of the freedmen, economic necessity at first asserted itself. Initially, the freedmen did sign wage agreements and went to work as plantation hands. Their experience with the wage system, however, reinforced rather than diminished their distaste for such an arrangement. The contracts signed were, in some cases, broken by the landowners. Accounts of planters who attempted to cheat or defraud their employees fill the reports filed with the Freedmen's Bureau in 1866.[42] In other cases, planters attempted to form collusive agreements to lower wages and restrict labor mobility.[43] It is likely that cases of outright dishonesty were the exception rather than the rule, and that the collusive agreements were frequently ineffective. They were, nevertheless, sufficiently noticeable to provoke widespread distrust of the new system. Though the Freedmen's Bureau did what it could to protect the rights of the freedmen, as General O. O. Howard noted in his report: "The fact cannot be concealed that the dispositon by so many employers, this early in the season, to reduce wages by community of action, tended seriously to lessen the confidence of the freed people in them and increased suspicion and prejudice."[44]

Dissatisfaction with the wage system not infrequently led to attempts to rectify the situation. Despite the common practice of withholding a portion of wages due until the picking had been completed, many workers apparently left the plantation in protest – temporarily or permanently – before the crop was harvested. The landowners sought protection from the competition of other employers through the passage of laws that restricted the mobility of the Negro. In late 1865 and early 1866, the legislatures of the southern states were controlled by the same white aristocracy that had ruled the South before the Civil War. They had been promptly recognized as legitimate governments under the reconstruction plan of President Johnson. Although these governments accepted the Thirteenth Amendment, they drafted and quickly passed the Black Codes – legislation that clearly defined an inferior status for the freedmen. Indeed, they made no pretense at hiding their intentions. An act of the South Carolina legislature in 1865 asserted that "persons of color . . . are not entitled to social or political equality with white persons."[45] A major goal of these acts was to restrict black mobility and to weaken the impact of competition in the labor market. For example, in February 1866 the Alabama Legislature passed an act that made it unlawful "for any person to interfere with, hire, employ, or entice away, or induce to leave the service of another, any laborer or servant who shall have stipulated or contracted, in writing, to serve for any given [period]."[46] A few months before, in December 1865, Louisiana had enacted a law that required all laborers to make contracts for the following year by

January tenth. The act stipulated that laborers leaving employers would forfeit all wages due them and could be imprisoned as a lien against any alleged losses. The law further stipulated

that any one who shall persuade or entice away, feed, harbor, or secrete any person who leaves his or her employer . . . shall be liable for damages to the employer, and . . . shall be subject to pay a fine of not . . . less than ten dollars, or imprisonment in the parish jail for not . . . less than ten days, or both.[47]

Another universally adopted provision of the Black Codes was a "vagrancy" statute. Under these acts, any freed person unable to prove in writing that he or she was employed was subject to arrest and fine. If the hapless "vagrant" was unable to pay the fine, he or she could be bound out to hire. Such laws had the effect of restricting the ability of blacks to quit their present employment in protest or to seek work elsewhere. Since there were sanctions against potential employers seeking to bid labor away, it was difficult for a freedman to find a new job without leaving his present employer.

Ironically, all these laws only increased the freedmen's dislike of wage labor contracts. Whitelaw Reid noted that the effect of such laws was "like the patent rat-trap. Nobody could make a safer contrivance. Rats could n't possibly get out of it. The only difficulty was that they declined to go in."[48] The Black Codes became one more reason for ex-slaves to insist that a new system of organization be instituted. Moreover, black workers soon discovered that they had acquired sufficient economic power to give weight to their demands. This power was an unexpected consequence of the blacks' decision to spend less time at work than they had been compelled to provide when slaves. They had created, as we saw in Chapter 3, a serious labor shortage.

The facts that laborers were free to contract and in relatively short supply gave them the power in the labor market to insist on alternative arrangements. One preferred alternative was sharecropping. D. Wyatt Aiken, a prominent South Carolina planter, noted the impact of the blacks' new market power on his own options: "In 1868, hands could not be hired for wages. The custom of the country was to 'give a part of the crop.' I had to yield, or lose my labor."[49] A report to the Pomological and Farmer's Club of Society Hill, South Carolina, comparing different forms of land tenure, made a similar observation concerning the blacks' insistence upon sharecropping:

It is regarded by the laborer as a higher form of contract, and is thereby more likely to secure labor especially in undesirable localities. It was this consideration more than any other, which at the outset led to the general adoption of the share contract. Then the colored laborer in the first flush of freedom . . . seemed disposed to withdraw himself altogether from hire; while the farmer deluded by the high price of cotton, and accepting the theory that *any* labor was better than none at all, was prepared to make every concession.[50]

The disappearance of the plantation

The disappearance of the plantation system after 1867 is evident in the statistics on farm size and organization collected for the 1880 Census of Agriculture. Table 4.3 presents the distribution of farms and farmlands in the cotton-growing areas of the South in 1880 categorized by the tenure arrangements, size, and form of labor organization.[51] Fewer than 1 percent of the farms in the region could be considered plantations even by our generous definitions. In fact, only 5.3 percent of all farms reported more than 100 acres in crops. We failed to find a single farm in our sample of 4,695 farms that could be designated a plantation when judged by the standards of the slave era, though over 4 percent of the farms operated in 1860 would have qualified.[52] The rise of the small farm is also evident in the 1880 statistics. Almost 80 percent of the farms reported 50 acres or less in crops. Most of these small farms were run exclusively with family labor; only 8 percent hired more than six man-months of labor per year. Approximately 60 percent of the small family farms were operated by tenants rather than owners.

The statistics of Table 4.3 make it clear that the plantation had disappeared before 1880. In fact most planters abandoned the wage system after only one or two seasons of trial. The Freedmen's Bureau report of 1867 comments for the first time on the rise of tenancy. The reports from the states of South Carolina, Florida, Mississippi, and Texas all mention the growing prevalence of tenant farming. In Mississippi a "majority" of black workers were reported as working on shares, and in the cotton districts of Texas about one-half were reported as sharecroppers.[53] In the same year, the federal commissioner of agriculture, discussing conditions in the South, stated that "the most prevalent and popular mode of contracting proprietors and laborers is *Working upon Shares.*"[54]

For a number of years after the war, the tax collectors in Georgia returned the "number of hands employed" by each taxpayer. These data, presented in Table 4.4, suggest a dramatic decline in wage labor in the late 1860s. From 1866 to 1869 the number of hands employed fell by 25 percent in the cotton regions of the state, and by over 30 percent in the Piedmont Plateau region. Neither the reports of the state's comptroller nor the tax laws define the concept of "hands employed" precisely enough to make its meaning unambiguous, but it is certain that the compilation includes hands working for wages. Since some hired hands were working in nonagricultural jobs, the estimates almost certainly exaggerate the extent of wage payments to workers in agriculture. While the data we have examined do not allow us to be certain of the matter, it is our impression that the disappearance of the plantation system was virtually complete by 1870. Certainly the size distribution of southern farms in that year reveals a dramatic shift when compared with 1860. Distributions for the Five Cotton States are presented in

Table 4.3. *Distribution of farms and farmland, Cotton South: 1880*

Type of farm[a]	Percent distribution of farms	Percent of all land in each class	Percent of all acres reported in crops in each class[b]
Small family farms	69.7	37.4	41.0
Owned	28.4	25.4	17.5
Tenanted	41.4	12.0	23.5
Rented	11.1	3.5	6.5
Sharecropped	30.3	8.5	17.0
Other small farms	8.5	8.5	6.1
Owned	4.7	6.5	3.6
Tenanted	3.7	2.1	2.6
Rented	0.9	0.7	0.6
Sharecropped	2.9	1.4	1.9
Medium-scale farms	16.5	33.4	26.5
Owned	10.8	26.6	17.4
Tenanted	5.7	6.9	9.1
Rented	2.1	3.1	3.4
Sharecropped	3.6	3.7	5.7
Plantations	0.9	6.8	8.9
Owned[c]	0.8	6.5	8.4
Tenanted[c]	0.1	0.3	0.5
Other large farms	4.4	13.9	17.4
Owned	3.8	11.6	14.1
Tenanted[c]	0.6	2.3	3.4
All farms	100.0	100.0	100.0
Owned	48.6	76.5	60.8
Tenanted	51.4	23.5	39.2
Rented	14.4	9.2	13.6
Sharecropped	37.0	14.3	25.6

[a] Definition of farm type is as follows: *small family farms,* farms reporting 50 acres or less in crops and 26 weeks or less of hired labor; *other small farms,* farms reporting 50 acres or less in crops and more than 26 weeks of hired labor; *medium-scale farms,* farms reporting more than 50 acres but 100 acres or less in crops; *plantations,* farms reporting 200 acres or more in crops, greater than 98 weeks of hired labor, and relying on hired labor for at least 60 percent of their requirements; *other large farms,* all farms not included in one of the above categories.
[b] Acres reported in crops are total acres harvested in 1879 planted with the following crops: rice, barley, buckwheat, Indian corn, oats, rye, wheat, cotton, flax, hemp, sugar cane, sorghum, tobacco, apples, and peaches.
[c] Figures reported are based on fewer than forty sample farms.
Source: Computed from a sample of farms from the 1880 Census of Agriculture. See Appendix G, Section 2, for details. See Chapter 5, Table 5.1 for racial breakdown.

Figure 4.2. The dramatic increase in the number of small farms is clearly evident. Table 4.5 presents the census statistics on farm size. The dramatic increase in the improved acreage organized in farms of less than 100 acres corresponds with an equally dramatic decline in the acreage organized in units of 500 or more improved acres.

Contemporary observers reported that the spectacular increase in the number of small farming units was accomplished by literally dividing the old plantation estates into numerous separate tenancies, one for each black family. The accompanying map of a plantation holding in northern Georgia depicts how this was accomplished in one such instance. The reorganization of this plantation took place at the outset of the 1869 season. It was in November of that year that the editor of the *Rural Carolinian* noted "as a matter of necessity" that the plantation system had already been "laid aside."[55]

The "matter of necessity" referred to was the insistence of the blacks that sharecropping replace the old arrangements. Nevertheless, it is important to emphasize that the blacks could not so easily have overthrown the plantation regime had the landowners felt substantial losses would accompany the fragmentation of the unit of production. Weakened by financial losses consequent upon the crop failures of 1867 and 1868, the planters were willing to accede to the blacks' insistence on tenant farming as an experiment. The process of transformation to tenancy was completed when it was discovered that small-scale operations produced rents at least equivalent to those anticipated under the plantation system.

Table 4.4. *Decline in "hands employed" in cotton regions of Georgia: 1866–1869*

Region number[a]	Region name	1866	1869	Percent decline
9	Central Cotton Belt	44,536	38,653	13.2
13	Piedmont Plateau[b]	66,902	46,286	30.8
18	Southwest Georgia	5,051	2,457	51.4
Total		116,489	87,396	25.0

[a] See Appendix G, Section 1, for a description of the economic regions of the South. See Roger L. Ransom and Richard Sutch, "Economic Regions of the South in 1880," *Southern Economic History Project Working Paper Series,* Number 3 (Berkeley: Institute of Business and Economic Research, March 1971) for a list of counties included in each region.
[b] Douglas, McDuffie, Oconee, and Rockdale Counties not reported.
Source: Georgia, Office of the Comptroller General, *Annual Report of the Comptroller General . . . October 16, 1866* (Macon: J. W. Burke & Co., 1866), Part 2, pp. 38–43; idem, *Annual Report . . . April 1, 1871* (Atlanta: Constitution Publishing Co., 1871), pp. 35–40.

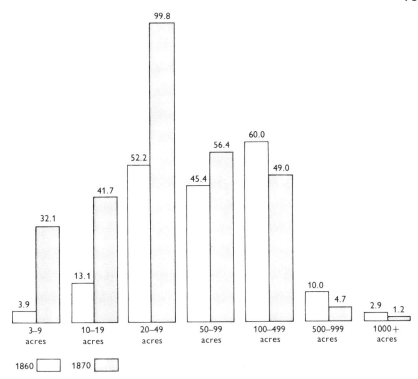

Figure 4.2 Thousands of farms in each size class, Five Cotton States: 1860 and 1870. (*Source:* U.S. Census office, Tenth Census [1880], *Report on the Production of Agriculture* [Washington: GPO, 1883], pp. 11, 16, 27.)

Table 4.5. *Farm size, Five Cotton States: 1860, 1870*

Number of improved acres	Thousands of farms		Percent of all farms in size class		Percent of improved land in size class[a]	
	1860	1870	1860	1870	1860	1870
3–49	69.2	173.6	36.9	60.9	7.4	20.2
50–99	45.4	56.4	24.2	19.8	12.0	19.6
100–499	60.0	49.0	32.0	17.2	47.6	49.1
500 and up	12.9	5.9	6.9	2.1	33.0	11.1
Total	187.6	284.9	100.0	100.0	100.0	100.0

[a] Percent of improved land was computed by estimating the mean size of farm for each size class up to 500 improved acres. Distribution of farms within size classes was approximated by fitting a continuous curve to the total distribution. Open interval was calculated as a residual left after the cumulative acreage organized in farms up to 500 acres was estimated.

Source: Data for both years are taken from U.S. Census Office, Tenth Census [1880], *Report on the Production of Agriculture* (Washington: GPO, 1883), pp. 11, 16, 27.

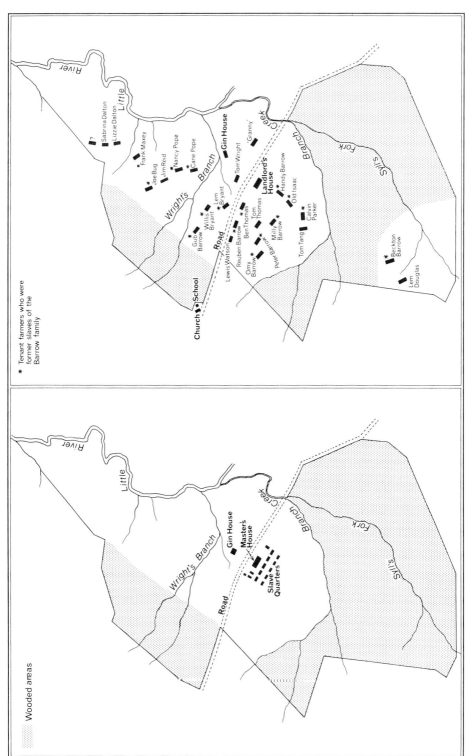

The Barrow plantation in 1860 and 1881. (*Source:* Adapted from *Scribner's Monthly*, XXI [April 1881], pp. 832–833.)

Economies of scale in cotton agriculture

It is frequently suggested that the large-scale plantation before the Civil War enjoyed substantial economies of scale. In other words, as both the number of acres and the number of slaves organized into a plantation were increased, the efficiency of the operation increased as well. These economies of scale have been offered by writers such as Lewis Gray as an explanation of the large size of antebellum cotton plantations and of the apparent tendency before the Civil War for the average size of farms to increase over time.[56] The question then arises whether the decline in farm size that accompanied the disappearance of the plantation had a significant impact on agricultural efficiency. We cannot employ aggregate data on total output and the stock of inputs to approach this question, for any observed change in productivity might easily be accounted for by the host of other simultaneously occurring phenomena that accompanied emancipation, reconstruction, and the rise of tenancy.

Yet, despite the difficulties in making a direct comparison between antebellum and postbellum agriculture, there is reason to doubt the premise that substantial scale-related economies existed in cotton agriculture before the war. Two recent studies that have employed the farm-by-farm data available in the Parker-Gallman sample of the Cotton South in 1860 have directed themselves to this question. Gavin Wright employed a regression technique to test whether output per hand was associated with the scale of the plantation after correcting for the influence of diversification, land quality, and capital intensity. He concluded that, with the exception of the alluvial regions along the Mississippi River, "economies of scale were limited, and that there is much evidence of *decreasing* returns."[57]

Robert Fogel and Stanley Engerman, using the same sample but somewhat different techniques, appear to have taken issue with Wright. They concluded that there were economies of scale in antebellum southern agriculture.[58] However, two qualifications need to be made immediately. According to Fogel and Engerman, the gains in efficiency were achieved when the farm size changed from the size class of one to fifteen slaves (fewer than eight hands) to the size class of sixteen to fifty slaves (between eight and twenty-five hands).[59] The largest farms (fifty-one or more slaves) were less efficient than the intermediate class, although more efficient than the small farms. Since fifty slaves was usually taken by contemporaries as a minimum size for a farm to deserve the title "plantation," these findings do not support without qualification the assertion that *plantations* enjoyed economies of scale. The Fogel-Engerman findings may also be influenced by the fact that 1859 was an exceptional year for cotton producers. The high yields and prices for that year would provide cotton growers with incomes well above the average from that crop and make such farms appear to be very "efficient," since output is measured by Fogel and Engerman in terms of total dollar value of production on the farm. Large cotton plantations devoted a larger share of their acreage to cotton and therefore received a greater windfall gain from the good crop year. A comparison based on the single year 1859, therefore, will exaggerate the "efficiency" of large plantations relative to a more typical crop year.[60]

It would be interesting to see the results obtained by applying similar techniques in an analysis of economies of scale in the postwar period. Unfortunately, several inherent difficulties preclude this approach. In the first place, the reorganization of agriculture was so complete that there were practically no large-scale farms remaining in 1880 that could be used to compare with the smaller-scale family farms. As we have already noted, not a single farm in our 1880 sample operated on a scale comparable to a slave plantation. Only 46 farms were discovered in our sample of more than 4,500 farms in 1880 that could be considered – even by the generous definition employed in Table 4.3 – as free plantations.[61] A second problem that would plague any attempt to measure economies of scale from data contained in the 1880 Census of Agriculture is the poor quality of the information available on labor input.[62] In light of these difficulties, we have not attempted to measure directly postwar economies of scale.

In any event, such a measure would not bear directly on the point at issue. We are not asking whether the few and atypical large farms that did survive into the postwar period were more or less efficient relative to the numerous small tenancies. What is at issue is whether the work-gang technology of the prewar plantation system, transplanted to the postwar context, was more or less efficient than family tenancy. This is a question that cannot be answered directly by econometric study. Nevertheless, it is possible to identify plausible explanations for the large scale of slave plantations and to ask whether they would have survived in the postwar environment. In this way, we are able to rule out the possibility that the South suffered a significant loss of efficiency simply because the plantation system disappeared.

There can be no question that the bulk of cotton production before the war took place on large holdings; 34.2 percent of the cotton output was produced on farms with fifty-one or more slaves, and 84.0 percent was produced on farms with more than ten slaves.[63] Clearly, there was some advantage to large-scale operation. A review of the literature suggests four possible explanations for the apparent advantage enjoyed by the larger slave farms.[64]

1. *Capital indivisibilities:* Large farms could make more efficient use of work stock, implements, and such machinery as cotton gins and presses than small farms, which might be forced to invest more heavily in capital than their scale of operation warranted.
2. *Division and specialization of labor:* Large farms, with their large labor force, could engage in greater specialization and routinization of tasks for unskilled labor, as well as make better use of skilled labor and management, than could small farms.

3. *Coercion of slave labor:* Large farms could afford to employ a highly coercive technology designed to produce a high intensity of work effort, while a small farm could not afford the supervision such techniques required.
4. *Financial and marketing advantages:* Plantation owners could command a higher price when selling cotton and arrange to pay a lower price when purchasing supplies, a market power not possessed by operators of smaller farms.

The econometric techniques employed by Wright and by Fogel and Engerman could measure economies arising from the sources listed in the first three points, but not those associated with the financial advantages of large scale mentioned in point four.[65] Wright, who failed to discover economies of scale, attributed the large size of antebellum plantations to this fourth cause, since the other three factors were ruled out.[66] Unfortunately, very little evidence has been uncovered that would indicate the magnitude of such financial and marketing gains in either the antebellum or postbellum period. In any case, to the extent that financial and marketing economies represented a substantial advantage of large scale, they would not necessarily have been lost with the decline in farm size following the war. Indeed, they might provide part of the explanation for the continued dominance of large landholdings in the postwar South. The large landholder would be able to continue to command these marketing advantages despite the fragmentation of production, since he could act as an agent for all his tenants. Even if the landowner did not act as an intermediary himself, the advantages of scale could have been retained for the South by the rural merchant. As we shall argue in subsequent chapters, this marketing function was taken over from the landowners by the rural merchants, who frequently acted as agents in the sale of cotton as well as serving as a provisioner. If so, the advantages of scale would not accrue to the landowners, but they would not be lost to southern agriculture either.

Fogel and Engerman identify the source of the scale economies they observed as the third point we mention: the coercion made possible by the work-gang system. As they put it: "Economies of scale in southern agriculture were achieved exclusively with slave labor."[67] They argue that "the organization of slaves into highly disciplined, interdependent teams capable of maintaining a steady and intense rhythm of work [was] the crux of the superior efficiency of large-scale operations on plantations, at least as far as fieldwork was concerned."[68] In their view, the key was coercion and the use of force, not the work-gang system per se, "for it was only by applying force that it was possible to get blacks to accept gang labor without having to pay a premium that was in excess of the gains from economies of scale."[69]

If this view of the matter is accepted, then the advantages of the plantation system disappeared with *emancipation* and could not have been regained with any system that denied landowners the right to apply force.

Reinstating the work-gang technology, substituting wages as an incentive rather than punishment as a disincentive, would not have replicated the efficiency of the slave plantation. By this argument postwar agriculture may have produced less output per man-hour than did slavery, but this cannot be properly counted as a welfare loss to the South as a whole, since the gain to the emancipated laborers produced by their release from physical coercion clearly exceeded the loss in output per man-hour attributable to removal of force. We know this because slaveowners before the war found that the premium they would have to pay free workers to agree to work as part of work gangs exceeded the gain from employing this method of organization and because plantation operators after the war found the blacks were unwilling to work in work gangs at a wage that would make this system of organization profitable.

The second point in our list of alleged advantages of large scale is the division of labor. There are two aspects to this argument: the routinization of and simplification of tasks possible with a large work force, and the large plantation's more efficient utilization of managerial skills. U. B. Phillips stated the case for the first of these points:

The great characteristic feature and the strength of the plantation method was in its division of labor and above all in its arrangement for the performance by the negroes of a labor nearly always of a routine character. The routine system was the only system by which the unintelligent, involuntary negro labor could be employed to distinct advantage; and, other things being equal, the most successful planter was always he who arranged the most thorough and effective routine. . . . [The] plantation system was probably the most efficient method ever devised for the use of stupid labor in agriculture on a large scale.[70]

One can reject Phillips's racist characterization of the Negro and still retain the essence of this argument for the issue of economies of scale. Indeed, Keith Aufhauser has recently emphasized the routine nature of plantation labor in his treatment of slave management.[71]

On the other hand, Robert Russel has argued that the division of labor was as much a difficulty as a boon. He pointed out that the routinization of agricultural tasks led to a boredom that reduced efficiency and that the division of labor led to an inflexibility that prevented its efficient redirection. "There would have been a moral difficulty about sending a dignified coachman to the field to plow or 'chop.'"[72] In addition to Russel's suggestion that there were counterbalancing tendencies that accompanied gang labor and routine tasks, we see three additional problems with Phillips's argument. If, as Phillips himself notes, routinization of tasks was associated with the "involuntary" nature of the labor, then the economies might more appropriately be attributed to coercion than to the simplification. Furthermore, it is not clear why the advantages of establishing a simple work routine come only with large scale. Even an individual working alone can adopt a repetitive routine. Finally, to the extent that specialization, as apart from routinization and simplification of tasks, for *unskilled* labor is the key, we simply note that none of the studies we have examined have made such an argument, nor have they presented evidence which suggests that such specialization took place.

Specialization of *skilled* labor and management is, of course, another matter. It is well known that most large plantations employed both slave and free labor in a variety of skilled tasks. Slaves were occasionally trained as carpenters or blacksmiths, and most large plantations hired overseers and employed, on an occasional basis, the services of such professionals as physicians, lawyers, and cotton factors. Moreover, it is alleged that managerial skills were in scarce supply and that the large scale of organization economized upon them.[73] To the extent that such economies of scale were significant, they, like the financial economies, would not be sacrificed by reorganizing production around family-oriented tenant farms. The landowner, as Joseph Reid has emphasized, retained substantial control over the tenant farm's operation and could, if it seemed desirable, apply his managerial skills to a large number of units.[74] Furthermore, small scale should not have precluded employing temporary services of artisans and professionals. We conclude that economies associated with the division of labor should not have been a barrier to the abandonment of the plantation system and the rise of tenancy.

This leaves what is, in other industries, the most frequently encountered advantage of large-scale operations: the gain from spreading the fixed costs of capital expenditure over large units. On the other hand, historians have argued that the capital required for cotton production involved such a small investment that it was available even to small producers. Very little machinery was required to grow cotton. Beyond teams, plows, and hoes, the only significant fixed capital outlay would be for the cotton gin and press. However, Russel insists that this equipment was available for a fee to all producers, either from a large planter in the region or from a public gin house.[75] In the postwar period, as we shall discuss in a subsequent chapter, public gin houses were located throughout the cotton regions. It would appear that the small farm did not operate under a disadvantage arising from capital indivisibilities. It was not until the early decades of the twentieth century that mechanization of cotton production became a reality and produced an economic advantage to consolidation.

Our review of each of the four alleged sources for economies of scale during the *prewar* period has led us to the conclusion that none of them would have operated as a deterrent to small-scale farming in the *postwar* period, whatever force they might have exerted before the abolition of slavery. This finding is of significance, since the absence of economies of scale facilitated the rise of tenancy by removing what would otherwise have been a serious economic objection to the fragmentation of production. Then, in the absence of this obstacle, the scarcity of labor gave blacks the economic power, and their newly acquired freedom of contract gave them the legal right, to insist upon new forms of economic organization.

The power to bring about institutional change is not, however, always sufficient to bring about significant realignment of economic status or significent redistribution of wealth. The blacks began freedom as the lowest class and as a landless class, and despite their success in bringing an end to the plantation they remained landless and economically subservient. The ownership of land remained concentrated in the hands of a few.

The concentration of landownership

The statistics on the change in the scale of farming units presented in Figure 4.2 and Table 4.5 clearly indicate that a new form of agricultural organization had arisen. It would be a mistake, however, to conclude from these numbers that a change in the ownership of land or its concentration had taken place.[76] Roger Shugg, using Louisiana tax records, has demonstrated that the size distribution of landownership did not shift toward equality after the war.[77] In fact, Shugg interpreted his data to show an increase in the concentration of landownership after the war:

Between 1860 and 1870 there was nearly a threefold increase in the number of [large landholdings] while the number of [owner-operated] farms actually decreased. The tendency of the larger properties to outstrip the smaller was strong between 1860 and 1873, and was only partially counteracted in the later years of reconstruction.[78]

Recently, a study by Jonathan Wiener has drawn from the manuscript Censuses of Population for 1850, 1860, and 1870 to study the persistence of the planter class over the Civil War decade in central Alabama. After a detailed study of the distribution of real estate in Marengo County, Alabama, in the heart of the black belt, Wiener concluded:

Between 1860 and 1870 the planter elite actually increased its relative wealth in real estate; it held a greater share of the real estate value five years after the war than it had when it began. The elite increased its share of the land value held by county residents by 8 per cent between 1860 and 1870, from 55 to 63 per cent.[79]

Our own examination of the real estate holdings reported by the census enumerators for Dallas County, Alabama, found a slight decrease in the concentration of landholdings between 1860 and 1870, but the two distributions presented in Table 4.6 are not dissimilar enough to warrant a conclusion that there was a trend toward equalization of landownership during the decade.[80]

The clear implication of the studies by Shugg, Wiener, and ourselves is that the ownership of land was not fragmented in the process of subdividing the holdings into tenant farms; rather, the landholdings remained extremely concentrated. Wiener reported that the largest landholders in Marengo County owned 63 percent of the real estate in 1870, despite the fact they represented only 10 percent of all landowners.[81] Our own estimates for Dallas County suggest that the wealthiest 10 percent owned 57 percent of the real estate of that county. What was lost was the plantation's system of

Table 4.6. *Distribution of real estate by landowners in Dallas County, Alabama: 1860, 1870*

Landowners ranked by value of real estate reported	Percent of all real estate held by each wealth class	
	1860	1870
Wealthiest 5%	47.2	43.1
Wealthiest 10%	60.4	57.0
Wealthiest 20%	75.1	73.0
Wealthiest 30%	84.3	82.7
Wealthiest 40%	91.1	88.7
Wealthiest 50%	93.8	93.0
Wealthiest 60%	96.3	95.8
Wealthiest 70%	97.9	97.7
Wealthiest 80%	99.1	98.8
Wealthiest 90%	99.8	99.7
100%	100.0	100.0

Source: Compiled from manuscript Population Census returns for Dallas County, Ala., 1860 and 1870. See Appendix G, Section 3, and Roger Ransom and Richard Sutch, "Tenancy, Farm Size, Self-Sufficiency, and Racism: Four Problems in the Economic History of Southern Agriculture, 1865–1880," *Southern Economic History Project Working Paper Series,* Number 8 (Berkeley: Institute of Business and Economic Research, University of California, April 1970), pp. 29–31.

Table 4.7. *Distribution of tenant farms classified by the number of tenancies per landowner, Five Cotton States: 1900*

	Percent of all tenant farms held by landowners with					Average number of tenants per owner of multiple tenancies
	1 tenant	2–4 tenants	5–9 tenants	10–19 tenants	20 or more tenants	
South Carolina	26.1	33.7	19.4	12.3	8.5	4.2
Georgia	31.7	35.9	17.0	9.6	5.9	3.8
Alabama	25.0	28.3	17.7	13.8	15.2	5.0
Mississippi	20.6	26.4	17.0	14.3	21.8	5.5
Louisiana	22.5	23.7	14.9	13.8	25.2	5.9
Five Cotton States	25.5	30.1	17.3	12.6	14.5	4.7

Source: U.S. Census Office, Twelfth Census [1900], *Census Reports . . . 1900,* Volume 6, *Agriculture,* 2 parts (Washington: GPO, 1902), Part 1, p. 312.

gang labor, not the plantation's concentration of control in the hands of the planter class.[82] A special study of landownership undertaken at the time of the 1900 Census confirms that landholdings remained concentrated even at the end of the century. In Table 4.7 the concentration of ownership is illustrated by the fact that 27.1 percent of all tenant farms in the Five Cotton States were owned by landlords who had ten or more tenants each in that year.

The concentration of landownership in the postwar period is significant because it meant that a small elite of white landowners controlled the employment opportunities for the majority of black workers. Moreover, as Jonathan Wiener has persuasively argued, this planter elite preserved intact the social and political hegemony of the antebellum era.[83] The reason, of course, that emancipation and the demise of the plantation did not destroy the planter class was that they retained firm control over the primary form of productive capital in the southern economy. Indeed, the only way the dominance of the planter class might have been ended would have been through a sweeping redistribution of land to the freedmen at the time of their emancipation. Although envisioned by Congress, such a redistribution did not take place. General O. O. Howard, superintendent of the Freedmen's Bureau, sadly observed the failure of such plans and lamented the lost opportunity: "Probably much more might have been done to develop the industry and energy of the colored race if I had been able to furnish each family with a small tract of land to till for themselves."[84] We believe it is entirely possible that Howard was right; in light of subsequent events, the failure to carry forward plans for land redistribution appears as a great tragedy of this era.

CHAPTER 5

AGRICULTURAL RECONSTRUCTION

The idea suggested itself of cutting the plantation up into numerous small farms, or rather patches. . . . It is no matter of surprise that this temptation proved irresistible. Every negro who procured one of these patches, saw himself at once in the light of an independent planter, placed upon an equal footing with his former master, and, looking into the future, beheld in himself a landed proprietor.

A. R. Lightfoot, "Condition and Wants of the Cotton Raising States," *De Bow's Review* 6 (February 1869), p. 153.

In an agricultural society the possession of land is the key to affluence, the source of economic security, and the basis of an estate to be passed on to one's children. Surrounded by an agrarian economy, the ex-slave felt that his economic independence required the acquisition of land. The Reverend Garrison Frazier, a Negro spokesman for a group of freedmen, at a meeting in Savannah told General Sherman and Secretary of War Stanton in 1864: "The way we can best take care of ourselves is to have land, and turn in and till it by our own labor. . . . We want to be placed on land until we are able to buy it and make it our own."[1] Whitelaw Reid related a conversation with an old man of sixty: "What's de use of being free if you do n't own land enough to be buried in? Might juss as well stay slave all yo' days."[2]

Yet the freedman's appetite for land by itself was not enough to secure a family homestead. The ex-slave faced three major obstacles: he had inherited nothing from slavery with which to purchase land, the disorganized state of the credit market made it difficult for him to borrow the necessary capital, and he found whites at best hesitant – and in many cases openly hostile – to the idea of Negro landownership.

The denial of black landownership

Our sources indicate that a great deal of land was put up for sale immediately after the war, and much of this land changed hands at a price substantially below its prewar level. *De Bow's Review* reported that, in 1866, land throughout the South was selling at from 16 to 25 percent of its assessed

Notes to Chapter 5 appear on pages 335–340.

prewar value and in December of that year published a list of eighty-one plantations offered for sale in the alluvial region of Mississippi and Louisiana.[3] John Dennett also commented on the "ruinously low" prices for good land in Georgia.[4] Nevertheless, only a few freedmen were in a position to take advantage of the low prices, for none had inherited money or other assets from slavery. Very few whites presented freedmen with gifts, and most blacks had been free too short a time to have earned income and saved enough to buy a homestead. A few blacks, who received income for work performed in areas controlled by the Union Army, did manage to save a limited amount of capital. Others received bounties from the United States government in recognition of military service during the war. Nevertheless, such cases were the exception. Only a handful were sufficiently endowed to afford the purchase of a farm, the work stock, and the tools necessary to support a family. A farm of 40 acres with one mule would cost in the neighborhood of $250 to $300. The major expenses would be for land (at $2 to $8 per acre) and for a mule ($50 to $60). The addition of a few farm implements, poultry, and some hogs would require another $30 or $40.[5]

Given the situation, the only practical way to assure the freedmen land would have been for Congress to have distributed acreage confiscated from former slaveowners. In March of 1865 Congress established the Bureau of Refugees, Freedmen, and Abandoned Lands to do exactly that. It was the original intention of Congress that the bureau would finance itself through confiscation of the land and property of rebels in the Confederate cause. The land was to be distributed to the freedmen, and the property sold to finance the construction of Negro schools and the provision of emergency relief. However, the intention of Congress was almost immediately thwarted by a general amnesty from confiscation ordered by President Johnson in May 1865.

Only on the Sea Islands, off the coast of South Carolina and Georgia, had blacks already been granted possessions of land prior to the Amnesty Proclamation.[6] On several islands, the blacks were allowed to retain possession of these land grants (the former owners were eventually compensated by Congress). Everywhere else land redistribution failed to materialize and remained an unfulfilled promise. Nevertheless, the freedmen's expectations that they might yet receive land from the government lingered for years. These hopes were rekindled as late as 1867 when Thaddeus Stevens introduced a bill in Congress that would have granted 40 acres and $50 to every former slave who was the head of a household.[7] The bill was defeated, and with it should have disappeared any further hope of congressional action to redistribute confiscated land. Yet in 1868 a representative to the constitutional convention in South Carolina insisted· "We all know that the colored people want land. Night and day they think and dream of it."[8]

Eventually, of course, it became clear to even the most optimistic blacks that land was not to be obtained without payment. Nevertheless, the extinction of that hope did nothing to stem the freedmen's appetite for landowner-ship. Land might still be secured through purchase. The first obstacle to be overcome was the ex-slave's lack of funds. In principle, a shortage of capital should not have forestalled the purchase of land. Pledging the land itself as collateral is a common device used to secure the loan of money necessary to pay for it. It would not be surprising, of course, if in the years immediately following the Civil War southern capital markets were in such a state of dis-array that no one could readily obtain a land mortgage. However, within five years, and certainly within fifteen, the South should have been able to reestablish a system of financial intermediaries. Indeed, given fifteen years, one might expect that even blacks who began freedom completely destitute would have managed to accumulate the means necessary for the purchase of land. With these presumptions, the blacks' strong desire for land would lead one to expect to find a rapid rate of land acquisition by blacks during the 1870s. In fact, this does not appear to have been the case. We estimate that, even as late as 1880, only 9.8 percent of the acreage actually cultivated in crops was owned and operated by blacks, who never-theless represented more than one-half of the agricultural population. This estimate, presented in Table 5.1, is based upon the census enumeration of acreage under cultivation.

When total acreage is considered, the extent of black landownership seems to have been even less impressive. At least this seems evident from the extensive study of Negro landownership in Georgia undertaken by W. F. B. Du Bois.[9] Using the annual reports of the state's comptroller general, Du Bois reported the total acreage in the state owned by Negroes beginning with the year 1874. These data, reproduced in Table 5.2, indicate that only a small fraction of the taxable land in Georgia was owned by blacks. In 1874, the first year included in the comptroller's statistics, the total acreage owned by Negroes was a mere 338,769 acres. Over the next six years less than 250,000 acres were added to this total. The acreage reported by black landowners in 1880 was only 1.6 percent of the total reported acreage in the state.[10]

Our own investigation of the Georgia tax records, reported in Table 5.3, revealed that blacks held a much smaller fraction of their total assets in land than did whites. Had they been free to buy land, their unusually strong desire to become landowners should have resulted in a higher fraction of their wealth being invested in real estate. The table presents the asset holdings of whites and blacks in the rural counties of Georgia for 1876 – the first year for which such a breakdown is possible. Whereas whites held about one-half their taxable net worth in land, blacks held less than one-fourth.[11] It is possible that this observed difference in the fraction of wealth held in the form of farmland was due to the fact that whites were relatively more wealthy than blacks. To check for the possibility that such a bias influenced the figures in Table 5.3, we have constructed the distribution of

Table 5.1. *Distribution of farms and farmland, by race of farm operator and form of land tenure and farm class, Cotton South: 1880*

Type of farm[a]	Percent distribution of farms		Percent of all land in each class		Percent of all acres reported in crops in each class[b]	
	White	Black	White	Black	White	Black
Small family farms	40.2	29.6	29.0	8.4	24.2	16.8
Owned	23.6	4.8	23.1	2.3	15.0	2.5
Tenanted	16.6	24.8	5.9	6.1	9.2	14.3
Rented	3.2	7.9	1.5	2.0	2.0	4.6
Sharecropped	13.4	17.0	4.4	4.1	7.2	9.8
Other small farms	5.9	2.6	7.5	1.0	4.4	1.7
Owned	4.4	0.3[c]	6.3	0.2[c]	3.3	0.2[c]
Tenanted	1.5	2.2	1.2	0.8	1.1	1.5
Rented	0.3[c]	0.6[c]	0.5[c]	0.1[c]	0.2[c]	0.4[c]
Sharecropped	1.2[c]	1.6	0.7[c]	0.7	0.8[c]	1.1
Medium-scale farms	12.3	4.2	29.2	4.2	19.9	6.6
Owned	9.4	1.4	25.1	1.5	15.2	2.2
Tenanted	2.9	2.8	4.2	2.7	4.8	4.4
Rented	1.0	1.1	2.0	1.2	1.7	1.8
Sharecropped	1.9	1.7	2.2	1.5	3.1	2.6
Plantations	0.8	0.1[c]	6.2	0.6[c]	7.7	1.2[c]
Owned	0.8[c]	0.1[c]	5.9[c]	0.6[c]	7.2[c]	1.2[c]
Tenanted	0.1[c]	0.0[c]	0.3[c]	0.0[c]	0.5[c]	0.0[c]
Other large farms	3.5	0.9[c]	11.4	2.5[c]	13.2	4.2[c]
Owned	3.1	0.7[c]	9.5	2.1[c]	10.4	3.7[c]
Tenanted	0.4[c]	0.2[c]	1.9[c]	0.4[c]	2.8[c]	0.5[c]
All farms	62.7	37.3	83.2	16.8	69.5	30.5
Owned	41.3	7.3	69.8	6.7	51.0	9.8
Tenanted	21.5	29.9	13.4	10.0	18.5	20.7
Rented	4.8	9.6	5.8	3.4	6.7	6.9
Sharecropped	16.6	20.3	7.6	6.7	14.8	13.8

[a] Definition of farm type is as follows: *small family farms*, farms reporting 50 acres or less in crops and 26 weeks or less of hired labor; *other small farms*, farms reporting 50 acres or less in crops and more than 26 weeks of hired labor; *medium-scale farms*, farms reporting more than 50 acres but 100 acres or less in crops; *plantations*, farms reporting 200 acres or more in crops, greater than 98 weeks of hired labor, and relying on hired labor for at least 60 percent of their requirements; *other large farms*, all farms not included in one of the above categories.

[b] Acres reported in crops are total acres harvested in 1879 planted with the following crops: rice, barley, buckwheat, Indian corn, oats, rye, wheat, cotton, flax, hemp, sugar cane, sorghum, tobacco, apples, and peaches.

[c] Figure reported is based on fewer than forty sample farms.

Source: Computed from a sample of farms from the 1880 Census of Agriculture. See Appendix G, Section 2, for details. Also see Chapter 4, Table 4.3, for totals.

Table 5.2. *Landownership by race in Georgia: 1874, 1876, 1880*

Year	Acres of land owned by		Percent of total acreage owned by blacks
	Whites	Blacks	
1874	34,196,870	338,769	1.0
1876	35,313,351	457,635	1.3
1880[a]	36,792,243	586,664	1.6

[a] The 1880 figures exclude Camden County. Apparently the county tax receiver did not report to the state in time for publication.
Source: Georgia, Office of the Comptroller General, *Report of the Comptroller General of the State of Georgia* for the years given as follows: *1874:* (Savannah: J. H. Estill, 1875), Tables 5, 13, pp. 14–17, 58–62. *1876:* (Atlanta: H. G. Wright, 1877), Tables 6, 7, 12, pp. 16–25, 46–50. *1880:* (Atlanta: Constitution Publishing Company, 1880), Tables 10, 16, pp. 123–127, 153–157.

Table 5.3. *Value of assets held in rural counties of Georgia, by race: 1876[a]*

Asset class	Whites		Blacks	
	Value (thousands of dollars)	Percent of all assets held	Value (thousands of dollars)	Percent of all assets held
Land	84,613	50.1	922	21.6
City and town property	15,906	9.4	441	10.4
Money and liquid assets	21,335	12.6	84	2.0
Kitchen and household furniture	8,279	4.9	450	10.6
Horses, mules, hogs, etc.	21,086	12.5	238	5.6
Plantation and mechanical tools	2,337	1.4	121	2.8
All other property	15,314	9.1	2,003	47.0
Aggregate taxable wealth	168,870	100.0	4,259	100.0

[a] "Rural counties" include all counties reporting to the comptroller that did not contain a city with 4,000 or more inhabitants in 1880.
Source: Georgia, Office of the Comptroller General, *Fourth Annual Report . . . for the Year 1876* (Atlanta: H. G. Wright, 1877), Table 6, pp. 16–20; Table 8, pp. 26–30; Table 9, pp. 31–35; Table 11, pp. 41–45; Table 12, pp. 46–50.

real estate holdings by wealth class for Coweta County, Georgia, from the original manuscript tax rolls for 1878.[12] As Table 5.4 shows, the lower levels of wealth reported by black landowners do *not* explain the difference in aggregate landholdings by race. For each and every wealth class, black owners of real estate held a smaller fraction of their wealth in land than did

Table 5.4. *Real estate holdings according to wealth class and race, Coweta County, Georgia: 1878.*

Aggregate taxable wealth ($)	Number of taxpayers		Number of taxpayers reporting real estate		Average value of real estate held by owner ($)[a]	
	White	Black	White	Black	White	Black
1–150	490	706	19	3	91.05	30.00
151–200	83	31	24	5	148.13	132.00
201–300	163	23	57	10	208.77	163.00
301–400	117	12	65	7	268.77	212.86
401 and up	1,022	9	756	8	1,424.43	607.50
Total	1,875	781	921	33	1,206.87	264.36

[a] Includes only taxpayers reporting landownership.
Source: Compiled from data in manuscript County Tax Digest for Coweta County, 1878.

their white counterparts. Table 5.4 also confirms that white taxpayers were much more successful than black taxpayers in becoming landowners, irrespective of their wealth class. Despite the fact that there were 737 black taxpayers with $200 or less of taxable wealth, only 8 of them – or just over 1 percent – held any land at all. Whites in this wealth class, by contrast, were almost seven times as successful in acquiring land.

Clearly, something other than mere poverty must explain the low level of black landownership. If contemporary witnesses are correct, the explanation is simply that whites denied blacks the opportunity of becoming a landowning class. The fundamental white objection to Negro ownership was rooted in the antagonism whites felt toward free blacks. Whites discouraged any sign of black independence that might have suggested a move toward social or economic equality. As one writer to the *Southern Cultivator* asked, "[What] will become of the present landholder, the upper strata of Society? They will suffer a degradation consistent with the elevation of the lower orders."[13] The tacit resistance to black landownership among the whites was usually sufficient to prevent such land sales. When it was not, whites who might agree to sell land to blacks were not uncommonly threatened with physical violence. Whitelaw Reid observed:

In many portions of the Mississippi Valley the feeling against any ownership of the soil by negroes is so strong, that the man who should sell small tracts to them would be in actual personal danger. Every effort will be made to prevent negroes from acquiring lands; even the renting of small tracts to them is held to be unpatriotic and unworthy of a good citizen.[14]

In fact, Mississippi went so far as to prohibit by law the right of blacks to "rent or lease any lands or tenements except in incorporated towns or cities."[15] While Mississippi was the only state to actually prohibit Negro proprietorship – and the Mississippi law was quickly overturned by the Freedmen's Bureau – white resistance did not need to rely upon the force of law. When threats and social pressure directed against white landowners did not suffice to curtail land sales to blacks, violence could be turned against the prospective black purchasers. As one observer noted:

As a general rule a man is very unpopular with his neighbors who will sell land to colored people; and then a colored man is in danger if he buys land. In Winston County [Mississippi] a dozen men were whipped, and the only charge against them was that they had bought land.[16]

The threat of violence did not completely prevent land sales to blacks, but it did substantially escalate the costs and risks faced by both the black buyer and the white seller. These added costs and risks were so great that they virtually eliminated a market in land accessible to blacks and priced most blacks out of even the thin market that remained. In the few cases in which a landowner was willing to risk retaliation and sell to a black, perhaps in the hope of receiving a price in excess of the market value, he would naturally insist upon payment in cash. Only blacks with cash on hand could avail themselves of such opportunities, for when the threats of white supremacists failed to frighten the landowner, they could be turned against any third party from whom the black sought financing. For all practical purposes, then, the option of owning agricultural land was one that may be disregarded when considering the situation faced by the freedmen in the Reconstruction Period. Agricultural reconstruction was in the hands of the landowners.[17]

The rise of tenancy

In January 1868 the agricultural land of the South was owned by the same class of white families who had owned both the South's land and its black labor before the war. While members of this elite had retained both ownership and control of the soil, they had lost the ownership of their labor with emancipation, and by 1868 it was clear that they were losing control over the labor as well. The shortage of agricultural workers, the blacks' distaste for the plantation regime, and the protection provided by the Freedmen's Bureau gave blacks the economic power, the will, and the courage to insist upon an end to the old plantation system.

As landowners, one by one, gave up the plantation system of organization, they divided their land into family-sized farms of between 30 and 50 acres each and rented them to freedmen, either for a fixed rent or, more typically, for a share of the crop. Each tenant farm was then operated as an independent unit, and each became the source of income for a single black family. So complete was this transformation that by 1880 only 8.9 percent of the agricultural land in crops in the Cotton South was still cultivated on farms that could, even by the most generous of definitions, be considered plantations. By contrast, over one-half the farms in the region were operated by tenants tilling 39.2 percent of the land in crops. About 72 percent of these farms were sharecropped; the rest were rented for a fixed cash rent.[18]

Family tenancy apparently emerged in the Cotton South as an almost unprecedented form of labor organization. It appears that, before the Civil War, almost all cotton farms were operated by owners or their managers. According to the studies made by Frank Owsley and his students of the manuscript Censuses of 1850 and 1860, approximately 80 percent of all farm operators owned real estate. This figure has been interpreted as a lower bound on the percentage of farms that were owner-operated.[19] In all probability the true figures would be closer to 90 percent. In any event, whatever the extent of prewar land renting, we can be confident that most if not all of it involved the leasing of plantations or medium-scale farms that were operated by the leaseholder on the plantation system.[20] There does not seem to have been any leasing of small land parcels to family tenants or sharecroppers aside from a very few isolated cases. Lewis Gray has argued that the scarcity of such references is strong evidence of the absence of family tenancy as a form of labor organization before the Civil War.[21]

Tenancy did not reflect a prewar form of agricultural organization; rather it seems to have emerged as the most practical of the many experimental systems tried by determined groups of planters who sought alternatives to the plantation system as early as 1865. Not all landowners were content to reestablish the plantation system after emancipation. Joseph Embree, for example, experimented with a form of the "task system" in Louisiana. His laborers were paid 50 cents upon completion of every stipulated assignment.[22] There is also an example of a London company that, having purchased land in South Carolina, contracted with local planters to cultivate it. Some thought was apparently given by Alabama legislators to chartering a farming corporation.[23] Another reported experiment was the "three-day system" in which each laborer was allotted a small plot to work on his own behalf (usually with the help of his family) and was furnished with the necessary work stock and implements. In exchange for this, he agreed to work on the landowner's plantation for three (or four) days of the week. With this sytem, the hand was usually provided with rations for himself, but not for the other members of his family, who presumably had to support themselves with the proceeds from the family plot.[24]

The significance of these labor experiments lies, not in the numbers involved (they were isolated cases attracting the attention of contemporaries because of their novelty), but in the fact that they illustrate that a wide variety of approaches were taken by landowners seeking a solution to "the labor problem." It appears that the most common form experimented with was family tenancy where the rent was a share of the crop. Many such sharecropping experiments must have proved successful, since by 1868 this new system began to gain wide popularity.[25]

The nature of a sharecropping agreement

Initially, the sharecropping contracts arranged varied considerably. The Department of Agriculture's report for 1867 asserted that "great diversity has existed in the form and character of [sharecropping] contracts."[26] Whitelaw Reid reports an early experiment where labor received 20 percent of the crop when they were provisioned by the landlord and one-fourth when they provided "a part of their own support."[27] A report to the Freedmen's Bureau indicated that laborers contracted in 1866 for as little as one-tenth or one-twentieth of the crop during "early attempts at this arrangement."[28] Very quickly, however, the sharecropping contract was standardized, and the fraction received by the laborer who was supplied with everything except food and clothing was increased to one-half the output. One of the interviewers for the Federal Writers Project on slavery reported an ex-slave's recollection of how the laborer's share came to be increased:

His father and mother rented a patch, mule and plow from Mr. Neal and the family was together. At first they gave the Niggers only a tenth of what they raised but they couldn't get along on it and after "a lot of mouthin' about it" they gave them a third. That wasn't enough to live on either so more "mouthin'" . . . until they gave them a half.[29]

It is extremely rare, after 1868, to find any terms other than equal division of the crops in a sharecropping contract. The universality of the fifty-fifty split is attested to by comprehensive surveys taken by Loring and Atkinson in 1869, the U.S. Department of Agriculture in 1876, and the Census Office in 1879.[30] Inasmuch as the demand for and supply of land typically vary from place to place and year to year, such uniformity in sharecropping rents throughout the South and over a long period of time seems surprising. Of course, the simplicity of the fifty-fifty split was appealing. Ruby Tartt recalled his parents' landlord "'vidin' de corn":

He'd take a bushel an' give 'em a bushel. When he mos' through he'd throw a ear of corn to dis one, an' give himse'f a ear; den he break a ear in two, an' he take part an' give dem part. Dat was close measurin', I tell you.[31]

But simplicity of contract terms alone cannot explain the uniform choice of a single rental share. The explanation lies in the fact that it proved unnecessary to bargain over the share. Adjustments to the contractual arrangement between landlord and laborer could be made by varying other contract terms. The critical variable appears to have been the number of acres allotted each tenant family. With a fixed share rent the laborer would seek to obtain as much land as he could in order to maximize his output and hence the return to his efforts. The landlord, on the other hand, would view the labor supply as fixed both in quantity and quality by the size and experience of the tenant's family. Therefore, he would wish to limit the amount of land granted so as to increase the yield per acre through more intensive cultivation. A small plot would yield high output per acre, but low yields per man.

Granting more land would increase the laborer's income, but simultaneously decrease the landlord's yield per acre.[32] The ultimate outcome of the bargaining process, of course, depended upon the market strength of the two parties, as well as the quality of the land and labor. Where a precise adjustment of the fixed share contract could not be reached by varying the size of the farm, adjusting the detailed terms of the agreement concerning such items as supplemental duties of the tenant and the allocation of minor expenses sufficed to adjust the "true" share rent per acre.[33]

With these sources of flexibility, it was unnecessary to bargain over the division of the crop as well. Despite occasional instances in which the sharecropping contract was complicated by side conditions, most sharecropping contracts were quite simple. They specified the amount of land to be tilled in each crop, the specific amount of capital to be supplied by the landowner, the proportion in which the crops were to be divided, the term of the lease (invariably one year), and a provision that the tenant should follow the landlord's direction concerning the management of the farm. Not all these provisions had to be spelled out in the contract. Thus, the provision regarding the division of land among crops was often implicit in the requirement that the seed be provided by the landowner. The sharecropper could plant only the crops for which he had been provided seed.

A contract typical of the agreements made is reproduced in its entirety as Figure 5.1. The landlord is the same Alonzo T. Mial whose wage contract for 1866 was reproduced as Figure 4.1 in Chapter 4. The tenant, Fenner Powell, was required to work "without any unnecessary loss of time [and] do all manner of work on Said farm as may be directed by Said Mial." In fact, sharecropping involved considerable direction by the landlord. Without such supervision the tenant might be tempted to put too large a portion of his time to an alternative use.

The sharecropping contract that had become standard by the early 1870s required the landlord to provide the land, housing, fuel, working stock, feed for the stock, farming implements, and seed. The freedman and his family provided the labor and fed and clothed themselves. If fertilizer was to be used, the landlord would choose the brand and amount and its cost was to be deducted from the final output before the crop was divided.[34]

Alternative share arrangements

Two other forms of contracting that were occasionally employed during this period are easily confused with sharecropping. One was the practice, described in Chapter 4, of paying workers on a plantation or large farm with a share of the crop rather than with a fixed money wage. The second alternative, called share *tenancy* (as opposed to share*cropping*) required the landowner to supply only the land, house, and (in most cases) fuel. The tenant provided his own work stock, implements, and provisions. For the use of the land the tenant paid a standard rent of one-third of the corn (or other

This contract made and entered into between A. T. Mial of one part and Fenner Powell of the other part both of the County of Wake and State of North Carolina—

Witnesseth—That the Said Fenner Powell hath barganed and agreed with the Said Mial to work as a cropper for the year 1886 on Said Mial's land on the land now occupied by Said Powell on the west Side of Poplar Creek and a point on the east Side of Said Creek and both South and North of the Mial road, leading to Raleigh, That the Said Fenner Powell agrees to work faithfully and dilligently without any unnecessary loss of time, to do all manner of work on Said farm as may be directed by Said Mial, And to be respectful in manners and deportment to Said Mial. And the Said Mial agrees on his part to furnish mule and feed for the same and all plantation tools and Seed to plant the crop free of charge, and to give the Said Powell One half of all crops raised and housed by Said Powell on Said land except the cotton seed. The Said Mial agrees to advance as provisions to Said Powell fifty pound of bacon and two sacks of meal pr month and occasionally Some flour to be paid out of his the Said Powell's part of the crop or from any other advance that may be made to Said Powell by Said Mial. As witness our hands and seals this the 16th day of January A.D. 1886

Witness   A.T. Mial [signed]   [Seal]

                                                        his
W. S. Mial [signed]   Fenner ✕ Powell   [Seal]
                                                       mark

Figure 5.1 Contract between Alonzo T. Mial and Fenner Powell; January 1886. (*Source: Alonzo T. and Millard Mial Papers, North Carolina Department of Archives and History.*)

grains) and one-fourth of the cotton – hence the colloquial expression "working on thirds and fourths."[35] All three forms of share contracting are contrasted in Table 5.5.

Of these three forms of share payments, by far the most common and widespread was sharecropping. This form of tenancy was established everywhere in the South. It flourished with all possible combinations of soil quality and labor conditions. It was observed on rich alluvial lands along the Mississippi River, throughout the length of the intensively cultivated black belt, on the exhausted soils of the Old South, and on the poor soils of the Appalachian hills. It was able to attract in many cases the most capable and experienced laborers, but it worked with the least efficient as well. Of the 493 counties in the United States that reported over 20 percent of their tilled land in cotton in 1880, only 1 – Issaquena County, Mississippi – reported no sharecropping, and only 11 reported less than 5 percent of the farms with this form of tenure.[36] The accompanying map portrays the prevalence of sharecropping reported in the county statistics of the 1880 Census.[37] It is immediately apparent that sharecropping was particularly common in the cotton-growing regions and less frequently employed in the

Table 5.5. *Contract provisions with three forms of share arrangements*

Factor of production	Contracting party responsible for furnishing factor with		
	Share tenancy	Sharecropping	Share wages
Land	Landlord	Landlord	Landlord
Housing	Landlord	Landlord	Landlord
Fuel	Landlord usually[a]	Landlord	Landlord
Work stock	Laborer	Landlord	Landlord
Wagons	Laborer	Landlord	Landlord
Implements	Laborer	Landlord	Landlord
Management	Laborer	Landlord	Landlord
Forage, feed	Laborer	Landlord	Landlord
Seed	Laborer	Landlord usually[b]	Landlord
Board	Laborer	Laborer	Landlord
Clothing	Laborer	Laborer	Laborer usually
Labor	Laborer	Laborer	Laborer
Fertilizer	Deducted from output	Shared	Landlord usually[b]
Ginning	Deducted from output	Shared	Landlord usually[b]
Baling	Deducted from output	Shared	Landlord usually[b]

Contracting party	Division of output with		
	Share tenancy	Sharecropping	Share wages
Landlord	One-fourth of cotton, one-third of grain	One-half of cotton and grain	Two-thirds to three-fourths of cotton and grain
Laborer	Three-fourths of cotton, two-thirds of grain	One-half of cotton and grain	One-third to one-fourth of cotton and grain

[a] Otherwise laborer. [b] Otherwise deducted from output.
Source: Based on numerous references in the contemporary literature. Particularly useful were F. W. Loring and C. F. Atkinson, *Cotton Culture and the South Considered with Reference to Emigration* (Boston: A. Williams, 1869), pp. 25–26; J. R. Dodge, "Report of the Statistician," in U.S. Department of Agriculture, *Report of the Commissioner of Agriculture . . . for the Year 1876* (Washington: GPO, 1877), pp. 131–135; Eugene W. Hilgard, ed., *Report on Cotton Production in the United States*, 2 vols. (Washington: GPO, 1884), 1, pp. 185, 356, 819; 2, pp. 250, 438, 517–522.

coastal rice or sugar regions. Other than this, no strong geographic patterns in the choice of tenure are apparent. The thirds and fourths system was practiced throughout the South, but it was much less common than sharecropping, particularly with black labor. Since it required a capital input on the part of the tenant, few freedmen were in a position to accept this form of renting immediately after the war, and the very slow rate with which freedmen accumulated capital impeded its use by blacks for many

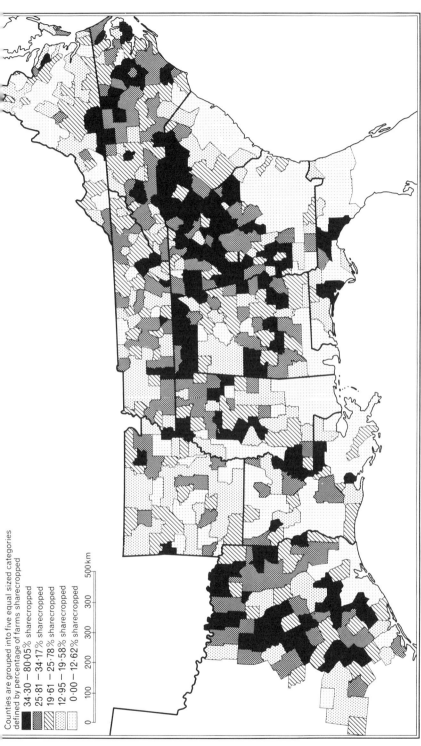

Counties are grouped into five equal sized categories defined by percentage of farms sharecropped

34·30 – 80·05% sharecropped
25·81 – 34·17% sharecropped
19·61 – 25·78% sharecropped
12·95 – 19·58% sharecropped
0·00 – 12·62% sharecropped

0   100   200   300   500km

The prevalance of sharecropping in the South, 1880. (*Source*: U.S. Census Office, Tenth Census [1880], *Report of the Production of Agriculture* [Washington: GPO, 1883], Table 5.)

years. Share wages, on the other hand, made only a brief appearance. With
the demise of the plantation and the restoration of a circulating currency,
this sytem all but disappeared.

The choice of tenure

In a sense, the adoption of sharecropping was the result of a compromise
between the laborers' pursuit of independence and higher incomes and the
landlords' desire to retain control and minimize risk. The blacks, seeking
independence, would have preferred to own the land outright. Their lack of
wealth and the barriers erected by hostile whites prevented any significant
number from doing so. With ownership ruled out, blacks would have preferred, in most cases, to rent for a fixed fee payable after harvest. In this
way, they would be free to organize their time and labor as they saw fit,
and, provided the rent charged was fair, they would receive the full benefit
of their productivity. Such an arrangement, however, did not always appeal
to landlords.[38] Though the tenant contracted to pay the rent regardless of
the outcome and would bear the brunt of any loss, a failure of the farm
would almost certainly result in a default of the rent and, as a consequence,
a loss to the landlord as well. The whites typically believed that without
supervision blacks would be certain to fail as independent farmers, and they
were, therefore, unwilling to rent land except when they could maintain
control of the labor.[39]

Contemporary accounts rarely mention renting to a freedman for a fixed
payment in the period immediately after the war.[40] Those few blacks who
attempted independent farming during this period frequently failed, thus
reinforcing, in the minds of those already prejudiced, the idea that "the
negro, left to himself, will barely do enough work to support existence."[41]
Even the U.S. commissioner of agriculture concurred:

The general tenor of information upon [planting by colored men] is that such efforts
have usually resulted in failure. . . . The difficulties to be encountered have been not
only worms, excessive rains, droughts, floods, and fields overrun with pernicious
growths of neglected years, but inexperience in business calculations [and] a pro-
verbial lack of foresight in the uneducated plantation negro.[42]

The commissioner did note that "failures have been more numerous than
successes among whites, as shown by the same returns," and that "there
are instances enough of thrift and foresight to refute the proposition that the
[colored] race is and must be incapable of business management."[43] However, this last point was almost certainly lost on the southern landlord. Even
if it had not been, in the years immediately following abolition blacks who
could farm successfully as independent farmers were sufficiently rare that
the cost of verifying their claims to success would have exceeded any expected gain from the possible higher rents that might be charged.

In this state of affairs, sharecropping appeared to the freedman as an attractive, though by no means perfect, substitute for owning or renting land. Compared with the plantation system it offered him more independence from white control, yet it secured him the capital necessary to engage in farming. Sharecropping also offered the potential of a higher income than could be obtained working for the fixed standard wage. This was particularly attractive to the man who possessed skills or who had gained experience beyond that of the average worker. Sharecropping, by paying him a fraction of the output, would reward his superior skills and diligence. By contrast, the laborers who worked on plantations were invariably offered a standard wage based solely upon their sex and age.[44] Placed in a work gang, they were able neither to demonstrate nor to benefit from superior performance. Because of the expense required to monitor each worker's individual performance, the incentives offered (if any) were to be shared by an entire gang. With no independent interest in the outcome, the individual laborer saw little reason to excel. Indeed, as a contributor to the *Rural Carolinian* observed: "Gang work requires the constant presence and pushing of the overseer . . . and it may be relied upon with certainty that the amount of work obtained from each will be measured by the capacity of the most inferior hand."[45] The adventuresome worker would obviously prefer to be rewarded on the basis of his own merit. Sharecropping offered him this opportunity.

Since the most capable workers would be the ones to benefit most from sharecropping, it is reasonable to suppose that those blacks who chose to remain at work for wages were seldom superior workers. This phenomenon was frequently commented on by contemporaries. The editor of the *Rural Carolinian* noted that "in many cases, a lack of ability to command the best negro labor, and to secure fidelity and efficiency" by the payment of fixed wages had made the plantation system "generally impracticable."[46] Ironically, the fact that the best workers adopted sharecropping, leaving the large plantation in the hands of the less capable, only reinforced the deprecatory characterization of the free black worker in the minds of many white observers of the wage system.

While it was the freedman who accepted sharecropping as a superior arrangement, even insisting upon this form of contract, the landlord also perceived a number of advantages in the new system. Chief among these was the incentive effect. Paid a share of the output, the laborer had a direct incentive to work well and protect the crop. The "constant presence and pushing of the overseer" was unnecessary, and therefore supervision was less costly than when paying fixed wages. Even left largely to himself, the sharecropper, in the view of many, worked harder and more diligently than when he was a member of a work gang. One landowner reported to Loring and Atkinson in 1868 that:

Cash wages to negroes, without very close overseeing, will not bring cheap produce.
Shares or renting is the only mode for the proprietor of plantations. The blacks must
be made to feel that they have a joint interest in the complete cultivation and thus be
induced to give their whole time.[47]

Another landlord ten years later concurred: "[Sharecropping] interests the
laborer, makes him dependent on the success of his management, and
enables him to work his entire family. I get more work done under this
system than for wages, and the work is much better done."[48]

The positive incentives offered by sharecropping had other implications
as well. A frequently mentioned effect of sharecropping was that the number of workers who deserted the farm before the cotton was picked was
substantially lower. This had been a recurring problem with the wage
system that even the practice of withholding a fraction of wages until December could not prevent.[49]

In addition to the incentive effect, an advantage of sharecropping as
perceived by the landlord was that it subjected him to less risk. If the crop
was poor, or the price of cotton low, his obligation to the laborers was
reduced accordingly. The landlord's share of the output, net of labor's
share, could never fall to less than nothing, which was not the case with
wage labor.[50] This factor seemed particularly influential in 1868 after two
years of widespread crop failures accompanied by a dramatic fall in cotton
prices. Writing in that year, W. H. Evans noted the risk-reducing aspects of
sharecropping and then added: "This advantage has assumed I think an
undue importance from the experience of last year. Such an extreme fluctuation in the value of our staple crop, is not likely to occur again."[51] Despite
Evans's optimistic outlook for future cotton prices, sharecropping must
have seemed a straightforward way to shift some of the potential risk to
laborers.

The sharing of risk implicit in the sharing of the crop, of course, cuts both
ways. While the landowner welcomed the opportunity to reduce his own
risk, the laborer might well have resisted assuming this added burden.
Robert Somers, viewing sharecropping in 1871, predicted difficulty on this
score for the future:

The negroes on the share system, . . . had a larger remuneration last year, when the
price of cotton was high, than they will have this year, when it has suffered a heavy
decline. Can the negro be expected to understand or be satisfied with this fluctuating
scale of remuneration for his toil? Is it desirable that he should be dragged, at his
present stage of progress, into all the ups and downs of cotton speculation? Is he
likely to comprehend that, while doing his best probably in both years, he should
have less this year than last, because France and Prussia have gone to war? And if
he cannot comprehend this, is there not a danger that he may be discontented, and
think himself the victim of some fraud or injustice nearer home?[52]

However, Somers's patronizing view of the freedman's ability to appreciate
the risks entailed in cotton production was unfair. The blacks did, of

course, perceive the added risk they were assuming. But, in their view, this was compensated for by the prospects of higher returns and the freedom from constant control by whites. In fact, the evidence is strong that the black worker would have willingly assumed all the risk, through either landownership or rental, in exchange for all the net proceeds, had this been possible.

Another point that needs to be emphasized is that the poor black was probably less averse to assuming risk than the comparatively wealthy landlord. Even in a good year the laborer could hope for little beyond the food and shelter necessary to sustain himself and his family. In a bad year, regardless of the form of his labor contract, he was unlikely to starve, since he could fall back on his landlord, merchant, or neighbors for assistance. A Georgia planter, describing an incident in which all but two of his sharecroppers had to apply to him for meat and corn, assumed the responsibility for assistance: "I furnished them, of course."[53] A contributor to the *Rural Carolinian* acknowledged the general responsibility of the community at large to support those in need.[54] When one has little to lose, one has little reason to avoid risk. Thus, the portion of the risk inherent in planting that was shifted from the landowner to the laborer with the adoption of sharecropping probably seemed more frightening to the landowner than to the freedman.[55]

The practical advantages of sharecropping were sufficiently apparent by 1870 to make it the preeminent form of contracting for black labor. Loring and Atkinson reported that nearly 200,000 out of the more than 250,000 acres owned by planters responding to their 1868 survey were cultivated under sharecropping arrangements.[56] Robert Somers, who traveled extensively throughout the South in 1870 and 1871, found sharecropping "to prevail so generally that any other form of contract is but the exception."[57] Apparently the landowners were convinced that their introduction of the new system was a sound decision. "The share system is so stoutly defended by many persons of practical experience that it requires some hardihood of conviction to avow an opposite opinion," said Somers, himself a critic of this form of contract.[58]

Sharecropping and labor control

Despite their stout defense of sharecropping, the planters nevertheless lamented the loss of control over their former slaves. Centuries of slavery had led them to believe that it was proper for the white man to control the black, and they resented the fact that they had been deprived of their status. After all, the transition from slavery to freedom had been forced upon the landowners, their legal right of control was removed by emancipation after the South's defeat in a war of rebellion, and their de facto control was eroded by the economic power acquired by blacks with the coincidence of high cotton prices and the labor shortage. The planters' frustration at this turn of events is evidenced in almost every contemporary newspaper, diary, or file of correspondence. The following extract from a letter signed "Hill-side" published in the *Rural Carolinian* of 1873, while it seems ludicrous today, nevertheless reflects the persistent desire of whites to assert their presumed authority:

A little plain talk too, to Sambo in the right way as soon as the bargain is made, as to the course of conduct by which the employer expects to be governed, and what he expects of him, is also productive of good. . . . We expect all orders to be promptly and cheerfully obeyed; that if we tell him to peel the bark off of a long, tall, sleek, slim pine sapling, grease it with tallow and climb it feet foremast, we will expect him to make a faithful effort to accomplish the undertaking, and that if he fails after a faithful trial, we will be satisfied.[59]

In the same year D. Wyatt Aiken spoke against sharecropping on precisely these grounds: "When the negro becomes a copartner in the plantation the employer sacrifices intelligence to ignorance, judgment to vanity, and self-respect to race and color."[60]

But the majority of planters were forced to face the realities of the time. While some landowners, like "Hill-side," continued to insist on obedience, most just grumbled about "the annoyance of having no one to cut and haul your family fuel, or go on errands, or haul anything for your family, or repair a gate, or hang a fallen door, or put up a fence blown down that does not enclose their crop, or do anything, except to cultivate the crop."[61]

While freedom for the blacks necessarily implied some loss of control over their destinies by their former masters, and sharecropping implied less control and supervision over labor than did the wage plantation, it should nevertheless be reemphasized that sharecropping required the constant attention of the landowner if he was to protect his own interest in the crop. Unlike renting for fixed payment, the proportion of the total output that the laborer receives is fixed and invariant. This reduces the incentive of the worker to exert himself. The problem was first rigorously analyzed by Alfred Marshall in his *Principles of Political Economy:*

For, when the cultivator has to give to his landlord half of the returns to each dose of capital and labour that he applies to the land, it will not be to his interest to apply any doses the total return to which is less than twice enough to reward him. If, then, he is free to cultivate as he chooses, he will cultivate far less intensively than upon the English plan [fixed cash rent].[62]

The southern landlord employed two devices to overcome this problem. First, he did not allow his tenant to be "free to cultivate as he chooses." As we have already noted, the sharecropping contract required the laborer to work under the direction of the landowner or his representative and to avoid any unnecessary loss of time. Second, the landlord prevented the land from being cultivated "less intensively than upon the English plan" by regulating the land-labor ratio (and the crop mix) at the time of contracting. As we have noted, the primary subject of negotiation between the landowner and the tenant was over the amount of land to be leased.[63]

Both the devices used by the landlord to prevent the sharecropper from misallocating resources had the effect of increasing the amount of labor effort expended upon each acre of land. But these devices worked in different ways. The control was exercised after the acreage was set to ensure that the sharecropper fulfilled his contractual obligation to work as intensively as agreed upon. This supervision was necessary because the worker would otherwise have an incentive to work less and take more free time than if he were renting the same acreage for a fixed fee. The supervision, therefore, increased the farm's output. The limitation placed upon farm size by the landlord, on the other hand, effectively lowered the return per worker because each family would have less acreage to cultivate. The lower the productivity of labor, the harder labor must work to maintain a standard of living. The effect of an acreage restriction would therefore be to increase the amount of effort the laborer was willing to exert.[64]

Since the two devices worked toward the same end – increasing the labor effort expended per acre – the landlord could adopt any number of possible combinations of control and farm size that would ensure that the expected return per acre was equivalent to that obtained from renting.

We conjecture, however, that when dealing with blacks the landowner – because of his racist views – would use more direct controls and supervision and rely less upon acreage restrictions than when his sharecroppers were white. This conjecture is confirmed by our study of white and black tenants in 1880. Black sharecroppers cultivated 10.5 percent more acreage per worker than black renters. On the other hand, white sharecroppers had 19.8 percent fewer acres per worker than their counterparts who rented.[65] In general, the land-labor ratio with sharecropping could have been less than, equal to, or greater than that chosen by tenants who were renting for fixed fee. Abstract theorizing can tell us little beyond the fact that there would be no automatic mechanism to ensure that the land-labor ratios would be similar with alternative forms of contracting. Except by coincidence, then, sharecropping would introduce a distortion into the allocation of resources and therefore reduce the efficiency of southern agriculture.

The efficiency of sharecropping

Although the information collected by the census in 1880 on agricultural inputs is admittedly deficient and could not sustain a detailed study of agricultural productivity, it might nonetheless be cautiously used to examine the extent to which the introduction of sharecropping distorted the allocation of resources. Table 5.6 presents several statistics for black-operated family farms in the Cotton South in 1880. According to our statistics, black sharecroppers averaged 8.0 acres of cropland, while the renters averaged only 7.3 The observed difference in land-labor ratios between sharecropped and rented farms implies that the agricultural system adopted in the postwar era created economic inefficiencies in the allocation of resources. Efficient use of resources would require equivalent factor ratios with various forms of contract. Although a precise estimate of the magnitude of this distortion is not presently possible, it is unlikely to have been substantial, probably reducing output by no more than a few percentage points.[66]

An interesting implication of the figures presented in Table 5.6 is that black tenants would have had little or no financial incentive to shift from sharecropping to renting. If we assume that the landlord received the same rent per acre from either form of contracting, the annual income earned per worker would have been virtually identical; $60.83 compared with $59.51. This observation bears on the topic of efficiency, since several economists

Table 5.6. *Comparison of factor ratios, productivity, and factor incomes on rented and sharecropped family farms operated by blacks, Cotton South: 1880*

| | Black-operated small family farms | |
	Rented	Sharecropped
Number of acres reported in crops per laborer[a]	7.25	8.01
Value of output per acre reported in crops ($)[a]	14.26	13.30
Assumed rent per acre received by landlord ($)[b]	5.87	5.87
Implicit annual income per laborer ($)[c]	60.83	59.51

[a] Figures reported are based on reporting farms only and are the mean of the variable averaged across farms using the weighting scheme described in Appendix G.

[b] We estimate in Appendix A, Table A.8, that the landlord received 44.1 percent of the total output produced by black families on small sharecropped farms. If this is correct, landlords received $5.87 per acre as the average share rent in compensation for the use of their land and capital. We assume that the land rent plus the return to capital per acre received by their owners when renting for cash was equal to this amount, since landlords were free either to rent or to sharecrop as they saw fit and therefore presumably expected approximately equal returns with each form of tenure.

[c] We calculated the implicit annual income per worker by first calculating the income per acre remaining to reward the labor effort of tenants after deducting the assumed rent paid the landlord. This figure was then converted to a per worker basis by multiplying by the number of acres reported in crops per laborer.

Source: Sample of farms from the 1880 Census of Agriculture.

have recently argued that the equality of returns from each form of tenure for both landlord and tenant would be sufficient evidence that a system including both forms of tenure would be economically efficient.[67] As the data of the table indicate, there is little empirical evidence to support such a contention in this case.

Of far greater significance than our argument that sharecropping introduced allocation inefficiencies into the southern agricultural system, and certainly of more concern to contemporaries, was the detrimental effect sharecropping had on efforts to enhance and improve soil quality. Despite its appeal to both labor and landowners, the consensus among contemporary agriculturalists, government officials, and prominent farmers was against sharecropping. They were not concerned with the issue of static efficiency; they feared that sharecropping was simply not compatible with scientific farming. "Who in the South," asked D. Wyatt Aiken, "ever saw a renter under-drain or horizontalize?"[68] Aiken had earlier provided an explanation of why so few "scientific" sharecroppers could be found:

Many, perhaps a majority of planters, contend that the stimulus of a portion of the crop is more effective than wages in money. This is undoubtedly erroneous. If the laborer is only stimulated by his share of the crop, the employer has no control of his time beyond his specific crop, else the laborer is more than worthy of his hire. Subsoiling, under-draining, making manure, purchasing fertilizers, erecting buildings, and general improvements, are all labors the "cropper" should never be expected to perform, unless he is paid a heavier percentage of the crop, than if he were employed simply to pitch, cultivate and harvest a certain crop.[69]

As Aiken recognized, both the landlord and the tenant were drawn by the nature of the sharecropping agreement to focus upon the present, rather than the future, needs of the farm.

One of the major obstacles to long-term investment in the farm was the invariable practice of annual contracting. Annual contracting and insecurity of tenure were important devices used by the landlord to ensure the faithful cultivation of the tenant farm. As D. Gale Johnson has argued, the sharecropper who performed poorly would not be rehired, and this threat was often sufficient to ensure that the work was well done.[70] Not surprisingly, the tenant insisted on maximizing the value of the current crop (to half of which he was entitled) and showed little interest in long-run investment prospects from which he would be unable to benefit unless he were allowed to continue to work the farm. Because of the fifty-fifty split inherent in sharecropping, the landlord had to exercise continual control just to keep the worker diligently attending to the current crop. To go beyond this and press his interests in future crops usually proved overly expensive. A Tennessee farmer noted:

It takes all that one or two hands and myself can make, (and we work day and night often,) to keep up the hands and teams of those that work on shares. The latter will not make a rail or a board, or clean off a ditch or do anything to keep up the place, unless they are paid extra.[71]

The ownership of the land, of course, entitled the landlord to the benefits forthcoming from improvements embodied in it. This made him the logical candidate to initiate and finance agricultural improvements. Yet, since the landlord would receive only half of the benefits of investments in the quality of his farm, his incentive to make such outlays would be reduced. Only if the return expected was worth twice what it cost would the landlord find a particular investment to his advantage. Thus, while landowners might pay their labor extra to make capital repairs or install capital improvements, they would invest less money in these projects than if they could anticipate receiving the full benefit from them. This impediment to capital formation ultimately worked to the detriment of both parties. One 1871 commentary agreed: "While this species of contract has an appearance of fairness for both employer and employed, yet it has grave objections. Virtually it is a partnership between capital and labor, deleterious to capital and prejudicial to production. Thus it injures both parties."[72]

The investments affected would not only be the more obvious capital improvements such as improved drainage, sturdy fencing, more elaborate outbuildings, and farm machinery, but also the voluntary reduction in current crop yields designed to improve or maintain the soil's fertility in the long run. Such practices as crop rotation, contour plowing, and fallowing might have produced significant long-run improvements in output per acre had the landlord been willing to make the short-run sacrifice of output they entailed. These practices proved profitable in northern agriculture and also on southern farms operated by the owner. Yet, from the perspective of an investor who would receive only one-half the benefits, this profitability apparently disappeared. As we have noted, contemporaries insisted that "no improvements can be made under this system."[73]

Cotton is an exhausting crop, and the failure to introduce improved agricultural practices and expand capital investment would have ultimately led to soil depletion and erosion with the inevitable decline in crop yields because of this neglect. This decline, however, could be checked by the use of fertilizer. Commercial fertilizer was the one means of improving the soil's productivity that was frequently agreed to by both parties to the tenure contract. To the sharecropper, expenditures on fertilizer brought immediate returns commensurate with the costs. To the landlord, the fertilizer not only increased the current output, but had the additional advantage of forestalling the depreciation of the farm. Of course, as southern agricultural journals were fond of pointing out, it would have been cheaper and more beneficial to have employed crop rotation and composting than to use commercial fertilizer. But this superior alternative was not compatible with sharecropping because it did not increase current yields. The result was that the South used commercial fertilizer in prodigious quantities, and as the years went by they used ever increasing amounts. While fertilizer prevented the worst effects of soil depletion from manifesting themselves, it was unable to increase agricultural productivity, and the failure of many landowners to make other capital improvements undoubtedly denied the South the dramatic improvements in agricultural productivity that accompanied the agricultural revolution in other regions of the United States.

The disincentive effects to investment inherent with sharecropping might have been overcome had the landowner found some way to capture fully the benefits of land improvements or, alternatively, to share the costs of them with the workers. The first possibility could not be easily accomplished as long as the rental share was fixed at the customary 50 percent, since superior land could not be rented for a greater share of the output than inferior land. Even more problematical would have been the difficulty of installing the improvement without interfering with the current productivity. As a practical matter, such investment required the participation of labor; contour plowing or underdraining are good examples. Yet the laborer would have no incentive to bear the cost of such improvements without additional compensation. One way to have provided such compensation would have been to guarantee security of tenure, either by tradition or by contract, so that the same tenant who shared in the cost of the improvement could share its benefits in future years. Alfred Marshall argued that the "virtual security of tenure" enjoyed by European métayers served this function.[74] But in the American South, there was no security of tenure for the laborer; as we have noted, insecurity of tenure was an important incentive to diligent labor.

Regardless of what might have been, the fact is that the southern landlord typically did not establish fixity of tenure, make side payments to sharecroppers to install improvements, or offer superior land on different terms than inferior land. The result was a lack of agricultural progress, a consequence that was foreseen from the outset. Robert Somers, an English visitor to the South in 1870, predicted that sharecropping's "incompatibility with progress will be seen more and more clearly as the Southern farmers proceed to keep live stock, to introduce deep or steam ploughing, to diversify their crops, or to carry out any improvement on their lands."[75]

Yet the pleas to abandon sharecropping went unheeded. This was not because the southern landlord lacked foresight, or even because the alternatives had other overruling disadvantages, but rather because within the context of the southern system there existed no visible incentive to change the form of tenure. From the perspective of the landlord, the current return to sharecropping was equivalent to any alternative available with other tenure arrangements and the expected return to investment was too low to encourage much capital improvement. Even the rational farsighted landowner understood the difference between advantages in principle and advantages in practice. In 1874 the Georgia Department of Agriculture made a survey of "intelligent and experienced" landowners of the state. Asked which form of tenure was superior, 66 percent responded in favor of wages, 11 percent for fixed rents, and 23 percent for sharecropping. Asked what proportion of black workers actually labored under each system, only 21 percent reported wages, 30 percent reported fixed rent, and fully 49 percent were leasing their land under sharecropping contracts.[76]

White tenants and white farmers

Up to this point, our narrative has focused upon the problems of black Americans in the postwar period, and our analysis has concentrated upon the adjustments necessitated by emancipation. But not all southerners were black, nor was agriculture before the war conducted solely on the plantation system. In fact, there were many small farms and many slaveless operations. These farms were owned by whites who cultivated their own crops and provided their own labor.[77] The owners of such farms were not required to reorganize their labor systems when emancipation came. But this does not mean they were unaffected by the changes that swept through the South.

The nonslaveholding whites can be roughly divided into two classes: the *poor whites* and *yeoman farmers.* Poor whites were families who subsisted at the fringe of antebellum society. They operated small, low-productivity farms, usually in the back country and hill counties. They were economically secure in that they were generally self-sufficient, but they produced little or no additional output for the market. Poor, illiterate, and ostracized from the plantation society, these marginal farmers found few opportunities for advancement in the pre-Civil War South. The road to success in that system seemed to be through the ownership of slaves and prime cotton land, and these farmers had little success in acquiring either.[78]

Although it is not at all certain, it appears that the rise of tenancy and the postwar labor shortage may have provided some of these poor whites with the opportunity to improve their situation within the southern economy for the first time. Statistics clearly reveal that tenant farms were taken up by whites as well as by blacks in the cotton regions. Table 5.1 details the distribution of farms and farmlands exhibited by our 1880 sample of farms, by race, tenure, and farm class. Of the operators of one-family tenant farms in that year, 40 percent were white, and a higher percentage of these (81 percent) were sharecroppers than was the case for black tenants (69 percent).

The antebellum South had, in addition to the slaveowners and the poor whites, an agrarian middle class. These whites owned and cultivated good land with their own labor (or with the assistance of at most one or two slaves). The farms of these yeomen tended to be located in the plantation regions, sandwiched between their larger slaveowning neighbors. They typically produced cotton or some other staple crop, and their owners may have aspired to eventual slaveownership and the life of a planter.[79]

This class of whites was apparently the least affected by emancipation. It is true that their ambitions to become slaveowners were foiled, but they were able to continue cultivating their land upon much the same plan as before the war. With a reasonable amount of luck and a normal amount of hard work they retained their farms. In 1880, 28 percent of all the farms in the Cotton South were operated by white owners who had 50 acres or less under cultivation. Many of these white owner-operators were undoubtedly the heirs of the prewar yeoman class, if they were not themselves the prewar owners of their land.

The emergence of a white tenant class and the acquisition of independent family farms by many blacks brought the blacks and the middle- and lower-class whites into a more parallel situation than most of these whites would have preferred. Before and during the Civil War nonslaveholding whites had generally defended slavery – even with their lives – partly at least because the inferior status of slaves minimized the competition between whites and blacks and provided every white an unquestioned touchstone of superiority no matter how mean or abject his situation.[80] After the war the similarity of their situations transformed the whites' proslavery sentiments into an open hostility toward the black population.

We have already emphasized the impact racism had upon the reorganization of southern institutions. But it would be a mistake to argue that the institutions were created primarily to serve racist ends. They were fashioned to solve real economic problems and to provide a framework within which the South could reestablish its economy. To be sure, racist attitudes precluded more satisfactory solutions. Nonetheless, it is more appropriate to think of racism as shaping the context within which the adjustments were worked out than as motivating the changes themselves. This point is well illustrated by the subject to which we now turn. The reorganization of southern financial institutions can be described almost without reference to the issue of race; yet probably no institutional change proved more detrimental to black progress than the rise of the rural merchant banker.

CHAPTER 6

FINANCIAL RECONSTRUCTION

> The scarcity of capital at the South can only be comprehended by one who has been through the country. . . . A few hundreds to some, or thousands to others, will make the difference of thousands of bales of cotton and millions of dollars in the result of this season's crop. . . . There has never been a time when so much general good could be done with so little capital at so small a risk.
>
> Theodore C. Peters, *A Report Upon Conditions of the South . . .*
> (Baltimore: H. A. Robinson, 1867), pp.7–8.

The elaborate financial and merchandising network developed to serve the antebellum cotton trade had to be completely rebuilt in the wake of the Civil War. With an institutional change as fundamental as the replacement of the slave plantation with family-operated tenant farms, it was inevitable that these financial institutions would have to be restructured and based upon an entirely new foundation. Unlike the reorganization of agriculture, which was discussed, debated, and deliberated, the evolution of the new financial and marketing institutions took place amid little contemporary notice, let alone debate. Although not as controversial as political reconstruction, or as dramatic as agricultural reconstruction, this financial reconstruction was to have even more far-reaching repercussions. In retrospect, we can see that the changes in this sector had a dominant influence upon the future course of southern agricultural development.

The antebellum financial system

The prewar cotton planter stood at the center of an extensive marketing and financial network that linked him with the cotton textile manufacturers of England and New England; with the importers, wholesalers, and manufacturers on the East Coast who furnished the plantation's needs; with the mule raisers of Kentucky, Missouri, and Tennessee; with the farmers of the Ohio and upper Mississippi basins who made up the deficiencies in southern supplies of barreled pork and cornmeal; and also with the bankers who

Notes to Chapter 6 appear on pages 340–343.

provided short-term credit. This elaborate network was presided over by a group of intermediaries and middlemen known as *cotton factors*.

The system worked well because the cotton factor could establish with the planters with whom he dealt a relationship "of an unusually intimate character." J. A. Ansley, an agent for cotton factors located in Augusta, Georgia, described this relationship in more detail:

For years [the planter and the factor] have done business together, and the factor knows fully the moral and pecuniary standing of his planting patron – his first inquiry being generally as to his reliability and integrity, then as to how many acres he is planting or preparing to plant, what force he has to depend upon, how his place is stocked, and all other questions necessary to his safety in making advances.[1]

Once the factor was assured that the farming operation was proceeding smoothly, he added his own endorsement to the planter's promissory note. Secured by both the growing crop and the planter's holdings of land and slaves, such notes could in turn be pledged as collateral by the factor at his own bank to obtain funds to purchase the supplies required by the plantation during the growing season. After the cotton was picked, ginned, and baled, the factor saw to the details of preparing the crop for market and shipping it to port. Once the crop was sold, the factor deducted from the proceeds the amount due him for supplies advanced and services rendered. With his share of the proceeds the factor could then repay the promissory note held by the bank.[2]

Southern banks, on their part, invested heavily in this *accommodation paper,* as it was called. They also purchased federal and state bonds and occasionally invested in the bonds of corporations promoting internal improvements. On the other hand, these banks rarely, if ever, invested in real estate mortgages, business loans, or personal notes. Largely because of the demand for their services by the factorage system, southern banks were able to achieve a size and financial sophistication appreciably greater than was common in other regions of the country. Estimates of the average size of antebellum banks in 1859 and 1860, based upon available statistics for chartered banks, are presented in Table 6.1.[3] As the estimates suggest, banks of the Five Cotton States surpassed those of all other regions in terms of the amount of capital invested, the quantity of notes in circulation, and the level of deposits per bank. The strength of southern banks depended upon the cotton factor, whose own financial power was derived from the plantation owner. The financial security of the planter in turn rested upon his collateral in land and slaves. When emancipation freed the slaves and depressed land values, the stability of the entire system was threatened.

The failure of the cotton factorage system to revive

Most of the prewar cotton factors attempted to reestablish business as usual after the Civil War. For several years they struggled, together with the

Table 6.1. *Average size of reporting banks, by region: 1859–1860*

| Region | Number of banks reporting | Thousands of dollars per bank | | | |
		Capital	Note circulation	Deposits	Total reported financial assets[a]
United States[b]	1,573	268	127	159	647
East[c]	1,035	285	108	186	659
West[d]	338	103	106	42	360
South[e]	200	460	263	217	1,073
Five Cotton States	69	883	563	434	2,232

[a] Total reported financial assets include loans and discounts, stocks, real estate, notes of other banks, due from other banks, and specie. [b] Total of East, West, and South. [c] Maine, New Hampshire, Vermont, Massachusetts, Rhode Island, Connecticut, New York, New Jersey, Pennsylvania, Delaware, Maryland, and Kentucky. [d] Ohio, Indiana, Illinois, Michigan, Wisconsin, Minnesota, Kansas, Iowa, Missouri, and the Nebraska Territory. [e] Virginia (including present-day West Virginia), North Carolina, Tennessee, Florida, Texas, Arkansas, and the Five Cotton States (South Carolina, Georgia, Alabama, Mississippi, Louisiana).

Source: U.S. Secretary of the Treasury, *Report of the Secretary of the Treasury on the State of the Finances, for the year Ending June 30, 1863,* House of Representatives, Executive Document Number 3, 38th Congress, 1st Session (Washington: GPO, 1863), Table 10, pp. 226–231; also see note 3 of this chapter.

landholders, to rebuild the marketing and financial network with which they were familiar. But as the plantation system began to succumb to the pressures placed upon it after emancipation, it became apparent that the factor could not possibly provide his traditional services to the multiplied numbers of farm operators who had gained control of cotton production. These farmers were typically tenants who owned neither the land they farmed nor much other capital. As a consequence, they could offer little collateral for a loan. In these circumstances, the landowner might have been expected to provide security on behalf of his tenants, but this practice did not develop. With emancipation, the landowner had lost his most important form of collateral: his slaves. All that remained was the growing crop and the land itself. However, the market value of land had plummeted, while the prices of food and other supplies remained relatively high. Frequently, the value of a family farm was insufficient to secure the necessary credit for the tenant who was to work it. The only form collateral could take was an interest in the growing crop. Yet, if the crop were to fail to live up to the tenant's expectations, there would be nothing more to ensure the debt. Given the uncertainty engendered by the widespread crop failures in 1866 and 1867, and the general skepticism on the part of whites that black farmers would work reliably on their own, it is not surprising that cotton factors did not view crop mortgages as adequate security. Later, local merchants would come to accept this form of collateral, but only when they could personally supervise the tenants throughout the year. To a businessman located in a seaport city dealing with numerous landowners, and thus potentially hundreds of tenants, such supervision was clearly out of the question.

The rise of tenancy by itself would probably have spelled the end of the factorage system, but many cotton factors did not even survive long enough to feel the effects of this change. The principal sources of the factor's credit – southern banks and cotton brokers – were financially ruined by the war, and the failure of the southern banking system to reestablish itself quickly left many factors without financial support. The extent to which the southern banking system suffered from the blows of the war is illustrated by the experience of Georgia and South Carolina. In 1860 these two states had forty-nine state-chartered banks. In South Carolina only one, the G. W. Williams Company, survived to reopen in 1865. In Georgia one bank in Augusta and two in Savannah weathered the war.[4] The other forty-five never reopened.

The resulting "credit shortage" kept many cotton factors from reestablishing their businesses and sharply curtailed the operations of those who did attempt to do so. The firm of Linton and Doughty, cotton factors in Augusta, complained of the shortage of capital in 1867:

An experience of fifteen years with a large list of cotton planters is sufficient to enable us to know very well the standing, means and integrity of each one of them; and we do not hesitate to say there are many among them that we would not require the "scratch of the pen" from, if we had the ready means at hand to supply them what is necessary to make the crops.[5]

The credit shortage seemed common throughout the South. "Everybody," a Mobile businessman told Whitelaw Reid, "wanted to buy, but nobody had any money."[6] James De Bow claimed that in April of 1867 the problem had "already reached the point when business becomes paralyzed."[7] Theodore Peters, who made extensive inquiries regarding this problem during his trip to the South in 1867, placed the blame for this state of financial affairs on the collapse of the rebel government:

[The Confederate] Government first absorbed all the realized capital that had been accumulated, and which was very large in the aggregate, and gave them in return its bonds, which have in turn become worthless, and are made so for all time to come. In the place, therefore, of an abundant cash capital for all the wants of legitimate business they are utterly worthless.[8]

Peters called upon northern capitalists to alleviate the shortage of credit, but his plea was largely unsuccessful. Communication with these potential suppliers of credit had been disrupted, and without the cotton factors' aid the channels of communication were slow to reopen.

The reestablishment of southern banking

The collapse of the antebellum banking system at first greatly hindered trade, but of course it was not long before attempts were made to organize new banks for the South. The reestablishment of a banking system, however, was obstructed by a number of changes in federal banking regulations. The National Banking Act, which completely rewrote the banking law of the United States, had been enacted during the Civil War. It established a minimum requirement of $50,000 in paid-in capital before a bank could obtain a national charter, and the act placed severe new restrictions on note issue and deposit creation. Restrictions on mortgage lending and other provisions of the act discouraged national banks from developing in agricultural regions throughout the country.[9] The extent to which these restrictive aspects of the law discouraged the formation of national banks and hindered their operation in the cotton regions is illustrated by the fact that only 20 of the 1,688 national banks organized during the first three years after the war were located in one of the Five Cotton States. Of these 20, 5 had already failed or closed by 1869.[10] All but 4 of the successful national banks in the Five Cotton States were located in one of the South's major commercial centers, and these exceptional 4 were located in cities with over 3,000 inhabitants. [11]

In order to discourage competition from state-chartered banks, Congress passed a 10 percent tax on the note issue of all nonnational banks in 1865.[12] This measure was so effective that it virtually eliminated state banknote issue throughout the country.[13] It also proved a severe obstacle to the establishment of state-chartered banks in the South. Had state banks been allowed to operate freely, they presumably would have relied heavily upon note issue. As it was, the 10 percent tax proved prohibitive, and the alternative – the introduction of checking accounts – was clearly impractical in the South at this time. The complexities of introducing a new form of money may well have posed as great an obstacle to deposit banking as the 10 percent tax posed to note issue.[14]

In any case, very few state banks were established in the South in the years immediately following the Civil War. In 1868, there were only 14 state-chartered banks in the Five Cotton States. Of these, 10 were located in New Orleans and 2 in Mobile, both large commercial centers where deposit banking apparently proved feasible. The only other 2 were savings banks chartered in Mississippi. No state banks at all were established in South Carolina or Georgia.[15]

Because of the early difficulty in establishing national and state banks, a number of "private" banks appeared in the major urban centers. Detailed figures are presented in Table 6.2. In July 1866, 67 unchartered banks had already been established in the major commercial centers of the South. By December 1868, the number had grown to 71. These firms were able to extend credit to factors and planters; however, they were restricted in their

Table 6.2. *Private banking in southern commercial centers: 1866, 1868*

	Number of private banks organized by July 1866		Total number of private banks operating, December 1868
	In operation July 1866	Still in operation December 1868	
New Orleans	18	7[a]	18
Charleston	12	4	12
Mobile	8	2	11
Augusta	8	4	6
Savannah	7	5[b]	12
Montgomery	7	3	5
Macon	4	2	5
Atlanta	3	1	2
Total	67	28	71

[a] Excludes one bank that moved to Baton Rouge, Louisiana. [b] One of the seven private banks in Savannah apparently split into two separate banks by 1868. We have counted this as a single survival.
Source: *1866:* I. Smith Homans, ed., *The Bankers' Magazine, and Statistical Register,* 21 (vol. 1, third series, August 1866), pp. 129–143. *1868:* I. Smith Homans, ed., *The Merchants & Bankers' Almanac for 1869* (New York: Office of the Bankers' Magazine and Statistical Register, 1869), pp. 53–75.

operation because they could not issue banknotes or create deposits without a charter. The majority of these were merchandising companies that seem to have been drawn into banking by the dearth of organized financial institutions in 1865 and 1866. The flurry of private banking activity in the South's larger cities was short-lived. Many of these firms dropped their banking business as soon as conditions became more settled. As is illustrated in the table, less than one-half the banks listed in 1866 were included in a comparable list drawn up one and one half years later. By 1880 the total number of private banks in these eight cities had fallen to only 24.

Despite the obstacles to obtaining a bank charter, an expansion of charter banking occurred after 1868. Table 6.3 compares the number of banks in 1868 and 1880 and is organized by the nature of the city in which the banks were located. The number of national banks in the Five Cotton States grew from 15 to 42 and the number of state-chartered banks from 14 to 49. Most of this expansion took place in the urban centers of the South. Of the 91 chartered banks in 1880, 47 were located in one of the eight major commercial centers, and another 25 were situated in one of the twenty-two urban cotton centers having a population greater than 3,000 in 1880. At the same time this expansion of chartered banking was taking place, private banking in these cities sharply declined. The number of private banks in urban centers fell from 98 in 1868 to only 44 in 1880.

Table 6.3. *Number of banks in Five Cotton States, by location and type of bank: 1868, 1880*

Class of city and type of bank[a]	1868		1880	
	Number of cities with banks	Number of banks	Number of cities with banks	Number of banks
Major commercial centers	8	94	8	71
National	7	11	8	20
State	2	12	7	27
Private	8	71	8	24
Urban cotton centers	13	32	22	45
National	4	4	12	14
State	1	1	10	11
Private	13	27	14	20
Rural cotton centers	12	13	76	90
National	0	0	8	8
State	1	1	11	11
Private	12	12	62	71
All cities	33	139	107	206
National	11	15	28	42
State	4	14	28	49
Private	33	110	84	115

[a] See Appendix G, Section 4, for a discussion of the procedure used to compile these statistics. *Major commercial centers* are Charleston, S.C.; Savannah, Augusta, Atlanta, and Macon, Ga.; Mobile and Montgomery, Ala.; and New Orleans, La. *Urban cotton centers* are towns of 3,000 or more people with substantial commercial and banking facilities which were prominent in the cotton trade. *Rural cotton centers* include all other towns with banking facilities in these states. For a complete list of cities and towns in 1880 according to these classifications, see Appendix G, Table G.16.
Source: 1868: I. Smith Homans, ed., *The Merchants & Bankers' Almanac for 1869* (New York: Office of the Bankers' Magazine and Statistical Register, 1869), pp. 47–75; U.S. Comptroller of the Currency, *Report of the Comptroller of the Currency,* House of Representatives, Executive Document Number 3, 41st Congress, 2nd Session (December 6, 1869) (Washington: GPO, 1869), pp. 558–593. *1880:* I. S. Homans, Jr., ed., *The Banker's Almanac and Register, January 1880* (New York: I. S. Homans, Jr., 1880), p. xviii; R. G. Dun and Company, *The Mercantile Agency Reference Book . . . January 1880,* 2nd ed. (New York: Dun, Barlow & Co., 1880); U.S. Comptroller of the Currency, *Annual Report . . . 1880,* House of Representatives, Executive Document Number 3, 46th Congress, 3rd Session (December 6, 1880) (Washington: GPO, 1880), pp. clxviii–clxxi.

The number of chartered banks in the Five Cotton States provides a misleading index to the recovery of urban banking in the South. We earlier noted that in the antebellum period the scale of bank operations in the South was very much larger than elsewhere in the United States (Table 6.1). Although we lack comprehensive data for the years immediately following the war, detailed information on national banks is available. As a class this

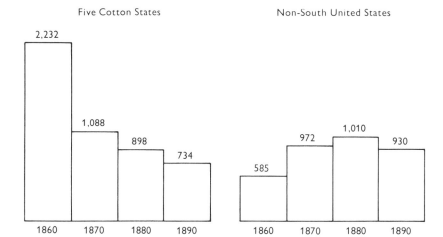

Figure 6.1 Total assets reported per bank by region: 1860, 1870, 1880, and 1890. (*Source:* Tables 6.1 and 6.4.)

surely included the largest banks of the South, so, if anything, data for these banks will exaggerate the size of a typical southern bank. Table 6.4 presents data on the size of national banks in the Five Cotton States, twelve southern states, and the balance of the United States between 1870 and 1890. According to each of several measures – banking capital, the total note issue, total deposits, and total assets reported by the banks – national banks in the twelve southern states were distinctly smaller than national banks in the rest of the country. While it is true that the size of banks in the Five Cotton States was approximately comparable to the size of the banks outside the South, this appearance is entirely due to the fact that we included New Orleans banks.[16] A comparison of the data in Tables 6.1 and 6.4 leaves no doubt that the scale of banking operations in the South fell substantially after 1860. This comparison is made in Figure 6.1. Despite the "recovery" of chartered banking noted above, the level of banking services available in the South was almost certainly lower for the balance of the nineteenth century than it had been in 1860.

The rural banker

The new banks located in the urban areas were able to serve the interests of the commercial establishments of the cities, but they were not well adapted to deal directly with agriculture. Without the factor as intermediary, the city banks had no established relationship with the rural areas. Not surprisingly, commercial banks in the urban centers showed no more interest in extending credit to small cotton farmers than had the factors. Even when national banks were established in a rural setting, they eschewed crop liens and land mortgages. Thus, for example, while the National Bank of Newberry, South Carolina (population 2,300), did three-fourths of its business

Table 6.4. *Characteristics of national banks, by region: 1870, 1880, 1890*

Year and region[a]	Total number of banks	Thousands of dollars per bank			
		Capital	Notes issued	Total Deposits	Total resources
1870					
Five Cotton States	14	304	192	507	1,088
Twelve southern states	69	176	126	276	636
Balance of United States	1,545	268	185	347	972
1880					
Five Cotton States	42	220	155	421	898
Twelve southern states	126	162	120	309	664
Balance of United States	1,935	224	159	424	1,010
1890					
Five Cotton States	101	144	35	413	734
Twelve southern states	386	131	27	297	562
Balance of United States	2,997	192	38	466	930

[a] The twelve southern states, in addition to the Five Cotton States, include Arkansas, Florida, North Carolina, Tennessee, Texas, Virginia, and West Virginia.
Sources: 1870: U.S. Comptroller of the Currency, *Report of the Comptroller of the Currency, December 5, 1870,* House of Representatives, Executive Document Number 3, 41st Congress, 3rd Session (Washington: GPO, 1870), pp. 566–573, 596–597. *1880:* U.S. Comptroller of the Currency, *Annual Report . . . 1880,* House of Representatives, Executive Document Number 3, 46th Congress, 3rd Session (Washington: GPO, 1880), pp. cl–cli, clxvii–clxxv. *1890:* U.S. Comptroller of the Currency, *Annual Report . . . 1890,* House of Representatives, Executive Document Number 3, Part 1, 51st Congress, 2nd Session (Washington: GPO, 1890), pp. 246–247, 262–273.

with farmers, their loans were made "purely on personal security or on collaterals; liens or mortgages are not asked for or given."[17] Despite the expansion of urban banking, the small farmer was left isolated from the financial centers by the collapse of the plantation and the disappearance of the cotton factor.[18]

The failure of large-city banks to develop ties directly to agriculture partially explains the dramatic increase in rural banks. According to Table 6.3, the number of small towns (with fewer than 3,000 people) that could provide banking services rose from 12 to 76 between 1868 and 1880. These towns, invariably located on a major transportation route, had become important terminuses in the marketing of cotton. With the factorage system largely gone by the 1870s, banking became an important service provided in these rural cotton centers. However, the banks that did business in such towns differed from their city cousins. Most small-town banks were un-chartered private banks. The data presented in Table 6.3 for the Five Cotton States show that only 21 percent of the rural banks in 1880 had obtained charters. Quite frequently, these private banking businesses appeared as an adjunct to some other business, most often a general store. Many of these bankers, judging by their advertisements appearing in the *Bankers' Magazine,* also served as collection agencies and insurance salesmen. R. G. Dun's Mercantile Agency, a firm that provided credit information on businessmen, prepared a business directory that included all the 71 private banks located in small towns. Table 6.5 displays the pecuniary strength and the occupation designated by Dun's reporters for each of these concerns; only 27 were listed simply as "bankers." The occupational designation for 19 others did not even indicate that banking was a sideline. The remaining 25 were described as combining some activity with banking. Table 6.5 also reveals that most of these private banks were quite small. Only 31 of the 71 bankers had a net worth that in Dun's judgment exceeded the $50,000-minimum capital required for a national bank charter in a small city, and 17 of these individuals had other interests outside their banks. Although state banking laws varied, we found that less than 4 percent of the state-chartered banks in the Five Cotton States were capitalized below $50,000 in 1880, and none were smaller than $25,000. Yet 28 of the 71 private bankers in Table 6.5 were assessed by Dun's agency as worth less than $25,000.[19] This measure of their net worth includes all the assets owned by the banker, not just those invested in banking.

Rural bankers provided a link to the more extensive financial services in the cities, and they invariably confined their banking operations to the

Table 6.5. *Occupation and pecuniary strength of private bankers in rural cotton centers: 1880*

Pecuniary strength[a]	Number with occupation listed as			
	Banker	Banker plus other occupation	Nonbanking occupation	Total
$250,000–500,000	3	2	—	5
$100,000–250,000	7	6	2	15
$50,000–100,000	4	6	1	11
$25,000–50,000	7	3	2	12
$10,000–25,000	3	4	4	11
$5,000–10,000	3	1	4	8
$2,000–5,000	—	1	3	4
Less than $2,000	—	1	2	3
Not reported	—	1	1	2
All classes	27	25	19	71

[a] The "pecuniary strength" is given by Dun's Mercantile Agency. This figure includes all assets owned by the banker, not just those invested in the banking business.
Source: R. G. Dun and Company, *The Mercantile Agency Reference Book . . . January 1880,* 2nd ed. (New York: Dun, Barlow & Company, 1880). See Appendix G, Section 4, for additional details, and Table G.16 for a list of rural cotton centers.

business of the large landowners and merchants in their area. Our examination of the records on these rural bankers in the Dun and Bradstreet Archives provides no evidence that these individuals provided short-term credit to small farmers unable to offer land or other assets as collateral.

The rise of the rural cotton center

The planters, cotton factors, and merchants who attempted to reestablish the antebellum financial and merchandising network after the war not only had to contend with the appearance of tenancy and the problems of a credit shortage, but in addition, they soon found that the cotton market was undergoing a drastic transformation. The major cotton entrepôts before the war had been either seaports such as New Orleans, Mobile, and Savannah, or cities situated on major rivers such as Vicksburg, Memphis, and Augusta. Improvements in transportation, especially the railroad, allowed a shift of cotton markets away from these waterports to towns and cities in the interior. Towns that before the war had played only a minor role in the marketing of the cash crop suddenly blossomed into major centers of the cotton trade. Dealers in Selma (Alabama), Rome (Georgia), Meridian (Mississippi), and a growing number of similar cities shipped cotton by rail directly to the North, bypassing the established river and sea routes.

The coming of the railroad was invariably coupled with another technological innovation – the telegraph. Rapid communication meant that information on distant market events could be supplied directly to even the smallest stop along the line without reliance upon a cotton factor and his business connections.

These developments in transportation and communication were coupled with yet other technological changes. On the antebellum plantation cotton was typically ginned and compressed into bales using machinery powered by animals or slaves. The resulting bale, however, usually required further compression at the wharf before it could be shipped by water economically. Following the war, improvements in small-sized compresses allowed the processing of cotton to shift away from the plantation to nearby cotton ginneries and warehouses, which had machinery powerful enough to obviate rebaling. Steam-operated gins and compresses could efficiently prepare the crop for market even in such small towns as Cheraw, South Carolina; Clinton, Mississippi; Newton, Alabama; and Bastrop, Louisiana. In 1870 none of these towns had a population larger than 1,000, yet all possessed ginning and marketing facilities for cotton.

Instead of relying on a broker in a major town to sell his crop, the postwar producer could sell it directly to a buyer at any one of dozens of small towns throughout the Cotton South. These rural cotton centers became the distributing centers for northern goods, as well as entrepôts of the cotton trade. In 1869, William B. Dana, editor of *Hunt's Merchant Magazine,* observed:

The minor villages, the corners and cross roads, buyers from which were heretofore unknown in Northern markets, familiar as they were in Southern centres like Mobile, Savannah, Macon, Charleston, &c., &c., now deal directly with the North; and there has also grown up a wider and more general system of commercial traveling than has ever before prevailed at the South. These travelers go from New York and Philadelphia, and from the manufacturing towns, and solicit direct trade with those with whom business was formerly done by the intervention of the Southern jobber or merchant.[20]

By examining the pattern of cotton shipments around 1880, together with the services offered by various towns in the Five Cotton States and the Cotton South, we have identified 158 towns that seem sufficiently important to warrant being called "rural cotton centers."[21] The accompanying map displays the transportation network of the South around 1880 and locates the cotton centers in relation to this network.

The reestablishment of southern merchandising

The sole survivor of the general collapse of the elaborate system of market intermediation that had developed before the war was the country store. However, these small furnishing merchants were hardly in a position to provision the entire South in 1865. In antebellum times such stores had existed only on the fringe of the plantation economy. Moreover, they had depended in large measure on the factorage system to provide them with their link to both financial markets and the wholesalers of merchandise.[22]

During the Civil War the country merchants were cut off from sources of external credit and supplies and were left without a market for agricultural staples. They were forced to close or sharply curtail operations. Of those few who did manage to survive or even to prosper on the wartime trade, most were wiped out by the collapse of the Confederate monetary system in 1865.

Following the war the high cotton prices and the attempts of planters to provision for the coming year attracted capital from the North. Prospective merchandisers appeared from all sides. Sidney Andrews found northern and western Georgia in December 1865 to be "full of 'runners' from Louisville and Cincinnati." In Charleston he estimated that "at least one half" of the stores were controlled by northern interests; in Savannah he found a similar situation.[23] Whitelaw Reid similarly described a Virginia town as "swarming with representatives of Northern capitalists, looking for investments."[24] The opportunities also attracted European immigrants and discharged soldiers from both armies. The southern merchants familiar with the antebellum trade frequently reentered the industry, joining their interests with those of newly arrived men who could bring capital or credit into the business. For a time these northern interlopers seemed to prosper. Andrews reported that northern agents were "getting many orders," and he was told that even more northerners were expected to come South before the

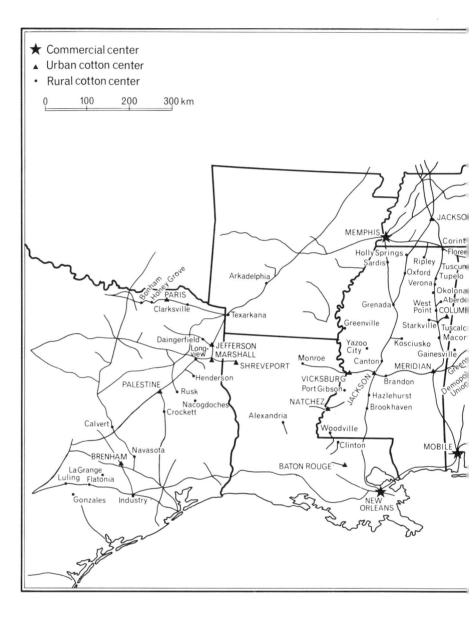

The railroads and the urban areas of the Cotton South, 1880. (*Source:* Based on maps in U.S. Cer Office, Tenth Census [1880], *Report on Cotton Production in the United States,* 2 vols. [Washing GPO, 1884], U.S. Census Office, Eleventh Census [1890], *Statistical Atlas of the United States* [W.

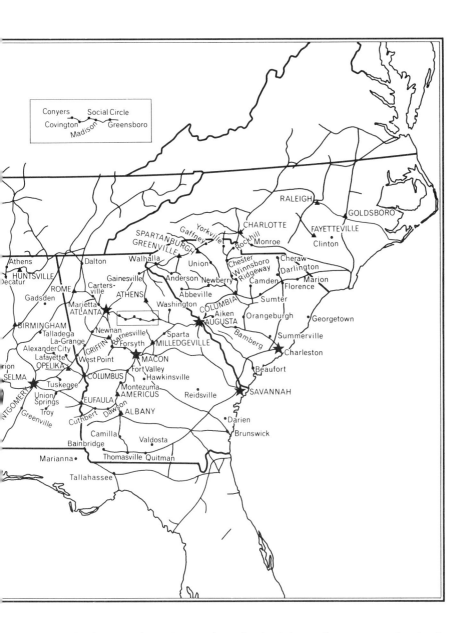

Conyers Social Circle
Covington Greensboro
Madison

RALEIGH
GOLDSBORO
CHARLOTTE FAYETTEVILLE
Gaffney Yorkville
SPARTANBURGH Rockhill Monroe Clinton
GREENVILLE Chester Cheraw
Athens Dalton Walhalla Union Winnsboro Darlington
HUNTSVILLE Anderson Newberry Ridgeway Marion
Decatur Gainesville Camden Florence
ROME Carters-ville Abbeville
Gadsden ATHENS Sumter
Marietta Washington
ATLANTA COLUMBIA
Aiken Orangeburgh Georgetown
BIRMINGHAM Newnan AUGUSTA
Talladega Barnesville Sparta Summerville
La-Grange Forsyth MILLEDGEVILLE Bamberg Charleston
AlexanderCity GRIFFIN
Lafayette West Point MACON Beaufort
OPELIKA COLUMBUS Fort Valley
rion SELMA Tuskegee Hawkinsville SAVANNAH
NTGOMERY Union Montezuma
Springs EUFAULA AMERICUS Reidsville
Troy Dawson Darien
Greenville Cuthbert ALBANY Brunswick
Camilla
Bainbridge Valdosta
Marianna Thomasville Quitman
Tallahassee

ton: GPO, 1898]. Plate 60; John F. Stover, *The Railroads of the South, 1865–1900* [Chapel Hill:
versity of North Carolina Press, 1955], p. 25; Ira G. Clark, *Then Came the Railroads: The Century
n Steam to Diesel in the Southwest* [Norman: University of Oklahoma Press, 1958], p. 148.)

next season began.[25] Early in 1866 Whitelaw Reid observed that in Natchez, Mississippi, "northern men had established themselves as commission merchants and dealers of plantation supplies, and were infusing new energy into the town. They said that they had all the business they could do."[26]

Yet the extent to which Yankees ultimately took over the southern furnishing business is greatly exaggerated by these reports. For the most part, the northerners stayed in the larger centers of trade, seldom venturing into the rural regions where a newcomer usually had to include a local partner in order to develop the contacts so essential to a successful operation. As one would-be merchant from the North lamented to John Dennett in 1865:

A Northerner needn't come into this country to go into business unless he . . . can buy into some Southern firm. You see if these people can trade with one of their own men, they're not going to trade with you and me. It's all natural enough – I don't blame them; but it puts you and me under an immense disadvantage there. Then New York is bound to favor the old houses in every kind of way, and we're under another disadvantage there. You know how it is with these countrymen and country dealers; they're used to coming in and hitching their horses to the same post year after year, and you can't change 'em to a new place; you couldn't if there hadn't been any trouble, and of course you can't now when they're down on us. I don't believe they'd speak to a man if they knew he'd ever passed through Boston.[27]

Outside the towns the merchandising business remained largely in the hands of southerners. A sample of 237 rural general store operators in business in 1880 revealed that only 3 had been born in nonslave states. Two-thirds of these merchants were born in the state of their residence; only 11 percent were foreign born (half of whom were German).[28] An examination of stores founded in Rankin County, Mississippi, between 1866 and 1870 revealed that of 22 merchants setting up businesses, 19 were southerners and 3 were immigrants. In only one case, where a firm was alleged to have a partner in the North, did we find evidence of northern involvement. The two firms that established themselves in business before 1868 were both operated by men who had been merchants in the county before the war.[29]

Once the immediate disruptions from the war subsided, the recovery of rural merchandising was quite rapid. By 1870 Dun's Mercantile Agency reported 290 general stores operating in the twenty-seven counties we selected to represent the Cotton South. Ten years later the number had grown to 860 stores.[30]

The rural merchant as a financial intermediary

In the cotton region the preparation of land began in January, planting usually commenced in March or April, and the crop did not reach market until November or December. During this long season the tenant farmer required food and other supplies for himself and his family, feed for his animals, fertilizer, and other inputs, as well as money to pay wages and board to any workers he might employ. To finance these expenditures, he invariably required some form of short-term credit.

It was the local furnishing merchants who became the suppliers, not only of food and materials, but of this credit as well. In the first years following the war this arrangement was established out of necessity. The landowners' shortage of ready cash and the disruption of the financial markets left no other source of credit. The merchants were able to extend credit at that time only because they, in turn, obtained financing from their northern suppliers. Wholesalers, eager to reestablish their southern business, were willing to ship goods on consignment, allowing the local merchant six months to a year before payment.

The merchant could not have adopted this role as financial intermediary had it not been for an innovation which, although of enormous significance, went virtually unnoticed: the creation of a centralized system of credit rating. The northern business community could not have been expected to provision the South on unsecured credit without some device by which wholesalers could establish the reliability and creditworthiness of their customers. This device was created by the R. G. Dun Mercantile Agency, which employed a surprisingly extensive army of "credit reporters" stationed in every county of the South to report information on local businessmen to the agency's New York office.

The Mercantile Agency had been founded in 1841 by Lewis Tappan, a New York merchant who foresaw the need for reliable credit information following the financial panic of 1837.[31] Tappan organized a network of correspondents, made up for the most part of local lawyers, who collected information on business firms throughout the United States. The information from the reports of these correspondents was carefully entered into a set of ledger books, which gradually accumulated a continuous file on each firm. Referring to these files, the Mercantile Agency was able to sell information on the creditworthiness of firms to whomever might be interested. During the years before the Civil War Tappan's agency had gradually expanded its interests beyond manufacturers and larger commercial establishments to include small merchants and traders in rural areas of the West and South.

In 1859 the Mercantile Agency was taken over by Robert G. Dun, who resolved to assemble the information collected in such a way that a "credit rating" and an index of "pecuniary strength" for each firm could be calculated and published. The outbreak of the Civil War delayed the implementation of these plans in the South, but upon cessation of hostility the agency was quick to reestablish and expand its southern reporting network hoping to take advantage of the scarcity of information in the North regarding southern business conditions and the progress being made in reestablishing trade. Dun employed local agents in virtually every county of the South as early as 1866, and he also established a number of roving credit reporters who traveled from county seat to county seat. These men specialized in making quick judgments based on whatever data were available. "I called on the storekeepers," explained one such investigator, "and usually paid a visit to the county seat to gossip with officials and to examine the assessment rolls for property descriptions."[32] Having formed his impression of the individual and his business, and after checking for any tangible property, the credit reporter forwarded his report to the home office.

Because each of the furnishing merchants in the South was investigated and rated by the agency, northern manufacturers and wholesalers were willing to provide credit through the consignment system – credit that the merchant in turn could pass on to the farmer. Without the obligation to pay the wholesalers until the end of the year, merchants could allow the cotton growers until the end of the season before settling their accounts. This arrangement soon became the established pattern. This development helps explain both the failure of the cotton factor to reappear and the limited scale of operation of the few existing rural banks. In the South the rural store handled those functions of the small country banks that were typical in western and midwestern agricultural regions.[33]

The limited market of the southern general store permitted the merchant to extend credit services to tenant farmers whom banks and other financial institutions avoided. Because his clientele was not numerous, the merchant could be quite familiar with each farmer requesting credit. With only a few customers, he could maintain a constant vigil throughout the year to ensure the safety of any advances. Edward King, traveling through the South in 1875, described the care with which merchants of the Mississippi Valley watched over their debtors:

They are obliged to watch both white and black planters who procure advances from them, to make sure that they produce a crop. If the merchant sees that there is likely to be but half a crop, he sometimes notifies the planters that they must thereafter draw only half the amount agreed upon at the outset. In short, in some sections the Hebrew is the taskmaster, arbiter and guardian of the planters' destinies.[34]

The effort required to maintain this supervision is illustrated by the response of a merchant in Mississippi to Robert Somers's inquiry concerning these practices:

I have three horses riding on saddle – my own one of de best pacers in de country; and when Sunday comes I say to my clerks, "Go you dis way and dat," and I go de other, and we see how de work is going on; and if negro is doing nothing we put them all . . . outside de store, of course.[35]

The customers of these small stores were, for the most part, family farmers. Their purchases seldom went beyond the bare necessities required to feed and clothe their own families and run the farm. Cornmeal, salt pork or "bacon," flour, lard, salt, coffee, and molasses accounted for most of the food purchases; shoes and calico cloth would provide clothing. Whiskey and tobacco were the only "luxury" items commonly ordered. Vegetables – particularly green vegetables – were rare. An occasional purchase of a ham or tinned fish might vary the basic diet. Corn or other feed for the animals, fertilizer for the crops, and farm implements such as a plow tip, took care of the farming needs. If the year had been good, some household items – a lantern, kitchen utensils, or perhaps a bolt of fancy cloth – might be entered on the account.[36]

Farmers rarely paid cash for the goods they bought. The general practice was for the merchant to "advance" the goods on credit up to a fixed amount established at the beginning of the season. The rule of thumb for such advances was $40 for each mule put to work.[37] This would imply that any amount over $80 would be unusual, for a tenant farm seldom harnessed more than two mules. Although Harry Hammond claimed that the debt held by merchants in the cotton areas of South Carolina in 1880 was "usually about $100" per farm, the average value of the liens reported in a survey of eleven South Carolina cotton counties taken by Hammond was only $78.[38] The purchases by the farmer throughout the year were debited to the farmer's account. Toward the end of the season, the books would be settled against the returns from the cash crop.

The merchant established two sets of prices: *cash prices* and *credit prices.* The cash price applied only if the goods were paid for when received. The credit price was always substantially above the cash price, thus assuring the merchant a rate of return on his loan.[39] The farmer, for his part, had little choice. By the middle of the growing season he was invariably out of cash and therefore had to charge his purchases. Sisk reports a store in Alabama whose cash sales for the month of June 1874 were $21.35, while credit sales for the same month totaled $1,191.46.[40] The Georgia State Department of Agriculture reported in 1875 and 1876 that only 20 and 28 percent of the farms in those years were able to avoid purchasing supplies on credit.[41]

The merchant required some sort of collateral for the loans he approved. The only asset a small-farm operator, particularly a tenant farmer, could offer was the forthcoming crop. To secure the loan, therefore, the merchant expected a *crop lien* on the farmer's future output. The enactment of crop lien laws in the early postbellum period permitted the merchant to enforce legally a contract binding the crop as security for the loan.[42] In addition to giving the merchant legal title to the farmer's crop, these liens normally required that the farmer pledge any other personal or real property he might own. Figure 6.2 reproduces a lien bond between Alonzo T. Mial and A. Robert Medlin, drawn up in Wake County, North Carolina, and dated February 29, 1876. The document was a printed form prescribed by "An Act to secure advances for Agricultural purposes" and seems typical of those used in other cotton states. According to the terms of the lien in Figure 6.2, Medlin agreed to give Mial a lien on "all of his crops grown"; and in further consideration signed over his rights to "All of his Stock horses, Cattle Sheep and Hogs – Carts and Wagons House hold and kitchen furnishings."

No. 123.—Lien Bond secured by Real and Personal Property.

STATE OF NORTH CAROLINA,

Wake County.

Articles of Agreement, Between _Alonzo T. Mial_ of said County and State, of the first part, and _A. Robert Medlin_ of the County and State aforesaid, of the second part, to secure an Agricultural Lien according to an Act of General Assembly of North Carolina, entitled "An Act to secure advances for Agricultural purposes":

Whereas, the said _A. R. Medlin_ being engaged in the cultivation of the soil, and being without the necessary means to cultivate his crop, _The Said A. T. Mial_ ~~have~~ has agreed to furnish goods and supplies to the said _A. R. Medlin_ to an amount not to exceed _One Hundred and fifty_ Dollars, to enable him to cultivate and harvest his crops for the year 1876.

And in consideration thereof, the said _A. R. Medlin_ doth hereby give and convey to the said _A. T. Mial_ a LIEN upon all of his crops grown in said County in said year, on the lands described as follows: _The land of A. R. Medlin adjoining the lands of Nelson D. Pain Samuel Bunch & others._

And further, in Consideration thereof, the said _A. R. Medlin_ for One Dollar in hand paid, the receipt of which is hereby acknowledged, have bargained and sold, and by these presents do bargain, sell and convey unto the said _A. T. Mial his_ heirs and assigns forever, the following described Real and Personal Property to-wit: _All of his Stock horses, Cattle Sheep and Hogs—Carts and Wagons House hold and kitchen furnishings._ To Have and to Hold the above described premises, together with the appurtenances thereof, and the above described personal property, to the said _A. T. Mial his_ heirs and assigns.

The above to be null and void should the amount found to be due on account of said advancements be discharged on or before the _1st_ day of _November_ 1876: otherwise the said _A. T. Mial his_ executors, administrators or assigns, are hereby authorized and empowered to seize the crops and Personal Property aforesaid, and sell the same, together with the above Real Estate, for cash, after first advertising the same for fifteen days, and the proceeds thereof apply to the discharge of this Lein, together with the cost and expenses of making such sale, and the surplus to be paid to the said _A. R. Medlin_, or his legal representatives.

IN WITNESS WHEREOF, The said parties have hereunto set their hands and seals this _29th_ day of _February, 1876._

his
A. Robert X _Medlin_ _____, [seal]
mark

Witness: _L. D. Goodloe_ [signed]   _A. T. Mial_ [signed], [seal]

Figure 6.2 A lien bond between A. Robert Medlin and Alonzo T. Mial; 1876. All italicized words were handwritten in the original. (_Source:_ Alonzo T. and Millard Mial Papers, North Carolina Department of Archives and History.)

The rural furnishing merchant: heir to the cotton factor

The development and widespread adoption of the crop lien was the last step in the process of restructuring the marketing and financial network that served southern agriculture. Before the Civil War this function had been performed by a complex of institutions presided over by the cotton factor. With the new arrangements, the local merchant inherited the factor's role. The new arrangements, however, differed in several important respects from the old. The large scale of antebellum plantations and the fact that they were managed by relatively sophisticated planter-businessmen had facilitated communication and commercial efficiency. The rise of tenant farming resulted in a dramatic multiplication of the number of farming units, many of which were operated by inexperienced and illiterate farmers. Since the distant cotton factor was not able to deal efficiently with so many producers, the country furnishing merchant was able to interpose himself and obviate the need for an intermediary such as the prewar factor. The local merchant could consolidate the cotton output as well as orders for merchandise from an even larger geographic area than that once controlled within a typical plantation unit. With the improvements in transportation and communication, these merchants dealt directly with textile manufacturers, importers, and wholesalers. In a sense, then, the merchant combined the consolidating role of the planter with the intermediary role of the factor. The economic efficiencies of the antebellum system could thus be preserved despite the structural transformation.

CHAPTER 7

THE EMERGENCE OF THE MERCHANTS' TERRITORIAL MONOPOLY

A new class of houses are springing up . . . whose conditions of advance are almost necessarily marked by a degree of rigour that was unknown in former times, and that will probably grind and impoverish the mass of poorer cultivators, white and black, for a long period to come.

Robert Somers, *The Southern States Since the War: 1870–1*
(New York: Macmillan & Co., 1871), p. 198.

The rapid ascendancy of the rural furnishing merchant and the importance of his economic role are dramatized by the fact that within several years of the war the merchant had come to dominate the territory in which he operated. His influence extended well beyond the strictly economic life of his corner of the country to all aspects of the rural culture. In fact, the storekeeper, according to Thomas Clark,

was all things to his community. . . . His store was the hub of the local universe. It was the market place, banking and credit source, recreational center, public forum, and news exchange. There were few aspects of farm life in the South after 1870 which were uninfluenced by the country store.[1]

The economic success of these rural stores had at first seemed to augur well for the farmers of the South. The advantages of having a local supplier were considerable amid the tumultuous changes of the years following the Civil War. But as the merchant consolidated his economic power, he began to be viewed in a different light. The storekeeper came to be seen as an oppressor who exploited and coerced his customers and who displaced the landowner as the leader of the community. George K. Holmes reflected the change in attitude when he described the new hierarchy that prevailed: "The merchants, who advance plantation supplies, have replaced the former masters and have made peons of them and of their former slaves."[2] It seemed to contemporaries that the South had traded black slavery for agricultural peonage.

Apparently the source of the merchant's power was his control over the new system of providing short-term agricultural credit. One of the unique characteristics that differentiated the new system of marketing and finance

Notes to Chapter 7 appear on pages 343–346.

from the factorage system of the Old South was the merchant's success in establishing and protecting what we shall call a *territorial monopoly*. This form of monopoly power was also the source of the merchant's ability to influence those economic, political, and social affairs that interested him. Within his sphere of influence the merchant could operate without serious competition, forcing local farmers to deal with him on his own terms.

The merchants' monopoly over credit

The rural merchant ran a truly *general* store. Yet the source of his monopoly power was his control over credit, only one of the many commodities he supplied. In the other branches of his business there were existing, or potential, alternative suppliers. Food might be purchased from farmers holding surpluses; hardware, drugs, and sundries were periodically available from itinerant peddlers; farm implements could be ordered directly from a manufacturer; livestock could be purchased from a drover. A trip of a day or two would enable a farmer to visit one of the many towns that, as we noted earlier, served as distribution centers of the cotton trade. There he could find a variety of mercantile establishments: dry goods dealers, druggists, smiths, wagon and harness makers, grocers, and typically a choice among several "general storekeepers." So long as he was prepared to pay cash, the southern farmer had a sufficient number of options to evade exploitation by any would-be monopolist.

The only branch of his business over which the general merchant had a monopoly was the supply of credit. However, this was all he needed to establish a more far-reaching control. Since credit was an absolute necessity for most small farmers, the merchant had only to insist that the farmer conduct all business at his store to ensure that his monopoly extended to every area of the furnishing business. In other words, the merchant predicated his willingness to extend credit on this condition, and the farmer who required credit had no alternative but to accede. Few farmers were able to buy regularly on a cash basis. As long as the merchant protected his control of credit from competitive pressures, he could maintain control over the farmer's commercial activities.

The storekeeper's position was in practice quite secure. As we argued in Chapter 6, the dominating constraint that limited the willingness of outsiders to offer credit in rural areas was the greater expense necessary for them to ascertain and control the risks involved in lending to small farmers. Though a nearby lender might afford the costs of supervision necessary to protect his equity, the expense to a city intermediary would have been considerably more, offsetting any advantages suppliers enjoying urban economies of scale might have had in rural markets. Perhaps the costs of monitoring rural loans could have been lowered through careful selection of borrowers. However, the difficulty in establishing "references" for such prospective borrowers would prove considerable for firms not in the immediate neighborhood. Information costs invariably placed the distant lender at a considerable disadvantage when competing with local sources of credit.

The storekeeper's economic dominance of his market also meant that, from the farmer's perspective, the acceptance of credit from an outsider might pose serious risks. If he alienated the local merchant by obtaining funds elsewhere, he could find himself cut off from even cash purchases in retaliation. The farmer also knew that he would require credit in future years as well as during the current season and that the vicissitudes of cotton farming might necessitate emergency aid at any time. The distant opportunist might not prove as reliable in these instances as the local merchant, who was an established community member and personal acquaintance. The merchant's social and political position in the local community posed an additional – and perhaps quite important – impediment to competition from those not located in the same area.

The merchant had little to fear, therefore, from the urban banker. The two businesses complemented, rather than competed with, each other. The banker provided banking services needed by the merchant; he accepted the merchant's note to finance inventory; he acted as the merchant's agent when dealing with wholesalers; on occasion he even assisted the merchant in the sale of cotton. But the banker left to the merchant the job of verifying the credit of farmers in his district and of bearing the risk of lending them money.

The price of credit

In the postwar South, contemporary observers of the rural furnishing merchant were quick to identify (and object to) the universal trademark of a monopolist: exorbitant prices. It was not the prices of supplies, foodstuffs, and fertilizers that were exorbitant, but the price of credit charged to all those without cash in hand. Henry Grady's report that "the cotton farmer has to pay the usurious percentage charged by his merchant broker, which is never less than thirty per cent., and frequently runs up to seventy per cent.," turns out, upon inspection of the available evidence, to be a rather accurate assessment of the price of credit prevailing in the Cotton South.[3]

The available data on prices charged by merchants for corn, bacon, and fertilizers bought on credit are surprisingly comprehensive. Between 1875 and 1896, Georgia and Louisiana, with varying degrees of regularity, conducted extensive surveys concerning the prices charged by local merchants. The most precise reports of this type were those made by Georgia's Department of Agriculture on the selling price of corn on May 1, beginning in 1881 and continuing on a regular basis through 1889. Georgia, following the example of the United States Department of Agriculture, established a corps of agricultural correspondents (apparently several in each of Georgia's 137 counties), to report regularly on the conditions of crops and other items of interest.[4] The correspondents were "carefully selected with reference to their intelligence, practical experience and sound judgment."[5] These

Table 7.1. *Corn prices in dollars per bushel, Georgia: 1881–1889*

Year	Farmgate selling price, December 1 of previous year, in currency	Purchase price charged by merchants, May 1 of given year		Ratio: purchase price to selling price	
		For cash	On credit	Cash	Credit
1881	0.69	0.89	1.12	1.29	1.62
1882	0.97	1.13	1.38	1.16	1.42
1883	0.65	0.72	0.95	1.11	1.46
1884	0.67	0.90	1.14	1.34	1.70
1885	0.70	0.74	0.98	1.06	1.40
1886	0.58	0.67	0.92	1.16	1.59
1887	0.60	0.68	0.92	1.13	1.53
1888	0.63	0.79	0.98	1.25	1.56
1889	0.60	0.66	0.87	1.10	1.45
Average				1.18	1.53

Source: *Farmgate selling price:* U.S. Department of Agriculture, "Prices of Farm Products Received by Producers," Volume 3, *USDA Statistical Bulletin,* Number 16 (Washington: GPO, 1927), p. 106. *Merchants' prices:* Taken from publications of the Georgia Department of Agriculture as follows: *1881:* "Quarterly Report . . . April 30th, 1881, "*Circular,* Number 17, ns (May 18, 1881), Table 1. *1882:* "Crop Report . . . April, 1882," *Circular,* Number 26, ns (May 15, 1882), p. 29. *1883:* "Crop Report . . . April 1883," *Circular,* Number 41, ns (May 14, 1883), p. 16. *1884:* "Crop Report . . . April, 1884," *Circular,* Number 53, ns (May 12, 1884), p. 11. *1885:* "Crop Report . . . May, 1885," *Circular,* Number 66, ns (May 12, 1885), p. 12. *1886:* "Crop Report . . . May, 1886," *Circular,* Number 79, ns (May 10, 1886), p. 11. *1887:* "Crop Report . . . May, 1887," *Circular,* Number 90, ns (May 9, 1887), p. 6. *1888:* "Crop Report . . . May, 1888," *Circular,* Number 104, ns (May 8, 1888), p. 7. *1889:* "Crop Report . . . May, 1889," *Circular,* Number 116, ns (May 1889), p. 7.

crop reporters were surveyed regularly throughout each year by the department, and in May of every year they were asked: "What is the cash price per bushel at which corn sells in your county May 1st?" and "What is the credit price paid per bushel at the same date?"[6] Their responses were tabulated and reported in departmental publications in extensive detail. We have consolidated and reproduced these data for the nine years of observation in Table 7.1, together with the farmgate *selling* price of corn during the previous December.

The cash price for corn a farmer would have to pay a merchant averaged 18 percent above the farmgate price of corn received by the farmers who had produced it. Since some local farmers might have stocks of corn to sell in May, the merchant would presumably not be able to sustain an exorbitant *cash* price for corn. Therefore, the 18 percent increase in corn prices between December and May probably represents a fair charge for the storage and related expenses incurred in inventorying the grain for five months.

On the other hand, the *credit* prices in May, according to the Georgia

Table 7.2. *Implicit interest charged*
by Georgia merchants: 1881–1889

Year	Annual rate of interest (%)
1881	51.7
1882	44.2
1883	63.9
1884	53.3
1885	64.9
1886	74.6
1887	70.6
1888	48.1
1889	63.6
Average	59.4

Source: Appendix D.

survey, ranged from 40 to 70 percent – and averaged 53 percent – above the December cash prices. In other words, an additional 35 percent was charged (above and beyond the legitimate costs incurred in storage) merely for credit. Of course, this premium could be thought of as representing a charge for interest on the credit extended.

In Appendix D we have computed the implicit interest rates charged by the merchants for the years 1881 through 1889; they are presented in Table 7.2. These rates range from a low of 44.2 percent to a high of 74.6 percent and averaged 59.4 percent per annum.

Interest rates in the neighborhood of 60 percent must be judged enormous when compared with credit charges at other times and other places in American history. Short-term interest rates in New York City during this period ranged generally from 4 to 6 percent and never ranged above 8 percent, we can safely assume 10 percent as the maximum cost of the funds involved.[7] The immediate presumption is that the lack of competition in southern financial markets explains this divergence. Before the merchant is made the villain of the piece, however, it should be noted in his defense that he operated in an environment that was not typical of other financial markets. Robert Somers alluded to the possibility that the terms upon which southern merchants advanced credit were "almost necessarily" severe.[8] Somers's own account suggests that the high risk of default and the high cost of supervision entailed in the granting of short-term credit to tenant farmers without real estate or collateral were reflected in the charges for such credit.

To be sure, there were risks involved in lending funds to farmers. On the other hand, it should be noted that these loans were made only after the merchant had assessed the creditworthiness of the prospective tenant, they were secured with a lien on the growing crop, and the merchant had legal right under terms of the lien to ensure that the crop was properly tended. Under these circumstances, it is likely that the merchant was able to reduce the risks to reasonably low levels. In any event, we can be sure that his credit charges cannot be justified by the risk of default alone. An anticipated default rate of over 30 percent would be necessary to justify a 60 percent charge for interest.[9] There is absolutely no evidence that actual default rates were ever of this order of magnitude. In fact, it is unlikely that more than 5 percent of the total investment was lost by default.[10]

Credit charges must also cover any legitimate costs involved in processing the loan and providing that level of supervision required to protect the merchant's investment. While the costs of processing a loan were likely to be trivial, particularly for a local farmer known to the merchant, supervisory costs were higher. Nevertheless, even an exaggerated estimate of such outlays cannot justify interest premiums of the magnitude reported in Table 7.2. As a hypothetical example, take the case of a merchant whose customers annually borrow $80 each. Suppose the merchant hires a full-time assistant, who is paid a generous $500 per year, to oversee 100 customers.[11] The annual supervisory costs per customer would then be $5 or 6.25 percent of the principal loaned. Taken together with a 10 percent opportunity cost of funds and a 5 percent risk of default, the supervisory costs in our example would justify no more than a 22.4 percent charge for interest, which, despite our exaggerated assumptions, is only about one-third the rate of interest charged by Georgia merchants.[12]

When assessing the magnitude of the supervisory costs and the risk of default, it should be recognized that the two costs were intimately related. The sole purpose of the supervision was to lower the risk of default. Our example implicitly allows for 5 percent of the borrowers to default completely on principal plus interest. It seems unlikely that the default rate would have been that high with a full-time overseer supervising the merchant's clients. We can only conclude that the interest charged southern farmers was exorbitant in the sense that it could not be justified by legitimate costs of providing credit.

There is a seeming paradox in our claim, however, that the merchant possessed a monopoly. Rural merchants were, after all, scattered ubiquitously over the southern countryside. In 1880 we have identified nearly 8,000 general stores located outside urban areas of the Cotton South.[13] Monopoly – the domination of a market by a single firm – might seem an unlikely phenomenon under these circumstances. The key to unraveling the paradox just posed lies in the fact that this monopoly was confined to the immediate neighborhood of the store; it was, as we have characterized it, a territorial monopoly.

The merchants' territorial monopoly

Why did the thousands of rural stores throughout the South not compete with each other? To come to grips with this question we turn to the records and published lists of the R. G. Dun Mercantile Agency. The agency maintained a file on virtually every store in the South. Any firm extending credit or sending goods on commission to rural merchants beyond its immediate locality required credit information on its customers. As a result of this necessity, the agency's *Reference Book* had become quite complete as early as 1870. For any given year thereafter a reasonably complete tabulation of enterprises can be reconstructed on the basis of the post office address of each store. The information collected by Dun's agency undoubtedly represents the most extensive, comprehensive, and accurate source of information available today on the pattern of southern merchandising after the Civil War.[14]

There were 7,977 general stores listed by the Mercantile Agency in the rural Cotton South in 1880, located at 2,937 separate postal addresses. Table 7.3 organizes these postal addresses by the number of stores sharing the same address. The actual number of separate store locations would be substantially understated by this definition, since only the post office name was provided in the Mercantile Agency's *Reference Books,* not the actual geographic location.[15] The table excludes those stores located in the thirty-one urban centers of the Cotton South, since stores in these towns were not likely to be catering to the farming community.[16]

That the general stores were ubiquitously scattered over the southern landscape is apparent from the accompanying map, which pinpoints each of the separate post office addresses. Over one-half of the 2,937 locations had only a single store; 70.5 percent of all locations had only one or two stores. Only 12.1 percent of all locations contained six or more stores with the same postal address. It should be noted immediately, however, that the number of stores sharing a single post office address provides a misleading index of the extent to which competition existed for the business of an area's farmers. In the first place, many of the post office addresses listing multiple stores referred to towns with populations of 1,000 to 3,000. It is likely that some of the stores included in such towns served an urban clientele rather than the farming community.[17] Second, in many cases a given postal address described a relatively large geographic area that incorporated the territories of more than one isolated merchant.[18] It should not be inferred that farmers living in these regions had an effective alternative to their neighborhood merchant or that a merchant in such a region was under more competitive pressure than one who was the only merchant listed at a given address.

We can assume at one extreme that each of the 7,977 stores we have identified was separately located in its own geographic territory. At the other extreme, there must have been a minimum of 2,937 distinct store locations, some of which were served by more than one store. The implications of

Table 7.3. *Rural general stores, Cotton South: 1880*[a]

Post Office addresses with	Number of locations	Percent of all locations	Cumulative percent of locations	Number of general stores	Percent of all stores	Cumulative percent of stores
1 store	1,597	54.4	54.4	1,597	20.0	20.0
2 stores	475	16.2	70.5	950	11.9	31.9
3 stores	260	8.9	79.4	780	9.8	41.7
4 stores	149	5.1	84.5	596	7.5	49.2
5 stores	98	3.3	87.8	490	6.1	55.3
6–10 stores	237	8.1	95.9	1,765	22.1	77.4
More than 10 stores	121	4.1	100.0	1,799	22.6	100.0
Total	2,937	100.0		7,977	100.0	

[a] General stores in towns and cities defined as commercial or urban cotton centers in Appendix G, Table G.16 are excluded from this tabulation. See note 16 of this chapter.

Source: R. G. Dun and Company, *Mercantile Agency Reference Book . . . January, 1880.* See Appendix G, Section 5, for a discussion of how "general store" is defined and the determination of a store "location."

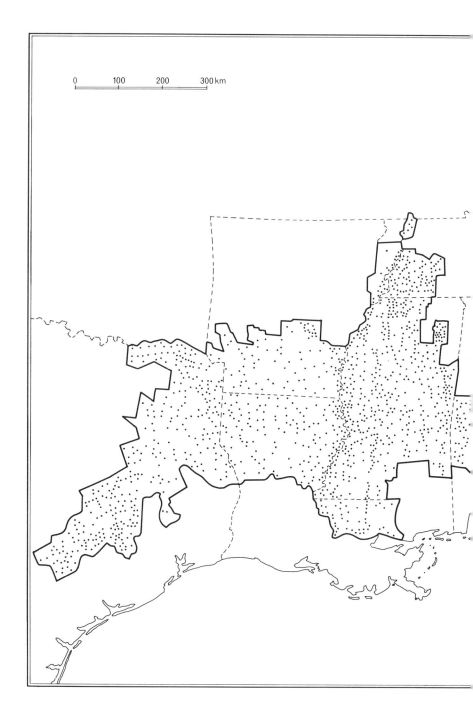

Post office addresses reporting at least one general store in the Cotton South, 1880.

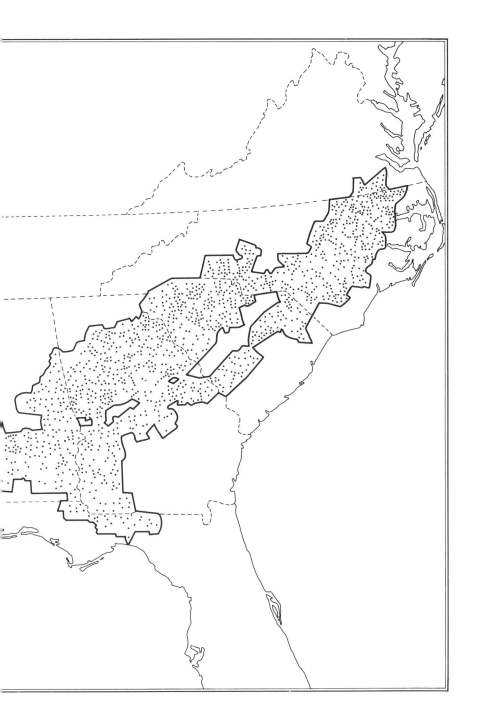

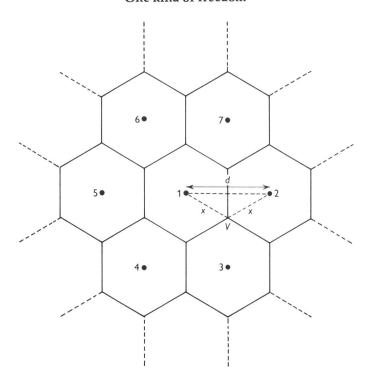

Figure 7.1 Hypothetical array of merchants' territorial markets.

these two alternative geographic dispersions are rather similar. This can be demonstrated by assuming that general store locations were "ideally dispersed," each in the center of a regular hexagon as depicted in Figure 7.1. Such a configuration would *minimize* the average distance between two adjacent store locations and thus represent the "best" possible situation that might have faced farmers scattered throughout the region. The minimum average distance between sites, d (the distance between points 1 and 2 in the figure), can be calculated from the total area of the Cotton South and the number of store locations it contained. If only 2,937 locations served the 206,419 square miles of the Cotton South, the most efficient spacing would give a market area of 70.3 square miles per location. From this we calculate d as 9.0 miles. On the other hand, with 7,977 locations d would be 5.5 miles.[19] Of course, in actuality, some of the stores were located farther apart. The hypothetical honeycomb pattern gives the *minimum* average distance between store locations. The true average was greater. Certainly, the average distance between store sites must have exceeded 5.5 miles, and even our alternative estimate of 9 miles may be too low.

By modern standards, 5.5 to 9 miles seem a short distance to travel. But in the rural South of 1880, such distances could represent a serious barrier to competition. For example, a farmer who wished to compare the prices and terms at two stores located 7 miles apart would have to undertake a trip of at least 14 miles, and possibly up to 24 miles.[20] Since even a 14-mile trip with a wagon and team would exhaust the better part of a day, the ubiquitous country store was not so common as to facilitate competition.[21]

These hypothetical calculations dramatize the fact that markets in the rural South were compartmentalized into relatively small areas of influence, within which each merchant held a virtual monopoly of credit. Transportation costs limited the ability of the merchant to attract distant customers. At a sufficiently great distance from the store, either agriculture would be unprofitable because of the expense of supplies or (more likely) farmers would find other stores closer to home. There must exist between any two stores, therefore, a distinct boundary on either side of which one store would have a competitive advantage over the other. These boundaries partitioned the South into literally thousands of separate territorial monopolies, each one dominated by a local merchant.[22]

The scale of the mercantile operation

As must be obvious at this point, territorial monopoly need not be synonymous with large scale of enterprise. The monopoly of the southern general store was small but secure. In the Cotton South, there averaged less than seventy farms per rural general store in 1880. Since a typical customer seldom generated more than $80 in credit business, this suggests a typical annual volume of not more than $5,600.[23] Inasmuch as most of the inventory was carried on commission, the investment required to conduct such a trade would be modest, a fact confirmed by the Mercantile Agency's 1880 *Reference Book.* Table 7.4 presents the agency's estimated pecuniary strength of general store merchants located in one of the tewenty-seven representative counties of our sample. Of all store operations, 48 percent were assigned a net worth of $5,000 or less. Only 7.3 percent of the merchants in our sample counties warranted a rating of $50,000 or better. Since these estimates represent the total estimated net worth of the *individual* who owned the business, the actual investment in the store would be overstated for any merchant who owned land or held other assets. Since a fraction of merchants owned more than one store, the possibility of a substantial exaggeration could be high. An owner of two stores, for example, would have his aggregate net worth entered twice, and both estimates would be roughly double the investment in a single store.

The small net worth of the South's furnishing merchants was a reflection of their small markets. Data from a sample of rural businesses in six counties of the Cotton South suggest that firms did not normally expand after they reached a capital investment of $5,000 to $10,000. Table 7.5 presents data on the changes in pecuniary strength of all the stores in these six

Table 7.4. *Pecuniary strength of rural general stores in twenty-seven representative counties, Cotton South: 1880*

Estimated pecuniary strength[a]	Number of stores	Percent of stores	Cumulative percent
Less than $2,000[b]	256	36.5	36.5
$2,000–$5,000	81	11.5	48.0
$5,000–$10,000	137	19.5	67.5
$10,000–$25,000	96	13.7	81.2
$25,000–$50,000	81	11.5	92.7
Over $50,000	51	7.3	100.0
All classes	702	100.0	

[a] "Pecuniary strength" is the estimated net worth of *the proprietor* of the general store as reported by the Mercantile Agency in 1880. In some cases the store owner had other occupations, and his pecuniary strength would include assets not involved in his mercantile operation.
[b] According to the key accompanying the *Reference Book,* concerns whose pecuniary strength was not reported should be considered as having less than $1,000 of net worth; accordingly firms in this category were placed in the class of stores with less than $2,000.
Source: R. G. Dun and Company, *Mercantile Agency Reference Book . . . 1880.* Also see Appendix G, Section 5.

counties over two five-year intervals. The table organizes firms according to their pecuniary strength at the outset of each period. The evidence suggests that firms whose initial estimated net worth was less than $5,000 tended to grow. Sixteen of the twenty-one firms that survived the first interval increased their net worth during the five-year period; thirty-one of the forty-nine small firms that survived the second interval moved to a higher rating. Larger firms, by contrast, did not grow. Only one large firm improved its pecuniary strength over the entire decade. Five of the twelve surviving large firms observed in the two intervals *declined* in strength. Optimally sized firms – those rated between $5,000 and $10,000 – showed no marked tendency to grow or decline. Had there been substantial economies associated with large scale, we would expect some firms to have consolidated and expanded their markets in order to realize these economies. Certainly there is no evidence that, beyond a scale represented by an investment of $10,000, economies of scale were present in southern merchandising.

The small scale of store operations in the South limited the total income that could be generated from a single store. We would not, therefore, expect to find massive accumulations of wealth generated from merchandising. Moreover, the profit that came into the hands of a successful merchant would not typically be reinvested in his store. Generally he would seek other investment opportunities – such as land or securities – to expand his portfolio. Several of the wealthier storekeepers in our sample provide examples of such diversification. Two of the stores in Tunica County, Mississippi, operated businesses with a capital investment of around $10,000; yet each proprietor was worth between $40,000 and $50,000. The balance of

Table 7.5. *Changes in pecuniary strength of general store operators, six southern counties: 1870–1875, 1875–1880*

Initial pecuniary strength[a]	January 1870–January 1875				January 1875–January 1880			
	Increased	No change	Declined	Disappeared	Increased	No change	Declined	Disappeared
Over $10,000	0	1	2	1	1	5	3	3
$5,000–$10,000	2	1	0	3	1	2	6	3
Less than $5,000	16	4	1	7	31	15	3	23
All firms	18	6	3	11	33	22	12	29

[a] The Mercantile Agency distinguished eleven categories of pecuniary strength, ranging from over $1,000,000 to less than $1,000. A complete list of these categories is given in Appendix G, Table G.18. All the stores examined fell into one of seven categories defined by the Mercantile Agency. Where no pecuniary strength was reported, the firm was assumed to be worth less than $1,000. A "change" in pecuniary strength is defined as a movement from one of the seven classes to another. As the pecuniary strength classes become higher, the class intervals rise in rough proportion, so that a one-step increase in pecuniary strength can be considered as a doubling in scale regardless of the initial size of the store.

Source: Compiled from R. G. Dun and Company, Mercantile Agency Credit Ledgers for six counties: Gwinnett, Worth, and Twiggs, Georgia; Russell, Alabama; Rankin and Tunica, Mississippi. See Appendix G, Section 5, for details of the sampling procedure. The pecuniary strength ratings were obtained from R. G. Dun and Company, *Mercantile Agency Reference Book* for January of the years indicated.

their assets was invested in various landholdings. A partner in one of these firms held extensive real property in Memphis. We also found that the less wealthy, but successful, store owners frequently invested their savings in local real estate rather than employing them to expand the store operation.[24] Occasionally investors put money into more than one store; however, there seems to have been a practical limit of two to three stores per owner all within the same or an adjacent county.

The limited size of the rural merchant's market actually helped protect it from outside interference. We found only a single case where a firm was controlled or backed by other than local individuals.[25] Outside investors would find the monopoly profits too small in the aggregate to be attractive. Despite the political and social power a merchant might exercise as a consequence of his economic power, his monopolistic practices were unlikely to cause much notice outside his own territory.

The appearance of new firms

The small scale and particularistic nature of the rural merchant's business meant that his territorial monopoly was left undisturbed. But it also served to check his ability to expand in response to a growing demand. As the markets for farm supplies expanded after the war, in part owing to increased population density and in part to a greater concentration on cotton production, the potential for new stores developed. This demand was met neither by the expansion of existing stores nor the arrival of outside entrepreneurs, but rather by local landowners or other men with local family or business connections. The number of stores in the South grew very rapidly in the years before 1885 in response to the growth of demand. In our twenty-seven representative counties, there were 290 stores in 1870; 678 in 1875; 860 in 1880; and 1,254 by 1885.

The new entrants were not interested in placing themselves in a location that would bring them into strong direct competition with existing firms. The costs of attracting a clientele in an established market would have been considerable. Since existing firms would be limited by the lack of scale economies, the geographic territory they served would actually be shrinking as the number of farm operators increased. Established merchants would be content simply to absorb new customers well within their existing market, abandoning to other merchants customers at the fringe of their domain. New stores, therefore, could best attract a clientele by locating on the boundary between two or more existing markets. Such a location would seem attractive whenever existing firms were far enough apart that spatial costs made each of them relatively expensive for farmers situated near the border of the competing markets.

Table 7.6 illustrates that the increase in the number of locations between 1870 and 1885 kept pace with the growth in the number of stores. As a result, a constant two-thirds of the post office addresses had only one or two

Table 7.6. *Number of general stores and general store locations in twenty-seven representative counties, Cotton South: 1870–1885.*

| Year | Number of stores | Number of locations | Percent of locations with | | |
			1 store	2 stores	3 or more stores
1870	290	110	51.8	15.5	32.7
1875	678	222	45.9	18.5	35.6
1880	860	265	44.9	19.6	35.5
1885	1,254	380	45.5	18.4	36.1

Source: R. G. Dun and Company, *Mercantile Agency Reference Book* for January of the years indicated.

stores throughout the fifteen-year interval, despite the great increase in the number of stores. This persistently high fraction of stores at isolated addresses is consistent with our expectation that new stores would locate at points not occupied by existing merchants. In order to confirm this implication, we carefully examined the pattern of entry for all stores established in six representative counties. Altogether, eighty-two new businesses were established between the end of 1870 and 1880 in the rural districts of these counties.[26] Thirty-five of them located in addresses occupied by no other earlier arrival; twenty-two more located where they shared a postal address with one other store. Thus, over the decade, forty-three percent of the new stores in the rural areas of these six counties had found a territory that clearly set them apart from their competition. We are confident, moreover, that a majority of the other stores also located themselves at unoccupied sites, despite the fact that they shared the same post office address with another store.

The appearance of new stores apparently had only a small effect on the business of existing stores. While the credit reporters were careful to inform the Mercantile Agency of even such minor causes for an alteration in a firm's financial position as changes in marital status, drinking and personal habits, we found no mention of threatened or actual competitive pressures in the files of the Mercantile Agency for any store in our sample.

The attractiveness of isolated locations, however, is not inconsistent with a rapid growth and influx of new stores locating in towns and cities. In fact, as we have seen, the period 1870–1880 saw the development throughout the South of a large number of small, dispersed shipping centers catering to the cotton trade. These trading towns developed modest populations and the retailing establishments to serve them. In our six-county sample, small towns such as Buford in Gwinnett County, Georgia, which listed no store in 1870, had fourteen by 1875. Less dramatic, but still impressive was the growth of general stores in Norcross, Georgia; Brandon and Austin, Mississippi; and Hurtville, Alabama. Table 7.7 summarizes the growth of

Table 7.7. *Number of general stores with addresses in towns located in four representative counties: 1870–1885*

Town, county, state	1870	1875	1880	1885
Brandon, Rankin, Mississippi	5	10	12	9
Austin, Tunica, Mississippi	1	2	7	4
Buford, Gwinnett, Georgia	0	14	11	13
Norcross, Gwinnett, Georgia	0	9	9	12
Hurtville, Russell, Alabama	1	4	8	12
Total, five towns	7	39	47	50

Source: Compiled from R. G. Dun and Company, *Mercantile Agency Reference Book* for January of the years indicated.

stores in these towns between 1870 and 1885. In all, fifty-three new stores, or 39 percent of all entrants in the six counties, had one of these five towns as address. The fact that the number of stores grew very rapidly in the early 1870s and much less so thereafter reinforces our suspicion that the large increase in general stores is associated with the development of trading towns throughout the South immediately after the war.

The disappearance of existing firms

One might expect that southern merchants, protected from competitive pressures, invariably prospered. Many did. But the lure of profits and low capital requirements encouraged many attempts to enter the furnishing business. It is not surprising that significant numbers failed to succeed. New entrants were often underfinanced or found the better territories already occupied.

That many firms "disappeared" is apparent from Table 7.8. The table traces the history of 173 firms in the six-county sample during two five-year intervals between January 1870 and January 1880. This number includes 38 firms that existed at the outset (31 rural firms and 7 town firms), 69 firms that entered business between January 1870 and January 1875, and 66 firms that opened for business between Janaury 1875 and January 1880. (Of the 135 new entrants, 82 were rural firms and 53 were town firms.) The disappearance rate is quite high: about 30 percent of the firms initially in business for each quinquennium ceased operations. However, not every disappearance represented financial failure. Table 7.9 summarizes the explanation given in the Credit Ledgers for the closing of the 40 disappearing firms listed in Table 7.8. Only 15, or about 14 percent of the 107 firms founded by 1875 included in Table 7.8, were clearly identified as having "failed" or "dissolved"; 9 more were listed as "out of business," a notation that might include any number of possibilities; 9 proprietors had "left" or

Table 7.8. *Reorganization and disappearance of general stores, six-county sample: 1870–1880*[a]

		Percent of	
	Number of firms	Initial firms	Remaining firms
Existing 1870 firms, 1870–1875			
Firms in 1870	38	100	—
Disappeared by 1875	11	29	—
Unchanged by 1875	15	39	56
Reorganized by 1875	12	32	44
Remaining 1870 firms in 1875	27	71	100
Established 1870 firms, 1875–1880			
Remaining 1870 firms in 1875	27	100	—
Disappeared by 1880	6	22	—
Unchanged by 1880	20	74	95
Reorganized by 1880	1	4	5
Remaining 1870 firms in 1880	21	78	100
Young firms, 1875–1880			
New entrants between 1870 and 1875[b]	69	100	—
Disappeared by 1880	23	33	—
Unchanged by 1880	25	36	54
Reorganized by 1880	21	30	45
Remaining 1875 firms in 1880	46	67	100
All firms, 1880			
Remaining 1870 firms in 1880	21	—	16
Remaining 1875 firms in 1880	46	—	34
New entrants between 1875 and 1880[b]	66	—	50
Total firms in 1880	133	—	100

[a] A firm is "reorganized" whenever it experienced some rearrangement of ownership. See text for a further discussion of both "disappearance" and "reorganization" of firms. [b] Includes only those new entrants still in operation at the end of the quinquennium.
Source: Compiled from the six-county sample of firms drawn from R. G. Dun and Company, Mercantile Agency Credit Ledgers; see Appendix G, Section 5.

"moved"; 4 had died or retired; and the files of 3 were discontinued without further explanation.

Although there were no legal barriers to entry into the mercantile business, in practice it would appear that substantial economic barriers were present. Not only was the rate of failure high, but it can be inferred that the primary cause for business failures was an inability to establish a sufficiently large clientele. Apparently those new entrants who were successful in establishing a business were those who were able to carve out a territory of influence within a relatively short time. Those who failed to do so succumbed within a few years.

The high risk of failure in the early years of operation of the store is apparent from Table 7.9. The median period in business before failing was only four years in the six-county sample. All but three of the failing firms were in business no more than five years; one-third of them were operating for three or fewer years. The fact that seven of the nine firms whose operators "moved" or "left," presumably to a new location, did so within three years also supports our contention that it was difficult for a new entrant to become established.

Disappearance was also associated with the size of capital investment, as is apparent from Table 7.10. The risk of outright failure was highest among small firms. Twelve of the fifteen failing firms, and all those described as "out of business," had a pecuniary strength of less than $10,000. Obviously, entering the merchandising business could be perilous – especially when attempted by a businessman who was underfinanced or unacquainted with his area. Occasionally, a well-established firm did fail. However, aspects of business that were unrelated to the provisioning trade seemed typically to blame. Table 7.10 includes three concerns with a pecuniary strength of over $10,000 that failed. One of these was a man who, in addition to a store, operated a wagon shop, a furniture factory, and a saw mill. His financial difficulties were largely a result of setbacks in these other ventures. A second store that failed was owned by a large landowner and his partners, who were apparently wiped out by the financial panic of 1873. The third failure of a concern with a high pecuniary strength involved two partners who had between them invested only about $2,000 to $3,000 in the store; the remaining capital was invested "in the north."[27]

The successful firm

As we noted at the outset, a strong prima facie case that southern merchants held a territorial monopoly can be pressed simply on the evidence that merchants charged rates of interest for credit that were far in excess of the opportunity cost of capital. As a consequence of the monopoly, successful firms were apparently able to earn high rates of return on their limited investment. Contemporaries reported that merchants did quite well, and frequently singled out spectacular examples. Charles Otken, writing in 1894, alleged that "everywhere are men engaged in the furnishing business whose [original] capital ranged from $500 to $5,000. In a period of twenty-five years, when southern planters were struggling with poverty, debts, and the labor system, they managed to accumulate handsome fortunes, varying from $10,000 to $200,000."[28] While the Mercantile Agency records do not specifically quote rates of return, they do contain evidence that supports the general impression given by contemporaries. The statistics on pecuniary strength presented in Table 7.5, for example, suggest that in fifty-one of the ninety-four successful businesses traced over the two five-year periods the firm increased its rating by at least one step. Since an increase of one step represents an approximate doubling of the owner's net

Table 7.9. *Causes for "disappearance" of general stores according to years in business, six-county sample: 1870–1880*

Years in business at time of disappearance	Failed or dissolved	Out of business	Left or moved	Died or retired	Not given	Total
1	0	0	1	0	2	3
2	2	1	4	1	0	8
3	4	1	2	0	0	7
4	3	3	1	0	0	7
5	3	1	0	1	0	5
6	1	0	0	1	1	3
7	0	1	0	0	0	1
8	0	2	0	0	0	2
9 or more	2	0	1	1	0	4
Total, all firms	15	9	9	4	3	40
Median number of years in business	4	4	3	5	1	4

Source: Compiled from R. G. Dun and Company, Mercantile Agency Credit Ledgers; see Appendix G, Section 5.

Table 7.10. *Causes for "disappearance" of general stores according to pecuniary strength, six-county sample: 1870–1880*

Pecuniary strength	Failed or dissolved	Out of business	Left or moved	Died or retired	Not given	Total
Over $10,000	3	0	1	0	0	4
$5,000–$10,000	4	2	0	0	0	6
Under $5,000	8	7	8	4	3	30
All firms	15	9	9	4	3	40

Source: Compiled from R. G. Dun and Company, Mercantile Agency Credit Ledgers; see Appendix G, Section 5.

worth in a five-year period, these entrepreneurs must have accumulated net worth at the rate of at least 15 percent per annum. In some instances these gains were achieved by attracting new partners, who brought new capital into the business; however, the ability to attract new capital is itself an indication of optimistic expectations.

The rewards to those who successfully operated general stores can be seen in the experiences of several Rankin County, Mississippi, storekeepers who survived the first years of business. One merchant who had "few [dollars] in the bank" in 1869 had $4,000 to $5,000 ten years later. Another who had "no capital" in 1867 was judged to be worth between $4,000 and $8,000 by 1878. Dun's agents estimated that two other merchants increased their net worth from an estimated $2,000 or $3,000 to the neighborhood of $6,000 or $8,000 in less than a decade. Finally, we note the experience of a partner who, when he became involved with the store in 1874, was worth "not more than" $3,000 or $4,000 and by 1878 held $15,000 in real estate and an additional $1,500 in personal property.[29]

These examples are not in themselves conclusive, nor does the structure of rural merchandising revealed by the Mercantile Agency Archives "prove" that all southern merchants were monopolists. What the archives present is a characterization of the business that is consistent with the notion that the merchants were able to acquire and maintain a territorial monopoly over the provision of credit. In our opinion, the historical evidence strongly supports the charge that the merchant possessed such a credit monopoly. The large number of stores and the small scale of their market, characteristics commonly associated with competitive markets, are in this instance manifestations of a territorial monopoly; the barriers to entry and competition, the exorbitant prices, and the high rates of return earned by successful business are universal signatures of monopoly power.

The merchant-landowner and the landlord-merchant

The economic gains that accrued to the merchant's monopoly were frequently invested in real estate. This development meant that over time those merchants who began business without landed assets gradually became landlords themselves. Typically, of course, the tenants of these acquired lands became the merchant's credit customers if they were not already so. When the roles of merchant and landlord were thus combined, the territorial monopoly of the merchant was made even more secure, and all possibility of dispute between landlord and merchant from which the tenant might benefit was extinguished.

While many merchants thus became landlords, it was also common for landowners to enter the furnishing business. In fact, most of the successful entrants into credit merchandising were local landowners who began to supply their own tenants (and others as well). Although the origins of these landlord-merchants was different from those of the merchant-landowners, the end result was much the same: the economic power of the credit monopolist and the landowner joined forces.

The statistical sources we have examined do not permit us to distinguish between tenants who were supplied by their landowners and those who dealt with a separate merchant and landlord. Nevertheless, it is worth noting that every merchant whose file we examined in the Mercantile Agency Archives and who persisted in business for at least five years owned at least some real estate; numerous others were reported to have quite substantial holdings of land. In Twiggs County, Georgia, two partners in a general store were said to "own more property than any man in the county."[30] A Tunica County, Mississippi, store was operated by A. A. Tate, whose real estate holdings were estimated at around $40,000 in Tunica, plus additional holdings in a neighboring county. Landowners often became silent partners in merchandising ventures. A Rankin County, Mississippi, firm reportedly had two such investors, each owning at least $10,000 in real estate; another Rankin firm was associated with a "planter" worth $20,000 in real estate.[31]

Glenn Sisk reports that in those cases where the tenant's merchant and landlord were not the same individual it was common practice throughout the black belt of Alabama for landlords to endorse the crop liens of their tenants.[32] This practice was probably a response to the change in Alabama's crop lien law in 1871, which made the landowner's lien superior to the merchant's.[33] With the landlord's endorsement, of course, the priority of the merchant's claim was maintained despite the intent of the 1871 law. The fact that in such cases the merchant could insist on the first claim to the crop is testimony to the power he possessed by virtue of his monopoly over credit when a conflict of interest arose with the merchant and landowner.[34] It would not be surprising if the exercise of the merchant's power over the landlord was frequently unnecessary, since, judging from the R. G. Dun Archives, many merchants who were not themselves landowners frequently had close family ties with planters. The father of H. H. Batte, a young storekeeper in Rankin County, had, according to the Dun reporter, "a fine plantation." A. A. Tate, the planter in Tunica County mentioned earlier, turned the mercantile business over to his son in 1873, yet his own connection with the business continued to be reported. In several instances mention was made by the Dun reporter of landed wealth on the part of a merchant's wife or father-in-law.

The close social ties between planters and merchants in many areas also suggest that competition between nearby merchants might be avoided by a tacit or explicit collusion. In areas where several merchants shared a territory, only one or two merchants needed to be party to a noncompetitive agreement. According to the *Montgomery Daily Advertiser* in 1868, some southerners felt that merchants colluded "for the purpose of fixing the value of their wares."[35]

The social relationship between the merchant and the remains of the old planter elite varied from locality to locality, and the devices used to protect the merchant's territorial monopoly also varied, reflecting local differences. However, the economic system that emerged was essentially the same throughout the cotton-producing regions of the South. Uniformly, the crop lien system was adopted and employed to exploit southern farmers by charging them exorbitant prices for supplies. To be sure, transportation and communications problems in the rural South would have made the prices of provisions and credit higher than they were in urban areas or the North even without exploitation. But one should not conclude that the merchant was merely providing a necessarily "expensive" service to his customers. There is no question that these rural merchants possessed monopoly power, that they recognized such power was theirs, and that they were not afraid to use it. Contemporary observers also perceived the advantage this system bestowed upon the storekeeper and worried aloud that such power might prove a corrupting influence. The *Mobile Daily Register* made the point in 1871:

A large number of young men, instead of cultivating their land with their own hands, always an honorable calling . . . have taken to little country stores, where the temptation to cheat the ignorant negro is too strong for the virtue of many, and they become degraded by consciousness of making money in unjust and low ways, lose their self-respect and sense of honor, form a low standard of virtue and honesty, and will soon become an inferior class of citizens.[36]

CHAPTER 8

THE TRAP OF DEBT PEONAGE

More evils have come to the farmers of the State on account of the mortgage and lien bond system than from any other, and indeed from every other source. It has proved a worse curse to North Carolina than drouths, floods, cyclones, storms, rust, caterpillars, and every other evil that attends the farmer.

W. N. Jones, Commissioner, Bureau of Labor Statistics, North Carolina, *First Annual Report of the Bureau of Labor Statistics* (Raleigh: Josephus Daniels, 1887), p. 76.

Contemporary critics insisted that the monopoly power of the merchant was used not only to exploit southern farmers but to control southern agriculture. The specific charge was made that the merchant forced the farmer into excessive production of cotton by refusing credit to those who sought to diversify production. Charles Otken, one of the most strident critics of the South's merchandising system, insisted that:

For years a class of merchants encouraged their credit customers to raise cotton exclusively, or very largely. They reasoned very naturally and very logically, that, the more goods sold to farmers, the greater their sales and the greater their aggregate profits. . . . The debts of the farmer bound him to cotton. He was powerless.[1]

Otken quoted Henry Grady, who, writing in 1889, had bluntly described how this was done: "When he [the farmer] saw the wisdom of raising his own corn, bacon, grasses, and stock, he WAS NOTIFIED that reducing his cotton acreage was reducing *his line of credit.*"[2]

Otken and Grady were journalists. George K. Holmes, an economist employed by the U.S. Department of Agriculture, made the same charge in an address delivered to the American Academy of Political and Social Science in 1893:

The merchants then took the helm. Such crops as they could most readily market must be produced under their orders, regardless of the fact that they might not be the ones most advantageous to their debtors. The kind of crop that best accorded with this requirement in the cotton regions was cotton.[3]

Notes to Chapter 8 appear on pages 346–353.

The ultimate damage wrought by reducing the farmer's right to choose his own crops was even more severe than this passage suggests. The merchant's "cry for cotton and more cotton" was viewed with alarm by southern critics of the system.[4] To them, more was at stake than the farmer's right to cultivate as he saw fit. Ending the South's dependence upon the single crop, cotton, was seen as an indispensable step in securing a prosperous future for the region. Therefore, they feared that the merchants' insistence upon cotton would doom the South to economic backwardness. Even before the Civil War, editorialist James D. B. De Bow saw the South's dependence upon cotton as a curse on southern development. He perceived that economic growth in the long run would have to be based upon a balanced expansion of industry, commerce, and agriculture. The single-minded concentration upon cotton, to his mind, was shortsighted and kept the South dependent upon the northern and European economies. De Bow wrote of the Cotton South:

No mind can look back upon the history of this region for the last twenty years, and not feel convinced that the labor bestowed in cotton growing during that period has been a total loss to this part of the country. It is true that some of the neighboring states have been benefited to some extent, and [the cotton trade] has served to swell the general commerce of the nation . . . but the country of its production has gained nothing, and lost much.[5]

The South's defeat in the Civil War and the end of slavery were viewed by these economic critics as offering an opportunity for the South to rebuild itself upon a new and sounder foundation fashioned from diversified agriculture and industrial enterprise. De Bow, writing on the future of the South in the first issue of his *Review* to appear after the war, struck a note of optimism and resumed his call for economic diversification:

The climates and soils of the vast region, which stretched from the Potomac to the Rio Grande, are favorable to every product upon which industry and capital are expended in any country. The vast mineral resources which geological surveys have divulged, which no hand of industry has yet attempted to develop; and the infinite number of manufacturing sites, all present the most tempting baits to enterprise, and will open up results for it, which nothing in the history of the times has equaled, dazzling and magnificent as have been its past achievements.[6]

Cotton might still play a prominent role, De Bow conceded, but " 'King' he may not be, in the sense in which many of us formerly recognized him."[7]

In the years immediately following the war, the tendency for farmers to purchase rather than to grow their own provisions was not considered unwise. High cotton prices were an obvious inducement to concentrate on cotton, and, as the *Southern Cultivator* noted in 1873, it was not uncommon for "men in other avocations" to purchase their supplies and provisions "and yet prosper."[8] However, when cotton prices returned to their normal level and the farmers continued to buy provisions on credit at premium prices, observers began to advocate that the farmer grow his own supplies.

"The South must prepare to raise her own provisions, compost her fertilizers, cure her own hay, and breed her own stock," claimed Henry Grady, editor of the *Atlanta Constitution*. "The farmers who prosper at the South are the 'corn raisers,' *i.e.*, the men who raise their own supplies, and make cotton their surplus crop."[9] Similar views were propounded on a monthly basis by editors of farm journals and local newspapers.[10] When farmers did not respond to what seemed a significant incentive to home production, these writers began to suspect that the merchant, through his insistence upon cotton, must be responsible for the farmer's dependence upon purchased supplies.

The decline in the production of food in the South

There is no question that the production of food and grain crops per capita fell dramatically in the southern states following the Civil War. We need only note the production statistics in 1870 to see that outputs of grains and meat sharply declined in the South after 1860.[11] Nor was this decline a temporary change. Table 8.1 summarizes the per capita production of food in the Five Cotton States from 1850 to 1890, and Figure 8.1 illustrates the enormous fall in food available from crops and swine. The per capita production of corn, by far the most important food crop, fell to one-half its prewar level in 1870, and did not appreciably improve thereafter. The loss in corn supply was not replaced by other crops. Table 8.1 shows that per capita outputs of ten other crops fell even more dramatically than did corn output. The total output of grains, expressed in units nutritionally equivalent to a bushel of corn, averaged one-half the prewar level in the thirty years following the Civil War.

The number of swine per capita similarly declined without subsequent recovery. Our examination of nineteenth-century animal husbandry suggests that neither the slaughter weight nor the ratio of animal slaughters to the stock of hogs in the South changed dramatically in the postbellum period.[12] Therefore, the amount of pork produced from a given swine population would not be substantially greater after the war. The implication of Table 8.1 must be that the available pork per capita declined by about one-half. Since roughly the same proportional decline occurred in per capita stocks of cattle and sheep, there could have been no marked increase in meat from these animals that would have offset the loss of pork after 1860. Of the remaining foodstuffs enumerated by the censuses, only the production of butter, which fell dramatically in 1870, showed a tendency to recover its prewar level of per capita production in the following years.[13]

The decline in food output was nearly 50 percent. It is conceivable that a portion of this decline could be explained by the reduced food requirements of the black population. Slaves required abundant calories to sustain their work effort. Following emancipation there was a reduction of work effort on the part of the black population that we have estimated to have been be-

Table 8.1. *Per capita production of food, Five Cotton States: 1850–1890*

Food	1850	1860	1870	1880	1890
Grains (corn-equivalent bushels)					
Corn	31.1	29.6	14.7	15.6	16.3
Other food crops[a]	6.7	6.3	2.6	3.9	2.7
Total grains	37.7	35.8	17.3	19.5	18.9
Livestock (number of head)					
Swine	2.11	1.64	0.73	0.88	0.73
Other cattle	0.73	0.51	0.29	0.31	0.30
Sheep	0.47	0.31	0.26	0.24	0.22

[a] Food crops, in addition to corn, were wheat, rye, rice, oats, cowpeas, beans, Irish potatoes, sweet potatoes, buckwheat, and barley. Outputs were converted to corn-equivalent bushels using the conversion ratios given in Appendix E, Table E.2.
Sources: Production of agricultural products: 1850: U.S. Census Office, Seventh Census [1850], *The Seventh Census of the United States* (Washington: Robert Armstrong, 1853), pp. 345–348, 377–384, 429–433, 456–460, 482–486. *1860:* U.S. Census Office, Eight Census [1860], *Agriculture in the United States in 1860* (Washington: GPO, 1864), pp. 2–5, 26–29, 66–69, 84–87, 128–131. *1870:* U.S. Census Office, Ninth Census [1870], *The Statistics of the Wealth and Industry of the United States* (Washington: GPO, 1872), pp. 81–85. *1880:* U.S. Census Office, Tenth Census [1880], *Report on the Production of Agriculture* (Washington: GPO, 1883), pp. 3–10. *1890:* U.S. Census Office, Eleventh Census [1890], *Reports on the Statistics of Agriculture* (Washington: GPO, 1895), pp. 74–83. Also see the historical summary in ibid., pp. 84–115. *Population for all years:* U.S. Bureau of the Census, *Historical Statistics of the United States* (Washington: GPO, 1960), Series A-155, A-156, A-161, A-162, A-165, pp. 12–13.

tween 28 and 37 percent (see Table 3.3). It follows that a reduction of food intake would accompany this reduction in work effort. However, the reduction in food requirements would be significantly less than the decline in the number of hours worked per capita. We estimate that for the population as a whole, the number of calories per capita required could not have fallen by more than 9.0 to 11.5 percent.[14] In fact, the fall in consumption of food should have been much less than this calculation of the decline in energy requirements. Free people opted for a diet with a greater proportion of meat than that provided by slave masters. To provide a given number of calories through meat would require more corn to be produced than if the calories were consumed in the form of cornmeal. Therefore, the shift in diet should have limited the decline in production of grains to something smaller than the fall in calories required. We conclude that the reduction in work effort might, at most, account for one-fifth of the decline in food output. The fall in production left unexplained is still enormous.

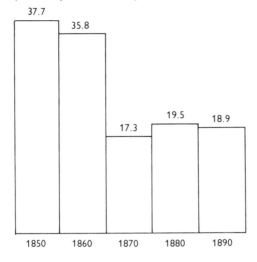

Per capita production of food crops
(in corn-equivalent bushels)

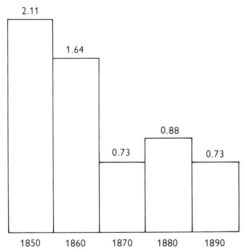

Number of swine per capita

Figure 8.1 Production of food in the five cotton states: 1850, 1860, 1870, 1880, and 1890. (*Source:* Table 8.1.)

The increased concentration upon cotton

The fall in food output seems to be associated with an equally dramatic shift in the composition of agricultural output. Figure 8.2 presents the ratio of cotton output to grain output for each census year from 1850 to 1890. Over the years, a shift toward cotton and away from grain is apparent.

This change cannot be adequately explained as a reaction to a shift in relative prices. Such prewar price data as are available suggest that the farmer received six to eight times the price of a pound of cotton for a bushel of corn.[15] Figure 8.3 displays the trends in the ratio of farmgate corn prices to cotton prices from 1869 to 1890. The cotton famine that accompanied the wartime disruption meant that corn prices were low relative to cotton prices, and this may have induced a shift of production into cotton. The ratio of corn prices to cotton prices was close to 5.5 in 1869, the first year for which we have farmgate prices of cotton.[16] By the mid-1870s, however, the ratio returned to its prewar level, and the value of a bushel of corn remained about six to eight times that of a pound of cotton for the next fifteen years. Since the prices displayed in Figure 8.3 represent the prices received by farmers who sold cotton or corn, they greatly understate the return to corn production for farmers who would otherwise have had to purchase corn at the credit prices charged by merchants.

If a sharp rise in cotton prices associated with the war is taken to be an explanation for the initial shift of acreage into cotton, the rapid return of relative prices to their prewar levels should have induced a rapid shift back to corn. As Figure 8.4 shows, there was a considerable shift of acreage from cotton to corn between 1866 and 1868. Thereafter, the trend was sharply reversed. There is no indication that a change in agricultural productivity took place that might explain an increased attention to cotton. Data on the

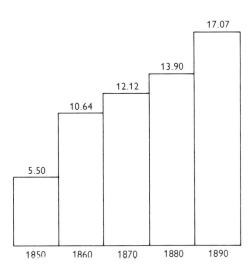

Figure 8.2 The number of pounds of cotton produced for each bushel of grain grown, Five Cotton States: 1850, 1860, 1870, 1880, and 1890. (*Source:* For grain production in corn-equivalent units, see sources to Table 8.1; For cotton production in pounds of lint, see the discussion in Appendix F.)

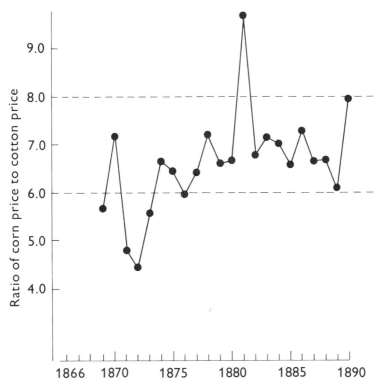

Figure 8.3 The ratio of the price of corn per bushel to the price of cotton per pound, Five Cotton States: 1869 to 1890. (*Source:* Note 16.)

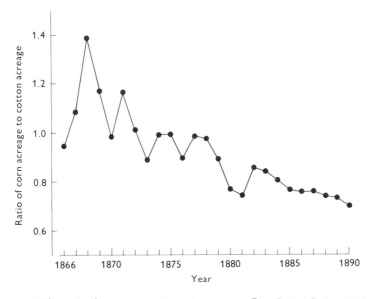

Figure 8.4 The ratio of corn acreage to cotton acreage, Five Cotton States: 1866 to 1890. (*Source:* Note 17.)

yields per acre in corn achieved in the Five Cotton States show that, relative to cotton yields, corn yields actually rose from 1869 to 1876. An improvement in the relative yield of corn, if anything, should have encouraged a relative increase in the acreage devoted to that crop.[17] In fact, as we have already noted, Figure 8.4 reveals that exactly the opposite took place. Corn acreage as a fraction of cotton acreage fell steadily from 1868 to 1890. Southern farmers were increasingly devoting their land to the staple crop, not foodstuffs.

The increasing concentration upon cotton appears even more puzzling when considered in light of the postwar labor shortage. The relative decline in labor could plausibly explain a shift toward land-intensive crops and away from those with high labor requirements. But there is no question that cotton was considerably *more* labor-intensive than were grain crops. It was commonly observed that twice as much labor was required to cultivate an acre of cotton as to cultivate an acre of corn. This being so, the labor shortage should have induced a shift toward corn, not cotton.[18]

The disappearance of self-sufficiency following the war

Before the enormous fall in food production, documented in Table 8.1, the South, particularly the Cotton South, produced very nearly enough food to meet all its needs. Sam Hilliard, in his comprehensive study of southern self-sufficiency before the war, cautiously concluded that the South as a whole was "largely feeding itself," but he noted that those areas of the South "in which commercial crops were important were also low in one or more of the basic commodities."[19] Other studies have supported this conclusion. They suggest that cotton producers were largely meeting their food needs.[20] On the other hand, the southern states, particularly in the Southeast, probably imported some food toward the end of the antebellum period to meet the needs of their urban populations and to fill deficits in the rice and sugar regions.[21]

If the South were only barely self-sufficient in food production before the war, the dramatic decline in per capita outputs of grain and pork can only imply that the South was unable to provision its own population in the postbellum period. Whatever the degree of dependence upon food supplied by the West or North before the war, there is little doubt that the South was a substantial net importer of food following the war.

The disappearance of self-sufficiency seems puzzling given the considerable change in the size distribution of farms. As Gavin Wright and Howard Kunreuther have demonstrated using the Parker-Gallman sample of farms, small farms before the Civil War had more swine per capita than large farms and devoted a relatively larger fraction of their acreage to corn production than to cotton production. If these patterns reflected a characteristic tendency for small farms to devote a greater fraction of their resources to food production, then, if anything, the switch to small-scale farms after the war should have resulted in an increased emphasis on food production, rather than the shift toward cotton that is observed.[22]

By 1880 the farms in the Cotton South were devoting 50 percent of their acreage to cotton. Table 8.2 shows that, as was the case before the Civil War, small farms planted a smaller fraction of their land in cotton than did the largest farms. Nevertheless, the lack of crop diversification among small farms is striking. Only 7.8 percent of the acreage on these farms was devoted to crops other than cotton and corn, while large farms reported 12.4 percent of their land in other crops. The table also reveals the greater number of crops reported by large farms compared with small farms. This lack of diversification was certainly puzzling to contemporaries. "It is a strange juncture of circumstances in which the great market staple of the State is selling at the cost of production, while everything else raised on the farm sells at a handsome profit," mused Thomas Janes, Georgia's commissioner of agriculture.[23] Janes condemned the increasing reliance on purchased foodstuffs, writing that he was "profoundly convinced that the

Table 8.2. *Percent of reported acres in crops devoted to cotton and to crops other than cotton and corn, and average number of different crops reported on farms, by tenure and farm type, Cotton South: 1880*

Farm size,[a] form of tenure	Percent of acreage in cotton[b]	Percent of reported acreage in crops other than cotton and corn[b]	Average number of different crops reported
Small farms	50.9	7.8	4.2
Owned	45.7	11.8	4.8
Rented	58.1	3.9	3.7
Sharecropped	53.6	5.2	3.8
Medium-scale farms	46.2	13.0	5.4
Owned	43.1	15.1	5.7
Rented	56.1	7.9	4.7
Sharecropped	50.0	4.5	5.1
Large farms	52.4	12.4	5.6
Owned	51.6	13.0	5.6
Rented	58.4	6.2	6.0
Sharecropped	57.1	10.4	5.2
All farms	50.2	8.9	4.5
Owned	45.7	12.6	5.0
Rented	57.8	4.6	3.9
Sharecropped	53.2	5.7	4.0

[a] Small farms reported 50 acres or less in crops, medium-scale farms reported more than 50 but 100 acres or less, large farms reported 100 acres or more.   [b] For cotton farms only.
Source: A sample of Cotton South farms drawn from the 1880 Census of Agriculture; see Appendix G, Section 2, for details.

greatest draw-backs to the prosperity of Georgia farming, is the mistaken policy of trying to make money with which to buy provisions, instead of raising provisions, not only for a support, but to make money."[24]

The advocates of self-sufficiency were not blind to the obvious economic advantage the South enjoyed in the cultivation of cotton. What they attacked was the practice of relying upon cotton to the exclusion of home-grown food. "Instead of cotton fields, and patches of grain, let us have fields of grain, and patches of cotton," was the advice of a Georgian quoted with approval by the *Southern Cultivator*.[25] James De Bow felt it was a "plain maxim of common sense" that a farmer should "make on the plantation everything that can be made suitable for man or beast."[26] The advice that filled the agricultural journals was to resist the "lure" of the staple crop and remain free from a dependence on others for supplies.[27]

Farmers were not unaware of these arguments, and some struggled to resist the trend toward increasing reliance upon cotton. "It should be the first object to raise all of the food necessary for man or beast," insisted a farmer's "study with a moral" that appeared in an 1871 issue of the *Rural Carolinian*.[28] Another article reasoned that "no planter can be in a bad condition, financially, with his barns filled with corn and his smoke-house filled with bacon."[29] A South Carolina farmer who signed himself "Panola" noted the advantages of cotton when a farmer took care to "feed himself and put his cotton crop in his pocket." In that way, he pointed out, "his surplus of grain will feed his family, and his cotton crop will allow them an occasional frolic."[30]

Despite these expressions of a desire for independence, southern farmers nevertheless were dependent on purchased, rather than farm-grown food-stuffs. To demonstrate just how great this reliance was, we have constructed estimates of the food remaining to farm families for consumption on farms in the Cotton South in 1879. Our estimating procedure, described in Appendix E, follows that of Robert Gallman and our own earlier estimates of southern self-sufficiency after the war.[31] For each farm in our 1880 sample, the outputs of food crops were converted to corn-equivalent units and then aggregated to determine the total food production. Allowances for seed were then subtracted, along with the corn-equivalent food needs for work stock and for hired labor. What remained was our estimate of grain available to the family either directly in the form of grain or indirectly as meat from animals slaughtered.[32] We report this residual in Table 8.3 as a per capita figure.

The estimates of Table 8.3 are based on what we consider to be conservative approximations of feeding and planting practices on southern farms.[33] We therefore expect that our estimates of residual food exaggerate the amount of food remaining for family members. The implication of the figures is immediately clear: small farms in the Cotton South did *not* produce enough grain to meet their food requirements. Small family farms reported

Table 8.3. *Per capita grain available to household members on farms, Cotton South: 1879*

Type of farm[a]	Bushels of grain per household member available as food	Percent of farms reporting deficits when consumption requirement per capita is		
		No bushels of corn	10 bushels of corn	15 bushels of corn
Small family farms	9.7	24.3	59.7	71.8
Other small farms	6.1	39.2	61.6	66.5
Medium-scale farms	34.5	16.1	28.5	37.0
Large farms	93.0	19.5	22.3	24.3
All farms	17.9	23.9	52.7	63.1

[a] See Chapter 4, Table 4.3 for definition of farm type.
Source: See Appendix E.

an average of only 9.7 bushels of grain per capita above the needs of the farm's work stock. Other small farms fared worse, producing only 6.1 bushels of corn per capita in residual grain production. One out of every four small farms was found to have a deficit of grain even if no allowance was made for human consumption.

At the very least, an average of 10 bushels of corn per year would be required to provide the minimal needs of each family member; a more plausible estimate would be 15 bushels per household member.[34] Figure 8.5 illustrates that almost 70 percent of the small farms produced insufficient grain to meet this standard. Our estimates confirm what many writers claimed at the time: the great majority of southern farmers had to purchase supplies. Indeed, even if we reduce the allowance for family consumption by one-third, 60 percent of the small farms would have produced inadequate supplies of corn and other grains.[35]

The impact of the cotton lien

The magnitude and pervasiveness of these food deficits throughout the Cotton South require explanation. What was the "lure" that made cotton so irresistible? The response given at the time by those farmers who were asked this question was invariably the same: cotton was required to secure a loan needed to finance the farm's operation.

Any lender requires collateral to secure the loans he makes. In the case of most tenants, what little personal property they possessed was typically insufficient to cover their credit needs. Additional security was required by

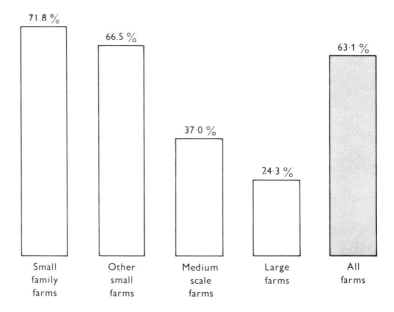

Figure 8.5 Percentage of farms reporting food deficits when per capita consumption of corn equivalents is 15 bushels: 1879. (*Source:* Table 8.3.)

the rural merchant in the form of a lien on the future crop output of the farm. In the view of the merchant, cotton afforded greater security for such loans than food crops. Cotton was a cash crop that could readily be sold in a well-organized market; it was not perishable; it was easily stored; and because its yield per acre and future price were more predictable, cotton entailed less risk than food crops.[36] For these reasons, the merchant frequently stipulated that a certain quantity of cotton be planted to further enhance the security of his loan.

This stipulation was not typically spelled out as part of the legal language of the crop lien contract, an omission that has led some historians to conclude that contemporary allegations that merchants refused credit to diversified farming operations were exaggerated.[37] But, of course, it was not necessary for this requirement to be a part of the contract. The lien was arranged and signed only after the merchant had assured himself that the stipulated crops had already been selected and that the work was well underway.[38] It was the universal complaint of the farmers that the rural merchant predicated his willingness to negotiate credit on the condition that sufficient cotton to serve as collateral had been planted.

It was obvious to the farmer that the merchant's requirements that he plant cotton had a less subtle motivation as well. The merchant's insistence on cotton had the convenient effect of driving the farmer into increased dependence upon *purchased* supplies. The more cotton the farmer had to grow, the fewer resources remained to produce food. Farmers perceived that a cotton lien enhanced the merchant's lucrative business of selling supplies at exorbitant credit prices, but they could do little about it. "We ought to plant less [cotton and tobacco] and more of grain and grasses," claimed a correspondent from Montgomery County, North Carolina, in 1887, "but how are we to do it; the man who furnishes us rations at 50 per cent. interest won't let us; he wants money crop planted."[39] This is not an isolated example. Other responses to a North Carolina survey confirm that farmers felt strong pressure to plant cotton at the expense of food crops:

The landlord and merchants who furnish supplies on time won't let [the tenants] sow much grain—they want cotton; and having to buy on time, they have to do as the merchant or landlord says, and the result is, they do not often pay out, and when they do they have nothing left.

We shall soon be swallowed up by the commission merchants and guano men. It is cotton! cotton! cotton! Buy everything and make cotton pay for it.

As a rule, tenants are forced to make a certain amount of cotton in order to get their supplies furnished them, and they cannot, therefore, pay the attention to making their bread and meat that they ought. . . . He is bound to feed his family, and not having anything, he is bound to buy on time. To do this he must promise the merchant to plant a certain amount of cotton.

We are obliged to buy on time and pay 50 or more per cent., hence are compelled to make money crop mostly to pay with.[40]

There is little question that the practice of merchants asking for crop liens from their customers was common throughout the South and that cotton was generally a requirement for extending such a lien.[41]

The monopolistic pricing system employed by merchants throughout the Cotton South would, by itself, allow merchants to exploit their customers. Any farmer lacking sufficient cash to buy all his supplies was forced to pay the exploitive credit prices. The additional insistence by the merchant that the farmer forgo self-sufficiency obviously increased the farmer's dependence on credit and served to inflate the merchant's profits. The exploitation was thus compounded.

Critics of southern merchants never tired of explaining the gains of being free from dependence on supplies sold at monopolistic prices. The formula for independence seemed simple enough, and the logic was compelling. As Mr. Hill of Jonesboro, Georgia, exhorted listeners at the county fair in August of 1873:

Make cotton your surplus crop! . . . Make your own fertilizers. . . . Thus you become independent of the Guano merchants. Raise your own provisions. Thus you become independent of the provision merchants. Your cheapest and safest line of transportation runs from your own fields and hog-pens to your own barn and meathouses! With no debts for your supplies, you will need no accommodation credits at two percent per month. Thus you can become independent of brokers, cotton factors and lien merchants. You can then sell your cotton at your own time, to your own chosen buyers, and will get your own money.[42]

It is important to realize that farmers who were initially paying monopolistic prices, and who then took this advice to become self-sufficient, would nevertheless have been adversely affected by the presence of the credit monopoly even though they might escape direct exploitation. Farmers who were being exploited by merchants' usurious interest rates had been initially forced into this position by their need for credit. Presumably, a comparison of the farmgate price of cotton with a cash farmgate selling price for corn had led them to prefer a crop mix that concentrated upon cotton and that therefore necessitated the purchase of food. It was this food deficit that produced a need for credit. By becoming self-sufficient, a farmer could avoid this necessity. But self-sufficiency would require a crop mix different from the one that would have maximized the farmer's income in the absence of a credit monopoly.

The existence of the monopoly of credit, coupled with the farmer's need for credit, invariably led to one of two outcomes. Either the farmer paid an exploitive price for supplies and was forced to grow even more cotton than he would have wished, or he chose self-sufficiency and grew less cotton than he would have wished. Either way, he would be unable to escape the adverse effects of the merchant's control of credit.[43] Of the two alternatives, the advice of Mr. Hill and many of his contemporaries was for farmers to choose the latter.[44]

The evidence is that southern farmers did not follow this advice. The advice went unheeded, but not because it was impossible to grow home supplies. Surely southern agricultural productivity on postbellum farms was high enough to provide amply for their needs and produce some cotton as a surplus crop as well. Farmers in the South had done so before the war, and they could do so after. The explanation for the persistent concentration upon cotton after 1865 is that cotton farmers were effectively prevented from practicing self-sufficiency as a means of escaping the merchant's power. They were locked in to cotton production.

The lock-in and persistence of cotton overproduction

In order to take the advice to provision his own farm and sever the relationship with the provisioning merchant, a farmer would have to alter his crop mix. The crop decisions could be made only at the beginning of a new season. If he had not produced sufficient food in the previous season to meet the needs of the farm for a full year, the typical farmer would not have sufficient stocks of foodstuffs to supply his farm over the coming season. Unless he had these stocks, or the cash to purchase them, he would be forced to borrow to cover the first year of his program of self-sufficiency. But this need for credit inexorably drove him back to the very merchant he sought to escape.[45]

The merchant had an obvious incentive to thwart the farmer's quest for independence. Moreover, he had the means to do so. The merchant simply refused to grant credit to a farmer who was not willing to accept a requirement that cotton be made the principal crop. Despite his desire to escape, the farmer was stilll locked into the production of cotton. His lack of self-sufficiency, of necessity, forced him to seek credit year after year, and the merchant's conditions for a loan ensured that the farm could not become self-sufficient. A farmer from Swain County, North Carolina, observed the plight of the cultivator. "The mortgage system," he wrote in 1887, "is working its deadly way into this county, and making sad havoc where its tempting offers are once entered into. Alas! one never gets out from its magic embrace until he dies out or is sold out."[46]

The farmer, faced with the prospect of continual seasonal indebtedness, might still hope eventually to save enough over several successive seasons to accumulate the cash necessary to purchase a year's supplies. But even this hope would be dashed. The low net income of the one-family farm severely limited the farm operator's ability to save, and misfortune or crop failure might wipe out his savings in a single season. Even if luck were with him, the merchant could eliminate the farmer's ability to save at any time. He could demand so much cotton that the cost of food at monopolistic prices would reduce the farmer's surplus income literally to a negative value. In this situation the farmer would end the year with insufficient output to pay his debt to the merchant. If the farmer's savings could not make up the difference, the merchant would have legal claim to part of the *next* crop, and the farmer would be required to sign a new lien contract for the coming year.

In most cases the storekeeper would not need to drive the farmer to this point. The merchant's territorial monopoly was effective enough that the need for credit on the part of a farmer was itself sufficient to guarantee his business for another year. The need for the extra insurance of an end-of-the-year debt would appear only if competition from nearby merchants threatened to lure the farmer away. In any case, the merchant would avoid driving the farmer so far into debt at the end of a season that he would become discouraged and work inefficiently or attempt to abscond without paying his debts. The merchant was compelled to provide for the needs of a farm, and once he had expropriated all the remaining income, there was no gain to creating additional debts that could never be repaid. An illustration of the merchants' cognizance of the dangers of accumulating debt is provided by the comment of the editor of the *Rural Carolinian* in regard to a merchant's reaction to some "unlucky" farmer confronted with serious losses: "Immediately [the farmer] is offered several cents a pound for his cotton more than it is worth. . . . [The merchant] offers this bonus to induce the rascally inclined customer to pay his debts."[47] In other words, if the occasion required, the merchant could simply adjust the price of cotton – and the farmer's income – to whatever level would keep the farmer at his job, but never free of the merchant's control. This ultimate trap of debt peonage, where the farmer ended the season still in debt to the merchant, was an extreme, probably resorted to in only a fraction of cases. But the lock-in mechanism, which held income sufficiently low to prevent an escape to self-sufficiency, undoubtedly kept a majority of small farmers in a perpetual cycle of cotton overproduction and short-term debt.

Contemporaries alleged that the lock-in was universal throughout the South. Charles Otken referred to it as the "vast credit system whose tremendous evils and exorbitant exactions have brought poverty and bankruptcy to thousands of families, . . . crushed out all independence and reduced its victims to a coarse species of servile slavery."[48] Agriculturalists, who employed less rhetoric and relied upon more careful observation, reached the same conclusion. Thomas Janes, commissioner of agriculture for Georgia during this period, conducted surveys which revealed that approximately 75 percent of the state's farmers were buying on credit.[49] Janes warned farmers against entering "the whirlpool of credit and debt which has engulfed so many, and from which so few have escaped unscathed."[50] Years later, a committee of the U.S. Congress reported on the "condition of the cotton growers." They concluded:

That generally the financial condition of the farmers is bad, a very large percentage insolvent, and that very few indeed are substantially increasing in the possesson of property. That the few who are actually solvent and making some increase in their estates are those who raise their own supplies, meat, corn, plow stock, producing cotton only as a surplus.[51]

From production statistics alone it is impossible to identify the farms which, by our definition, were gripped in the merchant's trap. But we can identify a large body of farms that must have been easy prey for the coercion of the credit monopolist. We know that at least three-fourths of all farms in Georgia purchased some fraction of their supplies on credit in the 1870s, and less precise reports elsewhere suggest that this figure was typical throughout the Cotton South. It seems likely that virtually every small farm required some credit. Those small farms that were unable to produce enough grains even to meet the needs of animals on their farms could hardly avoid seeking credit. Probably most of the farms that failed to produce 15 bushels of corn per family member (63.1 percent of all farms) were exploited through exorbitant credit prices and were susceptible to manipulations of the merchant. Even if no farms other than small farms with grain deficits were caught by the merchant, our self-sufficiency estimates suggest that 56 percent of all farms in the Cotton South would have been locked in. Over 300,000 farms and families paid homage to the merchant's power.[52]

The genesis of debt peonage

Our analysis of debt peonage and the power of the merchant to force farmers into overproduction of cotton has considerable appeal as an explanation of the persistent dependency on outside sources of foodstuffs displayed by the South throughout the latter part of the nineteenth century. The paradox of why free farmers in the New South ignored the widely publicized incentives to turn to self-sufficiency is easily resolved by an explanation that argues farmers were not, in fact, "free." Farmers grew cotton rather than food because the will of the merchant prevailed over the interests of the farmer.

Another aspect of the appeal of the lock-in argument is that the origins of this system and its emphasis on cotton are easily explained in terms of events immediately following the Civil War. The spectacularly high prices for cotton that followed the famine of the wartime period made farmers eager to plant as many acres of cotton as their labor allowed. In those halcyon days, there was no conflict between the farmer's interest and his supplier's interest on the question of growing cotton. The lure of cotton profits was so enormous that, despite a shortage of supplies and the collapse of southern banking and factorage systems, ways were found to finance the crops. To the small farmer, as we have seen, this invariably meant a crop lien from a local merchant or a wealthy planter. However, the famine prices were short-lived. By 1868 the trend in prices had already begun to favor a shift of production back to corn. Yet, for many small farms, the trap had by this time already been sprung. The collapse of the cotton prices made crop liens worth less than had been anticipated. Bad crops in 1866 and 1868 added to the difficulties. Saddled with debts incurred because of losses, farmers had no alternative but to accede to the merchants' demand that they grow cotton to repay their debts. Farmers soon found that this practice locked them into the continued need for credit to begin each new season. The merchant had been quick to seize an opportunity to prevent a shift to greater grain production.

The "profitability" of cotton

Economists are usually skeptical of arguments that seem so clearly to deny the power of competitive behavior. A simpler, more direct, reason for the southern farmer's perference for cotton could be posited: perhaps conditions following the war had changed to make it profitable to specialize in the cash crop and purchase supplies. Two critics of the debt-peonage argument have summarized this view:

> Farmers in Kansas grow wheat, not because local merchants force them, but because it is wealth-increasing to do so. The proceeds from wheat sales permit farmers to buy more food and other things (cotton goods) than "growing their own." Presumably the same mechanism operated in the South, but economic conditions were appropriate for cotton, not wheat.[53]

This argument apparently convinced these critics without any additional consideration. Yet the argument does not demonstrate that southern farmers were actually better off producing cotton rather than food or that they were free to grow food if they wished. To presume, as these economists have, all the necessary conditions for a competitive world begs the fundamental issue in question: did or did not the southern economy work in an efficient and nonexploitive way?

Whether or not economic conditions in the South "were appropriate for cotton" was a question contemporaries struggled to resolve without success. The editor of the *Rural Carolinian* expressed his puzzlement over this issue in 1874:

Figures do not lie, it is said. Well, perhaps they don't; but they sometimes tell the truth in such a way that it is more deceptive than a downright lie. Figures are made to say that cotton planting is the most profitable branch of agriculture. This is true, no doubt; but, then, these same figures are made to show that cotton planting is a losing business, and all the planters, or at the best, most of them, are becoming bankrupt. There is a good deal of truth in this too, we fear.[54]

The editor's confusion is easily understood in light of the serious obstacles to accurate estimation of the returns from various crops even on those farms that kept careful records of their costs and receipts.

The key to the problem lies in accurately establishing how many additional bushels of corn the farmer could expect to produce by shifting to corn raising the labor currently required to produce a given quantity of cotton. The answer to this question cannot be obtained from the census, since the census did not report the amount of labor expended upon each crop. A search of the agricultural literature makes it clear that cotton required considerably more labor and animal power per acre of land throughout the year than did the cultivation of corn:

The number of days' work needed upon an acre of cotton, from the first to the last, is greater than upon any other crop, and the other expenses bestowed upon it greater.[55]

Cotton culture requires more labor, more mules, more ploughs, and more expensive machinery (as gins and screws) than the growing of corn, oats, wheat, peas, clover and grasses.[56]

"Every observing farmer knows," remarked one contributor to the *Southern Cultivator*, "that for each additional acre of land planted in cotton, two must be deducted from the number in corn."[57] This rule of thumb is consistent with the statements of other contemporaries. Another writer in the *Southern Cultivator* presented statistics that imply that 3 acres of corn could be produced by giving up 1 acre of cotton.[58] He was criticized by a third correspondent of the agricultural journal who set the ratio at 1.67 acres of corn per acre of cotton forgone.[59] It does not seem unreasonable on the basis of these observations to assume that 1 acre of cotton would release sufficient labor and capital to cultivate between 1.67 and 2 acres of corn.

In 1879 the small-scale family-operated farms in our sample from the Cotton South averaged 178 pounds of cotton per acre. The same farms produced 11.3 bushels of corn per acre. Hypothesizing that the labor and other resources devoted to a parcel of average cotton land were diverted to corn production, we can calculate that the typical operator of a small family farm would obtain between 10.6 and 12.7 bushels of corn for every 100 pounds of cotton forgone.[60] We can ignore the production of cotton seed, since the seed would be used to pay for the ginning and bailing of cotton.[61] However, in addition to the output of grain, the corn crop yielded fodder.[62] The value of the corn fodder was equivalent to between 10 and 18 percent of the value of the grain.[63] We shall take the lower estimate of the fodder yield for the purposes of our calculation. This adjustment raises the corn-cotton trade-off to between 11.7 and 14.0 bushels of corn equivalents for every 100 pounds of cotton, or 12.85 bushels if we take the midpoint.

Given this physical trade-off between crops, we can ask whether the farmer who was buying corn at credit prices should have attempted to grow more corn. The value of the cotton he must forgo is easily estimated, since cotton prices were fairly uniform throughout the South, and frequent surveys by the U.S. Department of Agriculture provide reliable testimony concerning the farmgate price. Over the three crops of 1878, 1879, and 1880, the average December 1 farmgate price for cotton in the Cotton South was 9.5 cents per pound.[64] If the farmer were purchasing corn, as we assume, the relevent price for evaluating the additional corn output would be the purchase price rather than the selling price. The price the typical farmer paid for corn is less certain. The surveys taken in Georgia during these years suggest that the credit prices for corn charged by merchants were 53 percent above the farmgate prices farmers received when they sold corn the previous December (see Chapter 7, Table 7.1). There is no reason to believe that the statistics for Georgia exaggerate the situation throughout the South. We have therefore applied this markup to the average farmgate price of corn that prevailed in the Cotton South from 1878 through 1880 – 62.3 cents per bushel.[65] Our estimated credit price was therefore 95.3 cents per bushel. The answer to our question is thus clear. A farmer who could have traded between 11.7 and 14.0 bushels of corn worth $11.15 to $13.34, for 100 pounds of cotton worth $9.50 would have been well advised to do so. The fact that many did not is testimony to the coercive power of the merchant.

The farmer who paid credit prices for corn could have increased his income at the margin by approximately 29 percent simply by shifting resources from cotton to corn. This does not mean that the farmer who could obtain corn at the *cash* price was unwise to depend on purchased corn. Using the same procedure employed in the calculation above to estimate the trade-off when valued at cash prices, we find that 12.9 bushels of corn would be worth $9.45.[66] This amount almost exactly equals the value of the 100 pounds of cotton that could be produced from the same labor. As one would expect, the retail prices of corn and cotton reflected the relative productivity of labor in producing these two crops.[67]

These figures make clear the source of the confusion that troubled the editor of the *Rural Carolinian*. Calculated at cash prices, the farmer's dependence on cotton would not seem unwise. But in practice, the farmer who sought to produce cotton at the sacrifice of self-sufficiency was required to pay much higher prices for corn and was prevented from increasing his own corn production in response. As a result, he might very well have entered a losing business.

The burden of monopoly

The rural merchant of the Cotton South was a monopolist who held a local, territorial monopoly over credit. As a monopolist he exploited his customers by charging exorbitant prices. In the traditional economic analysis, a monopolist is condemned not merely for overcharging but also for underselling, since the quantity of the good demanded is typically lower as a consequence of its higher price. In this particular instance, however, the furnishing merchant was able to prevent the farmers' demand for credit from contracting in response to the exorbitant interest rates charged. The merchant compelled the farmer to plant and cultivate more cotton and less foodstuffs than he would have freely chosen to do given the high price of credit. Apparently the merchant used his control over the farmers' crop decisions not merely to maintain the balance between cotton and corn production that had existed before the appearance of the credit monopoly, but to push significantly beyond that point toward specialization in cotton. As we have seen, there was an otherwise inexplicable shift away from grain crops and animal husbandry and toward cotton in the Cotton States following the Civil War. The monopolist in this case both overcharged and oversold his product.

Every farmer in the Cotton South was harmed as a consequence of the merchants' coercion. Those who entirely avoided the need for credit by achieving self-sufficiency in grain and pork were making crop decisions that were less than optimal. In a free market they might well have chosen a crop mix that required the purchase of some corn. Their self-sufficiency in foodstuffs would represent, therefore, a self-imposed reduction in economic efficiency designed solely to evade exploitation by a monopolist. The farmers who avoided the credit system by accumulating sufficient cash to finance all their grain purchases without asking for credit were forgoing the interest such cash assets might have earned had they been productively invested.[68]

It would be presumptuous to attempt to quantify these economic losses. To do so would require more knowledge than we have about the nature of the demand for cotton, the efficiency of crop production, the productivity of alternative investments, and the numbers of farmers who were directly and indirectly affected by the system. One point is clear, however: the magnitude of the losses borne by the farmers exceeded the gains achieved by the merchants. The losses did not arise solely from the transfer of income from producers to the providers of credit. In particular, the crop mix chosen by most farmers was economically inefficient and therefore southern agriculture was less productive than it might have been. While we cannot measure the extent to which regional income was reduced in the aggregate by this imposed inefficiency, we can obtain a feeling for what the merchants' exploitation may have meant to the tenant farmers who were trapped within the system.

There were three direct effects of the credit monopoly: it reduced the farmer's income, it reduced the security of the farmer's livelihood, and it reduced the farmer's independence. The most obvious impact of the monopoly was to lower the real income of the farmer. One crude measure of the magnitude of this reduction can be gained by calculating the real income of black tenants operating family farms in 1879–1880. In Chapter 1 we calculated that the material income of black tenant-farm operators was about 29 percent above the consumption standard of slaves, or approximately $41.39 per year per capita in 1859–1860 prices. That calculation, however, assumed that there was no exploitation of farmers in the postwar era. In Appendix A an alternative cost-of-living index is presented for 1879–1880 on the assumption that 60 percent of the farm family's purchases were made on credit (Table A.9). When we use that index to recalculate the material income of black tenant families, the figure falls to $35.82 per capita, or 13.5 percent less than when we assumed all purchases were made for cash. Although a number of assumptions are required to make such a calculation, we believe our estimate provides an order of magnitude for the proportion of agricultural output that was diverted to the merchants.

A 13.5 percent rate of exploitation would be, of course, considerably less than the rate of exploitation of slave labor, which we have estimated at approximately 55 percent (Chapter 1, Table 1.1). According to our estimates, the material income of tenants who were exploited by merchants was nearly 12 percent above the consumption of slaves who were exploited by their masters. The fact that blacks were materially better off as freedmen than as slaves does not, of course, excuse the merchants' exploitation. Nor can a reduction in real income of 13.5 percent be dismissed as trivial, particularly when it is remembered how low were agricultural outputs per capita in the first place. In considering the fraction of output that was left to the farmer, it is also significant that the rate of exploitation could be adjusted by the merchant. In good years the tenant lost proportionately more than in years of poor harvests. The merchant not only impoverished his customers, he stifled their hopes and reduced their incentive as well.

The farmer caught up in this system also was compelled to take greater risks. Forced to plant cotton that would be sold after the harvest at a yet unknown price to finance the season's purchases of corn at prices also yet to be established, the farmer fulfilled his corn requirements on terms that embodied not only the risk attendant upon an uncertain crop yield but the risk inherent in the fluctuations of the relative price of corn and cotton as well. A glance at Figure 8.3 suggests that the year-to-year changes in the ratio of the price of corn to the price of cotton were not insignificant. Had the farmer grown his own corn, he would have faced only the crop risk of an uncertain corn yield.[69] The farmer had to be compelled by the merchant to assume the increased risks involved in the exchange of cotton for corn since he was not compensated for assuming this added burden by expectations of higher income.

The southern tenant was neither owner of his land nor manager of his business. Caught between requirements imposed by the landlord and those imposed by the merchant, his independent decision making was limited to the mundane and menial aspects of farming. The larger decisions – concerning land use, investments in the farm's productivity, the choice of technology, and the scale of operation – were all made for him. Undoubtedly, as a consequence, his pride, his ambition, and his efficiency as a tiller of the soil were reduced. The magnitude of these losses cannot, of course, be measured; but neither should such implications be ignored.

CHAPTER 9

THE ROOTS OF SOUTHERN POVERTY

Twenty-odd years ago . . . I fondly imagined a great era of prosperity for the South. Guided by history and by a knowledge of our people and our climatic and physicial advantages, I saw in anticipation all her tribulations ended, all her scars healed, and all the ravages of war forgotten, and I beheld the South greater, richer and mightier than when she molded the political policy of the whole country. But year by year these hopes, chastened by experience, have waned and faded, until now, instead of beholding the glorious South of my imagination, I see her sons poorer than when the war ceased his ravages, weaker than when rehabilitated with her original rights, and with the bitter memories of the past smouldering, if not rankling, in the bosoms of many.

Lewis H. Blair, *A Southern Prophecy: The Prosperity of the South Dependent upon the Elevation of the Negro,* 1889. Reprinted (Boston: Little, Brown & Co., 1964), p. 15.

No event was more significant to southern history than the Civil War. For generations southerners continually referred to The War, wrote of The War, even dated the events of their lives by the years elapsed since The War. It is easy, of course, to understand this preoccupation. The South's defeat in the Civil War destroyed much of the framework of antebellum southern society, and what replaced it was often designed on radically different lines. Gone was slavery. Gone were the plantations. Gone were the cotton factors. In their place were sharecroppers, tenant farms, and rural merchants. Whether or not it was a case of cause and effect, this transformation coincided with the virtual cessation of economic growth in the South. No wonder southerners found it difficult to put the "bitter memories of the past" behind them.

Nowhere was the disruption that accompanied the end of the war more complete or the reorganization required more sweeping than in the economic realm. But once the new economic institutions had been established, further institutional change ceased. It was as if the South, exhausted by the effort required to rebuild its economic institutions, had placed a moratorium on further development. It required a shock nearly equal to emancipation to jolt the agrarian South out of the routine it had followed for the four post-

Notes to Chapter 9 appear on pages 353–355.

emancipation decades. That shock was the coming of the cotton boll weevil. This small insect, only about 0.25 inch long, was unknown in the United States before 1892, although before that time it had spread to northern Mexico from its original habitat in Central America. When the westward march of cotton production in the United States ultimately reached southern Texas, and there came into contact with Mexican cotton culture, the weevil was afforded an entry into the American South. Within two years the pest had spread to half a dozen counties in southern Texas. Thereafter, year by year the boll weevil infestation slowly advanced eastward across the Cotton South. By 1903 it had reached the Texas-Louisiana border. By 1907 the alluvial country of Mississippi had been broached. The weevil had overrun half of Alabama's black belt by 1912 and almost all of Georgia by 1916. The next year it appeared in South Carolina. By 1921 virtually all the Cotton South had been infested. The weevil's march through the cotton belt is tracked on the accompanying map.

The adult female weevil lays her eggs in the buds and fruit of the cotton plant during the spring. The grubs that hatch feed upon the maturing cotton, destroying much of the crop. The new pest was potentially far more destructive than the worms and caterpillars that had previously plagued southern cotton fields. After the first report of the weevil reached Washington in 1894, the U.S. Department of Agriculture sent an entomologist, C. H. Tyler Townsend, to Brownsville, Texas, to investigate. He reported that in infested fields:

During the year 1894 in the Brownsville region (San Tomas) the loss of crop was estimated at over 90 per cent. In the San Diego region the loss was about 90 per cent. At La Rosita, 12 to 18 miles west of San Diego, the damage was estimated to be something over 75 per cent. At Rosita, on the Nueces, about 15 miles below Sharpsburg, 90 per cent of the crop was destroyed.[1]

Of course, not every farm was equally ravaged. The fall in crop output per acre in a countywide region overrun by the weevil was estimated by the Department of Agriculture to be in the neighborhood of 50 percent.[2] The figures in Table 9.1 present the volume of production of cotton in twenty Texas counties in 1899 and 1902. Ten of the counties were infested by the boll weevil during the two-year period. According to the Department of Agriculture there had been no significant decline in acreage or any unfavorable climatic conditions that might otherwise explain the contrast between the 53 percent decline in output of the infested counties and the 11 percent increase in the unaffected region.[3]

The impact of the cotton boll weevil on southern agriculture was immediate. An insect had finally accomplished what agriculturalists in the New South had been urging for years: southern farmers reduced their concentration upon cotton and shifted into other crops. Table 9.2 presents for each of the Five Cotton Sates the average acreage devoted to cotton over the four-

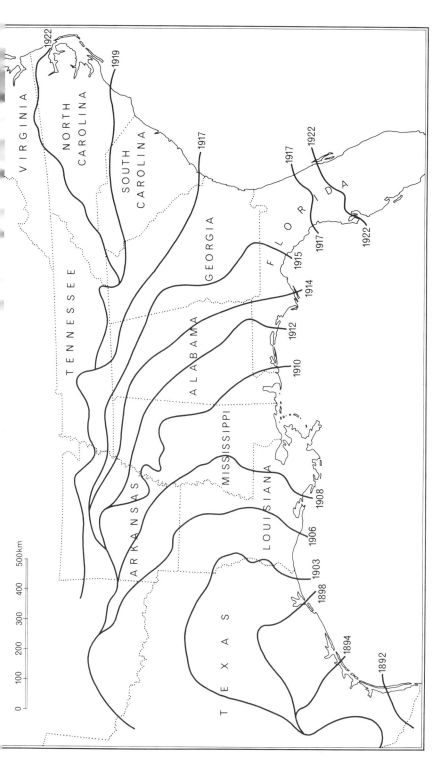

The spread of the cotton boll weevil in the United States, 1892–1922. (*Source:* Adapted from U.S. Department of Agriculture, W. D. Hunter and B. R. Coad, "The Boll-Weevil Problem," *USDA Farmers' Bulletin*, Number 1329 [June 1923] Figure 1, p. 3.)

Table 9.1. *Effect of the boll weevil on production of cotton in Texas: 1899,*
1902

Counties	Production (number of 500-lb bales)		Percent change
	1899	1902	
Infested between 1899 and 1902			
Caldwell	47,473	23,133	−51.3
Colorado	30,923	11,493	−62.8
Fayette	73,238	31,200	−57.4
Gonzales	44,131	25,351	−42.6
Grimes	26,541	12,135	−54.3
Lavaca	42,484	22,906	−46.8
Montgomery	10,272	3,660	−64.4
San Jacinto	8,826	3,044	−65.5
Travis	60,078	28,382	−52.8
Wharton	27,383	12,870	−53.0
Total	371,349	174,174	−53.1
Not yet infested in 1902			
Collin	49,077	47,344	−3.5
Cooke	11,905	11,012	−7.5
Delta	24,705	26,256	6.3
Denton	20,381	24,541	20.4
Fannin	59,802	70,540	18.0
Grayson	40,874	54,087	32.3
Hunt	50,317	49,713	−1.2
Lamar	49,193	59,269	20.5
Montague	15,064	16,981	12.7
Wise	17,556	18,869	7.5
Total	338,874	378,612	11.2

Source: U.S. Department of Agriculture, *Yearbook of the United States Department of Agri-*
culture, 1903 (Washington: GPO, 1904), p. 207.

year period immediately preceding the arrival of the boll weevil in each state
and the average cotton acreage over the four-year period immediately following the state's infestation. The decline in cotton acreage is dramatic; for
the five states taken together it averaged 27.4 percent. The 31.3 percent
decline in yields per acre explains why.

Thus, the boll weevil heralded the end of the era the Civil War had
introduced. The postemancipation era began with great gains and great
hopes, but those gains were never capitalized, and those hopes never materialized. The South of 1900 was poor. Relative to the entire United States,
per capita income was less than 50 percent of the national standard in the
South Atlantic and East South Central divisions.[4] The South of 1900 was
underdeveloped. It remained an agrarian society with a backward technology that still employed hand labor and mule power virtually unassisted by

Table 9.2. *Cotton acreage and crop yield before and after boll weevil infestation, Five Cotton States: 1889–1924*

State	Last year before infestation	First year of complete infestation	Acres in cotton (thousands)			Yield per acre (pounds of lint)		
			Average of 4 years before infestation	Average of 4 years after infestation	Percent decline	Average of 4 years before infestation	Average of 4 years after infestation	Percent decline
Louisiana[a]	1902	1908	1,523	1,030	32.4	245	156	36.4
Mississippi[a]	1907	1914	3,567	2,775	22.2	200	170	15.1
Alabama[a]	1909	1916	3,469	2,426	30.1	164	126	22.8
Georgia[b]	1914	1920	4,953	3,476	29.8	230	117	49.2
South Carolina[b]	1917	1921	2,500	1,924	23.1	231	176	24.0
Total			16,011	11,630	27.4	211	145	31.3

[a] Based on harvested acres and yield per harvested acre. Acreage cultivated is not available before 1909. [b] Based on acres under cultivation in July and yield per cultivated acre.

Source: U.S. Department of Agriculture, Agricultural Marketing Service, "Cotton and Cotton Seed: Acreage, Yield, Production, Disposition, Price, Value, by States, 1866–1952," USDA Statistical Bulletin, Number 164 (Washington: GPO, 1955), pp. 13, 14, 16, 24, 25, 28, 29, 31.

mechanical implements. The rural South of 1900 was stagnant. Crop outputs, yields per acre, and agricultural technology remained virtually the same year after year. Progress was nowhere in evidence.

The dynamics of southern poverty

Throughout this book we have examined the institutional structure of the postemancipation southern economy. Our objective has been to identify those institutional characteristics that might help us to understand the failure of the economy to produce the hoped-for era of prosperity. We have taken this approach because we believe that the core of the problem of underdevelopment is institutional. But a static analysis of economic institutions alone will fail to provide a full explanation of why any particular economy produced poverty or prosperity. Economic growth is a dynamic process; to examine the causes of southern poverty, we must identify the forces that worked over time to hinder capital formation, technological innovation, and industrial development.

Our study of the institutional mechanisms was a necessary prerequisite to any analysis of the dynamics of the South's economic system. It is through economic institutions that an individual's desire for self-advancement is translated into human behavior that actually generates and propels economic growth and development. We believe the institutional flaws of the southern economy reduced the anticipated returns and increased the effective costs of new investment, which in turn impeded capital formation. For the same reason, innovative changes in the production process were severely delayed. Furthermore, we believe that the rigidity of the South's economic institutions prevented the region from either capitalizing on its comparative advantage in cotton production or shifting to other crops and economic activities when that comparative advantage began to fade. We also believe that the rigidity of southern institutions helps to explain the lack of labor mobility that otherwise might have encouraged an outmigration of labor long before the twentieth-century Negro exodus to the North.

As we shall argue below, the impediments to capital formation, the South's subservience to cotton, and the barriers to interregional labor mobility were three of the roots of southern poverty. Each of these explanations can be considered as economic interpretations; these roots were buried deep in the South's economic institutions. There existed another dynamic factor impeding economic growth – one not normally considered as economic in nature – that also appeared during our examination of the South's economic structure. That factor was the pervasive influence of race relations. We believe that the animosity and mutual fear that existed between the races, and in particular the whites' antagonism toward the blacks' economic advancement, were at least as powerful as were economic incentives in motivating individual economic behavior. The effect of racism was felt throughout the entire system; it left no economic institution undistorted.

As a cause of southern poverty, racism may well have been preeminent. One way in which racial animosities restricted southern development is rather obvious. When whites used threats of violence to keep blacks from gaining an education, practicing a trade, or purchasing land, they systematically prevented blacks from following the three routes most commonly traveled by other Americans in their quest for self-advancement. With over half the population held in ignorance and forced to work as agricultural laborers, it is no wonder that the South was poor, underdeveloped, and without signs of economic progress.

While this point is obvious by itself, it is also misleading. If the direct coercive manifestations of racism were the only obstacles to progress, blacks might well have overcome them by outright defiance or, even more likely, they might have bypassed them by finding new roads for self-advancement. It would be presumptuous to argue that whites, by threat, bluster, and force alone, could have kept blacks from advancing their own cause. Moreover, if the impact of racism were restricted only to these direct influences, racism would not explain why southern whites (with presumably all the opportunities denied blacks) did not advance their own fortunes in the forty years following emancipation.

The racism that permeated the southern economy had a more subtle, yet more powerful, impact – more subtle and more insidious because it removed the incentive to self-advancement, not only for the blacks, but for the whites as well. Racism distorted the economic institutions of the South, reshaping them so that the market signals – which normally direct resources toward their most productive employment and provide the incentive to the investments and the innovations that propel economic growth – were either not generated or were greatly weakened. As an example of this mechanism, we shall consider first the case of education.[5]

The economic impact of racism: education

Slavery, as we have seen, produced a largely illiterate black population and left it an easy victim of racial oppression. Perhaps the vulnerability of an illiterate population was recognized, for black education became a primary target of white oppression. The costs of education and skill acquisition were increased by acts of violence and discrimination. A further obstacle to black education was that fewer schools were provided for black children, and these were of inferior quality compared with those provided for whites. Undoubtedly many blacks were discouraged from seeking an education. But what of the black man or woman who persevered, who educated himself, or who braved the whites' hostility and went to school? What did the education mean once it was acquired?

Most blacks who sought an education hoped that literacy and elementary education would make them better farmers or farm managers or open the possibility of becoming independent landowners or artisans. But such individuals were frequently disappointed, not because education was worthless for these pursuits, but rather because blacks were never allowed to pursue those occupations. A literate farmer may well be a better farm manager, but in a rural society where few blacks were educated and where landowners were invariably white, it was not easy for a black man to find employment as an overseer or farm manager. Nor was it easy to lease a farm on better terms than were standard. If a superior job could not be secured, the advantages of the education could not be fully utilized by the laborer. And if it was common knowledge that educated blacks were unable to find employment in occupations that made full use of their acquired skills, then the incentive for others to pursue education would be dampened considerably. With the apparent returns to education kept low by the agricultural system, the net investment in education remained low, the black population remained largely illiterate and the problem perpetuated itself.

The same phenomenon kept many blacks from seeking to acquire artisan or mercantile skills. If racist pressure kept blacks from practicing these skills or prevented them from earning the same incomes from their skills as similarly trained whites, then the incentive to apprentice themselves would be greatly diminished.

A critic of this line of argument might be prompted to suggest that a well-functioning market system would, despite racism, provide opportunities for educated or skilled blacks to earn the full income to which this productivity entitled them. While many landlords and white artisans were prejudiced and refused to hire blacks at a fair wage, there were, presumably, some who either were not prejudiced or who were unwilling to subordinate their interest in money to their interest in race. Such individuals would bid the superior worker away with higher wages; and competition between such individuals would soon ensure that incomes were commensurate with productivity.

This line of argument, however, is inapplicable to the southern case for a number of reasons. First, it overlooks the fact that, whatever the employer's racial attitude, he was living within a racist society. A white artisan would not hire a black artisan to assist him, whatever the salary, if doing so would significantly reduce his business from racist clients. Recall from Chapter 2 the South Carolinian who rejected the idea of putting Paschal in charge of his grain mill, since he feared white customers would cease to deal with him. A landowner would not hire a black manager if tradespeople and merchants would refuse to deal with him. Only when blacks were hired to fill "black jobs" and paid "black wages" would the general white population find their employment acceptable.

Second, blacks with superior skills would often discover it was difficult to convince potential employers that they actually possessed such skills. Even if the employer were not himself prejudiced, he would know that virtually every black in the post-Civil War period was in fact illiterate and unskilled. If he shared the opinions of many, he would also believe it unlikely that any black could achieve the capabilities of his white competitors. With such beliefs, it would have seemed a waste of time to assess a black worker's claim to superior skills. He would think that few, if any, would actually pass the test. The southern agricultural system was geared to operate with low-skilled laborers compensated under standard contracts. It made little sense for an individual employer to break away from the standard practice in the hope of attracting superior labor, since the number of such workers seemed so small.

A black worker had little incentive to obtain special skills since he would merely overqualify himself for the only jobs available. The difficulty of breaking into the market for educated and skilled workers – a market where blacks were extremely rare – makes it understandable why so few blacks sought education or special skills: the rewards would not have seemed certain enough and high enough to warrant the expense and effort. This discouragement further reinforced the problem. The absence of any skilled blacks, save the exceptional few, only strengthened the whites' confidence that the average black would never prove capable of advancing beyond a common laborer.

Those whites who competed in the same labor markets with unskilled blacks were similarly disadvantaged. The economic system that limited black education required an agricultural economy structured to utilize uneducated labor. Agriculture in the South generated no demand for skilled or literate workers of any color. Once established, such an agricultural system also left little room for educated whites. As a result, the poor white's incentive to educate himself was suppressed nearly as effectively as the black's.

The economic impact of racism: land tenure

We have already discussed how coercion was directly applied by white supremacists to deny blacks the right of landownership. With this alternative largely closed off, the majority of black farmers initially opted for sharecropping. This system gave them some measure of independence and allowed them to capture at least part of the rewards from superior performance. But southern sharecropping also placed an impediment in the path of further economic advancement for any unskilled laborer, white or black, who entered into it. Sharecropping failed to provide much opportunity to learn new skills by experience. Decisions concerning the crops to be raised, the inputs to be used, and the sale of the crop were all in the hands of the landlord or the merchant, not the tenant. Thus it was difficult for the sharecropper to prepare himself for more independent farming.

If the sharecropper was black, a continuously operating form of racism discouraged him from making use of even this limited experience to advance his skills or to acquire a talent for management. Despite a sharecropper's lack of opportunity to participate in managerial decisions, he might still learn by observation and inquiry. But a black sharecropper would find it difficult to benefit from such acquired knowledge. His present landlord would not alter the terms of the tenure arrangement in the worker's favor unless forced to do so by competitive pressures. But effective competition did not develop. If the black went elsewhere in search of a more attractive offer, he would find that, at best, he was regarded as only an average unskilled black worker. More likely than not, the very fact that a laborer was seeking work would be commonly taken as an indication that he was not reliable. The presumption would be that he was "let go" by his previous landlord, for, had he been a superior worker, he would have been retained.

The prospective employer most likely would be unwilling to incur costs to verify a claim of higher than average ability, and the previous employer would not see it in his own interest to vouch for the worker's productivity. Unable to bargain one employer off against another, the black worker who had gained experience would be exploited. As a consequence, other black workers would not see it as worthwhile to expend the effort necessary to gain skills that would go unrewarded. Therefore, few sharecroppers actually acquired managerial skills, and landowners were seldom wrong when they assumed that sharecroppers did not possess them. The system was self-reinforcing and self-perpetuating.

Whites could also be drawn into this trap. While a white laborer would not be viewed as obviously unskilled, a white who had previously been a sharecropper might have a difficult time arguing for more independence from a new landlord. The landlord would reason that, had the white laborer actually possessed managerial skills, he would have rented for a fixed fee. There is some evidence, which we offer in Table 9.3, that white sharecroppers were as a class less skilled than other white farm operators. White operators of small-scale family farms were generally able to read and write: only about 15 percent of the white owners, for example, were illiterate. Yet among white sharecroppers the illiteracy rate exceeded 25 percent. In sharp

Table 9.3. *Percent of operators of family farms who were illiterate, by race and tenure, Cotton South: 1880*

	Percent illiterate	
Form of tenure	White	Black
Owners	15.1	84.9
Renters	7.7	82.6
Sharecroppers	25.6	76.6
All operators	18.0	79.5

Source: Sample of Cotton South farms drawn from the 1880 Census of Agriculture.

Table 9.4. *Average age of farm operators in eastern Iowa and Cotton South, by tenure: 1880*

Form of tenure	Eastern Iowa			Cotton South		
	Native born	Foreign born	All	White	Black	All
Owners	46.9	48.0	47.4	43.6	45.5	43.9
Tenants	32.9	38.6	36.0	35.7	40.7	38.6
Renters	—	—	—	37.4	41.4	40.0
Sharecroppers	—	—	—	35.2	40.5	38.1
All operators	43.5	45.1	44.3	40.9	41.7	41.2

Source: Eastern Iowa: Seddie Cogswell, Jr., *Tenure, Nativity and Age as Factors in Iowa Agriculture, 1850–1880* (Ames: Iowa State University Press, 1975), p. 31. *Cotton South:* Sample of farms from the 1880 Census of Agriculture; see Appendix G, Section 2, for details.

contrast is the pattern of illiteracy displayed by black operators of family-sized farms. Among blacks illiteracy was lowest among sharecroppers. As we noted in Chapter 5, and as the figures in Table 9.3 reflect, sharecropping attracted the most able black workers.

The effectiveness of the trap created by sharecropping is illustrated by the fact that it did not serve as a stepping stone to more independent farming for most who entered into it. The agricultural ladder from wage labor to tenancy to ownership was much less common in the South and among blacks than it was in the American Midwest during this period.[6] According to the figures for 1880, reproduced in Table 9.4, owner-operators of farms in eastern Iowa were ten to fourteen years older on average than farm tenants, suggesting that tenancy there was a young man's institution. Once he had established himself and prospered as a tenant, he could advance up the ladder to farm ownership. In the Cotton South, by contrast, tenants averaged several years older than their counterparts in Iowa, despite the fact that the average age of southern farm operators was three years younger than that of Iowa farmers. The black tenants of the South were on average five years older than southern white tenants and nearly eight years older than native-born white tenants of eastern Iowa. The difference in age between tenants and owner-operators was also less marked in the South than in the Midwest.

The economic impact of racism: credit

The capital market was also adversely influenced by white appraisals of Negro ability. Lenders required information on a prospective borrower's assets, on his education, and on his ability as a farmer. Race, in each of these instances, seemed to be viewed as pertinent information by white leaders. Without further investigation, the lender might conclude that a black applicant was less creditworthy than a white. The costs of obtaining more accurate information would be high relative to the possible gains to the moneylender. As a result, the loan application of the black would be denied, limited to a lower amount, or offered at a higher interest rate than to whites.

Our study of the South's financial markets suggested that commercial and private banks did not make loans to small farmers regardless of their race and that the furnishing merchants who dominated the rural credit markets did not discriminate in the implicit interest they charged their credit customers. The device by which discrimination was applied, if it was applied, was by restricting the line of credit extended to blacks to something less than that allowed equally situated whites.

The discrimination against black farmers would have been greatest against the owner, inasmuch as he had only his own resources upon which to rely in establishing his credit rating. Moreover, the merchant probably shared the general opinion that an independent black farmer was not likely to be very successful. Black renters and sharecroppers would have fared better when seeking credit, since they could expect some assistance from the landlord, who would stand to gain from a more generous supply of credit to the worker. An increased quantity of capital would increase output per acre and reduce the risk of default.

We do not have direct evidence of discriminatory practices against blacks in the credit market. However, if blacks faced higher interest charges or if merchants rationed credit more severely to blacks than to whites, we should observe lower inputs of capital relative to land and labor on black-operated farms. Table 9.5 confirms this prediction. White farms reported a substantially higher value of farm implements per acre of crops than did black farms, particularly owner-operated family farms.[7]

Since the underlying difficulty, according to our analysis, was that in the minds of whites black skin implied inadequate managerial ability, we should find that the discriminatory effect would be most pronounced with regard to those types of capital that required considerable managerial skill to employ. A good example of this sort of capital input would be the untilled acres on the farm. Such land (including meadows, woodlands, unimproved land, and improved land not in cultivation) provided a very important stream of inputs to the farm, particularly the owner-operated farm. Fallowing was a common technique used to maintain soil quality. Meadows and other forms of unimproved land also provided feed for farm animals. Once again our expectations are confirmed. White-operated farms had, on the average, four times as much untilled land as black-operated farms. Among small family farms the ratio of untilled to tilled acres for white farmers was more than twice the ratio for black farmers, regardless of the form of tenure.

The racial prejudice of the merchant may also have worked to the detri-

Table 9.5. *Inputs of capital on farms, by race and tenure, Cotton South: 1880*

Type of farm[a]	Average value of farm implements per acre reported in crops ($)[b]		Number of untilled acres per tilled acre	
	White	Black	White	Black
Small family farms	1.80	0.79	2.72	0.63
Owned	2.25	1.28	4.01	2.02
Tenanted	0.90	0.66	0.88	0.37
Rented	0.80	0.64	1.65	0.42
Sharecropped	0.93	0.67	0.69	0.34
Other small farms	3.06	0.86	3.83	0.90
Owned	3.64	c	4.77	c
Tenanted	1.39	0.82	1.14	0.90
Medium-scale farms	1.08	0.69	3.92	1.40
Owned	1.15	0.67	4.43	1.58
Tenanted	0.83	0.71	2.23	1.31
Large farms	1.04	c	2.23	c

[a] For definition of farm types, see Appendix G, Section 2.   [b] Figures are only for farms reporting the value of farm implements.   [c] Estimates not reported for cells with fewer than forty sample observations.
Source: Sample of Cotton South drawn from the 1880 Census of Agriculture. Also see Roger Ransom and Richard Sutch, "The Ex-Slave in the Post-Bellum South: A Study of the Economic Impact of Racism in a Market Environment," *Journal of Economic History* 33 (March 1973), Table 2, p. 141.

ment of the black when he sought financing to purchase fertilizer. In the Cotton South 33.5 percent of the white-operated family farms purchased fertilizer; only 21.9 percent of the black-operated family farms did so. This is particularly surprising, since the black-operated farms should have had a greater need for commercial fertilizer. They had a relative shortage of untilled land, and they reported fewer animals that could provide manure. We estimate that on small family farms operated by whites there was an average of 1.9 work animals and 9.9 swine compared with only 1.3 work animals and 5.2 swine on black-operated farms. Black-run farms that did purchase fertilizer reported a higher expenditure per acre than their white counterparts, confirming their greater need for this input. Moreover, we suspect that this is also an indication that the black farmer whose need for commercial fertilizer was moderate or low was in many cases unable to obtain financing for this input.[8]

Discrimination in land tenure and labor arrangements and in the market for capital meant that black families had to support themselves with fewer acres of land than did white families. Table 9.6 illustrates the wide differences in the land-worker ratio reported in the census manuscripts we have

Table 9.6. *Number of acres of cropland per worker on family farms, by race and tenure, Cotton South: 1880*

	Acres of crops per worker[a]	
Form of tenure	White	Black
Owner-operated farms	12.5	6.6
Rented farms	14.5	7.3
Sharecropped farms	11.7	8.0
All farms	12.4	7.5

[a] Figures based only upon farms reporting both acreage and labor.
Source: Sample of Cotton South farms drawn from the 1880 Census of Agriculture.

Table 9.7. *Value of output per worker and value of output per family member on family farms, by type of farm, tenure, and race of farm operator, Cotton South: 1880*

Type of farm	Value of output per worker ($)[a]		Value of output per family member ($)[a]	
	White	Black	White	Black
Small family farms	255.74	159.62	81.35	63.57
Owned	283.70	155.78	88.12	58.11
Tenanted	212.47	160.40	70.87	64.67
Rented	260.19	159.51	88.02	67.63
Sharecropped	200.69	160.81	66.64	63.30
Other small farms	262.78	153.79	143.73	127.94
Owned	262.29	b	149.18	b
Tenanted	264.17	147.23	127.93	117.65

[a] Based only upon farms reporting the value of farm output.   [b] Estimates not reported for cells with fewer than forty sample observations.
Source: Sample of Cotton South farms drawn from the 1880 Census of Agriculture.

examined. While the small differences in labor intensity between renting, sharecropping, and owning were income equalizing, the differences in acreage per worker between whites and blacks were the direct result of discrimination and resulted in lower returns to black labor than to white.[9] Table 9.7 shows that gross returns to families on white farms were about 60 percent above those on black farms. The difference between white and black farms in output per family member is less pronounced; however, this reflects the fact that whites could afford greater leisure and have a smaller fraction of the family at work than could blacks.

Of course, the discrimination practiced against blacks would not have been tolerated by white landowners had their own incomes been adversely affected to any considerable extent. But this was not the case. The value of output per acre on white-operated sharecropped farms was $12.91 and that upon sharecropped farms operated by blacks was $13.30. Since in either case the landlord received approximately one-half the output, his returns per acre would be very nearly the same whether his labor was white or black. The small difference (about 3 percent) might be attributed to the fact that the landlord exercised greater supervision over black tenants than he did over whites and therefore required a slightly higher compensation per acre from black sharecroppers to reward his extra effort with them.

Racism in the capital markets meant that black farmers had less capital, smaller farms, and fewer acres of untilled land than whites. This meant that the typical black farmer was more dependent upon purchased supplies than his white counterpart and was thereby more susceptible to exploitation by the merchant's credit monopoly. If this was the case, we would expect black farmers to have been locked into cotton overproduction more frequently than whites and to be less self-sufficient. Some evidence that this was the case is offered in Table 9.8. Black operators of one-family farms devoted a higher percentage of their acreage to cotton, a lower percentage to crops other than cotton and corn, and reported fewer crops grown.

Emancipation removed the legal distinction between the South's two races, but it left them in grossly unequal economic positions. The blacks lacked assets; they lacked education; they lacked skills. From the outset

Table 9.8. *Percent of reported acres in crops devoted to cotton and to crops other than cotton and corn and average number of different crops reported by family farms, by race and tenure, Cotton South: 1880*

Form of tenure	Percent of reported acreage in cotton[a]		Percent of reported acreage in crops other than cotton and corn[a]		Average number of different crops reported	
	White	Black	White	Black	White	Black
Owned	44.8	51.9	11.8	5.7	4.9	4.2
Rented	50.3	60.2	6.6	3.1	3.9	3.6
Sharecropped	50.4	55.5	7.5	3.4	3.9	3.7
All farms	47.0	56.1	10.1	3.7	4.5	3.8

[a] For cotton farms only.
Source: Sample of Cotton South farms drawn from the 1880 Census of Agriculture.

there were whites who sought to preserve the social and political inequalities between the races, and these white supremacists perceived that to do so they would have to maintain the economic inequalities as well. When necessary, a campaign of violence was launched to prevent blacks from acquiring assets, education, or skills. But the violence was only the most visible way in which racial suppression worked. The most powerful and most damaging way was indirect. Southerners erected an economic system that failed to reward individual initiative on the part of blacks and was therefore ill-suited to their economic advancement. As a result, the inequalities originally inherited from slavery persisted. But there was a by-product of this effort at racial repression: the system tended to cripple all economic growth. It caught up whites in its trap, stifled their initiative, and curtailed their economic progress. Lewis H. Blair, a southerner from a prominent Virginia family, perceived this phenomenon and viewed it as the principal cause of the South's lack of prosperity in 1889: "Like a malignant cancer which poisons the whole system, this degradation [of the Negro] seems to intensify all the other drawbacks under which we labor."[10]

Capital formation and economic growth

Self-sustaining growth in per capita income is possible only if the productivity of labor can be made to grow. While it is often possible to increase productivity in the short-run through exertion of extra effort or by reorganizing production along more efficient lines, such gains cannot be made continuously. The key to self-sustaining growth is the establishment of a constantly growing ratio of capital to labor. With more capital per worker, labor is more productive. Therefore, since investment is the source of capital formation, continuing net investment is essential to maintaining economic growth. Technological progress can also sustain economic growth, but new processes and new technologies invariably are embodied in the form of physical and human capital. In order to apply an advanced technology, investment in new machines and training for the laborers is required. Either way, investment is essential.

Investment must be financed out of current income. What is not consumed can be invested. This simple fact explains why probably the most significant cause of persistent poverty in the world today is poverty itself. When an economy is very poor, it is difficult to save much from current income to finance the increase in capital that might improve incomes in the future. In part this was the South's problem. The poor tenant farmer, exploited by the merchant and held back by an inefficient tenure system, was often in no position to save and invest. On the other hand, if poverty invariably bred poverty, no economy would ever have been able to grow. The fact of the matter is that the South's institutions removed the incentive to invest.

The system of rural merchandising must accept much of the blame for the economic stagnation of the South. The merchants exploited most of the income generated in southern agriculture in excess of the minimum levels requisite for farm life. While they left the farmer with enough to survive, the merchants removed most of the gains from whatever growth took place and thereby removed the incentive that might otherwise have stimulted invest- ment. There seemed little reason for the cotton farmer, white or black, to struggle in order to excel or to deprive his family in order to save. No matter what the outcome of his investments, he could expect to retain little beyond his current level of consumption.

The merchant's monopoly over credit also discouraged growth by mak- ing the effective rate of interest exorbitantly high. It is not surprising that southern farmers made only minimal investments in new capital. Few op- portunities in southern farming were sufficiently profitable that the agricul- tural entrepreneur could afford to borrow at 25, 40, or 60 percent rates of interest to invest in his farm. Capital investment lagged in the rural South, and the monopolistic and inefficient southern capital markets were partly to blame. The failure of southern banking to concern itself with the South's agriculture hindered even owners of substantial landholdings from invest- ing in agricultural improvements.

The significance of the high southern interest rate is difficult to exagger- ate. It was essentially through investment in new capital that output per capita in American agriculture was accelerated so rapidly in the late nine- teenth and early twentieth centuries. Southern farmers, priced out of this market, never took part in the general expansion. They lagged far behind in the adoption of hybrid corn. Cotton was the last major American staple crop to be mechanized. The South was the last region of the country to improve its herds of dairy and meat cattle, swine, and sheep.

Tenancy, and particularly sharecropping, also militated against long-run investment in southern farms. Annual contracting was an essential feature of tenancy. The result may have been, as we have seen, to make tenancy relatively "efficient" to landlords, but it also removed the laborer's long-run commitment to soil productivity. The farm tenant or sharecropper was primarily interested in the immediate harvest; he or she had little incentive to invest time or money in practices without an immediate payoff. Crop rotation, contour plowing, animal husbandry, and scientific farming, with their short-run costs and only long-run benefits, were not adopted by southern tenants.

Not surprisingly, the South led the nation in fertilizer consumption. Fer- tilizer represented an annual expenditure with an immediate payoff the tenant was willing to share. The 1900 Census revealed the dramatic differ- ences in reliance upon commercial fertilizer among regions. Table 9.9 sum- marizes these statistics. In 1899 the Five Cotton States reported expendi- tures of 51 cents per improved acre for commercial fertilizer. This stands in contrast to the national average of only 13 cents and an expenditure of between 3 and 4 cents per acre in the farm states of the North Central and

Western divisions. These comparisons are even more striking when fertilizer consumption is computed as a ratio to the total value of farm output. The heavy expenditures for fertilizer documented in Table 9.10 prove that southern agriculture was not incapable of saving and investing when the returns were viewed to be high enough. But these expenditures did not serve to build up the South's resources, nor did they increase agricultural productivity. Their purpose was to forestall the soil deterioration that would otherwise have depressed productivity. Southern land was nevertheless eroded by wind and water, overcropped with cotton, rarely rejuvenated by fallowing or crop rotation. Commercial fertilizers only allowed farmers working this exhausted land to hold their own.

The world market for cotton

The South's link to the world's cotton market was another important dynamic factor in the story of southern growth and development. Since the early decades of the nineteenth century, the South's economy had been primarily based upon its exports of cotton. During the antebellum era the revenue received from England and the North for cotton crops allowed southerners to purchase the manufactured goods they did not produce. After the Civil War, the South's commitment to cotton was increased even further. Pushed by the merchants' insistence, the farmers of the postemancipation era devoted relatively more resources to cotton than they had before the war.

Southerners who thought about the role King Cotton played in securing the South's prosperity – and most southerners did think about it at one time or another – were of two minds about their monarch. Cotton seemed to be simultaneously a blessing and a curse. Southerners saw much truth in the commonsense explanation offered by political economists which maintained that the South's concentration upon cotton reflected the region's comparative economic advantage. The region's climate and soil gave this natural advantage and made the South the obvious source of the world's supply of textile fiber. Southern farmers could grow cotton and trade it for more of the things they did not produce – manufactured products and agricultural products other than cotton and corn – and in this way enjoy a higher standard of living than if they had established a more balanced economy. The South's failure to diversify agriculture or develop manufacturing could be explained and justified by this reasoning simply by noting that other crops and manufacturing would not have proved as profitable as cotton. The blessing of King Cotton was the prosperity he brought to southern farmers.

Yet many southerners saw as a curse the South's concentration upon cotton production and the dependency upon the world market for cotton this specialization implied. When cotton revenues were high, the South might prosper; when they were low, the South would be depressed. While it is true that the South's fortunes were linked to the world cotton markets, the dependency was an unusual one, since the American producers of cotton

Table 9.9. *Commercial fertilizer expenditures per improved acre and as percent of value of total output, by geographic regions: 1899*

| | Expenditures on commercial fertilizer | |
Region	Per improved acre (cents)	As percent of value of farm output
United States	12.6	1.10
North Atlantic division	40.2	2.35
North Central division	3.3	0.31
Western division	3.9	0.32
Five Cotton States	50.7	4.22
South Carolina	85.4	7.17
Georgia	55.6	5.45
Alabama	36.8	3.33
Mississippi	18.7	1.42
Louisiana	32.3	1.93

Source: U.S. Census Office, Twelfth Census [1900], *Census Reports . . . 1900: Agriculture,* Part I (Washington: GPO, 1902), Table 13, pp. 158–169.

Table 9.10. *Consumption of commercial fertilizers, Four Cotton States: 1875–1891*

| | Thousands of tons | | | |
Year	South Carolina	Georgia	Alabama	Louisiana
1875	—	48.6	—	—
1876	—	55.3	—	—
1877	—	75.8	—	—
1878	—	93.2	—	—
1879	—	85.0	—	—
1880	86.4	119.6	—	—
1881	109.3	152.4	—	—
1882	94.8	125.3	—	—
1883	100.4	125.4	—	—
1884	101.0	151.8	47.7	—
1885	—	170.2	49.1	—
1886	—	160.7	45.4	—
1887	—	166.1	49.3	6.7
1888	125.8	208.0	62.6	8.2
1889	132.0	202.9	71.6	10.2
1890	125.0	288.1	99.8	11.1
1891	130.0	306.7	115.8	11.4

Source: "The Commercial Aspect," *The American Fertilizer* 1 (August 1894), p. 101.

Table 9.11. *Wartime prices of cotton in Liverpool, England: 1860–1865*

Year[a]	Price (pence per pound)		Thousands of bales	
	Nominal	Deflated[b]	Exports of cotton from U.S.	Total imports of cotton into U.K.
1860–1861	5.97	4.98	3,774	3,376
1861–1862	8.50	7.39	3,128	3,036
1862–1863	18.37	15.31	645	1,445
1863–1864	22.46	18.56	11	1,932
1864–1865	27.17[c]	22.83	27	2,587

[a] The commercial year beginning September 1 and ending August 31 is used. [b] Gavin Wright deflated Watkins's Liverpool price using the Rousseaux price index (1879–1881 = 100). [c] The highest price paid for cotton in Liverpool in the 1864–1865 year was 31.25 pence.
Source: Nominal Liverpool prices and U.S. exports to all destinations: James L. Watkins, U.S. Department of Agriculture, "Production and Price of Cotton for 100 Years," *USDA Miscellaneous Bulletin,* Number 9 (Washington: GPO, 1895), Tables 7 and 8, pp. 10–11. *Deflated price:* Gavin Wright, "Cotton Competition and the Post-Bellum Recovery of the American South," *Journal of Economic History* 34 (September 1974), Table 1, p. 611. *Imports into United Kingdom from all sources:* Thomas Ellison, *The Cotton Trade of Great Britain* (New York: August Kelly, 1968), Table 1, originally published in 1886.

actually dominated the supply side of that market.[11] In principle, this dominance could have been employed to the South's advantage. No other country could come close to matching the South's ability to produce fiber efficiently in the volume necessary to supply the world's textile factories. The South might have dictated world cotton prices and thereby controlled the income generated by its production. The potential was obviously there. During the Civil War, when a Confederate embargo together with a Union blockade effectively shut off the supply of southern cotton, the world price soared. Table 9.11 presents statistics on average cotton prices in England during the war. In 1864 the Liverpool price of cotton was four and one-half times the price in 1860.

These price movements during the cotton famine suggest that the South might have benefited through a policy of restricting output during "normal" times. Gavin Wright has estimated that the nature of the demand for American cotton in the antebellum period was such that any price increase stimulated by a reduction in supply would have been approximately proportional in magnitude to the decline in output.[12] This means that a restriction in supply would have increased prices sufficiently so that the total revenue generated by cotton sales would remain largely unaffected despite the reduced volume of production. There would have been a large gain, nevertheless, from adopting a policy of output reduction. Resources would be freed from cotton production for use in other pursuits (such as food production and manufacturing) without reducing the revenue generated from cotton. Moreover, since the same total revenue would have been generated by a reduced quantity of inputs, the profit margin on cotton production would have risen.

Notwithstanding these potential gains, the South did not take control of the production or of the marketing of its staple, either before or after the war. Cotton was produced by hundreds of thousands of separate producers, each one making independent decisions on production, and it was marketed by thousands of separate merchants and brokers scattered throughout the South. The potential power the South's geographic and climatic advantage bestowed was never exploited. The world cotton price upon which southern fortunes depended so heavily was left to seek its own level.

Rather than reducing output and raising cotton prices, the economic institutions adopted by southerners after the Civil War had the effect of increasing output above, and lowering prices below, what they might otherwise have been. Because the price of cotton per pound was lower, the total revenue generated by the larger output was not substantially greater.[13] The obvious loss to the South was that resources were being used to produce cotton that might have been used elsewhere. While it is true that from the point of view of any single (nonexploited) farm operator, cotton seemed more profitable than diversified agriculture, and agriculture seemed more profitable than manufacturing, this view cannot be validly generalized to the entire economy. For the South as a whole, cotton specialization was *not* more profitable than diversified agriculture, and an agrarian economy was not superior to an economy with a balance between agriculutre and industry. The curse of King Cotton was the lack of prosperity he imposed upon the South.[14]

The South's dependence upon cotton had the added disadvantage of making the southern economy vulnerable to fluctuations in cotton prices, which from year to year were highly variable. In Figure 9.1 we have plotted the wholesale price of cotton in New York (deflated by a wholesale price index for all commodities to remove the effects of inflation and deflation in the general price level).[15] Actually the impact of price fluctuations is exaggerated by the price statistics presented in the figure. When the crop was poor, the resulting high price helped to maintain total revenues; low prices tended to correspond with high volumes of production.

Adverse long-run trends in world cotton demand posed a more serious threat than the short-run fluctuations. Throughout the postemancipation era, the demand for cotton was generally expanding.[16] However, the expansion was not always uniform and the total world supply of cotton was also growing. As a result relative price trends developed that did not always favor the South. For example, between 1869 and 1877 cotton prices fell faster than other wholesale prices. This trend was reversed in the 1880s, but it turned down again after 1890. A rising trend favored the South after 1898. These cycles in the terms of trade were beyond the influence of any single farmer, and as individual incomes rose and fell in step with these

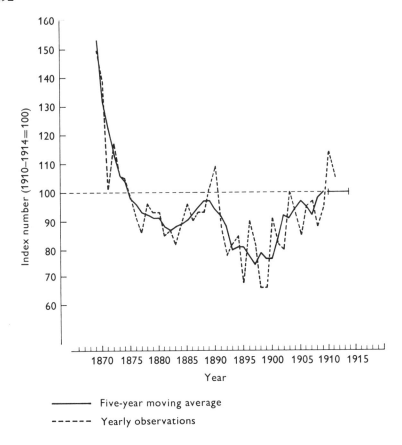

Figure 9.1 Deflated wholesale price of cotton: 1869 to 1911. (*Source:* Note 15.)

movements, the farmer came to view the rule of King Cotton as capricious.

The major impediment to economic development posed by the South's comparative advantage in cotton was not, however, the sensitivity of the southern economy to the cotton market or the capricious nature of cotton prices. Rather the curse of King Cotton that worried southerners the most was the lack of industrialization and economic diversification implied by a single-minded devotion to a cash crop. This concern was certainly justified. As economists today recognize, there can be little hope for sustained economic growth in an exclusively agricultural society.

Such an extractive economy has its natural limits. Increasing the quantity of land per worker is necessary if the productivity of agricultural labor is to be continuously expanded.[17] Yet, with a constant or growing population, the land-labor ratio can be increased (once all the arable land is taken up) only by removing labor from agriculture. In other words, if an agricultural economy is to grow continuously, it must either have a growing industrial sector to absorb the released labor or a continuing outmigration of labor to some other region. The South of the late nineteenth century was without a growing industrial sector and without significant outmigration. There were no employment opportunities for those who would be displaced by agricultural productivity advances.

The advocates of a New South argued that a manufacturing sector would stimulate growth and modernization of the southern economy and that agriculture would share in the expanding prosperity at the same time it released the labor necessary for industrial production. But appeals to develop manufacturing went unheeded despite the logic of the argument. Even without the stimulation of an expanding industrial sector, modernization and economic development might still have come to the South from another direction. If the agricultural sector had been able to improve labor productivity on its own, the expansion in agricultural incomes might have stimulated industrialization. But as we have already seen, agricultural productivity growth was held in check by the impediments to capital formation. The South had chosen its King, but Cotton had failed the South.

The South's link to the national economy

A remaining puzzle in the history of southern agriculture is the fact that the South's post-Civil War stagnation coincided with an era of rapid economic growth in the North and West. The period between the Civil War and World War I was a time of rapid development in the rest of the country. Table 9.12 presents estimates of the average per capita gross national product of the United States from 1869 to 1906. In Table 9.13 the rate of growth of national output is contrasted with the rate of growth of rural southern gross crop output per capita. As can be seen, national output per capita was considerably above rural southern crop output per capita throughout the entire period, and it grew at over two and one-third times the rate of southern agricultural output.

Regardless of the explanation for the slow rate of southern growth, these divergent trends within a unified national economy are surprising. If labor had been free to move to its most remunerative employment, the large gaps between southern and northern incomes should have attracted southern labor to the North. Despite a region's absolute advantage in the production of a particular commodity, divergent trends in productivity growth should ultimately shift the comparative advantage away from the depressed sector. Thus the relative backwardness of southern agriculture should have ultimately led to the development of a southern manufacturing sector.

The fact that neither a significant outmigration to the North nor a viable manufacturing sector in the South developed during the nineteenth century can only be explained by barriers to the mobility of factors of production.

Table 9.12. *Per capita gross national product of United States and per capita gross crop output of Five Cotton States: 1869–1906 by quinquennium*

| Quinquennium | Midyear point | Annual average per capita gross national product, 1902–1906 prices ($) | | Annual average per capita gross crop output, Cotton States, 1899–1908 prices ($)[a] |
		Kuznets's concept	Department of Commerce concept	
1869–1873	1871	116	—	39
1872–1876	1874	132	—	41
1877–1881	1879	170	—	44
1882–1886	1884	194	—	47
1887–1891	1889	202	—	52
1889–1893	1891	211	220	52
1892–1896	1894	—	226	52
1897–1901	1899	—	258	55
1902–1906	1904	—	296	57

[a] The southern crop output is divided by the rural population of the Five Cotton States.
Source: U.S. Bureau of the Census, *Historical Statistics of the United States, Colonial Times to 1957* (Washington: GPO, 1960), Series F-4, p. 139, and Appendix F, Table F.3.

Table 9.13. *Annual rates of growth in per capita value of United States gross national product and gross crop output of Five Cotton States: 1869–1906*

Mid-quinquennium to mid-quinquennium	United States gross national product (%)	Gross southern crop output (%)[b]
1871–1874	4.43	1.85
1874–1879	5.18	1.33
1879–1884	2.72	1.31
1884–1889	0.74	2.28
1889–1894	1.60[a]	−0.18
1894–1899	2.70	1.04
1899–1904	2.78	0.83
1871–1891	3.03	1.43
1891–1904	2.29	0.77
1871–1904	2.74[a]	1.17

[a] Calculated as the weighted geometric mean of the pre-1891 and post-1891 growth ratios.
[b] The southern crop output is divided by the rural population of the Five Cotton States.
Source: Table 9.12.

Labor was not attracted to the North nor capital to the South. We believe that, once again, the rigidities and racial barriers built into southern economic institutions are to blame.

Southern labor, particularly black labor, was largely illiterate. It was therefore difficult for black workers to learn about economic opportunities elsewhere. Without correspondence (not to mention remittances) from blacks who had successfully migrated North, it is not surprising that few southern blacks set out into what must have seemed a largely unknown country. Southern labor, particularly black labor, was poor, and migration was expensive as well as risky. Not only the costs of transportation, but also sufficient income to support the family during the move and the search for new employment would have to be saved in advance. To southern cotton farmers, who were often unable to save at all in their poor and exploitive economy, the costs of migration must have appeared enormous.

To many of these southerners, agriculture was the only profession they knew, and it was particularly expensive to move into a new agricultural region, since the income from crops planted on a new farm would not be forthcoming until at least a full season had passed. To move from southern to midwestern or western agriculture would have required a year's support for provisions. The situation would have been less difficult for those seeking work as wage laborers in northern cities. Although the prospect of industrial employment must have seemed more uncertain, it was no coincidence that when blacks did leave the South it was primarily to northern cities, not to northern agriculture, that they went.

If illiteracy, poverty, and indebtedness kept labor in the South, it was the unsuitability of southern financial institutions that kept capital in the North. Despite the fact that the physical rate of return to investment in the South was high, the inability to capture the full rewards from investment prevented a flow of capital from equalizing the return to investment in the South with the lower return that could be earned in the rest of the country's financial markets.[18]

The close of the postemancipation era

An outmigration of black labor from the Cotton South ultimately did take place. Figure 9.2 presents estimates of the gross outmigration of native nonwhites from the Five Cotton States to nonsouthern states for each census decade from the 1880s to the 1920s.[19] Throughout the first three decades there was a small but growing migration to the North and West. But it was not until after 1910 that the migration reached impressive proportions. Since there were approximately 4.6 million nonwhites in the Five Cotton States, nearly 15 percent of the black population must have left the Cotton South between 1910 and 1930. This black exodus was one of the largest migrations in human history.

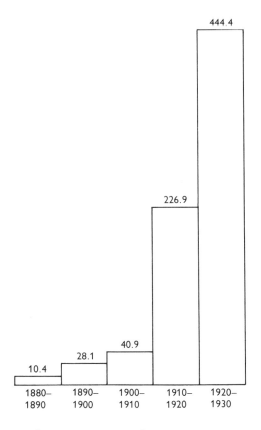

Figure 9.2 Native non-white outmigration (in thousands) to non-Southern states from the Five Cotton States: 1880 to 1930, by decades. (*Source*: William Edward Vickery, "The Economics of the Negro Migration, 1900-1960." Ph.D. dissertation, University of Chicago, December 1969, Table 42, p. 173.)

The outmigration of blacks did not accelerate until after the arrival of the boll weevil. The exodus began first in Louisiana, then spread to Mississippi and Alabama, and finally to Georgia and South Carolina. The eastward spread of the migratory impulse roughly corresponded with the eastward march of the boll weevil. There are other reasons, as well, to suggest that the post-1910 Negro exodus was stimulated by events and forces external to the southern economic system. The American involvement in World War I, the reduction in foreign immigration that produced labor shortages in the northern urban areas, and improvements in interregional transportation were undoubtedly all factors of importance. But none of these factors worked from within. It required a series of shocks from without to awaken the southern economy from the stupor into which it had fallen.

Changes other than the black migration also disturbed the economic quiet of the South. Here again it is worth noting that by and large they were

forces that impinged from the outside. Developments in local rural transportation, particularly the improvement to local roads induced by the inven-
tion of the automobile, threatened the merchants' previously secure territorial monopoly. The U.S. Post Office's inauguration of rural free delivery in
1896 and the establishment of parcel post service in 1913 facilitated the rise
of mail-order houses, most notably Sears-Roebuck and Montgomery
Ward, thus providing southern farmers with alternatives to the local furnishing merchant. The establishment of the postal savings system in 1910
provided a haven for savings in rural areas ill served by the South's urban-
oriented commercial banks. The institutional changes induced by these
developments had the effect of opening opportunities, increasing competition, and improving the economic condition of rural southerners. But there
was an ugly side to the changes in this period as well.

The economic system that was at last yielding to the pressures of change
had done more in its time than stifle economic progress. It had also served
the ends of race control. By defining a subordinate position for blacks and
by limiting black advancement, the postemancipation economy had served
white supremacists by keeping the Negro "in his place." The time elapsed
since the Civil War had done nothing to weaken or modify the racism
inherited from slavery. Indeed, a case can be made that the economic and
social system that arose reinforced those racist beliefs. The system muted
the economic incentives of blacks and preserved the economic inequalities
they inherited from slavery. The uncritical white racist needed no more
evidence than the lack of black progress to establish the inferiority of the
Negro race.

Once the economic system was threatened, the social structure based
upon white supremacy was also threatened. Perhaps it is significant that
legally enforced racial segregation appeared during the initial decades of the
twentieth century. Not until after the economic system began to lose its
power to ensure that the racial "inferiority" of blacks would remain well
established did southern states begin to pass Jim Crow laws. The first laws
of this type adopted in the South were those applying to railroad passen-
gers, and they did not come to South Carolina until 1898, to North Carolina
until 1899, and to Virginia until 1900. Separation of the races in railroad
stations, on street cars, and on steamboats was a twentieth-century innovation. Separate entrances to theaters, separate toilet facilities and drinking
fountains, ticket windows for "whites only" and "colored" were likewise
products of the period between 1900 and 1918. It was in 1915 that South
Carolina passed a law prohibiting black and white workers from sharing
the same room, entrance, exit, doorway, stairway, or window at the same
time and from using the same "lavatories, toilets, drinking water buckets,
pails, cups, dippers or glasses" at any time. Southern states established
separate hospitals, separate prisons, separate mental institutions, and separate orphanages. State parks and state colleges denied blacks admission to
facilities established for whites.[20]

One kind of freedom

In 1865 emancipation from chattel slavery permitted black Americans one kind of freedom. No one would deny that this freedom was a significant and meaningful one. With their freedom blacks advanced their material income and their economic welfare. They gained a degree of independence that was significantly greater than they were allowed in bondage. Yet this freedom was incomplete. Unlike the indentured servants of Colonial America, blacks received no freedom dues: land redistribution was aborted and the blacks were forced to begin their lives as free men and women without money, without tools, without work animals, without assets of any kind. Their economic, political, and social freedom was under constant attack by the dominant white society determined to preserve racial inequalities. The economic institutions established in the postemancipation era effectively operated to keep the black population a landless agricultural labor force, operating tenant farms with a backward and unprogressive technology. What little income was generated in excess of the bare essentials of life was exploited by monopolistic credit merchants.

In the early years of this century, the kind of freedom permitted blacks began to change. On the surface it was diminished; the color line was written into the laws and the attack on the political, economic, and social rights of blacks was intensified. But these devices coincided with, indeed may have been a reaction to, an increasing exercise of economic opportunity. Thus, the new kind of freedom was superior to the old in at least one respect: it was more amenable to black economic advancement and the development of black leadership.

Not until very recently, during the 1960s, did the elaborate system of racial segregation, degradation, and repression established in the early 1900s come under an attack sufficiently aggressive to force it into retreat. It is significant to our story that this attack was launched and largely carried out by black Americans themselves. Jim Crow had arisen as a form of race repression to replace an economic system that had earlier stifled black initiative, ensured black poverty, and demoralized black leaders. Despite the blatant hostility that motivated the Jim Crow movement and despite the viciousness of the legal devices used against blacks, blacks acquired education, literacy, and skills. In time some blacks were able to become landowners and many more left agriculture for urban occupations, particularly in the North. Slowly black incomes began to improve, black initiative was stimulated, and black leaders began to challenge the persistent white resistance and the legal restrictions that impeded further progress. The change that came to the South in the early years of this century set in motion the first significant forces for black advancement since emancipation.

Today, little remains to remind Americans of postemancipation economic institutions. Sharecropping has virtually disappeared from the South. Today more cotton is grown in California and Arizona than in the Five Cotton States put together. And now it is planted, cultivated, and harvested, not by black labor, but by machine. The rural merchant is gone, replaced by the supermarket and made unnecessary by the automobile. The rigidities, the exploitation, and the inefficiencies of the post-Civil War economy have vanished. Many see in the South of today a belated realization of the hopes for the New South that animated so many southern newspaper writers a century ago. The forces we believe explain the povery of the South in 1900 seem to have disappeared.

All but one. The legacy of slavery persists. Racism, racial phobia, racial prejudice, racial animosities still survive. They continue to poison our society and to weaken and distort our economy. The result of the economic advancements achieved by blacks since World War I is not, as we know all too well today, parity with whites. The progress made to date has been painfully slow. At every step it has been resisted by racists, impeded by the force of law, and held back by economic institutions that continue to discriminate on the basis of race. The kind of freedom permitted black Americans today is still incomplete. The promise of freedom and equality that accompanied emancipation remains as yet unfulfilled despite the lapse of more than a century. Surely the time has finally come to make good on this promise.

STATISTICAL APPENDIXES

Immobility, or even that slow advance which is perceptible to laborious statisticians only, and is unfelt and unseen by the masses, produces discouragement and discontent.

> U.S. Senate Committee on Agriculture and Forestry, "Present Conditions of Cotton-Growers of the United States Compared with Previous Years," Senate Report Number 986, 53rd Congress, 3rd Session (Washington: GPO, 1895), 1, p. iv.

CONSTRUCTION OF INCOME AND WELFARE ESTIMATES: 1859–1899

Calculation of the exploitation rate of slaves: 1859

We define the *rate of exploitation* as the ratio of the income expropriated from the slave population each year to the total value of the slave-produced output. The income expropriated is the total income produced by slaves less the value of the food, clothing, housing services, and other consumption items provided by their owners. We denote the rate of expropriation by ϵ, labor's share of total output by the fraction α, total output by Q, and the value of slave consumption by M. Thus:

$$\epsilon = \frac{\alpha Q - M}{\alpha Q}$$

In what follows we treat Q and M on an annual per slave basis. The value of labor's share, αQ, is equal to the gross value of all output produced per slave (say, on a cotton plantation) less the income properly attributable to other factors of production (principally land, work stock, and supervisory personnel).

For the purposes of our calculation we have made estimates of α, Q, and M for an average farm in the Cotton South and for a "typical cotton plantation" both in 1859. The primary source is a sample of 2,588 slave farms drawn from the enumerators' manuscripts of the 1860 Census of Agriculture. This sample was collected for the purposes of an unrelated series of studies by William Parker and Robert Gallman. However, it is well suited for our purposes since it represents a random sample of approximately 1.7 percent of all the farms located in the 413 counties that produced at least 1,000 bales of cotton in 1859. The 2,588 slaveowners together reported owning 40,576 slaves.[1]

Estimating farm output per slave

We have used the Parker-Gallman sample to estimate the average output of cotton and other farm products sold, consumed by resident whites, or fed to slaves. These estimates of output per slave are presented in Table A.1. Farm output fed to farm animals or used as seed is excluded as an intermediate product. So as not to exaggerate the estimate of the exploitation rate, we have deliberately underestimated the total output. When estimating deductions for animal feed, we deliberately chose high estimates of the feeding requirement. We have also restricted the total to include only fifteen farm products. Omitted products, had they been included, would raise the total output and the estimated rate of exploitation.

The value of housing services consumed by both whites and slaves is included in the total income estimates reported in Table A.1. In addition, we have estimated the value of the increase in livestock inventories from the average value of livestock per slave reported in the Parker-Gallman sample, based on the assumption that the livestock-slave ratio remained constant.

We have separately estimated the value of total output for plantations with fifty-one or more slaves[2] as well as for all slave farms in the sample. Since our estimates of the other parameters necessary to compute the exploitation rate are probably more reliable for large plantations than for the average of all farms, we feel this class of farms will yield the more precise estimate of the exploitation rate.[3]

Our estimate of the value of housing services, reported in Table A.2, is not directly based on the Parker-Gallman sample. Rather, we have made a number of assumptions based on contemporary accounts of living conditions on southern farms. Each farm with from one to fifty slaves was assumed to have a residence for the farm operator worth $200. Farms with fifty-one or more slaves were assumed to have one or more houses for white residents worth an aggregate of $400. We feel these estimates are quite conservative. Martin cites the *Southern Cultivator* for 1859 as describing a four-room, one-story wooden "cottage, suitable for a small planter or overseer" as worth $650 to $700.[4] We have lowered this figure substantially in light of the rude descriptions of some slaveowners' houses offered by Gray, Martin, and Olmsted.[5] For slaves, we assumed a value of housing of $10 per person. This implies that the average slave cabin was worth $50 to $60 and that the average farm possessed slave dwellings worth a total of $157.[6]

The value of the stock of dwelling units was converted to an estimated value of services produced per slave by assuming a 7 percent return on capital (see below) and depreciation rates based upon estimated half-lives for buildings that seemed roughly consistent with the description of these buildings offered by Gray, Martin, and Sutch.[7] Table A.2 also presents the estimated value of services per slave derived from the implicit rent on land and buildings other than dwellings and the implicit rent from farm implements and machinery reported by farms in the Parker-Gallman sample.

Estimating labor's share

Not all the output produced on slave farms is properly attributed to slave labor. Some fraction represents the contribution of nonlabor factors of production: land, work stock, farm capital, and supervisory personnel. There are two approaches to this problem of estimating labor's share. One in-

Table A.1. *Calculation of value of total output per slave on all slave farms and on large plantations: 1859*

Farm product	Unit	Output per slave — All farms	Output per slave — Plantations with 51 or more slaves	Percent deductions for — Seed	Percent deductions for — Feed	Price per unit ($)	Net output per slave ($) — All farms	Net output per slave ($) — Plantations with 51 or more slaves
Staples								
Cotton	400-lb bale	2.19	2.46	—	—	40.00	87.44	98.47
Molasses[a]	Gallon	3.90	5.35	—	—	0.333	1.30	1.78
Tobacco	Pound	5.01	0.91	—	—	0.078	0.39	0.07
Rice	Pound	6.02	7.48	10	—	0.020	0.11	0.13
Food crops								
Corn	Bushel	66.05	45.15	5	b	0.84	—	27.27
Meat products	Dollar	19.13	9.61	—	—	—	19.13	9.61
Sweet potatoes	Bushel	10.68	5.17	29.5	—	0.50	4.15	2.80
Irish potatoes	Bushel	0.93	0.43	18.0	—			
Wheat[c]	Bushel	3.29	1.21	14.5	—	1.30	3.66	1.34
Dairy products[d]	Hundredweight	3.49	1.52	—	—	0.83	2.90	1.26
Garden products	Dollar	1.00	0.93	—	—	—	1.00	0.93
Cowpeas, beans	Bushel	3.77	2.74	40	34.8	0.60	0.57	0.41
Other outputs								
Manufactured products	Dollar	2.04	0.70				2.04	0.70
Housing services[e]	Dollar	2.92	1.91				2.92	1.91
Increase in livestock inventory[f]	Dollar	1.94	1.25				1.94	1.25
Total							127.55	147.93

Notes and sources for Table A-1 are on pp. 206–7.

Notes and sources for Table A.1

[a] Molasses was the only sugar product reported in any quantity by farms included in the Parker-Gallman sample.

[b] Deductions for corn fed to animals were computed using Gallman's feeding requirements rather than as a percentage of the crop. See source notes below.

[c] Wheat was the only small grain crop of significance. We assume that the small amounts of oats, barley, rye, and buckwheat grown were fed to animals.

[d] Because our price quotation for dairy products is for hundredweights of "fluid milk equivalents," we have converted the butter output per slave to fluid milk equivalents using the assumption that 3 pounds of butter required 100 pounds of milk. This ratio was typical in southern states in 1889. (Richard Sutch, "The Treatment Received by American Slaves: A Critical Review of the Evidence Presented in Time on the Cross," Explorations in Economic History 12 [October 1975], p. 373). Cheese production was trivial, and milk production was not reported, although it is doubtful that much fluid milk was sold or consumed on southern farms.

[e] The value of housing services is the sum of the estimated value of housing services provided by dwellings for whites and slaves reported in Table A.2.

[f] The value of the increase in livestock inventories is estimated from the average value of livestock per slave in the Parker-Gallman sample (see Table A.3) and the assumption that the livestock population increased at the same rate as the increase in the slave population (2.15 percent per year); see Richard Sutch, "The Profitability of Slavery – Revisited," Southern Economic Journal 31 (April 1965), p. 367. This would keep the livestock-slave ratio constant.

Source: Outputs were computed from the Parker-Gallman sample of farms. Crop outputs are for the crop year 1859. Number of slaves and farm animals enumerated are for June 1860. We have adjusted these populations back to 1859 using an assumed growth rate of 2.15 percent (see note f).

Seed and feed deductions were estimated as follows:

Rice: In Appendix E, Table E.1, we report the seeding requirements for rice at 180 pounds per acre. Gray reports that 1,800 pounds per acre was considered a good crop in 1791 and that in 1857 the Savannah River region averaged 45 to 55 bushels per acre. At 40 pounds a bushel, this is a yield of 1,800 to 2,200 pounds per acre (Lewis Cecil Gray, History of Agriculture in the Southern United States to 1860, 2 vols. [Washington: Carnegie Institution, 1933], 2, p. 730). We take 1,800 pounds as an average yield since the Cotton South farmers were less productive on average than the Savannah River region plantations.

Corn: Robert Gallman assumes a 5 percent seeding requirement for corn ("Self-Sufficiency in the Cotton Economy of the Antebellum South," Agricultural History 44 [January 1970], p. 10, note 12). We used Gallman's feeding requirements for milch cows, sheep, and other cattle of 8.99, 0.6, and 2.6 bushels of corn per head, respectively (p. 10, note 13). Gallman argues that these estimates are upper bounds (p. 11) and they exceed the standards we estimate for 1880 in Appendix E. As we note in that appendix, however, Gallman's feeding requirements for horses, mules, and oxen may not be upper bounds. For this reason, we have employed a feeding allowance of 50 bushels for horses and oxen and 42 bushels for mules. See Table E.4. Following Sutch, we estimate that swine required 7 bushels per year ("Treatment," p. 379). Using these feeding standards, we estimate that 65.85 bushels of corn were required per slave to feed the livestock on all farms and 10.43 bushels on farms with 51 or more slaves. These feeding standards produced a small corn deficit for "all farms." For the purposes of our table we allocate the entire deficit. Also note that we allocate the entire crops of oats, barley, buckwheat, hay, and rye to animal feed, as well as fractions of the potato, cowpea, and wheat crops.

Sweet potatoes: Sutch, "Treatment," p. 374.

Irish potatoes: Sutch, "Treatment," p. 374.

Wheat: Marvin W. Towne and Wayne D. Rasmussen, "Farm Gross Product and Gross Investment in the Nineteenth Century," National Bu-

Sources for Table A.1 (cont.)

reau of Economic Research, Trends in the American Economy in the Nineteenth Century, (Princeton: Princeton University Press, 1960), p. 294.

Cowpeas and beans: Sutch, "Treatment," pp. 376–377.

Prices of crops were estimated as follows:

Cotton: The weighted yearly average wholesale price for cotton in New Orleans for the crop year 1859 was 10.8 cents per pound (Gray, History of Agriculture, 2, p. 1027). Alfred Conrad and John Meyer estimate the cost of transportation to New Orleans and marketing costs of from 0.7 cent to 0.8 cent per pound ("The Economics of Slavery in the Ante Bellum South," Journal of Political Economy 66 [April 1958], p. 105). Accordingly, we put the farmgate price at 10.0 cents per pound.

Molasses: The range of New Orleans wholesale price of molasses in 1859 is reported for each quarter in Charles E. Seagrave, "The Southern Negro Agricultural Worker: 1850–1870" (Ph.D. thesis, Stanford University, 1971), p. 112. The price used is the simple average of the midrange for each of the four quarters.

Tobacco: The wholesale price of leaf tobacco in New Orleans for 1859 is reported in Gray on the authority of George R. Taylor (Gray, History of Agriculture, 2, p. 1038).

Rice: Gray reports the export price of rice in 1859 at 3.2 cents per pound (History of Agriculture, 2, p. 1030) and notes that 162 pounds of paddy rice is equivalent to 100 pounds of milled rice (p. 730). This suggests a farmgate price of 2 cents per pound for paddy rice.

Corn: The quoted price for corn is a simple average of the local price of corn in Virginia and the wholesale price in New Orleans as reported by

Gray (History of Agriculture, 2, p. 1039). The Virginia corn price was taken by Gray from Arthur G. Peterson, "Historical Study of Prices Received by Producers of Farm Products in Virginia, 1801–1927," Virginia Agricultural Experiment Station, Technical Bulletin, Number 37 (March 1929), p. 168.

Irish and sweet potatoes: Potato prices are difficult to obtain, probably because there was little market for potatoes. In 1848 the U.S. Patent Office reported sweet potato prices ranging from 37.5 cents to $1 per bushel (Annual Report of the Commissioner of Patents for the Year 1848: Agriculture [Washington: Wendell & Van Benthuysen, 1849], p. 655). Towne and Rasmussen use a figure of 48 cents a bushel for "1860" for the nation as a whole and claim it is based upon Peterson's Virginia price of Irish potatoes (Towne and Rasmussen, "Farm Gross Product," p. 303). However, their source citation is in error. Peterson gives no potato prices for years prior to 1867 ("Prices Received"). In the 1880s potatoes were approximately 60 to 75 percent of corn prices, which suggests the 50 cents per bushel price employed in our calculations. We used the same price for Irish potatoes for lack of a better estimate.

Wheat: We have used the average annual local price of wheat in Virginia reported by Peterson for 1859 ("Prices Received," p. 168).

Dairy products: Towne and Rasmussen, "Farm Gross Product," p. 289.

Cowpeas and beans: Prices for cowpeas are difficult to find. Scattered reports by the U.S. Patent Office suggest that cowpeas sold for somewhat more than potatoes and less than corn. This suggests a price of 60 cents a bushel. This is somewhat lower than Towne and Rasmussen's 73 cents a bushel for peas and beans, which they based on 1900 prices for peas extrapolated backward by changes in Wisconsin dried pea prices (Towne and Rasmussen, "Farm Gross Product," p. 304).

Table A.2. *Estimates of value of, depreciation rate of, and implicit rent derived from residential structures, land, and farm implements and machinery on slave farms and plantations, per slave: 1860*

Type of asset	Average value per slave ($)		Rate of depreciation (%)[a]	Estimated value of services per slave ($)[b]	
	All farms	Plantations with 51 or more slaves		All farms	Plantations with 51 or more slaves
Farm lands and buildings[c]	498.77	559.30	—	—	—
Less					
Dwellings for whites[d]	13.48	4.70	4.5	1.55	0.54
Slave cabins	10.00	10.00	6.7	1.37	1.37
Land and outbuildings[e]	475.29	544.60	2.7	46.10	52.83
Farm implements and machinery[c]	21.71	24.24	15.0	4.78	5.33

[a] Rates of depreciation were calculated to give an estimated half-life for dwellings for whites of 15 years, for slave cabins of 10 years, and for land of 25 years. The rate of depreciation for farm implements is consistent with that we have estimated for southern agriculture circa 1870 (Roger Ransom and Richard Sutch, "The Impact of the Civil War and of Emancipation on Southern Agriculture," *Explorations in Economic History* 12 [January 1975], pp. 19–20) and is above the 10 percent assumed by Robert Fogel and Stanley Engerman (*Time on the Cross*, 2 vols. [Boston: Little, Brown & Co., 1974], 2, p. 133).

[b] Calculated assuming an interest rate of 7.0 percent and the rate of depreciation given in the table. See text for a justification of a 7 percent rate of interest.

[c] From the Parker-Gallman sample.

[d] Average value per slave is based on an assumed value of $200 per farm for farms with 1 to 50 slaves and $400 per farm for plantations with 51 or more slaves.

[e] The average value of the land and outbuildings per slave, which we compute as a residual, is generally consistent with Martin Primack's estimate of the ratio of the values of land to buildings in 1860 for the southeast and south central regions ("Farm Construction as a Use of Farm Labor in the United States, 1850–1910," *Journal of Economic History* 25 [March 1965], Table 2, p. 116). His ratio, applied to the value of farmlands and buildings reported in the Parker-Gallman sample, gives a figure 13 percent lower than our estimate for land and outbuildings. The difference is easily explained, since our estimate includes the value of outbuildings, whereas his does not.

volves the estimation of α directly through the specification and estimation of a production function; the other approach involves calculating the value of labor's share (αQ) indirectly as a residual.

Fogel and Engerman have employed the Parker-Gallman sample to estimate α directly by regression analysis. They report a labor share of 58 percent.[8] This estimate would imply that the income produced by slave labor amounted to $73.98 on all farms and $85.80 on large plantations. For a number of reasons, however, we have chosen to employ a different procedure to estimate these numbers. In the first place, we have reservations concerning the legitimacy of specifying the southern agricultural production function with the Cobb-Douglas form, which Fogel and Engerman employed. Furthermore, Fogel and Engerman describe their results as "quite preliminary" and "quite tentative."[9] Finally, the alternative procedure gives a lower estimate of output per slave and therefore yields a more conservative estimate of the exploitation rate. The procedure we employ involves estimating the value of the output attributable to all other factors of production and then computing the value of labor's share as a residual.

Beginning with Conrad and Meyer, a number of attempts have been made to estimate the value of all capital (land, work stock, farm implements) per slave typical of cotton production. In addition to Conrad and Meyer's estimates, those of Saraydar, Sutch, and Foust and Swan are the most important.[10] Our investigation of these estimates has convinced us that they rely on too fragmentary a data base to be reliable.[11] Our own estimates, detailed in Table A.3, are taken from the Parker-Gallman sample.

In Table A.4 we present our estimate of the value of labor's share obtained by subtracting from the value of output the charges for interest, depreciation, and supervisory costs. Ever since Conrad and Meyer first studied the issue, it has been acknowledged that "southerners and northerners alike considered 6–8 per cent a reasonable rate of return."[12] Since the

Table A.3. *Value of capital per slave, Parker-Gallman sample: 1860*

	Value per slave ($)	
Form of capital	All slave farms	Plantations with 51 or more slaves
Farmland and buildings[a]	498.77	559.30
Implements and machinery	21.71	24.24
Livestock	90.00	58.27
Total	610.48	641.81

[a] Includes value of residences of whites as well as slaves. For this reason we have included the value of living services for whites in our estimates of total income presented in Table A.1.
Source: Parker-Gallman sample. Also see Table A.2.

Table A.4. *Estimates of value of output per slave and labor's share: 1859*

	All farms	Plantations with 51 or more slaves
Total output (Q)($)	127.55	147.93
Less		
Interest due to capital[a]	9.46	6.80
Depreciation due to capital	4.53	4.52
Interest due to land	33.27	38.12
Depreciation due to land	12.83	14.71
Supervisory costs	5.00	5.00
Labor's share (αQ) ($)	62.46	78.78
Labor's share (α) (%)	49.0	53.3

[a] Includes value of dwellings, implements, machinery, and livestock and assumes a rate of interest of 7 percent.
Source: Tables A.1, A.2, A.3.

New York and Boston rates for 1859, which they quote, were 6.8 and 7.0 percent, respectively, we feel justified in using a 7.0 percent interest rate to compute the interest attributable to capital and land.[13] This rate applied to our estimated value of capital and land per slave (Table A.3) gives $42.73 for "all farms" and $44.92 for large plantations. To these interest costs we must add the depreciation costs associated with capital and land, which we computed using the rates given in Table A.2. The only other remaining drain on the total output is the income of supervisory personnel. Conrad and Meyer estimate this to have amounted to between $5 and $15 per *hand*.[14] Saraydar, Conrad and Meyer's sharpest critic, agreed that "on balance, an estimate for supervisory costs of $10 a hand does not seem unreasonable."[15] Accepting this figure, which implies a cost of $5 per slave, we obtain our estimates of the value of slave-produced output (αQ) presented in Table A.4: $62.46 per slave for all farms, $78.78 for plantations.

It is significant that the estimate of labor's share as a percentage of total output using this technique is similar for the "all farms" (49.0 percent) and for the "large plantation" (53.3 percent) categories. The estimates are also in general agreement with (though they are somewhat lower than) Fogel and Engerman's estimate of 58 percent based on the estimated coefficients of their Cobb-Douglas production function.

Estimating the value of slave consumption
To compute the exploitation rate, we need finally to estimate the value of the food, clothing, shelter, and other provisions consumed by slaves (M). Our range of estimates is given in Table A.5. As can be seen, the largest part of this "income" was in the form of food, most of which was produced by the slaves themselves.

Table A.5 *Value of slave consumption: 1859*

| | Range of estimates ($) | |
	Low	High
Food, farm-produced	16.00	17.00
Manufactured items, farm-produced	0.70	1.00
Purchased items	7.00	10.00
Housing services[a]	1.37	1.37
Physician's bills	2.50	2.75
Total	27.57	32.12
Weighted average	28.95	

[a] See Table A.2.
Source: See text.

There exists considerable evidence to support the proposition that the standard ration provided an adult farm hand consisted of 2 pounds of cornmeal and 0.5 pound of "salt pork" or "bacon" per day.[16] If we evaluate the cornmeal at 84 cents a bushel for shelled corn (as reported in Table A.1) and the pork at $6.00 per hundredweight,[17] this ration would cost approximately $21.92 per *hand* per year.[18] Fogel and Engerman report in one note that the ratio of food consumption for adult hands to food consumption for an average of all slaves was 1.28 and in another note that it was 1.41. The 1.28 ratio was identified as the "lowest of the conversion factors suggested by various studies of food consumption."[19] These two ratios suggest a range of food costs per *slave* of between $15.55 and $17.13. Fogel and Engerman's own estimate of the value of plantation-produced food consumed by slaves is $17.77.[20] However, it has been demonstrated that Fogel and Engerman's procedures for estimating the slave diet introduced a significant number of upward biases.[21] We therefore believe that a range of $16 to $17 per slave per year for the value of *plantation-produced* food would be a generous estimate.[22]

On some plantations much of the slaves' clothing was made by slaves on the premises. Other plantations, particularly large ones, purchased most of the clothing required. On average, $2.04 of manufactured products per slave was reported by the farms included in the Parker-Gallman sample. Most of these manufactured items must have been clothing. Only 70 cents worth of manufactured products per slave was reported by the large plantations (see Table A.1). For our purposes we adopt the expenditure estimates for plantations that purchase rather than make most of their clothing. (This will exaggerate the value of slave consumption.) Accordingly, we place the value of plantation-produced clothing (and other manufactures) consumed by slaves at between $0.70 and $1.00 per slave.

With regard to the costs of purchased clothing, foods, and other supplies, Gray reported:

Expense accounts of several plantations where practically all provisions and clothing were produced at home show an average annual out-of-pocket expense of $2.50 per slave, consisting chiefly of the purchase of shoes and materials for manufacturing clothing, together with a few delicacies for the hospital. . . . Plantations purchasing a portion of the clothing ready-made, together with fish or other meat and a few delicacies, averaged about $7 to $10 a slave.[23]

The latter range of figures seems reasonable, and we have employed them in our calculations. The one remaining cost is that for medical care, which we put at $2.50 to $2.75 per slave on the authority of Eugene Genovese.[24] (The costs of medical supplies and drugs – about 25 to 50 cents – are included in Gray's estimate of out-of-pocket costs.) This brings the total value of slave "income" to between $27.57 and $32.12, as reported in Table A.5.

Since there is reason to believe that slaves on large plantations were better cared for than those on small farms,[25] we have used the upper limit of this range to apply to the farms with fifty-one or more slaves. An average, weighted by the number of slaves, of the higher and lower limits gives the figure of $28.95, which we apply to the "all farms" category.

Table A.6 presents our estimates of the exploitation rate. According to our calculations, slaves had approximately 54 percent of the product of their labor taken from them without compensation; on large plantations the exploitation rate may have been slightly higher. We remind the reader that these are conservative estimates. We have attempted to make assumptions and select parameters that bias these rates downward.

Addendum on the profitability of slavery

Because of the extensive literature on the profitability of slavery, we thought it of interest to note that our estimates of the rate of exploitation can be used to make a new estimate of the rate of profit earned by slaveowners. At the

Table A.6. *Estimates of rate of exploitation of slaves: 1859*

	All farms	Plantations with 51 or more slaves
Labor's share (αQ) ($)	62.46	78.78
Slave consumption (M) ($)	28.95	32.12
Exploited income ($\alpha Q - M$)($)	33.51	46.66
Rate of Exploitation (ϵ)(%)	53.7	59.2

Source: Tables A.4, A.5.

same time, this calculation can be used to demonstrate the general consistency of our own estimates with the earlier findings.

The work on profitability began with the classic paper by Conrad and Meyer (1958), which soon spawned a host of imitators and critics. Chief among these were Yasuba (1961), Evans (1962), Saraydar (1964), Sutch (1965), Genovese (1965), Foust and Swan (1970), Butlin (1971), and Fogel and Engerman (1972 and 1974).[26] There was also a debate centered largely upon this issue at the 1967 meetings of the Economic History Association.[27]

We estimate that in 1859, the year of our output and slave consumption estimates, the average price of a slave was approximately \$865.00.[28] An optimistic purchaser of slaves in that year expected to be able to exploit the income from those slaves and their descendants in perpetuity. Thus, the price of the average slave should have approximated the present value of the expected stream of future exploitation. If the rate of profit earned is r, and the value of the exploited income from the purchased slaves and all their descendants in any year (t) is denoted by E_t, the present-value formula can be written:

$$P = \sum_{t=0}^{\infty} \frac{E_t}{(1+r)^t}$$

where P is the price of an average slave. If the expected rate of growth of the slave population is a, then E_t should be expected to grow at that appreciation rate. Thus:

$$E_t = E_0(1+a)^t$$

where E_0 is the average value of exploited income per slave in 1859 (that is, $E_0 = aQ - M$). Thus:

$$P = E_0 \sum_{t=0}^{\infty} \left(\frac{1+a}{1+r}\right)^t$$

or, replacing the infinite series by the value of its sum, and solving for E_0:

$$E_0 = P\left[1 - \left(\frac{1+a}{1+r}\right)\right]$$

Solving for r:

$$r = \frac{1+a}{1-(E_0/P)} - 1$$

Between 1850 and 1860, the slave population grew at the rate of 2.15 percent per year.[29] If we take E_0 to be \$33.51 – the average value of exploited income for all farms in 1859 (see Table A.6) – we have r equal to 0.063, or a rate of return of 6.3 percent. If we take E_0 to be \$46.66 – the average exploitation for slave plantations in Table A.6 – then r would rise to

8.0 percent. These figures are remarkably consistent with the rates of return reported by Foust and Swan. In 1859, with cotton at 10 cents a pound (cf. Table A.1), and assuming, as we have, that slave farms were producing a modest surplus of foodstuffs, Foust and Swan calculated a rate of return for "all regions" to have been 6.9 percent.[30]

Computation of labor's share of agricultural output: 1879

To compute labor's share of agricultural output in the Cotton South of 1879, we restrict our attention to the black tenants of small family farms. A *small family farm* is defined as a farm reporting 50 acres or less in crops and employing only twenty-six weeks or less of hired labor. This class of farm operator represented the poorest segment of the agricultural labor force.[31] Had we expanded our attention to include all black-operated farms, or white-operated farms, our estimate of the value of per capita output would be larger.

Estimating farm output: 1879

Our estimates are based on our sample of farms drawn from the manuscript Census of Agriculture for 1880. (This sample is described in detail in Appendix G, Section 2.) For 1879, the 1,310 black tenants of small family farms included in this sample reported an average value of farm output of $338.63 per farm to the census; sharecroppers reported $327.45 per farm.[32] These figures are adjusted in Table A.7 to provide an estimate of income comparable to that estimated for 1859 in Table A.1. To the value of census-reported income we have added our estimate of the value of housing services. In 1900 black tenants reported a value of buildings per farm of $80.22, and black sharecroppers reported $78.17 per farm.[33] Since the value of farm lands *and* buildings did not significantly change between 1880 and 1900, we have taken the value of a black tenant's dwelling in 1880 to be

Table A.7. *Estimates of value of farm output per farm on black-operated family farms: 1879*

	Value per farm ($)	
	All tenant farms	Sharecroppers
Agricultural output	338.63	327.45
Plus: housing services[a]	10.28	10.28
Less: purchased fertilizer	6.98	7.81
Total output	341.93	329.92

[a] Method of estimating is discussed in text.
Source: Sample of farms in the Cotton South from the 1880 Census of Agriculture.

$75.[34] Applying the same depreciation and interest rates employed in Table A.2 to estimate the value of housing services from slave cabins, we obtain an estimate of the value of housing services per farm in excess of $10. This implies a value per capita of $1.96 for all tenant farms and $1.99 for share-cropped farms. This estimate exceeds by 45 percent the value of housing services per capita for slaves given in Table A.5 ($1.37).[35]

We assume that the livestock inventories were not expanded between 1879 and 1880, and we probably understate total income slightly because of this omission. Finally, we have deducted the average expenditure on pur-chased fertilizers, which was the only significant purchased input. Our final estimate of the value of total output is $341.93 for all black-operated tenant farms and $329.92 for farms that were sharecropped.[36]

Estimating labor's share of output
Sharecropping contracts for farms where the landowner provided all capital and work stock traditionally called for 50 percent of the cotton and grain output to go to the landlord. As we discuss in Chapter 5, this traditional division was universally observed and seems to represent a reliable basis for estimating labor's share. Tenants who rented for cash (or a stipulated amount of cotton) on average probably received the same share of output as sharecroppers, although there might be substantial variation from case to case. A rough equality of shares would have to exist, since both labor and landowners were free to choose whichever form of tenure they wished, and fixed rents could not coexist with share rents if the returns to either party were substantially different. For this reason, we use the typical share con-tract as the basis for distributing the output of all tenant farms as well as sharecropped farms, though our results will obviously be more reliable for the second category.

To obtain our estimate of labor's share, the value of agricultural output is first adjusted to correspond to "contractual output" as defined by the typi-cal share contract. This adjustment is made in Table A.8. We begin with the value of total output reported in Table A.7 and then subtract the value of housing services, the value added from pork production, and the value of garden output. Labor's share of contractual output is exactly one-half the remaining total.

The tenants did not have to share the output of pork produced on the farm with the landlord, since they fed any swine from their own share of the corn output. Therefore, the value of pork production less the corn used as swine feed (in other words, the value added in pork production) has to be sub-tracted from agricultural output in the process of defining contractual out-put. The value added in pork production we estimate at 25 percent of the value of animals slaughtered.[37] We estimate the typical value of animals slaughtered in 1879 at $7.98.[38] The average annual slaughter we assume was 83 percent of the census enumeration of swine.[39] Since there was an average of 4.93 swine on black-operated tenant farms, and 4.85 swine on

Table A.8. *Estimates of contractual output and labor's share per farm on black-operated family farms: 1879*

	All tenant farms	Sharecroppers
Total output ($)[a]	341.93	329.92
Less		
Housing services[a]	10.28	10.28
Value added in pork production[b]	8.16	8.03
Garden produce[c]	20.96	20.68
Contractual output ($)	302.53	290.93
Labor's share of		
contractual output ($)[d]	151.27	145.47
Plus		
Housing, pork, and garden produce	39.40	38.99
Labor's income ($)	190.67	184.46
Labor's share (%)	55.8	55.9

[a] See Table A.7. [b] See Text. [c] Includes poultry, dairy, and orchard products. The value of these products was estimated at $4.00 per capita (see text). [d] One-half of contractual output.
Source: Based on sample of farms in the Cotton South from the 1880 Census of Agriculture.

black-operated sharecropped farms, $8.16 of the reported income was attributable to the production of pork on tenant farms and $8.03 on sharecropped farms.[40]

The value of garden produce, including potatoes and beans, poultry, dairy, and orchard products, is estimated at $4.00 per capita. No figure was provided by the census for the value of garden produce. The production of sweet potatoes, cowpeas, butter, milk and cheese, and eggs was reported. A conservative estimate of the value of these outputs exceeds $3.00 per capita. Since these products were all *excluded* from the 1859 figure for the value of garden produce per slave reported in Table A.1 ($1.00), we are confident that our $4.00 per capita estimate is conservative.

Finally, to labor's share of contractual output we must add back the value of housing services, pork production, and garden produce that was excluded from contractual income. This gives us the two estimates of total labor income per farm that are presented in Table A.8: $190.67 for black tenant farms and $184.46 for black sharecropped farms. This implies that labor's share of total output was slightly below 56 percent. This figure is very close to the 53.3 percent we estimated as labor's share on large slave farms in 1859 (Table A.4).

The cost of living: 1859, 1879

To facilitate comparison of the 1879 income estimates with those we have made for 1859, we have constructed a (necessarily crude) estimate of the relative cost of living that is applicable to the bulk of black agricultural laborers in the cotton regions of the South. The construction of any southern price index for this purpose is seriously hampered by the lack of data on retail prices, particularly for a number of miscellaneous items. Furthermore, because of the significant shifts in the composition of consumption that accompanied the blacks' acquisition of economic freedom, the traditional index number problem of establishing appropriate weights is even more severe in this instance than is typical in conventional comparisons. This shift in consumption patterns is significant for another reason as well. As slaves, the composition of the blacks' consumption was determined for them by their masters. As freedmen, they were able to make their own choices. Thus, even if real income remained the same, we would argue that any shift in consumption patterns represented an improvement in black welfare as they themselves perceived it. For this reason, we have chosen to use weights reflective of consumption patterns of slaves. With these weights, we will exaggerate any rise or underestimate any fall in the cost of maintaining the slave living standards.

An extensive literature exists on the consumption patterns of slaves. As mentioned above, the standard ration consisted of 1 peck of cornmeal and 3.5 pounds of "bacon" per week for an adult field hand. There is no question that substitutions of such foods as beef and molasses were occasionally made for the allowance of bacon, and substitutions of sweet potatoes, cowpeas, or small grains were made for the allowance of corn. Generally, however, the prices of meat substitutes moved with the price of bacon, and the price of grain substitutes moved with the price of corn. For this reason, the food component of our price index is taken to be the average of corn and bacon cash prices weighted using a ratio of 14 pounds of bacon to 1 bushel of corn. Table A.9 presents the corn and bacon prices and the food price index. It should be noted that our price quotations for corn and bacon in 1859–1860 are both wholesale, whereas the 1879–1880 prices are retail. Since retail prices are generally above wholesale prices, another source of upward bias is introduced into our cost-of-(slave)-living index.

Clothing provided slaves typically amounted to two or three pairs of pants and shirts, a pair of boots, and perhaps an occasional hat and coat.[41] An examination of the Weeks Report (an 1880 Census publication that collected a wide variety of local retail prices for 1880 and a number of years preceding it) indicated that there were no marked regional differences in the prices of clothing and boots or in the trends in these prices.[42] For this reason, we have adopted Ethel Hoover's national price indexes for clothing. Hoover's study relied heavily on the Weeks Report, but also made use of a variety of other data sources. Setting 1859–1860 at 100, Hoover's clothing index in 1879–1880 was 94.9.[43]

An important component in cost-of-living indexes is rent. There are no reliable statistics on rural rents in the South during this period. We note, however, that the general impression of economic historians has been that

Table A.9. *Price indexes for food and clothing: 1879–1880 with 1859–1860 as base*

	1859–1860	1879–1880 Cash prices	1879–1880 Credit prices
Food			
Shelled corn ($/bushel)	0.84[a]	0.7650[b]	0.9975[b]
Bacon ($/pound)	0.1102[c]	0.0800[b]	0.1015[b]
Food index (1859–1860 = 100)	100	79.1	101.5
Clothing index (1859–1860 = 100)	100	94.9	94.9[d]
Cost of living (1859–1860 = 100)	100	86.2	99.6

[a] Table A.1. [b] The average of 1879 and 1880 retail purchase prices of corn and bacon in Georgia reported in Appendix D, Table D.1. [c] The average New Orleans wholesale price of bacon in 1859–1860 as reported by Charles E. Seagrave, "The Southern Negro Agricultural Worker: 1850–1870" (Ph.D. thesis Stanford University, 1971), pp. 112–113. [d] We assume that clothing, housing, and manufactured items could all be purchased for cash.

property values, and therefore rents, fell throughout the South following the Civil War. In the absence of any clear data, we assume that the rent component of the index did not change. We also assume that the few manufactured items purchased by black laborers experienced modest price declines, comparable to Hoover's fall in clothing prices. For example, Hoover's fuel and light index was 94.4 in 1879–1880; soap was 86.1; starch was 89.8.[44]

We have estimated in Section 1 of this appendix that, at a minimum, food amounted to between 53 and 58 percent of the slave's consumption (Table A.5). Accordingly, we have assigned a weight of 60 to food in deriving our index. Hoover's clothing index is given a weight of 25 percent, since it stands as a proxy for manufactured products as well as clothing and boots. The remaining 15 percent of the budget was assumed to have experienced no price change between 1860 and 1880. The resulting index number for 1879–1880, with 1859–1860 as our base year, is 86.2

This suggests that the cost of living for black agricultural laborers fell by more than 13 percent over the twenty-year period. In Table A.10 we use this index to estimate the per capita value of black income on tenant farms in 1879 expressed in 1859–1860 prices. If we compare these estimates with the highest estimate of the value of slave consumption reported in Table A.5, we find that black tenant farmers and their families achieved a 31.4 percent increase in real income. Even black sharecroppers, the poorest class of agricultural laborers in 1880, saw a 28.9 percent increase in their material standard of living when compared with the most generously provided slaves.

If we calculate the real value of black income in 1879 assuming that all food was purchased at credit prices rather than cash prices, the figures for

Table A.10. *Comparison of per capita slave consumption on large planta-tions in 1859 with per capita income of black tenant farmers and their families in 1879.*

	All tenant farmers	Share-croppers	Slave plantations
Labor's income per farm, 1879 ($)[a]	190.67	184.46	
Average number of family members, 1880[b]	5.24	5.17	
Per capita income, 1879–1880 ($)	36.39	35.68	
Real per capita income, 1879–1880; 1859–1860 dollars ($)[c]	42.22	41.39	
Slave consumption, 1859 ($)[d]			32.12
Increase in real per capita income, 1859–1879 (%)	31.4	28.9	

[a] Table A.8. [b] Sample of southern farms from the 1880 Census of Agriculture. [c] See Table A.9 for price index at cash prices. [d] Table A.5 (high estimate).

all tenant farms in 1879 would be $36.54 in 1859–1860 prices. This would still represent an increase in material income of 13.8 percent. The corresponding figures for sharecroppers are $35.82 of income in 1879 measured in 1859–1860 prices. This class would have experienced an improvement of 11.5 percent in material income.

OCCUPATIONAL DISTRIBUTION
OF SOUTHERN BLACKS:
1860, 1870, 1890

Information on the occupational distribution of southern blacks is limited. The federal population censuses, generally the primary source of occupational data, did not record the occupations of slaves before the Civil War. The first two postwar censuses collected occupational data for blacks, but did not publish tabulations by race. Not until 1890 were published census figures for occupations of black Americans available.

The occupational distribution of slaves: 1860

Before the Civil War, the Census Office did not collect information on the occupations of slaves. The enumerators merely listed slaves by age, sex, color (black or mulatto), and owner's name. Not even the slave's name or family connections were recorded.[1] The only systematic bodies of data known to us that supply information on slave occupations are the Mortality Censuses of 1850 and 1860.[2] In both years the census enumerators, in addition to their regular duties of enumerating the population and collecting statistics on agriculture and manufacturing, were expected to ascertain from each household the particulars of each death that had occurred within the family during the preceding twelve months. Among the particulars requested was the occupation of the decedent.

Because the statistics collected by this procedure greatly underenumerated the actual number of deaths, they proved nearly worthless as a measure of mortality. "The Tables of the Census which undertake to give the total number of . . . Deaths," said the introduction to the 1850 Census volume, "can be said to have but very little value."[3] Accordingly, little attention was paid to these mortality data at the time, and little interest has been shown in them subsequently. In particular, the occupational data on the decedents were not even published in the official reports. The manuscript schedules of these censuses have been preserved for a number of states and, despite the deficiencies of the enumeration, can be used to

Notes to Appendix B appear on page 360.

reconstruct the occupational distribution of the population in 1850 and 1860.

Deaths among both the free and slave populations were recorded, and in many southern enumeration districts the "occupations" of the dead slaves were also recorded. A number of enumerators, however, either did not record slave occupations or reported "slave," "servant," or "laborer" indiscriminately for all slaves. Accordingly, only a fraction of the records is usable. Nevertheless, nearly one-half of the schedules appear to have been properly completed.

An occupational distribution of people who die is not the same as the occupational distribution of the living population of which the decedents had been members. Since deaths occur disproportionately among infants and among the aged, such a tabulation would underrepresent young adults. This problem, however, can be overcome if a sufficiently large number of observations is available. Since the census recorded the age of each decedent, an occupational distribution can be obtained for each age cohort separately. For example, the occupations of male slaves aged twenty to twenty-nine at the time of death can be collected from the manuscripts. If we assume that the members of each age-sex cohort who died in 1860 are a random sample of those who were alive that year, we can weight the occupational distribution for each age cohort by the fraction that represents that age-sex group's contribution in the entire population. In this way, an occupational distribution for the whole population can be reconstructed.

There are, however, at least two reasons to suspect that those people who die may not be a random sampling of their age-sex cohort's occupational distribution. The first is the problem posed by hazardous occupations. If some jobs are more likely than others to be the cause of their holder's death, such occupations would be disproportionately represented. What will be obtained by the procedure described is, not an occupational distribution of the population alive at a point in time, but the occupational distribution of all people ever born. While in one sense those who pursue dangerous or unhealthy careers will be overrepresented, in another sense it is appropriate that they should be, since more people ever born will pursue such occupations than is evident from the proportions alive at any point in time. For this reason, we have made no correction for this effect. In any case, it is unlikely to be of major importance, since none of the typical slave occupations seem to have been unusually hazardous.

The second potential source of divergence of an occupational distribution based upon those who die from one based upon those who live arises in the case of death preceded by protracted illness. If the malady was both sufficiently debilitating and sufficiently persistent, it might have influenced the occupation pursued. A slave too weak to work in the field might have been assigned lighter work, such as basket weaving. This problem should not be of major importance, and in this instance, the bias imparted, we suspect, would be to exaggerate the proportion of slaves reported as artisans.

There is yet another reason to suspect that the procedure we have adopted might overrepresent artisans. Since the occupations recorded were those reported by the deceased slave's owner to the enumerator, there may have been some tendency to exaggerate the number of artisans. The slaveowner presumably would tend to overstate the skill of slaves he owned who were actually only semiskilled artisans or part-time artisans. Such slaves would then enter the schedules as full-fledged craftsmen.

Counterbalancing these effects that tend to exaggerate the number of artisans at the expense of field hands is the fact that we have deliberately avoided including any major cities in our sample. Since we suspect that the proportion of slave artisans in urban areas exceeded those in rural areas, our procedure will understate the proportion of artisans among all slaves in the population. For this reason, we have identified the occupational sample as representing the rural slave population. It should be noted, however, that a number of towns and villages with populations under 3,000 were included in the rural sample. For this reason, our figures should still somewhat exaggerate the proportion of artisans working in rural districts.

We were forced to exclude the large cities from the tabulations because our procedure requires that a sufficiently large number of observations be collected within each age-sex class so that an accurate occupational distribution can be calculated. Even in the large southern cities, insufficient numbers of young adult slaves died to provide an adequately large sample. For example, in Charleston District, which includes Charleston, South Carolina, only eighty-three gainfully occupied male slaves were recorded in the Mortality Census of 1860.

We have been able to obtain microfilms of the 1860 mortality schedules from three of our five Cotton States: South Carolina, Georgia, and Louisiana. A careful examination was made of the returns for each county to ensure that only those counties in which the enumerators conscientiously reported the mortality statistics would be included. We selected ten districts of South Carolina, forty-five counties of Georgia, and nine parishes of Louisiana. Table G.15 of Appendix G lists those included. Table B.1 presents the distribution of the 4,106 observations on male slaves collected, by state and occupation, and also provides the specific definition of each occupational category.

For each of the three state samples the occupational distribution of each census age cohort was weighted by the cohort's contribution to the aggregate male slave population of the included counties. For the purposes of Table 2.1, Chapter 2, the three state samples were aggregated together using weights that reflected the size of the male slave population of the Five Cotton States. The Georgia sample was weighted by the aggregate of Georgia and Alabama, and the Louisiana sample was weighted by the population of Louisiana and Mississippi.

The occupational distribution were significantly different in the three states. A separate distribution for each sample is therefore given in Table B.2.

Table B.1. *Distribution of observations on occupations of deceased male slaves, Mortality Census sample: 1860*

Occupation	South Carolina	Georgia	Louisiana
Agriculture			
Field hand[a]	403	441	375
Driver[b]	6	—	2
Service			
House servant[c]	19	7	9
Nurse[d]	18	—	—
Cook	1	1	2
Gardener	1	1	—
Unskilled labor			
Laborer	1	14	—
Teamster[e]	4	2	5
Watchman	5	1	—
Boat hand[f]	5	—	—
Mill hand	1	3	—
Hostler	—	2	—
Miner	1	—	—
Turpentine hand	1	—	—
Woodcutter	—	1	—
Railroad hand	—	1	—
Artisan			
Blacksmith	11	16	4
Carpenter	31	5	7
Miller	3	3	—
Cooper	4	—	—
Shoemaker	2	1	1
Mechanic	2	2	—
Engineer	2	1	1
Mason[g]	2	2	—
Painter	—	2	—
Weaver	1	—	—
Mat maker	1	—	—
Musician	1	—	—
Carriage maker	—	1	—
Tailor	—	1	—
Brick maker	—	—	1
No occupation			
Not given	39	40	32
Dependent[h]	940	1,028	581
Illegible	4	—	—
Total decedents	1,509	1,577	1,020

[a] Includes plowboy, hoe hand, farm hand, stock minder, stock tender, and stock feeder. [b] Includes foreman. [c] Includes houseboy, servant, and butler. [d] Includes "child's nurse," a person who would be identified today as a baby-sitter. [e] Includes wagoner and carriage driver. [f] Includes fisherman, sailor, and ferryman. [g] Includes brick mason and bricklayer. [h] Includes children 14 years old and under without occupation. Also includes invalid, infirm, superannuated, idiot, and lunatic.

Source: Manuscript Census of Mortality, 1860. See Appendix G, Table G.15.

Table B.2. *Occupational distribution of male slaves, South Carolina, Georgia, and Louisiana samples: 1860*

Occupation	South Carolina	Georgia	Louisiana
Agriculture	81.7	87.6	92.7
Field hand	81.3	87.6	92.3
Driver	0.4	—	0.4
Service	4.2	2.1	3.1
Unskilled labor	3.2	4.1	1.2
Artisan	10.9	6.2	3.0
Blacksmith	2.3	3.0	0.9
Carpenter	5.3	1.1	1.5
Other	3.3	2.1	0.6
Total	100.0	100.0	100.0
Proportional population weight	.1899	.4320	.3781

Source: Manuscript Census of Mortality, 1860.

Black occupations: 1870

The tabulations presented in Chapter 2, Tables 2.5, 2.6, and 2.7, are based on a sampling of the manuscript Cenus of Population taken in 1870. This was the first census taken after the Civil War and the first to record the occupations of most black Americans. There is little question that the 1870 Census underenumerated the population of the South in that year, a problem we discuss in Chapter 3.[4] Nevertheless, the census returns may be sampled and the results used to reconstruct the occupational distribution of blacks. There is no reason to believe the undercount systematically or coincidentally excluded blacks with skilled occupations relative to those unskilled. Moreoever, we suspect the undercount was primarily the result of defective enumeration in some census districts, whereas most districts were thoroughly and accurately canvassed. To guard against difficulties that might arise from the undercount of 1870, we carefully selected for our sample only those districts where the enumerators' schedules or other evidence suggested consistent and thorough reporting.

The sample drawn from the 1870 Census is in reality two separate samples: a 10 percent sampling of selected rural areas and a 100 percent sampling of six southern cities. The rural sample was composed of the black population living in the rural areas of thirteen counties located in the Five Cotton States. These counties are listed in Table B.3. The table also gives the names of any towns excluded and the numbers of male workers in our sample.

The urban sample consisted of a complete tabulation of the working black populations of the six towns listed in Chapter 2, Table 2.6. It should be noted that all the towns are located in one of the thirteen counties chosen for

Table B.3. *Rural sample: 1870*

County, State	Number of gainfully occupied blacks in sample	Towns excluded from sample
Georgetown, South Carolina	925 (358)[a]	Georgetown Village
Coweta, Georgia	203	Newnan
Gwinnett, Georgia	48	
Tattnall, Georgia	43	Reidsville
Taylor, Georgia	101	
Thomas, Georgia[b]	187	Thomasville
Twiggs, Georgia	184	
Worth, Georgia	23	
Dallas, Alabama	1,863 (936)[a]	Selma and Cahawba
Attala, Mississippi	149	Kosciusko
Bolivar, Mississippi	175	
Calhoun, Mississippi	43	Pittsboro
Morehouse, Louisiana	192	Bastrop Town
Total sampled	4,136 (2,642)[a]	

[a] Small sections of Georgetown County, S.C., and Dallas County, Ala., were sampled at 100 percent rather than 10 percent. The figures given in this table are the total number of workers sampled. The figures from these two sections were reduced to 10 percent of their value before being added to the balance of the county. The numbers given in parentheses are the sizes of the completed 10 percent sample.

[b] One district of Thomas County, Ga., did not report occupations consistently. This section, constituting approximately 14 percent of the rural sections of the county, was excluded from the sample. Thus this county was sampled at approximately an 8.6 percent rather than a 10 percent rate.

our rural sample. In addition, the thirteen counties included the towns of Reidsville, Georgia, and Pittsboro, Mississippi. Reidsville had only three black male workers, and Pittsboro had only nine; none of the twelve were skilled workers.

Literacy was also reported by the census, which recorded the ability to read and write for all individuals over ten. This information was used to prepare the literacy statistics for Table 2.7 of Chapter 2.

Computation of racial balance index of occupations: 1890

After emancipation, the census takers recorded the occupations of all citizens ten years old and older, but not until 1890 were separate tabulations made for white and "colored" workers.[5] These figures for the South show a marked concentration of blacks in low-skilled occupations. Table B.4 gives the distribution of colored, native white, and foreign-born white males for the Five Cotton States in 1890. Over 70 percent of the blacks were engaged in agricultural occupations; more than one-half were farm laborers. Of those few who were in nonagricultural occupations, nearly three-quarters were in low-skilled occupations: common laborers, servants, and factory operatives.[6] If we combine the high-skilled, nonagricultural occupations with farm operators to define a "privileged class," the census tabulations of 1890 suggest that only 39 percent of the blacks would qualify (over 80 percent of whom were farm operators). Among whites, whether native, second generation, or foreign born, the corresponding percentage in privileged occupations is approximately 70. Our definition of *privileged class* is rather generous. While social scientists traditionally have regarded farm operators as members of a privileged class, most southern farm operators engaged in considerable manual labor, and it is questionable whether sharecropper and tenant farmers should be classed with owner-operators.

Black women fared even less well than the men. Table B.5 presents comparable figures for female workers. Only 8.9 percent held privileged jobs, compared with approximately 50 percent of white females. The occupational classifications of the published census were aggregated into the functional categories used in Tables B.4 and B.5 according to the scheme presented in Tables B.6 and B.7.

Table B.4. *Distribution of male workers, ten years old and older, by occupation, Five Cotton States: 1890*

| | Percent of each race and nativity class | | | | |
| | | Native whites | | | |
Occupation	All colored[a]	Native parents	Foreign parents	Foreign-born whites	Total
Agriculture	73.6	70.3	14.5	14.3	69.1
Laborer	41.9	22.1	4.3	5.5	31.5
Farm operator[b]	31.7	48.2	10.2	8.8	37.6
Nonagriculture	26.4	29.7	85.5	85.6	30.9
Low-skilled[c]	19.2	8.4	23.0	25.0	14.8
High-skilled[d]	7.3	21.3	62.5	60.6	16.1
Total	100.0	100.0	100.0	100.0	100.0
Lower class[e]	61.0	30.5	27.3	30.5	46.3
Privileged classes[f]	39.0	69.5	72.7	69.5	53.7
Number gainfully occupied	985,280	801,369	49,763	47,652	1,884,064

[a] Defined as "persons of negro descent, Chinese, Japanese, and civilized Indians." [b] Includes sharecroppers, tenant farmers, overseers, and farm managers. [c] Includes nonagricultural laborers, servants, and factory operatives. [d] Includes skilled artisans, managerial and commercial occupations, professionals, and occupations not specified. [e] Sum of agricultural laborers and low-skilled nonagricultural occupations. [f] Sum of farm operators and high-skilled nonagricultural occupations.

Source: U.S. Census Office, Eleventh Census [1890], *Report on the Population . . . 1890*, Part 2 (Washington: GPO, 1897), pp. 530, 548, 562, 574, 606.

Table B.5. *Distribution of female workers, ten years old and older, by occupation, Five Cotton States: 1890*

| Occupation | Percent of each race and nativity class | | | | |
| | All colored[a] | Native whites | | Foreign-born whites | Total |
		Native parents	Foreign parents		
Agriculture	62.2	51.4	6.1	6.2	58.8
Laborer	56.3	30.7	2.8	3.0	50.2
Farm operator[b]	5.9	20.7	3.3	3.2	8.6
Nonagriculture	37.8	48.6	93.9	93.8	41.2
Low-skilled[c]	34.8	23.0	30.7	42.0	32.6
High-skilled[d]	3.0	25.6	63.3	51.9	8.5
Total	100.0	100.0	100.0	100.0	100.0
Lower class[e]	91.1	53.7	33.5	45.0	82.9
Privileged classes[f]	8.9	46.3	66.5	55.1	17.1
Number gainfully occupied	515,894	120,750	10,076	6,189	652,909

[a] Defined as "persons of negro descent, Chinese, Japanese, and civilized Indians."   [b] Includes sharecroppers, tenant farmers, overseers, farm managers.   [c] Includes nonagricultural laborers, servants, factory operatives.   [d] Includes skilled artisans, managerial and commercial occupations, professionals, and occupations not specified.   [e] Sum of agricultural laborers and low-skilled nonagricultural occupations.   [f] Sum of farm operators and high-skilled nonagricultural occupations.

Source: U.S. Census Office, Eleventh Census [1890], *Report on the Population . . . 1890,* Part 2 (Washington: GPO, 1897), pp. 530, 548, 562, 574, 606.

Detailed data on the racial balance in various occupations in 1890 are provided in Chapter 2, Table 2.8, which presents an index of racial balance for approximately fifty separate occupations. This index was designed to range from a value of -1 (complete exclusion of blacks) through zero (exact integration) to $+1$ (complete exclusion of whites). In the following discussion we formally define the racial balance index. The following terms are defined:

p The fraction of the total number employed who are black ($0 < p < 1$)

x The number of blacks in a given occupational category

n The total number of individuals (white and black) in a given occupational category ($x < n$)

b The fraction of a given occupational category that is black ($= x/n$)

If there had been random assignment of gainfully employed persons to occupational categories, the expected number of blacks in a category with n positions would be pn. The actual number would be binominally distributed

Table B.6 *Occupations of males, ten years old and older, Five Cotton States: 1890*

Occupation	Number occupied	Comments
Laborer	805,080	
Agriculture	594,700	
Not specified	132,417	
Railroad employee	34,099	
Teamster	17,167	Includes draymen and hackmen
Lumberman	9,333	Includes woodchoppers and raftsmen
Other	17,364	Includes miners in Alabama, Georgia, and South Carolina; quarrymen in Alabama; dairymen in Louisiana; and sailors, boatmen, canal men, pilots, fisherman, and oystermen in all states but Georgia
Service	36,262	
Servant	23,336	
Porter	5,985	Includes messengers and packers
Gardener	3,566	Includes florists, nurserymen, and vinegrowers
Barber	3,475	Includes hairdressers
Factory operative	32,088	
Saw mill	13,197	Includes planing mill employees
Cotton mill	12,326	Includes woolen and other textile mill operatives
Iron and steel mill	4,487	In Alabama, Georgia, and Louisiana only
Other	2,078	Includes charcoal, coke, and lime burners in Alabama and Mississippi; and tobacco and cigar factory operatives in Louisiana
Skilled labor	95,982	
Carpenter	32,781	Includes joiners and woodworkers in Georgia and Mississippi; and cabinet makers and upholsterers in Louisiana
Blacksmith	10,769	Includes wheelwrights
Mason	7,503	Includes marble and stone cutters
Painter	6,663	Includes glaziers, varnishers, and in Alabama and Georgia plasterers
Engineer, and fireman	6,105	Excludes steam railroad employees
Machinist	4,947	
Shoemaker	4,463	Includes bootmakers and boot and shoe repairers
Printer	3,557	Includes engravers and bookbinders
Butcher	3,433	
Miller (flour, grist)	3,310	Excludes millers in Louisiana; probably includes millwrights
Other	12,451	Includes brick makers, potters, mechanics, and telegraph and telephone operators (except in Louisiana); coopers in Georgia, Louisiana, and South Carolina; tailors and bakers in Louisiana and South Carolina; and tinners and tinware makers in Louisiana and Mississippi
Farm operator	707,811	Includes farmers, planters, sharecroppers, tenant farmers, agricultural overseers, and farm managers

Table B.6 (*cont.*)

Occupation	Number occupied	Comments
Managerial, commercial	117,313	
Merchandiser	59,730	Includes merchants, dealers, peddlers, agents, salesmen, collectors, and commercial travelers
Bookkeeper, clerk	35,002	
Hotel, stable, saloon keepers	8,494	Includes restaurant and boardinghouse keepers, bartenders, and hostlers,coverage of all categories is complete only for Mississippi; excludes restaurant and saloon keepers in Alabama and South Carolina, bartenders in South Carolina; and hotel and boardinghouse keepers in Georgia, Louisiana, and South Carolina
Foreman, watchman	5,877	Includes policemen, detectives, and nonagricultural overseers; excludes foremen and overseers in Louisiana
Government official	4,837	
Banker	3,373	Includes officials of banks and brokers
Professional	37,695	
Clergyman	8,952	
Physician, surgeon	8,246	
Teacher, professor	8,049	
Lawyer	5,780	
Manufacturer	5,455	Includes publishers
Surveyor	1,213	Excludes Georgia and Mississippi; includes civil, mechanical, and mining engineers in the other states
Total specified	1,832,231	
Other	51,833	Computed as a residual
Total gainfully occupied	1,844,064	

Source: U.S. Census Office, Eleventh Census [1890], *Report on the Population . . . 1890,* Part 2 (Washington: GPO. 1897), pp. 530, 548, 562, 574, 606.

with *pn* as the mean. Binomial theory tells us that the standard error, σ, of this expectation is:

$$\sigma = \sqrt{np(1 - p)}$$

A measure of racial imbalance in a given occupation class is the number of standard errors the actual number of blacks holding that occupation is away from the expected number had no imbalance been present. This measure is given by v:

$$v = \frac{x - pn}{\sqrt{np(1 - p)}}$$

Table B.7. *Occupations of females, ten years old and older, Five Cotton States: 1890*

Occupation	Number occupied	Comments
Laborer	354,352	
Agriculture	327,820	
Not specified	26,319	
Other	213	Includes dairymaids in Georgia, Louisiana, and Mississippi; and employees of steam railroad companies in South Carolina
Service	174,801	
Servant	109,880	Includes stewardesses and professional housekeepers
Laundress	64,656	
Other	265	Includes gardeners (except in Mississippi) and barbers and hairdressers in Louisiana
Factory operative	11,787	
Cotton mill	11,374	Includes woolen and other textile mill operatives
Other	413	Includes tobacco and cigar factory operatives in Louisiana, and basket makers in Mississippi
Skilled Labor	27,413	
Seamstress	26,752	Includes dressmakers, tailoresses, and milliners
Other	661	Includes bakers in Louisiana and South Carolina; printers, engravers, and bookbinders (except in Louisiana); and telegraph and telephone operators in Alabama and Georgia
Farm operator	56,195	Includes sharecroppers, tenant farmers, planters, and overseers
Managerial, commercial	8,782	
Merchandiser	3,404	Includes merchants, dealers, peddlers, and saleswomen
Hotel, saloon keeper	3,101	Includes boardinghouse, lodginghouse, and restaurant keepers
Clerk, bookkeeper	1,916	Includes copyists, stenographers, typists, and accountants
Government official	361	
Professional	16,809	
Teacher	14,383	Includes artists, musicians, and teachers of art and music (except in Louisiana)
Nurse, midwife	2,426	
Total specified	650,139	
Other	2,770	Computed as a residual
Total gainfully occupied	652,909	

Source: U.S. Census Office, Eleventh Census [1890], *Report on the Population . . . 1890,* Part 2 (Washington: GPO, 1897), pp. 530, 548, 562, 574, 606.

Substituting bn for x and rearranging terms, we have:

$$v = \sqrt{\frac{n(b-p)^2}{p(1-p)}}$$

since b is bounded by zero and unity, the number of σ units is bounded by

$$-\sqrt{np/(1-p)} \quad \text{and} \quad \sqrt{n(1-p)/p}$$

Thus, v can be standardized so that it is bounded by -1 and $+1$ by dividing by:

$$\sqrt{\frac{n(1-p)\ p^{\,1-b}}{(1-p)^{1-b}p^{\,b}}}$$

After simplifying, the standardized index, which we denote as Ψ, is expressed as:

$$\Psi = \frac{b-p}{(1-p)^b\,p^{\,1-b}} = \frac{b-p}{p[(1-p)/p]^b}$$

Note that Ψ is independent of n and, therefore, can be used to compare the racial imbalance in occupational categories of different overall magnitudes.

ESTIMATES OF LABOR SUPPLIED
BY SLAVE AND FREE LABOR

Our conclusion that the supply of labor offered by the black population after emancipation declined by something between one-fourth and one-third the level supplied under slavery is based on a comparison of the relative amounts of labor offered under each system. Obviously, such a comparison is a generalization of many diverse situations reported. Our estimates accordingly are presented as rather broad intervals rather than as precise point estimates. They are intended to illustrate the effects of emancipation by establishing the change in labor supply between the last decade of slavery and the first decade and a half of freedom.

The procedure we employed was to use contemporary sources to judge the relative change in three of the four basic parameters that govern the labor supplied by any population: the fraction of the population at work, the average number of days worked, and the average number of hours worked each day. We were unable to make any judgment of the decline in the fourth factor, the intensity of the work effort per hour. We do, however, account for the differences between men, women, and children in this regard. With the coercion of slavery removed, freed blacks sought to lower each of these four factors determining the supply of labor effort. Table C.1 presents the detailed estimates we have constructed for each of the three changes and calculates the cumulative effect freedom had on the supply of man-hours per capita.

The estimates represent our judgment reached after a study of both systems of labor. Because our argument focuses on the effects of these changes on agriculture, we have confined our estimates to the participation of the rural population engaged in agricultural occupations. We shall consider each of each of the components of Table C.1 in turn.

Labor force participation

With slavery, a very high labor force participation ratio was obtained through compulsion. Even the aged, disabled, and very young were put to work. To account for those rural slaves who were not employed or who were

Table C.1. *Estimate of labor supply per capita by rural black population*

	Slaves (1850s)			Free labor (1870s)		
	Males 16 and over	Females 16 and over	Children 10–15	Males 16 and over	Females 16 and over	Children 10–15
1. Fraction of rural population engaged in agriculture	0.95–0.98	0.90–0.95	0.85–0.90	0.90–0.93	0.50–0.67	0.50–0.67
2. Average number of days worked per year	268–289	261–284	225–236	242–276	235–258	199–210
3. Average number of hours worked per day	12–14	11–13	10–12	11–13	10–12	9–11
4. Hours supplied to agriculture per person (1 × 2 × 3)	3,055–3,965	2,584–3,507	1,913–2,549	2,396–3,337	1,175–2,074	896–1,548
5. Effective value of one hour (adult male = 1)	1.00	0.75	0.67	1.00	0.75	0.67
6. Male-equivalent hours supplied per person (5 × 4)	3,055–3,965	1,938–2,630	1,282–1,708	2,396–3,337	881–1,556	600–1,037
7. Fraction of 1860 population	0.285	0.281	0.131	0.285	0.281	0.131
Total male-equivalent hours supplied to agriculture per capita	1,607–2,124			1,009–1,524		

engaged as personal servants, cooks, or in some other nonagricultural occupation, we have assumed that 2 to 5 percent of all adult males, 5 to 10 percent of all adult females, and 10 to 15 percent of all children aged ten to fifteen were not members of the agricultural labor force.

To estimate the labor force participation following emancipation, we examined the sample of occupations of blacks ten years or older from the manuscript census discussed in Appendix B. This study revealed that the proportion of the male population engaged in agricultural occupations in any one county ranged from 65 to 95 percent; the proportion of women at work in agriculture varied from 25 to 63 percent. At a minimum it seems reasonable that the reduction of labor force participation of men averaged at least 5 percentage points, the value assumed for Table C.1. We have also assumed a decline in the participation ratio for women to between 0.50 and 0.67. Such estimates are consistent with the tabulation of occupations presented in the 1870 Census.[1] That our assumed participation ratio for women in the postwar period may be too high is suggested by a survey taken by the Georgia State Department of Agriculture in July 1875, which revealed that only 28 percent of the "able-bodied negro women" were at work or on farms.[2]

The three labor force participation ratios given in line 1 of Table C.1 for 1870 together imply an *overall* labor force participation ratio for the black population in that year of between 46 and 54 percent. A survey of several hundred planters in Georgia, taken in October 1874, found that on their farms the labor force participation of resident Negroes was 42.5 percent.[3] A sample of nearly 2,000 black-operated farms in 1880 revealed an overall labor force participation rate among families of farm operators of 48.7 percent. On small family-operated farms, the labor force participation rate was lower yet. On those owned and operated by blacks the rate was 44.3 percent, and on black-operated tenant farms it was 48.1 percent.[4] The reductions in labor force participation presented in line 1 of Table C.1 alone would result in a 17 to 24 percent decline in the labor supply offered by a given population.

Average number of days worked per year

Based on a discussion by Lewis Gray, we estimate that male adult slaves worked 268 to 289 days of the year.[5] This estimate allows for 48 to 52 Sundays off, 13 to 26 Saturdays off, 12 days of illness, and 3 to 7 holidays per year.[6] Women worked the same number of days as the men except for relief during advanced pregnancy and recovery after delivery, which we estimate as averaging between 5 and 7 days per woman per year. This estimate is based on our assumption that slave women were typically released from farm work for 4 to 6 weeks per birth.[7] Assuming one live birth every 5 years from age sixteen on gives an average reduction of 5 to 7 days per woman per year. This is a generous allowance, since it implies a birth rate larger than that actually observed.[8] Children were, from all reports, put to work at ages varying from six to twelve and assigned field work along with their parents.[9] However, it is likely that slave children worked fewer days than did adults. We have therefore assumed they received every Saturday and Sunday off, were excused for illness for a total of 21 days, and received 10 to 21 holidays during the year.

After emancipation, blacks insisted on all or part of Saturday off, and usually demanded additional holidays as well. Testimony to these demands can be found in contemporary surveys and commentary.[10] The 1874 survey of Georgia planters revealed that Negro wage hands averaged 5.0 days per week (or 260 days per year, assuming a full 52-week year); "croppers" averaged 4.6 days per week (or 239 days per year); renters 4.4 days a week (or 229 days per year). The average for all blacks was given as 4.7 days per week (or 244 days a year). (The average for white workers was 4.8 days per week.) According to the report, "the remainder of the time is spent in visiting, hunting, idleness, etc."[11] Charles Seagrave's Louisiana study found that the typical Class I field hand averaged about 225 days worked in 1866–1867.[12] Based on these sources, we have conservatively assumed that the number of days worked per year by men ranged from 242 to 276, a reduction of between 13 and 26 days per year. For women and children, we assumed a 26-day reduction. These estimates are presented in line 2 of Table C.1. The implied decline in number of days worked per year would, by itself, account for an 8 to 11 percent decline in the labor supply.

Average number of hours worked per day

Eugene Genovese has devoted more attention to the length of the slaves' working day than any other scholar:

> To risk a generalization for the South as a whole: The slaves' workday, as perceived by their masters, averaged about twelve hours, and as perceived by the slaves, who calculated the extras and shared a portal-to-portal mentality with laborers else-where, averaged about fifteen hours. That is, the slave worked about twelve hours in the fields and a few hours more in getting to and from work and doing odd jobs.[13]

Gray gives an estimate of 15 to 16 hours of work per day for slaves during the busy season.[14] Fogel and Engerman imply a workday of 12.7 to 13.6 hours.[15] We assume that male slaves worked 12 to 14 hours per day. Since some of the extras and odd jobs were the types of chores "unemployed" women might have performed after the abolition of slavery and because women were allowed time off for child care – particularly nursing mothers – we have taken 11 to 13 hours as their average workday. Children over ten years of age were assumed to work 10 to 12 hours daily.

We assume that free laborers after the war uniformly worked 1 hour less per day than had been the practice under slavery. The Freedmen's Bureau in Louisiana set as a standard 10 hours per day in the summer, and 9 hours per

day in winter.[16] Complaints of substantially larger reductions voiced in the
Loring and Atkinson survey suggest that our assumed fall of 1 hour from
the prewar norm is probably quite modest. Such a 1-hour decline in the
working day would, by itself, reduce the available labor supply by 9 to 10
percent.

Relative efficiency of women and children

Women were usually regarded as three-fourths and children as two-thirds
as productive as men.[17] The rates charged to "rent" or hire slaves for a year
corroborate this rule of thumb. The annual hire rate of female slaves relative
to males in the Five Cotton States, according to the U.S. Department of
Agriculture, was 61.5 percent, and the weighted average relative for children was 44.2 percent.[18] After these figures are adjusted for the relatively
fewer hours worked per year by slave women and children (line 4), the per
hour productivity of women relative to men becomes 70 to 73 percent, and
that for children becomes 66 to 71 percent. The relative efficiency (line 5)
taken with our estimates of the number of hours supplied in the 1870s also
agrees closely with the differential rates of annual pay offered in 1867 to free
men and women.[19]

Population weights

The three cohorts' contributions were weighted by their respective share in
the population of 1860 (line 7).[20] The balance of the population (children
under ten) are assumed not to have worked under either slavery or freedom.
Had we weighted the free labor estimates using the population distribution
from 1870 Census, the decline in the effective labor supply would have been
even greater, though not markedly so.

CALCULATION OF INTEREST CHARGED FOR CREDIT IMPLICIT IN THE DUAL-PRICE SYSTEM

Rural furnishing merchants of the South provided supplies on credit payable after the harvest. Rather than establishing and calculating credit charges as an annual interest rate applied to the amount borrowed, merchants posted two prices on each item. The cash price was charged if the customer did not request credit; the credit price was charged, but, of course, deferred, when a loan was involved. For example, on July 1, 1878, the average cash price of corn in middle Georgia was 78 cents per bushel according to a survey conducted by the Georgia State Department of Agriculture. On the same date the credit price was $1.04 per bushel payable on November 1, 1878.[1] In effect, the farmer would pay 26 cents in November as interest on a four-month loan of 78 cents. Computed as simple interest, this amounts to 33.3 percent for one-third of a year or 100 percent per annum.[2] "'Time is money,'" an official of the Georgia Department of Agriculture remarked after reporting these figures, "in this case *time costs much money*."[3]

The Georgia surveys

The 1878 GDA survey was the first to report cash and credit prices for corn on a specific date.[4] The practice of conducting such retail price surveys annually was begun in 1881 and continued through 1889. The day on which price observations were to be collected was changed from July 1 to May 1 of each year. The observations were obtained by means of a questionnaire directed to the department's crop correspondents. There were typically two or three farmers located in each county who responded to these surveys.[5] They were regularly questioned by the department on the condition of local crops, weather, yields, and farming practices; and they seem to have taken their job seriously. In regard to the retail price surveys, the department noted:

The correspondents of the Department are composed of a number of the most intelligent practical farmers in each county, and while it is possible that they may sometimes err in their estimates of the yield of the crop of their counties, there is no room for error in their reports of the prices paid for corn and bacon.[6]

Notes to Appendix D appear on pages 361–362.

The statewide averages of the cash and credit prices published in the May crop reports of the department are reproduced in Chapter 7, Table 7.1.[7] There is little doubt that the credit extended was through November 1; this was the traditional repayment date and it is mentioned in the published crop reports throughout the period. Therefore, the credit referred to in the May reports was extended for six months. The simple-interest-rate equivalents of the credit markups shown in Table 7.1 are given in Table 7.2.

We have reported the May crop report figures and based our discussion in Chapter 7 on them because we believe they are the most comprehensive and precisely defined data on merchant charges that have been assembled. However, the GDA also collected similar information in its December crop reports for each year from 1879 through 1890, with the exception of 1881. The December surveys asked for the average cash and credit prices paid by farmers during the preceding year. The average length of time for which these loans were extended is not known. Since the bulk of the farmer's credit purchases would take place after May 1, a term of less than six months is probably correct. The GDA assumed a six-month period when discussing these prices in 1879, but noted that the loans referred to were for "less than an average of six months."[8] In 1883 the department asserted that the "time for which the credit is given will not, on an average, exceed five or six months."[9] By 1885 they had reduced this estimate to "not . . . over four months," the term to payment they consistently used throughout the balance of the period.[10]

We have reproduced the cash and credit prices for corn and bacon from the December reports in Table D.1 and present our calculations of the implicit rates of interest for assumed terms of both six and four months in Table D.2. It is probable that the true average length of loan lies within this range.[11] Comparison of the six-month interest rates for corn in Table D.2 with those in Table 7.2 for those years of overlap shows that except in 1885 and 1886 the December crop reports reported credit charges that exceed those from the May surveys. This suggests that merchants did not adjust the credit prices downward as the year progressed, at least not sufficiently to hold the implicit interest rate charged constant. In other words, the later in the season supplies were needed, the higher was the effective rate of interest charged.

The Louisiana surveys

Beginning in 1886 the Louisiana State Bureau of Agriculture also conducted annual surveys of its crop correspondents to obtain the cash and credit prices for corn in that state. Between 1886 and 1888 these surveys asked for the prices prevailing on May 1; after 1888 they asked for June 1 prices. The published tabulations did not report a statewide average, only parish-by-parish figures. We have taken a simple average of the prices reported. Only parishes in which both the cash and credit prices were given are included. The prices and the implicit interest rates are presented in Table D.3.

The opportunity cost of credit

C. Vann Woodward has suggested that the merchant should not be blamed for the high rates of interest he charged because he was merely passing on to his customers the high price he himself paid for credit:

Nor did [the merchant] pocket the take of his till. He in turn paid outrageous rates of interest to factors, who paid their tributes to the ultimate lords of credit. The merchant was only a bucket on an endless chain by which the agricultural well of a tributary region was drained of its flow.[12]

Table D.1. *Cash prices and credit prices charged by Georgia merchants for corn and bacon: 1879, 1880, 1882–1890*

	Corn (cents/bushel)		Bacon (cents/pound)	
Year	Average cash price	Average credit price	Average cash price	Average credit price
1879	75.0	97.5	7.00	9.50
1880	78.0	102.0	9.00	10.80
1881	—	—	—	—
1882	106.0	133.0	14.00	17.00
1883	67.0	94.0	10.21	12.95
1884	88.0	113.0	11.00	14.25
1885	76.0	99.0	8.00	10.50
1886	69.0	93.0	8.00	11.40
1887	72.0	98.0	8.89	11.60
1888	77.0	98.0	9.71	12.30
1889	66.0	87.0	7.91	10.38
1890	68.0	85.0[a]	7.50	9.75

[a] We have corrected a typographical error in the original source.

Source: Taken from Georgia, Department of Agriculture, *Publications of the Georgia State Department of Agriculture,* as follows: *1879:* "Supplemental Report–1879," *Circular,* new series, Number 4, pp. 6–7, in Volume 5 (Atlanta: Jas. P. Harrison & Co., 1880). *1880:* "Supplemental Report–1880," *Circular,* new series, Number 14½, pp. 6, 9, in Volume 6 (Atlanta: Jas. P. Harrison & Co. [1881]). *1882:* "Supplemental Report . . . 1882," *Circular,* new series, Number 34, pp. 10–11, 21, in Volume 8 (Atlanta: Jas. P. Harrison & Co., 1883). *1883:* "Supplemental Report . . . 1883," *Circular,* new series, Number 49, pp. 6, 13, in Volume 9 (Atlanta: Jas. P. Harrison & Co., 1884). *1884:* "Supplemental Report . . . 1884," *Circular,* new series, Number 61, pp. 6, 11, in Volume 10 (Atlanta: Jas. P. Harrison & Co., 1885). *1885:* "Supplemental Report . . . 1885," *Circular,* new series, Number 74, pp. 5, 9, in Volume 11, Part 1 (Atlanta: Jas. P. Harrison & Co., 1885). *1886:* "Supplemental Report . . . 1886," *Circular,* new series, Number 87, pp. 5, 10, in Volume 12 (Atlanta: Constitution Book & Job, 1886). *1887:* "Supplemental Report . . . 1887," *Circular,* new series, Number 100, pp. 5, 10, in Volume 13 (Atlanta: Constitution Book & Job, 1887). *1888:* "Supplemental Crop Report . . . 1888," *Circular,* new series, Number 113, pp. 2–4, in Volume 14 (Atlanta: W. J. Campbell, 1889). *1889:* "Supplemental Report–1889," *Circular,* new series, Number 124, p. 4, in Volume 15 (Atlanta: Constitution Book & Job, 1889). *1890:* "Supplemental Crop Report–1890," *Circular,* Third Series, Number 3, p. 10, in Volume 16 (Atlanta: Geo. W. Harrison, 1891).

Table D.2. *Implicit interest rate (percent) charged by Georgia merchants*
for corn and bacon bought on credit: 1879, 1880, 1882–1890

| | Assuming average loan period of: | | | |
| | Six months | | Four months | |
Year	For corn	For bacon	For corn	For bacon
1879	60.0	71.4	90.0	107.1
1880	61.5	40.0	92.3	60.0
1881	—	—	—	—
1882	50.9	42.9	76.4	64.4
1883	80.6	53.7	120.9	80.6
1884	56.8	59.1	85.2	88.7
1885	60.5	62.5	90.8	93.8
1886	69.6	85.0	104.4	127.5
1887	72.2	61.0	108.3	91.5
1888	54.5	53.3	81.8	80.0
1889	63.6	62.5	95.4	93.8
1890	50.0	60.0	75.0	90.0
Average, 11 years	61.8	59.2	92.8	88.9

Source: Table D.1.

Woodward provides no citation for this assertion, and we have found no
evidence that would support it. The wholesale business seems to have been
vigorously competitive in the nineteenth century;[13] the efficiency of the
credit rating and collection agencies reduced the risk to wholesalers selling
goods on consignment, and what scattered evidence we have found suggests that merchants were charged between 3 and 15 percent for trade
credit. Glenn Sisk, who has proved reliable in other regards, reports that
wholesale merchants generally charged retail merchants 6 percent interest
beginning after an initial "free" month.[14]

Whatever the actual charges made by wholesalers supplying the southern
merchant, it is important to make the theoretical point that the "opportunity
cost" of credit to the merchant that would be appropriate to compare with
the rates he charged southern farmers would be the going rate for short-
term loans. A merchant with reasonable credit should have been able to
borrow money at between 6 and 10 percent and use the principal to purchase his supplies for cash.[15] If, in dealing directly with the wholesale
merchants, he chose to pay markedly higher rates than this (and there is no
evidence that he had to do so), it was either because he valued the conve-
nience of a single transaction or because of his own inability to borrow at
more reasonable rates. But in either of these cases, it would have been the
rural merchant's monopoly position that allowed him to afford the higher

Table D.3. *Cash prices, credit prices, and implicit interest rates charged by Louisiana merchants for corn: 1886–1896*

Day of observation	Average cash price (cents/bushel)	Average credit price (cents/bushel)	Implicit interest rate (%)
May 1, 1886	67.5	97.0	87.4
May 1, 1887	66.5	91.9	76.4
May 1, 1888	73.4	95.7	60.8
June 1, 1889	65.6	87.6	80.5
June 1, 1890	64.5	86.4	81.5
June 1,1891	95.1	118.9	60.1
June 1, 1892	75.4	97.8	70.3
June 1, 1893	65.4	86.0	75.6
June 1, 1894	67.4	86.8	69.1
June 1, 1895	64.9	85.2	75.1
June 1, 1896	51.3	70.6	90.3
Average, 11 years			75.3

Source: Taken from Louisiana, Bureau of Agriculture, *Biennial Report of the Commissioner of Agriculture of the State of Louisiana,* as follows: *1886:* "Crop Report for the Month of May, 1886," *Circular,* Number 2, in *Biennial Report . . . May, 1888* (Baton Rouge: Leon Jastremski, 1888), table facing p. 32. *1887:* "Report for May, 1887," in ibid., table facing p. 94. *1888:* "Crop Report far [sic] May, 1888," *Circular Series of 1888,* Number 2, in *Biennial Report . . . April, 1890* (Baton Rouge: Truth Job Office, nd), table facing p. 20. *1889:* "Crop Report for May [1889]," *Circular Series of 1889,* Number 2, in ibid., table facing p. 150. *1890:* "Report . . . for May, 1890," *Circular Series of 1890,* Number 2, in *Biennial Report . . . April, 1892* (Baton Rouge: Truth Job Office, 1892), table facing p. 30. *1891:* "Crop Report for May, 1891," *Circular Series of 1891,* Number 3, in ibid., table facing p. 142. *1892:* "Report . . . May, 1892," *Circular Series of 1892,* Number 2, in *Biennial Report . . . April, 1894* (Baton Rouge: Truth Book & Job, 1894), np. *1893:* "Report . . . May, 1893," *Circular Series of 1893,* Number 2, in ibid., np. *1894:* "Crop Report for May, 1894," *Circular Series of 1894,* Number 2, in *Biennial Report . . . January, 1896* (Baton Rouge: Truth Book & Job, 1896), table facing p. 24. *1895:* "Crop Report for May, 1895," *Circular Series of 1895,* Number 2, in ibid., table facing p. 158. *1896:* "Crop Report for May, 1896," *Circular Series of 1896,* Number 2, in *Biennial Report . . . January, 1898* (Baton Rouge: Truth Book & Job, 1898), np.

charges. In a competitive market he would have to secure money at the going rate in order to remain in business and earn a normal rate of return. A credit charge is *exorbitant* (i.e., noncompetitive) when it exceeds the riskless default-free rate of interest, adjusted for the probability of default by the borrower plus any legitimate costs of processing the loan. This is true irrespective of the additional costs incurred by, or the economic efficiency of, the lender.

The risk of default

Some contemporary observers excused the magnitude of the interest rates charged by merchants by referring to the presumably high risks of the business. One of the crop reports of the Georgia Department of Agriculture commented:

> It is not altogether the merchants fault that such prices are demanded. . . . The risk on such sales is exceptionally hazardous, and the seller must charge such a percentage on time sales as will save him from loss at the hands of those who fail to pay, or pay at the end of expensive litigation.[16]

On the other hand, as we noted in Chapter 7, it is unlikely that the risks of default were so high that interest rates in the neighborhood of 60 percent could be justified. The implicit rate of default can be computed from the quoted rates. The total return to the merchant from his credit sales will be the time price charged, T, times the fraction of the amount owed that is actually paid. If d is the fraction of the accounts owed that is not paid, that is, the default rate, then $(1 - d)T$ is the net return on the investment. The loan advanced is equivalent to the cash price of the goods, C, and thus:

$$\frac{(1 - d)T - C}{C}$$

is the rate of return. This should be compared with the short-term interest rate of 10 percent per year or 5 percent for six months. From the figures in Table 7.1 we calculate that T/C averaged 1.297 between 1881 and 1889 in Georgia. Substituting these values into the formula gives $1.297(1 - d) - 1 = 0.05$. Solving for d gives 0.190.

This calculation implies that the merchant would have to have anticipated a loss of 19 percent of his loans over the forthcoming six months to justify charging a 59.4 percent rate of annual interest. This is an annual default rate of 38 percent. If merchants demanded a 50 percent markup on cash prices for extending six months of credit (100 percent interest), the default rate would have to have been 30 percent (60 percent annually). To justify a rate of only 40 percent, the anticipated annual default rate would have to have been 25 percent. If such high potential default rates actually prevailed, it is likely that merchants would have taken steps to reduce the actual rates of loss. This might have been done by discriminating against poor credit risks and by employing supervisory personnel to oversee the debtors' farms. There is evidence that merchants did both. Thomas Clark reports that good credit risks were charged less than poor ones,[17] and it was universal practice for the merchant to supervise his customers closely.

Supervisory costs

To compute the nonexorbitant rate of interest, which includes the cost of supervision, we must modify the formula already given. We use S to denote the outlay for supervision. Therefore:

$$\frac{(1 - d)T - C - S}{C} = 0.05$$

In Chapter 7 we calculate that an exaggerated allowance for supervision would be 6.25 percent of the principal loaned annually. Supposing the risk of default would have been, even with supervision, as high as 5 percent annually, we have for a six-month period:

$$0.975\,(T/C) - 1 - 0.03125 = 0.05$$
$$0.975\,(T/C) = 1.08125$$
$$T/C = 1.109$$

The highest rate a merchant could justifiably charge, even with these exaggerated assumptions concerning the expense and effectiveness of supervision, would be 10.9 percent for six months or 21.8 percent on an annual basis.

CALCULATION OF FOOD RESIDUALS ON SOUTHERN FARMS: 1880

The estimates of food surpluses and deficits on farms in the Cotton South presented in Table 8.3 are based on new estimates of the seeding practices and feeding practices on small southern farms around 1880. We constructed new estimates because of problems with our own earlier estimates and the inapplicability of the estimates of other writers who have examined self-sufficiency in the antebellum period.[1]

All the estimates in the earlier studies were deliberately biased against the hypotheses being tested. Such biases were introduced as a check against possible overstatement of the authors' cases. The antebellum studies attempted to establish the *presence* of self-sufficiency, and thus minimized food production and exaggerated consumption. Our earlier postbellum study attempted to demonstrate the *absence* of self-sufficiency, and therefore we deliberately understated the consumption requirements of the farm. Having demonstrated the absence of self-sufficiency employing extreme assumptions, we wished to construct more realistic estimates for the present study. Nevertheless, where doubt existed concerning actual practice, we have consciously attempted to make conservative judgments which, if they erred, would likely exaggerate food production and understate consumption.

Obviously, farm practices in any period vary a great deal from farm to farm and region to region. In our estimates we have tried to mirror what seem to be the normal habits of the southern cotton farmer who operated a one-family farm, since that class of farms is the focus of our analysis of the lock-in mechanism. As a result, our estimate of residual food on these farms is probably more accurate than on the larger farms or plantations in the South. The method used to calculate the residual grain production remaining for human consumption can be outlined in three steps:

1. The outputs of grain and other feed on the farm were adjusted to net outputs by subtracting allowances for seeding each crop.
2. The net feed outputs were then converted into corn-equivalent bushels using equivalence ratios based upon the nutritional value of each crop.

Notes to Appendix E appear on pages 362–363.

244

These corn-equivalent bushels of feed were then aggregated to obtain the total net grain production on the farm.

3. The net output was then reduced by the estimated amount of corn-equivalent bushels of feed consumed on the farm by work animals and animals raised for sale. Allowance was also made for rations provided hired workers employed during the year. Excluded from this calculation were swine and poultry, which were fed primarily in order to produce meat for the farm population.

Feed grains grown in the South

We have included the reported outputs for eleven feed crops grown on southern farms: corn, wheat, oats, rye, barley, buckwheat, cowpeas, dried beans, rice, Irish potatoes, and sweet potatoes. No other crops were commonly used as feed by southern farmers. Some additional food for farm families would have been available from garden vegetables and fruits; however, these could only have modestly supplemented the basic diet.[2]

We have tried, whenever possible, to derive estimates of the seed per acre commonly sown for these crops on southern farms. Seeding practices varied considerably. This is to be expected; there is a wide range where substitution of labor inputs for seed inputs is possible, particularly with corn, peas, and potatoes. The most important crop for our analysis is corn. Seed used for the corn crop ranged from as little as 0.125 bushel per acre when corn was planted sparingly in hills to as much as 3 bushels per acre when it was sown with drills. There is indication from the contemporary sources that planting both in hills and with drills was common. Editorial advice tended to favor planting in hills; however, the relatively low yields achieved per acre and the scarcity of labor at corn planting time (when the cotton crop also required attention) suggest that the practice of planting with drills was more common. Nevertheless, so that our estimates of net output will be on the generous side, we have taken the low figure of 0.25 bushel of corn per acre planted as the average for the Cotton South.

The practice for other crops in the South in 1880 was apparently based on rules of thumb that tended to be seed-intensive. Records of actual practices are not abundant, and those reported in experimental station reports were almost always exceptional cases. Table E.1 summarizes seed requirements collected from a review of the agricultural journals of the times. Since the suggested practices were those either recommended by the editors or reported by successful farmers, they stand as conservative estimates of the less efficient practices followed by the average farmer. To be even more cautious, we have employed for our calculations the *lowest* seed requirement in any case where a range of observations was reported. Because of the absence of reliable acreage data for the crops in beans, peas, and potatoes, the seed requirements of these crops have been expressed as a percentage of the achieved yields: 8 percent of the bean and pea crop was allocated for seed; 3 percent of the potato crop was reserved for future crops.[3]

Table E.1. *Seed requirements in the South: circa 1880*

Crop	Observed bushels per acre		Estimate used to calculate food residuals (bushels per acre)
	Mimimum	Maximum	
Corn (in hills)	0.125[a]	0.25 [b] ⎫	
Corn (with drills)	2.00[b]	3.00[b] ⎬	0.25
Oats	1.25[c]	2.00[a,b]	1.25
Wheat	1.50[a,b]	2.00[a,b]	1.50
Buckwheat	0.50[d]	1.00[d]	0.50
Rye		1.50[a,b]	1.50
Barley		2.00[a,b]	2.00
Rice		180 lb[e]	180 lb/acre

[a] "Timely Farm and Plantation Topics," *Rural Carolinian* 1 (June 1870), p. 573. [b] "Facts and Figures for Farmers," *Rural Carolinian* 1 (January 1870), p. 211. [c] *Southern Cultivator* 28 (August 1870), pp. 254–255. [d] *Southern Cultivator* 43 (1885), p. 235. [e] "Topics for Rice Farmers," *Rural Carolinian* 1 (July 1870), p. 607.

Our estimates of food production make no allowance for losses because of crop perishability, damage by insects and rodents, or losses in processing. Our desire to keep the final estimates of food deficits conservative dictated this neglect.

Corn-equivalent units

We have computed ratios to convert bushels of feed grains into their nutritional equivalence in bushels of corn. The ratios, presented in Table E.2, are based on the total digestible nutrients available to the animal. Wherever possible, we have relied upon the earliest estimates of the nutritional content of feeds, since the quality of the grains measured would have been closer to those available in 1880. For example, the food value of hybrid corn was about 10 percent less than that of the native variety grown in the nineteenth century.[4] To illustrate that equivalencies of the order of magnitude we have employed were appreciated by practicing farmers in the late nineteenth-century South, we have included in Table E.2 some comparative values of grains published in the *Rural Carolinian* in 1870. The values derived from this early source are remarkably close to the scientific estimates.

Feed requirements for livestock

To account for the feed required by work stock, we constructed estimates of the corn-equivalent bushels of feed required to maintain each work animal: horses, mules, asses, and oxen. Our estimates are based upon studies of

Table E.2. *Nutritional values of farm crops in corn-equivalent units*

Crop	Pounds per bushel[a]	Conversion ratio to bushels of corn[b]	Conversion ratios implied in 1870 *Rural Carolinian*[c]
Corn	56	1.000	1.00
Barley	48	0.866	0.94
Buckwheat	48	0.620	0.75
Oats	32	0.433	0.54
Rye	56	1.050	1.14
Wheat	60	1.104	1.40
Cowpeas	60	0.946	1.36
Dried beans	60	0.946	1.30
Irish potatoes	60	0.220	—
Sweet potatoes	60	0.362	0.31
Rice[d]	1	0.014	—

[a] Bushel weights are from "Facts and Figures for Farmers," *Rural Carolinian* 1 (January 1870), p. 211; they agree with those in B. F. Dancy, "Stock Feeding, as Practiced in North Carolina," *North Carolina Experiment Station Bulletin*, Number 66 (September 1889), p. 70. However, in the case of cowpeas, dried beans, and potatoes, the weights given most likely exaggerate the actual weight of bushels used at the time. Richard Sutch, "The Treatment Received by American Slaves: A Critical Review of the Evidence Presented in *Time on the Cross*," *Explorations in Economic History* 12 (October 1975), pp. 374, 377.
[b] Conversion ratios were computed from net energy values of feed given in W. A. Henry and F. B. Morrison, eds., *Feeds and Feeding: A Handbook for the Student and Stockman*, 17th ed. (Madison: Henry-Morrison Co., 1921), p. 121, for all crops except buckwheat, sweet potatoes, and rice, which were computed from net energy values given in F. B. Morrison, *Feeds and Feeding: A Handbook for the Student and Stockman*, 20th ed. (Ithica: Morrison Co., 1940). Morrison does not give nutritional value for dried beans. Since contemporaries viewed cowpeas and dried beans as roughly equivalent, we have used the same conversion ratio for both.
[c] Conversion ratios computed from nutritional equivalences and bushel weights published in *Rural Carolinian* 1 (January 1870), p. 211.
[d] The conversion ratio for rice is given in terms of pounds of rice to bushels of corn, since the census reported rice output in pounds.

nutritional needs reported by Morrison[5] and estimates of feeding practices reported by agricultural journals of the time.

The estimates of feed consumption of livestock constructed by Jennings for the U.S. Department of Agricultural form the basis of Robert Gallman's estimates of feed requirements used in his study of self-sufficiency in the antebellum South.[6] Gallman considered the Jennings estimates for 1909 to represent an upper bound to the grain fed southern animals fifty years previously. However, we feel Jennings's estimates are not applicable to small farms in the postbellum South. His estimates of feed consumption by livestock are constructed by dividing the total estimated feed consumed by livestock on farms in the United States by the stock of animals on farms that year. Such a procedure will obviously obscure any regional difference in feeding practices. Moreover, Jennings's estimates of the *grain* fed to animals assumes no differences between regions with regard to the use of pasturage, forage, and fodder as food for farm animals. Our extensive examination of southern practices suggests that cotton farmers relied more extensively than other regions on grain for feed.[7] We suspect, therefore, that the Jennings estimates for grain fed to animals could well be low, not high, when applied to southern farms. Finally, we note that Jennings's disaggregation of his data by class of animals was extremely crude. Detailed breakdowns by specific animal were obtained by applying broad allocative factors to the total fed to all animals. Thus, he notes: "If one class of livestock has been allocated too much feed, some other kind will have less. A large probable error should be allowed for, especially in the more detailed tables."[8]

Because our study is particularly sensitive to possible errors in one class of animals – work stock – Jennings's procedure is inappropriate. We have therefore chosen to construct our own estimates, based on the reports of contemporaries regarding actual practices and the necessary nutritional standards reported by experiments with animals.

A sampling of reported practices of southerners for feeding horses and mules is presented in Table E.3. The wide range of practices in the South is apparent from the table and illustrates the inherent problem of deriving an "average" level of feeding for work stock. Most of the estimates probably reflect practices that are above average for small farmers, who were notorious for their inadequate treatment of working stock. A survey of actual feeding practices of North Carolina farmers in 1889 gave 41 bushels as the "low" feeding practice for horses; the "average practice" was 68 bushels. For mules, Table E.3 reports one observation of 25 bushels for a one-year-old mule; the minimum reported for a fully grown animal was 36 bushels (required by an "idle mule"). The North Carolina survey reported a "low" practice of 29 bushels of corn and an "average" of 65 bushels for mules.

Of course, not all the animal feed was from the grains grown on the farm or purchased. Some roughage was always available from crops, and pasture could provide additional food as well. Nor were all the enumerated work stock adult animals; young animals required less food. However, for the consideration of work stock on the small cotton farms of the South, our sample of southern farms in 1880 suggests that most farms maintained only adult working animals throughout the year; breeding operations were not common on the small family farms that constitute the focus of our analysis of debt peonage.[9] Moreover, complaints in the agricultural journals suggest that not all farmers provided adequate feed for their stock throughout the year. To account for poor feeding practices, the presence of young work stock on the farm, and the presence of forage, we have adopted an estimate of average feed consumption of 35 bushels of corn for horses and oxen,[10] and 30 bushels of corn for mules (see Table E.4). We are confident that our estimates are conservative estimates of actual feeding practices for work stock on southern farms around 1880.[11]

Table E.3. *Observed feeding practices for livestock in the South*

Source[a]	Number of corn-equivalent bushels per year fed as grain	Comments[b]
Horses		
SC (Jan. 1868)	75	Plus fodder and pasture (p. 12)
L&A (1869)	75	Recommended average (pp. 145–146)
SC (Dec. 1870)	80	Practice of a Negro woman on a sharecropped farm (p. 418)
SC (1886)	50	"May appear small"; to be supplemented with peas, etc. (pp. 91–93)
Survey (1889)	41	"Low practice" at light work; plus estimated 19 bushels of corn-equivalent fodder (p. 70)
Survey (1889)	68	"Average practice" at light work; plus estimated 32 bushels of corn-equivalent fodder (p. 70)
Mules		
Peters (1867)	70	(p. 18)
RC (Nov. 1869)	125	"High culture" (p. 89)
SC (Nov. 1870)	82.5	"For the average cotton farm . . . if working *all* the time" (pp. 403–404)
SC (Sept. 1870)	90	For cotton work (p. 292) plus 2,000 pounds of hay
SC (Sept. 1870)	60	For "other" work; plus estimated 9 bushels of corn-equivalent fodder (p. 292)
SC (Nov. 1870)	75	"No mule will need more if otherwise attended to" (p. 374)
SC (Nov. 1870)	36	"For idle mule" (p. 374)
SC (Nov. 1870)	75	"For cotton work"; plus estimated 27 bushels of corn-equivalent fodder (p. 375)
SC (Nov. 1870)	60	"For half cotton/half corn work"; plus estimated 21 bushels of corn-equivalent fodder (p. 375)
SC (Dec. 1870)	80	A Negro woman's practice (p. 418)
SC (July 1870)	25	One year old (p. 208)
SC (July 1870)	50	Two year old (p. 208)
SC (June 1872)	100	(p. 218)
Survey (1889)	29	Ordinary work; lowest practice; plus 20 bushels of corn-equivalent fodder (p. 71)
Survey (1889)	65	Ordinary work; average practice; plus 31 bushels of corn-equivalent fodder (p. 71)

[a] Source abbreviations are: *SC, Southern Cultivator; RC, Rural Carolinian; L&A,* F. W. Loring and C. F. Atkinson, *Cotton Culture and the South Considered with Reference to Emigration* (Boston: A. Williams, 1869); Survey, B. F. Dancy, "Stock Feeding, as Practiced in North Carolina," *North Carolina Experiment Station Bulletin,* Number 66 (September 1889); Peters, Theodore C. Peters, *A Report upon Conditions of the South, with Regard to its Needs for a Cotton Crop and its Financial Wants in Connection Therewith* (Baltimore: H. A. Robinson for R. M. Rhodes & Co., 1867).

[b] When grain was supplemented with fodder pulled from cornstalks, we have converted them to corn-equivalent bushels using the ratio of 2 pounds of fodder equal to 1 pound of corn.

The other livestock enumerated on farms were swine, milch cows, other cattle, and sheep. Of these, swine were by far the most significant. Virtually every farm had at least one or two hogs; the average on small family farms was about ten swine. These animals consumed large amounts of food over the course of a year. On the other hand, swine also represented the supply of meat to the family. We noted in Chapter 8 that there is no evidence that the stock of swine per capita in the South increased between 1870 and 1890. Nor have we found any evidence that small cotton farmers were raising swine for sale off the farm. Thus it seems reasonable to suggest that all the corn fed to swine was ultimately consumed in the form of pork by the farm family. We have not allocated any of the grain production to swine in our feeding requirements, since we shall assume below that this grain was not lost as food, but merely consumed in a different form. The same argument applies with respect to "other cattle" on the farm and to any poultry. We allocate no grain to them on the assumption that such feed would eventually appear as meat (or eggs) for the farm family.

Milch cows and sheep must be fed in our model, since these animals were not frequently slaughtered. The dairy products would be consumed, but we have selected feeding requirements so low as to exclude the food energy required by an animal to produce milk. On the basis of available evidence, we estimate that farmers provided true milch cows with between 6.5 and 9 bushels of grain per animal.[12] For our purposes we have lowered this figure to 5 bushels per animal. Sheep were generally kept on pastureland, and required very little additional feed. We allocate 0.25 bushel of corn per year to sheep as feed.

Table E.4. *Feed allowances for animals on cotton farms (in corn-equivalent bushels)*

| Animal | Reasonable allowance, 1880[a] | Estimate, 1880 | | Gallman's allowance, 1860[c] |
		Lower bound[b]	Upper bound	
Horse	35.0	23.3	50.0	38.11
Ox	35.0	23.3	50.0	38.11
Mule	30.0	15.5	42.0	38.11
Milch cow	5.0	5.0	9.0	8.99
Other cattle	0.0[d]	1.0	2.6	2.60
Sheep	0.25	0.25	0.6	0.60

[a] These are the allowances used in Chapter 8; see text for a discussion.   [b] Roger Ransom and Richard Sutch, "Debt Peonage in the Cotton South after the Civil War," *Journal of Economic History* 32 (September 1972), p. 661.   [c] Robert E. Gallman, "Self-Sufficiency in the Cotton Economy of the Ante-bellum South," *Agricultural History* 44 (January 1970), pp. 10–11.   [d] See text.

A summary of our feeding requirements is presented in Table E.4. For comparative purposes, we have also reproduced the feed allowances used in Gallman's pre-Civil War study.

Human consumption needs

Once the output required for seed and animal feed is deducted, the residual constitutes food available to the farm population either in the form of grain or as feed for food-producing animals. There remains the question of how much grain was required for food by people on the farm. The absolute minimum measure of this requirement would seem to be the standard pork-corn ration fed to slaves, reduced to account for the lower energy needs of a free population. This figure, reported in Table E.5, is 21.1 bushels of corn (or its equivalent) per year per adult field hand. The more ample ration suggested by Fogel and Engerman would require 26.1 bushels. Observations of rations actually provided after the war, as might be expected, suggest that free laborers enjoyed a diet that contained relatively more meat than did the slave diet. Calories consumed in the form of meat require greater amounts of corn than calories consumed as corn or cornmeal. Widely scattered observations show that the amount of pork which could be produced from a bushel of corn ranged from 8.4 to 18.7 pounds.[13] We assume that the conversion of corn to pork took place at a ratio of 1 bushel of corn to 15 pounds of pork.[14]

Based on these figures, a reasonable measure of the food requirements of an adult hand in the postwar period would be 25 to 35 bushels of corn per year. However, it is clear from our calculations based on rations that, if necessary, workers could survive on 21 to 26 bushels. To account for the rations provided hired hands, we have subtracted 20 bushels of corn from the farm's net food supply for each full-time laborer employed during the year.

What remains after this subtraction for hired help constitutes the food available to the farm family. To estimate the family food requirements, we have employed the adult ration of 20 bushels of corn per year. Granting that a working adult requires greater caloric intake than the average for the entire population, we have taken 15 bushels to be our per capita ration for family members. This assumes that one-half the population received only a half ration.[15] Any farm producing less than this per capita amount would certainly have to purchase additional food away from the farm.

Tenure

One final adjustment in the estimated grain residual was required to account for differences in tenure among farms. Sharecropped farms were not responsible for feeding the working stock, which was the responsibility of the landlord (see Table 5.5). Therefore, on sharecropped farms, no output

Table E.5. *Rations provided free adult farm laborers, expressed as bushels of corn-equivalent grains required*

Source	Cornmeal[a]	Pork[b]	Other food[c]	Total corn-equivalent bushels required
Based on slave rations[d]				
Standard Rations[e]	11.1	10.0	—	21.1
Fogel and Engerman[f]	11.7	9.9	4.5	26.1
Observations of free labor				
Peters (1867)[g]	13.5	10.0	—	23.5
Capron (1867)[h]	13.5	12.2	—	25.7
Freedmen's Bureau (1865)[i]	13.5	17.4	—	30.9
Loring and Atkinson (1869)[j]	20.2	13.9	—	34.1

[a] Cornmeal rations were converted from meal back to unmilled corn applying the assumption that it required 1.037 bushels of corn to produce 1 bushel of cornmeal. This factor was determined from an examination of the manuscript returns of the 1880 manufacturing schedules for the 305 flour and grist mills reporting from our representative counties (see Appendix G, Section 2). The average for all mills was 51.32 pounds of meal from 1 bushel (56 pounds) of corn; however, the most common estimate of loss from milling was 2 pounds (reported by 103 of the mills). We used this estimate as our factor. It should be emphasized that, not only does this ratio of 54 pounds of meal for each bushel of corn imply a loss less than the average, it also neglects the costs of milling, which the farmer typically paid with a fraction of his crop.

[b] We assume that the conversion of corn to pork took place at a ratio of 15 pounds of pork to 1 bushel of corn. See discussion in text.

[c] For the purposes of converting the Fogel-Engerman diet to corn-equivalent units of production, we used the relationships in Table E.2 for potatoes, cowpeas, and grains. We assumed that beef could be produced as efficiently as pork, and we neglected outputs of dairy products. In every case, the assumptions biased the requirements downward.

[d] We have reduced the slave rations reported in our sources to reflect the lower energy requirements of free laborers, using the adjustment factors discussed in Chapter 8, note 14. The standard ration was reduced by 17.9 percent; the Fogel-Engerman ration by 22.7 percent.

[e] See Appendix A, note 16, for a list of references supporting this estimate.

[f] Because of a number of computational errors in the original source (Robert W. Fogel and Stanley L. Engerman, *Time on the Cross*, 2 vols. [Boston: Little, Brown & Co., 1974], 2, p. 97), we have employed the revised Fogel-Engerman diet calculated by Richard Sutch, "The Treatment Received by American Slaves: A Critical Review of the Evidence Presented in *Time on The Cross*," *Explorations in Economic History* 12 (October 1975), Table 2, pp. 380–381.

[g] Theodore C. Peters, *A Report upon Conditions of the South* (Baltimore: H. A. Robinson for R. M. Rhodes & Co., 1867), p. 18.

[h] Horace Capron, "Southern Agriculture," in *Report of the Commissioner of Agriculture for the Year 1867* (Washington: GPO, 1868), p. 416.

[i] This ration is the one the Freedmen's Bureau of Louisiana required in wage contracts for the 1866 season. The full reference is "Order of Brevet Major General A. Baird," *Circular*, Number 29, New Orleans, December 4, 1865. The document is reproduced in Charles L. Seagrave, "The Southern Negro Agricultural Worker: 1850–1870" (Ph.D. thesis, Stanford University, 1971), pp. 103–106.

[j] F. W. Loring and C. F. Atkinson, *Cotton Culture and the South Considered with Reference to Emigration* (Boston: A. Williams, 1869), p. 26.

was fed to the working stock (horses, mules, asses, or oxen). However, the sharecropper was committed to pay one-half of all output on the farm as rent. Therefore, the total food produced on the farm was divided by two before the portion that remained for the sharecropper's family was calculated. In all other respects, sharecropped farms were treated exactly as other farms.

ESTIMATES OF PER CAPITA GROSS CROP OUTPUT: 1859–1908

The only previous attempt of which we are aware to measure aggregate per capita agricultural income for the South in the late nineteenth century is Richard Easterlin's estimates of "agricultural service income per worker" for 1880 and 1900. Easterlin's calculations are based on Carol Brainerd and Ann Miller's estimates of the number of agricultural workers per state, on the census reports of the aggregate value of farm products produced in each state in 1879 and 1899, and on estimates of national agricultural service income for 1880 and 1900. The farm product figures from the census were used to partition and distribute to each state the estimate of the agricultural service income for the entire country. Agricultural service income for the United States was based upon Robert Martin's estimates.[1]

Easterlin's estimates put average agricultural service income in the Five Cotton States at $254.35 in 1880 and $258.30 in 1900, both measured in 1929 dollars.[2] This suggests that agricultural productivity in these states grew at a rate less than 0.08 percent per year during the last two decades of the century. Easterlin's estimates of per capita personal income in the Five Cotton States for 1880 and 1900 hardly present a more favorable view of southern development in this period. In 1929 dollars, per capita income increased from $156.06 to $185.25, representing a rate of growth of only 0.86 percent per annum, little more than one-half the national rate of growth.[3] While Easterlin's well-known estimates of regional personal income relatives suggest that the rate of growth for the "South" kept pace with that of the nation as a whole, inspection of his state-by-state figures demonstrate that this was true only because of the rapid economic growth experienced by Virginia, Florida, and Texas and the inclusion in the average for the South in 1900 of Oklahoma for the first time (that state's per capita income exceeded that of the Five Cotton States by 25 percent).[4]

Easterlin warned that his estimates of agricultural service income may be "liable to considerably more than 10 percent error."[5] Our own study suggests that the 1880 value of farm product Easterlin used to distribute Martin's aggregate was underestimated in the South relative to the other

Notes to Appendix F appear on pages 364–368.

states.[6] These inadequacies of Easterlin's estimates make them ill-suited for the purpose of measuring the rate of economic growth in the South's agricultural sector. Moreover, it is desirable to have more than two observations on income to calculate growth rates. As our own estimates later revealed, southern agricultural income in 1880 was abnormally high and in 1900 abnormally low; therefore, the rate of growth calculated between Easterlin's two dates is a poor estimate for the period they span.

For these reasons we have made our own estimates of agricultural output on an annual basis for the years 1866 through 1908 and have constructed a comparable measure for 1859. Our estimates incorporate the Five Cotton States: South Carolina, Georgia, Alabama, Mississippi, and Louisiana. Because of data limitations, we have restricted our estimates to aggregate crop output, a concept considerably more narrow than agricultural service income or personal income originating in agriculture.

Gross crop output: 1866–1908

Crop output is evaluated at farmgate prices and therefore is net of marketing, transportation, insurance, and storage charges. Our concept is gross of all farm expenditures except seed. Only crop outputs are included; therefore, our measure excludes value added in animal husbandry (both increases in the stock and the flow of animal and poultry products),[7] direct capital formation, and capital gains (or losses) arising from changes in land values. The most important of these omissions is value added in animal husbandry. Since the per capita stock of farm animals actually decreased during the period, this omission will bias the estimated growth rates upward. Our estimates also exclude the value of silk; turpentine; apiary products; forest, orchard, and nursery products; garden produce; and home manufacturing – all of which we define to be outside the farm sector.

The bases for most of our calculations are the annual "revised" estimates of crop output by state for 1866 through 1908 originally prepared by the U.S. Department of Agriculture's Bureau of Agricultural Economics (BAE) in the 1930s.[8] With the exceptions of cotton and sugar output, these crop estimates were based on the annual surveys of the U.S. Department of Agriculture's crop correspondents, a large corps of farmers located in each county of the country who reported on crop and weather conditions, acreage, yields, and prices on a regular basis. In preparing the revisions, the survey data were benchmarked by the BAE to census figures on crop output for each census year from 1879 to 1909. The annual estimates made for the first four years, 1866 through 1869, differ substantially from the original estimates made contemporaneously by the USDA.[9] The revisions drastically lowered the original estimates of crop output in the southern states. As extreme examples: the corn output for Alabama in 1866 was originally reported at 65 percent of the 1859 level, but was revised to 28 percent;[10] the 1866 production of oats in Louisiana was revised from parity

Table F.1. *Average farmgate prices: 1899–1908*

Crop	Unit	Price (dollars per unit) South Carolina	Georgia	Alabama	Mississippi	Louisiana
Cotton	Pound	0.0918	0.0920	0.0898	0.0910	0.0894
Sugar	Pound	0.0350	0.0350	0.0350	0.0350	0.0350
Rice	Pound	0.01596	0.01596	—	—	0.01596
Tobacco	Pound	0.0831	0.2215	0.2070	0.1994	—
Corn	Bushel	0.722	0.697	0.652	0.633	0.611
Oats	Bushel	0.594	0.58	0.549	0.544	0.490
Irish potatoes	Bushel	1.043	0.984	0.942	0.923	0.873
Sweet potatoes	Bushel	0.53	0.56	0.571	0.58	0.57
Rye	Bushel	1.177	1.111	1.111	—	—
Wheat	Bushel	1.09	1.052	0.976	0.900	—

Source: U.S. Department of Agriculture, Bureau of Agricultural Economics, "Prices of Farm Products Received by Producers," Volume 3, "South Atlantic and South Central States," *USDA Statistical Bulletin* Number 16, (Washington: GPO, 1927).

with 1859 to only 16 percent of that level;[11] and the wheat output of Mississippi in 1866, originally reported as 258,687 bushels, was revised downward to 120,000 bushels.[12] The reasons for these significant revisions is not given in any of the sources cited. Our own study has led us to suspect that the revised figures may exaggerate the initial decline in output and the subsequent rate of expansion in the immediate postwar recovery. Nevertheless, we have employed the revised rather than the original data. We have no reason to suspect that the revised series exaggerates the rate of growth of crop output for the period following 1879. For cotton and sugar the USDA estimates of annual output are based on marketing data. These series are discussed separately below.

The crops included in our estimate are cotton, sugar, rice, tobacco, corn, oats, Irish potatoes, sweet potatoes, rye, and wheat.[13] These ten crops accounted for 99.5 percent of the cultivated acreage in the Five Cotton States in 1879.[14] Three separate estimates were calculated: aggregate crop output evaluated at current farmgate prices, aggregate crop output evaluated at farmgate prices deflated to 1910–1914 dollars, and aggregate crop output evaluated at the average of farmgate prices for 1899–1908. For most of the crops the current farmgate prices were based on the USDA crop correspondents' reports of prices received by farmers in December of each year. These prices were compiled for the southern states in a 1927 *Statistical Bulletin*, Number 16.[15] *Bulletin 16* usually reported prices for the years before 1878 in terms of gold rather than currency. We have returned to the original reports for the currency prices reported in those years.[16] Therefore, our *current*-price series is a *currency*-price series throughout. We have used the Warren-Pearson-BLS wholesale price index for all commodities to deflate the *current*-price series to constant dollar terms.[17] For an index of physical crop output, we weighted the production of each crop using average farmgate prices from the ten-year period spanning 1899 through 1908. These fixed-price weights are given in Table F.1. Per capita estimates were obtained by dividing the aggregate output by our estimate of the rural population of the Five Cotton States for each year. This series is given in Table F.2. The three per capita output series are given in Tables F.2 and F.3. The specific procedures used to calculate the value of each crop and the size of the rural population are described below.

Detailed description of sources and procedures, crop estimates: 1866–1908

Cotton
The official USDA estimate of the annual output of lint cotton in pounds grown in each state is based on national marketing data originally compiled by Latham, Alexander, and Company, except for the years 1869, 1879, 1889, and 1899.[18] Inspection of the USDA data reveals that the total Latham-Alexander output (in thousands of pounds) was allocated by the BAE to the separate states in the same proportion as the states' contribution to the *preharvest* cotton crop predictions (in 400-pound bales) made each year by the USDA on the basis of the November crop reports received from the county correspondents.[19] The BAE departs from these sources and reports the Census of Agriculture estimates for census years. No attempt was made by the BAE to reconcile the differences between the Latham-Alexander figures and the census reports in those years. Our own study suggests that this presents a problem only for 1869. We reported in Chapter 3, note 59, that the census underenumerated actual cotton production in that year by approximately 12 percent. Accordingly we have adjusted the reported cotton output in that one year upward to correct for this underenumeration. No deduction was made for cotton seed, ginning, or baling since we do not include the value of cotton seed produced, most of which was typically paid to the gin operator to cover the costs of ginning and baling.

The prices of cotton received by farmers for the years 1879, 1880, and 1882 through 1908 are taken from *Bulletin 16*. Prices for 1876 and 1878 are also available and were taken from the USDA reports for those two years.[20] Farmgate prices are not available by state for earlier years or for 1877 and 1881. However, average farmgate prices for the United States have been published for the years beginning with 1869 in an early USDA report, compiled by George K. Holmes.[21] We have used Holmes's United States series to interpolate state prices for 1877 and 1881.[22] From the published sources it does not appear to be possible to make separate estimates of the farmgate price of cotton for each state for the years before 1876. We have therefore used the Holmes United States average prices for 1869–1875 and

Table F.2. *Estimates of value of crop output per capita, Five Cotton States: 1859, 1866–1908*

Year	Aggregate crop output evaluated at current prices (millions of dollars)	Rural population (thousands)	Per capita crop output current prices ($)	Deflated per capita crop output (1910–1914 dollars)
1859	318.1	3,747	84.89	89.36
1866	224.9	3,905	57.59	33.10
1867	276.7	3,991	69.33	42.80
1868	294.6	4,080	72.21	45.70
1869	307.8	4,170	73.81	48.88
1870	290.8	4,263	68.21	50.53
1871	269.6	4,358	61.86	47.58
1872	335.3	4,454	75.28	55.35
1873	282.5	4,553	62.05	46.65
1874	280.7	4,654	60.31	47.87
1875	279.4	4,758	58.72	49.76
1876	224.0	4,863	46.06	41.87
1877	246.6	4,971	49.61	46.80
1878	207.5	5,082	40.83	44.87
1879	271.7	5,194	52.31	58.12
1880	298.2	5,310	56.16	56.16
1881	274.1	5,378	50.97	49.49
1882	311.4	5,447	57.17	52.94
1883	255.3	5,517	46.28	45.82
1884	250.6	5,587	44.85	48.23
1885	255.9	5,659	45.22	53.20
1886	232.1	5,731	40.55	49.39
1887	274.5	5,804	47.29	55.64
1888	271.5	5,879	46.18	53.70
1889	303.6	5,954	50.99	62.95
1890	329.4	6,030	54.63	66.62
1891	292.5	6,129	47.72	58.20
1892	249.2	6,229	40.01	52.64
1893	259.8	6,332	41.03	52.60
1894	252.5	6,435	39.24	56.06
1895	261.8	6,541	40.02	56.37
1896	265.9	6,648	40.00	58.82
1897	309.7	6,757	45.83	67.40
1898	281.7	6,868	41.02	57.77
1899	283.0	6,981	40.54	52.65
1900	343.5	7,097	48.40	59.02
1901	337.9	7,171	47.12	58.17
1902	349.4	7,247	48.21	56.06
1903	431.0	7,323	58.86	67.66
1904	497.9	7,400	67.28	77.33
1905	465.1	7,477	62.20	70.68
1906	448.2	7,556	59.32	65.91
1907	499.9	7,635	65.47	68.92
1908	479.4	7,715	62.14	67.54

Table F.3. *Estimates of physical crop output per capita, Five Cotton States:*
1859, 1866–1908

Year	Aggregate crop output, evaluated at 1899–1908 prices (millions of dollars)	Per capita crop output, 1899–1908 prices ($)	Index of physical crop output per capita
1859	267.5	71.39	100.0
1866	83.0	21.25	29.8
1867	130.1	32.60	45.7
1868	131.6	32.25	45.2
1869	145.2	34.82	48.8
1870	189.0	44.34	62.1
1871	140.9	32.33	45.3
1872	186.6	41.89	58.7
1873	180.0	40.85	57.2
1874	180.4	38.76	54.3
1875	200.0	42.08	58.9
1876	202.6	41.66	58.4
1877	211.3	42.51	59.5
1878	209.1	41.15	57.6
1879	240.0	46.21	64.7
1880	258.2	48.63	68.1
1881	219.0	40.72	57.0
1882	297.4	54.60	76.5
1883	238.2	43.18	60.5
1884	243.5	43.58	61.0
1885	275.4	48.67	68.2
1886	251.8	43.94	61.5
1887	289.5	49.88	69.9
1888	285.0	48.48	67.9
1889	322.0	54.08	75.8
1890	328.3	54.44	76.3
1891	336.8	54.95	77.0
1892	280.5	45.03	63.1
1893	312.0	49.27	69.0
1894	383.4	59.58	83.5
1895	341.3	52.18	73.1
1896	355.2	53.43	74.8
1897	407.5	60.31	84.5
1898	414.6	60.37	84.6
1899	361.0	51.71	72.4
1900	348.6	49.12	68.8
1901	370.8	51.71	72.4
1902	352.2	48.60	68.1
1903	404.3	55.21	77.3
1904	503.0	67.97	95.2
1905	412.5	55.17	77.3
1906	436.7	57.80	81.0
1907	443.8	58.13	81.4
1908	462.0	59.88	83.9

applied them uniformly to each of the five states. It was necessary to convert Holmes's gold prices to currency prices using the November average price of gold. The reflated Holmes series was extrapolated backward for three years (1866, 1867, and 1868) using the average New York wholesale price of cotton as a guide.[23]

Sugar

Raw sugar production in (short) tons for Louisiana is taken from the 1923 *USDA Yearbook*. The yearbook also provides statistics for sugar produced in the balance of the United States, but this series is not disaggregated by state of origin.[24] The aggregate figures for United States production are apparently based upon the marketing data originally compiled by Willett and Gray. These figures are the basis of the U.S. Beet Sugar Association estimates used by Towne and Rasmussen and by Strauss and Bean.[25] The Willett and Gray estimates exclude sugar syrup, refined molasses, and by-product molasses. Production of molasses was reported in the censuses, and these figures were linearly interpolated to obtain annual molasses output.[26] Molasses production was converted to raw sugar equivalents at the rate of 9 pounds of sugar per gallon of molasses.[27] The non-Louisiana production of sugar and molasses was disaggregated into estimates for each of the other four Cotton States and a residual using linearly interpolated proportions based on census production statistics.

The farmgate price of sugar was estimated as 72.1 percent of the New York wholesale price published in *Historical Statistics*.[28] The same series was applied uniformly to each of the five states. The farmgate wholesale price ratio was estimated from data in the Aldrich reports and Lewis Gray's *History of Southern Agriculture*.[29]

Rice

Of the Five Cotton States only South Carolina, Georgia, and Louisiana grew significant amounts of rice.[30] For these three states, production in hundredweights for the years 1895–1908 has been estimated by the USDA.[31] For the commercial years before 1895, Holmes has prepared an annual series of national data reported in 162-pound barrels.[32] This series was converted to hundredweights and put on a crop year basis using the procedure, adopted by Strauss and Bean, of taking 40 percent of the commercial year production as output of the previous year's crop and 60 percent as the current crop.[33] The adjusted Holmes series was disaggregated into state estimates by using the proportions of national rice output reported for each state at the censuses linearly interpolated for the intercensual years. For every year the three states produced over 90 percent of national output A deduction of 5 percent was made for seed based on the seed requirements outlined in Appendix E, Table E.1.

Rice in all three states was evaluated using the Strauss and Bean series of farmgate prices, which they calculated as 30 percent of the New York wholesale price.[34]

Tobacco

Tobacco was not a major staple crop in any of the five states under consideration. What was grown was apparently produced in small amounts as a specialty crop or for local consumption. Annual production data are available only for South Carolina since 1889 and for Georgia since 1899.[35] The only other source of state-by-state production is the census. We have linearly interpolated the census data in pounds for each state as our measure of tobacco production. Louisiana grew negligible quantities of tobacco and was accordingly excluded from the estimates. No deduction was made for seed.

Tobacco prices per pound vary considerably by grade. For total United States production, Strauss and Bean used the national series published by the BAE.[36] However, the scattered statistics by states obtained from the USDA crop reporters suggest that the farmers of the Five Cotton States received considerably higher prices than those typical in the major tobacco-producing states.[37] This can be accounted for by the presumption that a higher fraction of the total crop in these states was specialty grades that commanded premium prices and by the fact that the local market for the common grades would presumably pay a better price than the commercial market of the tobacco states. The missing values in the incomplete farmgate price series for the cotton states were interpolated using the Virginia farmgate series as a guide.[38]

Corn

The BAE output estimates for Indian corn in bushels were used as our estimate of corn production. A deduction of 0.25 bushel per acre of corn harvested was made for a seed allowance (see Appendix E, Table E.1).[39]

Currency prices for each state for the years 1866 through 1877 were taken from the annual reports of the USDA. The prices for 1878 and all subsequent years were taken from *Bulletin 16*.[40]

Oats

Oat production in bushels was estimated for each year by the BAE. A deduction of 1.25 bushels per acre was allowed for seed (Table E.1).[41]

Oat prices were obtained from the same reports as corn prices, except that the oat price for 1868 for Louisiana had to be obtained from the USDA report for that year.[42] Missing prices for Louisiana for 1866, 1876, and 1877 were estimated by interpolation using Mississippi oat prices as a guide.[43]

Irish potatoes

White potato production in bushels has been estimated by the BAE.[44] A 3 percent deduction for seed was allowed (See Appendix E, note 3).

Farmgate prices were obtained from the same sources as corn prices. Missing price data for Georgia (1876–1878) and Louisiana (1877–1880) were interpolated using prices in neighboring states as a guide.[45]

Sweet potatoes

Sweet potato and yam production in hundredweights for 1868 and after has been estimated by the USDA.[46] A 3 percent deduction was made for seed (see Appendix E, note 3), and the series was converted to 55-pound bushels. No output figures are given for 1866 and 1867 or for Mississippi in 1868 by the USDA. These missing observations were filled in by extrapolating the 1869–1870 ratio of sweet potato output to all crop output backward to those years.

Bulletin 16 erroneously reports sweet potato prices that have not been converted to gold prices for the years before 1878.[47] Sweet potato prices were not reported for 1876–1878, 1882, 1893–1894, and 1898. These observations were interpolated using regression techniques that related observed sweet potato prices to corn, oat, and Irish potato prices in neighboring states and sweet potato production within the state.[48]

Rye

The BAE has made annual estimates of rye production for South Carolina and Georgia, but not for Alabama, Mississippi, and Louisiana.[49] The census statistics indicate that rye was an insignificant crop in Mississippi and Louisiana, but that 10,000 to 20,000 bushels per year were raised in Alabama. We excluded Mississippi and Louisiana rye from our estimates, but calculated our own series for Alabama by interpolating between the census figures using the BAE annual series for Georgia.[50] A deduction of 1.5 bushels per acre was made for seed (see Appendix E, Table E.1).[51]

Rye prices were obtained for all three states from *Bulletin 16* and the various reports of the USDA used for the other grain crops. We have interpolated estimates for the 1866 and 1876–1879 prices in Georgia and Alabama using South Carolina rye prices and within-state wheat and corn prices as a guide.[52]

Wheat

According to the decennial census, wheat was an unimportant crop in Louisiana. For the other four states the BAE estimates of wheat production were adjusted to deduct a 1.5-bushel per acre seed allowance (see Appendix E, Table E.1).[53]

Wheat prices were obtained from the same sources as corn prices.

Aggregate crop output: 1859

Production estimates for 1859 were taken from the Eighth Census reports and are reproduced in Table F.4. The same deductions for seed were made in 1859 as for the other years. Molasses was converted to sugar equivalents by the procedure already described.

Price estimates used to evaluate production are the same as those employed in Appendix A, Table A.1, except for sugar, oats, and rye. The sources of these price estimates are given in the notes to Table F.4.

Table F.4. *Production, price, and value of crop output, Five Cotton States:* 1859

Crop	Unit	Production (thousands)	Price per unit ($)[a]	Value (thousands of dollars)	
				Current prices	1899–1908 prices
Cotton	Pound[b]	1,610,181	0.10	161,018	145,947
Sugar	Pound[c]	383,870	0.07125[d]	27,351	13,435
Rice[e]	Pound	177,939	0.02	3,559	2,840
Tobacco[f]	Pound	1,416	0.078	110	292
Corn	Bushel	124,980	0.84	104,983	82,683
Oats	Bushel	3,162	0.40[g]	1,265	1,811
Irish potatoes	Bushel	1,731	0.50	866	1,638
Sweet potatoes	Bushel	22,689	0.50	11,345	12,754
Rye[h]	Bushel	277	0.84[i]	233	314
Wheat[f]	Bushel	5,637	1.30	7,328	5,797
Total				318,058	267,511

[a] Unless otherwise noted, see source notes for prices in Appendix A, Table A.1., for citation.

[b] Cotton was originally reported in 400-pound bales.

[c] Sugar was originally reported in hogsheads, which we have converted to pounds assuming a weight of 1,150 pounds each on the authority of Lewis Gray, *History of Agriculture in the Southern United States to 1860*, 2 vols. (Washington: Carnegie Institution, 1933), 2, p. 1033. Molasses was originally reported in gallons, which we have converted to sugar equivalents at the rate of 9 pounds of sugar per gallon of molasses.

[d] The wholesale price of sugar "on the plantation" is given by Gray, *History of Agriculture, 2*, p. 1034.

[e] Excludes Alabama and Mississippi.

[f] Excludes Louisiana.

[g] Oat prices are for "local markets" in Virginia and are taken from Arthur G. Peterson, "Historical Study of Prices Received by Producers of Farm Products in Virginia, 1801–1927," Virginia Agricultural Experiment Station, *Technical Bulletin*, Number 37 (Blacksburg: Virginia Polytechnic Institute, 1939), p. 169. The U.S. Patent Office (*Annual Report . . . for the Year 1848* [Washington: Wendell & Van Benthuysen, 1849]); shows no particular regional variation in oat prices (p. 651).

[h] Excludes Mississippi and Louisiana.

[i] The U.S. Patent Office suggests that rye and corn sold for approximately the same price (*Annual Report . . . 1848*, p. 651). Thus we have employed the corn price for rye.

Source: U.S. Census Office, Eighth Census [1860], *Agriculture of the United States in 1860* (Washington GPO, 1864), pp. lxxviii, xlvi, lxiv, xxix, 185. Also see U.S. Census Office, Ninth Census [1870], *The Statistics of the Wealth and Industry of the United States* (Washington: GPO, 1872), pp. xxix–xcix.

Rural population

The population figures were benchmarked to the census enumerations of the Five Cotton States in 1850, 1860, 1880, 1890, 1900, and 1910.[54] The 1870 population was adjusted upward by 7.07 percent to compensate for the

6.6 percent undercount of the population we estimated for that census year.[55] For the census years 1870 through 1910 the fractions of the total population living in towns and cities with a population of 2,500 or more were based on census figures.[56] For 1860, the urban population of towns and cities over 2,500 was compiled from Census Office sources.[57]

The annual rate of rural population growth between 1870 and 1880 was used to interpolate population figures between those two dates and to extrapolate backward to 1866. The annual growth rates during each of the following three decades were used to interpolate population figures after 1880. The 1860 rural population estimate was extrapolated to 1859 using the rate of growth of the aggregate population between 1850 and 1860.

Addendum on rates of growth in the antebellum South

Until recently there was little doubt that the cotton economy of the South before the Civil War was inefficient, grew less rapidly than the northern economy, and provided less income for its inhabitants than its natural resources and population should have been able to secure. There also seemed little question that the cause of this lackluster performance was the South's dependence upon slave labor.[58] Stanley Engerman, however, has raised doubts about these propositions by his reinterpretation of Richard Easterlin's work on regional income. Engerman first presented his reinterpretation in the course of a discussion of the effects of slavery upon the southern economy in 1967, and the argument was elaborated in a paper published in 1971. It was then taken up by Robert Fogel and Engerman that same year and further refined in their controversial two-volume study of slavery, *Time on the Cross*.[59] For the purposes of this reinterpretation, Engerman reworked the 1840 and 1860 regional estimates of personal income relative to the United States average that had been developed in a series of articles by Richard Easterlin.[60]

Easterlin's income estimates for the year 1840 were made on a state-by-state basis. His estimates for 1860, however, were for the broad geographic divisions defined by the Bureau of the Census. Easterlin's figures, expressed as a percentage of the United States average, are reproduced in Table F.5. They show that antebellum southern incomes (South Atlantic and East South Central states) were 45 to 49 percent below the levels achieved in the Middle Atlantic and New England states in 1840, and 50 to 55 percent below the per capita income of the two northeastern regions in 1860. These figures place southern incomes lower relative to the national average in 1860 than they had been in 1840. Easterlin's figures seem to support both the proposition that the South was less prosperous than the Northeast and that its rate of growth was less rapid than in the states of the North.

There is, moreover, reason to believe that Easterlin's calculations exaggerate the progress made in the South between 1840 and 1860. They are

Table F.5. *Personal income per capita as a percent of United States average, by geographic division: 1840, 1860*

Geographic division[a]	Relative personal income per capita (%)	
	1840	1860
United States	100	100
New England	132	143
Middle Atlantic	136	137
East North Central	67	69
South Atlantic	70	65
East South Central	73	68
West North Central	75	66
West South Central	144	115

[a] States included in each region are as follows: *New England:* Connecticut, Rhode Island, Massachusetts, Vermont, New Hampshire, and Maine. *Middle Atlantic:* New York, Pennsylvania, New Jersey, Maryland, and Delaware. *East North Central:* Ohio, Michigan, Indiana, Illinois, and Wisconsin. *South Atlantic:* Virginia (including present-day West Virginia), North Carolina, South Carolina, Georgia, and Florida. *East South Central:* Kentucky, Tennessee, Alabama, and Mississippi. *West North Central:* Iowa and Missouri. In 1860 Minnesota, Nebraska, and Kansas were also included in this division. *West South Central:* Arkansas and Louisiana. For the sake of completeness we have included the figures for the western regions (West North Central and West South Central). However, because of their frontier nature and the noncomparability of the regional definitions used by Easterlin for 1840 and 1860, we have not considered these regions in the text on the advice of J. R. T. Hughes, "[Book Review of] Robert W. Fogel and Stanley L. Engerman, eds., *The Reinterpretation of American Economic History . . .*," *Explorations in Economic History* 10 (fall 1972), p. 123.
Source: Richard A. Easterlin, "Regional Income Trends, 1840–1950," in Seymour E. Harris, ed., *American Economic History* (New York: McGraw-Hill, 1961), Table 1, p. 528; Figure 1, p. 526.

based primarily upon the census returns for the crops of 1839 and 1859, respectively, and the representativeness of both sets of figures has been questioned. In Chapter 1 we pointed out that 1859 was an unusually bountiful crop year for the South, and figures for that year undoubtedly overstate the normal productivity of late antebellum agriculture in the South. At the same time, there is evidence that suggests that the 1840 Census may underreport the true levels of southern agricultural production in that year without simultaneously underreporting the population.[61] If there was not a similar underenumeration at the 1860 Census (and there is no evidence that there was), Easterlin's estimates may seriously overstate the rate of antebellum southern growth. The 1840 figure would be too low, while the 1860 figure would be too high. Furthermore, as Easterlin himself noted, his treatment of the service component of personal income would tend to produce an underestimate of the rate of growth of per capita income in the Northeast relative to the rest of the country, which would in turn lead to an understatement of the degree to which the gap between the southern and northern economies had widened during the period.[62]

Engerman's reinterpretation of Easterlin's figures was accomplished by modifying Easterlin's original estimates. Engerman's calculations proceed in two steps, both of which we believe are inappropriate in the context of the argument he was making.

Engerman first converted the Easterlin per capita income relatives to estimates of per capita income. He multiplied the relatives by Robert Gallman's estimate of gross national product in 1839 and 1859, and then divided these figures by the population enumerated in 1840 and 1860. This procedure gives a national average (in 1860 prices) of $96 in 1840 and $128 in 1860.[63] These figures imply an average annual growth rate for the national economy of 1.45 percent. While this calculation still leaves the southern income at 45 to 55 percent of the northeastern income, the implied rate of national growth is high enough that, despite their relative decline, southern income levels rose in absolute terms from $66 to $84 in the South Atlantic, and from $69 to $89 in the East South Central, states.[64] These figures represent a growth rate of less than 1.3 percent in both regions. Engerman argued on the basis of these figures that "growth did occur within the period in each of the sections."[65]

We have no doubt that there was some improvement in southern per capita income between 1840 and 1860. However, we doubt that Engerman's procedure accurately measures the growth rates. The rates calculated by Engerman's procedure are extremely sensitive to small changes in the per capita income relatives, yet Easterlin reported his relatives only to the nearest percentage point.[66] Engerman relied upon Easterlin's work sheets to prevent rounding errors from disturbing his calculations, although it is extremely doubtful that the underlying data justify Engerman's confidence in them. Easterlin's original estimates were expressed as relatives because he believed the available data could only be used to express relative regional income levels.

Engerman next aggregated the two southern regions and the West South Central division into an aggregate described as "the South," and he combined the two northeastern divisions with the East North Central and the West North Central divisions into an aggregate called "the North." Engerman's figures are reproduced in Table F.6. The aggregation of the subregions causes the rate of growth of per capita income in the "South" to rise to 1.67 percent per year, and that in the "North" to fall to 1.30. "Comparing rates of growth of per capita income between 1840 and 1860," Engerman concluded, "the southern economy does not appear stagnant."[67] This striking reversal in conclusions comes about because the aggregate growth rate in the South exceeds the rate of growth in each of its three subregions, while, during the same period, the rate of growth in the North was lower

Table F.6. *Personal income per capita, by geographic division: 1840, 1860*

	Personal income per capita, 1860 prices ($)		Annual rate of growth (%)
Geographic division[a]	1840	1860	
United States	96	128	1.45
North	109	141	1.30
Northeast	129	181	1.71
New England[b]	126	186	1.97
Middle Atlantic[b]	130	178	1.58
North Central	65	89	1.58
East North Central[b]	64	90	1.72
West North Central[b]	72	86	0.89
South	74	103	1.67
South Atlantic	66	84	1.21
East South Central	69	89	1.28
West South Central	151	184	0.99
South less Texas[c]	72	96	1.45
West South Central less Texas[b]	140	165	0.82

[a] See Table F.5, note *a*, for regional definitions. Engerman adjusted the West South Central to include Texas in both years.
[b] Engerman did not report these divisional figures. We have calculated them on the basis of Easterlin's relatives in Richard A. Easterlin, "Regional Income Trends, 1840–1950," in Seymour E. Harris, ed. *American Economic History* (New York: McGraw-Hill, 1961), Table 1, p. 528.
[c] Based on Easterlin's relatives in ibid. and population figures in U.S. Bureau of the Census, *Historical Statistics of the United States: Colonial Times to 1957* (Washington: GPO, 1960), p. 13.
Source: Stanley L. Engerman, "Some Economic Factors in Southern Backwardness in the Nineteenth Century," in John F. Kain and John R. Meyer, eds., *Essays in Regional Economics* (Cambridge: Harvard University Press, 1971), Table 2, p. 287.

than in any of its four subregions. This counterintuitive phenomenon arises because of the westward migration of population during the period. In the South the westward migration was away from regions of relatively low per capita income to regions of high average per capita income, raising the southern average. Westward migration in the northern regions, on the contrary, was from areas of high per capita income to regions of low per capita income.

To argue from these figures that the South grew more rapidly than the North, however, is highly misleading. Viewed in this way, southern growth occurred primarily because of a continuous migration to more productive soils of the West. Yet within each geographic division southern growth was slow (and slower on the good lands of the West South Central than on the poorer soils of the South Atlantic region). Rather than refuting the arguments that the southern slave economy was moribund, the figures in Table F.6 support the notions that the South was indeed stagnating with respect to the North and that the only recourse left to white southerners who wished to better their positions was to move westward.[68]

The northern population also shifted westward during this period, but the movement was from a high income region (New England and the Middle Atlantic states) to a lower income region (the East North Central and West North Central states). This migration was not an irrational act of individuals giving up high income jobs for low income ones, however. Rather, the bulk of the westward migration was made up of individuals leaving northeastern agriculture for western agriculture. Richard Easterlin has recently computed estimates of agricultural income per worker by geographic division for 1840 and 1860. These figures are reproduced in Table F.7.[69] They show, for example, that agricultural productivity in the East North Central region was 45 percent greater than in New England in 1860. In both the southern and northern cases the westward migration generally improved the lot of those who took part in it. The difference, of course, was that in the South those who moved west left behind a backward, slowly growing economy, while those from the North left behind a low-productivity agricultural sector within a rapidly growing and highly prosperous economy. Indeed, it can be argued that the northern improvements in agricultural productivity produced by migration were an integral part of the mechanism of economic growth in the North. Rising agricultural productiv-

Table F.7. *Agricultural income per worker and its rate of growth, by geographic division: 1840, 1860*

Geographic division[a]	Income per worker, 1879 prices ($)		Annual rate of growth (%)
	1840	1860	
United States	203	234	0.71
New England	175	177	0.06
Middle Atlantic	214	242	0.62
East North Central	218	257	0.83
South Atlantic	167	181	0.40
East South Central	218	240	0.48
West North Central	207	202	-0.12
West South Central	319	327	0.12

[a] See Table F.5, note *a*, for a definition of the regions.
Source: Richard A. Easterlin, "Farm Production and Incomes in Old and New Areas at Mid-Century," in David C. Klingaman and Richard K. Vedder, eds., *Essays in Nineteenth Century Economic History: The Old Northwest* (Athens: Ohio University Press, 1974), Table B.1, p. 110.

ity in the North and West freed even greater fractions of the population from farm labor and thereby facilitated northeastern industrialization, while the simultaneous westward movement of southerners did nothing to improve economic conditions in the regions they left behind.

Table F.7 also presents the rates of growth of agricultural productivity in the various regions. As can be seen, the rates of growth in southern agriculture lag behind those of the southern economy in general (Table F.6) and far behind the rates of growth of New England, the Middle Atlantic states, and the East North Central division (Table F.6).

Gathering statistics among the cotton plantations, drawn by Herrick, engraved by H. B. Hall (1871). Photograph reproduced from *One Hundred Years' Progress of the United States by Eminent Literary Men* (Hartford: L. Stebbins, 1871).

DATA APPENDIX

It might perhaps be a good thing to say to anyone who has to make a large quantitative statement about a group or class, "do not guess, try to count, and if you can not count admit that you are guessing." . . . It is particularly healthy to ask of any generalization the questions of how many? how often? how much and in what proportion?

George Kitson Clark, *The Making of Victorian England*
(Cambridge: Harvard University Press, 1962), p. 14.

DESCRIPTIONS OF MAJOR COLLECTIONS OF DATA GATHERED BY THE SOUTHERN ECONOMIC HISTORY PROJECT

The Southern Economic History Project was established in 1969, with financial assistance from the National Science Foundation and the University of California, to collect and analyze several large bodies of data from unpublished archival material. In this appendix we wish to describe each of the major collections of data gathered by the Southern Economic History Project. We also wish to define more precisely the geographic and temporal limitations we have used to restrict our attention for the purposes of this book.

Our desire has been to examine the implications of economic freedom for the ex-slave and the steps by which the southern economy reorganized itself after the Civil War. The eleven states that together formed the Confederacy against the Union, and that harbored the bulk of American blacks at the time of emancipation, incorporated a wide variety of regional differences and local problems. Nevertheless, and somewhat to our surprise, it proved possible to establish boundaries to a relatively large geographic region within which economic and social conditions were sufficiently homogeneous to allow accurate generalizations. Because of an association with cotton agriculture, we have, throughout the book, identified this region as the *Cotton South*. This area, outlined in the map facing Chapter 1, incorporates 337 counties from the eleven former Confederate States. Covering over 200,000 square miles, the Cotton South consists of a wide swath of territory running from the cotton-growing lands of the Carolinas through the black belts of Georgia, Alabama, and Mississippi, including the alluvial valleys of the Mississippi and Red rivers, and the eastern prairies of Texas.

The focus of our work has been on the three decades that followed the Civil War. For that reason, we chose to construct the boundaries of the Cotton South using the year 1880 as a benchmark, relying heavily on the Census of Agriculture in 1880 for our primary data. In that year the Tenth Census Office commissioned Eugene Hilgard to undertake an exhaustive study of cotton production in the United States. Hilgard's report, which included detailed statistical evidence from every cotton-producing state, provides an invaluable base upon which to construct a regional breakdown

Notes to Appendix G appear on pages 368–373.

of the Cotton South. While the available data would doubtless have led us to 1880 in any event, that year happens to be a very useful vantage point for reflecting upon the changes of the Reconstruction Period. The physical damage from the Civil War had been repaired by that time, and the external influence of northern power had been diminished with the removal of federal troops four years earlier. The reorganization of the economy had been largely completed by 1880; yet the effects of emancipation and the Civil War were still visible. The census year, 1880, was well before the disrupting influences of the boll weevil and the agricultural depression of later decades produced an impetus for a new round of economic and social change.

1. The Cotton South

The procedure we adopted to define the Cotton South began with the partitioning of the 993 counties in the eleven former Confederate States into sixty-three *economic regions*, each composed of two or more counties that shared common agricultural, demographic, economic, physiographic, and historical characteristics.[1] Two regions of the Confederacy, southern Florida and western Texas, were immediately excluded from our analysis because they lacked an established agriculture in 1880. Soil type and climatic conditions in each of the remaining 870 counties were first examined to construct tentative regional boundaries. Information on soil characteristics and condition in 1880 was obtained from Eugene Hilgard's study, which distinguished twenty-eight soil categories throughout the South.[2] These are listed in Table G.1 and identified in the map accompanying the table. Hilgard's soil and climatic divisions were checked against similar regional definitions by Lewis Gray, Hugh Bennett, and the more recent work of Alan Bogue and Calvin Beale.[3] All these sources supported Hilgard's divisions and reinforced our confidence in the 1880 survey. Each county was assigned to a soil group, and these groups defined the first tentative boundaries for economic regions.[4] Economic and demographic characteristics for each county were then collected from the published volumes of the Tenth Census.[5] These data were used to redefine, partition, or combine the initial regions. This procedure produced our final total of sixty-one regions within the eleven states. These regions are listed in Table G.2 and the boundaries are delineated in the map accompanying the table.[6]

Once the regional distinctions had been established, the published data, which were collected on a county basis, were reaggregated into subtotals for each of the sixty-one economic regions included in our study. In addition to the wealth of published census data, an extensive sample of 11,202 farms was drawn from the manuscript schedules submitted by the census enumerators for the Agricultural Census of 1879. This sample was collected in a manner that allowed disaggregation of the data into the economic regions we have defined.[7]

All the statistical findings reported in this study were initially examined on a region-by-region basis, and it was examination of these detailed data that led us to the results we report in the book. By and large, the detailed data displayed a remarkable uniformity across the Confederate States. The only pronounced divergence from the general pattern was exhibited by regions characterized by diversified farming and the absence of a staple crop. These regions – concentrated for the most part in western Virginia, western North Carolina, and eastern Tennessee – were coincidently the areas of the antebellum South that made the least use of slave labor and that were thought of, both before and after the war, as the most backward. In regions whose agricultural economy was based upon a cash crop, our findings were remarkably uniform. Nevertheless, partly for expository reasons, but primarily to allow us the freedom to generalize accurately without noting minor deviations, we have chosen consistently to present our results for only those economic regions that concentrated upon the production of cotton. Because we have reason to believe that the patterns established in the Cotton South were the ones ultimately adopted by the balance of the ex-slave states, a concentration upon this region captures the ingredients necessary for an economic analysis of emancipation. The cotton region we have identified includes seventeen of the economic regions we initially defined. Table G.3 provides a list of those regions, together with the number of counties they contain and Hilgard's soil code for each region.

In a number of instances, special considerations or limitations of our data have led us to compile statistics on a state-by-state basis. In these instances we have, in every case, restricted our attention to the *Five Cotton States*: South Carolina, Georgia, Alabama, Mississippi, and Louisiana.

In most respects, agriculture in the Cotton South was typical of agriculture in all the former Confederate States. Table G.4 presents a comparison of the two regions. In 1880, the Cotton South included 43 percent of the population of former Confederate States and a slightly higher fraction of the South's tilled acreage and number of farms. Tables G.5, G.6, and G.7 provide more detailed data on the agricultural characteristics of the Cotton South. There were two respects in which the Cotton South differed from the rest of the South in 1879–1880. Almost three-fourths of the cotton grown in the United States was produced in the Cotton South. This emphasis on cotton as a staple is apparent from the very large fraction of tilled acreage devoted to cotton, rather than grains or other staples (Table G.5). Less obviously, the Cotton South had a relatively high proportion of the Negro population of the South. More than half of the southern black population lived in this region, whereas only about one-third of southern whites lived in the cotton area (Table G.4). It is, of course, precisely these unique characteristics that make the Cotton South interesting for our analysis. The emphasis on cotton and the large fraction of blacks reflect the legacy of the antebellum slave economy that reached its fullest development in the cotton-producing areas.

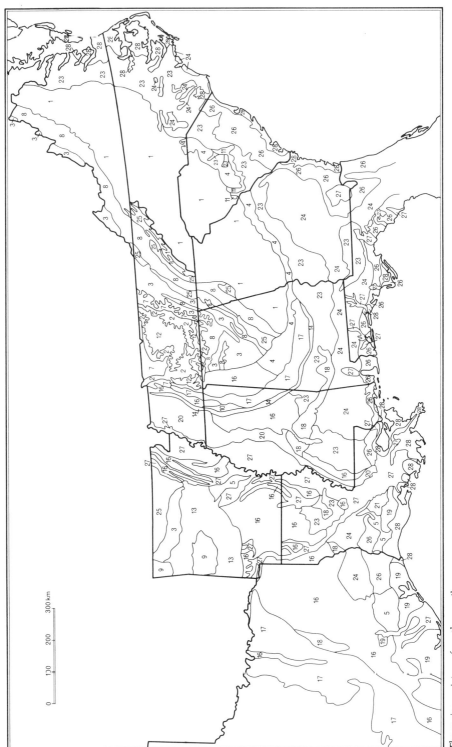

The major variet.es of southern soil.

Table G.1. *Major varieties of southern soil*

Code	Description of soil type	Code	Description of soil type
1	Granite and metamorphic gray and red lands of the Piedmont	17	Black, stiff calcareous (Cretaceous) prairies in Alabama, Mississippi, Arkansas, and Texas
2	Highland rim of the central basin of Tennessee	18	Calcareous prairie lands (Tertiary) in Alabama, Mississippi, Louisiana, and Texas
3	Siliceous and mountain lands in Tennessee, north Alabama, and north Arkansas	19	Black calcareous and coast prairies in Texas and Louisiana
4	Sand hills belt of North Carolina, South Carolina, Georgia, and Alabama	20	Brown loam bluff and tablelands in Tennessee and Mississippi
5	Gray silt prairies in Arkansas, Louisiana, and Texas	21	Brown loam prairies of Louisiana
6	Sand deserts of southwest Texas	22	Sandy prairies of Indian Territory
7	Red clay lands of middle Tennessee	23	Oak, hickory, and long-leaf pine hills in central belt extending from North Carolina to Louisiana
8	Valley lands with narrow cherty ridges in Tennessee, Georgia, and Alabama	24	Long-leaf pine hills and level wire-grass and pine barrens in Alabama, Florida. Georgia, North Carolina, Texas, and Mississippi
9	Clay and red loam prairies in Arkansas, Missouri, and Texas	25	Gray, gravelly ridges and magnesium limestone lands of Arkansas, Tennessee, and northwest Georgia
10	Red lands (Cretaceous) of the Pontotoc Ridge in Mississippi	26	Long-leaf pine flats and savannahs along the coast from Virginia to Texas
11	Red hills (Tertiary) of South Carolina	27	Alluvial lands and large upland swamps
12	Limestone lands of the central basin of Tennessee	28	Marshes, swamps, and live-oak lands of the coast
13	Red loam region of Arkansas		
14	Flatwood regions of Alabama, Mississippi, and Tennessee		
15	Gypsum prairies and arid plains of the Llano Estacado in Texas		
16	Oak, hickory, and short-leaf pine uplands in Mississippi, Tennessee, Arkansas, Texas, and Louisiana		

Source: Eugene W. Hilgard, U.S. Census Office, Tenth Census [1880], *Report on Cotton Production in the United States also Embracing Agricultural and Physico-Geographical Descriptions of the Several Cotton States and of California*, 2 vols. (Washington: GPO, 1884), "General Agricultural Map for all the states," opposite p. 3.

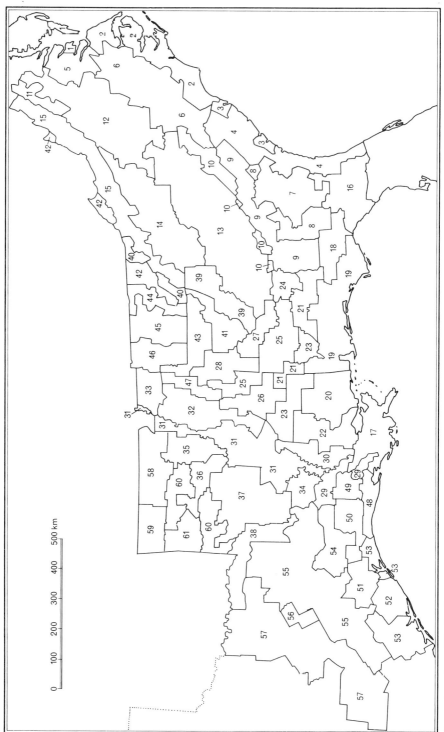

Economic regions of the South.

Table G.2. *Economic regions of the South: 1880*

Region number	Region name	Number of counties	Soil code[a]
1	Capes and coastal plains of Virginia	7	28
2	Seaboard region of North Carolina and Virginia	23	28
3	Sea Island district of South Carolina	2	28
4	Savannahs and palmetto flats along the lower Atlantic seaboard	14	26
5	Chesapeake rolling coastal plains of Virginia	20	23
6	Coastal plain of North and South Carolina and Virginia	31	23
7	Southern wire-grass and pine barrens of Georgia	14	24
8	Southern wire-grass and limesink region of Georgia	9	24
9	Central cotton belt of Georgia and South Carolina	28	23
10	Sand hills belt of South Carolina and Georgia	11	4
11	Northern Piedmont plateau of Virginia	8	1
12	Central Piedmont plateau	48	1
13	Southern Piedmont plateau	81	1
14	Blue Ridge	45	1
15	Appalachian valleys of Tennessee and Virginia	39	8
16	Long-leaf pine flats and savannahs of the Gulf Coast	12	24, 26
17	Rice and sugar lowlands of southeast Louisiana	12	27
18	Southwest Georgia and northern Florida	7	23
19	Rolling pine woods and limesink region of Alabama and Florida	15	24
20	Lower gulf coastal plain of Mississippi and Louisiana	9	24
21	Oak and hickory uplands of Alabama and Mississippi	9	23
22	Central gulf coastal plain of Mississippi and Louisiana	10	23
23	Central prairie region of Mississippi and Alabama	10	18
24	Tuskegee region of Alabama	4	17
25	Black belt of Alabama and Mississippi	15	17
26	Short-leaf pine uplands with oak and hickory, Mississippi	10	16
27	Gravelly hills of Alabama	5	4
28	Appalachian border of the coastal plain	9	16
29	Mississippi alluvial region south of the Red River	5	27
30	Old Natchez region	9	20
31	Mississippi-Yazoo delta north of the Red River	25	27
32	Brown loam tablelands and sandy oak uplands, Mississippi and Tennessee	17	20
33	Memphis region of Tennessee	7	20
34	Long-leaf pine hills and prairie region of Louisiana	4	23
35	Crowley's Ridge, Arkansas	8	16
36	Gray silt prairie of Arkansas	6	5
37	Red River rolling lands, Arkansas and Louisiana	22	16
38	Upper Red River region	10	16
39	Appalachian River valleys of Alabama and Georgia	15	8
40	Cumberland tablelands and Unak Mountains	8	3
41	Cumberland plateau region of Alabama	8	3
42	Cumberland plateau region of Tennessee and Virginia	9	3
43	Tennessee River valley of Alabama	9	8
44	Eastern highland rim of Tennessee	9	2, 7
45	Central basin of Tennessee	16	12
46	Western highland rim of Tennessee	12	2, 7
47	Summit watershed of Tennessee and Pontotoc Ridge of Mississippi	6	10

Table G.2. (*cont.*)

Region number	Region name	Number of counties	Soil code[a]
48	Tidewater region of Louisiana	4	28
49	Brown loam prairies of Louisiana	2	21
50	Long-leaf pine flats of Louisiana and Texas	3	26
51	Light prairies east of the Brazos River	4	5
52	Brazos sugar bowl region	4	27
53	Black calcareous and coast prairies of Texas	12	19
54	Long-leaf pine hills of Louisiana and Texas	6	24
55	Oak, hickory, and pine region west of the Red River	44	16
56	Minor black prairie region of Texas	2	18
57	Central black prairie region of Texas	40	17
58	Ozark plateau	13	25
59	Southern border of the Ozark plateau	6	3
60	Red loam region of the Arkansas River basin	12	13
61	Clay prairie country of Arkansas	6	9
62	Southern Florida[b]	12	—
63	Western Texas[b]	111	—
Total		993	

[a] For soil codes, see Table G.1.   [b] These regions were not included in our study.
Source: Roger Ransom and Richard Sutch, "Economic Regions of the South in 1880," *Southern Economic History Project Working Paper Series,* Number 3 (Berkeley: Institute of Business and Economic Research, 1971), Appendix B, pp. 64–100.

Table G.3. *Regions in the Cotton South: 1880*

Region number[a]	Region name	Number of counties	Soil code[b]
6	Coastal plain of North and South Carolina and Virginia	31	23
9	Central cotton belt of Georgia and South Carolina	28	23
13	Southern Piedmont plateau	81	1
18	Southwest Georgia and northern Florida	7	23
21	Oak and hickory uplands of Alabama and Mississippi	9	23
22	Central gulf coastal plain of Mississippi and Louisiana	10	23
23	Central prairie region of Mississippi and Alabama	10	18
24	Tuskegee region of Alabama	4	17
25	Black belt of Alabama and Mississippi	15	17

Table G.3. (*cont.*)

Region number[a]	Region name	Number of counties	Soil code[b]
26	Short-leaf pine uplands with oak and hickory, Mississippi	10	16
30	Old Natchez region	9	20
31	Mississippi-Yazoo delta north of the Red River	25	27
32	Brown loam tablelands and sandy oak uplands, Mississippi and Tennessee	17	20
34	Long-leaf pine hills and prairie region of Louisiana	4	23
37	Red River rolling lands, Arkansas and Louisiana	22	16
38	Upper Red River region	10	16
55	Oak, hickory, and pine region west of the Red River	44	16
Total		336	

[a] Region numbers correspond to those on the map accompanying Table G.2 [b] Soil codes are from Table G.1.

Table G.4. *Major demographic and agricultural characteristics, Confederate South and Cotton South: 1880*

	Confederate South[a] (thousands)	Cotton South (thousands)	Cotton South as percent of Confederate South
Population	12,733.6	5,514.6	43.3
Black[b]	5,333.1	2,998.7	56.2
White	7,400.5	2,515.9	34.0
Number of farms	1,230.9	546.3	44.4
Tilled acres	57,191.2	26,627.0	46.6
Total acres	187,819.2	81,606.0	43.5
Production of			
Cotton (bales)	5,697.0	4,141.0	72.7
Corn (bushels)	265,333.8	95,740.0	36.1

[a] The total for the Confederate South includes all eleven of the former Confederate States, but excludes those areas of Florida and Texas that were only sparsely settled in 1880 (see map accompanying Table G.2). [b] Includes trivial numbers of "civilized Indians," Chinese, and Japanese persons.
Source: U.S. Census Office, Tenth Census [1880], *Statistics of the Population of the United States at the Tenth Census (June 1, 1880)* (Washington: GPO, 1883); idem, *Report on the Production of Agriculture* (Washington: GPO, 1883).

Table G.5. *Farm output, Cotton South: 1879*

Crop (unit)	Output (thousands)	Acres (thousands)	Yield per acre	Percent of tilled land
Staple crops				
Cotton (bale)	4,141.0	10,460.5	0.396	39.3
Tobacco (pound)	2,559.3	5.5	469.1	a
Rice (pound)	9,176.2	21.3	431.5	a
Sugar (hogshead)	4.037	30.2	0.13	0.1
Total	—	10,517.5	—	39.5
Grain crops				
Corn (bushel)	95,740.0	8,748.3	10.94	32.9
Oats (bushel)	23,198.5	1,314.2	17.65	4.9
Wheat (bushel)	5,280.1	835.1	6.32	3.1
Rye (bushel)	141.0	36.3	3.88	0.1
Total	—	10,933.9	—	41.1
Total grain and staples	—	21,451.4	—	80.6

a Less than 0.1 percent.
Source: U.S. Census Office, Tenth Census [1880], *Report on the Production of Agriculture* (Washington: GPO, 1883).

Table G.6. *Farm characteristics, Cotton South: 1879–1880*

	Aggregate (thousands)	Per farm	Per total acre	Per tilled acre
Total acres	81,606	149.4	1.00	3.065
Tilled	26,627	48.7	0.326	1.000
Improved[a]	28,560	52.3	0.350	1.073
Unimproved	53,046	97.1	0.650	1.992
Value of farm ($)	459,432	840.99	5.63	17.25
Value of farm products ($)	286,028	523.57	3.51	10.74
Number of work animals[b]	1,366	2.50	0.017	0.051
Number of cattle[c]	3,191	5.84	0.039	0.120
Number of swine	5,794	10.61	0.071	0.218

[a] Includes permanent meadows, permanent pastures, orchards, and vineyards in addition to tilled acres.   [b] Includes mules, asses, horses, and working oxen.   [c] Includes milch cows and "other cattle."
Source: U.S. Census Office, Tenth Census [1880], *Report on the Production of Agriculture* (Washington: GPO, 1883).

Table G.7. *Size and tenure distribution of farms, Cotton South: 1880*

| | Number of acres | | | | | |
	Under 20	20–49	50–99	100–499	Over 500	Total
Number of farms						
Owned	10,600	31,010	61,786	159,118	26,669	289,183
Rented	18,403	43,112	14,373	12,668	1,604	90,160
Sharecropped	37,254	87,977	23,537	16,868	1,362	166,998
Total	66,257	162,099	99,696	188,654	29,635	546,341
Percent of each						
tenure class						
Owned	3.67	10.72	21.37	55.02	9.22	100.00
Rented	20.41	47.82	15.94	14.05	1.78	100.00
Sharecropped	22.31	52.68	14.09	10.10	0.82	100.00
Total	12.13	29.67	18.25	34.53	5.42	100.00
Percent of each						
size class						
Owned	16.00	19.13	61.97	84.34	89.99	52.93
Rented	27.78	26.60	14.42	6.71	5.41	16.50
Sharecropped	56.23	54.27	23.61	8.94	4.60	30.57
Total	100.00	100.00	100.00	100.00	100.00	100.00

Source: U.S. Census Office, Tenth Census [1880], *Report on the Production of Agriculture* (Washington: GPO, 1883).

2. The sample of southern farms in 1880

The decennial censuses published by the federal government are unquestionably the most comprehensive source of data for quantitative analysis of the postbellum South. Evidence taken from the published census reports from 1860 through 1900 can be found throughout our study. However, the published reports by themselves were not sufficient for our needs. Though the censuses were very complete in the data they collected, the published reports did not organize the data in a manner to facilitate direct investigation of a number of important issues. The published tabulations do not reveal, for example, production of farms disaggregated by the race of the farm operator or by the form of tenure; nor are production data available by the size class of farm.

Data on size of farm, crop acreage, and production were originally collected by the census enumerators and recorded by hand on printed forms designed for this purpose. The same enumerators also returned schedules, listing by full name all members of the population, together with information on race, sex, age, occupation, education, and other demographic characteristics.[8] The original manuscript returns of the 1860, 1870, and 1880 censuses are still available.[9] Thus, although not easily accessible, the data we wished to have still existed. To make this valuable information available in a form that would facilitate analysis, the Southern Economic History Project drew a sample of more than 11,000 farms from the manuscript Census of Agriculture for 1880.

We initially considered drawing this sample from the 1870 Census manuscripts, but except for a small sample described below, rejected this alternative for several reasons. The Ninth Census, in 1870, was deficient in several respects. The census in that year used forms for the enumeration of population, agriculture, and manufacturing similar to those employed in 1850 and 1860. As a result, data on farm tenure were not collected. Crop acreage was also omitted from these schedules, seriously constraining the scope of any productivity analysis based upon the enumeration. Finally, considerable problems were faced in the southern states in completing the enumeration. As a result, the population is certainly undercounted for that year, and we have found confusion in the entries for agricultural data as well.[10]

Collecting the sample

The information we wished to collect for each farm included in our sample was contained on two separately returned schedules. Information on farm production, inputs, size, and tenure was listed on the agricultural schedules under the name of the farm operator. The top panel of a sample page of these agricultural schedules is reproduced as Figure G.1. A full list of the information requested is given in Table G.8. Information on the age, race, and family of the farm operator was recorded on the population returns, one page of which is reproduced as Figure G.2. To obtain a complete picture of any farm, it was necessary to locate the name of the farm operator in the population schedules. As an example, consider the sharecropped farm of William Proctor, which appears on line 5 of Figure G.1. Proctor's name also appears on the population schedule (on line 38 of Figure G.2). To the information available on the production of Proctor's farm, it is possible to add that he was black, aged twenty-seven, and had a family of two children and a wife, Nancy. A similar collation of names is possible for Richard Adams whose name appears on both schedules reproduced here.

Unfortunately, the names on the population schedules are not alphabetized, nor has any index been prepared. The need to collate information from both schedules led us to concentrate our sampling to a limited geographic area. This was accomplished by selecting representative counties to reflect the characteristics of the economic region in which they were located. One or more counties were chosen to represent each of the regions identified.[11] A systematic sample, which caught approximately 11 percent of the farms listed in the agricultural schedules, was then drawn from each representative county.[12] The use of representative counties ensured that a sufficiently

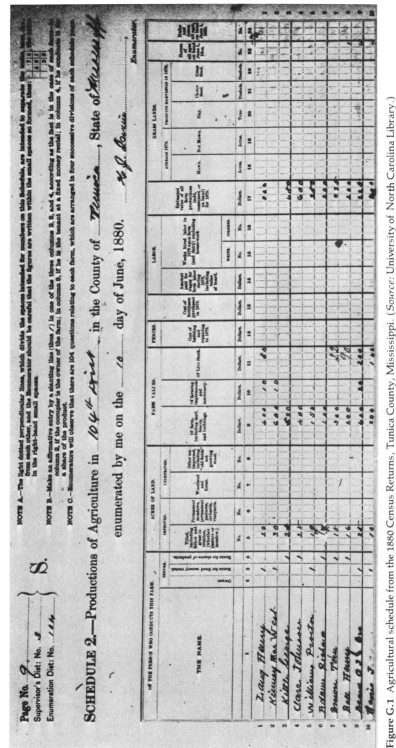

Figure G.1 Agricultural schedule from the 1880 Census Returns, Tunica County, Mississippi. (*Source*: University of North Carolina Library.)

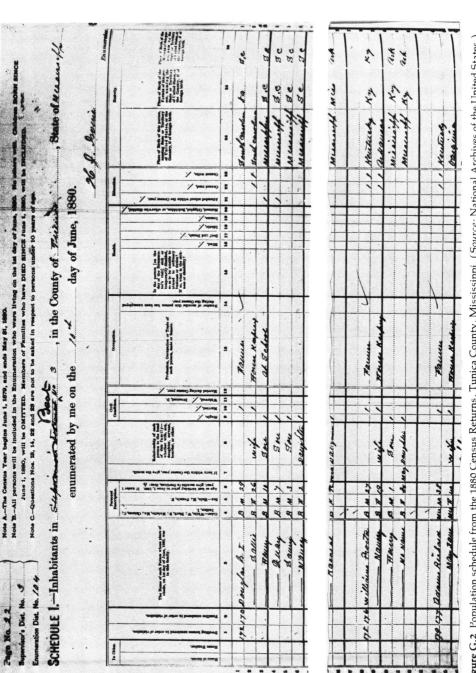

Figure G.2 Population schedule from the 1880 Census Returns, Tunica County, Mississippi. (*Source:* National Archives of the United States.)

large number of farms was drawn from each region to allow detailed disaggregation of results, yet at the same time, provided sufficient sampling density to facilitate the collation of data on different schedules.

In all, we drew sample farms from forty-nine of the sixty-one regions in the South; a total of seventy-three sample counties were included.[13] The full sample comprised 11,202 farms.

The data collected from the 1880 Census manuscripts
The Southern Economic History Project transcribed and coded in machine-readable language over forty items of information about each farm sampled. Table G.8 lists the items. A complete list of "additional crops" reported by the census is given in Table G.9. For each farm, the page and line citation of the schedules was recorded, making it possible subsequently to check any discrepancies or irregularities that might later appear. Any unusual feature that might prove of particular interest was recorded as a "footnote," and a "footnote tag" was added to the data for that farm.[14]

The data reported in the 1880 Census seem in most cases to be quite reliable. Our checks for errors and consistency in sample data revealed very few instances where the numbers reported seemed wholly unreasonable. There were, however, two sets of variables for which the sample data must be viewed with some caution. The "number of people who lived in same dwelling as farm operator" (item 9 in Table G.8) was determined by our data collectors by counting the number of people listed as residing in the same house as the farm operator. Only rarely were ambiguities encountered in determining this number.[15] However, calculation of the "number of people who worked on a farm" (item 10 in Table G.8) involved a degree of judgment by the collector of the data. A person was counted among those at work only if a farm-related occupation was listed for him or her in the population schedule.[16] We believe such a procedure probably tends to understate the true participation in farm labor, since we make no allowance for individuals not listing an agricultural occupation, but who nevertheless might have contributed some labor to the farm.[17]

This measure of agricultural labor is also subject to misinterpretation owing to two other possible situations. Household members listed "at work" on a farm could, in fact, have been employed on some farm other than the one operated by the head of household, thus causing our data to exaggerate the labor on the sample farm. On the other hand, laborers working on the sample farm might have lived in a house other than the farm operator's, in which case they would not be counted in the labor force by our procedure. We have no way of determining the presence of such misspecification of labor input for an individual farm. We note, however, that when data are aggregated, there is some tendency for the two biases to cancel each other.

We had originally hoped to be able to measure the amount of hired labor purchased by each farmer. The returns did ask for the amount of wages paid for labor over the year (item 22 in Table G.8) and for the number of

Table G.8. *Data collected for each sample farm*

1	State in which farm was located
2	County (parish) in which farm was located
3	Enumeration district in which farm was located
4	Page and line number of Agricultural Census manuscript identifying sample farm
5[a]	Page and line number of Population Census manuscript identifying farm operator
6[a]	Race of farm operator (white, black or mulatto, Chinese, Indian)
7[a]	Literacy of farm operator (recorded by defining an illiterate as a person whom the census recorded as unable either to read or write)
8[a]	Age of farm operator on June 1, 1880
9[a]	Number of people (including farm operator) who lived in same dwelling as farm operator on June 1, 1880
10[a]	Number of people living in farm operator's dwelling who worked on a farm on June 1, 1880
11[a]	Place of birth of farm operator (state or territory of United States, or country if of foreign birth)
12	Tenure of farm operator, June 1880 (owner, rents for fixed money rental, rents for share of products)
13	Number of tilled acres of land on farm, June 1880 (including fallow and grass in rotation, whether pasture or meadow)
14	Number of acres in permanent meadows, permanent pastures, orchards, and vineyards, June 1880
15	Number of acres in unimproved woodland and forest, June 1880
16	Number of acres in other unimproved land, including "old fields" not growing wood, June 1880
17	Value of farm, including land, fences, and buildings (in dollars), June 1880
18	Value of farming implements and machinery (in dollars), June 1880
19	Value of livestock (in dollars), June 1880
20	Cost of building and repairing fences (in dollars) during 1879
21	Cost of fertilizers purchased (in dollars) during 1879
22	Amount paid for wages for farm labor during 1879, including value of board (in dollars)
23	Man-weeks of hired white labor in 1879 on farm and dairy, but excluding housework
24	Man-weeks of hired colored labor in 1879 on farm and dairy, but excluding housework
25	Estimated value of all farm production (sold, consumed, or on hand) for 1879 (in dollars)
26	Number of horses of all ages on hand, June 1, 1880
27	Number of mules and asses of all ages on hand, June 1, 1880
28	Number of *working* oxen on hand, June 1, 1880
29	Number of milch cows on hand, June 1, 1880
30	Number of all other cattle on hand, June 1, 1880
31	Number of sheep on hand, June 1, 1880
32	Number of swine on hand, June 1, 1880
33	Number of acres of Indian corn planted in 1879
34	Number of bushels of Indian corn harvested in 1879
35	Number of acres of cotton planted in 1879
36	Number of 400-pound bales of cotton harvested from crop of 1879
37	Number of bushels of Irish potatoes harvested in 1879
38	Number of bushels of sweet potatoes harvested in 1879
39	Number of acres devoted to each additional crop reported in 1879[b]
40	Production of each of additional crops in 1879[b]

[a] Taken from population schedules, all other data were taken from agricultural schedules.
[b] See Table G.9 for list of additional crops.

Table G.9. *"Additional crops" for which
information was recorded*

Crop	Measure of output
Apples	Bushel
Barley	Bushel
Buckwheat	Bushel
Cane molasses	Gallon
Cane sugar	Hogshead
Cowpeas	Bushel
Dried beans	Bushel
Flax	Pound of fiber
Hemp	Ton
Maple molasses	Gallon
Maple sugar	Pound
Oats	Bushel
Peaches	Bushel
Rice	Pound
Rye	Bushel
Sorghum molasses	Gallon
Sorghum sugar	Pound
Tobacco	Pound
Wheat	Bushel

man-weeks of labor hired (items 23 and 24 in Table G.8). However, apparently because of ambiguities in the instructions issued to the enumerators, this question was frequently ignored or misinterpreted. As a result, in many cases the information was incorrectly recorded or incomplete; in others, the census taker simply failed to record the hiring of farm labor.[18] We transcribed the data as reported on the original form; however, they could not be used without some judgment regarding the reliability with which the enumerator collected the information. As it turned out, our staff responsible for collecting the data were often in a position to render such an appraisal at the time the coding was prepared. It became apparent that individual enumerators tended to record the data in a consistent – even if incorrect – manner for their enumeration district. Therefore, an examination of the schedules for the entire district usually allowed us to judge whether the wage information was or was not recorded accurately, and a code was assigned to each enumeration district to signal this judgment. This code was then used in subsequent analyses involving the use of labor data on the farms.[19]

The reliability and accuracy with which data were transposed from the manuscripts to the coding forms, and from there to punch cards, were checked using a variety of tests and checking programs. For example, the distribution of sample values was plotted, compared with the mean, and examined for extreme outliers. Crop data were examined for unusually high or low yields per acre. Search was made for inconsistencies in related variables using a variety of techniques. Ratios were tested for outliers, regressions were run, and scatter diagrams were studied to uncover discrepancies that might appear. Any extreme cases were checked against the original microfilms of the schedules for accuracy. The number of recording errors was surprisingly low. Those recording errors that were found were corrected. However, *we did not change any data that had been accurately transposed from the microfilms,* regardless of how unusual those data appeared.

Farms included in the original sampling frame were replaced only when they reported less than 3 acres of tilled land *and* less than $500 of output[20] or when the acreage data were illegible. All farms selected to replace originally sampled farms were so noted. A total of 162 farms, located in twenty-one of the representative counties, had to be replaced.

To check for any possible biases in our sampling procedure, we performed a series of consistency checks contrasting the sample with the published data for the county. These checks used chi-square tests for comparing distributions and Student's t tests to compare sample means with the published figures for twenty-five variables. The results of these tests convinced us that in all but a few counties there were no serious problems, and in no case did any systematic bias appear. Where any statistically significant differences between sample and published data were discovered, we examined the original manuscripts and the coding form to discern the possible cause of the divergence. In two cases, a major difference turned out to be a compilation error in the published data.[21] On the basis of these examinations, we accepted the validity of every county sampled.

The fact that two sets of data had to be collated for each farm led predictably to some instances of farms that were selected for the sample but whose operator could not be identified in the population schedules. Such unmatched farms were retained in the sample, though obviously they had to be excluded from certain analyses. In all, we matched 96.4 percent of the farms collected in the sample. To ensure that no bias was introduced in excluding unmatched farms from analysis, we carried out the consistency tests comparing the sample means for matched and unmatched farms. We found no significant differences in the sample values.[22]

As a final check of the accuracy of our transcribing and coding process, 2 percent (220) of the sample farms were randomly selected and then recoded from the original manuscripts by an individual other than the person who had transcribed the farm's data for the original sample. Over 8,000 separate entries were thus recoded. Only 23 discrepancies were found: 0.29 percent. Of these discrepancies, about two-thirds were coding errors committed by the second coder, an individual who had no previous coding experience. This excellently low error rate is evidence of the care our coding and keypunching staff took to ensure accuracy of results. We offer it here as testimony to their remarkable diligence – particularly remarkable given the difficulty of reading handwriting nearly 100 years old from microfilms that were not always of high quality.

Aggregating the sample for the Cotton South

Though we collected sample farms and data from the entire South, the results employed in this study are based only upon the farms located in the Cotton South. Twenty-seven of the representative counties, containing 5,318 sampled farms, were in the Cotton South. A list of these counties, and the number of farms sampled from each, is provided in Table G.10.

Table G.10. *Representative counties in sample of farms: Cotton South*

Region and representative counties	Number of farms in county or region	Number of farms sampled	Sampling rate (%)[a]
6. Coastal plain of North and South Carolina and Virginia	67,655	235	0.35
Nash, N.C.	2,130	235	11.03
9. Central cotton belt of Georgia and South Carolina	32,411	375	1.16
Barnwell, S.C.	3,474	195	5.61[b]
Twiggs, Ga.	863	96	11.12
Terrell, Ga.	707	84	11.88
13. Southern Piedmont plateau	140,825	655	0.47
Union, S.C.	2,524	280	11.09
Gwinnett, Ga.	2,498	140	5.60[b]
Coweta, Ga.	1,998	235	11.76
18. Southwest Georgia and northern Florida	10,787	180	1.67
Thomas, Ga.	1,588	90	5.67[b]
Gadsen, Fla.	1,555	90	5.79[b]
21. Oak and hickory uplands of Alabama and Mississippi	16,488	265	1.61
Pike, Ala.	2,389	265	11.09
22. Central gulf coastal plain of Mississippi and Louisiana	11,985	365	3.05
Pike, Miss.	1,471	175	11.90
Lincoln, Miss.	1,590	190	11.95
23. Central prairie of Mississippi and Alabama	17,027	227	1.33
Rankin, Miss.	1,727	227	13.14
24. Tuskegee region of Alabama	10,970	295	2.69
Russell, Ala.	2,607	295	11.32
25. Black belt of Alabama and Mississippi	38,794	930	2.40
Perry, Ala.	2,442	325[c]	13.31
Lowndes, Ala.	3,462	400	11.55
Clay, Miss.	1,507	205	13.60
26. Short-leaf pine uplands of Mississippi	15,613	305	1.95
Attala, Miss.	2,253	305	13.54

Table G.10. (*cont.*)

Region and representative counties	Number of farms in county or region	Number of farms sampled	Sampling rate (%) [a]
30. Old Natchez region	11,686	180	1.54
Jefferson, Miss.	1,551	180	11.61
31. Mississippi-Yazoo delta	16,742	139	0.83
Tunica, Miss.	608	74	12.17
Washington, Miss.	454	65	14.32
32. Brown loam tablelands and sandy oak uplands			
Mississippi and Tennessee	40,527	224	0.55
Yalobusha, Miss.	1,655	224	13.53
34. Long-leaf pine hills and prairie region of	2,848	60	2.11
Louisiana Grant, La.	521	60	11.51
37. Red River rolling lands	29,204	230	0.79
Claiborne, La.	2,008	230	11.45
38. Upper Red River region	15,095	266	1.76
Red River, Tex.	2,254	266	11.80
55. Oak, hickory, and pine region west of the			
Red River	67,675	387	0.57
Cherokee, Tex.	2,139	232	10.85
Robertson, Tex.	2,454	155	6.32 [b]
Cotton South			
County totals	50,429	5,318	10.55
Region totals	546,332	5,318	0.97

[a] Based on number of sampled farms and published census totals for each county.   [b] Target sampling rate of 5 farms out of 90 (5.56 percent).   [c] Thirty-five farms from enumeration district number 77 of Perry County, Alabama, were deleted from the sample of farms for the purpose of calculations reported in this study because of a failure of the enumerator to record the acres of land devoted to each crop.

Not all the 5,318 farms in the original sample were employed for the calculations reported in this book. Farms that exhibited serious data deficiencies and farms where ambiguities existed with regard to the definition of the farming unit were deleted from the sample. Data problems caused us to remove 387 farms. The most common reasons were inability to locate the farm operator's name in the population schedules and illegibility of the reported value of an important variable (race of the farm operator, tenure, number of tilled acres, or acreage and production of either cotton or corn). We also excluded farms that reported no labor at all and farms where the total of the family and hired labor was insufficient to provide at least one man-year for every 100 acres reported in crops. Finally, faulty reporting on the original manuscripts forced us to exclude 35 farms in Perry County, Alabama, from the sample. A total of 236 farms were excluded from the sample owing to ambiguities in ownership or tenure characteristics. These exclusions involved farms where more than one form of tenure was reported or where a single farm family operated more than one farm.

In all, 623 of the original farms in the sample were excluded from our analysis. The remaining 4,695 farms represent 0.86 percent of all farms in the Cotton South in 1880. The data for these farms can be aggregated to construct estimates that reflect the experience of the 546,332 farms in the Cotton South through the use of an appropriate weighting procedure. A weighting procedure is necessary because our sampling technique drew farms at differing sampling rates from each of the seventeen economic regions that together make up the Cotton South. The rate ranged from 0.35 percent in Region 6 to 3.05 percent in Region 22 (see Table G.10). The procedure we adopted for any statistic of interest began by computing that statistic for each farm in the sample. A simple average of the statistic was then computed for each representative county. We then weighted the sample mean in each representative county by the total number of farms reported for that county in the published census. The results so obtained for each representative county were then summed for all counties in each economic region and divided by the total number of farms in the representative counties. These regional means were then weighted by the total number of farms in the region to produce an aggregate estimate of the statistic for the Cotton South. Should the average value per farm be of interest, this aggregate value would then be divided by the total number of farms in the Cotton South – 546,332 in all.

Such a procedure assumes that the county samples do, in fact, reflect the county populations from which they were drawn and that the sampled counties were indeed accurate representatives of their regions. A measure of the accuracy of this procedure is provided in Table G.11, where the values

Table G.11. *Comparison of published census data and estimates from sample farms, Cotton South: 1880*

Variable	Published census value	Weighted sample estimate
Farm tenure (% in each class)		
Owned	52.93	50.43
Rented	16.50	14.16
Sharecropped	30.57	35.41
Total acres	149.4	153.6
Value of farm ($)	840.99	990.85
Value of farm output ($)	523.57	567.20
Number of work animals	2.50	2.52
Number of swine	10.61	10.57
Bushels of corn per acre	10.94	11.14
Bales of cotton per acre	0.396	0.379

Source: Published census figures are taken from Tables G.5, G.6 and G.7.

of several variables that can be obtained from the published census records are compared with the estimates based on the weighted sample.

Stereotyping southern farms

For many aspects of our study, it was convenient to group farms according to size and the amount and type of labor they used. We defined five classes of farms for analytical purposes. These stereotypes were based on prevailing practices as reported in the agricultural journals and are commonly alluded to in the historical literature. The actual classes delineated were defined using the data on labor employed and land use that we collected with our sample.[23] We estimated the labor input on farms that reported only the wage bill. In most instances, a county average for the weekly wage was available from other farms in the representative county. Where this was not the case, an average wage based upon the U.S. Department of Agriculture data for 1879 was employed.[24] The quantity of land reported in crops for 1879 was used as the criterion for farm size.[25]

Our definitions, which are employed consistently throughout this study, are as follows:

Family farms: Farms that reported 50 acres or less in crops and hired 26 man-weeks or less of labor

Small wage-paying farms: Farms that reported 50 acres or less in crops and hired more than 26 man-weeks of labor

Medium-scale farms: Farms reporting more than 50 acres but 100 acres or less in crops

Plantations: Farms reporting 200 acres or more in crops, hiring greater than 98 weeks of labor, and relying on hired labor for at least 60 percent of their requirement

Large farms: All farms not included in one of the above categories; that is, all farms with 100 acres or more in crops not designated as plantations

Table G.12 presents the number of farms included in the sample according to these categories, broken down by race and tenure.

3. Other uses of the manuscript census returns

Although the sample of farms drawn from the 1880 Census of Agriculture was by far the most important sample of data taken from the manuscript schedules, it was by no means the only data collection drawn from these documents by the Southern Economic History Project. The most important of the supplemental samples employed in this study are described briefly below.

Farm samples from eight counties: 1850, 1860, 1870

Despite the deficiencies and problems of the 1870 Census, it proved useful in several instances to have a sample of farms drawn from that source. A

Table G.12. *Number of farms in Cotton South sample, by type of farm, tenure, and race* [a]

Type of farm	Number of farms sampled		
	White	Black	Total
Family Farms			
Owned	1,152	297	1,449
Rented	173	462	635
Sharecropped	424	848	1,272
All family farms	1,749	1,607	3,356
Small Wage-Paying Farms			
Owned	195	23	218
Rented	17	33	50
Sharecropped	37	82	119
All small wage-paying farms	249	138	387
Medium-Scale Farms			
Owned	404	64	468
Rented	40	51	91
Sharecropped	63	94	157
All medium-scale farms	507	209	716
Other Large Farms			
Owned	140	22	162
Rented	12	3	15
Sharecropped	5	8	13
All large farms	157	33	190
Plantations			
Owned	36	2	38
Rented	5	0	5
Sharecropped	3	0	3
All plantations	44	2	46
All Farms			
Owned	1,927	408	2,335
Rented	247	549	796
Sharecropped	532	1,032	1,564
All farms	2,706	1,989	4,695

[a] This is an unweighted distribution of sample farms. A weighted distribution by tenure class is presented in Table 5.1.

careful examination of the manuscript returns for agriculture and population suggested to us that the bulk of the problems that plagued the published census returns arose from the faulty enumeration of occasional enumeration districts.[26] Because a majority of the assistant marshals who undertook the enumeration performed their job with diligence and care, it proved possible to select a number of counties where the censuses of population and agriculture appeared to be reasonably complete.[27]

A number of questions concerning the transition from slavery to freedom could be usefully approached by contrasting agricultural patterns before and after the Civil War. For this purpose, it seemed desirable to draw samples from the 1850 and 1860 manuscript schedules of agriculture and collate them with the data on the farm operator from the population schedules. So that the results across the census years would be comparable, only counties that did not experience boundary changes at any time between 1849 and 1880 were considered. This constraint, together with the deficiencies in the data for many counties in 1870, severely restricted our choice. We ultimately identified eight counties that met our criteria and that we felt reflected economic regions in which they were located. Six of the counties were representative counties included in our original 1880 sample, but Dallas, Alabama, and Madison, Louisiana, were not originally included and were later added to the complete 1880 sample. The eight counties are listed in Table G.13, together with the number of farms in the 1870 sample. The collection and checking procedures were similar to those employed in the 1880 sample.

The sample of farms for 1870 has been referred to several times in the present study. We were fortunate, however, to obtain a more extensive sample of southern farms from the 1860 manuscripts that had been collected by William Parker and Robert Gallman for an unrelated series of studies. This sample, described below, was both larger and more extensive than our own eight-county sample. Since it proved possible to utilize the Parker-Gallman sample for the purposes of this book, the 1850 and 1860 eight-county samples were not used.

Table G.13. *Counties in 1870 sample of farms*

County, State	Number of farms reported	Number of farms sampled	Percent of farms sampled
Attala, Mississippi	1,784	234	13.1
Coweta, Georgia	724	85	11.7
Dallas, Alabama	732	120	16.4
Georgetown, South Carolina	218	25	11.5
Halifax, Virginia	1,294	170	13.1
Madison, Louisiana	1,543	200	13.0
Red River, Texas	573[a]	180	31.4
Robertson, Texas	197	25	12.7
Total	7,065	1,039	14.7

[a] Examination of the manuscript Census of Agriculture reveals that this published figure for Red River County did not follow our definition of a farm. The official enumeration grouped tenant farms, which we treated as independent operations, together into a single holding; the calculated "sampling rate" is thus biased upward.

Samples from the 1880 manufacturing schedules

Information on employment, wages, and capital investment was collected for every establishment enumerated on the manufacturing schedules for each of our twenty-seven representative cotton counties. A detailed description of the data collected is presented in Part A of Table G.14.

Table G.14. *Data on manufacturing establishments: 1880*

A. Data collected for all manufacturing establishments
  1. Major product of establishment
  2. Value of capital invested
  3. Maximum employment between November 1879 and May 1880
  4. "Average" employment during same period
     a. For males under 16
     b. For females under 15
     c. For children
  5. Number of hours worked
     a. From May to November
     b. From November to May
  6. Average day's wage
     a. For skilled mechanics
     b. For ordinary laborers

B. Additional data collected for "flour and grist mills"
  1. Number of bushels and value of wheat purchased
  2. Number of bushels and value of corn purchased
  3. Number of bushels and value of other grain purchased
  4. Output produced
     a. Barrels of wheat flour
     b. Barrels of rye flour
     c. Pounds of buckwheat flour
     d. Pounds of barley meal
     e. Pounds of cornmeal
     f. Pounds of feed
     g. Pounds of hominy
  5. Value of all other products
  6. Value of all products produced

C. Additional data collected for "slaughtering and meatpacking" establishments
  1. Number of beeves slaughtered, gross weight, and total value
  2. Number of sheep slaughtered, gross weight, and total value
  3. Number of hogs slaughtered, gross weight, and total value
  4. Value of all animals slaughtered
  5. Whether or not establishment produced
     a. Fresh beef
     b. Canned beef
     c. Salted beef
     d. Mutton
     e. Fresh pork
     f. Salted pork
     g. Hams
     h. Lard
  6. Total value of all products produced

Census enumerators were asked to include additional information on "flour and grist mills" that was of substantial interest to our study. Therefore, we collected the additional information noted in Part B of Table G.14 for each of the 652 flour and grist mills located in the twenty-seven representative counties in the Cotton South.

"Slaughtering and meat-packing" establishments were asked at the time of the census to report the number and weight of animals slaughtered in 1879. These data, together with the other information listed in Part C of Table G.14, were collected for every slaughterhouse enumerated in one of the eleven former Confederate States, a total of 404 establishments located in 132 counties throughout the South.

A sample of black occupations: 1870

The manuscript population schedules in 1870 reported the occupation of each person enumerated. To obtain a distribution of occupations among blacks in 1870, we drew a sample from several counties in the Cotton South. For the rural enumeration districts in these counties, we collected a 100 percent sample of black men and women over the age of ten years. In the towns located in these counties, we collected a 10 percent sample of blacks. For each black person included in the sample, we recorded sex, age, occupation, and literacy from the population schedules.[28]

A sample of slave occupations: 1860

The 1860 Census did not report occupations of slaves. However, the mortality schedules for that census did, in certain instances, record the occupation of slaves who died in 1860. The 1860 Mortality Census schedules are available for South Carolina, Georgia, and Louisiana. We selected counties from these states where the enumerator of the mortality schedules accurately recorded both slave and free occupations. A list of these counties is presented in Table G.15. A 100 percent sample was collected, containing data on the occupation, sex, and age cohort of each deceased person.[29]

A sample of real and personal estate: 1860, 1870

Despite the difficulties surrounding the questions regarding the value of real and personal estate in the 1870 Census, we felt it might prove useful to obtain data on the reported wealth of persons in both 1860 and 1870. We therefore collected samples, including all heads of households in Dallas County, Alabama, for 1860 and for 1870. For each year we recorded the value of real estate, the value of personal estate, and the race of the individual enumerated.[30] No attempt was made to link individuals in the two samples.

The Parker-Gallman sample of farms from the Cotton Counties: 1860

The Southern Economic History Project's sampling from the Agricultural Census of 1880 had an important predecessor in the project conducted by

Table G.15. *Counties, parishes, and districts included in sample from Mortality Census of 1860*

Districts of South Carolina	Counties of Georgia, continued	Counties of Georgia, continued
Abbeville	Early	Stewart
Beaufort	Effingham	Talbot
Clarendon	Fayette	Taylor
Edgefield	Floyd	Thomas
Fairfield	Hancock	Upson
Georgetown	Harris	Walker
Laurens	Heard	Warren
Marlboro	Henry	Washington
Sumter	Jasper	Wayne
Union	Jefferson	Webster
	Laurens	Wilkinson
Counties of Georgia	Lee	
Baker	Lowndes	Parishes of Louisiana
Banks	Macon	Bossier
Bryan	Marion	Carroll
Burke	McIntosh	Catahoula
Calhoun	Monroe	Claiborne
Camden	Oglethorpe	Concordia
Carroll	Pierce	Franklin
Chattahoochee	Polk	Jackson
Clay	Putnam	Madison
Columbia	Schley	
Decatur	Screven	

William Parker and Robert Gallman. This study, which concentrated on the structure of the antebellum cotton economy, involved the collection of data for a sample of 5,230 farms located in one of the 413 counties which produced at least 1,000 bales of cotton in the aggregate in 1860. This sample, which was drawn from the 1860 Census of Agriculture manuscripts, also involved the collation of data from the agricultural schedules with information from the population schedules. In fact, it was the success of the Parker-Gallman project that inspired our own sampling from the 1880 manuscript schedules. Before we began our own work, we acquired a copy of the Parker-Gallman tape and discussed our proposed collection techniques with Robert Gallman and William Parker. These discussions provided invaluable guidance to our own efforts.

Because the Parker-Gallman sample concentrated on the slave economy in the cotton regions, we have been able, through the generosity of Professors Parker and Gallman, to employ their data for our own purposes. Full details on the Parker-Gallman sample are to be found in James Foust's dissertation.[31] A briefer description is provided in a volume edited by William Parker.[32]

4. The urban South

Throughout this study of the postbellum South, we have focused our attention on the agricultural sector of the economy. In our examination of the system of agricultural credit and furnishing business we were particularly concerned to limit the influences introduced by data from cities and towns.

Identifying cotton centers in the South

We identified 158 towns and cities in either the Cotton South or the Five Cotton States that seemed to play a prominent enough role in the commercial activity of their regions to warrant designation as at least "minor" cotton centers. Each of these towns was classified as a *commercial center,* an *urban cotton center,* or a *rural cotton center.* A complete list of the towns, located either in the Cotton South or in one of the Five Cotton States, that serve as the focus of our analysis is presented in Table G.16.

Four factors were considered in determining the importance of a town or city that might be placed in one of these categories: (1) the population reported in 1880 for that town,[33] (2) the presence of banking facilities,[34] (3) evidence that there were commercial facilities such as warehouses, public cotton gins, commission or factorage houses located in the town,[35] and (4) the proximity of transportation facilities and the pattern of cotton shipments.[36]

Commercial centers are nine cities that had a population in excess of 10,000 in 1880. Each of these cities had at least five banks, at least one of which was a national bank. Their commercial facilities and transportation links confirm that these cities were preeminent in the commercial economy of the South, serving as entrepôts and marketing centers for large regions. Three of these cities – Atlanta, Montgomery, and Memphis – were within the Cotton South.

Urban cotton centers include all the remaining cities and towns with a population of 3,000 or more in 1880. Each of these centers had at least one bank and extensive commercial facilities that made it the focus of regional activity in its surrounding area. We have identified thirty-two urban cotton centers, twenty-eight of which were located in the Cotton South.

Rural cotton centers are towns that catered to a more local trade, serving a single large county or perhaps two or more smaller counties. Included in this category are all towns with a population in 1880 of between 1,500 and 3,000, together with any other town that had a commercial bank. We identi-

Table G.16. *Urban areas of the Cotton South and the Five Cotton States: 1880*

City	County	Class of city[a]	Population (thousands)	Number of banks	Number of general stores[b]
Alabama					
Alexander City	Tallapoosa	III	0.8	1	10
Athens[c]	Limestone	III	1.0	1	8
Birmingham	Jefferson	II	3.1	1	14
Decatur[c]	Morgan	III	1.1	0	3
Demopolis	Marengo	III	1.4	1	5
Eufaula	Barbour	II	3.8	2	21
Florence[c]	Lauderdale	III	1.4	0	15
Gadsden[c]	Etowah	III	1.7	1	8
Gainesville	Sumter	III	1.0	1	13
Greensboro	Hale	III	1.8	2	15
Greenville	Butler	III	2.5	1	15
Huntsville[c]	Madison	II	5.0	2	13
Lafayette	Chambers	III	1.1	1	3
Marion	Perry	III	2.1	1	17
Mobile[c]	Mobile	I	29.1	8	4
Montgomery	Montgomery	I	16.7	6	43
Opelika	Lee	II	3.2	2	15
Selma	Dallas	II	7.5	2	20
Talladega[c]	Talladega	III	1.2	1	20
Tuscaloosa[c]	Tuscaloosa	III	2.4	2	11
Tuscumbia[c]	Colbert	III	1.4	0	7
Tuskegee	Macon	III	2.4	0	16
Troy	Pike	III	2.3	1	18
Union Springs	Bullock	III	1.9	1	17
Uniontown	Perry	III	0.8	0	9
Total, 25 cities			96.7	38	340
Georgia					
Albany	Dougherty	II	3.2	1	24
Americus	Sumter	II	3.6	2	5
Athens	Clarke	II	6.1	2	20
Atlanta	Fulton	I	37.4	8	12
Augusta[c]	Richmond	I	21.9	10	4
Bainbridge	Decatur	III	1.4	1	11
Barnesville	Pike	III	2.0	1	7
Brunswick[c]	Glynn	III	2.9	2	13
Camilla	Mitchell	III	0.7	1	7
Cartersville[c]	Bartow	III	2.0	1	9
Columbus[c]	Muscogee	II	10.1	4	14
Conyers	Rockdale	III	1.4	1	13
Covington	Newton	III	1.4	1	14
Cuthbert	Randolph	III	2.1	1	9
Dalton[c]	Whitfield	III	2.5	1	16
Darien[c]	McIntosh	III	1.5	0	28
Dawson	Terrell	III	1.6	1	7

Table G.16. (*cont.*)

City	County	Class of city[a]	Population (thousands)	Number of banks	Number of general stores[b]
Forsyth	Monroe	III	1.1	1	7
Fort Valley	Houston	III	1.3	1	6
Gainesville	Hall	III	1.9	2	6
Greensboro	Greene	III	1.6	1	9
Griffin	Spalding	II	3.6	2	8
Hawkinsville	Pulaski	III	1.5	2	7
La Grange	Troup	III	2.3	2	4
Macon[c]	Bibb	I	12.7	7	7
Madison	Morgan	III	2.0	2	14
Marietta	Cobb	III	2.2	1	7
Milledgeville	Baldwin	II	3.8	1	6
Montezuma	Macon	III	0.4	2	5
Newnan	Coweta	III	2.0	2	9
Quitman[c]	Brooks	III	1.4	1	14
Reidsville[c]	Tattnall	III	0.1	1	1
Rome[c]	Floyd	II	3.9	4	7
Savannah[c]	Chatham	I	30.7	5	5
Social Circle	Walton	III	0.6	1	7
Sparta	Hancock	III	0.8	1	7
Thomasville	Thomas	III	2.6	1	11
Valdosta[c]	Lowndes	III	1.5	1	11
Washington	Wilkes	III	2.2	1	14
West Point	Troup	III	2.0	1	9
Total, 40 cities			184.0	81	394
Louisiana					
Alexandria	Rapides	III	1.8	0	15
Baton Rouge	East Baton Rouge	II	7.2	2	27
Clinton	East Feliciana	III	1.1	0	7
Monroe	Quachita	III	2.1	1	15
New Orleans[c]	Orleans	I	216.1	14	1
Shreveport	Caddo	II	8.0	2	16
Total, 6 cities			236.3	19	81
Mississippi					
Aberdeen[c]	Monroe	III	2.3	2	5
Brandon	Rankin	III	0.9	0	11
Brookhaven	Lincoln	III	1.6	0	13
Canton	Madison	III	2.1	1	9
Columbus	Lowndes	II	4.0	2	10
Corinth[c]	Alcorn	III	2.3	1	7
Greenville	Washington	III	2.2	1	17
Grenada	Grenada	III	1.9	2	6
Hazlehurst	Copiah	III	1.3	0	12
Holly Springs	Marshall	III	2.4	1	10
Jackson	Hinds	II	5.2	2	19
Kosciusko	Attala	III	1.2	1	9

Table G.16. (*cont.*)

City	County	Class of city[a]	Population (thousands)	Number of banks	Number of general stores[b]
Macon	Noxubee	III	2.1	1	17
Meridian	Lauderdale	II	4.0	4	22
Natchez	Adams	II	7.1	1	16
Okolona	Chickasaw	III	1.9	2	8
Oxford	Lafayette	III	1.5	1	8
Port Gibson	Claiborne	III	2.0	0	10
Ripley[c]	Tippah	III	0.6	1	5
Sardis	Panola	III	1.0	1	8
Starkville	Oktibbeha	III	1.5	1	11
Tupelo	Lee	III	1.0	1	5
Verona	Lee	III	0.6	1	5
Vicksburg	Warren	II	11.8	2	20
West Point	Clay	III	1.8	2	8
Woodville	Wilkinson	III	1.0	1	10
Yazoo City	Yazoo	III	2.5	1	18
Total, 27 cities			67.8	33	299
South Carolina					
Abbeville	Abbeville	III	1.5	0	13
Aiken[c]	Aiken	III	1.8	1	11
Anderson	Anderson	III	1.9	1	17
Bamberg	Barnwell	III	0.6	1	14
Beaufort[c]	Beaufort	III	2.5	1	18
Camden[c]	Kershaw	III	1.8	0	27
Charleston[c]	Charleston	I	50.0	13	0
Cheraw[c]	Chesterfield	III	1.2[d]	1	21
Chester	Chester	III	1.9	1	10
Columbia	Richland	II	10.0	4	3
Darlington	Darlington	III	0.9	0	20
Florence	Darlington	III	1.9	0	17
Gaffney	Spartanburgh	III	0.4	0	14
Georgetown[c]	Georgetown	III	2.6	1	26
Greenville	Greenville	II	6.2	1	27
Marion	Marion	III	0.8	0	18
Newberry	Newberry	III	2.3	1	16
Orangeburgh	Orangeburgh	III	2.1	1	15
Ridgeway	Fairfield	III	0.5	1	6
Rock Hill	York	III	0.8	1	10
Spartanburgh	Spartanburgh	II	3.3	1	17
Summerville[c]	Colleton	III	2.0	0	10
Sumter	Sumter	III	2.0	1	23
Union	Union	III	1.3	1	14
Walhalla	Oconee	III	0.8	1	10
Winnsboro	Fairfield	III	1.5	1	6
Yorkville	York	III	1.3	1	7
Total, 27 cities			103.9	35	390

Table G.16. (*cont.*)

City	County	Class of city [a]	Population (thousands)	Number of banks	Number of general stores [b]
Cotton region of Arkansas					
Arkadelphia	Clarke	III	1.5	0	10
Texarkana	Miller	III	1.4	1	11
Total, 2 cities			2.9	1	21
Cotton region of Florida					
Marianna	Jackson	III	0.6	0	8
Tallahassee	Leon	III	2.5	1	15
Total, 2 cities			3.1	1	23
Cotton region of North Carolina					
Charlotte	Mecklenburg	II	7.1	4	23
Clinton	Sampson	III	0.6	1	13
Fayetteville	Cumberland	II	3.5	2	39
Goldsboro	Wayne	II	3.3	1	33
Monroe	Union	III	1.6	1	18
Raleigh	Wake	II	9.3	3	24
Total, 6 cities			25.4	12	150
Cotton region of Tennessee					
Jackson	Madison	II	5.4	2	8
Memphis	Shelby	I	33.6	8	6
Total, 2 cities			39.0	10	14
Cotton region of Texas					
Bonham	Fannin	III	1.9	1	3
Brenham	Washington	II	4.1	3	15
Calvert	Robertson	III	2.3	1	10
Clarkesville	Red River	III	1.5[d]	1	4
Crockett	Houston	III	0.6	1	10
Daingerfield	Morris	III	0.4	1	4
Flatonia	Fayette	III	0.9	1	11
Gonzales	Gonzales	III	1.6	1	10
Henderson	Rusk	III	1.7	1	5
Honey Grove	Fannin	III	0.9	1	6
Industry	Austin	III	N.A.	1	4
Jefferson	Marion	II	3.3	2	10
La Grange	Fayette	III	1.3	1	6
Longview	Gregg	III	1.5	1	6
Luling	Caldwell	III	1.1	1	10
Marshall	Harrison	II	5.6	2	16
Nacogdoches	Nacogdoches	III	0.3	1	4
Navasota	Grimes	III	1.6	1	14
Palestine	Anderson	II	3.0	1	7

304

Table G.16. (*cont.*)

City	County	Class of city [a]	Population (thousands)	Number of banks	Number of general stores [b]
Paris	Lamar	II	4.0	2	5
Rusk	Cherokee	III	0.6	1	3
Total, 21 cities			38.2	26	163
Total, Cotton South					
Commercial centers (3 cities)		I	87.7	22	61
Urban cotton centers (28 cities)		II	151.3	54	487
Rural cotton centers (94 cities)		III	129.6	89	975
Total (125 cities)			368.6	165	1,523
Total, Five Cotton States					
Commercial centers (8 cities)		I	414.6	71	76
Urban cotton centers (22 cities)		II	131.7	45	344
Rural cotton centers (95 cities)		III	142.4	90	1,084
Total (125 cities)			688.7	206	1,504

[a] Classes of city are: I, commercial center; II, urban cotton center; III, rural cotton center. For definitions of these classes, see text. [b] Includes all stores at this postal address, regardless of geographic location. [c] Cities in the state that were *not* in the region we define as the Cotton South. [d] Population estimated by R. G. Dun and Company, *The Mercantile Agency Reference Book . . . January 1880,* 2nd edition (New York: Dun, Barlow & Co., 1880).
Source: Population: U.S. Census Office, Tenth Census [1880], *Statistics of the Population of the United States at the Tenth Census (June 1, 1880)* (Washington: GPO, 1883), pp. 93–351. *Number of Banks in 1880:* See text discussion. *Number of general stores in 1880:* Compiled from R. G. Dun and Company, *The Mercantile Agency Reference Book . . . January 1880,* 2nd ed. (New York: Dun, Barlow & Co., 1880). Any store listed as "general store," "dry goods and groceries," or "dry goods, etc." was included in the list.

fied 106 such towns and we added 11 others that, despite their small population, seemed to be the focus of local commercial activity. Of these 117 towns, 94 were located in the Cotton South.

Our list does not, of course, include *every* town involved in some aspect of the cotton trade. As we emphasize in the study, farmers by 1880 were in a position to sell cotton to, and buy provisions from, a host of small traders and merchants throughout the South. The cotton centers we have identified were the first link between this network of small traders and northern manufacturing and commercial interests.

Banking statistics in the postbellum South
The information on banking for this study was collected from a variety of sources. Data for national banks are complete and were published annually in the reports of the comptroller of the currency. As regards other banks, there is some ambiguity about which nonnational banks had state charters,

and whether various "savings banks" and "trust companies" should be considered as commercial banks. We have, for the most part, relied upon the classifications provided by Homans's *Bankers' Almanac*. This annual publication, which presented address lists of "all" American bankers, was the standard banking reference of the times. It has been cited by monetary historians as the most comprehensive source available.[37] Unfortunately, the almanac's lists are not without error. Dun's Mercantile Agency also took pains to prepare lists of bankers for clients subscribing to their *Reference Book* of credit ratings for businesses. Comparing these two sources, we have made some minor adjustments to the Homans data, correcting for double counting and apparent misclassification. The figures presented in Chapter 6 and in this appendix, therefore, differ slightly from those we presented in our earlier work.[38] A summary of banks in the Five Cotton States in 1880, according to the type of bank and the class of city in which they were located, is presented in Table G.17.

5. The Dun and Bradstreet archives

The most comprehensive source of information on businesses in the South during the mid-nineteenth century are the extensive records of the R. G. Dun Mercantile Agency. That firm, forerunner of the present-day Dun and Bradstreet Companies, Inc., collected vast amounts of data on firms throughout the United States. The Southern Economic History Project has made extensive use of these archives.

In 1859, when the Mercantile Agency was taken over by Robert G. Dun, he decided to publish a reference book, a large volume loaned to subscribers and updated on a regular basis.[39] The *Mercantile Agency Reference Books* contained, according to their compiler, "ratings on the merchants, manufacturers and traders, generally, throughout the United States and Canada."[40] Since the information they contained was confidential, the books were loaned, not sold, to subscribers.[41] As a result, we know of only two reasonably complete sets of the books presently surviving: one at Dun and Bradstreet's New York office; the other at the Library of Congress in Washington.

Dun's reference books

By the 1870s the *Mercantile Agency Reference Book* was being issued at least twice a year. The book organized the names of businesses or individuals by city and state, according to post office address. The occupation or type of business was indicated, together with Dun's estimate of the "pecuniary strength" of the owner and the "credit rating" of the firm. In 1870, Dun's identified ten categories of pecuniary strength, ranging from over $1 million to less than $2,000; an eleventh – less than $1,000 – was added for 1875 and after. The agency had seven ratings for general credit, ranging from "unlimited" down to "fair." These definitions of credit and pecuniary

Table G.17. *Number of banks in Five Cotton States, by type of bank and class of city: 1880*

State and class of city	National banks	State-chartered banks	Private banks	All banks
Alabama				
Commercial centers	4	4	6	14
Urban cotton centers	4	2	3	9
Rural cotton centers	2	2	11	15
Total	10	8	20	38
Georgia				
Commercial centers	6	15	9	30
Urban cotton centers	6	5	4	15
Rural cotton centers	1	6	29	36
Total	13	26	42	81
Louisiana				
Commercial centers	7	4	3	14
Urban cotton centers	0	0	4	4
Rural cotton centers	0	0	1	1
Total	7	4	8	19
Mississippi				
Commercial centers	0	0	0	0
Urban cotton centers	0	4	7	11
Rural cotton centers	0	3	19	22
Total	0	7	26	33
South Carolina				
Commercial centers	3	4	6	13
Urban cotton centers	4	0	2	6
Rural cotton centers	5	0	11	16
Total	12	4	19	35
Five Cotton States				
Commercial centers	20	27	24	71
Urban Cotton Centers	14	11	20	45
Rural cotton centers	8	11	71	90
Total	42	49	115	206

Source: See text.

strength ratings are summarized in Table G.18. Where no estimate was provided in the book, Dun's advised their customers that the firm or individual should be regarded as belonging in the lowest category of credit (3+) or pecuniary strength (L).

In 1971, with the permission and cooperation of Dun and Bradstreet Companies, Inc., we examined those portions of the 1870, 1875, 1880, and

Table G.18. *Pecuniary strength and credit rating scale of Dun's Reference Book*

	Reference Book code	Reference Book key
Pecuniary strength	A+	$1 Million and over
	A	$500,000–$1,000,000
	B	$250,000–$500,000
	C	$100,000–$250,000
	D	$50,000–$100,000
	E	$25,000–$50,000
	F	$10,000–$25,000
	G	$5,000–$10,000
	H	$2,000–$5,000
	K	Less than $2,000
	L	Less than $1,000[a]
General credit	A1	Unlimited
	1 } 1+ }	High
	2 } 2+ }	Good
	3 } 3+ }	Fair

[a] This rating was initiated in 1875.

1885 *Reference Books* that covered businesses in the eleven southern states. For the twenty-seven representative cotton counties in our 1880 sample of farms, we coded every listing in these four *Reference Books* into machine-readable form. The name of the firm or person; the location of the business (including any notation that it was "near" or "*x* miles from" some postal address); the proprietor's occupation, pecuniary strength, and credit rating were all collected for the sample. We identified forty-three specific occupational categories, which are listed in Table G.19.

Dun's credit ledgers
The *Reference Books* enable the researcher to construct a very complete cross-section of businesses at some point in time. However, firms – particularly firms with poor credit ratings – frequently changed the name under which they did business. In some cases, these name changes reflected reorganization designed to improve the financial standing of the business; in others they were changes in name only, adopted in the hope that the new name would be better received than the old. A large part of Dun's business service involved keeping track of these changes in the "style" under which firms did business. Fortunately, the original files upon which the *Reference Books* are based have been preserved in the form of hand-written volumes, known as the Credit Ledgers, which have been deposited with the Baker

Table G.19. *List of occupations enumerated in Dun and Bradstreet*
Reference Book, twenty-seven representative cotton counties

Bakery	Justice of the peace, sheriff
Bank, banker, cashier, moneylender	Lawyer, judge
Blacksmith	Liquor, saloon, bar
Butcher	Livery
Carpentry	Lumber
Cigars, tobacco	Mechanic
Clothing	Millinery
Confection	Newspaper, editor
Cotton gin, cotton mill	Physician, dentist
Drugs	Farmer, planter
Dry goods	Postmaster
Fertilizer	Printer, publisher
Furniture	Restaurant
General store	Rice mill
Grist mill, mill	Saddlery
Grocery	Saw mill
Gunsmith	Shoemaker, boots and shoes
Hardware	Tailor
Harnesses	Tanning
Hotel	Tinware, tinner
Jeweler	Turpentine

Library at Harvard University. These ledgers, in which the reports from the field were copied, were maintained with great care by the clerks of the New York office from 1841 to around 1880. Beginning in 1875, the records were transferred to a new system that used the recently invented typewriter.[42]

Without the continuous record provided by the Credit Ledgers, it is impossible to trace firms or individuals through time. Although these volumes are not available for general use, we were able to arrange with Dun and Bradstreet Companies, Inc., to have access to them. With the assistance of the Baker Library staff, we examined the complete set of Credit Ledger entries for twenty-two rural southern counties.[43] A list of these twenty-two counties is provided in Table G.20.

The entries in the Credit Ledgers are organized according to the name of each individual or business. To show how entries were placed in the ledgers, we have reproduced as Figure G.3 a facsimile of one page from Rankin County, Mississippi. When the space alloted on the page to a given enterprise was exhausted, the entry was continued on a subsequent page of the ledger. Therefore, a complete set of reports on most businesses involved locating a series of separate entries in the volume. While some attempt was made by Dun's clerks both to index and to cross reference reports for related businesses, we have found these guides to be incomplete. To be certain that all related passages concerned with a particular business had been located, a thorough search of *all* entries in the county proved neces-

Table G.20. *Counties for which Dun's Credit Ledgers were examined*

Alabama	Georgia	Mississippi	South Carolina
Bibb	Coweta	Rankin[a]	Barnwell
Russell[a]	Gwinnett[a]	Tunica[a]	Beaufort
	Liberty	Yalobusha	Union
Florida	Tattnall		
Gadsen	Terrell	North Carolina	Tennessee
	Twiggs[a]	Nash	Scott
	Worth[a]		
			Texas
	Louisiana		Cherokee
	Plaquemines		
			Virginia
			Giles
			Halifax

[a] A sample of 173 firms was drawn from these six counties.

sary. Once all reports were gathered together, the continuous record of the firm, for as long as it appeared in the Credit Ledgers, could be examined.

The need for this extensive examination and organization of this hand-written material limited the number of counties for which information could be assembled. The data from the Credit Ledgers discussed in the present study are based on six of the twenty-two counties for which we obtained access: Gwinnett, Twiggs, and Worth, Georgia; Russell, Alabama; and Rankin and Tunica, Mississippi.

It is impossible to capture in only a few words the full flavor and variety of information contained in the Credit Ledger reports. To illustrate the nature of the information, and to point out some of the problems encountered in organizing data, we shall consider in some detail a typical set of entries: the reports provided on a general store opened in Chinquepin Grove, Gwinnett County, Georgia, by D. A. Farr and F. M. Wages in 1873 and operated by a number of persons thereafter.[44]

D. A. FARR & F. M. WAGES   CHINQUEPIN GROVE   GENERAL STORE

Sept. '73: Established but a short time, doing well, making money. Men of good character and habits, prudent and attentive to business. Wages is married and [a] farmer by occupation. Farr attends to the store. Wages owns real estate. The firm [is] estimated [to be] worth from $6,000–8,000. Good for moderate amounts.
Jan. '74: No change   *June '74:* Worth $6,000. Reliable.
Aug. '74: Dissolved. Succeeded by Farr and Smith.

FARR & SMITH   BUFORD   GENERAL STORE

Aug. 74: They are energetic, good standing and business capacity. Worth $3,000 or 4,000 but considered responsible.
March '75: Established several years and doing but small business, of good character, are steady and attentive to business and considered responsible for small amount. Farr attends to the store. Smith is the railroad agent. Have some real estate and are estimated worth $1,000 to 2,000. Farr married, age 40. Smith single, age 30.

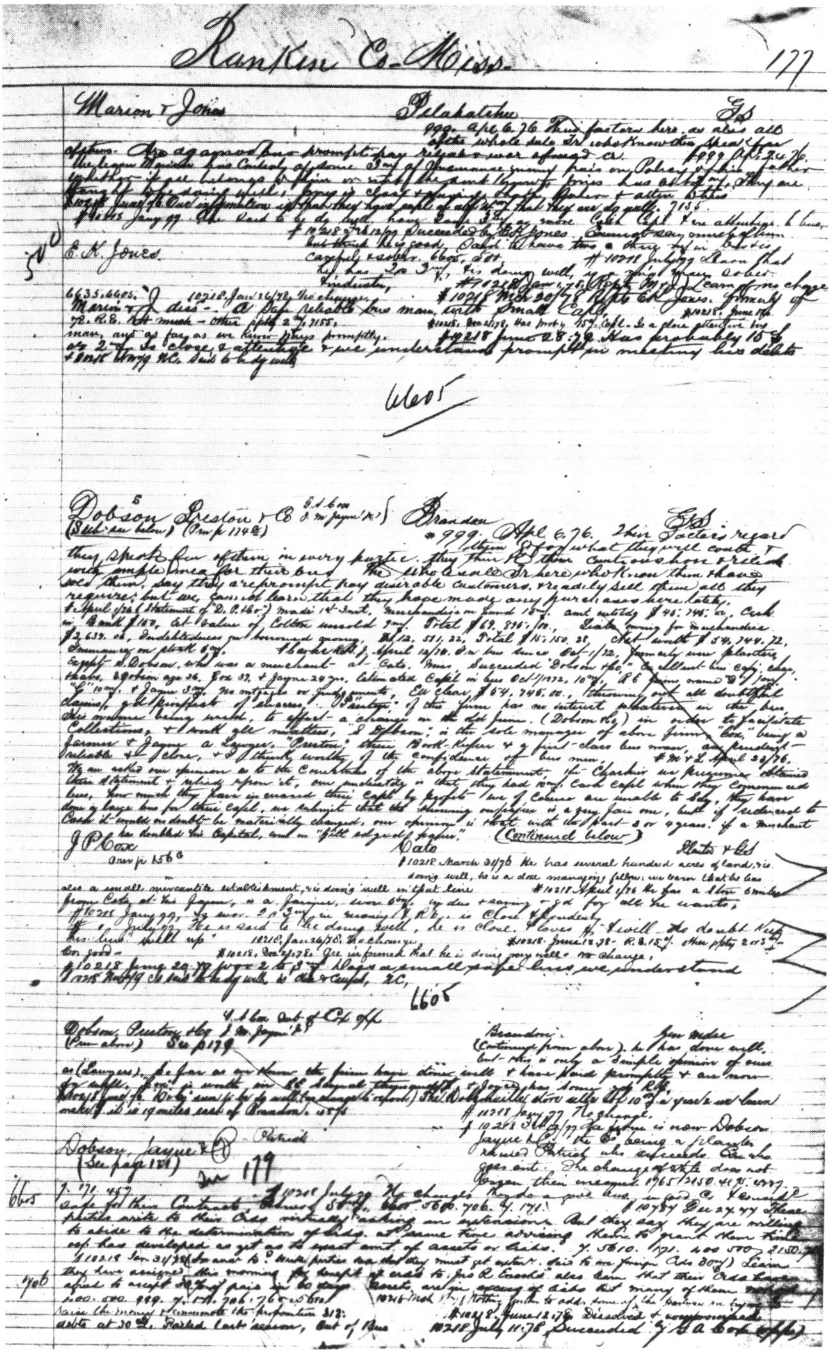

Figure G.3 A page from the R. G. Dun and Company Credit Ledger for Rankin County, Mississippi. (*Source:* Baker Library, Harvard University.)

June '75: Fair business capacity. Worth $3,000 or 4,000. Considered reliable.

Dec. '75: Considered reliable and estimated worth $3,000.

June '76: Good businessmen, considered reliable. Estimated worth $4,000.

Jan. '77: Worth $3,000 and considered reliable.

April '77: Reports Smith and Evans succeed Farr and Smith. Are not well established in business but are favorably spoken of.

J. P. SMITH AND EVANS

June '77: Don't know as to means or business ability.

Dec. '77: Estimated worth $3,000. Considered reliable.

March '78: Dissolved and succeeded by J. P. Smith. Good man, stands well at home. Looked upon as honest. Said to be close and will pay his bills, though [he] has very little business capacity and [is] not doing much. Owns real estate and estimated worth $2,000 or 3,000.

At this point the trail becomes obscured. There were a number of Smiths in Gwinnett County, and it is not clear which of them operated this store. One entry, for a J. T. Smith, described a general store that was in business from March 1878 through January 1880. The entry suggests that Dun's reporters had some problem determining Mr. Smith's standing:

J. T. SMITH   BUFORD   GENERAL STORE

March '78: Not well known. Business reputation not well established. Doubtful.

Sept. '78: Cautious and economical. Has a plantation in Jackson and a mill in Hall County. He is worth about $5,000. Owns some real estate in this place. Considered good for any amount that he would wish to buy.

May '79: Little or no means.

Jan. '80: Returns $700 real estate, $500 in good accounts and $500 stock of goods and $200 personal property. In very fair standing and credit with trade. Estimated worth $2,000 to $2,500.

Though the September 1878 entry is something of an anomaly, it seems highly likely that this is, in fact, the Smith who took over the business begun by Farr and Wages. The January 1880 report was the last filed on this store location. Though we have not reproduced the entries here, we note that both Farr and Evans became involved in other mercantile businesses elsewhere in the county.

As might be expected, careful attention was given by the reporters to all the assets owned by the firm and its partners. Any ownership of real estate (which could be checked at the county courthouse) by a partner of the firm was frequently noted. (Note the mention of real estate for each new partner in our example.) Some appraisal of the individuals' "worth," together with the amount of capital invested in the firm were often forwarded. Indications of the volume of business (usually in very general terms, but at times specifying the dollar volume) can be found in many entries. The business "capacity" of each partner and his role in the firm were typically evaluated. It is apparent from the sample entry that Farr was the storekeeper in the early partnerships, while Wages (a farmer) and Smith (a railroad agent) were less active in the day-to-day operations of the store. (Note that the favorable tone of the reports were affected by Farr's departure.)

Though the details and frequency with which these items are reported vary throughout the volumes we have examined, the sample presented above is a fair illustration of a typical entry in the records. The financial holdings of the firm and the reporter's judgment of the person's ability were the primary bases for the pecuniary strength and credit ratings. When information was available, additional consideration might be given to the promptness with which bills were paid. Even a well-to-do merchant occasionally drew complaints of tardy payments. "Just a little meaner than the Devil wants them to be," wrote a reporter of two prosperous Twiggs County partners, "[they] own more property than any man in the county, yet [are] in debt to everyone they can and never pay." Such instances were rare; as a rule, ownership of property ensured a good credit rating.

The comprehensiveness of the Mercantile Agency lists
It is important to establish that the records of the Mercantile Agency represent a complete enumeration of stores in the South. A priori there is good reason to expect the lists to be quite inclusive. Most merchants with sound businesses would want to be listed so they could obtain credit from commercial centers. Wholesalers buying Dun's service would expect comprehensive coverage, particularly including those firms with a marginal or unsound business. Our examination of the Credit Ledgers turned up a number of cases where it was clear that merchants establishing their businesses actually wrote to Dun's to announce their opening. In other cases, it was clear that clients of Dun's had inquired of the New York office for information regarding unlisted firms.

As an empirical check on the completeness of the lists, we have examined data on occupations reported in the manuscript population schedules for the censuses of 1870 and 1880 in our merchant sample. Lists were compiled from the census documents that included every person who reported an occupation related to merchandising. These lists were then compared with the names of merchants obtained from the corresponding *Reference Book* of 1870 or 1880 for those counties. The results of this comparison are summarized in Table G.21. We collected 243 names for this comparison, of which 186 (76.5 percent) were found both on the census and on Dun's list. The rest were about equally split between those found only on the census list

Table G.21. *Merchant names listed in censuses of 1870 and 1880 and in Dun and Bradstreet archives*

	Number of names located	Percent of total
Located both in census and Dun and Bradstreet	186	76.5
Listed in Dun and Bradstreet but not in census	32	13.2
Listed in census but not in Dun and Bradstreet	25	10.3
Total	243	100.0

(25) and those found only on Dun's list (32). In evaluating these results, it is important to note the inexactness inherent in such a matching of lists. The Dun's list included names of firms that could not always be unambiguously identified with individuals enumerated in the census. By the same token, not all owners of mercantile establishments identified themselves as such in the occupational designation of the census, and some people may have exaggerated the importance of their positions. Problems such as these probably account for our inability to match all the names in both lists.

In addition to this comparison with the census manuscripts, we compared the number of stores listed in the 1880 *Reference Book* for South Carolina with a list of stores we compiled from an independently prepared, comprehensive survey taken in 1882 by Harry Hammond.[45] Hammond's survey listed 2,462 stores in the state; Dun's list counted 2,245. The difference is less than 10 percent, a remarkably small discrepancy considering the two-year difference in dates of the two sources and the problems of accurately defining what constitutes a "store."

These checks have convinced us that the Mercantile Agency's pride that their lists represented a virtually complete enumeration of merchants throughout the South seems well founded.

The sample of firms from the credit ledgers
We analyzed a sample 173 firms which were "general stores" in the six counties included in the Credit Ledger sample. Because we included only firms in business during one of the years for which we had a *Reference Book* (1870, 1875, 1880), the sample does *not* include every general store in operation between 1870 and 1880.[46] For each store in the sample we recorded the date on which the store was opened; the number of reorganizations that occurred over the decade; and, for any store that disappeared, the reason for the disappearance. We also recorded the storekeeper's credit rating and pecuniary strength from the *Reference Book* for those years in which he was listed. Finally, whenever possible we located all partners involved with the firm in the manuscript schedules of either the 1870 or the 1880 Population Census and recorded the age, occupation, birthplace, and names and ages of family members living in the same household.

A major problem in using the information in the Credit Ledgers as a basis for studying merchant establishments is the definition of a "store." We wished to examine the operation of a store serving some market over a number of years. So long as service in a fixed location was maintained without interruption to the customers, we considered that business to be a single *store,* irrespective of who owned or operated it. Dun's, however, was primarily interested in the *people* involved in merchandising. In their eyes, every change in partners or backers of the store represented a new *firm,* even if the business had not changed with the new arrangement. It was not at all uncommon for rural stores to alter the composition of their partnerships. In the present study, we have treated a *store* as a single business establishment over any period of time which it remained open for business, irrespective of changes in the financial arrangement or partners. A *new store* was defined as the opening of a store with a new facility not currently used by an existing merchant. The date at which this new store "entered" the industry was determined as accurately as possible from the reports on the establishment in the Credit Ledgers. Thus, "Farr and Wages," having been "established but a short time," were presumed to have commenced business in 1873.[47]

We termed changes in the composition of the firm's ownership or financial backing that did not significantly alter the store's service a *reorganization* of the existing firm. Although "Farr and Wages," "Farr and Smith," "Smith and Evans" and "J. P. (or J. T.) Smith" were different partnerships, they all operated *the same store.* Smith was still in business in 1880. Therefore, we counted this succession of partnerships a single *store,* and noted that it had been *reorganized* three times.

When a firm ceased to have reports entered into the Credit Ledgers, we considered that it had *disappeared.* For the most cases, we were able to establish a definite reason for the closing of the file. For those few where the reports end abruptly and without explanation, we assumed that the store disappeared at the date of the last report. The case of "Dobson, Jayne & Co.," a general store in Rankin County, Mississippi, that encountered difficulties in early 1878, illustrates the difficulty that sometimes arose in determining the fate of a mercantile business:

DOBSON, JAYNE & CO.   BRANDON   GENERAL MERCHANDISE

Jan. '78: . . . Also learn that their creditors have agreed to accept 30% if paid in 60 days. Assets are in excess of liabilities, but many of them not good.
March '78: Nothing further to add. Some of the partners are trying to raise the money . . .
June '78: Dissolved and compromised debts at 30 cents. Failed last season. Out of business.
July '78: Succeeded by G. A. Cox.

Did the store *disappear* in June of 1878? (The *firm* had obviously failed financially.) Was *Cox* a new sotre? Our guideline suggests that an existing store was reorganized in June and July of 1878, and that G. A. Cox was *not* a new firm. A subsequent entry for Cox clearly indicated that, despite the financial embarrassment of the original firm, the general store remained in operation during 1878:

G. A. COX & CO.   BRANDON

June '79: . . . G. A. Cox undertook to settle the affairs of Dobson, Jayne & Co. and Dobson & Co. and did compromise and close much of their indebtedness of said firms but in the end fell through and was sold out.

The fact that this last entry also noted that the firm was out of business and that no subsequent firm undertook to maintain the establishment means that this store *disappeared* from our sample at that point.

NOTES

Chapter 1. What did freedom mean?

1 Slave prices for 1859 and 1860 in Georgia are given in Ulrich B. Phillips, "The Economic Cost of Slaveholding in the Cotton Belt," *Political Science Quarterly* 20 (June 1905), p. 267. The annual output per *slave* is calculated in Appendix A, Table A.1. To convert to a per hand basis, we assumed that the ratio of workers to slaves was 0.5. For support of this conversion ratio see Lewis Cecil Gray, *History of Agriculture in the Southern United States to 1860*, 2 vols. (Washington: Carnegie Institution, 1933), 1, p. 544; Kenneth M. Stampp, *The Peculiar Institution: Slavery in the Ante-Bellum South* (New York: Alfred A. Knopf, 1956), p. 57; and James D. Foust and Dale E. Swan, "Productivity and Profitability of Antebellum Slave Labor: A Micro-Approach," *Agricultural History* 44 (January 1970), pp. 42–43.

2 It has become common to define *economic exploitation* as occurring if, and only if, a worker is paid less than the value of his marginal product – that is, his or her incremental contribution to output measured with other factors unchanged. Joan Robinson is credited with developing this concept (*The Economics of Imperfect Competition,* 2nd ed. [London: Macmillan Co., 1969], pp. 281–283, 1st edition published in 1933).

3 For a more detailed discussion of the diet, shelter, and clothing provided slaves, see Richard Sutch, "The Treatment Received by American Slaves: A Critical Review of the Evidence Presented in *Time on the Cross,*" *Explorations in Economic History* 12 (October 1975), pp. 353–383. Other well-known discussions of these issues include Ulrich B. Phillips, *American Negro Slavery* (New York: D. Appleton & Co., 1918), Chapter 14; Kenneth M. Stampp, *The Peculiar Institution,* Chapter 7; and Eugene D. Genovese, *Roll, Jordan, Roll: The World the Slaves Made* (New York: Pantheon, 1974), pp. 540–561.

4 David C. Barrow, Jr., "A Georgia Plantation," *Scribner's Monthly* 21 (April 1881), p. 832.

5 Whitelaw Reid, *After the War: A Tour of the Southern States, 1865–1866* (New York: Harper & Row, 1965), p. 499, first published in 1866.

6 Reid, *After the War,* pp. 528–529.

7 In Appendix C, we discuss the derivation of this estimate of the decline in the number of hours worked by the black population. Also see the discussion in Chapter 3 and Table 3.3.

8 According to the U.S. Department of Agriculture estimates made by James Watkins, the 1859 crop was 2.241 billion pounds, worth $246.5 million; the crop of 1858 was 1.796 billion pounds. A simple least-squares estimate of the trend between 1849 and 1858 predicts that the 1859 crop would have been 1.707 billion pounds. James L. Watkins, U.S. Department of Agriculture, Division of Statistics, "Production and Price of Cotton for One Hundred Years," *USDA Miscellaneous Bulletin,* Number 9 (Washington: GPO, 1895), pp. 3, 8, 10.

9 Gavin Wright emphasized the extraordinary nature of the 1859 crop year ("Prosperity, Progress, and American Slavery," in Paul A. David et al., *Reckoning with Slavery: A Critical Study in the Quantitative History of American Negro Slavery* [New York: Oxford University Press, 1976], pp. 313–316).

10 In Chapter 3 we argue that it is probable that labor productivity for black farm workers actually did rise after the Civil War. We should note at this point, however, that in addition to the data problems suggested in the text, the inadequacy of our information on labor inputs, and in particular, on the intensity of the work effort per hour, makes a more precise calculation of the change in labor productivity beyond our reach. Furthermore, the problems inherent in estimating the level of labor productivity at any point in time go beyond inadequacies of the underlying data. Economists have not yet resolved certain theoretical and conceptual difficulties inherent in the notion of factor productivity. In many applications, these difficulties are not of serious consequence, but it is precisely when one comes to compare productivity in two widely different economic systems that these theoretical problems become crippling. See Evsey D. Domar, "On Total Factor Productivity and All That," *Journal of Political Economy* 70 (December 1962), pp. 598–600; and idem, "On the Measurement of Technological Change," *Economic Journal* 71 (December 1961).

11 See Appendix F, Table F.2, for estimates of the rural population of the Five Cotton States.

12 For the Five Cotton States (South Carolina, Georgia, Alabama, Mississippi, and Louisiana), Easterlin estimated per capita personal income in 1929 dollars at $156.06 in 1880. Twenty years later the average was only $184.51, an increase representing a rate of growth of 0.8 percent per year over the twenty years. Richard A. Easterlin, "Regional Growth of Income: Long Term Tendencies, 1880–1950," in Simon Kuznets and Dorothy Swaine Thomas, eds. *Population Redistribution and Economic Growth, United States, 1870–1950*, Volume 2 (Philadelphia: American Philosophical Society, 1960), Table A 4.1, p. 185. Easterlin's state estimates were weighted using the 1880 Census populations of the five states. U.S. Bureau of the Census, *Historical Statistics of the United States, Colonial Times to 1957* (Washington: GPO, 1960), Series A 155, 156, 161, 162, 165, p. 12. See Appendix F for a further discussion of Easterlin's estimates.

13 Before and after the Civil War, blacks represented approximately 52 percent of the rural population of the Five Cotton States (See Chapter 4, Table 4.1), but because of their higher labor force participation (and, when slaves, their longer work hours), they supplied approximately 70 percent of the South's total labor before the war and about 60 percent after the war. For an estimate of white and black labor force participation rates in 1879, see Roger Ransom and Richard Sutch, "The Ex-Slave in the Post-Bellum South: A Study of the Economic Impact of Racism in a Market Environment," *Journal of Economic History* 33 (March 1973), Table 3, p. 143. To calculate the aggregate decline in the rural labor supply, we assumed that the labor force particpation of whites before the war equaled their postwar rates. Our estimate is based on the assumption that white workers before and after the war worked as many hours per day on average as did free black workers. We have taken the midpoints of our estimates of the length of work year given in Appendix C, Table C.1.

14 These crop estimates are, of course, incomplete measures of the total agricultural output of the five states over the period. Sale of other crop outputs, and the value added from animal, dairy, and poultry products, would increase measured gross income over the estimates of Table 1.4. The portion of crops fed to animals and the costs of inputs such as purchased feed and fertilizer would reduce income received by a farmer. We are confident that the crop estimates exaggerate the rate of growth of aggregate agricultural income because the production of products excluded from our measure grew less rapidly than our measured crop output, and at the same time, the variable expenditures we ignored increased more rapidly than did measured crop output.

15 U.S. Census Office, Twelfth Census [1900], *Census Reports . . . Agriculture* (Washington: GPO, 1902), Part I, Table 14; Part II, Tables 8, 18, 19.

16 The rate of growth of agricultural output between 1879 and 1899 is calculated from the figures on per capita crop output measured in terms of 1899–1908 prices presented in Appendix F, Table F.3. The population used to deflate the aggregate output series was the rural population of the Five Cotton States.

17 Everett S. Lee estimates that in 1900, only 12.3 percent of the blacks in the Five Cotton States lived in cities or towns with a population of at least 2,500 ("Migration Estimates," in

Simon Kuznets and Dorothy Swaine Thomas, eds., *Population Redistribution and Economic Growth, United States, 1870–1950,* volume 1 [Philadelphia: American Philosophical Society, 1957], Tables P 4.A and P 4.B, pp. 349–356). This compares with 17.1 percent of the white population living in urban areas of that size in 1900. The census enumerated 1.3 million blacks who were farmers or farm workers in 1900. Of this total, 70.7 percent were "farmers" or laborers on home farms; 29.3 percent were agricultural workers not on home farms. U.S. Bureau of the Census, *Negro Population: 1790–1915* (Washington: GPO, 1918), p. 528.

18 W. O. Atwater and Charles D. Woods, U.S. Department of Agriculture, Office of Experiment Stations, "Dietary Studies with Reference to the Food of the Negro in Alabama in 1895 and 1896," *USDA Experiment Stations Bulletin,* Number 38 (Washington: GPO, 1897), p. 16.

19 Atwater and Woods, "Dietary Studies," p. 69.

20 Atwater and Woods, "Dietary Studies," pp. 62–63.

21 Atwater and Woods, "Dietary Studies," p. 21.

22 The examples cited by Carl Kelsey involve detailed records of expenditures by three families in Alabama over a two-year period (1900–1901). He stated that "all of these families are a little above the average" (*The Negro Farmer* [Chicago: Jennings & Pye, 1903], pp. 49–50). Conditions were apparently somewhat better in the alluvial region. Kelsey noted that the owners sampled in that region "make many efforts to get their tenants to improve their condition" (pp. 54–55).

23 Easterlin's estimates of regional income trends before the Civil War are discussed in Appendix F. We note here that a considerable debate has developed regarding the rate of growth of the slave economy. Our reliance upon Easterlin's figures reflects our conclusion that these numbers are the most reliable currently available. See our discussion in Appendix F.

24 Recent statements of this view are offered by Eugene P. Genovese, *The Political Economy of Slavery: Studies in the Economy and Society of the Slave South* (New York: Pantheon, 1965); and Douglas F. Dowd, "A Comparative Analysis of Economic Development in the American West and South," *Journal of Economic History* 16 (December 1956). Earlier treatments of the same theme that have been particularly influential include J. E. Cairnes, *The Slave Power: Its Character, Career, and Probable Designs: Being an Attempt to Explain the Real Issues Involved in the American Contest* (New York: Harper & Row, 1969), originally published in 1862; Phillips, "Economic Cost of Slaveholding"; Gray, *History of Agriculture* (1933), 2, Chapter 20; and Robert R. Russel, "The General Effects of Slavery upon Southern Economic Progress," *Journal of Southern History* 4 (February 1938). For a review of the literature, see Harold D. Woodman, "The Profitability of Slavery: A Historicial Perennial," *Journal of Southern History* 29 (August 1963).

Chapter 2. The legacy of slavery

1 Albert Taylor Bledsoe, *An Essay on Liberty and Slavery* (Philadelphia: J. B. Lippincott & Co., 1856), p. 299.

2 Chancellor Harper, "Harper on Slavery," in *The Pro-Slavery Argument; As Maintained by the Most Distinguished Writers of the Southern States, Containing the Several Essays, on the Subject by Chancellor Harper, Governor Hammond, Dr. Simms, and Professor Dew* (New York: Negro Universities Press, 1968), p. 95, originally published in 1852 by Walker, Richards & Co. This volume reprinted essays written in the late 1830s and early 1840s.

3 Richard C. Wade, *Slavery in the Cities: The South, 1820–1860* (New York: Oxford University Press, 1964), p. 91. Henry Bullock discusses the fears inspired by the Vesey and Turner revolts (*A History of Negro Education in the South from 1619 to the Present* [Cambridge: Harvard University Press, 1967], p. 14). On the rise of restrictive laws against education of slaves as a response to white fears, see Carter G. Woodson, *The*

Education of the Negro Prior to 1861 (New York: Arno Press, 1968), pp. 162–171, originally published in 1915; Wade, *Slavery in the Cities*, pp. 173–177; and Eugene D. Genovese, *Roll, Jordan, Roll: The World the Slaves Made* (New York: Pantheon, 1974), pp. 561–564.

4 Wade, *Slavery in the Cities*, pp. 90–93, 173–177.

5 An estimate of 2 to 3 percent is offered by Daniel C. Thompson without citation, but with the introduction that it was "according to the most reliable estimates" (*Sociology of the Black Experience,* Contributions in Sociology, Number 14 [Westport: Greenwood Press, 1974], p. 168). Woodson cites two contemporary estimates of slave literacy: one of "one out of every fifty" (2 percent) in the "Southwest," and another that "five thousand out of the four hundred thousand slaves of Georgia" (1.25 percent) were literate at the end of the slave era (*Education of the Negro Prior to 1861,* pp. 227–228). Joel Williamson puts the figure for South Carolina at "perhaps 5 per cent" (*After Slavery: The Negro in South Carolina During Reconstruction, 1861–1877* [Chapel Hill: University of North Carolina Press, 1965], p. 210). Genovese cites W. E. B. Du Bois's conjecture of 5 percent as "entirely plausible" (*Roll, Jordan, Roll,* p. 563).

6 These figures were collected in 1870 by the Census Office after there had already been several years of educational efforts aimed at blacks by the Freedmen's Bureau (U.S. Census Office, Ninth Census [1870], *The Statistics of the Population of the United States* [Washington: GPO, 1872], pp. 396–397, 560–567). Also see Table 2.4 for more detail.

7 These data are based on a sampling from the manuscript records of the 1860 Census of Mortality. See Appendix B for details.

8 See, for example, the arguments of Samuel Bowles, who insists that literacy was not a necessary prerequisite for the factory operatives in Massachusetts ("Unequal Education and the Reproduction of the Social Division of Labor," *Review of Radical Political Economics* 3 [fall and winter 1971]).

9 Woodson argues that masters in rural areas simply ignored the laws against education when it suited them to do so (*Education of the Negro Prior to 1861,* pp. 3, 13–15), and Genovese suggests the same (*Roll, Jordan, Roll,* pp. 561–566). Woodson also insists that what efforts were taken to enforce the regulations met with little success, even among the slaves of owners interested in prohibiting learning.

10 Both Woodson and Genovese point out the extent to which slaves depended upon clandestine means to obtain formal education (Woodson, *Education of the Negro Prior to 1861,* pp. 206–208, 216–219; Genovese, *Roll, Jordan, Roll,* pp. 561–566).

11 If the slaveholder shared the belief of many whites that the black race was mentally incapable of benefiting from education, he might not even acknowledge the small gains noted in the text. We shall return later in this chapter to the role this racist misconception played.

12 Lewis Cecil Gray, *History of Agriculture in the Southern United States to 1860,* 2 vols. (Washington: Carnegie Institution, 1933), 1, p. 549.

13 A closely related point, which reinforces the argument in the text, becomes relevant if the free workers have available educational facilities subsidized by the state. Public education would lower the cost of obtaining an education, increase the amount of education obtained, and put the slaveowner at a further competitive disadvantage.

14 An interesting implication of this argument is that many of these plantation craftsmen were underemployed, spending part of their time as field hands rather than practicing their craft.

15 An excellent discussion of European and American perceptions of Africans is given by Winthrop Jordan (*White over Black: American Attitudes Toward the Negro, 1550–1812* [Chapel Hill: University of North Carolina Press, 1968], Chapter 1). Also see Carl Degler, "Slavery and the Genesis of American Race Prejudice," *Comparative Studies in Society and History* 2 (October 1959).

16 Hollis Burke Frissell, "Popular Education in the South," in *Race Problems in the South: Report of the Proceedings of the First Annual Conference Held under the Auspices of the Southern Society* (New York: Negro University Press, 1969), pp. 83–97, originally published in 1900.

17 Robert W. Fogel and Stanley L. Engerman, *Time on the Cross,* 2 vols. (Boston: Little, Brown & Co., 1974), 1, pp. 5, 147, 231.

18 Herbert Gutman and Richard Sutch, "Sambo Makes Good, or Were Slaves Imbued with the Protestant Work Ethic?" in Paul A. David et al., *Reckoning with Slavery: A Critical Study in the Quantitative History of American Negro Slavery* (New York: Oxford University Press, 1976).

19 On slave productivity, see Appendix A and the literature on the profitability of slavery, especially the papers reproduced in Hugh G. Aitken, ed., *Did Slavery Pay?* (Boston: Houghton Mifflin Co., 1971). On the hours of work, see our Appendix C. On the caloric content of the diet, see Richard Sutch, "The Treatment Received by American Slaves: A Critical Review of the Evidence Presented in *Time on the Cross,*" *Explorations in Economic History* 12 (October 1975), pp. 384–386. Descriptions of the work gang are provided by Frederick Law Olmsted, *The Cotton Kingdom,* edited by Arthur M. Schlesinger (New York: Alfred A. Knopf, 1953), pp. 432–433, originally published in 1861, and by Kenneth M. Stampp, *The Peculiar Institution: Slavery in the Ante-Bellum South* (New York: Alfred A. Knopf, 1956), pp. 54–57, among many others. On physical punishment, see Stampp, *Peculiar Institution,* pp. 174–177, 186–187; and Gutman and Sutch, "Work Ethic," pp. 57–69.

20 Stampp, *Peculiar Institution,* pp. 100–104.

21 Sutch, "Treatment," pp. 384–386.

22 Paul A. David and Peter Temin, "Slavery: The Progressive Institution?" *Journal of Economic History* 34 (September 1974), p. 752.

23 Stampp, *Peculiar Institution,* pp. 164–170.

24 *Southern Cultivator* 23 (1865), p. 90.

25 Carl Schurz, *Report of Carl Schurz on the States of South Carolina, Georgia, Alabama, Mississippi, and Louisiana,* Senate, Executive Document Number 2, 39th Congress, 1st Session (Washington: GPO, 1865), p. 16.

26 *Southern Cultivator* 23 (1865), p. 134.

27 *Rural Carolinian* 1 (February 1870), p. 313.

28 Peter Kolchin, *First Freedom: The Response of Alabama's Blacks to Emancipation and Reconstruction* (Westport: Greenwood Press, 1972), p. 38.

29 Kolchin, *First Freedom,* pp. 38, 41. The first quote is from a manuscript diary entry of J. B. Moore, dated March 11, 1866; the second is from a letter from Spencer Smith to Colonel Cadle dated January 20, 1866; the third was taken from the *Daily Selma [Alabama] Messenger* of May 9, 1867.

30 Williamson, *After Slavery,* p. 164.

31 U.S. Bureau of Refugees, Freedmen, and Abandoned Lands, *Reports of the Assistant Commissioners of Freedmen . . . ,* Senate, Executive Document Number 6, 39th Congress, 2nd Session, December 1866 (Washington: GPO, 1867), p. 60.

32 Benjamin C. Truman, "Report of Benjamin C. Truman," Senate, Executive Document Number 43, 39th Congress, 1st Session (Washington: GPO, 1866), p. 10.

33 Despite some initial fears in the North that southerners would resist, the abolition of slavery was apparently quickly accepted in the South as one of the consequences of defeat. Among those who confirmed that the southerners' reaction to abolition was one of acceptance were journalists John R. Dennett (*The South As It Is: 1865–1866* [New York: Viking Press, 1967], pp. 360–361, originally published as a series of articles in *The Nation,* 1865–1866), and Sidney Andrews (*The South Since the War as Shown by Fourteen Weeks of Travel and Observation in Georgia and the Carolinas* [Boston: Houghton Mifflin Co., 1970], pp. 56–58, 154–162, 178, first published in 1866), as well as presidential envoy Carl Schurz (*Report,* pp. 8–10). Also see *De Bow's Review* 1 (January 1866), p. 92.

34 Dr. Joseph Warren to John Eaton, letter dated April 10, 1865, reproduced in John Eaton, *Grant, Lincoln and the Freedmen* (New York: Longmans, Greene & Co., 1907), pp. 208–209.

35 Whitelaw Reid, *After the War: A Tour of the Southern States, 1865–1866* (New York:

Harper & Row, 1965), pp. 302–303, first published in 1866. For other comments on the enthusiasm of freedmen for education, see the reports of the Freedmen's Bureau for 1867, in particular the comments by J. W. Alvord, in U.S. Bureau of Refugees, Freedmen, and Abandoned Lands, *Fourth Semi-Annual Report on Schools for Freedmen, July 1, 1867* (Washington: GPO, 1867), p. 4. Also see Kolchin, *First Freedom*, pp. 84–87.

36 John W. Deforest, *A Union Officer in the Reconstruction* (New Haven: Yale University Press, 1948), p. 116, first published in 1867.

37 Testimony of James Atkins, in U.S. Congress, *The Ku-Klux Conspiracy*, Report of the Joint Select Committee, House of Representatives, Report Number 22, 42nd Congress, 2nd Session (Washington: GPO, 1872), Part 6, p. 524.

38 The report of the superintendent of public schools in South Carolina in 1869 noted that the following societies were active in black education in that year: Pennsylvania Association of the Freedmen's Bureau, American Missionary Association, Southern Educational Association of Saint Louis, New England Freedmen's Aid Society of Boston, New England Freedmen's Union Mission, Presbyterian Committee of Home Missions of New York, the Protestant Episcopal Home Missionary Society, and the Methodist Episcopal Church. Cited in Edgar Wallace Knight, *The Influence of Reconstruction on Education in the South* (New York: Arno Press, 1969), p. 76, originally published in 1913.

39 U.S. Bureau of Refugees, Freedmen, and Abandoned Lands, "Report of the Commissioner" (November 1866), in *Report of the Secretary of War, 1866*, House of Representatives, Executive Document Number 1, 39th Congress, 2nd Session (Washington: GPO, 1866), p. 716.

40 The data are from U.S. Bureau of Refugees, Freedmen, and Abandoned Lands, "Report of the Commissioner" (October 20, 1869), in *Report of the Secretary of War, 1869*, House of Representatives, Executive Document Number 1 (Part 2, Volume 1), 41st Congress, 2nd Session (Washington: GPO, 1869), pp. 516–517.

41 Oliver Otis Howard, Commissioner, U.S. Bureau of Refugees, Freedmen, and Abandoned Lands, "Report of the Commissioner" (December 19, 1865), *Message from the President . . . Transmitting Report . . .*, House of Representatives, Executive Document Number 11, 39th Congress, 1st Session (Washington: GPO, 1866), p. 13.

42 For reports of such violence in each of the Five Cotton States, see U.S. Bureau of Refugees, Freedmen, and Abandoned Lands, "Report of Major General O. O. Howard, Commissioner" (October 14, 1868), in *Report of the Secretary of War, 1868*, House of Representatives, Executive Document Number 1 (Part 1), 40th Congress, 3rd Session (Washington: GPO, 1869), pp. 1040–1052. There is also testimony covering this period given by witnesses during the Ku-Klux conspiracy hearings (U.S. Congress, *Ku-Klux Conspiracy*).

43 Testimony of John A. Minnis, in U.S. Congress, *Ku-Klux Conspiracy*, Part 8, p. 552.

44 U.S. Bureau of Refugees, Freedmen, and Abandoned Lands, "Report . . . 1868," p. 1047.

45 In 1869 the bureau reported 924 schools and 52,051 students enrolled in the Five Cotton States (U.S. Bureau of Refugees, Freedmen, and Abandoned Lands, "Report . . . 1869," p. 518). The 1870 Census reported 747,273 black children aged five to seventeen (U.S. Census Office. Ninth Census [1870], *The Statistics of the Population of the United States* [Washington: GPO, 1872], p. 618). The maximum level of school operation by the bureau was reached in 1869. By the end of that year, the states had begun to take over part of the burden of education; see (U.S. Bureau of Refugees, Freedmen, and Abandoned Lands, "Report of the Commissioner" (October 20, 1870), in *Report of the Secretary of War, 1870*, House of Representatives, Executive Document Number 1 (Part 2, Volume 1), 41st Congress, 3rd Session (Washington: GPO, 1870), pp. 322–323.

46 Oliver O. Howard, Commissioner, U.S. Bureau of Refugees, Freedmen, and Abandoned Lands, "Report of the Commissioner" (October 20, 1871), in *Report of the Secretary of War, 1871*, House of Representatives, Executive Document Number 1 (Part 2, Volume 1), 42nd Congress, 2nd Session (Washington: GPO, 1871), p. 451.

47 The major exception appears to be the city of New Orleans, where integration was actually accomplished for a period of six or seven years. See Louis R. Harlan, "Desegregation in

New Orleans Public Schools During Reconstruction," *American Historical Review* 67 (April 1962).

48 This issue was the subject of inquiry by the congressional committee investigating the Ku Klux conspiracy in 1871. See U.S. Congress, *Ku-Klux Conspiracy,* Part 11, pp. 284–285, 304–305, 352–353, 367–370.

49 Testimony of Cornelius McBride, in U.S. Congress, *Ku-Klux Conspiracy,* Part 11, pp. 336–337.

50 Testimony of Joseph H. Speed, in U.S. Congress, *Ku-Klux Conspiracy,* Part 8, p. 426.

51 Testimony by witnesses before the joint congressional committee investigating the Ku Klux conspiracy provides documented instances of outrages by the Klan against schoolteachers in every southern state visited by the committee (U.S. Congress, *Ku-Klux Conspiracy*).

52 Testimony of William T. Blackford, in U.S. Congress, *Ku-Klux Conspiracy,* Part 9, p. 1288.

53 Knight, *Education in the South,* p. 47. Data on North Carolina expenditures and school enrollment by race are given for "teachers" and for "schoolhouses" between 1871 and 1875. White expenditures per student averaged $2.05 for teachers and 19 cents for schoolhouses; black expenditures per student averaged $1.54 for teachers and 17 cents for schoolhouses. While these estimates are probably only approximate, they do suggest the magnitude of the differential in expenditures on white and black pupils.

54 Testimony of Cornelius McBride, in U.S. Congress, *Ku-Klux Conspiracy,* Part 11, pp. 338–342. First-class teachers were, according to McBride, paid $100 per month; and third-class teachers $40 per month (p. 334).

55 George P. Rawick, ed., *The American Slave: A Composite Autobiography,* 19 vols. (Westport: Greenwood Publishing Co., 1972), 4, p. 113. This nineteen-volume collection reproduces the ex-slaves' narratives collected by the Federal Writers Project of the Works Progress Administration in the 1930s.

56 Testimony of James Atkins, in U.S. Congress, *Ku-Klux Conspiracy,* Part 6, p. 524.

57 Our findings confirm those of Kolchin, *First Freedom* (p. 147, note 20). He found that in Beat Number 1 of Lowndes County, Alabama, and in Township 3, Range 2 West of Madison County, Alabama, 1.1 percent of the "working Negroes over eighteen years old" were artisans. Kolchin defined "artisan" to include all "skilled workers and members of certain service occupations, such as barbers."

58 Our procedure for estimating the urban black population is discussed in Chapter 4 (see Table 4.1).

59 This proportion is obtained by projecting both our rural and urban samples to the black population of the Five Cotton States.

60 David Golightly Harris, manuscript diary, entry for December 23, 1867, quoted by Williamson, *After Slavery,* p. 162.

61 W. E. Burghardt Du Bois, *The Negro Artisan: A Social Study* (Atlanta: Atlanta University Press, 1902), pp. 20–21.

62 Du Bois, *The Negro Artisan,* p. 15.

63 Du Bois, *The Negro Artisan,* p. 22. Emphasis in the original.

64 Williamson, *After Slavery,* p. 161.

65 Edward McPherson, *The Political History of the United States of America During the Period of Reconstruction (from April 15, 1865, to July 15, 1870) . . .,* 3rd ed. (Washington: James J. Chapman, 1880), p. 36.

66 James G. Blaine, *Twenty Years of Congress: From Lincoln to Garfield,* 2 vols. (Norwich: Henry Bill, 1886), 2, p. 100.

67 See Du Bois, *Negro Artisan,* and Lorenzo J. Greene and Carter G. Woodson, *The Negro Wage Earner* (Washington: Association for the Study of Negro Life and History, 1930), Chapters 9 and 10, for a description of the devices – both legal and illegal – used late in the nineteenth century to exclude blacks from various skilled occupations.

68 Exceptions are female nurses and midwives, male schoolteachers, foremen, and watchmen. All of these occupations were nevertheless dominated by whites.

Chapter 3 The myth of the prostrate South

1 Among the traditional historians who have emphasized the damage from the war are
   Walter L. Fleming, *The Sequel of Appomattox* (New Haven: Yale University Press, 1919),
   p. 87; James L. Sellers, "The Economic Incidence of the Civil War in the South," *Mississippi Valley Historical Review* 14 (September 1927); Fred A. Shannon, *The Farmer's Last
   Frontier* (New York: Holt, Rinehart & Winston, 1945), pp. 78–79; E. Merton Coulter, *The
   South During Reconstruction, 1865–1877* (Baton Rouge: Louisiana State University Press,
   1947), Chapter 1; and Paul W. Gates, *Agriculture and the Civil War* (New York: Alfred A.
   Knopf, 1965), pp. 108, 371–373. Though not rejecting the earlier view, some recent works
   have treated the subject more cautiously. For example, see James G. Randall and David
   Donald, *The Civil War and Reconstruction* (Boston: D. C. Heath & Co., 1961), and
   Hodding Carter, *The Angry Scar: The Story of Reconstruction, 1865–1877* (New York:
   Doubleday & Sons, 1959), pp. 35–44. The most detailed study by an economist is probably
   Eugene M. Lerner, "Southern Output and Agricultural Income, 1860–1880," *Agricultural
   History* 33 (July 1959). The extensive debate on the economic impact of the Civil War
   initiated by Charles Austin Beard and Mary R. Beard (*The Rise of American Civilization*
   [New York: Macmillan Co., 1927], Chapter 18) and carried forward by Louis Hacker (*The
   Triumph of American Capitalism* [New York: Columbia University Press, 1940], Chapter
   24) deals almost exclusively with the war's effect on the industrial North. A collection of
   the most important essays in this debate is reprinted in Ralph Andreano, ed., *The Economic Impact of the Civil War* (Cambridge: Schenkman, 1964).

2 Sellers, "Economic Incidence," p. 191. It appears that most economic historians would
   accept Sellers's argument that the effects of the war were long standing. Richard Easterlin
   mentions the impact of the war as a possible cause of the decline in commodity income of
   the South ("Interregional Differences in Per Capita Income, Population, and Total Income,
   1840–1950," in National Bureau of Economic Research, *Trends in the American Economy
   in the Nineteenth Century* [Princeton: Princeton University Press, 1960], p. 85). Robert
   Gallman, in a summary of the patterns in American growth, has argued that "the heavy
   and enduring impact of the war on the South was an important factor in the widening of
   regional income differences after 1860." (Lance E. Davis et al., *American Economic
   Growth: An Economist's History of the United States* [New York: Harper & Row, 1972],
   p. 57.). A recent economic history text written "from an economist's perspective" suggests
   that the damage to the South from the war was quite severe and the consequences on
   economic growth very pronounced (Albert W. Niemi, Jr., *U.S. Economic History: A
   Survey of the Major Issues* [Chicago: Rand McNally, 1975], pp. 166–170). Also see
   Robert Higgs, *The Transformation of the American Economy, 1865–1914: An Essay in
   Interpretation* (New York: John Wiley & Sons, 1971), p. 114.

3 John Stuart Mill, *Principles of Political Economy*, 2 vols. (Boston: Charles C. Little &
   James Brown, 1848), 1, Chapter 5, Section 7.

4 Donald F. Gordon and Gary M. Walton offer a discussion of the West German experience
   and a hypothesis that suggests that the rapid growth following wartime destruction should
   be regarded as typical ("A New Theory of Regenerative Growth and the Post-World War
   II Experience of West Germany" [Unpublished paper, Indiana University and the University of Rochester, November 1973]).

5 Sidney Andrews, *The South Since the War as Shown by Fourteen Weeks of Travel and
   Observation in Georgia and the Carolinas* (Boston: Houghton Mifflin Co., 1970), p. 30,
   originally published in 1866.

6 Whitelaw Reid, *After the War: A Tour of the Southern States, 1865–1866* (New York:
   Harper & Row, 1965), p. 324, originally published in 1866. Sidney Andrews and John
   Dennett, as well as Reid, made frequent references to the conditions of railroads during
   their trips in 1865 and early 1866. See Andrews, *The South Since the War*, pp. 30, 108–109,
   201, 230–231, 288–289, and 365; and John R. Dennett, *The South As It Is: 1865–1866*
   (New York: Viking Press, 1967), pp. 34–37, 231, 266, originally published as a series of
   articles in *The Nation*, 1865–1866. Also see Reid, *After the War*, pp. 324–325, 328, 330–

331, 355–356, 401–402, 425. James De Bow, who traveled extensively by rail in 1866, was impressed with the recovery of southern railroads (*De Bow's Review* [February 1866], pp. 217–219).

7 *De Bow's Review* 3 (February 1867), p. 216.

8 John F. Stover, *The Railroads of the South: 1865–1900* (Chapel Hill: University of North Carolina Press, 1955), p. 58.

9 As we note below, there is considerable reason to believe that the Ninth Census under-enumerated statistics of population and agriculture in the South for 1869–1870. To our knowledge, no one has investigated the extent to which the 1870 Manufacturing Census in the South embodied similar deficiencies. A casual perusal of the manuscripts indicates to us that the southern manufacturing returns contain many irregularities.

10 There was no major shift in the composition of southern manufacturing between 1859 and 1869. In both years, the major industries were lumber products, flour and grist milling, cotton goods, machinery, and boots and shoes. Together, these five industries accounted for 51.0 percent of the total value added in manufacturing in the Five Cotton States in 1859 and 46.8 percent in 1869. See the sources listed for Table 3.1.

11 Richard A. Easterlin's estimates of output, capital investment, and value added in manu-facturing by state, which were used to prepare Table 3.2, extend back only to 1869. Other than the figures we have presented in Table 3.1, there are no consistent estimates of manufacturing activity for the South that span the antebellum and postbellum years. Therefore, the 1869 figures presented in Tables 3.1 and 3.2 are not exactly comparable. Our estimates in Table 3.1, based on the census reports, follow the guidelines indicated by Easterlin and by Robert Gallman ("Commodity Output, 1839–1899," in National Bureau of Economic Research, *Trends in the American Economy in the Nineteenth Century* [Prin-ceton: Princeton University Press, 1960]) regarding the definition of manufacturing activ-ity. Some minor discrepancies, however, remain.

12 Ideally, one would like estimates of the level of manufacturing activity in real terms. However, no satisfactory regional price indexes for manufacturing output have been devel-oped and the use of national indexes, weighted by national composition of manufacturing output, would greatly distort the southern series. Since we know that the entire postwar period was generally one of declining prices, the data presented understate the rate of manufacturing expansion in the Five Cotton States.

13 The manufacturing employment was estimated by Richard Easterlin ("Estimates of Manu-facturing Activity," in Simon Kuznets and Dorothy Swaine Thomas, eds., *Population Redistribution and Economic Growth, United States, 1870–1950,* Volume 1 [Philadelphia: American Philosophical Society, 1957], p. 684); total employment was estimated by Ann R. Miller and Carol P. Brainerd, "Labor Force Estimates," in Kuznets and Thomas, *Population Redistribution and Economic Growth,* Volume 1, pp. 609–621.

14 This withdrawal of labor was an inevitable result of any emancipation scheme. That such a withdrawal of labor on the part of freed slaves is not unusual following emancipation is suggested by the experiences of other slave economies where slavery was peacefully abol-ished. In her review of slavery throughout the world, Willemina Kloosterboer found that a "shortage" of labor followed emancipation in the British West Indies, Mauritius, and the Portuguese colonies (*Involuntary Labour Since the Abolition of Slavery* [Leiden: E. J. Brill, 1960], pp. 191–194). Also see Alan H. Adamson's excellent discussion of emancipation in British Guiana (*Sugar Without Slaves: The Political Economy of British Guiana, 1838–1904* [New Haven: Yale University Press, 1972]).

15 The white population engaged in agriculture worked primarily on small family farms growing food for their own consumption both before and after the war. This class of white farmers produced only a limited fraction of the total cotton output of the South. Apparently the per capita output of these white family farms was not significantly affected by either the war or emancipation. While this group sustained the heaviest casualties in the fighting, it seemed able to carry out agriculture on much the same pattern after as before the war.

16 Frederick Law Olmsted, *The Cotton Kingdom,* edited by Arthur M. Schlesinger (New York: Alfred A. Knopf, 1953), p. 19, first published in 1861.

17 Olmsted, *Cotton Kingdom*, p. 87.

18 F. W. Loring and C. F. Atkinson, *Cotton Culture and the South Considered with Reference to Emigration* (Boston: A. Williams & Co., 1869), p. 123. Emphasis in the original.

19 Theodore C. Peters, "Report of an Agricultural Survey of the South," letter to Isaac Newton, U.S. Commissioner of Agriculture, dated June 1, 1867, printed in U.S. Department of Agriculture, *Monthly Report* (May/June 1867), pp. 192–203.

20 Loring and Atkinson, *Cotton Culture*, p. 21.

21 *Rural Carolinian* 1 (May 1870), p. 510.

22 A possible response to the labor shortage might have been a shift away from the cultivation of labor-intensive crops such as cotton and into less demanding crops such as small grains and grasses. However, the spectacularly high price for cotton at this time, and possibly the inexperience of southern farmers with these alternative crops, dictated against such a shift.

23 If the factor ratios were not fixed, so that work stock or other forms of capital could have been substituted for the scarce black labor, then the effect of the labor shortage might have been partially offset by changing the factor ratios. This might have been precluded if during the course of the Civil War the stock of capital had been reduced sufficiently that such substitution was not possible. In this case, and only in this case, could the destruction produced by the Civil War be said to have been a contributing factor in retarding economic recovery. On the other hand, if short-term flexibility had existed in production arrangements, the same regenerative mechanism that rebuilt manufacturing capital should have operated to quickly restore agricultural capital. See Table 1.4 for the estimated decline in per capita output between 1859 and 1878–1880.

24 The argument of the text can be formalized using the following notation. Let output, Q, be regarded as a function of labor, L; land, T; work stock, W; and other agricultural capital, K:

$$Q = F(L, T, W, K)$$

Assuming this production function is homogeneous with respect to labor, and dividing both sides of the equation by the population, P, we can write:

$$(Q/P) = (L/P) F' (T/L, W/L, K/L)$$

If we can establish that none of the factor ratios (T/L, W/L, or K/L) fell, and assuming no shift in the production function, a decline in the labor supply per capita, L/P, could help explain the decline in per capita output, Q/P. Moreover, if it can be established that the factor ratios do not increase, as would be the case with a fixed-coefficient technology, the decline in per capita labor supply could explain the entire fall in per capita crop output.

25 Gordon and Walton ("Theory of Regenerative Growth") elaborate this mechanism in some detail and point out that the rate of return on capital would be further enhanced when labor and capital are not readily substitutable in the short run.

26 If the factor-labor ratios actually rose, and if the production technology remained unconstrained by emancipation, the relative increase in the nonlabor factors of production should have increased or at least held constant output per man-hour. In this regard, the estimates of productivity per man-hour in Appendix A, imply that a small increase in productivity may have actually occurred. We note there, however, that such estimates are of necessity rather imprecise.

27 The only notable exception was those areas along the Mississippi River where levees had broken during the war, flooding land that had previously been cultivated (*De Bow's Review* 1 [April 1866], p. 434). The number of acres involved did not account for a significant fraction of the prewar cotton production.

28 Loring and Atkinson, *Cotton Culture*, pp. 10, 12, 84–85.

29 Data for 1860 and 1870 are summarized in U.S. Census Office, Tenth Census [1880], *Report on the Production of Agriculture* (Washington: GPO, 1883), pp. 11, 16.

30 During the decade before the Civil War wholesale cotton prices in New York varied from a low of 8.5 cents per pound to a high of 15.75 cents and averaged just over 11 cents. In 1866 the average New York price of cotton was 43.2 cents; in 1867 it was 31.6 cents; and in 1868 a typical pound of cotton traded hands at 24.9 cents. It was not until 1876, ten years after

the Civil War, that the average price fell below 15 cents per pound (James L. Watkins, "Production and Price of Cotton for One Hundred Years," *USDA Miscellaneous Bulletin*, Number 9 [Washington: GPO, 1895], pp. 10–12). Even after these prices are discounted to correct for the inflated postwar currency prices, the wholesale prices of cotton during this period can be said to have been spectacularly high. Deflated to their "gold" values, the 1866 price becomes 30.7 cents per pound; the 1867 price becomes 22.9 cents; and the 1868 price falls to 17.8 cents. We have converted the currency prices reported in Watkins ("Production and Price of Cotton") to gold prices using the annual average gold value of the dollar as reported in Ainsworth R. Spofford, ed., *American Almanac and Treasury of Facts . . . 1889* (New York: American News Co., 1889), p. 341. The gold premium during the greenback period lasted until December 1878.

31 There remains the fact that some fraction of the land planted had to be restored, since many acres had stood uncultivated for several years. The resulting overgrowth and soil erosion posed a greater problem in preparing the land for planting than would have been the case in a normal year. However, our estimate sets the loss of value attributable to wartime neglect at no more than 4 to 7 percent (Roger Ransom and Richard Sutch, "The Impact of the Civil War and of Emancipation on Southern Agriculture," *Explorations in Economic History* 12 [January 1975], p. 17). Moreover, the lower rate of land utilization accompanying the postwar labor shortage would mean that there would be no need to reclaim some of the overgrown land.

32 The officers were asked to discriminate between "the rich, who are usually hostile, and the poor or industrious, usually neutral or friendly" (William Tecumseh Sherman, "Special Field Order No. 120 . . . Kingston, Georgia, November 9, 1864," in U.S. Congress, House of Representatives, Miscellaneous Document Number 233, Part 3, 52nd Congress, 1st Session [Washington: GPO, 1892], p. 713).

33 Data for 1860 and 1870 are summarized in U.S. Census Office, Tenth Census [1880], *Agriculture*, pp. 12, 16–17.

34 Prewar mule prices are reported in Lewis Cecil Gray, *History of Agriculture in the Southern United States to 1860*, 2 vols. (Washington: Carnegie Institution, 1933), 1, p. 542; James L. Watkins, "The Cost of Cotton Production," *USDA Miscellaneous Bulletin*, Number 16 (Washington: GPO, 1899), p. 46; U.S. Patent Office, *Report of the Commissioner of Patents for the Year 1853: Agriculture* (Washington: Nicholson, 1854), pp. 28–34; idem, *Report . . . 1854: Agriculture*, pp. 22–25; and idem, *Report . . . 1855: Agriculture*, pp. 38–40. Also see *The American Farmer*, Fourth Series 14 (1858), p. 196; and idem, Fourth Series 15 (1859), p. 251, which report sales in the breeding states of mules that were undoubtedly destined for the southern market and that had probably not been broken to the draft (Robert B. Lamb, *The Mule in Southern Agriculture* [Berkeley: University of California Press, 1963], Chapters 2, 3; and Ulrich Bonnell Phillips, *Life and Labor in the Old South* [Boston: Little, Brown & Co., 1963], p. 134, originally published in 1929). When well trained, a mule would have apparently sold for $15 to $20 more than when unbroken (U.S. Patent Office, *Report . . . 1853: Agriculture*, p. 23).

35 Postwar mule prices are reported in U.S. Department of Agriculture, Bureau of Agricultural Economics, *Livestock on Farms, January 1, 1867–1919* (Washington: USDA, January 1937), pp. 94, 96, 104, 106, 110. The prices given in this source have been deflated to gold values from the currency values originally obtained through surveys of the department's crop correspondents. The 1868 Mississippi price was $72 in currency, and the South Carolina price was originally reported as $85 (U.S. Department of Agriculture, *Report of the Commissioner of Agriculture for the Year 1867* [Washington: GPO, 1867], p. 92). The year 1870 stands as the postwar price peak, whether currency or gold prices are consulted.

36 Mule prices are reported in Table 3.4; cotton prices in December 1858 are taken from Gray, *History of Southern Agriculture*, 2, p. 1027. The price reported by Gray was reduced by 0.75 cent per pound for transportation, brokerage fees, insurance, etc., on the authority of Alfred Conrad and John Meyer, "The Economics of Slavery in the Ante Bellum South," *Journal of Political Economy* 66 (April 1958), p. 105. Cotton prices in December 1870 are

taken from U.S. Bureau of the Census, *Historical Statistics of the United States, Colonial Times to 1957* (Washington: GPO, 1960), Series K303, p. 302. This source reports the farmgate price in gold.

37 Loring and Atkinson, *Cotton Culture*, p. 54.

38 Again, Sherman's march through Georgia would be the most extreme case of military destruction. Except where some "local hostility" was encountered, the army was expected to limit its confiscation to food and animals. In his orders Sherman was quite explicit regarding the destruction of property: "To army corps commanders alone is intrusted the power to destroy mills, houses, cotton-gins, &c." (Sherman, "Special Field Order No. 120," p. 713). Nevertheless, some Confederate observers insisted that the destruction of property was widespread. See, for example, the colorful descriptions provided by Coulter, *South During Reconstruction*, pp. 2–3.

39 Gray, *History of Agriculture*, 1, p. 542.

40 See Appendix A, Table A.2.

41 D. Wyatt Aiken, "Does Farming Pay in the South?" *Rural Carolinian* 2 (March 1871), pp. 323–324.

42 U.S. Department of Agriculture, *Report of the Commissioner . . . 1867*, pp. 102–119. Prices in South Carolina and Alabama fell 60 percent and in Mississippi, according to the *Report*, the decline was about 65 percent (p. 119). The loyal states, over the same period, without exception, saw farms increase in value. The figure for Georgia is confirmed by the Georgia State Comptroller General, who presented data based on property tax returns, implying an average decline of 42 percent in the value of an acre of land between 1860 and 1867. The figures include "wild" lands as well as "improved" acreage. Georgia, Office of the Comptroller General *Annual Report of the Comptroller . . . October 16, 1866* (Macon: J. W. Burke & Co., 1866), Table A, p. 7; idem, *Report . . . August 11, 1868, to January 1, 1869* (Atlanta: Samuel Bard, 1869), Table C, n.p.

43 U.S. Department of Agriculture, *Report of the Commissioner . . . 1867*, p. 105.

44 The survey by Loring and Atkinson makes numerous references to the price of land following the war *(Cotton Culture*, pp. 101–126). The highest price mentioned was from Crawford County, Georgia, where "at private sale land will bring from $5 to $10 per acre. Choice places $12, or perhaps $15, though that would be an exception" (p. 112).

45 Georgia, Office of the Comptroller General, *Report of the Comptroller . . . for the Year Ending September 30, 1884* (Atlanta: Jos. P. Harrington & Co., 1884), pp. 128–132.

46 Gates, *Agriculture and the Civil War*, p. 379.

47 Gray, *History of Agriculture*, 1, p. 542.

48 In Appendix A we estimated the average price of a slave at $865 in 1859 and the average value of capital per slave on slave farms at $610.48 (Table A.3).

49 This estimate was made using the same procedure employed to estimate the 1859 price of slaves reported in Appendix A, note 28. In this case, however, we have used a more conservative benchmark price of $1,500, and we have not adjusted the estimate upward to account for slaves with special skills. The slaves from South Carolina and Georgia were evaluated using the Fogel-Engerman data for the "Old South"; those from Mississippi, Alabama, and Louisiana were evaluated using the "Louisiana" series.

50 Lerner's widely cited study is particularly vulnerable to this criticism. He relied heavily upon the 1870 Census to support his conclusion that "wherever war touched the South . . . the aftermath was disorganization, ruin, and suffering" ("Southern Output," p. 117). Some historians who have written on the economic impact of the Civil War have also relied on aggregate census data for evidence that there was considerable destruction; for example, see Gates, *Agriculture and the Civil War*, pp. 372–379.

51 U.S. Census Office, Ninth Census [1870], *The Statistics of the Population of the United States* (Washington: GPO, 1872), p. xviii.

52 Howard's estimate was quoted by a contributor to the *Rural Carolinian* 1 (April 1870), p. 433. Also see the comments made by the editor of *De Bow's Review* 1 (March 1866), p. 304, and by the editor of the *New Orleans Times* as quoted in *De Bow's Review* 1 (April 1866), pp. 433–434.

53 Loring and Atkinson, *Cotton Culture*, p. 8; also see pp. 3, 9, 16, 106.

54 The problem of this undercount is discussed in U.S. Census Office, Tenth Census [1880], *Compendium of the Tenth Census (June 1, 1880)* (Washington: GPO, 1883), pp. liv–lxxvi; and U.S. Census Office, Eleventh Census [1890], *Compendium of the Eleventh Census: 1890*, 3 parts (Washington: GPO, 1892–1897), Part 1, pp. xxxv–xliii. Also see Francis A. Walker, "Statistics of the Colored Race in the United States," in 2 parts, *Publications of the American Statistical Association*, New Series, 2 (September and December 1890). In 1890 the Census Office set the "official" estimate of the undercount of the 1870 Negro population of the United States at 9.5 percent, and of the white population of the United States at 2.2 percent (U.S. Census Office [1890], *Compendium*, pp. xxxv–xliii). As we note elsewhere, the official adjustment of the black population is almost certainly too large (Ransom and Sutch, "Civil War," pp. 8–10). It was made by assuming a constant rate of increase between 1860 and 1880 in the eleven Confederate States plus West Virginia and Kentucky.

55 Ransom and Sutch, "Civil War," Table 1, p. 8. Because of the difficulty of adjusting for interstate migration of the white population and the allocation of the estimated war-related deaths of whites between southern and northern states, we have not attempted to compute similar estimates for the white population. However, there can be no doubt that the official revision of the 1870 Census of the white population was also too high.

56 See Ransom and Sutch, "Civil War," p. 8, for details. The wartime deaths were apparently concentrated among teenagers and young adults. The highest war-related mortality was recorded for blacks who were ten to nineteen years old in 1860.

57 U.S. Census Office, Ninth Census [1870], *The Statistics of the Wealth and Industry of the United States* (Washington: GPO, 1872), p. 72.

58 Our 1870 sample of farms, discussed in Appendix G, revealed the following rates of nonreporting among farms that did report the number of acres: value of the farm, 3 percent; value of the farm implements, 16 percent; value of livestock, 7 percent.

59 Latham, Alexander and Company, *Cotton Movement and Fluctuation: 1903–1908*, 35th ed. (New York: Latham, Alexander & Co., 1908), p. 131; U.S. Census Office [1870], *Wealth and Industry*, p. 76. By contrast with the large indicated undercount for 1870, the Latham-Alexander figures imply that the Census of 1860 underenumerated the crop of 1859 by less than 4 percent, and the 1880 Census undercounted the 1879 crop by only 0.1 percent. The superintendent of the 1880 Census reported that special care was taken that year to enumerate the cotton crop accurately (U.S. Census Office [1880], *Agriculture*, p. 18). Incidentally, the Latham-Alexander estimates were reprinted by the U.S. Department of Agriculture and have been accepted by the department as the primary source for "official" annual cotton statistics. Watkins, "Production and Price of Cotton," pp. 10–12; U.S. Department of Agriculture, Bureau of Statistics, George K. Holmes, "Cotton Crops of the United States, 1790–1911," *USDA Bureau of Statistics Circular*, Number 32 (Washington: GPO, 1912); U.S. Department of Agriculture, Agricultural Marketing Service, "Cotton and Cotton Seed: Acreage, Yield, Production, Disposition, Price, Value, by States, 1866–1952," *USDA Statistical Bulletin*, Number 164 (Washington: GPO, 1955).

60 Reid, *After the War*, p. 363. Emphasis in the original.

61 *De Bow's Review* 1 (June 1866), p. 659.

62 *De Bow's Review* 1 (April 1866), p. 417.

Chapter 4. The demise of the plantation

1 D. H. Jacques, "Future of Southern Farming," *Rural Carolinian* 1 (November 1869), p. 113.

2 David Barrow, "A Georgia Plantation," *Scribner's Monthly* 21 (April 1881), p. 831.

3 On the rewards offered slaves, see Kenneth Stampp, *The Peculiar Institution: Slavery in the Ante-Bellum South* (New York: Alfred A. Knopf, 1956), pp. 164–170. Whitelaw Reid mentions the use of daily rewards in 1865 to revive "drooping energies" (*After the War: A*

Tour of the Southern States, 1865–1866 [New York: Harper & Row, 1965], p. 505, first published in 1866).

4 On the use of corporal punishment, see Carl Schurz, "Report of Carl Schurz on the States of South Carolina, Georgia, Alabama, Mississippi, and Louisiana," Senate, Executive Document Number 2, 39th Congress, 1st Session (Washington: GPO, 1865), pp. 17–20. For descriptions of the role of the "overseer" in the new regime, see D. Wyatt Aiken, "Alabama from an Agricultural Point of View," *Rural Carolinian* 1 (April 1870), p. 406; Reid, *After the War*, pp. 483–490, 495–498; and Barrow, "A Georgia Plantation," p. 831.

5 Whitelaw Reid describes the "negro quarters" on the river plantations in Mississippi, which were probably above average in the South at that time (*After the War*, pp. 482–483, 492–493). David Barrow discusses the use of the old slave cabins in his portrayal of the shift to free labor in Georgia ("A Georgia Plantation," p. 832).

6 Lewis Cecil Gray, *History of Agriculture in the Southern United States to 1860*, 2 vols. (Washington: Carnegie Institution, 1933), 1, p. 563. Commissioner Horace Capron of the U.S. Department of Agriculture gave the same rations for slaves in his 1867 report (Horace Capron, "Southern Agriculture," in U.S. Department of Agriculture, *Report of the Commissioner of Agriculture for the Year 1867* [Washington: GPO, 1868], p. 416). Also see the references in Appendix A, note 16.

7 F. W. Loring and C. F. Atkinson, *Cotton Culture and the South Considered with Reference to Emigration* (Boston: A. Williams & Co., 1869), pp. 26–27.

8 A. H. Arminton's contract with Calvin, January 1, 1866, in the Southern Historical Collection, University of North Carolina Library.

9 Reid, *After the War*, p. 499; U.S. Bureau of Refugees, Freedmen, and Abandoned Lands, *Report by the Commissioner of the Freedmen's Bureau of all Orders Issued by Him or Any Assistant Commissioner (March 1866)*, House of Representatives, Executive Document Number 70, 39th Congress, 1st Session (Washington: GPO, 1866), p. 319.

10 Reid, *After the War*, p. 561.

11 Loring and Atkinson, *Cotton Culture*, pp. 26–27.

12 U.S. Bureau of Refugees, Freedmen, and Abandoned Lands, *Reports of the Assistant Commissioners of Freedmen . . . (January 1867)*, Senate, Executive Document Number 6, 39th Congress, 2nd Session (Washington: GPO, 1867), pp. 50, 84.

13 U.S. Department of Agriculture, *Report . . . 1867*, p. 416; J. R. Dodge, "Report of the Statistician," in U.S. Department of Agriculture, *Report of the Commissioner of Agriculture . . . for the Year 1876* (Washington: GPO, 1877), pp. 130–131.

14 The *Rural Carolinian* advocated the practice of withholding wages, and it seems to have been widely adopted (1 [June 1870], p. 571). Note the inclusion of such a condition in the Mial contract reproduced as Figure 4.1.

15 The collapse of the southern banking system at the end of the war contributed to this problem. The difficulties encountered in reestablishing the banks will be taken up in Chapter 6.

16 See the reports of the Freedmen's Bureau, particularly U.S. Bureau of Refugees, Freedmen, and Abandoned Lands, *Reports of the Assistant Commissioners . . . 1867*, pp. 50, 84; and the comments in *Rural Carolinian* 5 (March 1874), pp. 353–354.

17 U.S. Bureau of Refugees, Freedmen, and Abandoned Lands, *Reports of the Assistant Commissioners . . . 1867*, pp. 4, 43, 98, 104, 118–119, and 161–162. In addition to obviating the need for currency, this arrangement had the advantage of reducing the risk borne by the planter, since the impact of a poor crop or a low price would be shared by the workers. The risk was a matter of some concern to those planters attempting for the first time to work with free laborers (*Southern Cultivator* 23 [1865], p. 180). They did not know how satisfactorily these laborers would work, and their prejudices inherited from the period of slavery made them unduly pessimistic.

18 A. R. Lightfoot, "Condition and Wants of the Cotton Raising States," *De Bow's Review* 6 (February 1869), p. 153.

19 Lightfoot, "Condition and Wants," p. 153. Emphasis in the original.

20 Nevertheless, this system remained sufficiently popular to warrant several references in two surveys of land tenure arrangements conducted in 1876 and 1879. See Dodge, "Report," pp. 131–135; and Eugene W. Hilgard, Special Agent, Tenth Census [1880], *Report on Cotton Production in the United States*, 2 vols. (Washington: GPO, 1884), 1, pp. 185, 356, 819; and 2, pp. 250, 438.

21 Support by the bureau for wage contracts is explicitly noted in U.S. Bureau of Refugees, Freedmen, and Abandoned Lands, *Reports of the Assistant Commissioners . . . 1867* from Alabama (p. 4), Mississippi (pp. 97–98), North Carolina (p. 104), South Carolina (pp. 118–119), and Virginia (pp. 161–162). Sample contracts were supplied to employers by the regional offices of the bureau (ibid., p. 51). An example of such a form contract can be found in Charles E. Seagrave, "The Southern Negro Agricultural Worker: 1850–1870" (Ph.D. thesis, Stanford University, 1971), pp. 36, 103–106.

22 U.S. Bureau of Refugees, Freedmen, and Abandoned Lands, *Reports of the Assistant Commissioners . . . 1867*, p. 98.

23 Reid, *After the War*, Chapter 52, p. 572.

24 John Townsend Trowbridge, *The Desolate South, 1865–1866* (Boston: Little, Brown & Co., 1956), pp. 195, 204. Originally published in 1866 as *The South . . . A Journey Through the Desolated States.*

25 Schurz, "Report," p. 15.

26 John Richard Dennett, *The South As It Is: 1865–1866* (New York: Viking Press, 1967), p. 364, originally published as a series of articles in *The Nation,* 1865–1866. For a discussion of the destructive impact of the slave trade on the black family during the late antebellum period, see Herbert Gutman and Richard Sutch, "The Slave Family: Protected Agent of Capitalist Masters or Victim of the Slave Trade?" in Paul A. David et al., *Reckoning with Slavery: A Critical Study in the Quantitative History of American Negro Slavery* (New York: Oxford University Press, 1976), pp. 94–133.

27 Loring and Atkinson, *Cotton Culture,* p. 6.

28 Reid, *After the War*, p. 389.

29 U.S. Bureau of Refugees, Freedmen, and Abandoned Lands, *Reports of the Assistant Commissioners . . . 1867*, p. 272.

30 The preference of blacks for the larger towns may reflect the almost total lack of employment opportunities for Negroes in small towns. An inspection of the manuscript censuses for 1870 for a sample of small towns revealed only a tiny fraction of blacks engaged in nonagricultural trades (see Chapter 2, Table 2.6, for several illustrations).

31 We know of no evidence that the thirty-nine cities without 1860 population data differed from those cities reporting for both years. If we assume that all cities in each 1870 size class in Table 4.1 had population changes corresponding to those reporting for both years, then the total implied increase in black urban population in towns over 1,000 would be 75,000 (a 50.7 percent increase). This would be 3.7 percent of the 2.02 million rural blacks in 1870.

32 Loring and Atkinson, *Cotton Culture,* p. 3.

33 The rate of increase of the black population was 36 percent for Texas and 46 percent for Florida, well above our estimate of an average increase of 17.6 percent for the black population in the United States between 1860 and 1870. The Census of Nativity that accompanied the 1870 Census is the source for our estimate of migration away from the Cotton South (U.S. Census Office, Ninth Census [1870], *The Statistics of the Population of the United States* [Washington: GPO, 1872], pp. 328–342). See Roger Ransom and Richard Sutch, "The Impact of the Civil War and of Emancipation on Southern Agriculture," *Explorations in Economic History* 12 (January 1975), pp. 9–10. On the migration of slaves, see Richard Sutch, "The Breeding of Slaves for Sale and the Westward Expansion of Slavery, 1850–1860," in Stanley L. Engerman and Eugene D. Genovese, eds., *Race and Slavery in the Western Hemisphere: Quantitative Studies* (Princeton: Princeton University Press, 1975).

34 Dennett, *The South As It Is,* p. 365.

35 On the optimism of planters immediately after the war, see the remarks by Reid (*After the*

War, pp. 414–416), and the comments of the editor in *De Bow's Review* 1 [January 1866], pp. 8–9).

36 The New York average prices are from James L. Watkins, U.S. Department of Agriculture, Division of Statistics, "Production and Price of Cotton for One Hundred Years," *USDA Miscellaneous Bulletin*, Number 9 (Washington: GPO, 1895), p. 11.

37 Capron, "Southern Agriculture," p. 417. Other accounts of the drought of 1866 can be found in D. Wyatt Aiken, "Does Farming Pay in the South?" *Rural Carolinian* 2 (March 1871), p. 323; and U.S. Bureau of Refugees, Freedmen, and Abandoned Lands, *Reports of the Assistant Commissioners . . . 1867*, pp. 52, 97, 118.

38 *Rural Carolinian* 5 (April 1873), pp. 353–354. Emphasis in the original.

39 Capron, "Southern Agriculture," p. 416.

40 There was no general deflation of currency prices or gold that might account for this substantial decline in wages. Indeed, had we expressed the wages in terms of gold dollars, the difference would appear still larger. For the gold values employed by the U.S. Department of Agriculture in deflating their annual wage series between 1866 and 1878, see U.S. Department of Agriculture, Bureau of Statistics, "Wages of Farm Labor," *USDA Bureau of Statistics Bulletin*, Number 99 (Washington: GPO, 1912), p. 25.

41 *Southern Cultivator* 27 (1869), p. 302.

42 See U.S. Bureau of Refugees, Freedmen, and Abandoned Lands, *Reports of the Assistant Commissioners . . . 1867*.

43 See *Rural Carolinian* 2 (May 1871), p. 572; Lightfoot, "Condition and Wants," p. 153; and Schurz, "Report," pp. 21–22.

44 Oliver Otis Howard, Commissioner, U.S. Bureau of Refugees, Freedmen, and Abandoned Lands, "Report of the Commissioner" (November 1866), in *Report of the Secretary of War, 1866*, House of Representatives, Executive Document Number 1, 39th Congress, 2nd Session (Washington: GPO, 1866), p. 706.

45 Edward McPherson, *The Political History of the United States of America During the Period of Reconstruction*, 3rd ed. (Washington: James J. Chapman, 1880), p. 34. McPherson's "history" is really a digest of federal and state legislation in this period that provides a useful and reliable compendium.

46 McPherson, *Political History*, pp. 33–34.

47 McPherson, *Political History*, p. 43.

48 Reid, *After the War*, p. 291.

49 Aiken, "Does Farming Pay?" p. 324.

50 W. H. Evans, "The Labor Question," *Southern Cultivator* 27 (January 1869), p. 54. Emphasis in the original.

51 The data are based on a sample of farms discussed in Appendix G, Section 2. The characterization of a farm as either a "small family farm" or a "plantation" is intentionally designed to reflect two stereotypes that emerge both from historians' treatment and the 1880 Census of Agriculture. The specific definitions are included in the notes to Table 4.3.

52 Twenty-five hands was usually set as the minimum for a small plantation. Calculating that there was roughly one working hand for every two slaves, and assuming that all slaveholdings of fifty or more slaves were held for agricultural purposes in the Five Cotton States, the 7,898 slaveholders who owned fifty or more slaves represented 4.2 percent of the 187,605 farms reported (U.S. Census Office, Eighth Census [1860], *Agriculture of the United States . . .* [Washington: GPO, 1864], p. 234; U.S. Census Office, Tenth Census [1880], *Report on the Production of Agriculture . . .* [Washington: GPO, 1883], p. 11). Note that in Table 4.5 we estimate that the largest 6.9 percent of the farms in 1860 controlled one-third of the total improved acreage in the Five Cotton States. In 1870 the same size class accounted for only 2.1 percent of all farms and 11.1 percent of the total improved acreage.

53 U.S. Bureau of Refugees, Freedmen, and Abandoned Lands, "Report of the Commissioner of the Bureau . . ." (November 1867), in *Report of the Secretary of War, 1867*, House of Representatives, Executive Document Number 1, Part 1, 40th Congress, 2nd Session (Washington: GPO, 1868), p. 681.

54 Capron, "Southern Agriculture," p. 417. Emphasis in the original.

55 Jacques, "Future of Southern Farming," p. 113.

56 Gray, *History of Agriculture,* 1, pp. 478–480.

57 Gavin Wright, "The Economics of Cotton in the Antebellum South" (Ph.D. dissertation, Yale University, 1969), p. 147. Emphasis in the original.

58 Robert W. Fogel and Stanley L. Engerman, *Time on the Cross,* 2 vols. (Boston: Little, Brown & Co., 1974), 1, p. 192.

59 Fogel and Engerman, *Time on the Cross,* 1, p. 193.

60 See Gavin Wright, "Prosperity, Progress, and American Slavery," in Paul A. David et al., *Reckoning with Slavery: A Critical Study in the Quantitative History of American Negro Slavery* (New York: Oxford University Press, 1976), pp. 316–318. A further difficulty with the Fogel-Engerman findings is that they combined all the observations from the Cotton South to reach their conclusions. Wright, on the other hand, made separate studies of each major region, and he found regional differences ("Economics of Cotton"). It is possible, therefore, that the Fogel-Engerman results reflect these regional differences more than they reflect true economies associated with farm size.

61 This definition includes farms reporting as few as 200 acres in crops. For a complete tabulation of the farms in our 1880 sample, see Appendix G, Table G.12. There were other farms with over 200 acres reported in crops, but they were cultivated primarily with family labor.

62 This problem is discussed more fully in Appendix G, Section 2. A third consideration that would complicate a study of economies of scale was pointed out in Chapter 3. It is apparent from our analysis of the labor shortage that the substitutability of other factors of production for labor was limited in the short run. This suggests that the cross-section production function that characterized *postwar* agriculture may not have been of the flexible type usually assumed in the analyses of production efficiencies. While not insurmountable, this characteristic introduces significant problems that are seriously aggravated by the dearth of observations on large-scale agriculture. For a recent attempt to grapple with these problems, see Arden R. Hall, who tentatively concluded that an assumption of no economies of scale was supported by his econometric results ("The Efficiency of Post-Bellum Southern Agriculture [Ph.D. dissertation, University of California, Berkeley, 1975], pp. 136–139).

63 These percentages were calculated from the Parker-Gallman sample of farms in the Cotton South in 1860.

64 The best discussion of the sources of the economies of scale on large plantations can be found in Gray's monumental study of southern antebellum agriculture (*History of Agriculture,* 1, pp. 478–480). Other treatments of the problem by historians include Ulrich Bonnell Phillips, "The Origin and Growth of the Southern Black Belts," *American Historical Review* 11 (July 1906); Robert R. Russel, "The Effects of Slavery upon Nonslaveholders in the Ante-Bellum South," *Agricultural History* 15 (April 1941); and Stampp, *Peculiar Institution,* pp. 30–32, 52–54. Economic studies include those of Wright, "The Economics of Cotton"; idem, "Prosperity, Progress and American Slavery," pp. 317–318; Fogel and Engerman, *Time on the Cross,* 1, pp. 191–196, and 2, pp. 141–149; Keith Aufhauser, "Slavery and Scientific Management," *Journal of Economic History* 33 (December 1973); and Jacob Metzer, "Rational Management, Modern Business Practices, and Economies of Scale in the Ante-Bellum Southern Plantations," *Explorations in Economic History* 12 (April 1975).

65 This is so because these studies evaluated outputs and inputs at prices that did not vary across the sample, a procedure necessitated by the lack of data on the actual prices received and paid by the farms in the sample.

66 Wright, "The Economics of Cotton," pp. 147–148.

67 Fogel and Engerman, *Time on the Cross,* 1, p. 234.

68 Fogel and Engerman, *Time on the Cross,* 1, p. 204.

69 Fogel and Engerman, *Time on the Cross,* 1, p. 237.

70 Phillips, "Origin and Growth," pp. 804–805.

71 Aufhauser, "Slavery and Scientific Management," pp. 815–818.

72 Russel, "Effects of Slavery," p. 115.

73 Jacob Metzer ("Rational Management") seems to have carried this argument further than anyone else.

74 Joseph D. Reid, Jr., "Sharecropping as an Understandable Market Response: The Post-bellum South," *Journal of Economic History* 33 (March 1973).

75 Russel, "Effects of Slavery," p. 115.

76 Such a mistake seems to have given rise to one of the myths associated with the New South rhetoric of the late nineteenth century. The belief that a redistribution of land ownership took place appears to have originated in an article published in 1881 by Henry W. Grady, editor of the *Atlanta Constitution* ("Cotton and Its Kingdom," *Harpers New Monthly Magazine* 63 [October 1881], pp. 721–723). Grady was cited by M. B. Hammond in his influential history of the cotton industry. Hammond buttressed the argument by presenting census statistics similar to those displayed in Table 4.5. See (Mathew B. Hammond, *The Cotton Industry* (New York: Macmillan Co., 1897), pp. 457–458; also see idem, "The Southern Farmer and the Cotton Question," *Political Science Quarterly* 12 (September 1897), pp. 127–130. Hammond in turn became a source cited by subsequent historians. For example, see Philip Alexander Bruce, "Social and Economic Revolution in the Southern States," *Contemporary Review* 78 (July 1900), p. 19; idem, *The Rise of the New South* (Philadelphia: G. Barrie, circa 1905), p. 59; and Emory Q. Hawk, *Economic History of the South* (New York: Prentice-Hall, 1934), p. 429. This interpretation also spread to such general history texts as Charles Austin Beard and Mary R. Beard, *The Rise of American Civilization* (New York: Macmillan Co., 1927), p. 269; and Samuel Eliot Morison and Henry Steele Commager, *The Growth of the American Republic* (New York: Oxford University Press, 1930), p. 627.

77 Roger W. Shugg, "Survival of the Plantation System in Louisiana," *Journal of Southern History* 3 (August 1937); idem, *Origins of Class Struggle in Louisiana: A Social History of White Farmers and Laborers During Slavery and After, 1840–1875* (Baton Rouge: Louisiana State University Press, 1939). The argument that the broadening of landownership accounted for the fall in farm size was earlier challenged by Alfred Holt Stone, "The Negro in the Yazoo-Mississippi Delta," *American Economic Association Publications*, 3rd Series, Volume 3 (1902). Paul Taylor noted that Stone's criticism helped convince the Census Bureau to change its procedure for classifying farms in 1910 (Paul S. Taylor, "Plantation Agriculture in the United States: Seventeenth to Twentieth Centuries," *Land Economics* 27 [August 1951], pp. 141–142). Also see Robert Preston Brooks, "The Agrarian Revolution in Georgia, 1865–1912," *Bulletin of the University of Wisconsin*, History Series, 3 (1914), pp. 41–45.

78 Shugg, *Origins of Class Struggle*, p. 241.

79 Jonathan M. Wiener, "Planter Persistence and Social Change: Alabama, 1850–1870," *Journal of Interdisciplinary History* 7 (autumn 1976), pp. 240; Idem, "Planter–Merchant Conflict in Reconstruction Alabama," *Past and Present* 68 (August 1975). Wiener defines the planter elite as the top 10 percent of all landowners ("Planter Persistence," p. 240).

80 The total value of reported real estate in Dallas County in 1860 was $15.7 million, reported by 1,070 individuals. In 1870 the total value was $6.0 million, reported by 1,109 individuals. The decline in value is attributable to the postwar depression of land prices, noted in Chapter 3, and perhaps the underreporting of real estate values in 1870. At the time of the 1870 Census, the data were questioned on grounds that persons were unwilling to respond to the question and that they tended to underreport real estate owing to fear of increased property taxation. For these reasons, the 1870 data were not published, and the questions were omitted in 1880. See our discussion of these census data in Appendix G, Section 3.

81 Wiener, "Planter Persistence," p. 240.

82 The failure to make this distinction between the plantation as a system of labor organization and the plantation as a large landholding has led to some confusion. Thus, when Shugg, C. Vann Woodward, and others argue for the "persistence of the plantation pat-

tern" into the late nineteenth century, they are referring to landownership patterns and they are not in conflict with our own interpretation that the plantation "system" had disappeared by 1880 (C. Van Woodward, *Origins of the New South, 1877–1913* [Baton Rouge: Louisiana State University Press, 1951], p. 178).

83 Wiener, "Planter Persistence," pp. 255–257.

84 Oliver Otis Howard, Commissioner, U.S. Bureau of Refugees, Freedmen, and Abandoned Lands, "Report of the Commissioner" (October 20, 1869), in *Report of the Secretary of War, 1869*, House of Representatives, Executive Document Number 1, 41st Congress, 2nd Session, Volume 1, Part 2 (Washington: GPO, 1869), p. 10.

Chapter 5. Agricultural reconstruction

1 Edwin D. Hoffman, "From Slavery to Self-Reliance," *Journal of Negro History* 41 (January 1956), p. 20.

2 Whitelaw Reid, *After the War: A Tour of the Southern States, 1865–1866* (New York: Harper & Row, 1965), p. 564, first published in 1866.

3 *De Bow's Review* 1 (May 1866), p. 543; idem, 2 (December 1866), pp. 667–668.

4 John Richard Dennett, *The South As It Is: 1865–1866* (New York: Viking Press, 1967), p. 265, originally published as a series of articles in *The Nation*, 1865–1866. Also see our discussion of postwar land prices in Chapter 3.

5 See Chapter 3 for citations on land, mule, and implement prices.

6 These islands had been occupied by Federal forces early in the war. After the exodus of the white population, the army had to deal with a large influx of black "refugees" from the mainland. The solution was to grant each family 20 to 40 acres and a mule. These land grants were confirmed by order of General Sherman in January 1865 in his famous "Special Field Order Number 15," which was issued with the knowledge of the secretary of war, Edwin Stanton. Eventually, 480,000 acres of land on these islands were distributed to about 40,000 blacks. For the history of the Sea Islands episode, see Willie Lee Rose, *Rehearsal for Reconstruction: The Port Royal Experiment* (New York: Alfred A. Knopf, 1964); W. L. Fleming, "Forty Acres and a Mule," *North American Review* 183 (May 1906); and Hoffman, "Slavery to Self-Reliance." For a discussion of the Sea Islands off Georgia, see Manuel Gottlieb, "The Land Question in Georgia During Reconstruction," *Science and Society* 3 (summer 1939), pp. 364–369.

7 Stevens's plan involved the confiscation of land belonging to some 70,000 Confederate officials amounting to about 394 million acres. On the issue of land confiscation, see Kenneth M. Stampp, *The Era of Reconstruction 1865–1877* (New York: Alfred A. Knopf, 1966), pp. 122–130.

8 Speech of C. P. Leslie, cited by Walter L. Fleming, ed., *Documentary History of Reconstruction*, 2 vols. (Gloucester: Peter Smith, 1960), 1, pp. 451–452, originally published in 1906. The comment was made in regard to the possibility that the state government would provide homesteads for freed slaves. For discussion of the South Carolina situation, where the persistence of Negro beliefs that land would be redistributed was particularly strong, see Joel Williamson, *After Slavery: The Negro in South Carolina During Reconstruction, 1861–1877* (Chapel Hill: University of North Carolina Press, 1965), pp. 80–90. Fleming argues that the debates in Congress over the Reconstruction Acts of 1867 and 1868 served to rekindle these hopes for land throughout the southern states ("Forty Acres," pp. 732–734).

9 W. E. B. Du Bois, "The Negro Landholder in Georgia," *Bulletin of the Department of Labor* 6 (July 1901).

10 Incidentally, the comptroller's figures will exaggerate the number of acres under cultivation by Negroes, since they include land not under cultivation and land owned by blacks and cultivated by someone else.

11 The 1876 property tax in Georgia was based on the full market value of all assets held within the state.

12 The original manuscript *Tax Digests* are stored in the Georgia State Archives in Atlanta.

We chose Coweta County as typical of the Piedmont region of Georgia. The year 1878 is the earliest possible date for which such a tabulation proved feasible.

13 *Southern Cultivator* 27 (1869), p. 373.

14 Reid, *After the War*, pp. 564–565.

15 Edward McPherson, *The Political History of the United States of America During the Period of Reconstruction*, 3rd ed. (Washington: James J. Chapman, 1880), p. 31.

16 Testimony of Cornelius McBride, schoolteacher, Chickasaw County, Mississippi, in U.S. Congress, *The Ku-Klux Conspiracy: Report of the Joint Select Committee*, House of Representatives, Report Number 22 (4 volumes, 13 parts), 42nd Congress, 2nd Session (Washington: GPO, 1872), Part 11, p. 335.

17 There is some evidence that pressures against black landownership were less severe in the larger cities. Most southern towns contained a "black quarter" in which Negroes owned property. The data of Table 5.3 suggest that in rural areas of Georgia the proportion of black-owned wealth invested in real estate in towns exceeded the fraction of white-owned wealth so invested.

18 See Table 4.3 and the discussion in Chapter 4.

19 See Frank L. Owsley, *The Plain Folk of the Old South* (Baton Rouge: Louisiana State University Press, 1949), Chapter 5; Frank L. Owsley and Harriet C. Owsley, "The Economic Basis of Society in the Late Ante-Bellum South," *Journal of Southern History* 6 (February 1940); Herbert Weaver, *Mississippi Farmers, 1850–1860* (Nashville: Vanderbilt University Press, 1945), pp. 63–67; H. L. Coles, Jr., "Some Notes on Slave Ownership and Land Ownership in Louisiana, 1850–1860," *Journal of Southern History* 9 (August 1943); and Blanche Henry Clark, *The Tennessee Yeomen, 1840–1860* (Nashville: Vanderbilt University Press, 1942), p. 28. Owsley's technique of estimating the extent of tenancy provides an upper bound, since it would include farms operated by relatives of the owner, hired managers, and also those operated by owners who, for one reason or another, declined to answer the question on real estate ownership.

20 Marjorie Stratford Mendenhall argues, rather unconvincingly, that the leasing of plantations before the war served as a model for postwar tenancy ("The Rise of Southern Tenancy," *Yale Review* 27 [autumn 1937], pp. 111–113).

21 Lewis Cecil Gray, *History of Agriculture in the Southern United States to 1860*, 2 vols. (Washington: Carnegie Institution, 1933), 1, pp. 406–408; and 2, pp. 646–667. Joseph Reid recently observed that a number of antebellum share tenancy contracts have been preserved which are similar in some respects to those characteristic of the postwar period. However, he was unable to demonstrate that such arrangements were at all common (all his examples are drawn from Haywood County, North Carolina, which grew no cotton and little tobacco). It would be difficult to prove that they inspired postwar emulation. See Joseph D. Reid, Jr., "Antebellum Southern Rental Contracts," *Explorations in Economic History* 13 (January 1976).

22 The Embree contract, dated January 26, 1866, is among the Joseph Embree papers, Louisiana State University, Department of Archives, Baton Rouge. We are grateful to Stanley Engerman for bringing this document to our attention.

23 The London company is discussed in *Rural Carolinian* 1 (March 1870), p. 384. Joseph Reid discovered in the Henry Watson, Jr., papers at Duke University Library the 1866 draft of an act intended to be submitted to the state legislature of Alabama that would have incorporated the Alabama Cotton Planters Association to engage in cotton cultivation. It is not known whether the act was introduced, but apparently the company was never chartered. We are grateful to Reid for bringing this document to our attention.

24 Thomas J. Edwards, "The Tenant System and Some Changes Since Emancipation," *Annals of the American Academy of Political Science* 49 (September 1913), p. 39.

25 See the discussion in Chapter 4 on the rapid introduction of sharecropping in 1867 and 1868.

26 U.S. Department of Agriculture, *Report of the Commissioner of Agriculture for the Year 1867* (Washington: GPO, 1867), p. 417.

27 Reid, *After the War*, p. 572.

28 U.S. Bureau of Refugees, Freedmen, and Abandoned Lands, *Reports of the Assistant Commissioners of Freedmen . . . (December 1867)*, Senate, Executive Document Number 6, 39th Congress, 2nd Session (Washington: GPO, 1867), p. 316.

29 George P. Rawick, ed., *The American Slave: A Composite Autobiography*, 19 vols. (Westport: Greenwood Publishing Co., 1972), 13, Georgia, Part 3, p. 204.

30 See F. W. Loring and C. F. Atkinson, *Cotton Culture and the South Considered with Reference to Emigration* (Boston: A. Williams & Co., 1869), pp. 25–26; J. R. Dodge, "Report of the Statistician," in U.S. Department of Agriculture, *Report of the Commissioner of Agriculture . . . for the Year 1876* (Washington: GPO, 1877), pp. 131–135; and Eugene W. Hilgard, Special Agent, Tenth Census [1880], *Report on Cotton Production in the United States*, 2 vols. (Washington: GPO, 1884), 1, pp. 185, 356, 476, 526, 641, 819; and 2, pp. 165, 250, 438, 516–522, 609, 643. Discussions of contracting terms can also be found in Robert Somers, *The Southern States Since the War, 1870–1* (New York: Macmillan & Co., 1871), pp. 128, 146–147; Enoch Marvin Banks, "The Economics of Land Tenure in Georgia," *Studies in History, Economics, and Public Law* 23 (1905); Edwards, "Tenant System"; and Joseph D. Reid, Jr., "Sharecropping as an Understandable Market Response: The Post-bellum South," *Journal of Economic History* 33 (March 1973). Exceptions to the fifty-fifty split can, of course, be found. The USDA survey noted that five counties reported deviations from the standard: De Kalb and Shelby in Alabama; Thomas, Harris, and Dooly in Georgia. In all but one of these reported deviations (De Kalb) the laborer received something less than one-half (Dodge, "Report," pp. 132–135). The census survey turned up only two reports of sharecropping with other than a fifty-fifty split, both in South Carolina. In the lower pine belt region of South Carolina "very few farms are worked on shares; when it is done, the landholder usually furnishes all supplies, and takes one-third of the cotton and one-half of the provision crop." In Aiken, Greenville, and portions of Fairfield and Spartanburg counties of South Carolina, the census reported the laborer's share as one-third of the crop (Hilgard, *Cotton Production*, 2, pp. 518, 520, 522).

31 Rawick, *American Slave*, 6, Alabama, p. 27.

32 It should be noted that the point being argued in the text assumes that the laborer is not free to seek part-time work off the tenant farm without the landlord's permission. This seems to have been the case, since the amount of labor to be applied was either explicitly or implicitly agreed to by both parties as part of the contract (see the sample contract reproduced as Figure 5.1).

33 Joseph Reid cites examples of rental contracts that embody such side adjustments ("Sharecropping as an Understandable Market Response," pp. 116–120). It is interesting to note in this context that in several of the cases cited by Reid it is clear that the size of plot was not easily amenable to adjustment. See his references to the "Scott Place" and the "Burnt Mill Pond Field" contracts (pp. 116–117).

34 An exception to the rule of equal division of all the crop output was cotton seed. The Mial-Powell contract reproduced as Figure 5.1 explicitly exempts cotton seed from the division. Since the seed was customarily given to the cotton gin operator in payment for ginning and baling the cotton, this exception was equivalent to deducting the cost of preparing the cotton for market from the output before dividing the crop. *Southern Cultivator* 29 (November 1871), p. 410. *Rural Carolinian* 6 (February 1875), p. 231.

35 We conjecture that the rental difference between cotton and corn in the thirds and fourths system was due to the different intensity of work effort involved in cultivating the two crops. Cotton required considerably more labor per acre than did corn for economically efficient operation (see notes 55–59 of Chapter 8 for references). Accordingly, labor expended upon cotton received a greater fraction of the product than labor expended upon corn. If we assume that the thirds and fourths system implies that one-quarter of the marginal product of land in growing cotton was equal to one-third of the marginal product of corn land and that likewise three-fourths of the marginal product of labor and capital used for cotton was equal to two-thirds of their marginal product in corn, then it can be shown that

with a homogeneous neoclassical production relationship the ratio of land to labor in corn should have been at least 1.5 times that in cotton. In fact, the rule of thumb applied by southern farmers seems to have been that 2 acres of corn had to be given up to release the labor needed for 1 acre of cotton (*Southern Cultivator* 28, [1870], p. 82). If that ratio is correct, then southern landlords got slightly too much of the cotton (25 percent instead of 22.6 percent) and too little of the corn (one-third rather than 36.8 percent) grown with this system. For this reason, we can guess there was a tendency for the labor to devote relatively too much attention to the corn and not enough to cotton with this system.

36 U.S. Census Office [1880], *Agriculture,* pp. 30–101.

37 The map places each county in 1880 into one of five equally sized categories defined by the percentage of farms sharecropped.

38 In 1880, only 26.6 percent of the small tenant farms were rented for fixed payment (see Chapter 4, Table 4.3). The proportion was higher (31.5 percent) among black tenants (Table 5.1).

39 The use of fixed rents by blacks was further curtailed by the unwillingness of most whites to extend credit to an independent black operator. The ability of the renter to meet his debts would depend upon his success as an independent farmer. But the potential lender, like the landlord, would likely have a low opinion of the black's ability to farm without supervision. Nearly 54.4 percent of black farm operators in the Cotton South were sharecroppers in 1880, while only 26.5 percent of whites farmed for a share of the crop (Table 5.1).

40 The U.S. commissioner of agriculture, however, mentions the occasional use of rents, fixed in terms either of money or of pounds of cotton, in his discussion of several alternatives to the wage labor system (Horace Capron, "Southern Agriculture," in U.S. Department of Agriculture, *Report . . .1867,* p. 417).

41 A. R. Lightfoot, "Condition and Wants of the Cotton Raising States," *De Bow's Review* 6 (February 1869), p. 153.

42 Capron, "Southern Agriculutre," p. 420.

43 Capron, "Southern Agriculture," p. 420.

44 According to the wage contract reproduced as Figure 4.1, all male workers over eighteen years old were paid a uniform $10 per month. Teenage males were paid $6 per month. The one woman who worked was twenty years old and was paid $6. The only exceptions listed in the contract seem to be for Amanda and Mary Whitley, who were offered only $5 each. Perhaps it is significant that neither woman signed the agreement.

45 *Rural Carolinian* 4 (June 1873), p. 458.

46 *Rural Carolinian* 5 (April 1874), p. 354.

47 Loring and Atkinson, *Cotton Culture,* p. 31.

48 J. N. Montgomery, "Farm Management," speech delivered February 12, 1878, at Americus, Georgia, in *Transactions of the Georgia State Agricultural Society, from August, 1876, to February, 1878* (Atlanta: James P. Harrison, 1878), p. 397. For other expressions of this impression, see the responses of landowners to the Loring and Atkinson survey (*Cotton Culture,* pp. 28, 31). Also see W. H. Evans, "The Labor Question," *Southern Cultivator* 27 (January 1869), p. 54. Robert Somers, who was critical of sharecropping for other reasons, conceded its incentive effect (*Southern States,* p. 146).

49 *Southern Cultivator* 27 (1869), p. 181; and Somers, *Southern States,* p. 60.

50 Comments on the risk-reducing appeal of sharecropping are found throughout the responses to the surveys by Loring and Atkinson (*Cotton Culture,* pp. 28, 31) and the Tenth Census Office (Hilgard, *Cotton Production*). Also see the judgment of a contributor in *Rural Carolinian* 4 (January 1873), p. 182. Joseph Reid, Jr., has emphasized the risk-reducing role of sharecropping in his discussion of tenure choice and makes a useful distinction between those risks that cannot be influenced by economic behavior and those risks whose impact can be partially offset by appropriate responses ("Sharecropping in History and Theory," *Agricultural History* 49 [April 1975]).

51 Evans, "The Labor Question," p. 54.

52 Somers, *Southern States,* p. 31.

53 U.S. Department of Agriculture, *Report . . . 1867*, p. 419.

54 *Rural Carolinian* 1 (April 1870), p. 392.

55 This point was suggested to us by Gavin Wright ("Comment on Papers by Reid, Ransom and Sutch, and Higgs," *Journal of Economic History* 33 [March 1973], pp. 175–176) and later developed into a more general model of agricultural decision making in Gavin Wright and Howard Kunreuther, "Cotton, Corn and Risk in the Nineteenth Century," *Journal of Economic History* 35 (September 1975).

56 Loring and Atkinson, *Cotton Culture*, p. 33.

57 Somers, *Southern States*, p. 128. Unfortunately, the 1870 Census did not collect data on farm tenure. In fact, the instructions to the enumerators were sufficiently confused that some reported each tenant farm separately, while others aggregated the reports of many tenant farms under the name of the landowner. Thus neither the size distribution of farms nor the more sophisticated technique used by Owsley on the prewar censuses can be used to estimate the extent of farm tenancy in that year (Owsley, *Plain Folk*, Chapter 5).

58 Somers, *Southern States*, p. 281.

59 Letter from a planter in Calhoun County, South Carolina, in *Rural Carolinian* 4 (January 1873), p. 183.

60 D. Wyatt Aiken, "Farming as Adapted to Middle South Carolina," *Rural Carolinian* 3 (February 1872), p. 229.

61 *Southern Cultivator* 27 (1868), p. 133.

62 Alfred Marshall, *Principles of Political Economy*, 1st ed. (London: 1890), p. 644.

63 Note the contrast with fixed renting, where the rent per acre is the subject of negotiation, but once set the renter may in principle take on as many acres as he wishes.

64 Since the marginal return to labor is reduced in the case under discussion relative to the marginal value of free time, the incentive to labor would be reduced at the margin. However, we are not considering a change so small relative to total income that we can safely use a marginal analysis. The relatively low levels of income generated in southern agriculture meant that the marginal utility of income was high relative to leisure. In other words, the supply of labor effort per family was negatively sloped with respect to its remuneration. This point was first made in an economic analysis of sharecropping by D. Gale Johnson, "Resource Allocation Under Share Contracts," *Journal of Political Economy* 58 (April 1950), p. 119.

65 Roger Ransom and Richard Sutch, "The Ex-Slave in the Post-Bellum South: A Study of the Economic Impact of Racism in a Market Environment," *Journal of Economic History* 33 (March 1973), p. 143.

66 Without more knowledge than we have concerning the relationship between inputs and outputs, and particularly without more information on the intensity of work effort that accompanied various land-labor ratios and contractual arrangements, it is not possible to calculate precisely the magnitude of the welfare loss. A crude estimate, based on the output per acre in Table 5.6, sets an upper limit of the loss at 7 percent by assuming that all the losses fell on sharecroppers. Since the loss was distributed among all farms, the total effect on the Cotton South would have been well below that number.

67 This is our interpretation of the arguments made by Joseph Reid, Jr., "Sharecropping as an Understandable Market Response"; Stephen DeCanio, *Agriculture in the Postbellum South: The Economics of Production and Supply* (Cambridge: MIT Press, 1974), pp. 123–130; and Robert Higgs, *Competition and Coercion: Blacks in the American Economy, 1865–1914* (New York: Cambridge University Press, 1977). Each of these writers was apparently influenced by the theoretical model of sharecropping advanced by Steven Cheung in his study of Taiwanese rice culture *(The Theory of Share Tenancy, with Special Application to Asian Agriculture and the First Phase of Taiwan Land Reform* [Chicago: University of Chicago Press, 1969]). Cheung's inference that sharecropping was efficient is valid provided landowners and workers bargain over the rental share. Such a model cannot be applied to the southern experience since, as we have seen, it was the land-labor ratio, and not the rental share, that was negotiated by the parties to the contract.

68 D. Wyatt Aiken, "Alabama from an Agricultural Point of View," *Rural Carolinian* 1 (April 1870), p. 406.

69 D. Wyatt Aiken, "Southern Farming and Farm Labor," *Rural Carolinian* 1 (December 1869), p. 141.

70 D. Gale Johnson, "Resource Allocation Under Share Contracts," pp. 119–120.

71 *Southern Cultivator* 29 (March 1871), p. 90.

72 "Southerner," "Agricultural Labor in the South," *Galaxy Magazine* 12 (September 1871), p. 331.

73 Loring and Atkinson, *Cotton Culture,* p. 32.

74 Marshall, *Principles,* p. 536.

75 Somers, *Southern States,* p. 281.

76 Thomas P. Janes, Commissioner, Georgia, Department of Agriculture, *Annual Report for the Year 1875* (Atlanta: J. H. Estill, 1876), pp. 87–88.

77 The small farmers of the antebellum South were the focus of extensive research by Frank Owsley; a summary of this work is in Owsley, *Plain Folk.* Owsley and his students examined the economic structure of farming in four states: Louisiana (Coles, "Slave Ownership"); Mississippi (Weaver, *Mississippi Farmers);* Tennessee (Clark, *The Tennessee Yeoman);* and Alabama (Owsley and Owsley, "Economic Basis"). Though subsequent criticism of Owsley's techniques by Linden and more recent work by Wright have cast considerable doubt on some of the conclusions regarding the importance of these small farmers in the economic and social affairs of the South, the presence of a very substantial number of slaveless farms, most of which were probably owner-operated, has not been disputed. See Fabian Linden, "Economic Democracy in the Slave South: An Appraisal of Some Recent Views," *Journal of Negro History* (April 1946); and Gavin Wright, "'Economic Democracy' and the Concentration of Agricultural Wealth in the Cotton South, 1850–1860," *Agricultural History* 44 (January 1970).

78 The ownership of slaves and land, as Gavin Wright's analysis of the Parker-Gallman sample of 1859 farms has shown, was extremely concentrated among the larger planters (Wright, "Economic Democracy"). Both Wright and Linden ("Economic Democracy") present persuasive arguments that most small farmers in the antebellum South did not control appreciable amounts of good cotton land or slave capital.

79 Owsley *(Plain Folk)* presents the most complete description of this type of farming. Though he exaggerated their importance in the economy of the antebellum South, the presence of many small cotton farms in the plantation regions cannot be denied.

80 Eugene Genovese has made this point in an essay that goes into many other social and economic links between nonslaveholding whites and slavery ("Yeoman Farmers in a Slaveholders' Democracy," *Agricultural History* 49 [April 1975], pp. 331–342).

Chapter 6. Financial reconstruction

1 J. A. Ansley, letter dated February 21, 1867, addressed to T. C. Peters, in Theodore C. Peters, *A Report upon Conditions of the South, with Regard to Its Needs for a Cotton Crop and Its Financial Wants in Connection Therewith* . . . (Baltimore: H. A. Robinson for R. M. Rhodes & Co., 1867), p. 15.

2 For a more thorough discussion of the role of the cotton factor and a more detailed description of the financial and marketing network of the antebellum era, see Harold Woodman's excellent study, *King Cotton and His Retainers* (Lexington: University of Kentucky Press, 1967).

3 Table 6.1 is based upon the returns of those state banks that reported to the United States secretary of treasury. No banks were reported from Texas or Arkansas. As nearly as can be determined, only chartered banks were included in the Treasury Department's lists. Moreover, since reporting was not required, the figures may not be comprehensive. The date for the balance sheet items varied slightly from state to state. We have taken the observation closest to January 1, 1860. U.S. Secretary of the Treasury, *Report of the*

Secretary of the Treasury on the State of the Finances, for the Year Ending June 30, 1863, House of Representatives, Executive Document Number 3, 38th Congress, 1st Session, (Washington: GPO, 1863), pp. 226–231.

4 U.S. Comptroller of the Currency, *Annual Report . . . December 4, 1876,* House of Representatives, Executive Document Number 3, 44th Congress, 2nd Session (Washington: GPO, 1876), p. 110; John Jay Knox, *A History of Banking in the United States* (New York: Bradford Rhodes & Co., 1903), pp. 568–569, 582. It is interesting to note that two of the surviving Georgia banks, the Georgia Railroad and Banking Company and the Central Railroad and Banking Company, had roughly one-half of their chartered assets committed to banking and the other half invested in transportation.

5 Peters, *Conditions of the South,* pp. 16–17.

6 Whitelaw Reid, *After the War: A Tour of the Southern States, 1865–1866* (New York: Harper & Row, 1965), p. 206, first published in 1866.

7 *De Bow's Review* 3 (May/June 1867), p. 485.

8 Peters, *Conditions of the South,* p. 7.

9 National banks were prohibited from making mortgage loans for a period longer than five years (George P. Sanger, ed., *The Statutes at Large, . . . of the United States of America,* Volume 13, December 1863 to December 1865 [Boston: Little, Brown & Co., 1866], p. 108). Richard Sylla presents a persuasive argument that the restrictions of the National Banking Act effectively curbed entry into southern banking ("Federal Policy, Banking Market Structure, and Capital Mobilization in the United States, 1863–1913," *Journal of Economic History* 29 [December 1969], pp. 659–665).

10 The failure rate among southern banks by 1869 had been 25 percent. In the rest of the country, only 3.3 percent of the national banks organized had failed in so short a time (U.S. Comptroller of the Currency, *Annual Report . . . 1876,* pp. 262–269, 274).

11 The note to Table 6.3 provides a list of the major commercial centers. The four smaller cities, each with one national bank, were Athens and Columbus, Georgia; Huntsville, Alabama; and Columbia, South Carolina.

12 George P. Sanger, *The Statutes at Large. . . ,* Volume 13, p. 484.

13 The circulation of all state banknotes is given by the U.S. Treasury Department as: $142.9 million in 1865; $20 million in 1866, $4.5 million in 1867, and $3.2 million in 1868. (U.S. Secretary of the Treasury, *Annual Report . . . 1928* [Washington: GPO, 1929], p. 552).

14 The use of individual deposit accounts necessitates an ability to keep rudimentary financial records. Yet, as we have seen, nearly all the freedmen were illiterate, as were a good many whites.

15 I. Smith Homans, ed., *The Merchants & Bankers' Almanac for 1869* (New York: Office of the Bankers' Magazine and Statistical Register, 1869), pp. 47–52. The information on banking in this period was obtained through a careful examination of the available primary sources on banking before 1880. See Appendix G, Section 4, for details on banking statistics.

16 Because there were so few national banks in the Five Cotton States after the war, the data from seven large New Orleans banks distort the average measure for the regions outside New Orleans. As an example of this tendency, we note the following differences in bank size for 1880 (in thousands of dollars):

	Capital per bank	Notes plus Deposits per bank	Total resources per bank
New Orleans	531	1,295	2,012
Five Cotton States less New Orleans	156	478	688

17 U.S. Census Office, Tenth Census [1880], *Report on Cotton Production in the United States*, 2 vols. (Washington: GPO, 1884), 2, p. 521.

18 For a more complete analysis of the high costs both commercial banks and factors faced when dealing with small tenant farmers, see Roger Ransom and Richard Sutch, "Debt Peonage in the Cotton South After the Civil War," *Journal of Economic History* 32 (September 1972), pp. 650–651.

19 Two of the bankers were not given a pecuniary strength rating. Following Dun's procedure, we interpret this to imply a pecuniary strength of less than $1,000.

20 William P. Dana, "Business Changes at the South – The Past and Future," *Hunt's Merchants' Magazine and Commercial Review* 61 (November 1869), p. 364.

21 A complete list of the commercial centers, the cotton centers, and the rural cotton centers located in one of the Five Cotton States or in the Cotton South is presented in Appendix G, Table G.16, together with data on population, number of banks, and number of general stores in each town or city in 1880. It should be noted that our criteria for a town to be classed as a rural cotton center were quite strict. For example, of the four towns mentioned in the text, only Cheraw, South Carolina, was selected as a rural cotton center. See Appendix G, Section 4, for a more complete discussion of our selection criteria. The four towns used as examples were selected, not from the list in the appendix, but from the *Reference Book* of Dun's Mercantile Agency for 1870.

22 For a discussion of the rural merchandising system before the war see Lewis E. Atherton, *The Southern Country Store, 1800–1860* (Baton Rouge: Louisiana State University Press, 1949).

23 Sidney Andrews, *The South Since the War as Shown by Fourteen Weeks of Travel and Observation in Georgia and the Carolinas* (Boston: Houghton Mifflin Co., 1970), pp. 365, 3–4, 366, first published in 1866.

24 Reid, *After the War*, p. 332.

25 Andrews, *The South Since the War*, pp. 365–366.

26 Reid, *After the War*, p. 481.

27 John Richard Dennett, *The South As It Is: 1865–1866* (New York: Viking Press, 1967), pp. 264–265, originally published as a series of articles in *The Nation*, 1865–1866.

28 The sample included all general stores operating in the counties of Barnwell, South Carolina; Coweta, Twiggs, Gwinnett, and Worth, Georgia; Bibb and Russell, Alabama; Rankin and Tunica, Mississippi. The merchants in these counties were identified from the list of businesses compiled from R. G. Dun and Company, *The Mercantile Agency Reference Book. . . January 1880,* 2nd ed. (New York: Dun, Barlow & Co., 1880). The birthplaces were determined by consulting the manuscript returns of the 1880 Census of Population.

29 These figures were collected from the files on Rankin County in R. G. Dun and Company, Mercantile Agency Credit Ledgers (unpublished, Dun & Bradstreet Archives, Baker Library, Harvard University).

30 The development of rural merchandising is examined in greater detail in Chapter 7. The figures in the text are from Table 7.6. See Table G.10 for a list of the twenty-seven counties.

31 The history of the Mercantile Agency, and its subsequent development into Dun and Bradstreet, Inc. (now Dun and Bradstreet Companies) is reported in Roy A. Foulke, *The Sinews of American Commerce* (New York: Dun & Bradstreet, 1941). Foulke's study was commissioned by Dun and Bradstreet, but it remains the only extensive treatment of the early role of credit reporting in the American economy.

32 Foulke, *Sinews of American Commerce*, p. 335.

33 We have discussed elsewhere the contrast between the South and the agricultural West in the use of banks. One striking measure is the fact that in 1880 banks in the Five Cotton States held less than $5 in deposits per capita, compared with nearly $20 of deposits per person for banks in the eighteen westernmost states (Ransom and Sutch, "Debt Peonage," Table 2, p. 649).

34 Edward King, *The Southern States of North America* (London: Blackie & Son, 1875), p. 274. King's reference to Jewish merchants reflects the fact that his observations were made

in the Mississippi River basin, an area that particularly attracted Jewish immigrants after the war. Throughout the South, Jews apparently constituted only a small minority of the merchants, and even in the Mississippi delta they did not dominate the furnishing business. This conclusion is based on a perusal of the surnames of merchants in Dun's *Reference Book* and is confirmed by a careful examination of the names and birthplaces of a sample of general store operators throughout the cotton region (see note 28, above).

35 Robert Somers, *The Southern States Since the War, 1870–1* (New York: Macmillan & Co., 1871), pp. 241–242.

36 The descriptions of this section draw heavily on the excellent study of Alabama merchants in the black belt region by Glenn Sisk ("Rural Merchandising in the Alabama Black Belt," *Journal of Farm Economics* 37 [November 1955], pp. 711–713), and on the descriptions of rural stores throughout Thomas Clark (*Pills, Pettticoats, and Plows: The Southern Country Store* [Indianapolis: Bobbs-Merrill, 1944]).

37 Sisk, "Rural Merchandising," p. 707.

38 Tenth Census, *Cotton Production*, 2, pp. 520, 521. Hammond reported the average lien was $77. The precise mean, however, was $77.95.

39 The two-price system probably developed as a device to avoid the letter, but not the spirit, of the laws against usury common in southern states. As we discuss in Chapter 7, the implicit interest rates charged for credit invariably exceeded 40 percent, and in some instances exceeded 70 percent, per year. Of course, the system also possessed the advantage that it was simpler to explain and easier to keep books on than the quotation and computation of interest charges would have been.

40 Sisk, "Rural Merchandising," p. 710.

41 Georgia, Department of Agriculture, "Consolidation of the Reports of Crops, &c." (August 15, 1875), p. 9; and idem, "Consolidation of the Reports of Crops, etc., for the Month of August, 1876," p. 2, both in *Publications of the Georgia State Department of Agriculture from September, 1874, to January, 1878.* (Atlanta: J. P. Harrison & Co., 1878), Volumes 1,2.

42 On the early passage of the lien laws, see Enoch Marvin Banks, "The Economics of Land Tenure in Georgia," *Studies in History, Economics, and Public Law* 23 (1905), Chapter 3; Robert Preston Brooks, "The Agrarian Revolution in Georgia, 1865–1912," *Bulletin of the University of Wisconsin, History Series* 3 (1914), Chapter 3; Mathew B. Hammond, *The Cotton Industry* (New York: American Economic Association and Macmillan Co., 1897), Chapter 5; and Oscar Zeichner, "The Legal Status of the Agricultural Laborer in the South," *Political Science Quarterly* 55 (September 1940). There can be little doubt that the lien system was widespread. See J. C. Hemphill, U.S. Department of Agriculture, "Climate, Soil, and Agricultural Capabilities of South Carolina and Georgia," *USDA Special Report*, Number 47 (Washington: GPO, 1882); and Thomas P. Janes, Georgia Department of Agriculture, *Annual Report . . . for the Year 1875* (Atlanta: J. H. Estill, 1876).

Chapter 7. The emergence of the merchants' territorial monopoly

1 Thomas D. Clark, *Pills, Petticoats, and Plows: The Southern Country Store* (Indianapolis: Bobbs-Merrill, 1944), pp. vii–viii.

2 George K. Holmes, "The Peons of the South," *Annals of the American Academy of Political and Social Science* 4 (September 1893), p. 67.

3 Henry W. Grady, "Cotton and Its Kingdom," *Harper's New Monthly Magazine* 63 (October 1881), p. 723.

4 In 1884 Georgia's commissioner of agriculture, J. T. Henderson, wrote to Louisiana's commissioner, T. J. Bird, that Georgia had "from three to five or more" correspondents in each county, selected "from different parts of the counties," (letter dated November 10, 1884, in Louisiana, Bureau of Agriculture, *Biennial Report of the Commissioner of Agriculture . . . 1886* [Baton Rouge: Leon Jastremski, 1886], pp. 4–5).

5 Thomas P. Janes, Georgia, Department of Agriculture, *Annual Report . . . for the Year 1875* (Atlanta: J. H. Estill, 1876), p. 130.

6 Georgia, Department of Agriculture, "Quarterly Report," *Circular*, Number 17, ns (May 18, 1881), p. 31, in *Publications of the Georgia State Department of Agriculture*, Volume 7 (Atlanta: J. P. Harrison & Co., 1882).

7 Commercial paper rates in New York of 60 to 90 days, maturity are given in Frederick R. Macauley, *Some Theoretical Problems Suggested by the Movements of Interest Rates, Bond Yield and Stock Prices in the United States Since 1856* (New York: National Bureau of Economic Research, 1938), Table 10, pp. A141–A161. Our maximum allows for at least a 3-percent differential between New York and the Cotton South. Richard Sylla calculated an average difference in gross earnings between national banks in New York City and those in the South to range from 2.33 to 3.33 percent in the interval 1888–1900 ("Federal Policy, Banking Market Structure, and Capital Mobilization in the United States, 1863–1913," *Journal of Economic History* 29 [December 1969], p. 672). Lance Davis provides detailed figures behind Sylla's calculations and additional data on mortgage returns suggesting a 3-percent differential is most generous ("The Investment Market, 1870–1914: The Evolution of a National Market," *Journal of Economic History* 25 [September 1965], pp. 360–365, 375).

8 Robert Somers, *The Southern States Since the War 1870–1* (New York: Macmillan & Co., 1871), p. 198.

9 The calculation of the default rate that might justify charging an interest rate of 60 percent when the risk-free rate of interest is 10 percent is presented in Appendix D.

10 It may be relevant to point out that a survey of general merchandise stores in Louisiana in 1926 revealed that the default rate on credit sales was 5.4 percent (Sherrod D. Morehead, *Merchant Credit to Farmers in Louisiana* [Russellville: privately printed, 1929], p. 41). Note, however, that this observation is quite late, after the appearance of mail-order houses and chain stores stores altered the general pattern of merchandising in the rural South considerably and undoubtly *increased* the risk to merchandising carried out under the old pattern.

11 We noted in Chapter 6 that an $80 debt would be a reasonable figure for most cotton farms. One-hundred farmers would not be too many to superintend, since a short visit once or twice a month should have been sufficient to ensure that a farmer was not falling behind in his work; that the crop was maturing as expected; and that the merchant's interest was not being jeopardized. A $500 salary would equal or exceed that of the typical overseer before the war (James L. Watkins, U.S. Department of Agriculture, Division of Statistics, "The Cost of Cotton Production," *USDA Miscellaneous Bulletin* Number 16 [Washington: GPO, 1899], p. 44.). According to Lewis C. Gray, "typical" salaries for overseers before the war were from $400 to $600 (*History of Agriculture in the Southern United States to 1860*, 2 vols. [Washington: Carnegie Institute, 1933], 1, p. 545).

12 The calculation of a "justified" rate of interest under the assumptions noted in the text is explained in Appendix D.

13 A discussion of the procedures used to identify and enumerate general stores is presented later in this chapter.

14 A detailed discussion of the records of the R. G. Dun Mercantile Agency appears in Appendix. G, Section 5.

15 Occasionally there are notations to the effect that a store was "near" or "*x* miles from" the listed address, in which cases those stores were treated as isolated locations. An examination of the Credit Ledgers convinces us that such notations were incompletely recorded in the *Reference Books*.

16 A list of these centers, together with the number of stores they contained, is included in Appendix G, Table G.16. Taken together, there were 540 stores excluded from Table 7.3.

17 Examples of such urban locations are the Class III towns listed in Table G.16. These rural cotton centers are listed along with their populations and number of general stores reported at their postal addresses.

18 One example is the town of San Augustine, Texas, in San Augustine county. As the only post office in the county, it is not surprising to find all eleven general stores in the county shared the same postal address. Similarly, Eaton, Georgia, in Putnam County, had eleven general stores, but its post office had to serve the entire county with the exception of a railroad station, whose post office was the address of a single general store.

19 The minimum average distance between sites (d in Figure 7.1) can be calculated from the relationship between the side, x, and the area, A, of each hexagon. Since $x = d/\sqrt{3}$ and the area of each hexagon is given by $A = (3xd)/2$, we can eliminate x and solve for d:

$$d = \sqrt{\frac{2\sqrt{3}\,A}{3}} = \sqrt{1.1547\,A}$$

The area of the Cotton South was computed from the official census figures of the area of each county in 1880. U.S. Census Office, Tenth Census [1880], *Report on Cotton Production in the United States . . . ,* 2 vol. (Washington: GPO, 1884).

20 If the farmer were conveniently located on a perfectly straight road connecting two stores 7 miles apart, he would require the 14-mile round trip mentioned in the text. If he were disadvantageously located equidistant from three stores (i.e., at point V in Figure 7.1), but still able to travel on straight roads to the first store (equal to a distance of x in the figure), then directly to the second store (a distance of d), then back home again (along a road of length x); the total distance traveled would be 15.1 miles ($x = 4.04$ miles). These calculations are extremely conservative, since no roads in the South were perfectly straight. Robert Fogel, using modern highway maps, estimated that the ratio of "highway distance" to straight-line distance is 1.6 (*Railroads and American Economic Growth: Essays in Econometric History* [Baltimore: Johns Hopkins Press, 1964], p. 67).

21 According to the editor of the *Rural Carolinian,* an ox team would travel 20 miles a day and a horse team 25 miles (*Rural Carolinian* 1 [January 1870], p. 208).

22 For an economic model of the behavior of these merchants and the workings of a territorial monopoly, see Roger Ransom and Richard Sutch, "Documenting Monopoly Power in the Rural South: The Case of the General Store," *Southern Economic History Project Working Paper Series,* Number 15 (Riverside: Center for Social and Behavioral Science Research, June 1975).

23 Scattered estimates of the annual volume of trade enjoyed by general stores described in the Mercantile Agency's Credit Ledgers indicate that an annual business in excess of $10,000 was considered quite substantial, and a volume of $4,000 to $5,000 seems typical.

24 The two examples of wealthy merchants in Tunica County, Mississippi, refer to the firms of "Tate and Son" and "Lowenhoupt and Kahn." The generalizations concerning the less wealthy merchants were based on an examination of Dun's Credit Ledger entries for firms in our six-county sample discussed in Appendix G, Section 5.

25 The single case noted in the text was a Mr. Washburn, of the firm Washburn and Runge in Rankin County, Mississippi, who was reported as living in Ohio. In every other instance of a direct involvement outside the immediate vicinity of the store, the partner lived no further away than an adjacent county.

26 The counties included in this analysis were Rankin and Tunica, Mississippi; Gwinnett, Worth, and Twiggs, Georgia; and Russell, Alabama. Stores establishing themselves in one of five towns (Brandon in Rankin County; Austin in Tunica County; Buford and Norcross in Gwinnett County; Hurtville in Russell County) were excluded.

27 The firms were Dwyer and Nash in Yellow River (Gwinnett County); Rhoades, Williams, and Meyers in Brandon (Rankin County); and Washburn and Runge in Brandon (Rankin County).

28 Charles H. Otken, *The Ills of the South* (New York: G. P. Putnam's Sons, 1894), p. 80.

29 The examples are all taken from the Credit Ledgers for Rankin County, Mississippi. Not all reports included sufficient detail to allow the estimates of net worth of the owners over a period of years. The five examples presented in the text were selected as representative of firms that were successful. While a detailed tabulation of changes in wealth was not

undertaken for firms in the other five counties in our sample, a preliminary review of these counties convinces us that the Rankin examples are typical of successful merchant experiences in other cotton counties.

30 Firm of B. H. and H. D. Tarver, Buzzard's Roost Station, Twiggs County, Georgia.

31 Firms of S. Dobson and Busik and Stevens, both of Brandon, Rankin County, Mississippi.

32 Glenn N. Sisk, "Rural Merchandising in the Alabama Black Belt," *Journal of Farm Economics* 37 (November 1955), p. 706.

33 *Acts of Alabama,* cited by Jonathan Wiener, "Planter-Merchant Conflict in Reconstruction Alabama," *Past and Present* 68 (August 1975), p. 88.

34 Wiener discusses the political conflict between a merchant class and a planter elite that occurred in Alabama during this period. He distinguishes differences in the outcome of this conflict between the black belt region – where most tenants were black and the planter elite came to dominate merchandising – and the hill counties – where tenants were more often white and the merchant class took control (Wiener, "Planter-Merchant Conflict"). While such conflicts were of important social and political consequence, we do not see that they had much economic significance, other than in determining which class background would typify the families that came to control the territorial monopolies.

35 *Montgomery [Alabama] Daily Advertiser,* July 11, 1868. Cited by Wiener, "Planter-Merchant Conflict," pp. 86–87.

36 *Mobile [Alabama] Daily Register,* February 26, 1871. Cited by Wiener, "Planter-Merchant Conflict," p. 87.

Chapter 8. The trap of debt peonage

1 Charles H. Otken, *The Ills of the South* (New York: G. P. Putnam's Sons, 1894), p. 57.

2 Otken, *Ills of the South,* p. 57. Emphasis in the original. Quoted from the *New York Ledger* (1889).

3 George K. Holmes, "The Peons of the South," *Annals of the American Academy of Political and Social Science* 4 (September 1893), p. 66.

4 Holmes, "Peons of the South," p. 67.

5 James D. B. De Bow, *The Industrial Resources, Statistics, &c. of the United States, and More Particularly of the Southern and Western States,* 3rd ed. 2 vols. (New York: A. M. Kelly, 1966), 2, p. 114, first edition published in 1852. For an excellent summary of similar complaints, and the attempts at correcting the South's "dependence" upon the North, see Harold D. Woodman, *King Cotton and His Retainers* (Lexington: University of Kentucky Press, 1967), pp. 139–153.

6 James D. B. De Bow, "The Future of the South," *De Bow's Review* 1 (January 1866), pp. 8–9.

7 De Bow, "Future of the South," p. 9.

8 *Southern Cultivator* 31 (September 1873), p. 343.

9 Henry W. Grady, "Cotton and Its Kingdom," *Harper's New Monthly Magazine* 63 (October 1881), pp. 723–724.

10 To illustrate the concern of periodicals, consider the following citations from four years of the *Rural Carolinian,* all of which urge more diversified farming: *Rural Carolinian* 1 (1869), pp. 11–12, 114, 182; idem, 1 (1870), pp. 376, 398–399; idem, 2 (1871), pp. 265–267, 388–389, 489–493; idem, 3 (1871), pp. 13–14; idem, 3 (1872), pp. 286–287, 377, 627–628; and idem, 4 (1872), p. 171.

11 We can make use of the 1870 data in this context despite the underenumeration in that year (discussed in Chapter 3), since we have reason to believe that both population and production were underreported by roughly the same proportion.

12 There is an extensive debate concerning the slaughter weights of hogs on antebellum plantations. The consensus that seems to be emerging is that the median dressed weight was in the neighborhood of 140 pounds, and the live weight approximately 185 pounds. Robert E. Gallman, "Self-Sufficiency in the Cotton Economy of the Antebellum South,"

Agricultural History 44 (January 1970), pp. 15–16; Eugene D. Genovese, *The Political Economy of Slavery: Studies in The Economy and Society of the Slave South* (New York: Pantheon, 1965), pp. 115, 122–123; Sam Bowers Hilliard, *Hog Meat and Hoecake: Food Supply in the Old South, 1840–1860* (Carbondale: Southern Illinois University Press, 1972), pp. 102, 261; and Richard Sutch, "The Treatment Received by American Slaves: A Critical Review of the Evidence Presented in *Time on the Cross,*" *Exploration in Economic History* 12 (October 1975), pp. 367–369. Our survey of the production statistics for slaughterhouses available in the manuscript returns to the Census of Manufacturing for all eleven southern states in 1880 revealed that the average live weight in that year was 185 pounds. There is also evidence to suggest that hogs slaughtered by commercial slaughterhouses weighed on average more than those slaughtered on the farm. A study by Sutch of the slaughter ratio, which surveyed sources for both the pre- and postwar periods, concluded that killings as a ratio to the June inventory held constant at approximately 80 percent throughout the period in question (Sutch, "Treatment," pp. 369–370).

13 Outside the Five Cotton States, the decline in beef production was less marked. Nevertheless, even in Texas, which was the state where cattle production was most pronounced, the per capita stock of "other cattle" declined. The average output of butter per capita in 1860 was 5 pounds; in 1870 it dropped to 2.7 pounds; by 1880 it was back to 4.6 pounds. See the sources for Table 8.1.

14 There is some disagreement concerning the diet of slaves. At one extreme, the standard daily slave ration of 0.5 pound of pork and 2 pounds of cornmeal for an adult field hand implies a caloric intake of 4,056 per day, and is probably a minimum (see the source references in Appendix A, note 16). At the other extreme is the suggestion by Robert William Fogel and Stanley L. Engerman that supplements to the pork and corn ration raised the daily caloric consumption of adult field hands to 5,357 calories (*Time on the Cross,* 2 vols. [Boston: Little, Brown & Co., 1974] 2, p. 97). As Richard Sutch argued, this figure exaggerates the true diet because of biases and errors involved with Fogel and Engerman's estimating procedure ("Treatment," pp. 394–396; also see Sutch for the sources and procedures used to estimate the caloric content of these diets). A plausible estimate of energy requirements for a typical adult suggests that 1,200 calories would be expended merely in sleeping, resting, and light personal activity, such as dressing and eating (ibid, p. 385; J. V. G. A. Durnin and R. Passmore, *Energy, Work and Leisure* [London: Heinemann Educational Books, 1967], pp. 31, 39, 46). A slave restricted to 4,056 calories per day could then be expected to work at a rate requiring approximately 4.8 calories per minute over a ten-hour period. Slaves provided 5,357 calories could be expected to work at tasks requiring 7 calories per minute. Assuming the maximum reduction in work effort was 37 percent, the implied decrease in the calorie requirements for adults who expended 4.8 calories per minute at work would be 17.9 percent; for adults expending 7 calories per minute at work, the reduction implies a 22.7 percent decline. Since approximately half the population was black, the net reduction in energy requirements that could be explained by the reduction of black work effort could not have exceeded 9 to 11.5 percent. There are a number of reasons for believing that the actual decline was less than this. First, it is not obvious that the fall in energy requirements for children would parallel that for adults, as implicitly assumed in the above calculations. Second, our estimates assume that the time released by the reduction in adult work effort was spent in sleep or rest. Had the released time instead been spent in recreation, housekeeping, or child care, the energy requirements of free blacks would have been higher.

15 Wholesale cotton prices are available from Lewis Cecil Gray, *History of Agriculture in the Southern United States to 1860,* 2 vols. (Washington: Carnegie Institution, 1933), 2, p. 1027. We adjusted Gray's figures downward by 0.75 cent per pound to reflect Alfred Conrad and John Meyer's estimate of the cost of transportation and marketing ("The Economics of Slavery in the Ante Bellum South," *Journal of Political Economy* 66 [April 1958], p. 105). Prices received by farmers for corn in Virginia are available from Arthur G. Peterson, "Historical Study of Prices Received by Producers of Farm Products in Virginia,

1801–1927," Virginia Agricultural Experiment Station, *Technical Bulletin* 37 (Blacksburg: Virginia Polytechnic Institute, 1929), pp. 168–169. Gray (*History of Agriculture*) presents wholesale prices for corn in New Orleans comparable to those he collected for cotton. Farmgate prices of corn by state for 1848 can be found in U.S. Patent Office, *Annual Report of the Commissioner of Patents, for the Year 1848* (Washington: Wendell & Van Benthuysen, 1849), p. 653. The corn prices per bushel ranged from 5.1 to 9.2 times the cotton price per pound; ten years later the same ratio ranged from 6.4 to 8.4.

16 The average ratio for all five states, displayed in Figure 8.3, is a weighted average, computed by weighting the ratio of prices for each state by the total value of corn and cotton production for that state in 1879. The corn and cotton price series and their sources are described in Appendix F.

17 The discussions in the text concerning cotton and corn yields and acreage are based on data reported in U.S. Department of Agriculture, Agricultural Marketing Service, "Corn: Acreage, Yield, and Production of All Corn . . . 1866–1943," *USDA Statistical Bulletin*, Number 56 (Washington: GPO, 1954), pp. 9, 10, 13, 14, 16; and U.S. Department of Agriculture, Agricultural Marketing Service, "Cotton and Cottonseed: Acreage, Yield, Production, Disposition, Price, Value, by States, 1866–1952," *USDA Statistical Bulletin*, Number 164 (Washington: GPO, 1955), pp. 17, 18, 20–22. Our conclusion takes into consideration the fact that corn prices did not fall relative to cotton prices during the period when relative yields were shifting.

18 We fail to see the force in the argument, advanced by Gavin Wright and Howard Kunreuther, which relates the shift toward cotton to a "land constraint" ("Cotton, Corn and Risk in the Nineteenth Century," *Journal of Economic History* 35 [September 1975], pp. 538, 549–550). It seems to us that they erroneously interpret the microeconomic effect of the landlords' use of acreage restriction to control sharecroppers as a macroeconomic "land shortage." Since renters of small farms devoted a larger fraction (58.1 percent) of their acreage reported in crops to cotton than did sharecroppers (53.6 percent), the acreage restrictions imposed upon sharecroppers do not seem to have biased their crop mix toward cotton (see Table 8.2).

19 Hilliard, *Hog Meat and Hoecake*, pp. 235, 234.

20 See Gallman, "Self-Sufficiency"; and William K. Hutchinson and Samuel H. Williamson, "The Self-Sufficiency of the Antebellum South: Estimates of the Food Supply," *Journal of Economic History* 31 (September 1971).

21 The theme of a South importing foodstuffs from the North and West is an old one. Guy S. Callender ("The Early Transportation and Banking Enterprises of the States in Relation to the Growth of the Corporation," *Quarterly Journal of Economics* 17 [November 1902]) argued this case. Louis B. Schmidt ("Internal Commerce and the Development of a National Economy before 1860," *Journal of Political Economy* 47 [December 1939]) and Douglass C. North (*The Economic Growth of the United States, 1790–1860* [Englewood Cliffs: Prentice-Hall, 1961], Chapter 9) based their models of national economic development on the importance of an interregional trade of foodstuffs. Albert Fishlow, on the other hand, disputed the Schmidt-North thesis that southern food imports played a leading role in western development, though he conceded that the South received some imports of meats and grains from the West ("Antebellum Interregional Trade Reconsidered," *American Economic Review* 54 [May 1964]; idem, *American Railroads and the Transformation of the Ante-Bellum Economy* [Cambridge: Harvard University Press, 1965], Chapter 7). More recently, Stanley Engerman computed self-sufficiency estimates for the South in 1840, 1850, and 1860 and found that the South Atlantic area and the four-state area comprising Alabama, Arkansas, Louisiana, and Mississippi were deficit regions in grain and meat in 1860; but he noted that his calculations were based upon very generous estimates of food requirements ("The Antebellum South: What Probably Was and What Should Have Been," *Agricultural History* 44 [January 1970], Table 1, pp. 134–136). The analysis of trade patterns in the 1850s by Robert W. Fogel emphasizes the growing rail traffic to the southeastern states in that decade ("American Interregional Trade in the Nineteenth Cen-

tury" and "A Provisional View of the 'New Economic History,'" both in Ralph L. Andreano, ed., *New Views on American Economic Development* [Cambridge: Schenkman, 1965]). Diane Lindstrom has suggested that the cotton areas largely fed themselves; the food imports mainly provisioned the cities and the rice and sugar regions ("Southern Dependence upon Interregional Grain Supplies: A Review of the Trade Flows, 1840–1860," *Agricultural History* 44 [January 1970]).

22 Wright and Kunreuther, "Cotton, Corn and Risk," pp. 526–529. As Wright and Kunreuther point out, William Brown and Morgan Reynolds ("Debt Peonage Re-examined," *Journal of Economic History* 33 [December 1973]) are incorrect to infer from the Gallman study that small farms were less diversified than large farms before the Civil War (Wright and Kunreuther, pp. 528–529, note 6).

23 Thomas P. Janes, Georgia Department of Agriculture, *Annual Report . . . for the Year 1875* (Atlanta: J. H. Estill, 1876), pp. 54–55.

24 Janes, *Annual Report*, p. 90.

25 *Southern Cultivator* 28 (November 1870), p. 379.

26 *De Bow's Review* 3 (April-May 1867), p. 365.

27 Frequent reference to the "profitability" of cotton in the South can be found in the journals we cite, and many observers were quite sanguine (though often incorrect) about the prospect of favorable cotton prices in the future. However, support for growing *some* cotton should not be taken as refuting or disavowing advice favoring diversified farming for individual farmers. Stephen J. DeCanio is surely mistaken when he suggests that there was about equal sentiment for and against diversified farming in the postbellum literature (*Agriculture in the Postbellum South: The Economics of Production and Supply* [Cambridge: MIT Press, 1974], pp. 94–118). He has, we think, seriously misinterpreted the viewpoints of writers who, while strongly favoring production of home supplies, concede the obvious advantage of raising some cotton. It is difficult to reconcile DeCanio's characterization of Henry Grady's endorsement of diversification as "half-hearted" (p. 104) with Grady's original comment (Grady, "Cotton and Its Kingdom," pp. 723–724).

28 "A Lesson for Cotton Planters," *Rural Carolinian* 3 (December 1871), pp. 125–126; reprinted from *The Plantation*.

29 *Rural Carolinian* 2 (April 1871), p. 397.

30 *Southern Cultivator* 29 (March 1871), p. 97.

31 Gallman, "Self-Sufficiency"; Roger Ransom and Richard Sutch, "Debt Peonage in the Cotton South After the Civil War," *Journal of Economic History* 32 (September 1972), pp. 659–664.

32 The crops included in our calculation were corn, rice, barley, buckwheat, oats, rye, wheat, cowpeas, dried beans, and Irish and sweet potatoes. The equivalence ratios used to convert these crops to corn equivalents are given in Appendix E, Table E.2. The animals included as feed-consuming units on the farm were horses, oxen, mules, milch cows, and sheep. See Appendix E for a discussion of feeding practices for these animals; the requirements are summarized in Table E.4. Since we express all food available to the family – including meat – as corn-equivalent grain, we allocate no food to the swine on the farm. This assumes that the farmer had the option of consuming his "surplus" either directly as grain or indirectly as slaughtered hogs fed from the surplus food available.

33 Gallman, in his study of antebellum self-sufficiency, employed estimates that he believed *over*stated actual feed and seed practices ("Self-Sufficiency," p. 19). We employed feed estimates in our earlier paper that, we felt, *under*stated the actual needs of the farm (Ransom and Sutch, "Debt Peonage," pp. 660–662). For our purposes here, we have revised our earlier estimate to reflect more realistic standards for the South around 1880. Nevertheless, we have kept our estimates conservative.

34 We estimate in Appendix E that an average working adult would require at least 20 bushels of corn per year to meet direct and indirect food needs; a child would need about half that amount. Considering that children constituted approximately one-half of the population, an average of 15 bushels of corn per capita would provide adequate food for the typical farm

family. Hired farm labor, if any, was assumed to require 20 bushels of corn-equivalent grain per capita as board annually.

35 It should not be assumed from the fact that the "all farms" category averaged 17.9 bushels of grain per household member that the South, or even the rural South, was self-sufficient, since family members living in separate dwelling units were not included in the farm household population, nor were the family members of hired laborers. For the same reasons, we suspect that the food requirements of the largest farms have been understated relative to the small farms.

36 Our sample of farms illustrates the greater predictability of cotton yields per acre across farms in the year 1879. In each of the counties sampled, the proportional variance in the physical yields per acre was higher for corn than for cotton. Throughout the period 1867 to 1890, farmgate prices for corn fluctuated far more widely than did farmgate prices for cotton. The total effect was to make raising corn for sale a more risky prospect in the view of the merchant. This does not mean, however, that from the perspective of the farmer who was purchasing corn the risks would be viewed the same. As Wright and Kunreuther have pointed out, in that case the farmer must sell cotton at an uncertain future price and use the proceeds to purchase corn at an uncertain future price. The combination of these market uncertainties with the usual risks in growing crops made growing cotton to purchase corn appear more risky than corn production (Wright and Kunreuther, "Cotton, Corn and Risk," Table 5, p. 537).

37 Thomas D. Clark, "The Furnishing and Supply System in Southern Agriculture since 1865," Journal of Southern History 12 (February 1946), pp. 36–37; Jacqueline P. Bull, "The General Merchant in the Economic History of the New South," Journal of Southern History 18 (February 1952), pp. 41–42.

38 Crops were pitched in January or February. See Rural Carolinian 4 (January 1870), p. 247; Southern Cultivator 30 (February 1872), p. 41. Note that the crop lien contract reproduced in Chapter 6 as Figure 6.2 does not stipulate the amount of cotton to be grown. The contract is dated February 29, 1876; yet the preparation of the cotton land was usually begun in January.

39 North Carolina, Bureau of Labor Statistics, First Annual Report . . . for the Year 1887 (Raleigh: Josephus Daniels, 1887), pp. 131–132.

40 Ibid., pp. 88–89, 92, 111, 129.

41 Additional testimony to the fact that merchants insisted upon cotton to secure their liens can be found in Mathew B. Hammond, The Cotton Industry (New York: American Economic Association and Macmillan Co., 1897), pp. 150–152; Eugene W. Hilgard, U.S. Census Office, Tenth Census [1880], Report on Cotton Production in the United States, 2 vols. (Washington: GPO, 1884), 1, p. 357; 2, p. 251; Otken, Ills of the South, pp. 54–64; and A. B. Hurt, U.S. Department of Agriculture, "Mississippi: Its Climate, Soil, Productions, and Agricultural Capabilities," USDA Miscellaneous Special Report, Number 3 (Washington: GPO, 1883).

42 B. H. Hill, "The True Policy of the Southern Planter," Rural Carolinian 5 (April 1874), p. 398.

43 For a more rigorous development of the argument presented in the text, see Roger Ransom and Richard Sutch, "The 'Lock-in' Mechanism and Overproduction of Cotton in the Postbellum South," Agricultural History 49 (April 1975).

44 We recognize that self-sufficiency would not invariably be superior to exploitation by the merchant. However, as we shall elaborate later in this chapter, there is reason to expect that the merchant would pursue his advantage to a point where self-sufficiency would be the farmer's preferred alternative. We interpret the advice of Mr. Hill and his contemporaries as evidence that the merchant's monopoly was, in fact, fully exploited.

45 In fact, a move to self-sufficiency might not be enough to free the farmer completely from the grips of the merchant. If the discussion is extended to include the farm's needs for supplies in addition to foodstuffs, then the farmer must clear enough cash from the sale of cotton to pay off his debt due on the past season's purchases and to purchase all the

supplies required for the coming season. In other words, the cotton crop must finance two years of food deficits and purchased supplies if the farmer is to escape the merchant's control.

46 North Carolina Bureau of Labor Statistics, *Annual Report . . . 1887,* p. 135.

47 *Rural Carolinian* 7 (April 1876), p. 178.

48 Otken, *Ills of the South,* p. 11.

49 Georgia, Department of Agriculture, "Consolidation of the Reports of Crops, &c," (August 15, 1875), p. 9; and idem, "Consolidation of the Reports of Crops, etc., for the Month of August, 1876," p. 2; both in *Publications of the Georgia State Department of Agriculture from September, 1874 to January, 1878* (Atlanta: J. P. Harrison & Co., 1878), volumes 1, 2.

50 Thomas P. Janes, "Report of the Commissioner," in Georgia, Department of Agriculture, *Annual Report . . . 1875,* p. 54.

51 U.S. Congress, Senate, Committee on Agriculture and Forestry, "Present Condition of Cotton-Growers of the United States Compared with Previous Years," *Report of the Committee . . . (February 23, 1895),* Senate, Report Number 986, 53rd Congress, 3rd Session, 2 vols. (Washington: GPO, 1895), 1, p. iii.

52 There were 546,332 farms in the Cotton South in 1880. The estimate that 56 percent of these farms were locked in was obtained by multiplying the fraction of farms under 50 acres (0.782) times the fraction of small farms which had grain deficits assuming a human requirement of 15 bushels per capita (0.713). See Chapter 4, Table 4.3, and Figure 8.5 in this chapter.

53 Brown and Reynolds, "Debt Peonage Re-examined," p. 868. Others emphasizing pecuniary motives to specialize are Robert Higgs, *Competition and Coercion: Blacks in the American Economy 1865–1914* (New York: Cambridge University Press, 1977), and Stephen DeCanio, "Cotton 'Overproduction' in Late Nineteenth-Century Southern Agriculture," *Journal of Economic History* 33 (September 1973), pp. 611–615; idem, *Agriculture in the Postbellum South,* pp. 12–15, 261.

54 *Rural Carolinian* 5 (April 1874), p. 353.

55 *Southern Cultivator* 33 (February 1875), p. 54.

56 *Southern Cultivator* 33 (December 1875), p. 462.

57 *Southern Cultivator* 28 (March 1870), p. 82.

58 *Southern Cultivator* 28 (September 1870), p. 292. The correspondent discusses a hypothetical farm of 200 acres. A switch from all cotton to one-half cotton and one-half corn reduced the labor requirements from fifteen hands to ten hands.

59 *Southern Cultivator* 28 (November 1870), pp. 374–376.

60 We assume that the average yield of corn and cotton per acre is achieved with the resources shifted between crops. Actually a farmer would choose to shift those resources that would maximize the yield difference. Since the marginal yield differential would be equal to or greater than the average differential, our assumption minimizes the gain expected from such a shift. Wright and Kunreuther have suggested that our calculation of the trade-off between cotton and corn is "inappropriate because it ignores the land constraint" ("Cotton, Corn and Risk," footnote 26, p. 538). In note 18 of this chapter we point out what seems to be an error in their argument that there was a macroeconomic land constraint. In any case, in this instance we fail to see the force of Wright and Kunreuther's objection, since our calculation is made for the hypothetical shift of a *marginal* amount of land, labor, and work stock from one crop to another in a *microeconomic* context. Our purpose is merely to demonstrate that a move towards self-sufficiency, if possible, would have been desirable.

61 *Southern Cultivator* 29 (November 1871), p. 410; *Rural Carolinian* 6 (February 1875), p. 231. The cotton prices given below are for cotton ginned and baled.

62 It was common southern practice, not employed elsewhere, to strip the green leaf blades from the growing cornstalks around August to be used as fodder. This practice was "well nigh universal in the leading cotton states" (R. J. Redding, "Culture Experiments on Corn," *Georgia Agricultural Experiment Station Bulletin,* Number 10 [December 1890],

p. 140). According to experiments run at a number of the southern Agricultural Experiment Stations, this practice reduced corn yields between 10 and 18 percent. Nevertheless, the pulling of fodder was practiced apparently because of the shortage of animal feed and the relative amount of free labor time available in August (*Southern Cultivator* 29 [August 1871], p. 283). Moreover, according to the calculations of the Experiment Stations, the value of the fodder collected more than made up for the loss in corn yield. See R. J. Redding, "Culture Experiments," pp. 140–141; idem, "Culture Experiments on Corn," *Georgia Agricultural Experiment Station Bulletin*, Number 15 (December 1891), p. 105; idem, "Fertilizer, Culture and Variety Experiments on Corn," *Georgia Agricultural Experiment Station Bulletin*, Number 23 (December 1893), p. 82; idem, "Fertilizer, Culture & Variety Experiments on Corn," *Georgia Agricultural Experiment Station Bulletin*, Number 27 (December 1894), p. 191; William C. Stubbs, "Report," *North Louisiana Experiment Station Bulletin*, Number 22 (January 1889), p. 310; S. M. Tracy and E. R. Lloyd, "Corn," *Mississippi Agricultural and Mechanical College Experiment Station Bulletin*, Number 33 (March 1895), p. 64.

63 As a southern rule of thumb, each bushel of shelled corn produced as a by-product approximately 10 to 14 pounds of pulled fodder. Numerous citations suggest that the market value of 100 pounds of pulled fodder equaled or exceeded the price of a bushel of corn. Therefore, each bushel of corn produced was accompanied by 10 to 14 percent of a bushel of corn equivalents in the form of fodder (see *Southern Cultivator* 28 [March 1870], p. 82; [September 1870], p. 292; 29 [July 1871], p. 249; [November 1871], p. 409; *Rural Carolinian* 6 [February 1875], p. 232; R. J. Redding, "Corn Culture," *Georgia Agricultural Experiment Station Bulletin*, Number 30 (November 1895), pp. 373–374; idem, *Georgia Agricultural Experiment Station Bulletin*, Number 10 [December 1890], p. 142; Number 15 [December 1891], p. 105; Number 23 [December 1893], p. 82; Number 27 [December 1894], p. 191). This ratio reflects the relative value of fodder as an animal feed relative to corn (Redding, *Georgia Agricultural Experiment Station Bulletin*, Number 30, p. 378; W. A. Henry, *Feeds and Feeding* [Madison: W. A. Henry, 1898], pp. 631–633). The yield of fodder would be considerably increased if the stover were harvested or if livestock were pastured in the cornfield after the harvest. The value of the tops and tassels of the cornstalk was placed at 8 percent of the value of the grain by Redding (*Bulletin*, Number 30, p. 378). This brings the value of the by-products to over 18 percent of the corn. A correspondent of the *Rural Carolinian* noted that the value of blades and shucks was 17.7 percent of the value of the corn grown (6 [February 1875], pp. 232–233).

64 Cotton prices for each state in the Cotton South are available from U.S. Department of Agriculture, Bureau of Agricultural Economics, "Prices of Farm Products Received by Producers," Volume 3, "South Atlantic and South Central States," *USDA Statistical Bulletin*, Number 16 (Washington: GPO, 1927). The prices for each state included in our definition of the Cotton South were weighted by the number of farms in the state. The 1878 prices were reported in gold value and were converted to currency following the practice noted in Chapter 3, Table 3.1.

65 The farmgate prices of corn for each state in the Cotton South were taken from U.S. Department of Agriculture, "Prices of Farm Products," and were weighted by the number of farms in that state.

66 The Georgia data suggest that cash prices for corn sold by merchants were 18 percent above the farmgate price from the previous December (see Chapter 7, Table 7.1). Applying this factor to the established farmgate price (62.3 cents) gives a cash price of 73.5 cents, making 11.7 to 14.0 bushels of corn worth between $8.60 and $10.29. The midpoint yield of 12.85 bushels would have been worth $9.45.

67 The figures presented in this section to support our conclusions are revised from earlier estimates presented in Roger Ransom and Richard Sutch, "The 'Lock-in' Mechanism and Overproduction of Cotton in the Postbellum South," *Agricultural History* 49 (April 1975), pp. 423–424. The adjustments are quantitatively small and do not change the conclusions.

68 In addition to the microeconomic losses discussed in this chapter, there were macroeconomic losses that fell upon the southern economy as a whole. As we shall discuss in

Chapter 9, the increased production of cotton induced by the credit system lowered world cotton prices sufficiently that the additional output of cotton forced upon each farmer did not contribute to his total revenue.

69 Wright and Kunreuther have emphasized the increased risk imposed upon the farmer who was forced to exchange cotton for corn. They go on to argue that this increase in riskiness may have induced some farmers to plant even more cotton than required by the merchant in a hope that a good crop would be sufficiently remunerative to allow them to escape the cycle of annual debt in the future. This suggestion is intriguing. However, at present very little evidence exists that a significantly large class of "gambler farmers" actually arose. See Wright and Kunreuther, "Cotton, Corn and Risk."

Chapter 9. The roots of southern poverty

1 C. H. Tyler Townsend, U.S. Department of Agriculture, Division of Entomology, "Report on the Mexican Cotton-Boll Weevil in Texas (Anthonomus grandis Boh.)," Insect Life 7 (March 1895), p. 303. The first report of the boll weevil in the United States was made by the USDA's Division of Entomology in 1894 (U.S. Department of Agriculture, Division of Entomology [L. O. Howard], "A New Cotton Insect in Texas," Insect Life 7 [December 1894], p. 273).

2 U.S. Department of Agriculture, Yearbook of the United States Department of Agriculture: 1903 (Washington: GPO, 1904), p. 208.

3 The two years, 1899 and 1902, were selected because they were "very similar in amount and distribution of rainfall and in other essential crop conditions." The report notes that "the two regions are close together, and that a careful examination of the records shows that the climatic conditions were remarkably alike in all important respects; but, on the other hand, it is the tendency of planters, as soon as the weevil becomes a serious menance, to devote more of their land to other crops. Accurate figures are not available, but on the whole an allowance of a reduction of acreage of this kind that would account for a 10 percent decrease in production would be ample" (U.S. Department of Agriculture, Yearbook . . . 1903, pp. 207–208).

4 Regional income relatives in 1900 are given by Richard A. Easterlin, "Regional Income Trends, 1840–1959," in Seymour E. Harris, ed. American Economic History (New York: McGraw-Hill, 1961), Table 1, p. 535. See Appendix F for a fuller discussion of these figures.

5 The economic analysis sketched below was inspired by "market signaling" models proposed by George Akerloff, "The Market for Lemons," Quarterly Journal of Economics 84 (August 1970); Kenneth J. Arrow, "Models of Discrimination," in A. H. Pascal, ed. Racial Discrimination in Economic Life (Lexington: D. C. Heath, 1972); and A. Michael Spence, Market Signalling: Informational Transfer in Hiring and Related Screening Processes (Cambridge: Harvard University Press, 1974). Also see Roger Ransom and Richard Sutch, "The Ex-Slave in the Post-Bellum South: A Study of the Economic Impact of Racism in a Market Environment," Journal of Economic History 33 (March 1973).

6 On the belief that a ladder existed in midwestern farming, which allowed farmers to climb from tenant to owner, see Allan G. Bogue, From Prairie to Corn Belt: Farming on the Illinois and Iowa Prairies in the Nineteenth Century (Chicago: University of Chicago Press, 1963), pp. 62–64.

7 The differences in the value of implements per acre reported between owner-operated farms and tenanted farms may be exaggerated by the census statistics. Some of the implements used on tenant farms may have gone unreported, since they were supplied by the landowner. Tenants who were responding to the census taker may have forgotten to report the value of such implements. This effect, if it does distort the between-tenure comparison, should not bias the racial comparison made in the text.

8 For more detail on fertilizer use by tenure, race, and farm size see Ransom and Sutch, "Ex-Slave," Table 2, p. 141.

9 See our discussion in Chapter 5 on labor intensity with various forms of tenure. Table 9.6

also provides evidence of another type of discrimination against black workers. Notice that where white sharecroppers had less land to work per laborer than did white cash renters, the reverse was true when comparing black sharecroppers with black renters. Since landowners believed that blacks required close supervision, black sharecroppers were likely to be more closely supervised than white sharecroppers. As a result black sharecroppers required a higher land-labor ratio relative to renting (we noted this point in Chapter 5). The white sharecropper, on the other hand, was typically under less supervision, and the landlord restricted the land-labor ratio granted white sharecroppers relative to white renters accordingly. These small differences in labor intensity between the forms of tenure were necessary to equalize returns to both landowners and labor; but, as we saw in Chapter 5, they are also manifestations of the inefficiency introduced into the system by the fixed-share contract.

10 Lewis H. Blair, *A Southern Prophecy: The Prosperity of the South Dependent Upon the Elevation of the Negro*, edited with an introduction by C. Vann Woodward (Boston: Little, Brown & Co., 1964), p. 26, originally published in 1889.

11 In the 1850s England imported 72 percent of its cotton from the United States; in 1860 England supplied 77 percent of its needs with American cotton. In the decade spanning 1875–1884, two-thirds of England's cotton imports were from the United States (Gavin Wright, "Cotton Competition and the Post-Bellum Recovery of the American South," *Journal of Economic History* 34 [September 1974], Table 1, p. 611).

12 In other words, the demand for cotton exhibited approximately unitary elasticity (Wright, "Cotton Competition," Table 6, p. 629; pp. 626–630).

13 Wright has estimated that the elasticity of demand for American cotton rose from approximately 1.0 before the Civil War to approximately 1.5 after the war (Wright, "Cotton Competition," Table 6, p. 629, 630). Any elasticity greater than 1.0 would imply that increases in output would raise total revenue.

14 The recognition by agriculturalists in the South that the nature of the demand for cotton implied a rough constancy of the gross value of cotton output also tended to work against efforts to enhance the productivity of labor in cotton production. The various state departments of agriculture in the South saw little reason to push experiments in cotton productivity. In marked contrast to the zeal with which agricultural experiment stations in the North and West promoted their major crops, those of the southern states were more interested in promoting diversification than in devising superior techniques for cultivating cotton.

15 The wholesale price of cotton for 1867–1895 comes from James L. Watkins, U.S. Department of Agriculture, "Production and Price of Cotton for 100 Years," *USDA Miscellaneous Bulletin*, Number 9 (Washington: GPO, 1895), pp. 11–14. Watkins's price is the average price per pound of middling upland cotton in New York for the commercial year ending August 31 of the year following the date given. For the years 1896–1914 the wholesale spot price (New York, upland middling) comes from U.S. Bureau of the Census, *Historical Statistics of the United States, Colonial Times to 1957* (Washington: GPO, 1960), Series E-104, p. 123. The bureau used Watkins's figures to extend this post-1890 series back to 1821. The cotton prices were deflated using the Warren-Pearson-BLS wholesale price index of all commodities (George F. Warren and Frank A. Pearson, *Prices* [New York: John Wiley & Sons, 1933], Table 3, p. 26). The terms of trade were adjusted to set 1910–1914 equal to 100. The five-year moving average is centered on the year given.

16 See Wright, "Cotton Competition," for a discussion of this expansion and for econometric estimates of its magnitude. Wright also points out that the expansion of cotton demand in the postwar era was less rapid than it had been in the antebellum era.

17 In principle, productivity per worker could be increased without an increase in the land-labor ratio by increasing the ratio of capital to labor (or the ratio of some other nonland input, such as fertilizer, to labor). In practice, however, the ability to base a continuous growth of agricultural productivity on increases in capital per acre without changing the quantity of human effort expended per acre is limited. Even the most intensively cultivated acre has an upper limit to the quantity of output it can produce. This limit is fixed by the

biology of the plant life cultivated and the amount of sunlight that falls upon the field. If this limit has been reached, output per worker could be further increased only by increasing the land-labor ratio. In practice, of course, this biological limit is not typically encountered, since diminishing returns to the expansion of the capital-land ratio would set in well before it is reached.

18 Lance Davis offers a discussion of the trends in regional rates of return in financial markets and of the South's failure to attract northern capital despite persistently high interest rates ("The Investment Market, 1870–1914: The Evolution of a National Market," *Journal of Economic History* 25 [September 1965], pp. 388–392). Robert Fogel and Jack Rutner have estimated that the physical rate of return produced by agricultural capital in the South was approximately twice that earned in the North ("The Efficiency of Federal Land Policy, 1850–1900: A Report of Some Provisional Findings," in William O. Aydelotte, Allan G. Bogue, and Robert W. Fogel, eds. *The Dimensions of Quantitative Research in History* [Princeton: Princeton University Press, 1972], Table 4, p. 398).

19 The figures come from William Vickery, "The Economics of the Negro Migration, 1900–1960" (Ph.D. dissertation, University of Chicago, December 1969). Nonwhite includes American Indians and Asians; only native-born nonwhites are included. The non-South is defined as the United States less the Five Cotton States (South Carolina, Georgia, Alabama, Mississippi, and Louisiana) and less Virginia, West Virginia, North Carolina, Florida, Kentucky, Tennessee, Arkansas, Oklahoma, and Texas.

20 We have drawn upon C. Vann Woodward for the details presented in this paragraph, and specifically for the quotation from the South Carolina law (*The Strange Career of Jim Crow*, revised edition [New York: Oxford University Press, 1966], pp. 97–109).

Appendix A. Construction of income and welfare estimates: 1859–1899

1 See Appendix G, Section 3, for details and source references to the Parker-Gallman sample. A distribution by state of the slaveholders contained in the sample is given in Richard Sutch, "The Breeding of Slaves for Sale and the Westward Expansion of Slavery, 1850–1860," in Stanley L. Engerman and Eugene D. Genovese, eds., *Race and Slavery in the Western Hemisphere: Quantitative Studies* (Princeton: Princeton University Press, 1975), Table 8, p. 187.

2 There are 144 such farms, with 12,314 slaves, included in the sample.

3 Incidentally, it is interesting to note that the large farms produced more staple output per slave than did all farms, but considerably less food (other than corn). Large plantations apparently produced significant surpluses of corn after allowances for animal feed are subtracted, while slave farms as a group appear to have had a corn deficit if animals were fed according to the requirements we suggest.

4 Edgar W. Martin, *The Standard of Living in 1860: American Consumption Levels on the Eve of the Civil War* (Chicago: University of Chicago Press, 1942), pp. 423–427.

5 Lewis Cecil Gray, *History of Agriculture in the Southern United States to 1860*, 2 vols. (Washington: Carnegie Institution, 1933), 1, p. 540; Martin, *Standard of Living in 1860*, pp. 128–131; Frederick Law Olmsted, *A Journey in the Seaboard Slave States* (New York: Dix & Edwards, 1856), pp. 17, 321, 330, 335, 384, 385, 392, 575; idem, *A Journey Through Texas* (New York: Dix, Edwards & Co., 1857), pp. 47, 48, 60; and idem, *A Journey in the Back Country* (New York: Mason Brothers, 1860), p. 233.

6 This implies a value of housing services for slaves of $1.37 per slave (see Table A.2). Robert Fogel and Stanley Engerman put the value of shelter (and fuel) at $6.95 per slave on farms with fifty-one or more slaves (*Time on the Cross*, 2 vols. [Boston: Little, Brown & Co., 1974], 2, p. 117). However, we believe this number is greatly exaggerated. Fogel and Engerman's estimate of the value of shelter is keyed to their estimate of the amount of food consumed by slaves, which Richard Sutch has demonstrated is exaggerated ("The Treatment Received by American Slaves: A Critical Review of the Evidence Presented in *Time on the Cross*," *Explorations in Economic History* 12 [October 1975], pp. 360–383). Fur-

thermore, it is based upon the fraction of income spent on housing in the "budgets of Massachusetts laborers in 1875" (Fogel and Engerman, *Time on the Cross*, 2, p. 117). Since there is no reason to expect this source to provide reliable estimates of the housing *provided* slaves, we have made our own crude estimate. If Fogel and Engerman's figures were credited (and assuming a depreciation rate of 6.7 percent and an interest rate of 7 percent), they would suggest that the value of slave housing was $50.73 per slave. Since they report there was an average of 5.2 persons per slave cabin on large farms, their estimate would value the slave cabin (and the woodlot that provided the fuel) at $263.80, 30 percent higher than the value we estimate for a white slaveowner's house.

7 Gray, *History of Agriculture*, 1, pp. 540, 562–563; Martin, *Standard of Living in 1860*, pp. 123–134; and Sutch, "Treatment," pp. 353–357.

8 Fogel and Engerman, *Time on the Cross*, 2, Table B.21, p. 135; equation 6.17, p. 143.

9 Fogel and Engerman, *Time on the Cross*, 2, p. 143.

10 Alfred H. Conrad and John R. Meyer, "The Economics of Slavery in the Ante Bellum South," *Journal of Political Economy* 66 (April 1958); Edward Saraydar, "A Note on the Profitability of Ante Bellum Slavery," *Southern Economic Journal* 30 (April 1964); Richard Sutch, "The Profitability of Slavery – Revisited," *Southern Economic Journal* 31 (April 1965); James D. Foust and Dale E. Swan, "Productivity and Profitability of Antebellum Slave Labor: A Micro-Approach," *Agricultural History* 44 (January 1970).

11 The most recent estimate is that by Foust and Swan ("Productivity and Profitability," Table 3, p. 51), who based their figures on Sutch's estimate for 1849. Sutch ("Profitability") drew his estimates from Saraydar ("Note"), who had revised Conrad and Meyer's figures ("Economics of Slavery"). Conrad and Meyer drew their support from scattered comments in Gray (*History of Agriculture*). The only apparently independent estimate of capital costs is that of Fogel and Engerman, who estimate the value of total capital in 1859 at $444.60 per slave (*Time on the Cross*, 2, Table B.11, pp. 78,79). However, they do not explain how this number was defined or calculated (Fogel and Engerman, *Time on the Cross*, 2, pp. 132 – 133).

12 Conrad and Meyer, "Economics of Slavery," p. 101.

13 Fogel and Engerman's argument that Conrad and Meyer's interest rate should be increased by 30 to 60 percent to compensate for the risk involved in cotton planting, while well taken in context, is not relevant here (*Time on the Cross*, 2, p. 70). We wish to measure only capital's share calculated at its opportunity cost, not the return to risk taking. On a southern plantation the "return to risk bearing" should be credited to the entrepreneur, not to capital per se. We include this amount in the total of income exploited from the slaves. This is proper since, once free, black farmers would have to bear the risks of southern agriculture themselves and they would earn the "returns to risk bearing." To suggest that exploited income justly belonged to the slaveowner because he bore the risks and responsibilities of agriculture overlooks the fact that these slaves were not free to assume those risks and responsibilities (and earn the associated income) themselves.

14 Conrad and Meyer, "Economics of Slavery," Table 5, p. 104.

15 Saraydar, "Note," p. 214. This figure is based on the assumption that one overseer would be needed for every 50 hands or one for every 100 slaves. In the South as a whole there were 110 slaves per overseer (Sutch, "Treatment," p. 352).

16 There seems to be almost unanimous agreement that this was the standard ration for slaves. See Ulrich Bonnell Phillips, *American Negro Slavery* (New York: D. Appleton & Co., 1918), pp. 265–266, 277, 279; Charles S. Sydnor, *Slavery in Mississippi* (New York: Appleton-Century, 1933), pp. 31–32; Rosser H. Taylor, "Feeding Slaves," *Journal of Negro History* 9 (April 1924), pp. 139–143; Gray, *History of Agriculture*, 1, p. 563; Kenneth M. Stampp, *The Peculiar Institution: Slavery in the Ante-bellum South* (New York: Alfred A. Knopf, 1956), pp. 283–289; Sam Bowers Hilliard, *Hog Meat and Hoecake: Food Supply in the Old South, 1840–1860* (Carbondale: Southern Illinois University Press, 1972), pp. 104–105, 157, 272; and Sutch, "Treatment," pp. 360–361.

17 The $6 price is typical of wholesale prices quoted for Cincinnati during the late 1850s

(Thomas Senior Berry, *Western Prices Before 1861: A Study of the Cincinnati Market* [Cambridge: Harvard University Press, 1943], Table 24, p. 571). We make no allowance for the cost of curing the pork or milling the corn. These tasks were typically performed by slaves on the farm. Since we have not included the value added by this activity in the total output given in Table A.1, it would be inappropriate to include these charges in the cost of the slave ration. Our use of wholesale prices already introduces an upward bias to the cost of provisioning the slaves, since the wholesale prices (in Cincinnati and New Orleans) exceeded the farmgate prices actually received by planters who sold surplus pork and corn.

18 Gray reports that in 1855 the cost of food, "everything being purchased," provided slave hands hired to work on the construction of Virginia canals was $25 per year (*History of Agriculture*, 1, p. 544). Since we are estimating only that fraction of the food produced on the plantation, this figure appears to be consistent with the one reported in the text.

19 Fogel and Engerman, *Time on the Cross*, 2, pp. 98, 117.

20 They report the diet in their Table B.13 (Fogel and Engerman, *Time on the Cross*, 2, p. 97). Elsewhere they evaluate the cost of that diet "at farm prices" as $21.25, however, this figure includes an allowance for "omitted foods" (that is, foods purchased or omitted from the census tabulations) of 19.6 percent (ibid., pp. 117, 97).

21 Sutch, "Treatment."

22 This figure is meant to include the food grown by slaves in plots they were allowed to cultivate on their own. The output of these slave plots was included in total output in Table A.1 and in Fogel and Engerman's estimate of plantation-produced food. Note that Fogel and Engerman's estimate of per capita income of slaves involves double counting of the output produced on slave plots (*Time on the Cross*, 2, p. 159).

23 Gray, *History of Agriculture*, 1, p. 544.

24 Eugene D. Genovese, "The Medical and Insurance Costs of Slave Holding in the Cotton Belt," *Journal of Negro History* 45 (July 1963), p. 155.

25 See Stampp, *Peculiar Institution*, p. 288; Sutch, "Treatment," p. 364; and Olmsted, *Journey in the Back Country*, p. 65.

26 Conrad and Meyer, "Economics of Slavery"; Yasukichi Yasuba, "The Profitability and Viability of Plantation Slavery in the United States," *Economic Studies Quarterly* 12 (September 1961); Robert Evans, Jr., "The Economics of American Negro Slavery," in Universities-National Bureau Committee for Economic Research, *Aspects of Labor Economics* (Princeton: Princeton University Press, 1962); Saraydar, "Note"; Sutch, "Profitability"; Eugene D. Genovese, *The Political Economy of Slavery: Studies in the Economy and Society of the Slave South* (New York: Pantheon, 1965); Foust and Swan, "Productivity and Profitability"; N. G. Butlin, *Ante-bellum Slavery: Critique of a Debate* (Canberra: Department of Economic History, Australian National University, 1971); Robert W. Fogel and Stanley L. Engerman, "The Economics of Slavery," in *The Reinterpretation of American Economic History* (New York: Harper & Row, 1971); and idem, *Time on the Cross*.

27 Alfred Conrad et al., "Slavery as an Obstacle to Economic Growth in the United States: A Panel Discussion," *Journal of Economic History* 27 (December 1967). While there still is a good deal of interest in this issue, it should be emphasized that neither a proof nor a disproof that slavery was profitable in any given year would have the significance that Conrad and Meyer originally thought it had. Sutch pointed out that the *viability* of slavery was more relevant than the *profitability* to the central concern of the debate (Sutch, "Profitability," pp. 365–366). For a fuller discussion of this issue, see Stanley Engerman, "The Effects of Slavery on the Southern Economy," *Explorations in Entrepreneurial History*, 2nd series, 4 (winter 1967), pp. 314–317; and Conrad et al., "Slavery as an Obstacle," pp. 278–280.

28 This estimate is based upon the age and sex composition of the slave population reported on the farms in the Parker-Gallman sample and the average price of slaves for each age and sex cohort relative to the prices of male slaves, twenty to twenty-nine years old. It is keyed to an 1859 price for prime-age field hands of $1,690. The relative price of slaves for each age

and sex cohort relative to that for prime-aged males was based on New Orleans data provided by Stanley Engerman and Robert Fogel (for more details see Robert W. Fogel and Stanley L. Engerman, "The Market Evaluation of Human Capital: The Case of Slavery," paper delivered at the Annual Cliometrics Conference, University of Wisconsin, Madison, April 1972; and idem, *Time on the Cross*, 1, pp. 72–76, and 2, pp. 79–80). The benchmark price of slaves is taken from Conrad and Meyer ("Economics of Slavery," p. 170), but is based on a study of Georgia and New Orleans slave prices by Ulrich B. Phillips (*Life and Labor in the Old South* [Boston: Little, Brown & Co., 1963], originally published in 1929, p. 177; also see idem, "The Economic Cost of Slaveholding in the Cotton Belt," *Political Science Quarterly* 20 [June 1905], p. 267). A rough adjustment for the premiums due on skilled slaves was made by assuming that 10 percent of the adult male population and 2 percent of the adult female population possessed skills that commanded an average premium of 60 percent. Fogel and Engerman report that the premiums paid for blacksmiths varied from 59 to 90 percent, depending upon age; the price of carpenters ranged from 39 to 73 percent above their field hand counterparts; and the price for cooks exceeded that for female hands by 48 to 190 percent ("Market Evaluation of Human Capital"). See Appendix B for our discussion of the proportion of skilled slaves in the South.

29 Sutch, "Profitability," p. 367.

30 Foust and Swan, "Productivity and Profitability," Table 6, p. 55. Conrad and Meyer ("Economics of Slavery") and Saraydar ("Note") did not make estimates of the rate of return for 1859. Sutch ("Profitability") reports an average rate of return for the South in 1859 (with 10-cent cotton) of 6.3 percent, but as Foust and Swan note, his rate is biased downward by an error in estimating capital costs in that year. Evans and Fogel and Engerman have estimated a 10 percent rate of return "on average" for the end of the 1850s (Evans, "The Economics of Slavery," p. 217; Fogel and Engerman, *Time on the Cross*, 1, p. 70, and 2, p. 78). However, their estimates are likely to be biased upward relative to the others by a number of oversights and inadequacies of their data. Specifically, both estimates exaggerate the typical life-span of the average slave and neglect to provide adequately for the dependent slave population, primarily the children and the superannuated.

31 In Chapter 4 and 5 we discuss in greater detail the relative economic position of differing tenure and labor arrangements following emancipation.

32 These output estimates are based on the value of farm output reported to the census. The instructions asked for the "estimated value of all farm production (sold, consumed, or on hand) for 1879." We interpret this figure to *include* the value of feed grains produced on the farm and fed to animals. If this interpretation is incorrect, our estimate of farm output and labor's share will be too low.

33 See U.S. Census Office, Twelfth Census [1900], *Census Reports: Twelfth Census . . . 1900: Agriculture* (Washington: GPO, 1902), Part I, Table 14, pp. 172–185. The figures reported in the text are only for farms that reported the value of buildings and represent a weighted average of the reports from eleven southern states. The weights used were the percentage of farms in our 1880 sample of the Cotton South that was located in each state.

34 The census in both years reported the total value of farmlands and buildings per farm. A general decline in both building values and land values seems to be suggested by general price movements in the United States. This implies that a farm dwelling of a quality comparable to the average 1900 black tenant's home would have been valued at somewhat more than $80. Offsetting this, however, is the inclusion of outbuildings in the 1900 data, which while undoubtedly of little value, would, nevertheless, exaggerate the value of the tenant's home. Another possible offsetting consideration is the observation by Martin L. Primack that the ratio of the value of buildings to land rose between 1880 and 1890 in South Carolina ("Farm Construction as a Use of Farm Labor in the United States, 1850–1960," *Journal of Economic History* 25 [March 1965], Table 1, p. 115). Primack's argument, we feel, has less force when applied to black tenant farms than to all farms in the state. Nevertheless, there may have been some tendency for the real value of tenant's dwellings to have risen between 1880 and 1900. For these reasons, we have reduced our estimate of the value of tenant's dwelling from the $80 reported at the turn of the century to $75 in 1880.

35 The number of family members per household was 5.24 for all tenants and 5.17 for sharecroppers in our 1880 sample of black-operated farms. We assume no need to adjust the figure on the value of housing for a change in price levels. See our discussion of the cost of living in 1859 and 1879.

36 However, note that we have not made a deduction for purchased feed. In Chapter 8 we argue that many tenant farmers were not self-sufficient in grain and would have to purchase corn. On the other hand, only the feed for work animals is an input to the production process. Our estimates suggest that most farms were able to feed their working stock. The food deficits arose because the farms were unable to provide for the swine and human requirements for grain. Also note that on sharecropped farms, the feed for work animals was the responsibility of the landlord (see the discussion of tenure in Chapter 5).

37 Each bushel of corn fed to a hog produced approximately 15 pounds of pork (see Appendix E, note 13). The manuscript census of slaughterhouses in 1879 reported the average price paid for swine was 4.314 cents per pound of live weight. Since the dressing yield for swine is 76.1 percent (U.S. Department of Agriculture, Economic Research Service, "Conversion Factors and Weights and Measures for Agricultural Commodities and Their Products," *USDA Statistical Bulletin*, Number 362 [Washington: GPO, 1965], p. 9), the farmgate price of pork implied would be 5.669 cents a pound. The swine slaughtered in 1879 were fed on corn produced in 1878 and 1879. The weighted average farmgate price of corn for those two years averaged over the Five Cotton States was 64.0 cents per bushel (see the references for corn production and prices given in notes 39 and 40 of Appendix F). Therefore, 1 bushel of corn could be converted into 11.3 pounds of pork at market prices. Since home production yielded 15 pounds per bushel the difference (3.7 pounds or 25 percent) must represent the value added in pork production.

38 The 118 slaughterhouses that reported the number, gross weight, and price paid for 25,450 swine to the census in 1879 suggest an average live weight of 185 pounds per animal and a farmgate price of $7.98. See Appendix G, Section 3, for a description of the sample drawn from the manuscript census of slaughterhouses.

39 The average slaughter ratio in 1879 was probably the same as antebellum practice, the best estimate of which seems to be 0.83 (Fogel and Engerman, *Time on the Cross*, 2, p. 95; Sutch, "Treatment," pp. 369–370).

40 These figures on value added in pork production imply that 9.4 bushels of corn were fed each hog during its lifetime, or 7.8 bushels per year. This estimate is somewhat above Sutch's figure for corn consumption per hog in the antebellum period of 7.0 bushels per year ("Treatment," p. 379). Had we used that standard, the value of corn fed to hogs would have been $5.40 per animal, value added would have been $2.58 per head, and the contribution to income $10.55 per tenant farm. Labor's share would in that case have been 56.1 rather than 55.8 percent.

41 See William Dosite Postell, *The Health of Slaves on Southern Plantations* (Baton Rouge: Louisiana State University Press, 1951), p. 39; Ralph Betts Flanders, *Plantation Slavery in Georgia* (Chapel Hill: University of North Carolina Press, 1933), pp. 160–161; Charles S. Davis, *The Cotton Kingdom in Alabama* (Montgomery: Alabama State Department of Archives and History, 1939), pp. 84–85; and James Benson Sellers, *Slavery in Alabama* (University: University of Alabama Press, 1950).

42 Joseph D. Weeks, U.S. Census Office, Tenth Census [1880], *Report on the Statistics of Wages in the Manufacturing Industries; with Supplementary Reports on the Average Retail Prices of Necessities of Life . . .* (Washington: GPO, 1886).

43 Ethel D. Hoover, "Retail Prices after 1850," in National Bureau of Economic Research, *Trends in the American Economy in the Nineteenth Century* (Princeton: Princeton University Press, 1960), p. 142. If anything, this underestimates the decline in the cost of clothing purchased by black laborers, since prices of the cheaper grades of cloth fell more rapidly than did the overall index. For example, in 1879–1880 the price of bleached shirting was 83.9 percent of its 1859–1860 level and prints were only 64.8 percent as expensive (pp. 172–173).

44 Hoover, "Retail Prices," pp. 142, 176.

Appendix B. Occupational distribution of southern blacks: 1860, 1870, 1890

1 Southern free blacks, a comparatively tiny minority in the Cotton States, did have their occupations recorded by the censuses of 1850 and 1860. But neither Census Office published an occupational distribution that separated the free blacks from the white population. An important beginning on the study of the occupations of southern free blacks, employing the manuscript census returns, has been made by Ira Berlin, *Slaves Without Masters: The Free Negro in the Antebellum South* (New York: Pantheon, 1974), Chapter 7.

2 Robert W. Fogel and Stanley L. Engerman have made use of probate records to estimate an occupational distribution for slaves *(Time on the Cross,* 2 vols. [Boston: Little Brown & Co., 1974], 1, p. 39; 2, pp. 37–40). However, their computation was marred by calculation errors and other difficulties that invalidate their results. See Herbert Gutman and Richard Sutch, "Sambo Makes Good, or Were Slaves Imbued with the Protestant Work Ethic?" in Paul A. David et al, *Reckoning with Slavery: A Critical Study in the Quantitative History of Slavery* (New York: Oxford University Press, 1976), pp. 74–89.

3 U.S. Census Office, Seventh Census [1850], *The Seventh Census of the United States: 1850* (Washington: GPO, 1853), p. xxxix.

4 See Chapter 3, note 54, for references to more extensive discussion of the 1870 undercount.

5 "Colored" workers included "persons of negro descent, Chinese, Japanese, and civilized Indians" (U.S. Census Office, Eleventh Census [1890], *Report on the Population of the United States . . . 1890,* Part 2 [Washington: GPO, 1897], p. 520).

6 Note that the tabulations made by the census are not entirely satisfactory for categorizing workers as low-skilled. For example, employees of steam railroad companies included skilled as well as unskilled workers. The occupational group of nurses and midwives undoubtedly included "nurses" who would more properly be regarded as servants than professionals.

Appendix C. Estimates of labor supplied by slave and free labor

1 U.S. Census Office, Ninth Census [1870], *The Statistics of the Population of the United States* (Washington: GPO, 1872).

2 Georgia, Department of Agriculture, *Annual Report . . . for the Year 1875* (Atlanta: J. H. Estill, 1876), p. 109.

3 Ibid., p. 88.

4 Roger L. Ransom and Richard Sutch, "The Ex-Slave in the Post-Bellum South: A Study of the Economic Impact of Racism in a Market Environment," *Journal of Economic History* 33 (March 1973), Table 3, p. 143.

5 Lewis Cecil Gray, *History of Agriculture in the Southern United States to 1860,* 2 vols. (Washington: Carnegie Institution, 1933), 1, pp. 556–557.

6 Our source for the estimated number of days lost due to illness is Robert William Fogel and Stanley L. Engerman, *Time on the Cross,* 2 vols. (Boston: Little, Brown & Co., 1974), 1, p. 126; 2, pp. 100–101. That theirs is a conservative estimate is argued by Richard Sutch ("Care and Feeding of Slaves," in Paul A. David et al. *Reckoning with Slavery: A Critical Study in the Quantitative History of American Negro Slavery* [New York: Oxford University Press, 1976], pp. 282–283).

7 Gray, *History of Agriculture,* 1, p. 562.

8 Averaging men and women together, our estimates put the adult work year at 265–287 days. Fogel and Engerman, certainly the most sanguine interpreters of slavery, put the adult work year at 265–275 days *(Time on the Cross,* 1, p. 208).

9 Gray, *History of Agriculture,* 1, p. 549.

10 F. W. Loring and C. F. Atkinson, *Cotton Culture and the South Considered with Reference to Emigration* (Boston: A. Williams & Co., 1869); *Rural Carolinian* 1 (April 1870), p. 407.

11 Georgia, Department of Agriculture, *Annual Report . . . 1875,* pp. 87–89.

12 Charles E. Seagrave, "The Southern Negro Agricultural Worker: 1850–1870" (Ph.D. thesis, Stanford University, 1971), pp. 43, 45.

13 Eugene D. Genovese, *Roll, Jordan, Roll: The World the Slaves Made* (New York: Pantheon, 1974), p. 60.

14 Gray, *History of Agriculture*, 1, p. 557.

15 Fogel and Engerman, *Time on the Cross*, 1, p. 208.

16 Seagrave, "Negro Agricultural Worker: 1850–1870," p. 103.

17 Gray, *History of Agriculture*, 1, pp. 548–549.

18 U.S. Department of Agriculture, *Report of the Commissioner of Agriculture for the Year 1867* (Washington: GPO, 1868), p. 416.

19 Ibid., p. 416.

20 U.S. Census Office, Eighth Census [1860], *Population of the United States in 1860* (Washington: GPO, 1864), pp. 616–623.

Appendix D. Calculation of interest charged for credit implicit in the dual-price system

1 Georgia, Department of Agriculture, "Consolidation of the Reports of Crops, etc., for the Month of June, 1878," *Circular*, Number 55, p. 11, in *Publications of the Georgia State Department of Agriculture*, Volume 4, "For the Year 1878" (Atlanta: Jas. P. Harrison & Co., 1879).

2 We have used simple interest in these computations because it is conventional to do so. Continuous compounding of interest at a given rate would increase the charge for credit over simple interest, since interest would then be paid on interest as well as the principal. In the example given the compound rate of interest would be 86.3 percent.

3 Georgia, Department of Agriculture, *Circular*, Number 55, p. 11. Emphasis in the original.

4 Twice before the department had asked its correspondents what annual rate of interest was paid by those purchasing on credit. In 1875 the average of the responses was 44 percent, and in 1876 the average reported was 62 percent. See Georgia, Department of Agriculture, "Consolidation of the Reports of Crops, &c. [August 15, 1875]," *Circular*, Number 16, p. 9, and "Consolidation of the Reports of Crops, etc., for the Month of August, 1876," *Circular*, Number 30, p. 2, both in *Publications of the Georgia State Department of Agriculture*, Volume 1, "September, 1874, to January, 1876," and Volume 2, "For the Year 1876" (Atlanta: James P. Harrison & Co., 1878).

5 In 1876 over 200 responses were obtained. In some counties as many as five respondents were noted. Georgia, Department of Agriculture, *Circular*, Number 30, pp. 4–9.

6 Georgia, Department of Agriculture, "Supplemental Report . . . for the Year 1882," *Circular*, new series, Number 34, p. 11, in *Publications of the Georgia State Department of Agriculture*, Volume 8, "For the Year 1882" (Atlanta: Jas. P. Harrison & Co., 1883).

7 A May price survey was also conducted in 1892. The simple averages of the regional figures published for that year are 66 cents on cash sales and 84 cents on credit per bushel of corn. These prices imply a 54.5 percent rate of interest. Georgia, Department of Agriculture, "Crop Report for the Month of May, 1892," *Circular*, fourth series, Number 1, p. 37, in *Publications of the Georgia State Department of Agriculture*, Volume 18, "For the Year 1892" (Atlanta: Geo. W. Harrison, 1892).

8 Georgia, Department of Agriculture, "Supplemental Report – 1879," *Circular*, new series, Number 4, pp. 6–7, in *Publications of the Georgia State Department of Agriculture*, Volume 5, "For the Year 1879" (Atlanta: Jas. P. Harrison & Co., 1880).

9 Georgia, Department of Agriculture, "Supplemental Report . . . for the Year 1883," *Circular*, new series, Number 49, p. 6, in *Publications of the Georgia State Department of Agriculture*, Volume 9, "For the Year 1883" (Atlanta: Jas. P. Harrison & Co., 1884).

10 Georgia, Department of Agriculture, "Supplemental Report . . . for the Year 1885," *Circular*, new series, Number 74, p. 5, in *Publications of the Georgia State Department of Agriculture*, Volume 11, "For the Year 1885" (Atlanta: Jas. P. Harrison & Co., 1885), Part 1.

11 The interest rates of Table D.2 differ from those presented by Mathew Hammond, whose numbers are based on the same sources, because of rounding and arithmetic errors evident in Hammond's calculations. Mathew B. Hammond, *The Cotton Industry* (New York: American Economic Association and Macmillan & Co., 1897), p. 153.

12 C. Vann Woodward, *Origins of the New South, 1877–1913* (Baton Rouge: Louisiana State University Press, 1951), pp. 184–185.

13 There was apparently an attempt to organize a price-fixing combination of wholesale grocery houses in 1903, but before that date there is no evidence of a lack of competition. See Glenn N. Sisk, "The Wholesale Commission Business in the Alabama Black Belt, 1875–1917," *Journal of Farm Economics* 38 (August 1956), p. 800.

14 Sisk, "Wholesale Commission Business," p. 801. After a price-fixing agreement arranged in 1903, rates apparently rose to 10 to 15 percent (p. 802). In another article Sisk reports that "wholesale commission merchants in Selma charged one dollar to $1.50 on each ten dollars worth of merchandise advanced by them, unless a bale of cotton was delivered to them for each ten dollars advanced; then a commission of 2¹/₂ per cent was charged for selling the cotton." It is unclear from the context to which date these practices refer. Glenn N. Sisk, "Rural Merchandising in the Alabama Black Belt, 1875–1917," *Journal of Farm Economics* 37 (November 1955), p. 708. Thomas D. Clark reports that a drug and notions wholesaler made no charge for credit but gave a 3 percent discount from net for settlement within ninety days ("The Furnishing and Supply System in Southern Agriculture since 1865," *Journal of Southern History* 12 [February 1946], footnote 13, pp. 30–31).

15 See Chapter 7, note 7.

16 Georgia, Department of Agriculture, "Supplemental Report . . . for the Year 1887," *Circular*, new series, Number 100, p. 5, in *Publications of the Georgia State Department of Agriculture*, Volume 13, "For the Year 1887" (Atlanta: Constitution Book & Job, 1887). Also see idem, *Circular* 55, p. 11. The suggestion that risk of default loomed large has also been made by a number of historians. See Clark, "Furnishing and Supply System," p. 30, and Woodward, *Origins of the New South*, p. 184.

17 Clark, "Furnishing and Supply System," p. 28.

Appendix E. Calculation of food residuals on southern farms: 1880

1 Roger Ransom and Richard Sutch, "Debt Peonage in the Cotton South After the Civil War," *Journal of Economic History* 32 (September 1972); Robert E. Gallman, "Self-Sufficiency in the Cotton Economy of the Ante-Bellum South," *Agricultural History* 44 (January 1970); Raymond C. Battalio and John Kagel, "The Structure of Antebellum Southern Agriculture: South Carolina, A Case Study," *Agricultural History* 44 (January 1970); William K. Hutchinson and Samuel H. Williamson, "The Self-Sufficiency of the Antebellum South: Estimates of the Food Supply," *Journal of Economic History* 31 (September 1971).

2 We base this assertion on a review of available studies of the postbellum southern diet. In particular, see Sam Bowers Hilliard, *Hog Meat and Hoecake: Food Supply in the Old South, 1840–1860* (Carbondale: Southern Illinois University Press, 1972). Numerous diet studies by Atwater and his associates in the 1890s provide more detail. See, for example, W. O. Atwater and Charles D. Woods, U.S. Department of Agriculture, Office of Experiment Stations, "Dietary Studies with Reference to the Food of the Negro in Alabama in 1895 and 1896," *USDA Experiment Stations Bulletin*, Number 38 (Washington: GPO, 1897). A further study of the diets of Negro tenants in the 1920s was made by Dorothy Dickins, "A Nutrition Investigation of Negro Tenants in the Yazoo Mississippi Delta," *Mississippi Agricultural and Mechanics College Experiment Station Bulletin*, Number 254 (August 1928).

3 The percentages reflect the lowest conceivable requirements. A discussion of the seed requirements for cowpeas is in Richard Sutch, "The Treatment Received by American Slaves: A Critical Review of the Evidence Presented in *Time on the Cross*," *Explorations in Economic History* 12 (October 1975), p. 376. Seed requirements per acre for beans are found in references cited in notes *a* and *b* of Table E.1. A report to the *Southern Cultivator* in 1870 claimed that 5 percent of the potato crop was needed for seed, which suggests our figure is quite conservative (*Southern Cultivator* 28 [June 1870], p. 184).

4 U.S. Department of Agriculture, Bureau of Agricultural Economics, *Livestock on Farms, January 1, 1867–1919* (Washington: USDA, 1937), p. 25.

5 F. B. Morrison, *Feeds and Feeding*, 20th ed. (Ithaca: Morrison Co., 1940).

6 Ralph Dickieson Jennings, U.S. Department of Agriculture, "Consumption of Feed by Livestock, 1909–1956," *USDA Research Production Report*, Number 21 (Washington: GPO, 1958); Gallman, "Self Sufficiency," pp. 10–11.

7 Jennings estimates that in the decade 1909–1919, 27.6 percent of all feed for horses and mules was from pasture; 31.6 percent was straw and hay; the remaining 39.8 percent was in grains ("Consumption of Feed," Table 3, p. 14). The pasturage seems particularly high for small southern farms in 1880, since our sample of 1880 farms indicates very few family farms has significant pasturage. According to a North Carolina survey in 1889, the average feed from nongrain sources was only about one-third of the total (B. F. Dancy, "Stock Feeding, as Practiced in North Carolina," *North Carolina Experiment Station Bulletin*, Number 66 [September 1889], pp. 70–71).

8 Jennings, "Consumption of Feed," pp. 39–40.

9 On this point see the discussion in Robert B. Lamb, *The Mule in Southern Agriculture* (Berkeley: University of California Press, 1963), Chapters 2 and 3.

10 Oxen were allocated the same feed as horses on the basis of a few scattered observations reporting between 60 and 80 bushels of corn per year. W. A. Henry gives roughly equivalent rations for oxen and horses (*Feeds and Feeding, A Handbook for the Student and Stockman* [Madison: W. A. Henry, 1898], p. 636).

11 These feeding requirements are still below the average grain fed to horses as estimated by Jennings. His total feed requirement was 100 bushels per horse, however only 38 bushels were in the form of grain. The revised estimates are substantially higher than those of our earlier study (see the lower bound estimates in Table E.4). It should be noted that those estimates required the farm to provide a substantial part of the animal feed from forage and crop fodder; an assumption deliberately made to introduce a downward bias into those requirements.

12 Dancy ("Stock Feeding") reports a minimum practice for milch cows of around 6.5 bushels of corn per year – assuming liberal forage allotments. Morrison suggests an absolute minimum of about 8 bushels per year (*Feeds and Feeding*, p. 1008), and Jennings's 1958 estimate for milch cows is 8.99 bushels per year in 1904–1914 ("Consumption of Feed").

13 Henry and Morrison estimate that a 200-pound hog consumed during his life about 10 bushels of corn as feed (*Feeds and Feeding*, p. 574). Since the loss of weight in slaughter was apparently about 20 to 25 percent (*Rural Carolinian* 7 [October 1875], p. 21; Sutch, "Treatment," pp. 361–368), a 200-pound hog would provide about 150–160 pounds of pork. This implies that 15–16 pounds of pork were produced from each bushel of corn. In 1875 an observer reported a ratio of 8.4: 1 (*Rural Carolinian* 7 [October 1875], p. 22); two other experiments in hog raising reported yields of 14.7: 1 (*Southern Cultivator* 28 [February 1870], p. 48) and 18.7: 1 (*Rural Carolinian* 1 [March 1870], pp. 366–367).

14 The ratio of corn prices to pork prices was approximately 11:1 (see Appendex A, note 37). Over the decade of the 1880s, the average price for a bushel of corn in Georgia was 8.1 times the average price of a pound of bacon, when both were purchased with cash. The ratio of credit prices was 8.4:1 (See sources to Table 7.1). It would appear that 1 bushel of corn could be converted into pork at market prices on less favorable terms than through meat production on the farm. Of course, the market prices must cover the costs of labor, slaughtering the animal, and processing the meat.

15 Robert W. Fogel and Stanley Engerman suggest that the adult field hand ration averaged, at a minimum, 28 percent more than the average for the entire slave population (*Time on the Cross*, 2 vols. [Boston: Little, Brown & Co., 1974], 2, p. 98). Applying this ratio to 20 bushels of corn would imply an average of 15.6 bushels of corn per capita for the population as a whole.

1 Richard Easterlin, "State Income Estimates," in Simon Kuznets and Dorothy Swaine Thomas, eds., *Population Redistribution and Economic Growth, United States, 1870–1950*, Volume 1 (Philadelphia: American Philosophical Society, 1957), pp. 714–717; Ann Ratner Miller and Carol P. Brainerd, "Labor Force Estimates," in ibid.; Robert F. Martin, *National Income in the United States, 1799–1938* (New York: National Industrial Conference Board, 1939).

2 Richard A. Easterlin, "Regional Growth of Income: Long Term Tendencies, 1880–1950," in Simon Kuznets and Dorothy Swaine Thomas, eds., *Population Redistribution and Economic Growth, United States, 1870–1950*, Volume 2 (Philadelphia: American Philosophical Society, 1960), Table A 4.3, p. 187. The figures for each state were weighted by the rural population as estimated by Everett S. Lee, "Migration Estimates," in Kuznets and Thomas, *Population Redistribution*, 1, pp. 96–98, 349, 353.

3 Easterlin, "Regional Growth of Income," Table A 4.1, p. 185. The figures for each state were weighted by the total population in the two years (Lee, "Migration Estimates," p. 349). The 1900 estimate calculated using the 1880 population weights given in Chapter 1, note 12, is lower.

4 Easterlin's personal income relatives are given in "Regional Income Trends, 1840–1950," in Seymour E. Harris, ed., *American Economic History* (New York: McGraw-Hill, 1961), Table 1, pp. 528, 545. Also see Stanley L. Engerman "Some Economic Factors in Southern Backwardness in the Nineteenth Century," in John F. Kain and John R. Meyer, eds., *Essays in Regional Economics* (Cambridge: Harvard University Press, 1971). Easterlin's relatives are based upon state data presented in his "State Income Estimates," and the personal income estimates in 1929 dollars in "Regional Growth of Income," Table A 4.1, p. 185.

5 Easterlin, "State Income Estimates," p. 707.

6 In 1880 6 percent of our sample of farms from the Cotton South did not report the value of farm products.

7 Our estimate does include the value of grains, etc., produced in the Five Cotton States and fed to meat animals, but we omit the value of feeds purchased from other states and the value added by the labor devoted to raising meat animals.

8 These data were originally published in mimeographed releases of the Bureau of Agricultural Economics. See, for example, U.S. Department of Agriculture, Bureau of Agricultural Economics, "Revised Estimates of Oats Acreage, Yield and Production, 1866–1929" (Washington: USDA, July 1934). We have drawn our numbers, however, from the latest publication of the U.S. Department of Agriculture. Specific references will be given for each crop.

9 The contemporaneous estimates have been collected in a convenient form in a series of Bureau of Statistics bulletins that appeared in 1907 and 1908. See, for example, U.S. Department of Agriculture, Bureau of Statistics, Charles C. Clark, "Oat Crops of the United States, 1866–1906," *USDA Bureau of Statistics Bulletin*, Number 58 (Washington, GPO, 1907).

10 U.S. Department of Agriculture, *Monthly Report* (November-December 1866), p. 445; U.S. Department of Agriculture, Bureau of Statistics, Charles C. Clark, "Corn Crops of the United States, 1866–1906" *USDA Bureau of Statistics Bulletin*, Number 56 (Washington, GPO, 1907), p. 7; U.S. Department of Agriculture, Bureau of Agricultural Economics, "Revised Estimates of Corn Acreage, Yield and Production, 1866–1929" (Washington: USDA, May 1934, mimeographed); and U.S. Department of Agriculture, Agricultural Marketing Service, "Corn: Acreage, Yield, and Production of All Corn, Corn for Grain, Corn for Silage, and Acreage for Forage; by States, 1866–1943," *USDA Statistical Bulletin*, Number 56 (Washington: USDA, June 1954), p. 20.

11 U.S. Department of Agriculture, *Monthly Report* (October 1866), p. 391; U.S. Department of Agriculture, Bureau of Agricultural Economics, "Revised Estimates of Oats," p. 44; and U.S. Department of Agriculture, Agricultural Marketing Service, *Oats:*

Acreage, Yield, Production, by States, 1866–1943 (Washington: USDA, June 1954), p. 22.

12 U.S. Department of Agriculture, *Monthly Report* (October 1866), p. 391; U.S. Department of Agriculture, Bureau of Statistics, Charles C. Clark, "Wheat Crops of the United States, 1866–1906," *USDA Bureau of Statistics Bulletin*, Number 57, revised (Washington: GPO, 1908), p. 5; U.S. Department of Agriculture, Agricultural Marketing Service, "Wheat: Acreages, Yield, Production, by States, 1866–1943 . . ." *USDA Statistical Bulletin*, Number 158 (Washington: GPO, February 1955), p. 18.

13 For reasons discussed later in this appendix, rice grown in Alabama and Mississippi, rye grown in Mississippi and Louisiana, and tobacco and wheat grown in Louisiana are excluded.

14 U.S. Census Office, Tenth Census [1880], *Report on the Production of Agriculture* (Washington: GPO, 1883), pp. 9–10.

15 U.S. Department of Agriculture, Bureau of Agricultural Economics, "Prices of Farm Products Received by Producers," Volume 3, "South Atlantic and South Central States," *USDA Statistical Bulletin*, Number 16 (Washington: GPO, 1927).

16 The BAE converted the currency prices to gold prices using the average gold value of a dollar of "greenback" currency in New York for the month of November of each year. These conversion ratios can be found in Ainsworth Spofford, ed., *Almanac and Treasury of Facts, Statistical, Financial and Political, for the Year 1889* (New York: American News Co., 1889), p. 341. It should be noted, however, that the conversion ratios used for cotton in 1878 and for all crops in 1875 by the BAE were in error. We have used the originally reported currency prices for the years 1866 through 1878 consistently. These currency prices are found for 1866 through 1873 in U.S. Department of Agriculture, *Report of the Commissioner of Agriculture for the Year 1873* (Washington: GPO, 1874), pp. 36–47. For the years 1874 through 1878, consult the respective USDA annual reports as follows: *1874*, p. 33; *1875*, p. 31; *1876*, pp. 102–138; *1877*, p. 168; and *1878*, p. 269.

17 George F. Warren and Frank A. Pearson, *Prices* (New York: John Wiley & Sons, 1933), Table 3, p. 26.

18 Latham, Alexander, and Company, *Cotton Movement and Fluctuation: 1903–1908*, 35th ed. (New York: Latham, Alexander & Co., 1908). We have used the figures in U.S. Department of Agriculture, Agricultural Marketing Service, "Cotton and Cottonseed: Acreage, Yield, Production, Disposition, Price, Value; by States, 1866–1952," *USDA Statistical Bulletin*, Number 164 (Washington: GPO, 1955).

19 See U.S. Department of Agriculture, *Monthly Report* (November-December 1866), p. 444; idem (November-December 1867), p. 357; idem (November-December 1868), p. 424; and idem (November-December 1870), p. 459.

20 U.S. Department of Agriculture, *Report of the Commissioner . . . 1876*, p. 138; and idem, *Report . . . 1878*, p. 269.

21 U.S. Department of Agriculture, Bureau of Statistics, George K. Holmes, "Cotton Crop of the United States, 1790–1911," *USDA Bureau of Statistics Circular*, Number 32 (Washington: GPO, 1912), p. 7.

22 See Arden Hall ("The Efficiency of Post-Bellum Southern Agriculture" [Ph.D. thesis, University of California, Berkeley, 1974], p. 170) for the details of this interpolation.

23 These wholesale prices are reported in U.S. Department of Agriculture, Division of Statistics, James L. Watkins, "Production and Prices of Cotton for One Hundred Years," *USDA Miscellaneous Bulletin*, Number 9 (Washington: GPO, 1895), pp. 11–12. Prices are reported there for the commercial year (p. 3). We have applied them to the appropriate crop years. The Watkins prices were reported in currency. For the years 1869 through 1876, the Holmes farmgate price averaged 1.27 cents below the New York wholesale price per pound. This constant differential was used in the backward extrapolation.

24 U.S. Department of Agriculture, *Agricultural Yearbook, 1923* (Washington: GPO, 1924), p. 845.

25 Marvin W. Towne and Wayne D. Rasmussen, "Farm Gross Product and Gross Investment in the Nineteenth Century," in National Bureau of Economic Research, *Trends in the American Economy in the Nineteenth Century* (Princeton: Princeton University Press,

1960), p. 300; U.S. Department of Agriculture, Frederick Strauss and Louis H. Bean, "Gross Farm Income and Indices of Farm Production and Prices in the United States: 1869–1937," *USDA Technical Bulletin*, Number 703 (Washington: GPO, 1940).

26 Molasses output was reported in the agricultural censuses of 1870, 1880, and 1890 for the preceding crop years. The 1900 and 1910 censuses separately reported on-farm production in the agricultural censuses and refinery production in the manufacturing censuses. However, only Louisiana and Texas had cane sugar refineries in 1910 (U.S. Bureau of the Census, *Thirteenth Census . . . Manufactures, 1909, Reports by States* [Washington: GPO, 1912], p. 426). The refinery output of those states was added to the on-farm production. The refinery production for 1899 had to be estimated, since state data were not published.

27 Towne and Rasmussen, "Farm Gross Product," p. 301.

28 U.S. Bureau of the Census, *Historical Statistics of the United States, Colonial Times to 1957* (Washington: GPO, 1960), Series E-103, p. 124.

29 U.S. Congress, Senate, *Wholesale Prices, Wages, and Transportation*, Senate Report Number 1394, 52nd Congress, 2nd Session, Part II (Washington: GPO, 1893), pp. 113–114; and Lewis Cecil Gray, *History of Agriculture in the Southern United States to 1860*, 2 vols. (Washington: Carnegie Institution, 1933), 2, p. 1030.

30 Only 3 percent of the rice acreage in 1879 in the Five Cotton States was located in Alabama and Mississippi (U.S. Census Office, Tenth Census [1880], *Agriculture*, p. 9).

31 U.S. Department of Agriculture, Agricultural Marketing Service, "Rice, Popcorn, and Buckwheat: Acreage, Yield, Production, Price, Value; by States, 1866–1953," *USDA Statistical Bulletin*, Number 238 (Washington: GPO, 1958).

32 U.S. Department of Agriculture, Bureau of Statistics, George K. Holmes, "Rice Crop of the United States, 1712–1911," *USDA Bureau of Statistics Circular*, Number 34 (Washington: GPO, 1912), p. 4.

33 Strauss and Bean, "Gross Farm Income," p. 69.

34 Strauss and Bean, "Gross Farm Income," p. 69. The gold prices of 1866 through 1878 were converted to currency prices.

35 U.S. Department of Agriculture, "Fluctuations in Crops and Weather, 1866–1948," *USDA Statistical Bulletin*, Number 101 (Washington: GPO, 1951).

36 Strauss and Bean, "Gross Farm Income," Table 27, pp. 67–68; U.S. Department of Agriculture, Bureau of Agricultural Economics, "Tobaccos of the United States: Acreage, Yield per Acre, Production, Price, and Value; by States, 1866–1945, and by Types and Classes, 1919–1945," *CS Series*, Number 30 (Washington: GPO, 1948).

37 U.S. Department of Agriculture, *Statistical Bulletin*, Number 16; and idem, *Report of the Commissioner*, as follows: 1867, pp. 80–86; *1868*, pp. 31–33; *1869*, pp. 24–31; *1870*, pp. 26–33; *1871*, p. 29; *1872*, pp. 20–22; *1873*, pp. 26–28; *1874*, pp. 30–32; *1875*, pp. 28–30; *1876*, pp. 99–101; *1877*, pp. 165–167.

38 Hall, "Efficiency of Post-Bellum Agriculture," pp. 211, 213–216.

39 U.S. Department of Agriculture, *Statistical Bulletin*, Number 56. The acreage harvested is also reported in this source.

40 U.S. Department of Agriculture, *Statistical Bulletin*, Number 16. Prices for 1866 through 1873 can be found in idem, *Report of the Commissioner . . . 1873*, p. 42. Estimates for 1874 through 1877 come from the respective USDA reports, as follows: *1874*, pp. 30–32; *1875*, pp. 28–30; *1876*, pp. 99–101; *1877*, pp. 165–167.

41 U.S. Department of Agriculture, Agricultural Marketing Service, *Oats*.

42 U.S. Department of Agriculture, *Report of the Commissioner . . . 1868*, p. 28.

43 Hall, "Efficiency of Post-Bellum Agriculture," pp. 177, 182.

44 U.S. Department of Agriculture, Bureau of Agricultural Economics, "Potatoes: Acreage, Production, Value, Farm Disposition, Jan. 1 Stocks (1866–1950)," *USDA Statistical Bulletin*, Number 122 (Washington: GPO, 1953).

45 Hall, "Efficiency of Post-Bellum Agriculture," pp. 183, 186, 188.

46 U.S. Department of Agriculture, Agricultural Marketing Service, "Sweet Potatoes: Esti-

mates in Hundredweight; by States, 1868–1953, Acreage, Yield, Production, Price, Value, Farm Disposition," *USDA Statistical Bulletin*, Number 237 (Washington: GPO, 1958). It should be noted that the prices reported in this bulletin are in error.

47 This can be confirmed by referring to the U.S. Department of Agriculture, *Monthly Reports*, for January 1869, p. 6; January 1870, p. 17; January 1871, p. 8; January 1872, p. 9; November-December 1872, p. 484; January 1874, p. 12; January 1875, p. 26; and January 1876, p. 29.

48 Hall, "Efficiency of Post-Bellum Agriculture," pp. 198–203.

49 U.S. Department of Agriculture, Agricultural Marketing Service, "Flaxseed and Rye: Acreage, Yield, Production, Price, Value; by States, 1866–1953," *USDA Statistical Bulletin*, Number 254 (Washington: GPO, 1959).

50 Hall, "Efficiency of Post-Bellum Agriculture," pp. 194–195.

51 Acreage figures for South Carolina and Georgia are given in *USDA Statistical Bulletin*, Number 254. They were estimated for Alabama assuming the same yeild per acre in that state as in Georgia.

52 Hall, "Efficiency of Post-Bellum Agriculture," pp. 194–196.

53 U.S. Department of Agriculture, *Statistical Bulletin*, Number 158.

54 U.S. Bureau of the Census, *Historical Statistics*, pp. 12–13.

55 Roger Ransom and Richard Sutch, "The Impact of the Civil War and of Emancipation on Southern Agriculture," *Explorations in Economic History* 12 (January 1975), Table 1, p. 8.

56 Lee, "Migration Estimates," pp. 96–98.

57 U.S. Census Office, Eight Census [1860], *Population of the United States in 1860 . . .* (Washington: GPO, 1864), pp. 9, 74, 195, 271, 452; U.S. Census Office, Ninth Census [1870], *Statistics of Population of the United States . . . 1870* (Washington: GPO, 1872), pp. 77–83, 99–107, 154–158, 182–186, 258–260. The towns included were Charleston and Columbia, South Carolina; Athens, Atlanta, Augusta, Columbus, Macon, Marietta, Newnan, Newton, Rome, and Savannah, Georgia; Huntsville, Mobile, Montgomery, Selma, and Tuscaloosa, Alabama; Columbus, Holly Springs, Jackson, Natchez, and Vicksburg, Mississippi; Algeres, Baton Rouge, Donaldsonville, Jefferson, New Orleans, and Saint Landry, Louisiana. Their aggregate population in 1860 was 483,824.

58 An eloquent statement of this view is provided by Eugene D. Genovese, *The Political Economy of Slavery* (New York: Pantheon, 1965). This interpretation has a long and distinguished historiographical pedigree. In a review of this tradition, Robert Fogel and Stanley Engerman cite U. B. Phillips, Guy S. Callender, Lewis C. Gray, Robert R. Russel, and Douglass C. North (Robert W. Fogel and Stanley L. Engerman, "The Economics of Slavery," in idem, eds., *The Reinterpretation of American Economic History* [New York: Harper & Row, 1971], pp. 318–320). Also see the references we have provided in Chapter 1, note 24.

59 Stanley Engerman, "The Effects of Slavery upon the Southern Economy: A Review of the Recent Debate," *Explorations in Entrepreneurial History*, second series 4 (winter 1967); idem, "Some Economic Factors in Southern Backwardness in the Nineteenth Century," in John F. Kain and John R. Meyer, eds., *Essays in Regional Economics* (Cambridge: Harvard University Press, 1971), pp. 284–289; Robert Fogel and Stanley Engerman, "The Economics of Slavery," pp. 333–336; idem, *Time on the Cross*, 2 vols. (Boston: Little, Brown & Co., 1974), 1, pp. 247–257; and 2, pp. 162–165. Also see Stanley Engerman, "The Economic Impact of the Civil War," *Explorations in Entrepreneurial History*, second series 3 (spring 1966).

60 Richard A. Easterlin, "State Income Estimates" (1957); idem, "Regional Growth of Income" (1960); idem, "Interregional Income Differences" (1960); and idem, "Regional Income Trends" (1961).

61 Gerald Gunderson, "Southern Ante-Bellum Income Reconsidered," *Explorations in Economic History* 10 (winter 1973). Also see Robert Gallman, "Southern Ante-Bellum Income Reconsidered," and Gerald Gunderson, "Southern Income Reconsidered: A Reply," *Explorations in Economic History* 12 (January 1975); and Marvin Fischbaum and Julius

Rubin, "Slavery and the Economic Development of the American South," *Explorations in Entrepreneurial History*, second series 6 (fall 1968).

62 Easterlin, "Regional Income Trends," pp. 530, 533–534.

63 Engerman, "Southern Backwardness," Table 2, p. 287. Also see Robert Gallman, "Gross National Product in the United States, 1834–1909," in National Bureau of Economic Research, *Output, Employment, and Productivity in the United States After 1800* (New York: Columbia University Press, 1966), Table A-1, p. 26. Engerman adjusted Gallman's 1859 estimate of the gross national product to remove the product of the Mountain and Pacific states, apparently by assuming a per capita income in those regions of $265.00.

64 Engerman, "Southern Backwardness," Table 2, p. 287.

65 Engerman, "Effects of Slavery," p. 318.

66 As an illustration of how sensitive the calculated growth rates are to small adjustments in the relatives, we take the case of the South Atlantic region. Easterlin reported relatives for 1840 and 1860 as 70 percent and 65 percent. Gallman's gross national product per capita grew from $94.91 in 1839 to $130.39 in 1859 ("Gross National Product," p. 26; and U.S. Bureau of the Census, *Historical Statistics*, p. 8), suggesting a South Atlantic annual growth rate of 1.224 percent. However, if the true 1840 relative had been 70.5 and the 1860 relative 64.5, then the growth in that region would have been 1.149. And if the true relatives were 69.5 and 65.5, the growth would have been 1.299 percent, which is 13 percent higher than the lower estimate. Both these estimates are within the rounding error implicit in Easterlin's numbers.

67 Engerman, "Effects of Slavery," p. 318.

68 This point has been forcefully made by Harold Woodman, "Economic History and Economic Theory: The New Economic History in America," *Journal of Interdisciplinary History* 3 (autumn 1972), pp. 336–340. Fogel and Engerman have challenged Woodman's interpretation, but they have not addressed the point at issue: the dynamic capacity of the slave economy to sustain economic growth (*Time on the Cross*, 1, pp. 252–253).

69 The existence of these figures was noted by Fogel and Engerman, but they do not discuss their implications (*Time on the Cross*, 2, pp. 162–163).

Appendix G. Descriptions of major collections of data gathered by the Southern Economic History Project

1 The regional definitions, of necessity, follow county boundaries, since the census data upon which we relied were not disaggregated below this level.

2 Eugene W. Hilgard, U.S. Census Office, Tenth Census [1880], *Report on Cotton Production in the United States*, 2 vols. (Washington: GPO, 1884).

3 Lewis Cecil Gray, *History of Agriculture in the Southern United States to 1860*, 2 vols. (Washington: Carnegie Institution, 1933); Hugh Hammond Bennett, *The Soils and Agriculture of the Southern States* (New York: Macmillan Co., 1921); Donald J. Bogue and Calvin L. Beale, *Economic Subregions of the United States*, U.S. Bureau of Agricultural Economics and U.S. Bureau of the Census Series, Number 19 (Washington: GPO, 1953).

4 Naturally, there were cases where a county encompassed more than one type of soil, and these counties were provisionally placed in the region that corresponded to the most prevalent soil type in the county. A total of 210 counties had mixed soil types.

5 Ten variables from the census volumes were used to describe the economic and demographic characteristics of each county: (1) percentage of tilled land in cotton or other staple crops, (2) average yield of cotton per acre, (3) percentage of population that was black, (4) percentage of farmers who owned their farms, (5) percentage of farmers renting, (6) percentage of farmers sharecropping, (7) percentage of farms with less than 50 tilled acres, (8) percentage of farms with more than 500 tilled acres, (9) average number of acres per farm, (10) average population per tilled acre.

6 For a more detailed description of the techniques employed to establish the regional boundaries, and a list of the counties in each region, see Roger Ransom and Richard Sutch, "Economic Regions of the South in 1880," *Southern Economic History Project, Working*

Paper Series, Number 3 (Berkeley: Institute of Business and Economic Research, March 1971), pp. 64–84.

7 A detailed description of the sampling procedure and the data collected is provided in Section 2 of this appendix.

8 For a brief history of the decennial censuses and a fuller description of the enumeration procedures at each census, see Carroll D. Wright, Commissioner of Labor, U.S. Department of Labor, and William C. Hunt, Chief Statistician, Twelfth Census, *The History and Growth of the United States Census, Prepared for the Senate Committee on the Census* (Washington: GPO, 1900).

9 These manuscripts were originally placed in the National Archives together with the returns from other censuses (see Katherine H. Davidson and Charlotte M. Ashby, compilers, "Records of the Bureau of the Census," *The National Archives, Preliminary Inventories*, Number 161 [Washington: GPO, 1964]). The population schedules are available on microfilm for each of the censuses from 1790 to 1880. Information regarding these films can be found in Arthur F. Sampson, *Federal Population Censuses, 1790–1890: A Catalogue of Microfilm Copies of the Schedules* (Washington: National Archives and Records Services, 1974). The nonpopulation manuscript schedules for these years were returned to the states in 1919. For the fifteen southern states, the original schedules of manufacturing and agriculture for 1850, 1860, 1870, and 1880 have been collected and microfilmed by the University of North Carolina Library. Information on these films is available in Samuel M. Boone, *Agriculture and Manufacturing Census Records of Fifteen Southern States for the Years 1850, 1860, 1870, and 1880* (Chapel Hill: University of North Carolina, 1966). The original manuscripts of the 1890 Census were destroyed in a fire, and except for a few scattered counties, the schedules are lost. The enumeration schedules for the 1900 Census were released as this book was in preparation and were unavailable for public use at the time the Southern Economic History Project was established. Subsequent census manuscripts are not yet available for public examination.

10 The problem associated with underenumeration of population and other items on the census are noted in Chapter 3 and in Roger Ransom and Richard Sutch, "The Impact of the Civil War and the Emancipation on Southern Agriculture," *Explorations in Economic History* 12 (January 1975), pp. 6–11. Our examination of the agriculture schedules suggests an additional difficulty with those returns. Enumerators occasionally did not consider sharecroppers or renters as "farm operators." In such cases information for these farms was aggregated and recorded within a single entry under the landowner's name, thus mistaking the actual size of farming operation.

11 County data were employed to select which county (or counties) were to represent each region. A full discussion of how representative counties were selected is in Ransom and Sutch, "Economic Regions." The procedure of using county characteristics to reflect regional traits was employed before with considerable success by Gray in his exhaustive study of antebellum southern agriculture (*History of Agriculture*).

12 The "basic sample" in each county was obtained by choosing the first five farms in each group of forty-five farms listed on the agricultural schedules. The starting point was selected randomly from the first eight blocs of five farms. Replacements were systematically chosen for farms where illegibility was a major problem. In a few cases, a target sampling rate of five farms out of ninety was employed.

13 A full list of the counties sampled can be found in Ransom and Sutch, "Economic Regions" (Table D.2, pp. 118–120). Of the twelve regions not sampled, six had representative counties that were in Arkansas. Microfilms of the agricultural schedules for this state could not be obtained by the Southern Economic History Project. The original manuscripts for Arkansas have been destroyed, and the microfilm copy at the University of North Carolina was of such poor quality that the film could not be reproduced. One Arkansas region (number 35, Crowley's Ridge) might be legitimately considered a part of the Cotton South; however, we did not include it in our definition partly because we were unable to draw a sample from this region. The other six regions not sampled were relatively unimportant and sparsely settled areas in 1880. In addition to the representative counties selected to reflect

regional characteristics, a few counties were included in the full sample owing to features of particular interest. None of these additional counties were included in the Cotton South Sample that was used to prepare the statistics reported in this volume.

14 These footnotes are on file with the Southern Economic History Project and are available to those using these sample data.

15 The census enumerator was instructed to number both the dwelling units and the "families" as he came to them. Thus, if two families were living together, it was normally possible to note this, and such cases were identified in our footnotes. In a few cases the enumerators did not always follow these rules. In cases where dwelling units were not identified in the schedules, the "number of people who lived in same dwelling as farm operator" was calculated by counting all the people with the same surname appearing in consecutive spaces above or below the name of the farm operator. Here again, such cases were noted in our footnotes.

16 In a few instances, the individual listed as the farm operator on the agricultural schedules had a nonagricultural occupation (such as physician or sheriff) on the population schedules. Such individuals were *not* counted as working on the farm.

17 Two possibilities come to mind. Since the census recorded occupations only for persons aged ten or over, child labor would be unrecorded. Women and other individuals who were primarily engaged in housework and child care typically contributed seasonal labor to the farm, though the enumerator was instructed to describe such persons as "keeping house."

18 Because of these problems, the published census volumes made no attempt to report the information collected on hired labor.

19 If the enumerator consistently reported reasonable answers to the labor questions, this was noted and the data were considered good. Blank entries in these districts were assumed to represent farms hiring no labor. In other enumeration districts, where the question was ingored altogether, this fact was noted and the data were considered missing on all farms. In those districts where the wage bill seemed to have been entered consistently and correctly, but the man-weeks incorrectly, the former data were coded as accurate. In those few instances where the wage data seemed inconsistent with our other estimates, but the man-weeks of labor seemed reasonable, the data were coded to indicate valid data on labor input. In these last two cases (where only one of the labor questions was judged accurate) we are nevertheless reasonably certain that *some* labor was hired during the year, and we can use the data that were deemed valid to estimate the amount of labor employed.

20 Such farms were excluded from the census definition of a "farm," and their outputs were not included in the published tabulations of the returns. In other words, such farms were excluded because officially they were nonfarms.

21 We found that in Washington County, Mississippi, the enumerators had erroneously attributed the value of farm, and several other variables, to the owner of the farm, rather than to the farm operator. However, agricultural data for each of the tenanted farms were provided. Thus, although our sample correctly treated these farms as individual units, our result was a much lower size of farm than that reported in the published returns. In Angelina, Texas, the published census apparently omitted from its tabulations several pages of agricultural forms that had been separated from the balance of the county's returns.

22 Although it was not statistically significant, there was a systematic tendency for the unmatched farms to be larger than average and to be operated by owners rather than by tenants.

23 A total of 138 farms was excluded from our analysis owing to absence of reliable labor data.

24 U.S. Department of Agriculture, Bureau of Statistics, "Wages of Farm Labor," *USDA Bureau of Statistics Bulletin 99* (Washington: GPO, 1912).

25 The number of "reported acres" is the sum of the acres harvested in 1879 with the following crops: rice, barley, buckwheat, Indian corn, oats, rye, wheat, cotton, flax, hemp, sugar cane, sorghum, tobacco, apples, and peaches. It is not equivalent to the number of acres tilled because it omits all other crops and all acreage planted but not harvested.

26 Our examination revealed a significant number of enumeration districts where only a half-

hearted attempt had been made to produce a comprehensive and accurate enumeration. Census officials later explained these deficiencies as resulting from the frictions that still persisted between the local populace and the federal government and also the lack of adequate compensation for the assistant U.S. marshals, who were expected to collect the census in addition to their other duties.

27 Nevertheless, even these counties were plagued by a problem that was common throughout the South in 1870. A combination of events made the population reluctant to answer questions concerning the value of real and personal estate and may have induced them to underreport farm size and holdings of animals. Unlike modern censuses, the individual returns of the census were public record and were on file in every county seat. The 1870 Census requested information on the dollar value of real and personal estate, of the farm and its holdings, of the livestock and of agricultural output. Republican state governments had moved to increase taxation of real and personal estate, much to the displeasure of a substantial part of the population. (For a discussion of the taxes and opposition to such measures in South Carolina, see Joel Williamson, *After Slavery: The Negro in South Carolina During Reconstruction, 1861–1877* [Chapel Hill: University of North Carolina Press, 1965], pp. 156–159). As an indication of how serious a problem was raised by asking these questions, we note that underreporting in the counties we have sampled is quite high. Even among those farms in 1870 that did report acreage, the rate of nonreporting for the value of the farm was 3 percent, the value of farm implements 16 percent, and the value of livestock 7 percent; 20 percent of the farm operators in our sample reported no personal estate, while 55 percent claimed to have no real estate. While the latter figure may reflect the prevalence of tenancy, the high proportion of operators without any personal estate must be attributed to underreporting of property.

28 This sample is discussed more fully in Appendix B.

29 This sample is discussed more fully in Appendix B.

30 In cases where no entry was entered for the question of real or personal estate, it was assumed that the value of the person's estate was zero.

31 James D. Foust, "The Yeoman Farmer and Westward Expansion of U.S. Cotton Production" (Ph.D. dissertation, University of North Carolina, 1967).

32 William N. Parker, ed., *The Structure of the Cotton Economy of the Antebellum South* (Berkeley: University of California Press, 1970). See in particular the chapters by Robert Gallman ("Self-Sufficiency in the Cotton Economy of the Ante-bellum South"), James D. Foust and Dale E. Swan ("Productivity and Profitability of Antebellum Slave Labor: A Micro Approach") and Gavin Wright ("Note on the Manuscript Census Samples Used in These Studies"). Also see Robert Gallman, "Efficiency and Farm Interdependence in an Agricultural Export Region: Sampling Procedure and Tests of the Sample" (unpublished paper, University of North Carolina, October 20, 1965), and, for a distribution of slaveholdings in the sample, Richard Sutch, "The Breeding of Slaves for Sale and the Westward Expansion of Slavery, 1850–1860," in Stanley L. Engerman and Eugene D. Genovese, eds., *Race and Slavery in the Western Hemisphere: Quantitative Studies* (Princeton: Princeton University Press, 1975).

33 The Census Office enumerated separately the "Populations of Civil Divisions less than Counties" in 1880 (U.S. Census Office, Tenth Census [1880], *Statistics of Population of the United States [June 1, 1880]*, 1 [Washington: GPO, 1888], pp. 93–351). The population of all but 3 of the 158 towns were given in this source. Our population estimates for Clarkesville, Texas, and Cheraw, South Carolina, were taken from R. G. Dun, *Mercantile Agency Reference Book* (New York: Dun, Barlow & Co., 1880). We have found no population estimate for Industry, Texas, in 1880.

34 The evidence we have collected on banking is discussed in the next section of this appendix.

35 Our principal source for establishing the presence of commercial establishments in a town was R. G. Dun, *Mercantile Agency Reference Book* (1880). We also employed an 1883 study by Harry Hammond for South Carolina (*South Carolina: Resources and Population, Institutions and Industry* [Charleston: Walker, Evans and Cogswell, 1883]).

36 Evidence on which towns served as local cotton markets was obtained from the reports of

county correspondents summarized by Eugene Hilgard in his study for the Tenth Census (*Cotton Production*). Additional evidence was obtained from Latham, Alexander and Company, *Cotton Movement and Fluctuation: 1903–1908*, 35th ed. (New York: Latham, Alexander & Co., 1908).

37 George E. Barnett, *State Banks and Trust Companies Since the Passage of the National Bank Act*, Volume 7 of the *Publications of the National Monetary Commission* (Washington: GPO, 1911); A. Piatt Andrew, "Statistics for the United States, 1867–1909," in *Statistics for the United States, Great Britain, Germany, and France*, Volume 21 of the *Publications of the National Monetary Commission* (Washington: GPO, 1911); David I. Fand, "Estimates of Deposits and Vault Cash in the Non-National Banks in the Post Civil War Period in the United States: 1876–1896" (Ph.D. dissertation, University of Chicago, March 1954); and Milton Friedman and Anna J. Schwartz, *Monetary Statistics of the United States:Estimates, Sources, Methods* (New York: National Bureau of Economic Research, 1970), volume 2.

38 Roger Ransom and Richard Sutch, "Debt Peonage in the Cotton South After the Civil War," *Journal of Economic History* 32 (September 1972), p. 666.

39 This first edition of the *Reference Book* had over 20,000 names of persons or firms (Roy A. Foulke, *The Sinews of American Commerce*, [New York: Dun & Bradstreet, Inc., 1941] p. 298). Dun's volume was not the first of its kind. Two years earlier, a rival credit agency, founded in 1855 by J. M. Bradstreet, had issued a smaller listing of credit ratings that concentrated on nine large cities. These two agencies continued as rivals until they were merged into Dun and Bradstreet, Inc., in 1931 (ibid., pp. 296–297). Dun's ratings are of greater interest to the present study because the Mercantile Agency concentrated on *rural* businesses in the West and South.

40 *The Mercantile Agency Reference Book*, 1880, title page.

41 The confidentiality of the records was impressed upon subscribers. The *Reference Book* was, according to Foulke, "bound in dark sheepskin and was closed with a bulky lock so that the subscriber might retain the key and thus keep its confidential contents from the prying eyes of subordinates and visitors (*Sinews of American Commerce*, p. 298).

42 The Mercantile Agency placed the very first commercial order for typewriters in 1875 with E. Remington and Sons (Foulke, *Sinews of American Commerce*, p. 374). The advantage of the new machines was their ability to produce legible carbon copies of reports. Predictably, the change was not well received by Dun's clerks. "The early ledgers reveal the Spencerian skill of these copyists," claimed Foulke, "who looked upon the introduction of the typewriter in later years as an offense against the age-old chirographic art" (p. 335). The "offense" was doubtless all the more serious inasmuch as many of the clerks were apparently very poor typists (pp. 374–375). The switch to typewritten records was initiated for firms located in large cities. The handwritten volumes were retained to at least 1880 in all the southern counties we have examined.

43 In selecting which counties to include in our study, we were constrained to some extent by the conditions of the ledgers. Of the twenty-two counties chosen, fourteen were representative counties in the Cotton South, a concentration that reflects our interest in that region.

44 In this section of the text, and elsewhere in this appendix, we have reproduced the entries from the Credit Ledgers verbatim except for spelling out some obvious abbreviations. Foulke provides additional background and examples of entries in the Credit Ledger volumes for firms located outside the southern states (*Sinews of American Commerce*, pp. 370–376). The ledgers also included coded notations indicating the credit reporter who supplied the information. No code books have been located to supply the names of these reporters. Accordingly, we have eliminated these notations from the text reproduced here.

45 We have retabulated the data from Hammond (*South Carolina*) because of numerous errors in the original tabulation. To allow the greatest degree of consistency in the definition of what constituted a "store" in the two lists, we aggregated all firms listed as a "general store," a "dry goods" store, or a "grocery store" in either list. The results reported exclude Charleston.

46 The firms were selected for the sample from the *Reference Book* lists of 1870, 1875, and 1880. Any firm not doing business in one of those years was excluded. The final tally of firms in each of the benchmark years was adjusted in some instances from data in the Credit Ledgers. Two firms that began operations in 1880 and were not in the 1880 *Reference Book* list were included for that year. The number of firms listed in 1870 and 1875 in the *Reference Book* was adjusted for firms that entered business in those years (and were thus not in the January list), and for a few instances where entries in the Credit Ledgers indicated that firms had been in business even though the *Reference Book* did not pick them up for that year.

47 If the first report on a firm gave no indication of how long it had been in business, we assumed that the firm commenced business in the year of the first report.

BIBLIOGRAPHY

Abbott, Martin. "Free Land, Free Labor, and the Freedman's Bureau." *Agricultural History* 30 (October 1956):150–156.

Adamson, Alan H. *Sugar Without Slaves: The Political Economy of British Guiana, 1838–1904.* New Haven: Yale University Press, 1972.

Aiken, D. Wyatt. "Alabama from an Agricultural Point of View." *Rural Carolinian* 1 (April 1870):405–408.

"Does Farming Pay in the South?" *Rural Carolinian* 2 (March 1871):323–324.

"Farming as Adapted to Middle South Carolina." *Rural Carolinian* 3 (February 1872):225–229.

"Southern Farming and Farm Labor." *Rural Carolinian* 1 (December 1869):140–142.

Aitken, Hugh G., editor. *Did Slavery Pay?* Boston: Houghton Mifflin Company, 1971.

Akerloff, George. "The Market for Lemons." *Quarterly Journal of Economics* 84 (August 1970):488–500.

The American Farmer. Fourth Series, Volumes 14 and 15 (1858 and 1859).

American Fertilizer. Volume 1 (August 1894).

Andreano, Ralph L., editor. *The Economic Impact of the Civil War.* Cambridge: Schenkman, 1964.

editor. *New Views on American Economic Development.* Cambridge: Schenkman, 1965.

Andrew, A. Piatt. "Statistics for the United States, 1867–1909." In *Statistics for the United States, Great Britain, Germany, and France.* Volume 21 of the Publications of the National Monetary Commission. Washington: GPO, 1911.

Andrews, Sidney. *The South Since the War as Shown by Fourteen Weeks of Travel and Observation in Georgia and the Carolinas.* Boston: Houghton Mifflin Company, 1970. Originally published in 1866.

Arrow, Kenneth J. "Models of Discrimination." In A. H. Pascal, editor. *Racial Discrimination in Economic Life.* Lexington: D. C. Heath, 1972.

Atherton, Lewis E. *The Southern Country Store, 1800–1860.* Baton Rouge: Louisiana State University Press, 1949.

Atwater, W. O., and Woods, Charles D. See U.S. Department of Agriculture, Office of Experiment Stations.

Aufhauser, Keith. "Slavery and Scientific Management." *Journal of Economic History* 33 (December 1973):811–823.

Banks, Enoch Marvin. "The Economics of Land Tenure in Georgia." *Studies in History, Economics, and Public Law* 23 (1905):1–142.

Barnett, George E. *State Banks and Trust Companies Since the Passage of the National Bank Act.* Volume 7 of the Publications of the National Monetary Commission. Washington: GPO, 1911.

Barrow, David C., Jr. "A Georgia Plantation." *Scribner's Monthly* 21 (April 1881):830–836.

Battalio, Raymond C., and Kagel, John. "The Structure of Antebellum Southern Agriculture: South Carolina, A Case Study." *Agricultural History* 44 (January 1970):25–37.

Beard, Charles Austin, and Beard, Mary R. *The Rise of American Civilization*. New York: Macmillan Company, 1927.

Bennett, Hugh Hammond. *The Soils and Agriculture of the Southern States*. New York: Macmillan Company, 1921.

Berlin, Ira. *Slaves Without Masters: The Free Negro in the Antebellum South*. New York: Pantheon, 1974.

Berry, Thomas Senior. *Western Prices Before 1861: A Study of the Cincinnati Market*. Cambridge: Harvard University Press, 1943.

Blaine, James G. *Twenty Years of Congress: From Lincoln to Garfield*. 2 volumes. Norwich: Henry Bill Publishing Company, 1884–1886.

Blair, Lewis H. *A Southern Prophecy: The Prosperity of the South Dependent upon the Elevation of the Negro*. Edited with an introduction by C. Vann Woodward. Boston: Little, Brown & Company, 1964.

Bledsoe, Albert Taylor. *An Essay on Liberty and Slavery*. Philadelphia: J. B. Lippincott & Company, 1856.

Bogue, Allan G. *From Prairie to Corn Belt: Farming on the Illinois and Iowa Prairies in the Nineteenth Century*. Chicago: University of Chicago Press, 1963.

Bogue, Donald J., and Beale, Calvin L. *Economic Subregions of the United States*. U.S. Bureau of Agricultural Economics and U.S. Bureau of the Census Series, Number 19. Washington: GPO, 1953.

Bond, Horace Mann. *The Education of the Negro in the American Social Order*. New York: Prentice-Hall, 1934.

Boone, Samuel M. *Agriculture and Manufacturing Census Records of Fifteen Southern States for the Years 1850, 1860, 1870, and 1880*. Chapel Hill: University of North Carolina, 1966.

Bowles, Samuel. "Unequal Education and the Reproduction of the Social Division of Labor." *Review of Radical Political Economics* 3 (fall and winter 1971):1–26.

Brooks, Robert Preston. "The Agrarian Revolution in Georgia, 1865–1912." *Bulletin of the University of Wisconsin,* History Series 3 (1914):393–521.

Brown, William W., and Reynolds, Morgan O. "Debt Peonage Re-examined." *Journal of Economic History* 33 (December 1973):862–871.

Bruce, Phillip Alexander. *The Rise of the New South*. Philadelphia: G. Barrie, circa 1905.

"Social and Economic Revolution in the Southern States." *Contemporary Review* 78 (July 1900):58–73.

Bull, Jacqueline P. "The General Merchant in the Economic History of the New South." *Journal of Southern History* 18 (February 1952):37–59.

Bullock, Henry Allen. *A History of Negro Education in the South from 1619 to the Present*. Cambridge: Harvard University Press, 1967.

Burns, John T. See Georgia, Office of the Comptroller General, 1866.

Butlin, N. G. *Ante-bellum Slavery: Critique of a Debate*. Canberra: Department of Economic History, Australian National University, 1971.

Cairnes, J. E. *The Slave Power: It's Character, Career, and Probable Designs: Being an Attempt to Explain the Real Issues Involved in the American Contest*. New York: Harper & Row, 1969. Originally published in 1862.

Callender, Guy S. "The Early Transportation and Banking Enterprises of the States in Relation to the Growth of the Corporation." *Quarterly Journal of Economics* 17 (November 1902):111–162.

Campbell, Sir George. *White and Black: The Outcome of a Visit to the United States [in 1878]*. London: Chatto & Windus, 1879.

Capron, Horace. See U.S. Department of Agriculture.

Carter, Hodding. *The Angry Scar: The Story of Reconstruction, 1865–1877*. New York: Doubleday & Sons, 1959.

Cheung, Steven N. S. *The Theory of Share Tenancy, with Special Application to Asian Agriculture and the First Phase of Taiwan Land Reform*. Chicago: University of Chicago Press, 1969.

Clark, Blanche Henry. *The Tennessee Yeomen, 1840–1860.* Nashville: Vanderbilt University Press, 1942.

Clark, Ira G. *Then Came the Railroads: The Century from Steam to Diesel in the Southwest.* Norman: University of Oklahoma Press, 1958.

Clark, Thomas D. "The Furnishing and Supply System in Southern Agriculture Since 1865." *Journal of Southern History* 12 (February 1946):24–44.

"Historical Aspect of Imperfect Competition in the Southern Retail Trade After 1865." *Journal of Economic History* 3 (December 1943):38–57.

Pills, Petticoats, and Plows: The Southern Country Store. Indianapolis: Bobbs-Merrill, 1944.

Cogswell, Seddie, Jr. *Tenure, Nativity and Age as Factors in Iowa Agriculture, 1850–1880.* Ames: Iowa State University Press, 1975.

Coles, H. L., Jr. "Some Notes on Slave Ownership and Land Ownership in Louisiana, 1850–1860." *Journal of Southern History* 9 (August 1943):381–394.

Conrad, Alfred; Dowd, Douglas; Engerman, Stanley; Ginzberg, Eli; Kelso, Charles; Meyer, John R.; Scheiber, Harry N.; and Sutch, Richard. "Slavery as an Obstacle to Economic Growth in the United States: A Panel Discussion." *Journal of Economic History* 27 (December 1967):518–560.

Conrad, Alfred H., and Meyer, John R. "The Economics of Slavery in the Ante Bellum South." *Journal of Political Economy* 66 (April 1958):95–130.

Coulter, E. Merton. *The South During Reconstruction, 1865–1877.* Volume 8 of Wendell Holmes Stephenson and E. Merton Coulter, editors. *A History of the South.* Baton Rouge: Louisiana State University Press, 1947.

Cox, Lawanda F. "Promise of Land for the Freedman." *Mississippi Valley Historical Review* 45 (December 1958):413–440.

Cox, Lawanda F., and Cox, John H., editors. *Reconstruction, the Negro, and the New South.* Columbia: University of South Carolina Press, 1973.

Dana, William P. "Business Changes at the South: The Past and Future." *Hunt's Merchants' Magazine and Commercial Review* 61 (November 1869):363–366.

Dancy, B. F. "Stock Feeding, as Practiced in North Carolina." *North Carolina Experiment Station Bulletin,* Number 66. Raleigh: 1889. This North Carolina Experiment Station study reports the results of an extensive survey of feeding practices throughout the state.

David, Paul A.; Gutman, Herbert G.; Sutch, Richard; Temin, Peter; and Wright, Gavin. *Reckoning with Slavery: A Critical Study in the Quantitative History of American Negro Slavery.* New York: Oxford University Press, 1976.

David, Paul A., and Temin, Peter. "Slavery: The Progressive Institution?" *Journal of Economic History* 34 (September 1974):739–783.

Davidson, Katherine H., and Ashby, Charlotte M., compilers. "Records of the Bureau of the Census." *The National Archives, Preliminary Inventories,* Number 161. Washington: GPO, 1964.

Davis, Charles S. *The Cotton Kingdom in Alabama.* Montgomery: Alabama State Department of Archives and History, 1939.

Davis, Lance E. "The Investment Market, 1870–1914: The Evolution of a National Market." *Journal of Economic History* 25 (September 1965):355–399.

Davis, Lance E.; Easterlin, Richard A.; and Parker, William N., editors. *American Economic Growth: An Economist's History of the United States.* New York: Harper & Row, 1972.

De Bow's Review, Devoted to the Restoration of the Southern States, and the Development of the Wealth and Resources of the Country. After the War Series. Volumes 1ff. Nashville, New Orleans, and New York: J. B. De Bow.

De Bow, James D. B. "The Future of the South." *De Bow's Review* 1 (January 1866):6–16.

The Industrial Resources, Statistics &c. of the United States, and More Particularly of the Southern and Western States. 3rd edition. 3 volumes. New York: A. M. Kelly, 1966. Originally published in 1852.

DeCanio, Stephen J. *Agriculture in the Postbellum South: The Economics of Production and Supply.* Cambridge: MIT Press, 1974.

"Cotton 'Overproduction' in Late Nineteenth-Century Southern Agriculture." *Journal of Economic History* 33 (September 1973):608–633.

"Productivity and Income Distribution in the Post-Bellum South." *Journal of Economic History* 34 (June 1974):422–426.

Deforest, John W. *A Union Officer in the Reconstruction*. New Haven: Yale University Press, 1948. Originally published in 1867.

Degler, Carl N. "Slavery and the Genesis of American Race Prejudice." *Comparative Studies in Society and History* 2 (October 1959):49–66.

Dennett, John Richard. *The South As It Is: 1865–1866*. New York: Viking Press, 1967. Originally published as a series of articles in *The Nation*, 1865–1866.

Dew, Charles B. "Critical Essay on Recent Works." In C. Vann Woodward. *Origins of the New South*. Baton Rouge: Louisiana State University Press, 1971, pp. 517–628.

Dickins, Dorothy. "A Nutrition Investigation of Negro Tenants in the Yazoo Mississippi Delta." *Mississippi Agricultural and Mechanical College Experiment Station Bulletin*, Number 254 (August 1928).

Dodge, J. R. See U.S. Department of Agriculture.

Domar, Evsey D. "On the Measurement of Technological Change." *Economic Journal* 71 (December 1961):709–729.

"On Total Factor Productivity and All That." *Journal of Political Economy* 70 (December 1962):597–608.

Dowd, Douglas F. "A Comparative Analysis of Economic Development in the American West and South." *Journal of the Economic History* 16 (December 1956): 558–574.

Du Bois, W. E. Burghardt. *The Negro Artisan: A Social Study*. Atlanta: Atlanta University Press, 1902.

"The Negro Farmer." In U.S. Bureau of the Census. *Special Reports, Supplementary Analysis and Derivative Tables, Twelfth Census of the United States: 1900*. Washington: GPO, 1906, pp. 511–579.

"The Negro Landholder of Georgia." *Bulletin of the Department of Labor* 6 (July 1901): 647–677.

R. G. Dun and Company. Mercantile Agency Credit Ledgers. Unpublished. Dun and Bradstreet Archives, Baker Library, Harvard University. These Credit Ledgers contain synopses of reports from the Mercantile Agency's agents in the field. The reports are described in Appendix G, Section 5.

The Mercantile Agency Reference Book (and Key), Containing Ratings on the Merchants, Manufacturers and Traders Generally, Throughout the United States and Canada: January 1870. 2nd edition. New York: Dun, Barlow & Company, 1870. The Mercantile Agency, beginning in 1859, issued *Reference Books* to subscribers which provided information on businesses. This information is discussed in Appendix G, Section 5.

The Mercantile Agency Reference Book (and Key), Containing Ratings on the Merchants, Manufacturers and Traders Generally, Throughout the United States and Canada: January 1875. 2nd edition. New York: Dun, Barlow & Company, 1875.

The Mercantile Agency Reference Book (and Key), Containing Ratings on the Merchants, Manufacturers and Traders Generally, Throughout the United States and Canada; January 1880. 2nd edition. New York: Dun, Barlow & Company, 1880.

The Mercantile Agency Reference Book (and Key), Containing Ratings on the Merchants, Manufacturers and Traders Generally, Throughout the United States and Canada; January 1885. Volume 67. New York: R. G. Dun & Company, 1885.

Durnin, J. V. G. A., and Passmore, R. *Energy, Work and Leisure*. London: Heinemann Educational Books, 1967.

Easterlin, Richard A. "Estimates of Manufacturing Activity." In Simon Kuznets and Dorothy Swaine Thomas, editors. *Population Redistribution and Economic Growth, United States, 1870–1950*, Volume 1, *Methodological Considerations and Reference Tables*. Philadelphia: American Philosophical Society, 1957, pp. 634–701.

"Farm Production and Income in Old and New Areas at Mid-Century." In David C. Klingaman and Richard K. Vedder, editors. *Essays in Nineteenth Century Economic*

History: The Old Northwest. Athens: Ohio University Press, 1975, pp. 77–117.

"Interregional Differences in Per Capita Income, Population, and Total Income, 1840–1950." In National Bureau of Economic Research. *Trends in the American Economy in the Nineteenth Century.* Studies in Income and Wealth, Volume 24. Princeton: Princeton University Press, 1960, pp. 73–140.

"Regional Growth of Income: Long Term Tendencies, 1880–1950." In Simon Kuznets and Dorothy Swaine Thomas, editors. *Population Redistribution and Economic Growth, United States, 1870–1950,* Volume 2, *Analyses of Economic Change.* Philadelphia: American Philosophical Society, 1960, pp. 140–287.

"Regional Income Trends, 1840–1959." In Seymour E. Harris, editor. *American Economic History.* New York: McGraw-Hill Company, 1961.

"State Income Estimates." In Simon Kuznets and Dorothy Swaine Thomas, editors. *Population Redistribution and Economic Growth, United States, 1870–1950,* Volume 1, *Methodological Considerations and Reference Tables.* Philadelphia: American Philosophical Society, 1957, pp. 703–757.

Eaton, John. *Grant, Lincoln and the Freedmen.* New York: Longmans, Greene & Company, 1907.

Edwards, Thomas J. "The Tenant System and Some Changes Since Emancipation." *Annals of the American Academy of Political Science* 49 (September 1913):38–46.

Ellison, Thomas. *The Cotton Trade of Great Britain.* New York: Augustus Kelly, 1968. Originally published in 1886.

Engerman, Stanley L. "The Antebellum South: What Probably Was and What Should Have Been." *Agricultural History* 44 (January 1970):127–142.

"The Economic Impact of the Civil War." *Explorations in Entrepreneurial History,* Second Series 3 (spring 1966):176–199.

"The Effects of Slavery on the Southern Economy." *Explorations in Entrepreneurial History,* Second Series 4 (winter 1967):71–97.

"Some Economic Factors in Southern Backwardness in the Nineteenth Century." In John F. Kain and John R. Meyer, editors. *Essays in Regional Economics.* Cambridge: Harvard University Press, 1971, pp. 279–306.

Evans, Robert, Jr. "The Economics of American Negro Slavery." In Universities-National Bureau Committee for Economic Research. *Aspects of Labor Economics.* Princeton: Princeton University Press, 1962, pp. 185–243.

Evans, W. H. "The Labor Question." *Southern Cultivator* 27 (1869):54–55.

Fand, David I. "Estimates of Deposits and Vault Cash in the Non-National Banks in the Post Civil War Period in the United States: 1876–1896." Ph.D. dissertation, University of Chicago, March 1954.

Fischbaum, Marvin, and Rubin, Julius. "Slavery and the Economic Development of the American South." *Explorations in Entrepreneurial History,* Second Series 6 (fall 1968): 116–127.

Fishlow, Albert. *American Railroads and the Transformation of the Ante-Bellum Economy.* Cambridge: Harvard University Press, 1965.

"Antebellum Interregional Trade Reconsidered." *American Economic Review* 54 (May 1964):352–364.

Flanders, Ralph Betts. *Plantation Slavery in Georgia.* Chapel Hill: University of North Carolina Press, 1933.

Fleming, Walter L., editor. *Documentary History of Reconstruction: Political, Military, Social, Religious, Educational and Industrial: 1865 to the Present Time.* 2 volumes. Gloucester: Peter Smith, 1960. Originally published in 1906.

"Forty Acres and a Mule." *North American Review* 183 (May 1906):721–737.

The Sequel of Appomattox. New Haven: Yale University Press, 1919.

Fogel, Robert W. "American Interregional Trade in the Nineteenth Century." In Ralph L. Andreano, editor. *New Views on American Economic Development.* Cambridge: Schenkman, 1965, pp. 213–224.

"A Provisional View of the 'New Economic History.'" In Ralph L. Andreano, editor. *New Views on American Economic Development*. Cambridge: Schenkman, 1965, pp. 201–209.

Railroads and American Economic Growth: Essays in Econometric History. Baltimore: Johns Hopkins Press, 1964.

Fogel, Robert W., and Engerman, Stanley L. "The Economics of Slavery." In Robert W. Fogel and Stanley L. Engerman, editors. *The Reinterpretation of American Economic History*. New York: Harper & Row, 1971, pp. 311–341.

"The Market Evaluation of Human Capital: The Case of Slavery." Paper delivered at the Annual Cliometrics Conference, University of Wisconsin, Madison, April 1972.

Time on the Cross. 2 volumes. Boston: Little, Brown & Company, 1974. Volume 1, *The Economics of American Negro Slavery*; Volume 2, *Evidence and Methods: A Supplement*.

Fogel, Robert W., and Rutner, Jack L. "The Efficiency of Federal Land Policy, 1850–1900: A Report of Some Provisional Findings." In William O. Aydelotte, Allan G. Bogue, and Robert W. Fogel, editors. *The Dimensions of Quantitative Research in History*. Princeton: Princeton University Press, 1972, pp. 390–418.

Foulke, Roy A. *The Sinews of American Commerce*. New York: Dun & Bradstreet, Inc., 1941. A history of Dun and Bradstreet, this book provides valuable information on the materials in the R. G. Dun and Company Credit Ledgers and Reference Books.

Foust, James D. "The Yeoman Farmer and Westward Expansion of U.S. Cotton Production." Ph.D. dissertation, University of North Carolina, 1967.

Foust, James D., and Swan, Dale E. "Productivity and Profitability of Antebellum Slave Labor: A Micro-Approach." *Agricultural History* 44 (January 1970):39–62.

Franklin, John Hope. *Reconstruction After the Civil War*. Chicago: University of Chicago Press, 1961.

Friedman, Milton, and Schwartz, Anna J. *Monetary Statistics of the United States: Estimates, Sources, Methods*. New York: National Bureau of Economic Research, 1970.

Frissell, Hollis Burke. "Popular Education in the South." An address before the Montgomery [Alabama] Conference of the Southern Society for the Promotion of the Study of Race Conditions and Problems in the South, May 9, 1900. In *Race Problems in the South: Report of the Proceedings of the First Annual Conference Held Under the Auspices of the Southern Society*. New York: Negro University Press, 1969. First published in 1900.

Gallman, Robert E. "Commodity Output, 1839–1899." In National Bureau of Economic Research. *Trends in the American Economy in the Nineteenth Century*. Studies in Income and Wealth, Volume 24. Princeton: Princeton University Press, 1960, pp. 13–67.

"Efficiency and Farm Interdependence in an Agricultural Export Region: Sampling Procedure and Tests of the Sample." Unpublished paper, University of North Carolina, October 20, 1965. This paper describes the procedures used to collect and check the data from a sample of 5,230 farms drawn by Gallman and William Parker from the 1859 manuscript census returns.

"Gross National Product in the United States, 1834–1909." In National Bureau of Economic Research. *Output, Employment, and Productivity in the United States After 1800*. Studies in Income and Wealth, Volume 30. New York: Columbia University Press, 1966, pp. 3–76.

"Self-Sufficiency in the Cotton Economy of the Ante-bellum South." *Agricultural History* 44 (January 1970):5–23.

"Southern Ante-Bellum Income Reconsidered." *Explorations in Economic History* 12 (January 1975):89–99.

Gates, Paul W. *Agriculture and the Civil War*. New York: Alfred A. Knopf, 1965.

Genovese, Eugene D. "The Medical and Insurance Costs of Slaveholding in the Cotton Belt." *Journal of Negro History* 45 (July 1963):141–155.

The Political Economy of Slavery: Studies in the Economy and Society of the Slave South. New York: Pantheon Books, 1965.

Roll, Jordan, Roll: The World the Slaves Made. New York: Pantheon Books, 1974.

"Yeoman Farmers in a Slaveholders' Democracy." *Agricultural History* 49 (April 1973): 331–342.

Georgia, Department of Agriculture. *Annual Report of Thomas P. Janes, Commissioner of Agriculture of the State of Georgia for the Year 1875.* Atlanta: J. H. Estill, 1876. The Georgia Department of Agriculture conducted regular surveys of its county correspondents regarding prices, production, and credit conditions of farmers. The results of these surveys were regularly reported in the annual report or other department publications. This is the most comprehensive source for credit and cash prices charged by rural merchants in the South.

Publications of the Georgia State Department of Agriculture [From September 1874 through 1890]. 16 volumes. Atlanta: J. P. Harrison & Company, 1878–1891.

Georgia, Department of Education. *Report of the State School Commissioner of Georgia to the General Assembly [1877/1878].* Atlanta: James P. Harrison & Company, 1881.

Georgia, Office of the Comptroller General. *Annual Report of the Comptroller General of the State of Georgia . . . October 16, 1866.* Macon: J. W. Burke & Company, 1866. The Georgia comptroller general published statistics on landownership, ownership of other taxable assets, and employment. The tax ledgers for some Georgia counties, which contain the original data, are accessible through the Georgia State Archives in Atlanta, Georgia.

Report of Madison Bell, Comptroller General of the State of Georgia Covering the Period from August 11, 1868 to January 1, 1869. Atlanta: Samuel Bard, 1869.

Annual Report of the Comptroller General of the State of Georgia in 1870. Atlanta: 1871.

Annual Report of the Comptroller General of the State of Georgia . . . April 1, 1871. Atlanta: Constitution Publishing Company, 1871.

Annual Report of the Comptroller General of the State of Georgia for the Year 1874. Atlanta: J. H. Estill, 1875.

Fourth Annual Report of the Comptroller General of the State of Georgia for the Year 1876. Atlanta: H. G. Wright, 1877.

Report of the Comptroller General of the State of Georgia from January 1st to October 1st, 1878. Atlanta: J. P. Harrison, 1878.

Report of the Comptroller General of the State of Georgia from October 1st, 1879, to October 1st, 1880. Atlanta: Constitution Publishing Company, 1880.

Report of the Comptroller General of the State of Georgia for the Year Ending September 30, 1884. Atlanta: J. P. Harrington & Company, 1884.

Gordon, Donald F., and Walton, Gary M. "A New Theory of Regenerative Growth and the Post-World War II Experience of West Germany." Unpublished paper, Indiana University and the University of Rochester, November 1973.

Gottlieb, Manuel. "The Land Question in Georgia During Reconstruction." *Science and Society* 3 (summer 1939):356–388.

Govan, Thomas P. "Was Plantation Slavery Profitable?" *Journal of Southern History* 8 (November 1942):515–535.

Grady, Henry W. "Cotton and Its Kingdom." *Harper's New Monthly Magazine* 63 (October 1881):719–734.

Gray, Lewis Cecil. "Economic Efficiency and Competitive Advantages of Slavery Under the Plantation System." *Agricultural History* 4 (April 1930):31–47.

History of Agriculture in the Southern United States to 1860. 2 volumes. Washington: Carnegie Institution, 1933.

Greene, Lorenzo J., and Woodson, Carter G. *The Negro Wage Earner.* Washington: Association for the Study of Negro Life and History, 1930.

Gunderson, Gerald. "Southern Ante bellum Income Reconsidered." *Explorations in Economic History* 10 (winter 1973):151–176.

"Southern Income Reconsidered: A Reply." *Explorations in Economic History* 12 (January 1975):101–102.

Gutman, Herbert, and Sutch, Richard. "Sambo Makes Good, or Were Slaves Imbued with the Protestant Work Ethic?" In Paul A. David, Herbert G. Gutman, Richard Sutch, Peter

Temin, and Gavin Wright. *Reckoning with Slavery: A Critical Study in the Quantitative History of American Negro Slavery*. New York: Oxford University Press, 1976, pp. 55–93.

"The Slave Family: Protected Agent of Capitalist Masters or Victim of the Slave Trade?" In Paul A. David, Herbert G. Gutman, Richard Sutch, Peter Temin, and Gavin Wright. *Reckoning with Slavery: A Critical Study in the Quantitative History of American Negro Slavery*. New York: Oxford University Press, 1976, pp. 94–133.

"Victorians All? The Sexual Mores and Conduct of Slaves and Their Masters." In Paul A. David, Herbert G. Gutman, Richard Sutch, Peter Temin, and Gavin Wright. *Reckoning with Slavery: A Critical Study in the Quantitative History of American Negro Slavery*. New York: Oxford University Press, 1976, pp. 134–162.

Hacker, Louis C. *The Triumph of American Capitalism*. New York: Columbia University Press, 1940.

Hall, Arden R. "The Efficiency of Post-Bellum Southern Agriculture." Ph.D. dissertation, University of California, Berkeley, 1975.

Hammond, Harry. "Cotton Production in South Carolina." In Eugene W. Hilgard, Special Agent, Tenth Census [1880]. *Report on Cotton Production in the United States also Embracing Agricultural and Physico-Geographical Descriptions of the Several Cotton States and of California*. Volume 2. Washington: GPO, 1884.

South Carolina: Resources and Population. Institutions and Industry. Charleston: Walker, Evans & Cogswell, 1883. Hammond compiled statistics for each town in South Carolina. Data on population, commerce, and transportation are given for each town, and more extensive information is provided for major cities.

Hammond, Mathew B. *The Cotton Industry: An Essay in American Economic History*, Part I, *The Cotton Culture and the Cotton Trade*. New York: American Economic Association and Macmillan Company, 1897.

"The Southern Farmer and the Cotton Question." *Political Science Quarterly* 12 (September 1897):450–475.

Harlan, Louis R. "Desegregation in New Orleans Public Schools During Reconstruction." *American Historical Review* 67 (April 1962):663–675.

Harper, Chancellor. "Harper on Slavery." In *The Pro-Slavery Argument, As Maintained by the Most Distinguished Writers of the Southern States, Containing the Several Essays, on the Subject, by Chancellor Harper, Governor Hammond, Dr. Simms, and Professor Dew*. New York: Negro Universities Press, 1968. Originally published in 1852 by Walker, Richards & Company.

Hawk, Emory Q. *Economic History of the South*. New York: Prentice-Hall, 1934.

Hemphill, J. C. See U.S. Department of Agriculture.

Henry, W. A. *Feeds and Feeding: A Handbook for the Student and Stockman*. Madison: W. A. Henry, 1898.

Henry, W. A., and Morrison, F. B., editors. *Feeds and Feeding: A Handbook for the Student and Stockman*. 17th edition. Madison: Henry-Morrison Company, 1921.

Higgs, Robert. *Competition and Coercion: Blacks in the American Economy, 1865–1914*. New York: Cambridge University Press, 1977.

The Transformation of the American Economy, 1865–1914: An Essay in Interpretation. New York: John Wiley & Sons, 1971.

Hilgard, Eugene W. See U.S. Census Office, Tenth Census [1880].

Hill, B. H. "The True Policy of the Southern Planter." *Rural Carolinian* 5 (April 1874): 398–399.

Hilliard, Sam Bowers. *Hog Meat and Hoecake: Food Supply in the Old South, 1840–1860*. Carbondale: Southern Illinois University Press, 1972.

Hoffman, Edwin D. "From Slavery to Self-Reliance." *Journal of Negro History* 41 (January 1956):8–42.

Holmes, George K. "The Peons of the South." *Annals of the American Academy of Political and Social Science* 4 (September 1893):65–74.

Also see U.S. Department of Agriculture, Bureau of Statistics.

Homans, I. Smith, editor. *The Bankers' Magazine and Statistical Register.* 21 [1, 3rd series] (August 1866). Homans's *Almanac* is the most comprehensive index of bankers available. Published annually, it lists the address and organization of each bank, organized by city and state.

—— editor. *The Merchants & Bankers' Almanac for 1869.* New York: Office of the Bankers' Magazine and Statistical Register, 1869.

—— editor. *The Banker's Almanac and Register, January 1874.* New York: Homans, Jr., 1874.

Homans, I. Smith, Jr., editor. *The Banker's Register, January 1880.* New York: I. S. Homans, Jr., 1880.

Hoover, Ethel D. "Retail Prices After 1850." In National Bureau for Economic Research. *Trends in the American Economy in the Nineteenth Century.* Studies in Income and Wealth, Volume 24. Princeton: Princeton University Press, 1960.

Howard, L. O. See U.S. Department of Agriculture, Division of Entomology.

Howard, Oliver Otis. "Address before the Cooper Institute of New York on the Freedmen Question." *De Bow's Review* 1 (March 1866):324.

—— Also see U.S. Bureau of Refugees, Freedmen, and Abandoned Lands.

Hughes, J. R. T. "[Book Review of] Robert W. Fogel and Stanley L. Engerman, editors, *The Reinterpretation of American Economic History.*" *Explorations in Economic History* 10 (fall 1972):119–127.

Hurt, A. B. See U.S. Department of Agriculture.

Hutchinson, William K., and Williamson, Samuel H. "The Self-Sufficiency of the Antebellum South: Estimates of the Food Supply." *Journal of Economic History* 31 (September 1971):591–612.

Jacques, D. H. "Future of Southern Farming." *Rural Carolinian* 1 (November 1869): 113–114.

Janes, Thomas P. See Georgia, Department of Agriculture.

Jennings, Ralph Dickieson. See U.S. Department of Agriculture.

Johnson, D. Gale. "Resource Allocation Under Share Contracts." *Journal of Political Economy* 58 (April 1950):111–123.

Jones, W. N. See North Carolina, Bureau of Labor Statistics.

Jordan, Winthrop D. *White over Black: American Attitudes Toward the Negro, 1550–1812.* Chapel Hill: University of North Carolina Press, 1968.

Kelsey, Carl. *The Negro Farmer.* Chicago: Jennings & Pye, 1903.

King, Edward. *The Southern States of North America: A Record of Journies. . . .* London: Blackie & Son, 1875.

Kitson Clark, George. *The Making of Victorian England, Being the Ford Lectures Delivered Before the University of Oxford.* Cambridge: Harvard University Press, 1962.

Kloosterboer, Willemina. *Involuntary Labour Since the Abolition of Slavery.* Leiden: E. J. Brill, 1960.

Knight, Edgar Wallace. *The Influence of Reconstruction on Education in the South.* New York: Arno Press, 1969. Originally published in 1913.

Knox, John Jay. *A History of Banking in the United States.* New York: Bradford Rhodes & Company, 1903.

Kolchin, Peter. *First Freedom: The Response of Alabama's Blacks to Emancipation and Reconstruction.* Westport: Greenwood Press, 1972.

Kuznets, Simon, and Thomas, Dorothy Swaine, editors. *Population Redistribution and Economic Growth, United States, 1870–1950.* 3 volumes. Philadelphia: American Philosophical Society, 1957, 1960, and 1964.

Lamb, Robert B. *The Mule in Southern Agriculture.* Berkeley: University of California Press, 1963.

Latham, Alexander and Company. *Cotton Movement and Fluctuation: 1903–1908.* 35th edition. New York: Latham, Alexander & Company, 1908. Latham, Alexander and Company compiled statistics on the cotton trade for each year since 1859. These figures have been accepted as the "official" annual cotton statistics by the U.S. Department of Agriculture.

Lee, Everett S. "Migration Estimates." In Simon Kuznets and Dorothy Swaine Thomas, editors. *Population Redistribution and Economic Growth, United States, 1870–1950*, Volume 1, *Methodological Considerations and Reference Tables*. Philadelphia: American Philosophical Society, 1957, pp. 9–362.

Lerner, Eugene M. "Southern Output and Agricultural Income, 1860–1880." *Agricultural History* 33 (July 1959):117–125.

Lightfoot, A. R. "Condition and Wants of the Cotton Raising States." *De Bow's Review* 6 (February 1869):151–154.

Linden, Fabian. "Economic Democracy in the Slave South: An Appraisal of Some Recent Views." *Journal of Negro History* (April 1946):140–189.

Lindstrom, Diane. "Southern Dependence upon Interregional Grain Supplies: A Review of the Trade Flows, 1840–1860." *Agricultural History* 44 (January 1970):101–113.

Loring, F. W., and Atkinson, C. F. *Cotton Culture and the South Considered with Reference to Emigration*. Boston: A. Williams & Co., 1869. The Boston firm of Loring and Atkinson undertook an extensive survey of cotton planters in 1868–1869.

Louisiana, Bureau of Agriculture. *Biennial Report of the Commissioner of Agriculture of the State of Louisiana [1886 through 1896]*. Baton Rouge: Leon Jastremski, 1886–1896. The Louisiana Bureau of Agriculture collected data on prices, production, and credit conditions of farmers. This information was summarized each year from 1886 through 1896 in the biennial reports of the commissioner.

Macauley, Frederick R. *Some Theoretical Problems Suggested by the Movement of Interest Rates, Bond Yields and Stock Prices in the United States Since 1856*. New York: National Bureau of Economic Research, 1938.

Marshall, Alfred. *Principles of Political Economy*. 1st edition. London: 1890.

Martin, Edgar W. *The Standard of Living in 1860: American Consumption Levels on the Eve of the Civil War*. Chicago: University of Chicago Press, 1942.

Martin, Robert F. *National Income in the United States, 1799–1938*. New York: National Industrial Conference Board, 1939.

McPherson, Edward. *The Political History of the United States of America During the Period of Reconstruction (from April 15, 1865, to July 15, 1870)*. . . . 3rd edition. Washington: James J. Chapman, 1880. McPherson's "history" is actually a digest of laws and extracts of statutes passed in the southern states during the period 1865–1870.

Mendenhall, Marjorie Stratford. "The Rise of Southern Tenancy." *Yale Review* new series 27 (autumn 1937): 110–129.

Metzer, Jacob. "Rational Management, Modern Business Practices, and Economies of Scale in the Ante-Bellum Southern Plantations." *Explorations in Economic History* 12 (April 1975):123–150.

Mill, John Stuart. *Principles of Political Economy, with Some of Their Applications to Social Philosophy*. 2 volumes. Boston: Charles C. Little & James Brown, 1848.

Miller, Ann Ratner, and Brainerd, Carol P. "Labor Force Estimates." In Simon Kuznets and Dorothy Swaine Thomas, editors. *Population Redistribution and Economic Growth, United States, 1870–1950*, Volume 1, *Methodological Considerations and Reference Tables*. Philadelphia: American Philosophical Society, 1957, pp. 362–633.

Montgomery, J. N. "Farm Management," speech delivered February 12, 1878, at Americus, Georgia. In *Transactions of the Georgia State Agricultural Society, from August 1876 to February 1878*. Atlanta: James P. Harrison, 1878, pp. 396–409.

Morehead, Sherrod D. *Merchant Credit to Farmers in Louisiana*. Russellville: privately printed, 1929.

Morison, Samuel Eliot, and Commager, Henry Steele. *The Growth of the American Republic*. New York: Oxford University Press, 1930.

Morrison, F. B. *Feeds and Feeding: A Handbook for the Student and Stockman*. 21st edition. Ithaca: Morrison Company, 1940.

Myrdal, Gunnar. *An American Dilemma*. 2 volumes. New York: Harper & Row, 1944.

National Bureau of Economic Research. *Output, Employment, and Productivity in the United States after 1800*. Studies in Income and Wealth, Volume 30, by the Conference on

Research in Income and Wealth. Princeton: Princeton University Press, 1966

    Trends in the American Economy in the Nineteenth Century. Studies in Income and Wealth, Volume 24, by the Conference on Research in Income and Wealth. Princeton: Princeton University Press, 1960.

Niemi, Albert W., Jr. *U.S. Economic History: A Survey of the Major Issues.* Chicago: Rand McNally College Publishing Company, 1975.

Nimmo, Joseph, Jr. *First Annual Report on the Internal Commerce of the United States . . . for the Fiscal Year Ending June 30, 1876.* House of Representatives, Executive Document Number 46, Part 2, 44th Congress, 2nd Session. Washington: GPO, 1877.

North, Douglass C. *The Economic Growth of the United States, 1790–1860.* Englewood Cliffs: Prentice-Hall, 1961.

North Carolina, Bureau of Labor Statistics. W. N. Jones, Commissioner. *First Annual Report of the Bureau of Labor Statistics of the State of North Carolina, for the Year 1887.* Raleigh: Josephus Daniels, 1887. The report by Commissioner Jones included the results of a comprehensive survey of North Carolina taken in 1886–1887. Landlords, tenants, and laborers were included, and a large number of extracts from each class of respondent was printed in the report.

Olmsted, Frederick Law. *The Cotton Kingdom.* Edited, with an introduction, by Arthur M. Schlesinger. New York: Alfred A. Knopf, 1953. Originally published in 1861.

    A Journey in the Back Country. New York: Mason Brothers, 1860.

    A Journey in the Seaboard Slave States. New York: Dix & Edwards, 1856.

    A Journey Through Texas. New York: Dix, Edwards & Company, 1857.

Otken, Charles H. *The Ills of the South, or Related Causes Hostile to the General Prosperity of the Southern People.* New York: G. P. Putnam's Sons, 1894.

Owsley, Frank L. *The Plain Folk of the Old South.* Baton Rouge: Louisiana State University Press, 1949.

Owsley, Frank L., and Owsley, Harriet C. "The Economic Basis of Society in the Late Ante-Bellum South." *Journal of Southern History* 6 (February 1940):24–45.

Parker, William N., editor. *The Structure of the Cotton Economy of the Antebellum South.* Berkeley: University of California Press, 1970. Also printed as *Agricultural History* 44 (January 1970):1–182.

Peters, Theodore C. "Report of an Agricultural Survey of the South." Letter to Isaac Newton, U.S. Commissioner of Agriculture, dated June 1, 1867. Printed in U.S. Department of Agriculture, *Monthly Report* (May-June 1867):192–203.

    A Report Upon Conditions of the South, with Regard to Its Needs for a Cotton Crop and Its Financial Wants in Connection Therewith as Well as the Safety of Temporary Loans. Baltimore: H. A. Robinson for R. M. Rhodes & Company, 1867. Peters toured the major cities of the Southeast on behalf of the Baltimore firm of R. M. Rhodes. His report was addressed to General Grant and included, together with his own impressions of the financial state of the South, letters from leading southern businessmen and planters commenting on the South's need for capital.

Peterson, Arthur G. "Historical Study of Prices Received by Producers of Farm Products in Virginia, 1801–1927. Virginia Agricultural Experiment Station, *Technical Bulletin,* number 37. Blacksburg: Virginia Polytechnic Institute, 1929.

Phillips, Ulrich Bonnell. *American Negro Slavery: A Survey of the Supply, Employment and Control of Negro Labor as Determined by the Plantation Regime.* New York: D. Appleton & Company, 1918.

    "The Economic Cost of Slaveholding in the Cotton Belt." *Political Science Quarterly* 20 (June 1905):257–275.

    Life and Labor in the Old South. Boston: Little, Brown & Company, 1963. Originally published in 1929.

    "The Origin and Growth of the Southern Black Belts." *American Historical Review* 11 (July 1906):798–816.

Postell, William Dosite. *The Health of Slaves on Southern Plantations.* Baton Rouge: Louisiana State University Press, 1951.

Primack, Martin L. "Farm Construction as a Use of Farm Labor in the United States, 1850–1960." *Journal of Economic History* 25 (March 1965):114–125.

Randall, James G., and Donald, David. *The Civil War and Reconstruction.* Boston: D. C. Heath & Company, 1961.

Ransom, Roger L., and Sutch, Richard. "Debt Peonage in the Cotton South After the Civil War." *Journal of Economic History* 32 (September 1972):641–669.

"Documenting Monopoly Power in the Rural South: The Case of the General Store." *Southern Economic History Project Working Paper Series,* Number 15. Riverside: Center for Social and Behavioral Science Research, June 1975.

"Economic Regions of the South in 1880." *Southern Economic History Project Working Paper Series,* Number 3. Berkeley: Institute of Business and Economic Research, March 1971.

"The Ex-Slave in the Post-Bellum South: A Study of the Economic Impact of Racism in a Market Environment." *Journal of Economic History* 33 (March 1973):131–148.

"The Impact of the Civil War and of Emancipation on Southern Agriculture." *Explorations in Economic History* 12 (January 1975):1–28.

"The 'Lock-in' Mechanism and Overproduction of Cotton in the Postbellum South." *Agricultural History* 49 (April 1975):405–425.

"The Rise of Sharecropping in the American South, 1865–1900: A Preliminary Report." *Southern Economic History Project Working Paper Series,* Number 1. Berkeley: Institute of Business and Economic Research, University of California, July 1969.

"Tenancy, Farm Size, Self-Sufficiency and Racism: Four Problems in the Economic History of Southern Agriculture, 1865–1880." *Southern Economic History Project Working Paper Series,* Number 8. Berkeley: Institute of Business and Economic Research, University of California, April 1970.

Ransom, Roger L.; Sutch, Richard; and Boutin, George. "A Sample of Southern Farms in 1880: Sampling Procedure." *Southern Economic History Project Working Paper Series,* Number 2. Berkeley: Institute of Business and Economic Research, University of California, September 1969.

Rawick, George P., editor. *The American Slave: A Composite Autobiography.* 19 volumes. Westport: Greenwood Publishing Company, 1972. Rawick has compiled volumes reprinting interviews taken in the 1930s with ex-slaves, as part of the Federal Writers' Project of the Works Progress Administration.

Redding, R. J. "Corn Culture." *Georgia Agricultural Experiment Station Bulletin,* Number 10 (December 1890); Number 15 (December 1891); Number 23 (December 1893); Number 27 (December 1894); and Number 30 (November 1895).

Reid, Joseph D., Jr. "Antebellum Southern Rental Contracts." *Explorations in Economic History* 13 (January 1976):69–83.

"Sharecropping as an Understandable Market Response: The Post-Bellum South." *Journal of Economic History* 33 (March 1973):106–130.

"Sharecropping in History and Theory." *Agricultural History* 49 (April 1975):426–440.

Reid, Whitelaw. *After the War: A Tour of the Southern States, 1865–1866.* New York: Harper & Row, 1965. Originally published in 1866.

Robinson, Joan. *The Economics of Imperfect Competition.* 2nd edition. London: Macmillan Company, 1969. First edition published in 1933.

Rose, Louis A. "Capital Losses of Southern Slaveholders Due to Emancipation." *Western Economic Journal* 3 (fall 1964):39–51.

Rose, Willie Lee. *Rehearsal for Reconstruction: The Port Royal Experiment.* New York: Alfred A. Knopf, 1964.

The Rural Carolinian: An Illustrated Magazine of Agriculture, Horticulture and the Arts, Volumes 1ff. Charleston: Walker, Evans & Cogswell, and D. Wyatt Aiken.

Russell, Robert R. "The Effects of Slavery upon Nonslaveholders in the Ante-Bellum South." *Agricultural History* 15 (April 1941):112–126.

"The General Effects of Slavery upon Southern Economic Progress." *Journal of Southern History* 4 (February 1938):34–54.

Salutos, Theodore. *Farmer Movements in the South, 1865–1933.* Berkeley: University of California Press, 1960.

Sampson, Arthur F. *Federal Population Censuses, 1790–1890: A Catalogue of Microfilm Copies of the Schedules.* Washington: National Archives and Records Services, 1974.

Sanger, George P., editor. *The Statutes at Large, Treaties, and Proclamations, of the United States of America,* Volume 12, *December 1859 to March 1863.* Boston: Little, Brown & Company, 1863.

———, editor. *The Statutes at Large, Treaties, and Proclamations, of the United States of America,* Volume 13, *April 1863 to December 1865.* Boston: Little, Brown & Company, 1866.

Saraydar, Edward. "A Note on the Profitability of Ante Bellum Slavery." *Southern Economic Journal* 30 (April 1964):325–332.

Schmidt, Louis B. "Internal Commerce and the Development of a National Economy Before 1860." *Journal of Political Economy* 47 (December 1939):798–822.

Schurz, Carl. "Report of Carl Schurz on the States of South Carolina, Georgia, Alabama, Mississippi, and Louisiana." In *Message of the President of the United States, Communicating . . . Information in Relation to the States of the Union Lately in Rebellion (December 19, 1865).* Senate, Executive Document Number 2, 39th Congress, 1st Session. Washington: GPO, 1865. Schurz was sent to the South by President Johnson in 1865. His report of his trip stresses the political situation in the South and the problems encountered in guaranteeing ex-slaves' rights as freedmen.

Seagrave, Charles Edwin. "The Southern Negro Agricultural Worker: 1850–1870." Ph.D. thesis, Stanford University, 1971.

Sellers, James Benson. *Slavery in Alabama.* University: University of Alabama Press, 1950.

Sellers, James L. "The Economic Incidence of the Civil War in the South." *Mississippi Valley Historical Review* 14 (September 1927):179–191.

Shannon, Fred A. *The Farmer's Last Frontier: 1860–1897.* New York: Holt, Rinehart & Winston, 1945.

Sherman, William Tecumseh. "Special Field Order No. 120 . . . Kingston, Georgia, November 9, 1864." In U.S. Congress, House of Representatives, Miscellaneous Document Number 233, Part 3, 52nd Congress, 1st Session. *The War of the Rebellion: A Compilation of the Official Records of the Union and Confederate Armies.* Series 1, Volume 39, Part 3, Correspondence. Washington: GPO, 1892.

Shugg, Roger W. *Origins of Class Struggle in Louisiana: A Social History of White Farmers and Laborers During Slavery and After, 1840–1875.* Baton Rouge: Louisiana State University Press, 1939.

———. "Survival of the Plantation System in Louisiana." *Journal of Southern History* 3 (August 1937):311–325.

Sisk, Glenn N. "Rural Merchandising in the Alabama Black Belt." *Journal of Farm Economics* 37 (November 1955):705–715.

———. "The Wholesale Commission Business in the Alabama Black Belt, 1875–1917." *Journal of Farm Economics* 38 (August 1956):799–802.

Somers, Robert. *The Southern States Since the War, 1870–1.* New York: Macmillan & Company, 1871.

Southern Cultivator: A Practical and Scientific Magazine for the Plantation, the Garden and the Family Circle. Volumes 27–42. Athens, Georgia.

The Southern Cultivator and Dixie Farmer. Volumes 43ff. Atlanta, Georgia.

"Southerner." "Agricultural Labor at the South." *Galaxy Magazine* 12 (September 1871): 330–338.

Spence, A. Michael. *Market Signalling: Informational Transfer in Hiring and Related Screening Processes.* Cambridge: Harvard University Press, 1974.

Spofford, Ainsworth R., editor. *American Almanac and Treasury of Facts, Statistical, Financial, and Political, for the Year 1889.* New York: American News Co., 1889.

Stampp, Kenneth M. *The Era of Reconstruction, 1865–1877.* New York: Alfred A. Knopf, 1966.

The Peculiar Institution: Slavery in the Ante-Bellum South. New York: Alfred A. Knopf, 1956.

Stone, Alfred Holt. "The Negro in the Yazoo-Mississippi Delta." *American Economic Association Publications,* Third Series 3 (1902):235–278.

Stover, John F. *The Railroads of the South: 1865–1900.* Chapel Hill: University of North Carolina Press, 1955.

Strauss, Frederick, and Bean, Louis H. See U.S. Department of Agriculture.

Stubbs, William C. "Report." *North Louisiana Experiment Station Bulletin.* Number 22 (January 1889).

Sutch, Richard. "The Breeding of Slaves for Sale and the Westward Expansion of Slavery, 1850–1860." In Stanley L. Engerman and Eugene D. Genovese, editors. *Race and Slavery in the Western Hemisphere: Quantitative Studies.* Princeton: Princeton University Press, 1975, pp. 173–210.

"The Care and Feeding of Slaves." In Paul A. David, Herbert G. Gutman, Richard Sutch, Peter Temin, and Gavin Wright. *Reckoning with Slavery: A Critical Study in the Quantitative History of American Negro Slavery.* New York: Oxford University Press, 1976, pp. 231–301.

"The Profitability of Slavery – Revisited." *Southern Economic Journal* 31 (April 1965): 365–377.

"The Treatment Received by American Slaves: A Critical Review of the Evidence Presented in *Time on the Cross.*" *Explorations in Economic History* 12 (October 1975):335–438.

Switzler, William F. *Report on the Internal Commerce of the United States . . . 1886.* House of Representatives, Executive Document Number 7, Part 2, 49th Congress, 2nd Session. Washington: GPO, 1886.

Sydnor, Charles S. *Slavery in Mississippi.* New York: Appleton-Century, 1933.

Sylla, Richard. "Federal Policy, Banking Market Structure, and Capital Mobilization in the United States, 1863–1913." *Journal of Economic History* 29 (December 1969):657–686.

Taylor, Paul S. "Plantation Agriculture in the United States: Seventeenth to Twentieth Centuries." *Land Economics* 27 (August 1951):141–152.

"Slave to Freedman." *Southern Economic History Project Working Paper Series,* Number 7. Berkeley: Institute of Business and Economic Research, University of California, January 1970.

Taylor, Rosser H. "Feeding Slaves." *Journal of Negro History* 9 (April 1924):139–143.

Thompson, Daniel C. *Sociology of the Black Experience.* Contributions in Sociology, Number 14. Westport: Greenwood Press, 1974.

Towne, Marvin W., and Rasmussen, Wayne D. "Farm Gross Product and Gross Investment in the Nineteenth Century." National Bureau of Economic Research. *Trends in the American Economy in the Nineteenth Century.* Studies in Income and Wealth, Volume 24. Princeton: Princeton University Press, 1960, pp. 255–312.

Townsend, C. H. Tyler. See U.S. Department of Agriculture, Division of Entomology.

Tracy, S. M., and Lloyd, E. R. "Corn." *Mississippi Agricultural and Mechanical College Experiment Station Bulletin,* Number 33 (March 1895).

Trowbridge, John Townsend. *The Desolate South, 1865–1866.* Boston: Little, Brown & Company, 1956. Originally published in 1866 as *The South . . . A Journey Through the Desolated States.*

Truman, Benjamin C. "Report of Benjamin C. Truman (April 9, 1866). "In *Message of the President of the United States, Communicating . . . a Report . . . Relative to the Condition of the Southern People and the States in Which the Rebellion Existed.* Senate, Executive Document Number 43, 39th Congress, 1st Session. Washington: GPO, 1866. Truman was sent to the South by President Johnson in 1865. His report includes detailed remarks on the "freedmen and their affairs."

U.S. Bureau of the Census. *Historical Statistics of the United States, Colonial Times to 1957.* Washington: GPO, 1960.

Negro Population: 1790–1915. Washington: GPO, 1918.

Thirteenth Census . . . Manufactures, 1909, Reports by States. Washington: GPO, 1912.

U.S. Bureau of Refugees, Freedmen, and Abandoned Lands, J. W. Alvord. *Fourth Semi-Annual Report on Schools for Freedmen, July 1, 1867.* Washington: GPO, 1867. Alvord's report contains extensive data on schools operated by the Freedmen's Bureau.

Oliver Otis Howard, Commissioner. *Report by the Commissioner of the Freedmen's Bureau of All Orders Issued by Him or Any Assistant Commissioner* (March 1866). House of Representatives, Executive Document Number 70, 39th Congress, 1st Session. Washington: GPO, 1866.

39th Congress, 1st Session, Washington: GPO, 1866. O. O. Howard's annual reports from 1865 to 1871 provide innumerable pieces of information gathered through the operation of the Freedmen's Bureau. Frequently, extracts from reports of other bureau officials are included to support the superintendent's points.

Oliver Otis Howard, Commissioner. "Report of the Commissioner of the Bureau of Refugees, Freedmen, and Abandoned Lands" (November 1866). In *Report of the Secretary of War, 1866.* House of Representatives, Executive Document Number 1, 39th Congress, 2nd Session. Washington: GPO, 1866.

Oliver Otis Howard, Commissioner. *Report by the Commissioner of the Freedmen's Bureau of All Orders Issued by Him or Any Assistant Commissioner* (March 1866). House of Representatives, Executive Document Number 70, 39th Congress, 1st Session. Washington: GPO, 1866.

Oliver Otis Howard, Commissioner. "Report of the Commissioner of the Bureau of Refugees, Freedmen, and Abandoned Lands" (November 1867). In *Report of the Secretary of War, 1867.* House of Representatives, Executive Document Number 1, Part 1, 40th Congress, 2nd Session. Washington: GPO, 1867.

Oliver Otis Howard, Commissioner. "Report of Major General O. O. Howard, Commissioner of Bureau of Refugees, Freedmen, and Abandoned Lands, to the Secretary of War" (October 14, 1868). In *Report of the Secretary of War, 1868.* House of Representatives, Executive Document Number 1, Part 1, 40th Congress, 3rd Session. Washington: GPO, 1869.

Oliver Otis Howard, Commissioner. "Report of the Commissioner Bureau of Refugees, Freedmen, &c." (October 20, 1869). In *Report of the Secretary of War, 1869.* House of Representatives, Executive Document Number 1, Part 2, Volume 1, 41st Congress, 2nd Session. Washington: GPO, 1869.

Oliver Otis Howard, Commissioner. "Report of the Commissioner Bureau of Refugees, Freedmen, Etc." (October 20, 1870). In *Report of the Secretary of War, 1870.* House of Representatives, Executive Document Number 1, Part 2, Volume 1, 41st Congress, 3rd Session. Washington: GPO, 1870.

Oliver Otis Howard, Commissioner. "Report of the Commissioner Bureau of Refugees, Freedmen, Etc." (October 20, 1871). In *Report of the Secretary of War, 1871.* House of Representatives, Executive Document Number 1, Part 2, Volume 1, 42nd Congress, 2nd Session. Washington: GPO, 1871.

Reports of the Assistant Commissioners of Freedmen, and a Synopsis of laws Respecting Persons of Color in the Late Slave States (January 1867) Senate, Executive Document Number 6, 39th Congress, 2nd Session. Washington: GPO, 1867. These reports from the assistant commissioners provide data and observations on the issues of schools, contracts, and attitudes of both blacks and white in each state.

U.S. Census Office, Seventh Census [1850]. *The Seventh Census of the United States: 1850.* Washington: Robert Armstrong, 1853.

Mortality Statistics of the Seventh Census of the United States, 1850. Washington: A. O. P. Nicholson, 1855.

U.S. Census Office, Eighth Census [1860]. *Agriculture of the United States in 1860, Compiled from the Original Returns of the Eighth Census.* Washington: GPO, 1864.

Manufactures of the United States in 1860, Compiled from the Original Returns of the Eighth Census. Washington: GPO, 1865.

Population of the United States in 1860, Compiled from the Original Returns of the Eighth Census. Washington: GPO, 1864.

Statistics of the United States (Including Mortality, Property &c.) in 1860, Compiled from the Original Returns and Being the Final Exhibit of the Eighth Census. Washington: GPO, 1866.

U.S. Census Office, Ninth Census [1870]. *The Statistics of the Population of the United States, Compiled from the Original Returns of the Ninth Census (June 1, 1870).* Washington: GPO, 1872.

The Vital Statistics of the United States, Compiled from the Original Returns of the Ninth Census (June 1, 1870). Washington: GPO, 1872.

The Statistics of the Wealth and Industry of the United States, Compiled from the Original Returns of the Ninth Census (June 1, 1870). Washington: GPO, 1872.

U.S. Census Office, Tenth Census [1880]. *Statistics of the Population of the United States at the Tenth Census (June 1, 1880).* Washington: GPO, 1883.

Report on the Manufactures of the United States at the Tenth Census (June 1, 1880). Washington: GPO, 1883.

Report on the Production of Agriculture in the United States at the Tenth Census (June 1, 1880). Washington: GPO, 1883.

Compendium of the Tenth Census (June 1, 1880). Washington: GPO, 1883.

Eugene W. Hilgard, Special Agent. *Report on Cotton Production in the United States also Embracing Agricultural and Physico-Geographical Descriptions of the Several Cotton States and of California.* 2 volumes. Washington: GPO, 1884. The Tenth Census commissioned Hilgard to supervise an exhaustive study of cotton production. This two-volume report is the most detailed and comprehensive source available for statistics on production and physical description of the cotton regions. Separate reports are presented for the cotton regions of each state.

Weeks, Jos[eph] D., Special Agent. *[Report] on the Statistics of Wages in the Manufacturing Industries, with Supplementary Reports on the Average Retail Prices of Necessaries of Life, and on Trade Societies, and Strikes and Lockouts.* Washington: GPO, 1886. Weeks' study was commissioned by the Tenth Census and remains the most comprehensive survey of prices and wages available for this period. His data relate primarily to cities, with only limited attention to the rural sector.

U.S. Census Office, Eleventh Census [1890]. *Report on the Population of the United States at the Eleventh Census: 1890.* 2 parts. Washington: GPO, 1895, 1897.

Reports on the Statistics of Agriculture in the United States. Washington: GPO, 1895.

Compendium of the Eleventh Census: 1890. 3 parts. Washington: GPO, 1892–1897.

Statistical Atlas of the United States. Washington: GPO, 1898.

U.S. Census Office, Twelfth Census [1900]. *Census Reports: Agriculture.* 2 parts. Washington: GPO, 1902.

U.S. Census Office, Thirteenth Census [1910]. *Thirteenth Census of the United States . . . 1910, Population.* Washington: GPO, 1913.

Thirteenth Census of the United States . . . 1910, Agriculture. Washington: GPO, 1913.

U.S. Comptroller of the Currency. *Report of the Comptroller of the Currency . . . (December 6, 1869).* House of Representatives, Executive Document Number 3, 41st Congress, 2nd Session. Washington: GPO, 1869.

Report of the Comptroller of the Currency, December 5, 1870. House of Representatives, Executive Document Number 3, 41st Congress, 3rd Session. Washington: GPO, 1870.

Annual Report, 1874. House of Representatives, Executive Document Number 3, 43rd Congress, 2nd Session. Washington: GPO, 1874.

Annual Report of the Comptroller of the Currency . . . December 4, 1876. House of Representatives, Executive Document Number 3, 44th Congress, 2nd Session. Washington: GPO, 1876.

Annual Report of the Comptroller of the Currency, 1877. House of Representatives, Executive Document Number 3, 45th Congress, 2nd Session. Washington: GPO, 1877.

Annual Report of the Comptroller of the Currency, 1880. House of Representatives, Executive Document Number 3, 46th Congress, 3rd Session. Washington: GPO, 1880.

Annual Report of the Comptroller of the Currency, 1881. House of Representatives, Executive Document Number 3, 47th Congress, 1st Session. Washington: GPO, 1881.

Annual Report of the Comptroller of the Currency, 1890. House of Representatives, Executive Document Number 3, Part 1, 51st Congress, 2nd Session. Washington: GPO, 1890.

U.S. Congress, *The Ku-Klux Conspiracy.* Report of the joint select committee appointed "to inquire into the condition of affairs in the late insurrectionary states." House of Representatives, Report Number 22, 42nd Congress, 2nd Session. 4 volumes, 13 parts. Washington: GPO, 1872. The joint select committee collected thirteen volumes of testimony from witnesses in every southern state. The testimony was particularly addressed to the problem of violence against Negroes.

Senate Committee on Agriculture and Forestry. "Present Condition of Cotton-Growers of the United States Compared with Previous Years." *Report of the Committee on Agriculture and Forestry on Condition of Cotton Growers in the United States, the Present Prices of Cotton, and the Remedy; and on Cotton Consumption and Production [February 23, 1895].* Senate, Report Number 986, 53rd Congress, 3rd Session. 2 volumes. Washington: GPO, 1895. The report details the problems of cotton growers in the late 1890s, including considerable testimony from growers and cotton merchants or agents.

Senate Committee on Finance. *Wholesale Prices, Wages, and Transportation.* Senate, Report Number 1394 (March 3, 1893), Part 2, 52nd Congress, 2nd Session. Washington: GPO, 1893.

U.S. Department of Agriculture. "Fluctuations in Crops and Weather, 1866–1948." *USDA Statistical Bulletin,* Number 101. Washington: GPO, 1951.

Monthly Reports of Department of Agriculture [1866–1870].

Report of the Commissioner of Agriculture for the Year [1867 through 1878]. 12 volumes. Washington: GPO, 1867–1878.

"Statistical Data Compiled and Published by the Bureau of Crop Estimates." *Department Circular,* Number 150. Washington: GPO, 1921.

Yearbook of the United States Department of Agriculture: 1903. Washington: GPO, 1904.

Agricultural Yearbook, 1923. Washington: GPO, 1924.

Horace Capron. "Southern Agriculture." In U.S. Department of Agriculture. *Report of the Commissioner of Agriculture for the Year 1867.* Washington: GPO, 1868.

J. R. Dodge. "Report of the Statistician." In U.S. Department of Agriculture. *Report of the Commissioner of Agriculture . . . for the Year 1876.* Washington: GPO, 1877. Dodge reported the results of a comprehensive survey of tenure practices in the South in 1876, as reported by the USDA correspondents in each county.

J. C. Hemphill, Special Agent. "Climate, Soil, and Agricultural Capabilities of South Carolina and Georgia." *USDA Special Report,* Number 47. Washington: GPO, 1882. One of several USDA reports dealing with the cotton states at this time. Hemphill collected evidence on the cost and extent of the cotton lien system.

W. D. Hunter and B. R. Coad. "The Boll-Weevil Problem." *USDA Farmers' Bulletin,* Number 1329 (June 1923).

A. B. Hurt. "Mississippi: Its Climate, Soil, Productions, and Agricultural Capabilities." *USDA Miscellaneous Special Report,* Number 3. Washington: GPO, 1883. One of several USDA reports dealing with the cotton states at this time. Includes data on extent and cost of cotton liens.

Ralph Dickieson Jennings. "Consumption of Feed by Livestock, 1909–56; Relation Between Feed, Livestock, and Food at the National Level." *USDA Research Production Report,* Number 21. Washington: GPO, 1958.

Frederick Strauss and Louis H. Bean. "Gross Farm Income and Indices of Farm Production and Prices in the United States, 1867–1937." *USDA Technical Bulletin,* Number 703. Washington: GPO, December 1940.

U. S. Department of Agriculture (*cont.*)

Agricultural Marketing Service. "Corn: Acreage, Yield and Production of All Corn, Corn for Silage, and Acreage for Forage, by States, 1866–1943." *USDA Statistical Bulletin,* Number 56. Washington: GPO, 1954.

Agricultural Marketing Service. "Cotton and Cottonseed: Acreage, Yield, Production, Disposition, Price, Value, by States, 1866–1952." *USDA Statistical Bulletin,* Number 164. Washington: GPO, 1955.

Agricultural Marketing Service. "Flaxseed and Rye: Acreage, Yield, Production, Price, Value, by States, 1866–1953." *USDA Statistical Bulletin,* Number 254. Washington: GPO, July 1959.

Agricultural Marketing Service. *Oats: Acreage, Yield, Production, by State, 1866–1943.* Washington: USDA, June 1954.

Agricultural Marketing Service. "Potatoes: Estimates in Hundredweight, by States, 1866–1953; Acreage, Yield, Production, Price, Value, Farm Disposition, Total Stocks." *USDA Statistical Bulletin,* Number 251. Washington: GPO, July 1959.

Agricultural Marketing Service. "Rice, Popcorn, and Buckwheat: Acreage, Yield, Production, Price, Value, by States, 1866–1953." *USDA Statistical Bulletin,* Number 238. Washington: GPO, 1958.

Agricultural Marketing Service. "Sweet potatoes: Estimates in Hundredweight, by States, 1868–1953; Acreage, Yield, Production, Price, Value, Farm Disposition." *USDA Statistical Bulletin,* Number 237. Washington: GPO, September 1958.

Agricultural Marketing Service. "Wheat: Acreage, Yield and Production by States, 1866–1943." *USDA Statistical Bulletin,* Number 158. Washington: GPO, 1955.

Bureau of Agricultural Economics. *Livestock on Farms, January 1, 1867–1919: Revised Estimates: Number, Value per Head, Total Value, by State and Divisions.* Washington: USDA, January 1937.

Bureau of Agricultural Economics. "Prices of Farm Products Received by Producers." Volume 3: "South Atlantic and South Central States." *USDA Statistical Bulletin,* Number 16. Washington: GPO, 1927.

Bureau of Agricultural Economics. "Potatoes: Acreage, Production, Value, Farm Disposition, January 1 Stocks: 1866–1950." *USDA Statistical Bulletin,* Number 122. Washington: GPO, March 1953.

Bureau of Agricultural Economics. "Revised Estimates of Corn Acreage, Yield and Production, 1866–1929." Mimeographed,USDA, 1934.

Bureau of Agricultural Economics. "Revised Estimates of Oats Acreage, Yield and Production." Mimeographed, USDA, 1934.

Bureau of Agricultural Economics. "Tobaccos of the United States: Acreage, Yield per Acre, Production, Prices, and Value, by States, 1866–1945, and by Types and Classes, 1919–1945." *CS Series,* Number 30. Washington: GPO, 1948.

Bureau of Statistics, Charles C. Clark. "Corn Crops of the United States, 1866–1906." *USDA Bureau of Statistics Bulletin,* Number 56. Washington: GPO, November 1907.

Bureau of Statistics, George K. Holmes. "Cotton Crops of the United States, 1790–1911." *USDA Bureau of Statistics Circular,* Number 32, Washington: GPO, 1912.

Bureau of Statistics, Charles C. Clark. "Oat Crops of the United States, 1866–1906." *USDA Bureau of Statistics Bulletin,* Number 58. Washington: GPO, November 1907.

Bureau of Statistics. "Rice Crops of the United States, 1712–1911." *USDA Bureau of Statistics Circular,* Number 34. Washington: GPO, 1912.

Bureau of Statistics. "Wages of Farm Labor: Nineteenth Investigation, in 1909, Continuing a Series That Began in 1866." *USDA Bureau of Statistics Bulletin,* Number 99. Washington: GPO, 1912.

Bureau of Statistics, Charles C. Clark. "Wheat Crops of the United States, 1866–1906." *USDA Bureau of Statistics Bulletin,* Number 57, revised. Washington: GPO, 1908.

Division of Entomology, [L. O. Howard]. "A New Cotton Insect in Texas." *Insect Life 7*

U. S. Department of Agriculture (*cont.*)
(December 1894):273.

    Division of Entomology, C. H. Tyler Townsend. "Report on the Mexican Cotton-Boll Weevil in Texas (Anthonomus grandis Boh.)" *Insect Life* 7 (March 1895):295–309.

    Division of Statistics, James L. Watkins. "The Cost of Cotton Production." *USDA Miscellaneous Bulletin*, Number 16. Washington: GPO, 1899.

    Division of Statistics, James L. Watkins. "Production and Price of Cotton for One Hundred Years." *USDA Miscellaneous Bulletin*, Number 9. Washington: GPO, 1895.

    Economic Research Service. "Conversion Factors and Weights and Measures for Agricultural Commodities and Their Products." *USDA Statistical Bulletin*, Number 362. Washington: GPO, June 1965.

    Office of Experiment Stations, W. O. Atwater and Cha[rle]s D. Woods. "Dietary Studies with Reference to the Food of the Negro in Alabama in 1895 and 1896." *USDA Experiment Stations Bulletin*, Number 38. Washington: GPO, 1897.

U.S. Department of the Interior. "Report of the Commissioner of Education." In *Report of the Secretary of the Interior, 1880.* House of Representatives, Executive Document Number 1, Volume 3, Part 5, 46th Congress, 3rd Session. Washington: GPO, 1882. The 1880 report includes a summary of enrollment data by states for each previous year in which figures were reported.

U.S. Patent Office. *Annual Report of the Commissioner of Patents for the Year 1848.* Washington: Wendell & Van Benthuysen, 1849.

    Report of the Commissioner of Patents for the Year 1849, Part 2, *Agriculture.* Washington: Office of Printers to U.S. House of Representatives, 1850.

    Report of the Commissioner of Patents for the Year 1851, Part 2, *Agriculture.* Washington: Robert Armstrong, 1852.

    Report of the Commissioner of Patents for the Year 1852, Part 2, *Agriculture.* Washington: Robert Armstrong, 1853.

    Report of the Commissioner of Patents for the Year 1853: Agriculture. Washington: Nicholson, 1854.

    Report of the Commissioner of Patents for the Year 1854: Agriculture. Washington: Nicholson, 1856.

    Report of the Commissioner of Patents for the Year 1855: Agriculture. Washington: GPO, 1856.

U.S. Secretary of the Treasury. *Report of the Secretary of the Treasury on the State of the Finances, for the year ending June 30, 1863.* House of Representatives, Executive Document Number 3, 38th Congress, 1st Session. Washington: GPO, 1863.

    Annual Report of the Secretary of the Treasury on the State of the Finances for the Fiscal Year ended June 30, 1928. Washington: GPO, 1929.

Vason, D. A. "The Fallacy of the Credit System, as Applied to Agriculture." Speech delivered August 15, 1877, at Newnan, Georgia. In *Transactions of the Georgia State Agricultural Society, from August, 1876 to February, 1878.* Atlanta: James P. Harrison, 1878, pp. 353–357.

Vickery, William Edward. "The Economics of the Negro Migration, 1900–1960." Ph.D. dissertation, University of Chicago, December 1969.

Wade, Richard C. *Slavery in the Cities: The South, 1820–1860.* London: Oxford University Press, 1964.

Walker, Francis A. "Statistics of the Colored Race in the United States." 2 parts. *Publications of the American Statistical Association* new series 2 (September and December 1890):91–106.

Warren, George F., and Pearson, Frank A. *Prices.* New York: John Wiley & Sons, 1933.

Watkins, James L. See U.S. Department of Agriculture, Division of Statistics.

Weaver, Herbert. *Mississippi Farmers, 1850–1860.* Nashville: Vanderbilt University Press, 1945.

Weeks, Joseph D., See U.S. Census Office, Tenth Census, [1880].

Wharton, Vernon Lane. *The Negro in Mississippi, 1865–1890.* New York: Harper & Row, 1965. Originally published in 1947.

Wiener, Jonathan M. "Planter-Merchant Conflict in Reconstruction Alabama." *Past and Present* 68 (August 1975):73–94.

"Planter Persistence and Social Change: Alabama, 1850–1870." *Journal of Interdisciplinary History* 7 (autumn 1976):235–260.

Williamson, Joel. *After Slavery: The Negro in South Carolina During Reconstruction, 1861–1877.* Chapel Hill: University of North Carolina Press, 1965.

Woodman, Harold D. "Economic History and Economic Theory: The New Economic History in America." *Journal of Interdisciplinary History* 3 (autumn 1972):323–350.

King Cotton and His Retainers. Lexington: University of Kentucky Press, 1967.

"The Profitability of Slavery: A Historical Perennial." *Journal of Southern History* 29 (August 1963):303–325.

Woodson, Carter G. *The Education of the Negro Prior to 1861: A History of the Education of the Colored People of the United States from the Beginning of Slavery to the Civil War.* New York: Arno Press, 1968. Originally published in 1915.

Woodward, C. Vann. *Origins of the New South, 1877–1913.* Volume 9 of Wendell Holmes Stephenson and E. Merton Coulter, editors. *A History of the South.* Baton Rouge: Louisiana State University Press, 1971. Originally published in 1951.

The Strange Career of Jim Crow. Revised edition. New York: Oxford University Press, 1966.

Wright, Carroll D., Commissioner of Labor, U.S. Department of Labor, and Hunt, William C., Chief Statistician, Twelfth Census. *The History and Growth of the United States Census, Prepared for the Senate Committee on the Census.* Washington: GPO, 1900.

Wright, Gavin. "Comment on Papers by Reid, Ransom and Sutch, and Higgs." *Journal of Economic History* 33 (March 1973):170–176.

"Cotton Competition and the Post-Bellum Recovery of the American South." *Journal of Economic History* 34 (September 1974):610–635.

" 'Economic Democracy' and the Concentration of Agricultural Wealth in the Cotton South, 1850–1860." *Agricultural History* 44 (January 1970):63–93.

"The Economics of Cotton in the Antebellum South." Ph.D. dissertation, Yale University, 1969.

"Note on the Manuscript Census Samples Used in These Studies." *Agricultural History* 44 (January 1970):95–100. A brief discussion of the Parker-Gallman sample of farms drawn from the 1859 manuscript census returns.

"Prosperity, Progress, and American Slavery." In Paul A. David, Herbert G. Gutman, Richard Sutch, Peter Temin, and Gavin Wright. *Reckoning with Slavery: A Critical Study in the Quantitative History of American Negro Slavery.* New York: Oxford University Press, 1976, pp. 302–336.

Wright, Gavin, and Kunreuther, Howard. "Cotton, Corn and Risk in the Nineteenth Century." *Journal of Economic History* 35 (September 1975):526–551.

Yasuba, Yasukichi. "The Profitability and Viability of Plantation Slavery in the United States." *Economic Studies Quarterly* 12 (September 1961):60–67.

Zeichner, Oscar. "The Legal Status of the Agricultural Laborer in the South." *Political Science Quarterly* 55 (September 1940):412–428.

"Transition from Slave to Free Agricultural Labor in the Southern States." *Agricultural History* 13 (January 1939):22–32.

INDEX

Page numbers in italic refer to maps, tables, or figures

Mississippi *(cont.)*
    173, 196, 222, *255, 256,* 260, 261, 262,
    273, 275, *276, 278*
Missouri, 49
Mobile, Alabama, 110, *111,* 116, 117, *118–*
    19, 301
Mobile Daily Register, 148
molasses production, *205,* 207, 260
monopoly, *see* credit, crop lien, merchandis-
    ing and merchants, territorial monopoly
Montgomery, Alabama, *111, 118–19,* 300,
    301
Montgomery Daily Advertiser, 147
Montgomery, J. N., 338n
Montgomery Ward, 97
Morehead, Sherrod D., 344n
Morison, Samuel Eliot, 334n
Morrison, F. B., 247, 363n
mule(s)
    feed requirements, 246–8, *249, 250,* 363 n7
    prices, 48–*9,* 327 n30 n34 n35
    raising, 48–9

Nash County, North Carolina, *xx,* 57, *291*
Natchez, Mississippi, *118–19,* 120, *303*
National Banking System, *see* banks
National Science Foundation, xi, 273
Negro, *see* blacks
New Orleans, 110, 111, 113, 116, *118–19,*
    302
New York City, 117, 210, 260
Newberry, South Carolina, 113, *118–19, 303*
Newton, Alabama, 116
Niemi, Albert, W., Jr., 324n
Norcross, Georgia, 141, *142*
North, Douglass C., 348n, 367n
North Carolina, *xx,* 27, *93, 118–19,* 123–4,
    134–5, 161, *173,* 197, 248, 273, 275, *276,*
    278
North Carolina Bureau of Labor Statistics,
    reports cited, 350n, 351n
North Carolina Department of Agriculture,
    survey, 248
note issue, *108,* 110, *114,* 341 n13 n16; *see*
    also banks

oats
    nutritional value, *247*
    output, 261, *263*
    prices, *256, 261, 263*
    seed requirements, *246*
occupations
    of blacks, *31, 32–3,* 34, *35,* 36, *37–8,* 224,
    225, 226, 298

    listed by Mercantile Agency, *308*
    and literacy, *35*
    of males and females, 34, *37–8, 226, 227,*
    228–9, 230
    and racial balance, 36, *37,* 38, 225–31
    of rural bankers, *115*
    of slaves, 15–*16,* 220–2, *223, 224,* 298
    see also artisans, blacks, literacy
Olmstead, Frederick Law, 46, 204, 321n,
    357n
orchard products, 216
Otken, Charles H., 144, 149, 164, 350n
output
    gross crop estimates, 9, *10,* 193, *194,* 254–
    7, *259,* 318 n14, 364 n7; antebellum, 6–7,
    263, 264–5, 318 n8; per capita, 9, *10,*
    193; growth in, 9, *10,* 194, 318 n16;
    USDA estimates of, 255–61, 364 n8 n9
    n10 n11
    gross national, 193, *194,* 266
    on postbellum farms, 11, *214–*15, *216,* 282,
    293, 358 n32: per acre, *100,* 185; per
    family member, *184;* per worker, *184*
    on slave plantations, 2, *3, 5,* 203–4, *205:*
    per slave, 209, *210*
    of southern manufacturing, 41–2, *43*
    see also gross crop output, income, *entries*
    for specific crops
overseer, 57
Owsley, Frank L., 88, 336n, 339n, 340n
Owsley, Harriet C., 336n
oxen, feed requirements, 246–8, *250,* 363 n10

Parker, William, N., 203, 299, 300
Parker-Gallman sample of farms, 1860, 73,
    156, 203, 204, *209,* 211, 296, 299, 300,
    371 n32
Passmore, R., 347n
Pearson, Frank A., 354n, 365n
pecuniary strength, 306 (def.), *308,* 313, 314;
    see also Dun's Mercantile Agency
Perry County, Alabama, *xx, 291,* 292
Peters, Theodore C., 106, 109, *249n, 252n,*
    326n, 340n
Peterson, Arthur G., 207n, 263, 347n
Phillips, Ulrich Bonnell, 76, 317n, 319n,
    327n, 333n, 356n, 358n, 367n
Pike County, Alabama, *xx, 291*
Pike County, Mississippi, *xx, 291*
Pittsboro, Mississippi, 225
plantation
    antebellum: definition of, 73, 332 n52; use
    of slave labor, 56, 75–6